APPRECIATING ART

2ND EDITION

LEAVING CERTIFICATE HIGHER AND ORDINARY LEVELS

Áine Ní Chárthaigh & Aidan O'Sullivan

Gill Education
Hume Avenue
Park West
Dublin 12
www.gilleducation.ie

Gill Education is an imprint of M.H. Gill & Co.

ISBN: 978-0-7171-74386

Design: Anú Design (www.anu-design.ie)

Illustrations: Oxford Illustrators and Designers, Sarah Wimperis and Keith Barrett

Front cover images:

The Artist's Garden at Vetheuil, 1880 (oil on canvas), Claude Monet (1840–1926) / National Gallery of Art, Washington DC, USA / Bridgeman Images

Statue of Michelangelo's David © lillisphotography/iStockphoto

Harry Clarke (1889–1931), The Garden of Paradise, Ink graphite, watercolour, gouache and glazes with body colour highlights / National Gallery of Ireland Collection / Photo © National Gallery of Ireland

Back cover image:

Paris Street; Rainy Day, 1877 (oil on canvas), Gustave Caillebotte / Heritage Image Partnership Ltd / Alamy Stock Photokar

The paper used in this book is made from the wood pulp of managed forests. For every tree felled, at least one tree is planted, thereby renewing natural resources.

Contents

Section 1: Art in Ireland

Section 2, Part 1: Medieval Art and Architecture

Section 2, Part 2: The Renaissance

Section 2, Part 3: The High Renaissance (Cinquecento)

Section 2, Part 4: Art in 19th-Century France and 20th-Century Europe

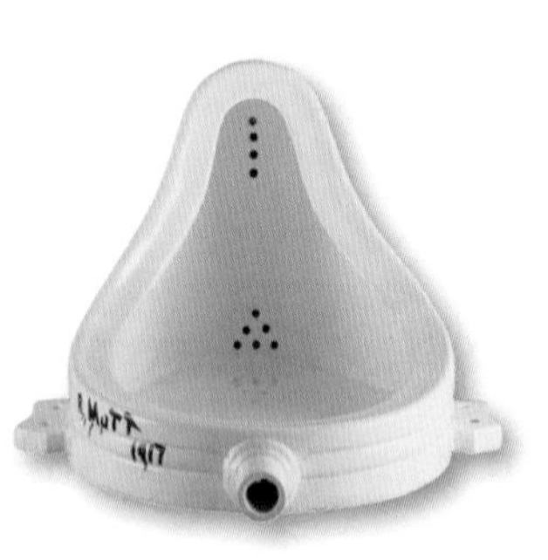

Section 3: Appreciation of Art

Section 4: Preparing for the Written Exam 465

Online material

The following chapters are accompanied by **bonus online material** on **www.gillexplore.ie**:

Chapter 5: The 11th and 12th Centuries: The Irish Romanesque Period (Hiberno-Romanesque)

You will find extra content on Romanesque art, including the monasteries, architecture, high crosses, manuscripts and metalwork.

Chapter 7: Irish Art in the 19th and 20th Centuries

In addition to the artists featured in the book, you will find extra content on the following:

John Hogan (1800–58)
James Arthur O'Connor (1792–1841)
Frederick William Burton (1816–1900)
Nathaniel Hone (1831–1917)
Walter Osborne (1859–1903)
William John Leech (1881–1968)
Paul Henry (1876–1958)
Seán Keating (1889–1977)
Evie Hone (1894–1955)
Mainie Jellett (1897–1944)
Norah McGuinness (1901–80)
Patrick Scott (1921–2014)
Gerard Dillon (1916–71)
Robert Ballagh (1943–)
John Behan (1938–)
Dorothy Cross (1956–)
Eilis O'Connell (1953–)
Michael Quane (1962–)

Chapter 34: Twentieth-Century Art in Europe

In addition to the artists featured in the book, you will find extra content on the following:

Emil Nolde (1867–1956)
Franz Marc (1880–1916)
Georges Rouault (1871–1958)
Georges Braque (1882–1963)
Kazimir Malevich (1878–1935)
Piet Mondrian (1872–1944)
Joan Miró (1893–1983)
René Magritte (1898–1967)
Le Corbusier (Charles-Édouard Jeanneret) (1887–1965)
Francis Bacon (1909–92)

Chapter 35: Design

You will find extra content on: origins of the designer, the basic rules of good design, The Deutscher Werkbund, Bauhaus, The International Style, new technology, computer technology and design, and on:

Henry Ford (1863–1947)
Eileen Gray (1878–1976)
Henry Dreyfuss (1904–72)

Chapter 39: Film Studies

You will find extra content on: the technology of film and the language of film.

Introduction

Looking at art

Looking closely at and thinking carefully about a work of art can be a meaningful and lasting experience.

Works of art can be seen at school, in books, on the internet, on television, in public places or in galleries, but learning to look takes time.

By the end of this chapter, I will...

* Be familiar with each of the art elements.
* Know how to analyse a painting.
* Be able to research background and context.
* Be able to evaluate a work of art.
* Know how to use art vocabulary and visually descriptive language.
* Know why sculpture had such an important role in the history of Western art.
* Be able to identify a sculpture in the round as distinct from a relief sculpture.
* Be able to compare a contemporary work with a work from the past.
* Be able to evaluate sculpture using appropriate art vocabulary.
* Know how to prepare an art history essay.
* Know how to write a good introduction.
* Know how to combine the description of art works with formal analysis.
* Know how to conclude an essay.
* Be able to illustrate your answer to support your points.

To fully appreciate a work of art, it is important to build up an understanding of art and learn the skills and vocabulary to make observations. Knowing how to 'read' art can completely change how you experience it.

Appreciating art

One of the best ways to appreciate a work of art is to investigate the art elements, context and background.

Elements of art

The elements of art serve as the building blocks for creating something. They are line, shape, form, space, texture, tone and colour.

Artists manipulate these seven elements and mix them with the principles of design to make a work of art. Not every work contains every element, but at least two will always be present.

Context and background

Finding out when and why the work was created will give you a clue as to what the artist might have had in mind. This, in turn, will help you to enjoy and appreciate the work more.

Appreciating Irish painting

Look at the works of Irish art on the following page. Explore and evaluate one or more of them using the four suggested steps in the next section.

Fig. 1 (left)
A Connemara Village, 1933–4, by Paul Henry, National Gallery of Ireland, Dublin

Fig. 2 (right)
The Goldfish Bowl, 1900, by Walter Osborne, 76cm x 64cm, Crawford Art Gallery, Cork

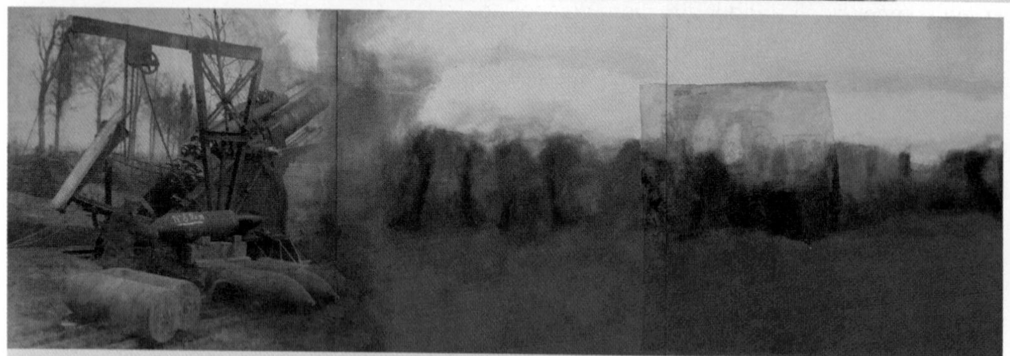

Fig. 3 (left) *Wasteland*, 2016, by Hughie O'Donoghue
Fig. 4 (right) *Berry Dress*, 1994, by Alice Maher, Irish Museum of Modern Art, Dublin

* *A Connemara Village* by Paul Henry (Fig. 1)
* *The Goldfish Bowl* by Walter Osborne (Fig. 2)
* *Wasteland* by Hughie O'Donoghue (Fig. 3)
* *Berry Dress* by Alice Maher (Fig. 4)

Four ways to look at a work of art

1. Look

* Look carefully at the work, paying close attention to details. What do you notice? Make some quick notes.
* Look again for 30 seconds and then turn away. Try remembering what you noticed. What details do you remember?
* Look back again. What did you overlook?

2. Describe

Describe what you see in detail, making reference to the subject matter and some of the art elements, like line, shape, colour, composition and materials.

Subject matter

What is the painting about? What do you see?

Composition

How have the different art elements been put together? What way is your eye drawn?

Ask yourself:

* Is the composition landscape or portrait (vertical or horizontal)?
* Does the composition follow the rule of thirds (Fig. 5)?

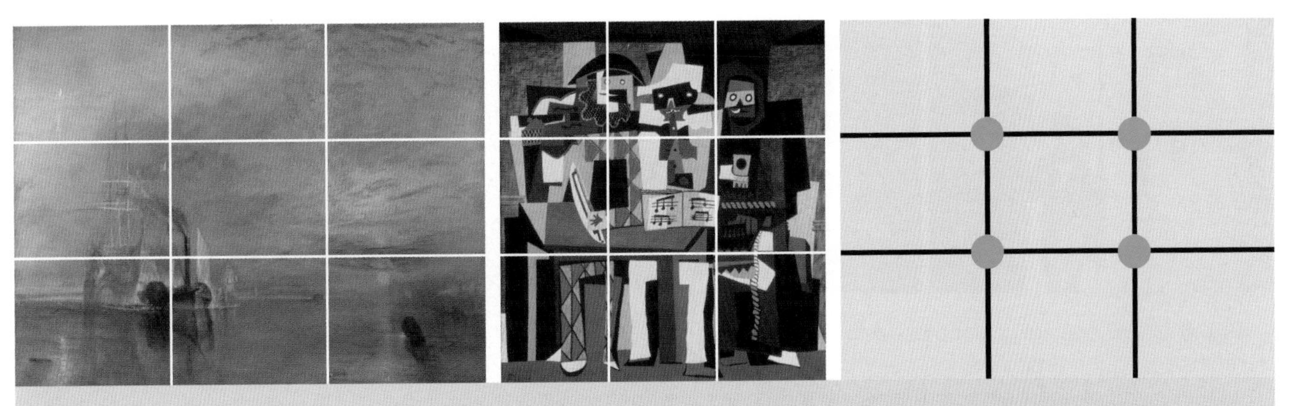

Fig. 5 The rule of thirds is more of a guideline than a rule. It helps the artist with the placement of focal points within the composition. Placing these at the intersections of any of the nine rectangles gives the picture counterbalance, making the composition stronger and more compelling.

Other elements in the picture can also be used to draw the eye around. For example, using the corners can draw the viewer's eye from one focal point to the other to create movement and life.

Fig. 6 The triangle or pyramidal composition is used to draw the viewer's attention to a figure or to give an impression of stability. To construct a pyramidal composition, an artist places objects and figures within the outline of an imaginary triangle or pyramid on the picture plane. It was very popular with Renaissance artists.

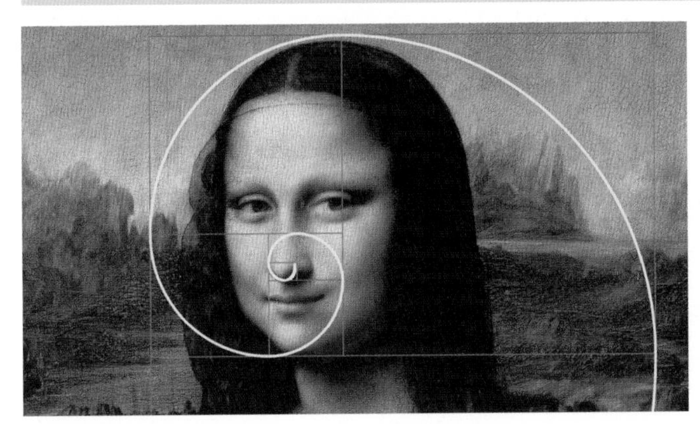

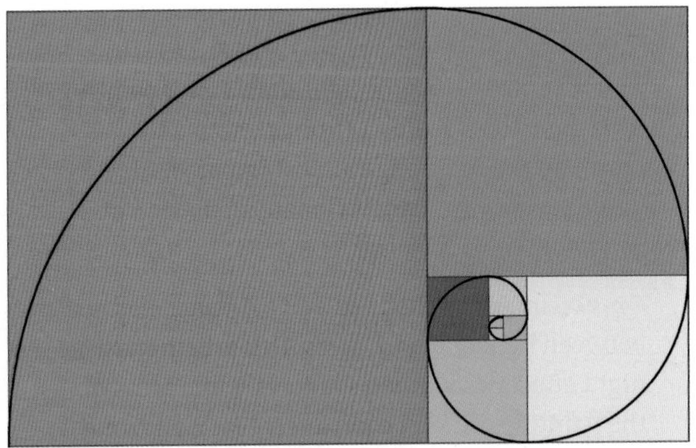

Fig. 7 Based on an ancient mathematical ratio that can be found in nature, the golden mean is used to create balance and harmony in the arts. A line or rectangle is divided into two unequal parts so that the ratio of the smaller part to the larger part is the same as the ratio of the larger part to the whole line or rectangle (1:1.618, see graphic above). A square taken from the rectangle creates a smaller rectangle of the same proportion. The relationships of the squares, rectangles and curves created by the formula are considered to be harmonious, based on nature and mathematics. The rule of thirds above is a simplification of this formula.

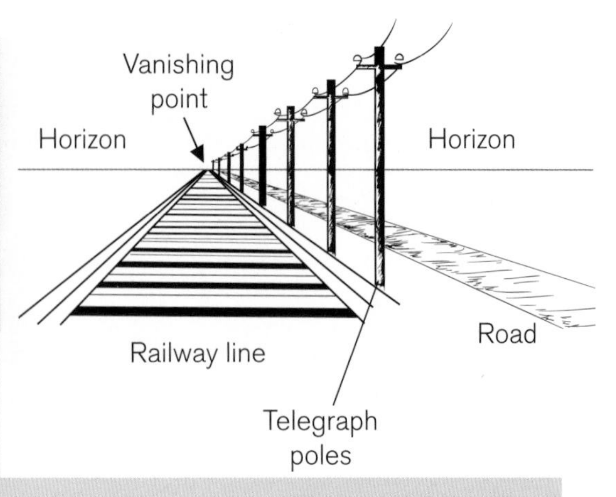

Fig. 8 Linear or single point perspective is a way of representing three-dimensional objects on a two-dimensional picture plane. In linear perspective, all parallel edges and lines converge towards a single vanishing point.

* Is the composition in a triangular shape (Fig. 6)?
* Is the composition based on the golden mean or section (Fig. 7)?

Lines

Look at the directions of lines. Are they horizontal, vertical or at other angles? Are they straight or curved, continuous or broken, thick or thin, long or short?

Perspective

Is there perspective in the painting? Does it suggest depth or distance and give the impression of three dimensions on a flat, two-dimensional surface (Fig. 8)?

Chiaroscuro: Italian for 'light-dark'. It is a painting technique that creates a strong contrast of light and shade through almost imperceptible gradations. Deep shadows create an illusion of three-dimensional forms.

Tenebrism: Deep shadows and a distinct contrast between light and dark areas. This art emphasises night effects and strong shadows. Some areas of the painting are kept completely black, allowing one or more areas to be strongly lit from a single source of light.

Sfumato: From the Italian word *fumo*, meaning 'smoke'. It is a technique in oil painting used to blend colours or tones so subtly that they melt into one another without perceptible transitions, lines or edges.

Shapes

Are the shapes rounded, rectangular, triangular, regular or irregular, symmetric or asymmetric?

Light

Look at light and dark, shadows and highlights. Has the artist used:

* Chiaroscuro to enhance the tones?
* Tenebrism to put the spotlight on certain parts of the picture?
* Sfumato to blend colour?

Tone

Are the tones pale, dazzling, dim, harsh, subtle? Are the contrasts high or low?

Tone: The lightness, intensity or brilliance of a colour. It can also refer to the prevailing hue in a picture.

Colour

Are the colours natural or exaggerated, intense or soft, dull or bright, warm or cool, complementary (opposite each other on the colour wheel) or harmonious (near each other on the colour wheel)?

Pattern

Are the patterns bold or subtle, simple or intricate, geometric or regular, rich or sparse?

Texture

What is the surface texture like? Is it even or uneven, smooth or coarse, shiny or matte? Can you see brushstrokes?

Process and technique

* What type of art work is it? For example, is it a painting, drawing, sculpture, photograph, video or installation?
* How do you think it was made?
* Can you see how the artist worked?
* Do you think the artist worked slowly and carefully or quickly and energetically?
* How long do you think it took to make?
* Do you think other people may have helped the artist?
* How is it displayed? If it is in a frame, what is the frame like?

Language of art

Try using visually expressive language. For example, when describing *A Connemara Village* by Paul Henry in the National Gallery of Ireland (see Fig. 1), instead of saying:

In the lower half of the painting there are mounds of turf, houses and a mountain. In the upper half there is a cloudy sky…

You could say:

The upper half of the composition is given over to the sky, which is filled with soft white clouds. A row of tiny whitewashed cottages is clearly outlined in sunshine on a little hill against a backdrop of deep blue mountains. This is highlighted by a large area of shadow crossing the foreground diagonally, balanced by the dark shapes of three mounds of turf.

3. Interpret

* What is this work of art about?
* What is the setting?
* Is a time and place depicted?
* Is there a narrative?
* What mood does the work convey or how does it affect your emotions?
* Do you think the artist is trying to communicate a message? What might it be? Why do you think this?

4. Research

* In what period in history did the artist live?
* How do you think the artist's social or historical background influenced the subject, style or technique?
* Was the work originally created as a piece of art or do you think it had some other purpose, such as religious, ceremonial or practical?
* Do you think it was originally intended for display in a private home, an art gallery or for another space, such as a palace, temple or church?
* Is this work typical of a particular period of the artist's career?
* Compare the work to another by the same artist.
* How does it relate to the work of other artists from the same period?
* Does knowing more about what the artist was trying to convey help you to enjoy it more? Why is that?

NOTE! Finding out more about the life of the artist and the period during which he or she lived can greatly help you to appreciate their art.

Figurative or abstract art

Painting and sculpture can be figurative or abstract.

An element of abstraction is *simplification*.

Figurative art

* Figurative art simply means that it is based on real object sources and is therefore **representational**.
* A **non-representative** painting has no resemblance to any real object. It may just be geometric shapes, bands of colour, etc.

Abstract art

* **Abstract works** can be based on real objects that have been changed, simplified or distorted.
* Non-representational abstract works are made from compositional elements that are not directly related to the visual world.

How to look at an abstract painting

What to look at first

* Look at the shapes and forms.
* Is space represented, or not?
* Is there an emotional effect through colours or marks?
* How has the surface been treated? Is it rough or smooth?
* Has the artist left marks that suggest expression or direction?

Look at the colour

* Does the colour convey emotion, time of day, distance or some other special feature?
* What kind of paint has been used?
* Can you see brushstrokes in the work?
* Do these brushstrokes convey movement?

Look again

* Where is the focal point?
* Why is your eye led there?
* Is your mind looking for objects and ideas, but is your eye attracted to areas of high contrast?

NOTE! Your eye is part of your brain! Allow it to do its work and lead your mind through the work.

Evaluate the work

Once you have looked at, investigated and researched the context of the work of art, you can begin to evaluate it.

* What do you think is successful about this work of art? What is not as successful?
* Would you recommend that other people see this work? What do you think they might say about it?
* What would you do with this work if you owned it?
* What do you think is worth remembering about this work?

NOTE! Art evaluation is not just about liking or disliking the art. The real point is to explain *why* you like or dislike something, not simply *whether* you like it or not.

Looking at paintings in the National Gallery of Ireland

The National Gallery of Ireland has numerous works of art on display. The main emphasis is on Irish art, but it also has very fine examples of European painting in its collection.

The paintings are divided into schools of painting based on the different forms and genres in Western European painting. We will look at two examples here: one from the Italian school and one from the Dutch school.

The Italian School

The Taking of Christ by Caravaggio

The National Gallery's greatest treasure is *The Taking of Christ*, a wonderful work by the 16th-century Italian master, Caravaggio.

The large painting is on long-term loan to the National Gallery. It was discovered by chance in a Jesuit refectory in Dublin in 1992.

Several copies of the work were well known for many years, but art historians believed the original was lost. In fact, it had been labelled under the name of another artist and had come to Dublin in the early 1930s from Scotland.

It was sold to a British art collector in Italy in the 18th century as a work by Gerard van Honthorst, also known as Gerard of the Night. He was one of Caravaggio's Dutch followers.

A masterpiece revealed

When the National Gallery was asked to clean the painting, the Italian art restorer Sergio Benedetti immediately recognised the work as the lost Caravaggio. As he carefully removed layers of dirt and discoloured varnish, the supreme technical quality of the painting was revealed.

Caravaggio

The name of the artist was changed because Caravaggio had become unpopular and the painting would therefore have been less valuable.

Michelangelo Merisi, called Caravaggio, was a controversial artist. He was violent and difficult and his paintings were intensely controversial.

The artist used real-life models, but instead of changing them to traditional 'holy' and idealised images, his religious figures were real, ordinary people. They were shown in life settings like that of the street and were even dirty and ragged.

Dramatic use of light and dark

His paintings are highly dramatic. The figures are shown from an extremely close viewpoint, almost like in a close-up film shot.

His techniques include tenebrism, or dramatic illumination, which is an intense form of chiaroscuro. This darkness became a dominating feature. A spotlight effect is achieved by a single source of light adding drama to the image.

Caravaggio became popular again in the 19th century. He is now regarded as a major figure in Western art.

Evaluate the work

Look at *The Taking of Christ* (Fig. 9).

* What is this painting trying to say? Note what you have discovered or decided about the work.
* How does the painting make you feel? Note your deep feeling and reaction to the work.
* Is the impact of the painting mostly visual or is it mostly what you think? Work this out.
* Where should the painting hang? Would you like it to hang on a wall in your school? Would you like to have it in your home? Would this make you look at the work in a different way?
* Would you like to see more paintings like this? Would you like to visit the National Gallery in Dublin to see it for yourself?
* Where would you see other paintings by this artist?

The Dutch School

The Dutch school is one of the strongest in the gallery. The paintings are from the 17th and 18th centuries, often thought of as the 'Golden Age' of Dutch painting.

The 17th century was a time of great wealth in Holland. There was a strong middle-class demand for art.

Genre painting was very popular. These were scenes of everyday life, like peasants at work, the aristocracy at leisure, community activities and simple domestic settings.

Which figure is central to the composition?

The figures are shown in half-length, like a film still. The soldiers are in contemporary costume. Judas's action has the effect of pushing Christ sideways. The dark red cloth behind forms a frame like an arc behind them. The juxtaposition (putting together) of both heads is the focal point of the composition. The contrast could not be starker. Judas, driven by greed, leans forward to kiss his master. The loving greeting instantly changes to an aggressive act. Jesus remains calm. His hands, clasped in faith, are a prominent feature at the bottom of the picture. His distress is seen only in his furrowed brow and downturned eyes.

> **Juxtapose:** Place close together for a contrasting effect.

How tenebrism contributes to the drama of the event

Caravaggio's use of extreme chiaroscuro creates intensity and vibrancy. The darkness is contrasted by the intensity of the colours, particularly the deep red and shiny blue-grey metal, which adds to the richness of the visual impact. Behind the group in the top right, a man in a red cloak carries a lantern. He is thought to have the features of Caravaggio, but the lantern has no role because the light source is high on the left, beyond the view of the spectator.

How does the artist convey the moment of chaos and commotion?

Judas stretches out to grab Jesus' sleeve. The cold, shining metal armour of the soldier's hand further highlights Christ's vulnerability. These lines indicate that the crowd is rushing in to capture him. The enormous punching force of the composition is pushing towards the left. Jesus alone, in passive resistance, faces the other way.

What is the painting about?

The painting depicts the chaotic moment of treachery in the Garden of Gethsemane after Judas has identified his master by kissing him. The soldiers push forward to arrest Jesus, who accepts his fate with humility.

Fig. 9 *The Taking of Christ*, 1602, by Caravaggio, oil on canvas, 133.5cm x 169.5cm, on indefinite loan to the National Gallery of Ireland from the Jesuit Community, Leeson St, Dublin, who acknowledge the kind generosity of the late Dr Marie Lea-Wilson, 1992

Johannes Vermeer

Johannes Vermeer was one of the foremost painters of the time. His genre paintings stand out for their simplicity and style. He worked slowly and meticulously and produced only a small number of works in his lifetime.

> **Genre:** Painting style that depicts scenes from ordinary life, typically domestic situations, associated particularly with 17th-century Dutch and Flemish artists.

His compositions often include objects or still life that hint at the prosperity and status of the people. His paintings have a distinctive style and are characterised by soft textures.

Evaluate the work

Look at *A Lady Writing a Letter with Her Maid* (Fig. 10).

- How big is the painting?
- What medium has been used?
- Is the surface smooth or textured?

* What do you know of the artist and similar art of the time?
* Does the title help you to understand the painting better?
* Is this a realistic depiction of the scene?
* Is there a theme or a message?
* Does the work create an atmosphere?

Is there a clear narrative?

The artist has avoided any narrative or story. The picture is unrelated to any specific situation. This creates its timeless, serene image.

What is happening in the picture?

A woman sits at a table writing a letter and a maid calmly looks out the window. She crosses her arms and waits.

How has the artist used colour?

Vermeer has used the hugely expensive pigment of lapis lazuli (natural ultramarine) in the most lavish way throughout his paintings. This was unusual among his contemporaries. He used it not just where blue is the obvious colour. It is part of the mix in the green of the chair fabric and the rich blue-grey shadows in the white linen sleeves.

How are the lines used?

Lines of perspective join the two figures. They extend from the upper and lower window frames across the maid's folded arms and forehead to the vanishing point of the mistress's left eye. This effectively means that the viewer's eye is drawn first to the maid, but it quickly passes to the woman at the table. She is the real focal point of the painting.

Which of the figures is the focal point?

The figures are a key aspect of the composition. The maid is the central figure. She is anchored by the picture frame behind her. She stands calm, still and straight, like a column. The fold in her skirts leads the eye to the floor. In marked contrast, her mistress is deeply engrossed in the intense activity of writing. She leans forward on her left forearm and the bright light falls on her writing arm. The angular folds on the pure white sleeve are sharply defined against background shadows.

How has the scene been composed?

Strong verticals and horizontals, particularly the heavy black frame on the wall behind, establish the space. The elegant interior features a black and white marble floor with a skirt of tiles and a large painting. The scene is set in the corner of a room, with light coming from a tall window on the left wall. A long, dark green curtain on the left is drawn back. A translucent lace curtain hangs down from the leaded glass window. The light and the pattern are carefully distributed by the closed shutter on the right pane.

What viewpoint is the composition from?

The artist has chosen a low viewpoint, scarcely higher than the top of the table. This adds to the figures' monumentality and enhances the height of the space.

Is the scene calm or lively?

The muted colours and strong composition contribute to the quiet mood of stillness. It suggests that no activity will interrupt the scene.

What does the painting mean?

The painting offers small clues to its meaning with some objects on the floor before. A crumpled letter, a stick of sealing wax and a bright red seal could either be a letter that the lady has received or a discarded draft of a letter. The red wax seal indicates that the crumpled letter was received. As letters were prized in the 17th century, it must have been thrown aside in anger. The empty chair at the table suggests someone has recently been sitting there, since chairs of this type were placed against the wall when not in use.

Fig. 10 *A Lady Writing a Letter with Her Maid*, c. 1670, by Johannes Vermeer, oil on canvas, 71.cm x 60.5cm, National Gallery of Ireland, Dublin, presented, Sir Alfred and Lady Beit, 1987 (Beit Collection)

Looking at sculpture

Sculpture had a major role in Western culture. The great sculptural figures of Ancient Greece and Rome (Fig. 11) were an important influence on the development of Renaissance art. In addition, architectural sculpture was one of the main forms of monumental religious art (Fig. 12) in Europe.

Fig. 11 *Apollo Belvedere*, Vatican Museum, Rome. Pope Julius II had this and other Roman statues transferred to the Vatican, where it has remained since at least 1508. The god Apollo moves forward majestically. He seems to have just released an arrow from the bow that he originally carried in his left hand. The work has been dated to midway through the 2nd century AD but owes its fame to the German art historian Johann Joachim Winckelmann. He believed this statue represented 'the highest ideal of art'.

Great leaders and important events are often commemorated in sculptural works. These works can be interesting, but abstract sculpture allows for a wide variety of thoughts and emotions.

We identify with sculpture in quite a different way compared to painting because it is three-dimensional and more interactive.

Sculpture is bold and noticeable and occupies space in much the same way as humans do (Fig. 13). It changes as we move around it. We can feel its various textures and forms, but each of us sees it in a different way.

Fig. 12 *Ecstasy of Saint Teresa*, 1647–52, by Gian Lorenzo Bernini, Cornaro Chapel, Santa Maria della Vittoria, Rome. Bernini's sculptural group shows a cupid-like angel holding an arrow. Teresa herself collapses, overcome with the feeling of God's love. Her body appears to have dissolved into the twisting folds of the drapery. Despite being made of heavy marble, saint and angel, set upon a cloud, appear to float weightlessly.

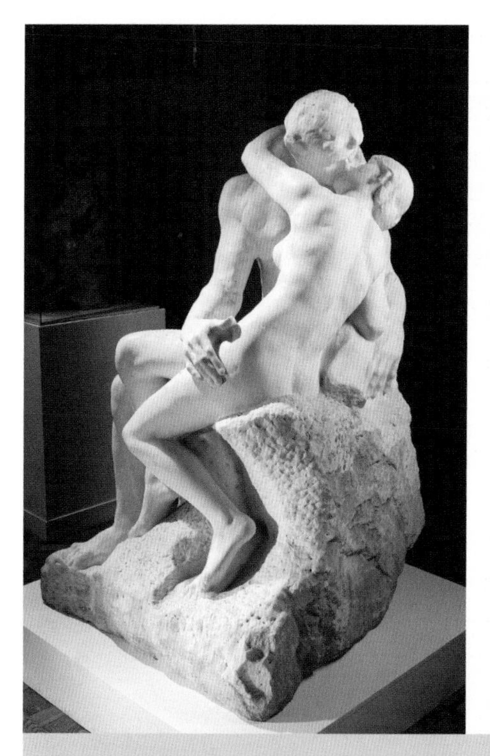

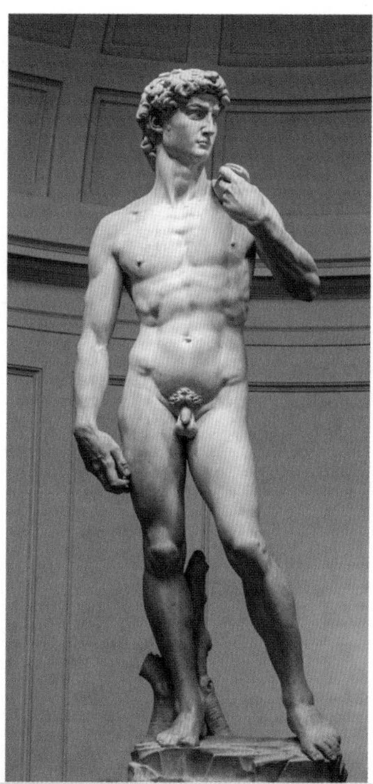

Fig. 13 (left) *The Kiss*, 1889, by Auguste Rodin, Musée Rodin, Paris. This work shows Rodin's unique ability to express intense emotion through the medium of sculpture.

Fig. 14 (centre) *David*, 1501, by Michelangelo, Galleria dell'Accademia, Florence. Michelangelo was only 26 years old when he carved the statue of David. The Renaissance sculpture is 4.2 metres high and depicts the biblical hero David, represented as a standing male nude. Originally commissioned for one of the niches in the Cathedral of Florence, it was carved from a single block of marble.

Fig. 15 (right) *Cantoria* (detail), 1431–8, by Luca della Robbia, marble relief for the Cathedral of Santa Maria dell Fiore, Florence. This is an organ loft, called a cantoria. Ten low relief panels are set in two rows. They depict boys and girls and little putti (winged cherubs or cupids) singing in harmony, playing instruments and dancing. To show perspective, the artist carved the foreground figures well out from the background and barely raised those behind.

Traditional sculpture

Form

In the past there were only two forms of sculpture:

* Sculpture in the round, also called freestanding (Fig. 14)
* Relief sculpture, which remained attached to a solid background (Fig. 15)

Techniques

Sculptors used only three main techniques:

* Carving
* Modelling
* Casting

Characteristics

The following were the main characteristics of sculpture:

* It was the only three-dimensional art form.
* It was representational (it was about something).
* It was an art of solid form. Empty spaces did not have a role in and of themselves.
* It had no moving parts.

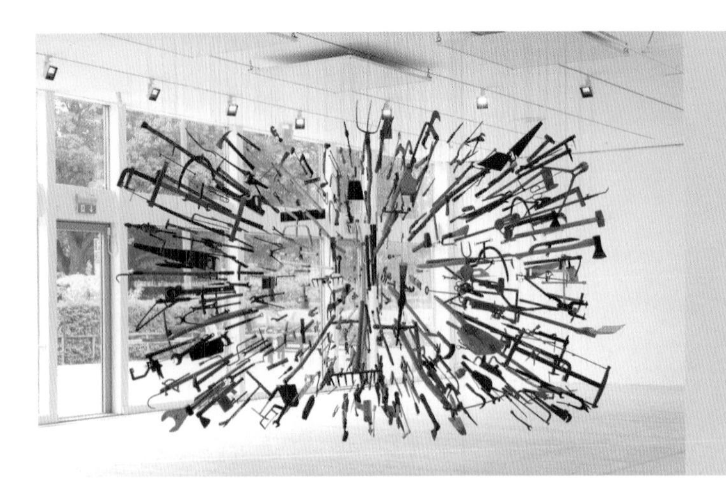

Fig. 16
Controller of the Universe, 2007, Damián Ortega, found tools and wire, Malmö Konsthall. During a stay in Berlin, the artist collected various tools in the city's flea markets. These are assembled in an installation of free-floating objects. The arrangement of the tools follows the idea of an exploded drawing. Each element seems to be propelled outwards from an invisible centre into the surrounding space.

Modern and contemporary sculpture

Today's sculptural concepts, materials or methods of production are free from the restrictions of the past.

Contemporary sculpture is often abstract and uses negative space in interesting and imaginative ways (Fig. 16).

It is often capable of movement. As well as being carved, modelled or cast, it can be assembled, glued, projected or constructed in a wide variety of ways.

How to look at sculpture

As with painting, having the tools and vocabulary to describe sculpture will help you to look at it with a more critical and appreciative eye.

Elements of sculpture

The two main elements of sculpture are mass and space.

* Mass is the actual solid bulk of the sculpture.
* Space is the air around it.

Some sculptors focus on mass. Others are more concerned with how it relates to the space. This space defines the edges of the sculpture and can be enclosed, for example in a hollow.

Fig. 17 *Parachute* by Dorothy Cross, Irish Museum of Modern Art, Dublin. *Parachute* is a good example of bricolage (artwork composed of different and unusual materials that happen to be immediately available). These objects may be considered old, useless, devalued and of no particular value. Cross reclaims these and creates unusual juxtapositions in new and different ways.

Dorothy Cross describes her art objects (in the case of *Parachute*, a dead bird) as 'characters'. What do you think the artist is trying to communicate to us in relation to nature and our role in and with nature?

Surface

A modelled surface can convey strong dark or light effects, almost like a painter uses chiaroscuro.

Light

Light creeping around the edge of a sculpture can produce amazing outlines. Light shining on the

NOTE! To find out more about a piece of art, try looking up the artwork on the museum website. Does knowing more about what the artist had in mind help you to appreciate the work?

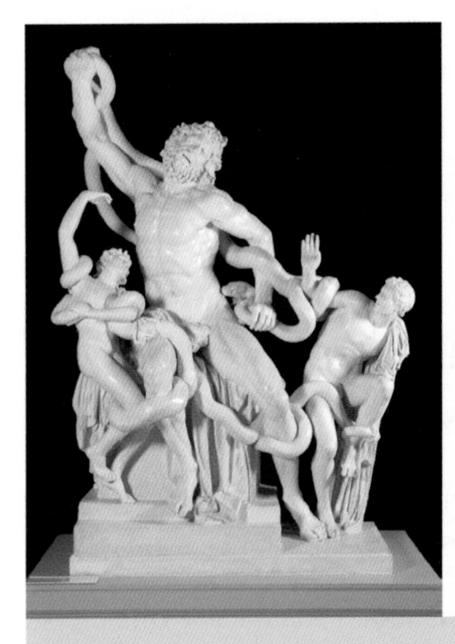

Fig. 18 (left) *The Laocoön and His Sons*, plaster casts by Antonio Canova, c. 1816 (copy from the Vatican Museums, Rome), 240cm x 141cm x 83cm, Crawford Art Gallery, Cork. The group features Laocoön, the Trojan priest of Apollo, and his sons. They were punished by the gods for warning the city of Troy against the wooden horse of the Greeks.

The statue was found in pieces, with parts of the serpent's coils and the three right arms of the figures missing. It was inaccurately restored in the 16th century.

These restorations are faithfully preserved in the Crawford cast, which was made around 1816 by Canova in the Vatican Museum. The Roman original has since been restored correctly.

Fig. 19 (centre) *Maman*, 1999, by Louise Bourgeois, Tate Modern Gallery, London. The great steel spider is so large that it can only be displayed outside or in a huge industrial-sized building (see Fig. 22.18 in Chapter 22).

It stands on eight slim, sharply pointed legs and has a ribbed spiral body. Standing underneath it, the viewer becomes aware of 17 heavy marble eggs hanging in a meshed sac overhead.

Maman was made for the opening of the Tate Modern in May 2000. It refers to emotional development in relation to motherhood, a central theme in the artist's work.

Fig. 20 (right) *My Bed*, 1998, by Tracey Emin, Tate Modern, London. *My Bed* was made in 1998, when the artist was living in a council flat in Waterloo. It shows her real bed at the time, with every kind of intimate and embarrassing object scattered across the crumpled, stained sheets.

It was made following a traumatic relationship breakdown, but, in her more mature years, Emin sees it as a portrait of a younger woman and reflects on how time affects all of us.

It first displayed at the Tate in 1999, when it was nominated for the Turner Prize. It was considered very shocking and attracted scores of visitors to the museum. It was bought by a private collector but is now on permanent loan to the Tate.

surface can bring out beautiful, exquisite colours, even on a plain surface.

Changes of light make outdoor sculpture all the more exciting, but in a museum it entirely depends on the curator's choice of lighting.

Touch

Textures in sculpture greatly appeal to the sense of touch, helping us to interact with it in a tactile way.

Sculptural works

Look at and evaluate the various sculptural works shown here from different times and places. Use some of the headings and questions in the next section to help with your analysis.

Key questions to ask when looking at sculpture

* **Subject:** What is the subject of this sculpture? What is happening in the work? What might it represent?
* **Form:** Does this sculpture have a strong presentation? Why do you think this? Does it look best directly from the front? Would it look good from different sides? Where do you see angles? Is the work well lit? Is the lighting picking up the subtleties of the surface?
* **Context or location:** Do you think this work was planned for this space? Would it feel different to look at it in another setting? Can you think of somewhere the work would have more/less impact?
* **Positive and negative space:** How does the sculpture react with the space inside and around it?
* **Scale:** Do you think the size of the sculpture affects the way it is perceived? Would the piece still work at a much larger or a much more intimate scale?
* **Material:** Why do you think the artist chose this material? How have the materials been used? Do you think these decisions affect the content?
* **Function:** Does this sculpture have a purpose or a function?

Writing about art

Writing an art history essay is similar to writing an essay for English or history. It just needs a slightly different approach and different observational skills. You need visual vocabulary to convey visual impressions, but the writing itself can be quite individual.

Planning and writing an art history essay

'It can be argued that the most impressive early tombs in Ireland were passage graves.'

Discuss this statement with reference to **one** named passage grave and **two** other types of named tombs from either the mesolithic or neolithic periods. In your answer, describe and discuss their structure, decoration and location.

and

Briefly discuss what you know about the people who built these tombs and their spiritual beliefs.

Illustrate your answer.

To prepare this essay from the 2014 Higher Level paper, you first need to establish what you need to know and then how to discuss these facts.

Discuss

The task is to **discuss**, so you need to:

* **Explore:** What is the reason? Why did this happen?
* **Study:** Study the facts: who, what, where, when, why and how.

* **Analyse:** What can you conclude from this? What does it mean? Why do you think that?
* **Compare:** Compare by using words like *similarly, likewise, also, like, just as, just like, similar to, the same as, compared to.*
* **Contrast:** Contrast by using words like *however, nevertheless, nonetheless, still, although/even though, though, but, yet, despite/in spite of, in contrast (to)/in comparison, while, whereas, on the other hand, on the contrary.*

Research

Research the facts for your essay by studying the Stone Age in Ireland in this textbook and check the suggested websites for additional information.

You will need to:

* Know **how** people lived in the Neolithic period, **what** we think their spiritual beliefs were and **why** we think that.
* Know **how** Stone Age people developed new technologies that helped their building methods.
* Know **what** structures have survived from this time (tombs).
* Know **where** to find these tombs, **how** they were constructed and **what** function they served.
* Be able to **compare** these tombs.
* Understand **why** passage graves were impressive by examining the location, structure, function and decoration in detail.
* Make notes of the relevant facts.
* Make an essay plan.
* Write the essay.

Planning the essay

* **Read the essay question carefully.** Highlight key words.
* **Identify the task words** of what needs to be done, e.g. discuss, explain, compare.
* **Identify the topic words** that indicate the subject of the essay, e.g. 'the most impressive early tombs in Ireland were passage graves', 'the people who built the tombs and their spiritual beliefs'.
* **Make notes in response to the question.**
* **Develop the key elements of your discussion.** Spend time on this, because it is the backbone of the essay. State it in the introduction and in the main body of the essay. Return to it in the conclusion.
* **Draw sketches.** Decide on the sketches that will best support your points. Sketches generally carry 10 marks (or 5 marks for questions with accompanying illustrations). They should be clearly labelled and annotated. If you like, use different colour pens to create impact.

Writing the essay

The introduction

Your introductory paragraph should accomplish two tasks:

* It should get the reader's interest so that they will want to read more.
* It should let the reader know what the writing is going to be about.

Avoid phrases like:

* I'm not sure about this, but...
* In this essay I will...
* I agree with the statement...

Your opening statement should be strong. For example:

Ireland has a wealth of neolithic and megalithic monuments, ranging from standing stones, dolmens and court cairns to the great burial mounds of Newgrange, Knowth and Dowth at Brú na Bóinne in Co. Meath.

Or quote an opening phrase from the Newgrange website itself:

'Newgrange is a neolithic monument in the Boyne Valley, County Meath. It is the jewel in the crown of Ireland's Ancient East.'

Then continue:

It is the best example of a Stone Age passage tomb in Ireland. It is one of several others in Brú na Bóinne, one of the most remarkable prehistoric sites in Europe.

The exact purpose of the mound is unknown. Little evidence survives, but early records describe the area as the home of the Tuatha Dé Danann, the ancient Irish gods who descended from the skies to inhabit Ireland.

In later generations it was thought to be the burial place of kings, but designs found on the stones also suggest it may relate to the movements of the sun. In other words, it may have been a kind of ancient astrological calendar.

The main body of the essay

Now that your topic has been introduced, you can begin a detailed analysis of **why** 'the most impressive early tombs in Ireland were passage graves'.

Do this in separate points. Give each point a new paragraph. Use headings if you like. Leave a line between each paragraph.

Address the **location**, **structure**, **function** and **decoration** in separate points, but link back at all times to the 'most impressive' theme.

Give general information on Newgrange and emphasise its impressive quality. For example:

Newgrange is the best example of a Stone Age passage tomb in Ireland. The burial mound is 80m in diameter and 13m high. Over 200,000 tons of earth and stone were used in its construction. The people must have also had quite sophisticated boat-building skills because it is thought that the stones were quarried in Wicklow and even in the Mourne Mountains before being transported by sea and upriver.

Lead on to the next paragraph that describes the **location** on a hill overlooking the river (an impressive setting). Describe the bend of the River Boyne. Include a sketch showing the other tombs.

As you go on, your points can become more specific. Outline the **structure** and the skills of corbel vaulting, the passage, etc. Make sketches.

Continue with the **function**, e.g. calendar, burial site, the roof box and the winter solstice. Make sketches.

Move on to a detailed account of the **decoration**. Give several examples of the 'impressive' art found on the stones. Write about at least three in detail and make sketches.

Use words or phrases at the start of each paragraph that show your reader how it relates to the previous paragraph. Use words like *however*, *in addition to* and *nevertheless*.

Provide supporting evidence for each point that you make – in other words, **why** this is so.

Revisit the theme ('the most impressive early tombs in Ireland were passage graves') and find other ways to express it. This emphasises how the question is being addressed.

Briefly compare the great burial tombs to the more basic structures of the dolmen and court cairn somewhere in the body of the essay.

The conclusion

Summarise the main ideas.

Finish with an interesting or thought-provoking, but relevant, comment. For example:

The art of Newgrange took time and effort to carve, so it must have had deep significance for the artists and those around them. It is certainly likely that this related to spiritual beliefs, but we know so little about the language and lives of the people that we can only guess at its meaning. However, this makes it all the more impressive, and as we look at those silent stones, we can begin to imagine what the people might have believed.

Check your essay!

* Does it show understanding of the question?
* Does it adequately discuss the topic?
* Does it address part (b) of the question?
* Does it show knowledge of the subject matter?
* Does it convey enthusiasm for the subject?
* Does it use references well without using chunks of text directly from the sources?
* Does it express ideas fluently, imaginatively and in an individual way?
* Does it include sketches that support your points?

Writing about art

Formal analysis

This may sound intimidating, but exam questions commonly ask you to discuss a statement referring to subject, style, colour, etc.

Analysis of the visual elements is simply writing about what you can see. You also need some knowledge of the subject, but your focus should be on the visual elements. These are aspects like line, colour, composition and style, and a description of the effects that these have on the viewer.

Each point should tie back to the overall theme of the essay.

Note how the following paragraphs respond to a question from the Higher Level paper from 2014.

'Giotto (c.1267–1337) created an illusion of depth on a flat surface and portrayed dramatic events as if they were happening on a stage.'

Discuss this statement with reference to a named work by Giotto, commenting on subject matter, composition, style and the techniques used in his work.

Sample answer:

In The Lament for Christ, *Giotto used dramatic foreshortening, correct proportions and a balanced composition to present lifelike figures set against a realistic background.*

Skilled use of light and shade makes the figures look real and three-dimensional, but the characters have individual facial expressions and gestures. They are like actors in a silent drama and show real and deep human emotion.

These grief-stricken friends and apostles of Jesus are gathered around to mourn his death after he has been removed from the cross. In the sky above, angels wring their hands and cry out in grief. This focuses even more attention on the scene.

The angels would have probably been even more prominent originally against the blue of the sky, but the colour has faded somewhat because Giotto used azurite rather than the more expensive lapis lazuli to make blue. This was not compatible with lime in the wet plaster and was applied dry, or a secco.

The hills, trees and rocks in the background, however, create the impression of real depth in the scene, like a backdrop on a stage. The composition has been cleverly organised so that the slope of the hill brings the eye directly to Christ's head, which is cradled so gently in the arms of his mother. This sharp diagonal line of the hill is balanced on the left by two upright figures. Two other figures in the foreground sit with their backs towards us. This

has the effect of excluding us, the viewer, from the intimate group. At the same time, though, it draws our eye around the mourners. Like the audience at a drama, we are observers, not partakers in the scene.

The answer includes a description of the work, but this is balanced by the use of the vocabulary of artistic techniques and visual elements. It also addresses the effect of these artistic techniques on the viewer.

Note in particular how the **main theme** of the essay – 'a drama on a stage' – acts as the driving force behind all the descriptive observations.

Comparative analysis

Comparisons of two works of art often appear as exam questions. Begin with these questions:

* What aspects of the two works stand out?
* Are the characteristics similar in both?

Your answer will typically start with the similarities:

* Are the two works by the same artist?
* Are the two works made of similar materials?
* Are they alike in style and approach?
* Are they from the same period of art history?
* Do they depict the same subject?

Indicate how differences in style between the two works can highlight the difference between periods of art history.

Writing an art appreciation essay

The most popular essay topic is probably a visit to an art exhibition or gallery.

Sample question

'Architecture, floor plan, lighting and display techniques all influence the overall visitor experience and appreciation of works of art in a gallery or museum.'

Discuss this statement with reference to a named gallery or museum you have visited. Describe in detail **two** named works you found interesting and discuss how these works were displayed.

and

In your opinion, briefly outline **two** initiatives that would encourage young people to engage with works of art on display in museums or galleries.

Illustrate your answer.

Introduction

The introduction to this question could begin with something quite straightforward like:

I visited the National Gallery of Ireland in Dublin recently with my teacher and our art class. I had really hoped to be able to see a wide variety of art, but unfortunately the main building is closed for renovation. As it turned out, this made the visit more interesting and enjoyable because although we saw quite a small number of works, we looked at them in great detail. We were also not as tired because we didn't have to walk through so many floors.

Main body

Our visit was concentrated in the Millennium Wing of the gallery. This bright, new, modern building won architectural awards when it was designed in 2002. The extension, which fronts onto Clare Street, was constructed in high-quality white concrete and adds a good deal of extra space to the gallery. It provided suites for the permanent collection and exhibitions, as well as a gallery shop and café.

The first thing I noticed was a most impressive long white staircase. This takes visitors to the galleries on the first floor, but it also creates an air of grandeur and expectation. Upstairs the rooms are divided between the European collection in part of the older building and the Irish collection in the new extension. I was delighted to leave my coat and bag downstairs in the cloakroom and noted that one could also access the galleries by the lift.

Continue with a description of the layout of the works. Mention the rooms and the lighting, and describe how the work is displayed based on your own individual experience:

I found low lighting made the rooms very peaceful and created a special atmosphere. In fact, I entirely forgot that it was artificial light because it allowed me to look at the works in such detail.

The time passed quickly as I wandered from room to room. Sometimes I sat for a while in front of the paintings on the long leather seats with my friends to enjoy works by Irish artists such as William Orpen, Paul Henry, William Leech and Jack B. Yeats. The European works included Impressionism and Post-Impressionism by artists such as Claude Monet, Auguste Renoir and Vincent van Gogh, but for me, two paintings really stood out.

One of those was Ecce Homo *by the Renaissance artist Titian from Venice. I found this image of a gentle Christ bound, tortured, beaten and crowned with thorns very moving. I was interested to learn that Titian painted it when he was almost 80.*

The soft painterly textures and feathery brushstrokes bring this painting to life. The artist used transparent coloured glazes to create an almost translucent effect, and the bright yellow glow behind Jesus' head places his face in shadow. The downcast eyes show his sorrow and torment, but the brightness of the halo suggests that while the human body is easily destroyed, the spirit cannot be reached so easily.

The essay should continue with a description of how the painting was displayed in the room itself, the space between other paintings, wall colour, etc.

Another example should be analysed in the same way.

Initiatives to engage young people

The second part of the question offers you a chance to put some individual ideas forward. Try to think of some imaginative ways to interest young people. Would written questions or drawings help? Or would a phone app or a short audio visual presentation be better? What do you think?

Conclusion

The essay should conclude with one or two sentences that bring the points together nicely.

Always emphasise your personal response to art.

Chapter review

* Taking the time to learn the elements and language of art can completely change your experience of it. What are the important art elements of painting and sculpture?
* A significant part of your art history exam must focus on facts, elements of art and the analysis of a work of art, but never lose sight of your own reaction to art. Have you included your own special and individual enthusiasm?

FURTHER RESEARCH

www.wga.hu – Caravaggio

www.wga.hu – Vermeer

www.crawfordartgallery.ie – Greco-Roman Sculpture

www.imma.ie – Dorothy Cross

www.tate.org.uk – Louise Bourgeois

www.traceyeminstudio.com – My Bed returns to Tate Britain for the first time in 15 years

www.nationalgallery.ie – A Connemara Village by Paul Henry

www.crawfordartgallery.ie – The Goldfish Bowl by Walter Osborne

www.youtube.com – Hughie O'Donoghue: One Hundred Years and Four Quarters at Galway International Arts Festival 2016

www.imma.ie – Hughie O'Donoghue

alicemaher.com – Alice Maher's Materials

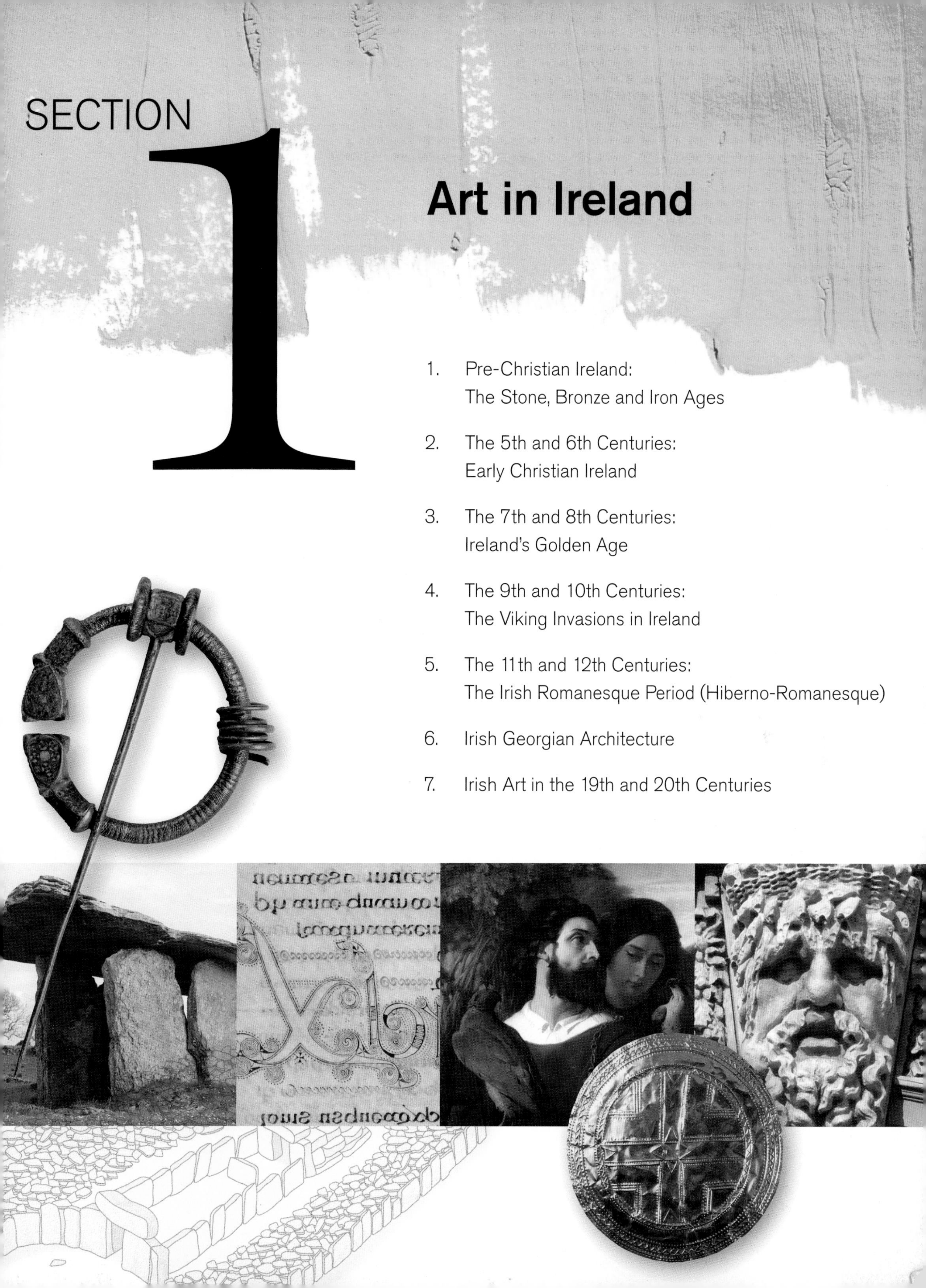

SECTION 1

Art in Ireland

Chapter 1

Pre-Christian Ireland: The Stone, Bronze and Iron Ages

Most art in pre-Christian Ireland was abstract. It reflected the technical, social and intellectual developments of the time. The pace of change in art and technology was slow at first. It took 7,000 years from the arrival of the first Stone Age people for metal technology to be developed in Ireland with the introduction of copper and bronze, another 1,500 years for iron technology to arrive, and 500 years for the major social and intellectual changes that came with Christianity.

One can see the increasing pace of change as each major technical and cultural innovation was built on the knowledge and experience of previous generations.

1. The Stone Age (10,500–2000 BC)

Human settlement began in Ireland around 10,500 BC, during the palaeolithic period of the Stone Age. (Research published in 2016 put the confirmed date of human activity in Ireland back 2,500 years earlier than had previoulsy been thought.) The earliest people were hunter-gatherers.

Neolithic: The New Stone Age (neolithic) was from 3700 to 2000 BC in Ireland. The word comes from the Greek words *neo*, meaning 'new', and *lithos*, meaning 'stone'. It refers to the time when farming and tool-making evolved and people began to settle in permanent communities.

Arrival of the first builders

Stone Age structures (architecture)

The works of art and construction that survive from the Stone Age are generally associated with ritual sites and places of importance to these first Irish people. Little evidence of their everyday lives or language survives, but we can find remains of the tombs they built to glorify their dead. They had

By the end of this chapter, I will...

* Be able to draw and describe a dolmen, a court cairn and a passage mound.
* Know the elements of Stone Age designs and techniques.
* Be able to draw and describe the entrance stone at Newgrange and a few other objects.
* Have opinions that I can back up on the meaning of Stone Age structures and designs.

enough spare time to think out, plan and build large structures, which can still dominate their local landscape.

Megalithic: Comes from the Greek words *mega*, meaning 'large', and *lithos*, meaning 'stone'. Megalithic builders used large stones to construct their tombs and monuments.

Stone Age technology

NOTE! Wood and stone were the only materials available for building and making tools and weapons during the Stone Age. Some hard stones, like flint, could be broken and shaped to produce sharp edges that could be used as knives, scrapers, chisels, axes, spears and arrowheads.

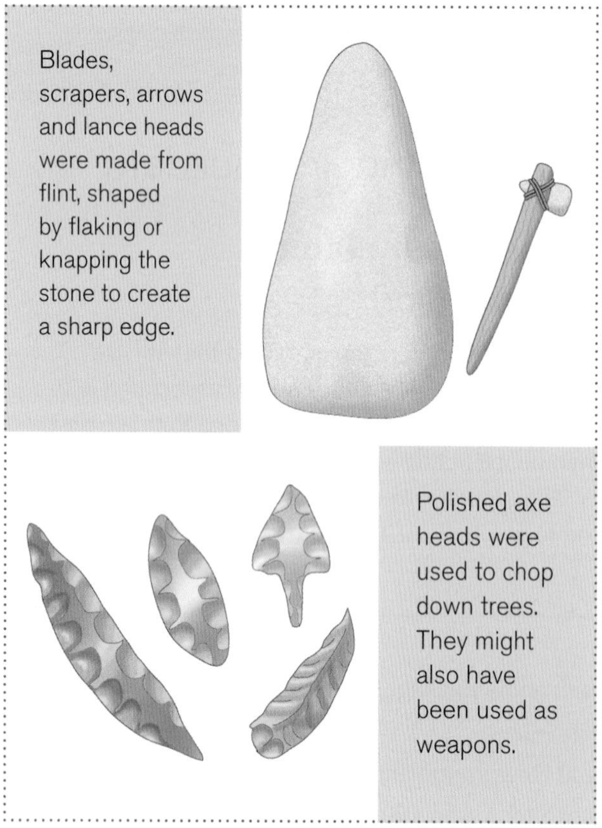

Blades, scrapers, arrows and lance heads were made from flint, shaped by flaking or knapping the stone to create a sharp edge.

Polished axe heads were used to chop down trees. They might also have been used as weapons.

Fig. 1.1 Stone Age tools and weapons

Fig. 1.2 Examples of Stone Age pottery

Pottery

Clay was dug and built into a variety of simple pots, which were probably fired on an open fire (Fig. 1.2).

Houses

Domestic buildings were generally round in plan. They were probably made with stone, wood and mud, with thatched roofs.

NOTE! Stones for large structures would have been moved by dragging and levering, possibly using logs as rollers to ease the progress of the largest stones. Beasts of burden and the wheel were not yet available.

Burial structures and monuments

Dolmens

Dolmens were the simplest megalithic structures. They were identified as tombs because human remains from cremations and burials were found within them, along with some Stone Age artefacts.

The stones at the back of the tombs are generally lower than those at the front. Some archaeologists believe that this suggests the capstones may have been dragged up an earthen ramp to rest on the uprights. There are dramatic examples at

Poulnabrone in the Burren in Co. Clare and at Kilcooley in Co. Donegal. There are 170 or so portal dolmens in Ireland (Fig. 1.3).

Dolmens are constructed of between three and seven stone legs supporting one or two large capstones. They are also known as portal dolmens because the entrance can look like a doorway (from the Latin *porta*, for 'gate').

Fig. 1.3 Poulnabrone portal dolmen in the Burren, Co. Clare

Court cairns

The covered chamber was sometimes divided by upright stones and sills or lintels, creating 'doorways' between spaces. Outside, a semi-circular area created a formal entrance or ceremonial area (Fig. 1.4).

Court cairn: A combination of a burial chamber inside a mound or cairn of stones with an open court in front of it.

NOTE! Dolmens and court cairns have no added decoration, but they were built as the result of an idea, which puts them in the realm of art.

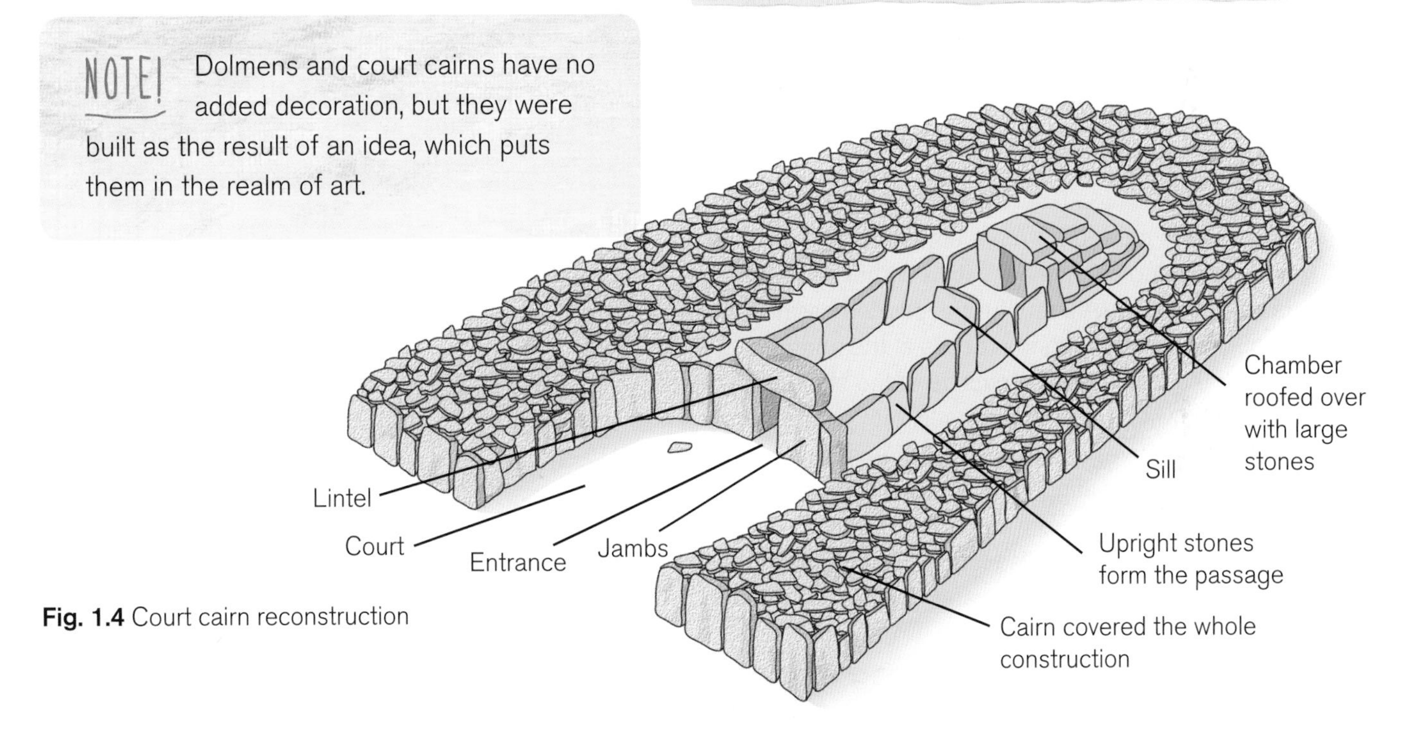

Fig. 1.4 Court cairn reconstruction

Passage mounds (graves)

There is a growing preference for the term *passage mound* rather than *passage grave* as the understanding of their function grows. There are over 200 known passage mounds in Ireland, in a variety of layouts and sizes. Many have decorated stones as part of their construction. There is a concentration of these structures in Co. Meath, particularly at Brú na Bóinne, an area 4km long and 3km wide that is enclosed by a bend in the River Boyne in Co. Meath. The site is 8km east of the town of Drogheda, 40km north of Dublin (Fig. 1.5). There are close to 40

Passage mounds are made by building a stone-lined passage, sometimes with a chamber at the end, and covering it with a mound of earth and stones.

mounds in this area, including three large mounds at Knowth, Dowth and Newgrange, with smaller satellite tombs surrounding them.

Knowth (c. 4000 BC)

The oldest and largest of these mounds is at Knowth (Fig. 1.6). It has two passages, one facing east and one facing west. It is surrounded by a kerb of 127 large stones, most of which are decorated. The mound covers an area of 1.5 acres and is the largest man-made roofed structure from the Stone Age in Western Europe (Fig. 1.7).

The western passage is 34m long and is of the undifferentiated type, that is, there is no clearly separate chamber at the end of the passage. A basin stone with remains of cremation burials and some grave goods were found in the passage. The grave goods included stone balls and pendants, coloured beads, shell necklaces and stone tools such as arrowheads, knives, chisels and scrapers. A number of the orthostats (upright stones) in the passage are decorated.

The eastern passage is more elaborate. At 40m long, it has a cruciform chamber with a corbelled vault 7m tall at the centre. A beautifully decorated basin stone (Fig. 1.8) was found in the recess at the northern side of the chamber. The outside of the stone is decorated with horizontal grooves, with concentric circles and curves at the centre. Inside it is decorated with arcs and radiating lines. A mace head carved from a piece of flint from the Orkney Islands off the coast of Scotland was also found (Fig. 1.9 and 1.10). It is a remarkably well-made and finely finished piece

Fig. 1.6 Aerial view of Knowth

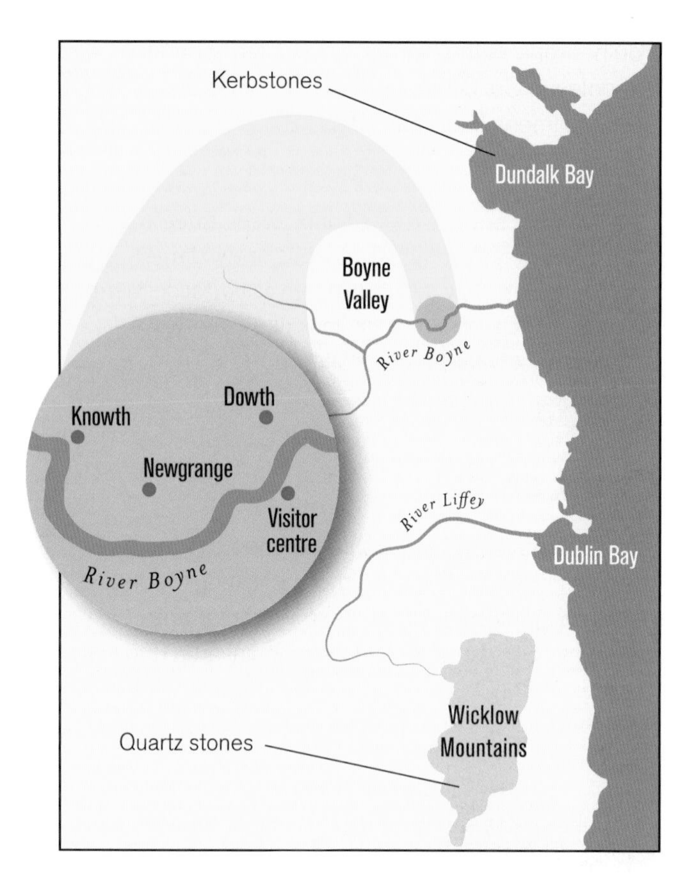

Fig. 1.5 Brú na Bóinne, Co. Meath

Basin stone: A large, almost circular, low profile stone hollowed out to create a kind of basin. They seem to have been used in passages to hold the cremated remains of the dead and small offerings.

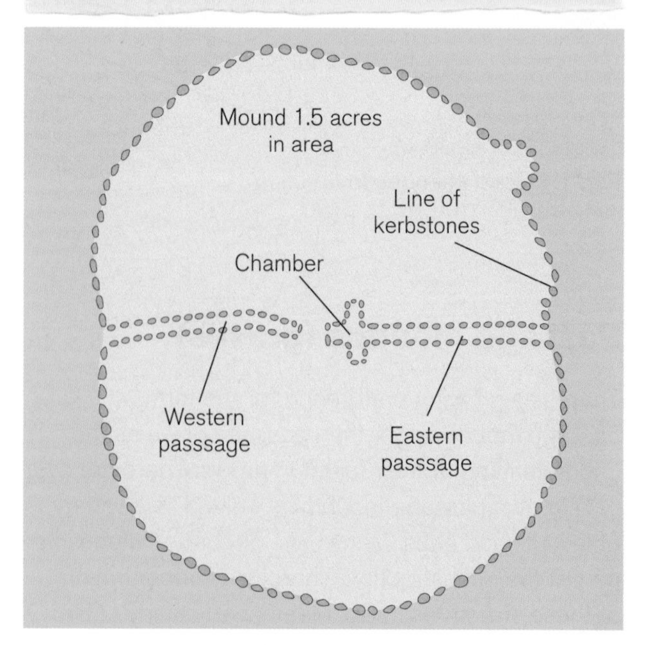

Fig. 1.7 Plan of Knowth

Fig. 1.8 Knowth basin stone

Kerbstones: The large stones laid end to end surrounding the base of many of the passage tombs. Some of these stones are 3m to 4m long and over 1m high. The kerb may have been laid out to define the shape of the mound and to retain the filling material that formed the mound.

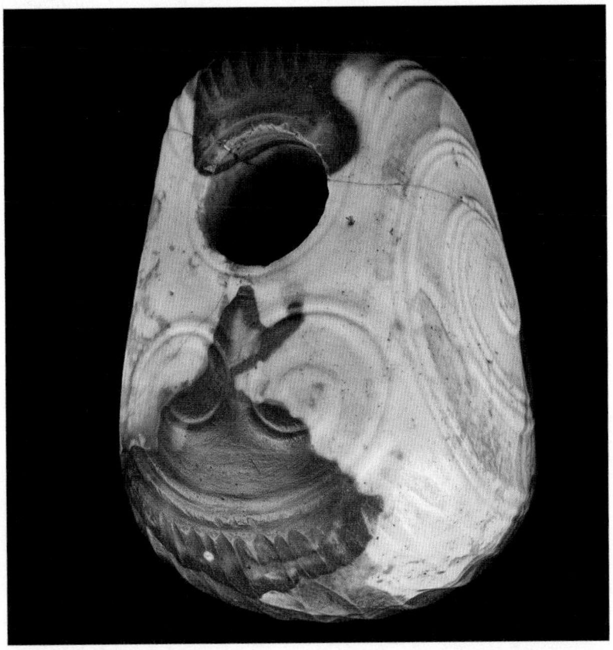

Fig. 1.9 Knowth mace head, carved from flint

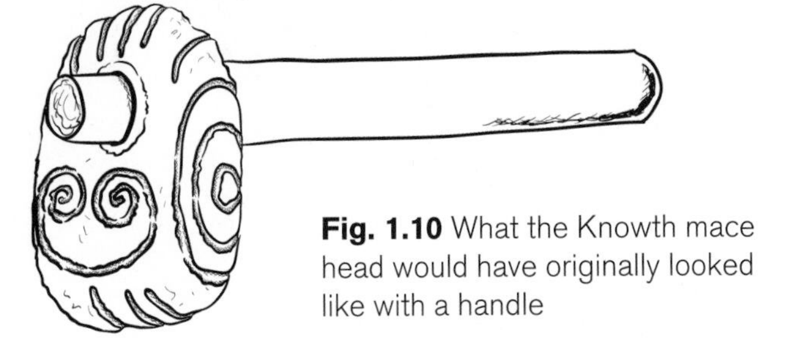

Fig. 1.10 What the Knowth mace head would have originally looked like with a handle

for such an early date. A mace is a type of hammer, so the heavy end is at the bottom. This mace has often been illustrated upside down because it looks a bit like a face from that angle.

White quartz stones are laid on the ground in front of the eastern entrance, creating a ceremonial or restricted area. This is a different interpretation of the purpose of the quartz stones to the arrangement made at Newgrange during its construction.

Many of the kerbstones that surround the base of the mound at Knowth are elaborately decorated with patterns that have been interpreted as relating to the phases of the moon and movements of the planets.

Dowth (c. 3200 BC)

Dowth has not been thoroughly excavated yet, but it has two passages facing west. One is a short passage with a circular chamber. The other has a longer passage with a cruciform chamber containing a large basin stone. There are many decorated stones in this mound as well. We will know more when a complete survey has been done.

Newgrange (c. 3200 BC)

The most famous of the Boyne Valley mounds is noted for the following.

* The 'roof box' over its entrance allows the sun to shine down the long passage into the furthest recesses of the chamber (a total of 24m) on the days around 21 December (the midwinter solstice, the shortest day) each year. Between the first and second roof slabs of the passage, over the entrance, is the rectangular opening built in stone, which forms the roof box. The upper lintel stone of this opening is carved to a depth of about 2mm with a series of triangles, which create a pattern of raised X shapes separated by vertical lines. The large flat slab of stone seen beside the entrance was used to block it, so the light box was the only source of light inside.
* The passage, which is 18.7m long, is formed by upright stones: 22 on the left (west) side and 21 on the right (east) side. These uprights are roofed with flat stones near the entrance and then a corbelled section at the chamber end.

* The chamber is roughly 6m in diameter and 6m tall. It has three recesses, which create a cruciform plan like the east passage at Knowth. There is a basin stone in each of the recesses, which contained ash from human cremations.

Newgrange was built about 3200 BC. It was excavated from 1967 to 1975, when it was reconstructed into the shape that we see today.

The wall of white quartz stones and grey, water-worn granite stones stands on the row of kerbstones at the front of the structure. The quartz came from Wicklow, 80km away, and the granite beach stones came from Dundalk Bay, which is 50km away.

The white stones were arranged as we see them today on the instructions of Professor O'Kelly, the chief archaeologist. Based on his research, he imagined that the mound had been built with a facing of white and grey stones when it was first constructed. There is some dispute about this theory and the archaeologists at Knowth came to a different conclusion.

What do you think the Stone Age builders intended by using the quartz stones?

* Ninety-seven kerbstones surround the base of the mound at Newgrange. Many have decorations, ranging from simple lines and spirals to fully decorated stones like the beautifully patterned entrance stone (Fig. 1.12) and kerbstone 52 on the opposite side of the mound. The kerbstones near the entrance are the largest – they are between 3m and 4m long and 1.2m high. They are greywacke stone, which is found at Clogherhead, Co. Louth, about 30km away. The 97 stones had to be transported by boat or raft along the coast and up the Boyne River to a point near Newgrange and then moved uphill to the site.

Fig. 1.12 Newgrange entrance stone and light box

Fig. 1.11 Newgrange

* The Great Circle is a ring of standing stones that surrounds the mound, 7m to 12m outside it. Only 12 undecorated stones remain standing out of the original 35. This ring of standing stones may be more modern than the mound, possibly from the Bronze Age.

Construction

The mound at Newgrange is 11m tall and between 79m and 85m in diameter.

Building large structures like this was a heroic task for Stone Age people. Their technology was limited to what they could carry, pull or lever into place, yet they moved large stones up to five tons in weight across country that may have been forested.

Layout

Construction probably began with the layout of the passages, as their orientation to the sun or moonlight was an essential part of the purpose of the structure. The line of the kerb would need to be laid out early on, as it was the retaining structure for the stones, sods and earth that made up the body of the mound. The corbelled roof over the chamber might have been constructed as the level of the mound built up, allowing access to gradually higher levels.

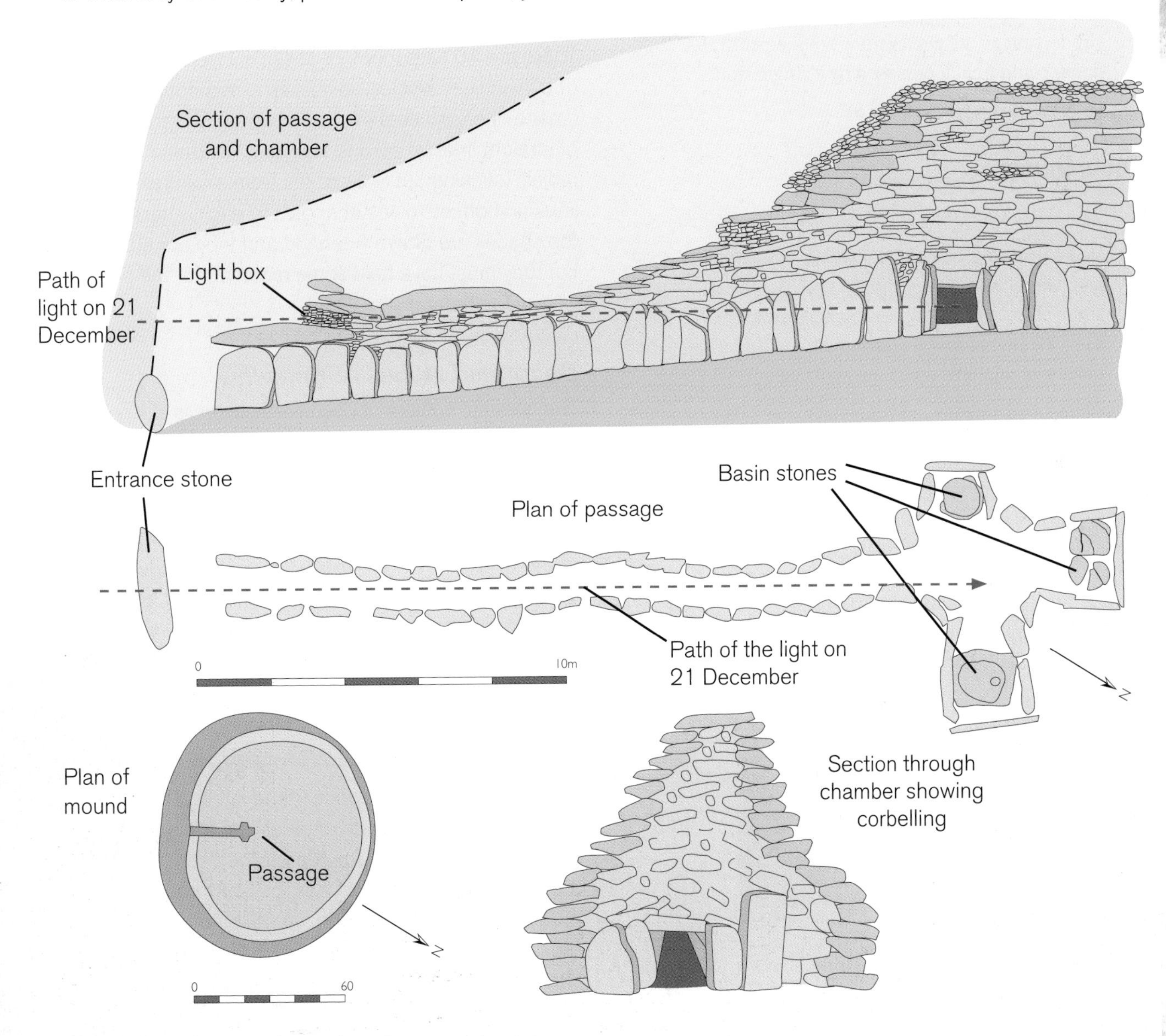

Fig. 1.13 Newgrange plan and section

Corbelling

These corbelled chambers are the oldest roofed structures still standing in Western Europe.

At Newgrange, grooves were cut in the top surface of the stones to help shed any water that might have trickled down into the mound. This outward lean of the stones would also help to distribute the weight away from the centre, thus reducing the risk of a collapse (Fig. 1.13).

Corbelled vaults were built on the standing stones of the chamber in gradually decreasing circles of large flat stones sloping slightly outwards. These rings of stones became self-supporting as the circles grew smaller, until the dome could finally be closed by a single stone.

Techniques

Stone dressing: Most of the stones at Knowth and Newgrange have been dressed, that is, a stone chisel or point driven by a hammer was used to remove rough areas and to take away a thin layer of stone and improve its colour.

Incision: Simple cuts or deep scratches are made in the less elaborately carved stones.

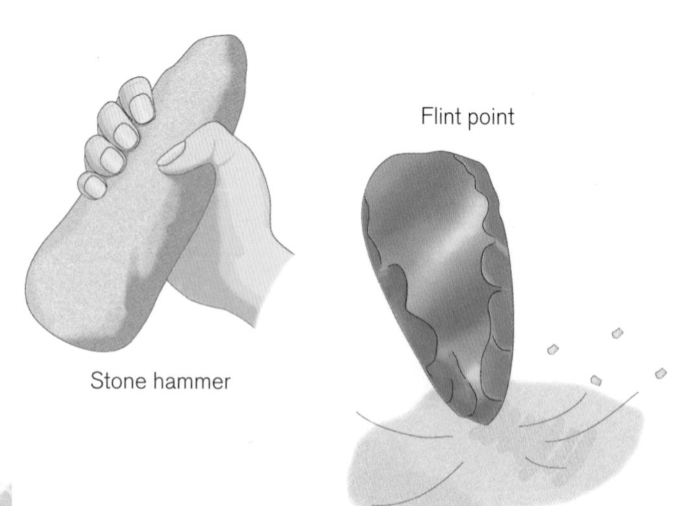

Fig. 1.14 Chip carving

Chip carving

The lines and patterns on the stones were made by cutting into the stone with a sharp flint or obsidian edge, or by picking or pecking with a stone chisel or point driven by a hammer (Fig. 1.14). This technique was used to create areas of low relief.

Smoothing

The surface of the stones sometimes may have been smoothed out by hammering or by rubbing with a rough-textured stone. The lines on the entrance stone at Newgrange were smoothed and deepened in this way.

Decoration

There are 10 categories of designs. Five are made of curved lines: circles, spirals, arcs, serpentiniforms (snake-like) and dots in circle shapes. Five are made of straight lines: chevrons, lozenges (diamond shapes), radials (sticking out like spokes from a centre), parallel lines and offsets (lines at angles to each other). All the shapes are drawn freehand and they are abstract, but they must have held some meaning for the people who made them (Fig. 1.15).

Decorated stones at Knowth

The greatest number of decorated stones is at Knowth – about half of all the Stone Age art in Ireland. Many of the 127 stones in the kerb are elaborately patterned. Kerbstone 15, which looks like a sundial, can be interpreted as a lunar calendar recording the phases of the moon (Fig. 1.16). Kerbstone 78 (Fig. 1.18) is also supposed to refer to the phases of the moon. It has a range of designs quite different from kerbstone 15. Wavy lines and circles dominate the pattern, which flows over the whole surface of the stone.

Decorated stones at Newgrange

At Newgrange the entrance stone is covered in a curvilinear pattern, which emphasises the size of the stone. A groove at the top centre lines up with the entrance and the roof box. Left of the groove is a triple spiral and beyond this a series of lozenges covers the end of the stone. Right of the centre, two double spirals sit on top of a wave pattern that connects back to the triple spiral. Lozenges, curves and zigzags cover the right-hand end of the stone.

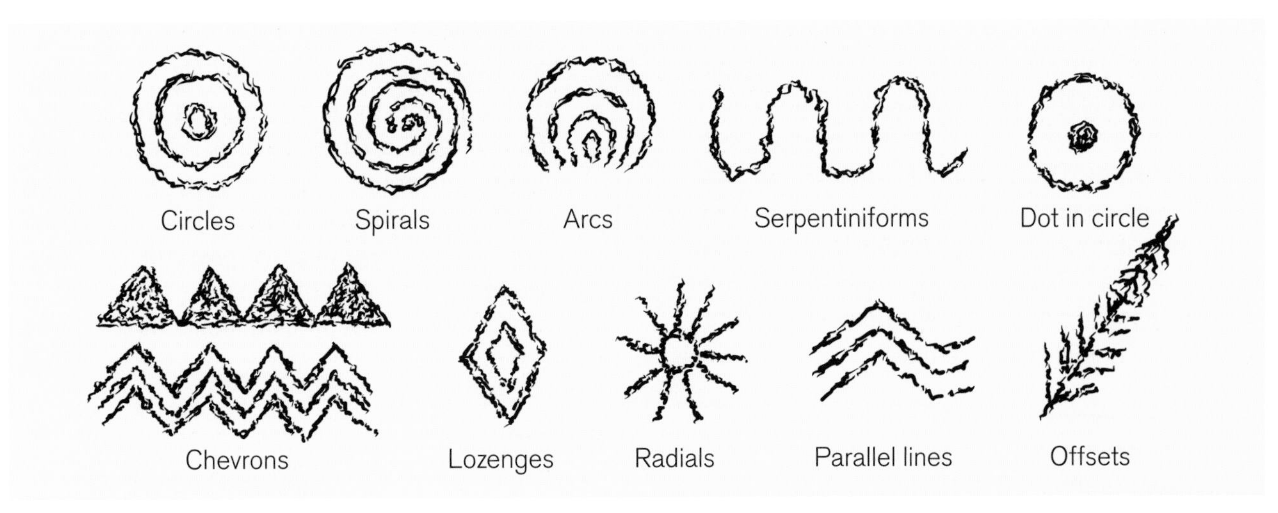

Fig. 1.15 Range of Stone Age designs

Kerbstone 52, on the opposite side of the mound, has a more varied range of patterns. It is divided into two parts by a groove down the centre. The upper half of the left side has a large double spiral and a small spiral and arcs with a cup mark on either side. On the lower part, lozenges have been carved into the surface, leaving raised outlines. A row of chevrons makes a border at the bottom. The right-hand side is dominated by three ovals with alternately raised and hollowed outlines, each with three cup marks across their centres. Series of arcs that connect with these ovals spread over most of the surface of the stone (Fig. 1.17).

Fig. 1.16 Knowth kerbstone 15, the sundial stone

NOTE! Sketching is a good way to help your memory. Practise things like the entrance stone at Newgrange. Begin your sketch with the groove that marks the entrance, near the top centre of the stone. Draw the three spirals to the left, then the group of spirals to the right of the groove. Finally, fill in the lozenges and curves at the ends of the stone. Write notes on your sketches pointing out the important features of the design.

Fig. 1.17 Newgrange kerbstone 52

Interpretation: What was the meaning of passage mounds?

Passage mounds seem to have been so much more than graves for ancestors. The sheer scale of the commitment from the Stone Age people who spent generations constructing them must have made them the most important thing in the lives of the community. They were the largest structures in the country for thousands of years and were the source of legends.

The earliest records describe Brú na Bóinne as the home of the Tuatha Dé Danann, the ancient Irish gods descended from the skies to inhabit Ireland. In later generations they were thought to be the burial places of ancient kings. The number of cremated remains inside the passage mounds is relatively small in relation to the size of the community and the length of time for which the mounds were used. This might mean that only very special members of the community were buried there or that they were ritual or sacrificial burials.

Astronomy

There is a growing body of support for the theory that designs on the stones relate to movements of the sun, moon and planets, which would be a way to keep track of the seasons and important community events. Kerbstones at Knowth in particular can be interpreted as recording lunar events and patterns. A full lunar cycle takes over 18 years, so Stone Age observers must have had ways to remember the phases of the moon.

* The passages at Knowth received the light of the rising and setting sun at the equinoxes, around 21 March and 23 September. The spring and autumn were important seasons for planting and harvesting in a farming community.
* At Newgrange, the light of sunrise enters the chamber on the winter solstice, the shortest day of the year, around 21 December. This may have celebrated the death of the old year and the beginning of the new. Other passage mounds also receive the light of the sun or the moon at significant seasons and are the focus of ongoing research.

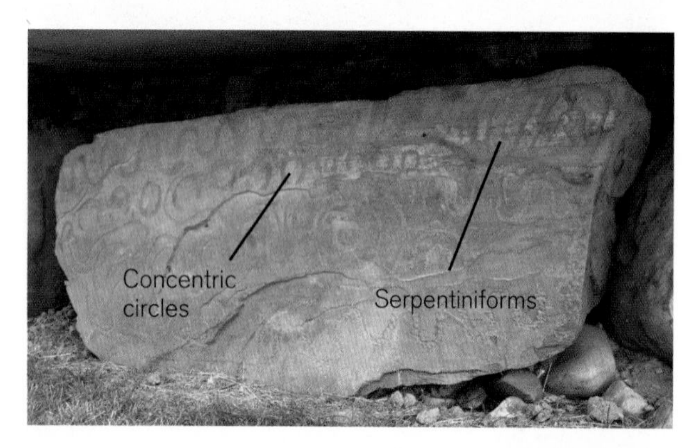

Fig. 1.18 Knowth kerbstone 78

Rituals

Rituals and ceremonies might have been held in procession around the mounds, stopping at significant stones relevant to the season.

NOTE! Areas outside the east and west entrances at Knowth are paved with quartz and granite stones like those on the front of the mound at Newgrange. These areas may have been the focus of ceremonies or they might have marked forbidden areas.

Review

* Based on your observations of Stone Age construction and design, do you think Stone Age people were intelligent and resourceful?
* What motivated Stone Age people to build large structures?
* What range of tools did Stone Age people have? What do you think they used them for?

EXAM QUESTIONS

Ordinary Level (2015)

The site illustrated in Fig. 1.11 is from the neolithic period. Answer (a), (b) and (c).

(a) Name the site.

(b) Describe and discuss the site under the following headings:

- Location
- Structure
- Function

(c) Sketch, describe and discuss the decoration on one of this site's main features.

Illustrate your answer.

Higher Level (2014)

'It can be argued that the most impressive early tombs in Ireland were passage graves.'

Discuss this statement with reference to **one** named passage grave and **two** other types of tombs from either the mesolithic or neolithic periods. In your answer, describe and discuss their structure, decoration and location.

and

Briefly discuss what you know about the people who built these tombs and their spiritual beliefs.

Illustrate your answer.

FURTHER RESEARCH

www.megalithicireland.com

www.sacred-destinations.com/ireland

www.archaeology.ie/nationalmonuments

www.newgrange.com

www.knowth.com

2. The Bronze Age (2500–500 BC)

During the Early Bronze Age, Stone Age culture survived for some time in the south and west of the country, while the Beaker people (so called because of their cremation burials found under upturned 'beaker'-shaped pots – see Fig. 1.19) brought Bronze Age society and technology to the north, east and midlands.

Fig. 1.19 Bronze Age beaker pottery

By the end of this chapter, I will...

* Know what bronze is and how it was made.
* Be able to draw and describe a sun disc, a lunula, a torc, a fibula, a gorget and a lock ring.
* Know the progression of design from the Early to the Late Bronze Age.
* Know the progression of techniques from the Early to the Late Bronze Age.
* Have opinions on Bronze Age craftsmanship that I can back up with facts.

Change in style

The clear differences between mechanically made Bronze Age art and freehand Stone Age art suggest that the people who developed metal technology in Ireland had a different culture than the Stone Age people. The Beaker people originated in mainland

Bronze Age design is the result of combining basic geometric shapes created with a compass and straight edge with the most up-to-date technology of the time. Metal was cast, hammered, twisted and cut to shape to create the range of forms preferred by the Bronze Age artists (Fig. 1.20).

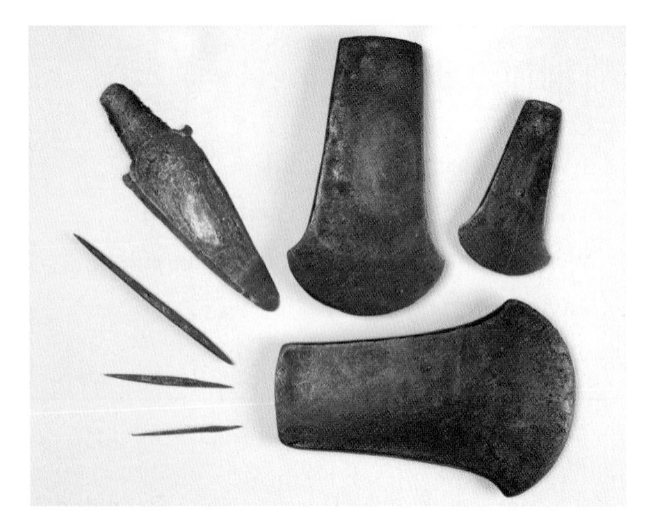

Fig. 1.20 Early Bronze Age objects

Fig. 1.22 Rock art, Derrynablaha, Co. Kerry

Europe and probably came in search of copper and gold deposits. There is certainly evidence of Irish gold and copper being traded into Europe and Britain, which suggests links with the wider European community.

Bronze Age structures (architecture)

Tomb design changed during the Bronze Age. In most of the country the dead were laid to rest in pits or cists. In the West of Ireland, wedge tombs, which were related to the court cairns from the Stone Age, were still being built. None of these burial sites had the drama of the Stone Age monuments.

Ceremonial sites made of circular earthen banks or standing stones and hilltop forts once thought to have been from the Iron Age are now believed to be Bronze Age structures, which continued in use into the Iron Age (Fig. 1.21). Stone carving seems to have been little practised except for a few examples of rock art found in counties Cork, Kerry and Donegal. Designs were very simple, mainly little hollow 'cup marks' surrounded by circles, sometimes with radiating lines (Fig. 1.22). Remains of Bronze Age human settlements (houses and fences) seem to have been made of wood that rotted away over the centuries, though evidence of a widespread population has survived through burial sites and finds of Bronze Age objects.

Metalwork

Mining for gold and copper was carried out at a number of locations in Ireland during the Bronze

Fig. 1.21 Drombeg stone circle, Co. Cork

Age. Evidence of Bronze Age metalworking has been found at Mount Gabriel in Co. Cork, the Vale of Avoca in Co. Wicklow and in the Mourne Mountains.

Low-technology mining

Gold

Gold was probably found in nuggets or by panning alluvial deposits in rivers. In the panning technique, a mixture of sand, gravel and gold particles is dug up from a riverbed and gradually washed with water, leaving the heavier parts (the gold) in the pan while the lighter material is washed away. The gold particles could be melted and cast into suitable-sized pieces to be worked on later.

Copper

Copper was mined by roasting ore-bearing rock with fire and cracking it by throwing cold water on it. The broken stone was then dug out with wooden shovels and crushed with stone hammers. The bits with the highest concentration of copper oxides would be selected and smelted over a charcoal fire. The resulting molten copper was poured into stone or sand moulds and cast into the shapes of axes, knives, sickles or whatever shape was required (Fig. 1.23).

Fig. 1.23 Bronze axe in a stone mould

Bronze is an alloy (mixture) of copper and tin, which is harder than copper and can hold a sharp edge for longer. In Ireland it was made from native copper and tin imported from Cornwall in England.

The Early Bronze Age (2500–1500 BC)

Decorative gold objects

Early Bronze Age objects were made from a single piece of gold, as the technology for joining pieces together with gold solder had not developed yet in Ireland. Craftsmen hammered gold into thin flat sheets and cut it to shape.

Early Bronze Age gold objects were decorated with simple abstract geometric patterns, such as circles, triangles, dots and straight lines. Repeated and combined in various ways, they made up the design repertoire of the first goldsmiths in Ireland (Fig. 1.25).

Tedavent Sun Discs

The Tedavent Sun Discs (Fig. 1.24) from the Early Bronze Age (c. 2000 BC) are circular in shape.

* **Form:** The discs are about 11cm in diameter. They are cut from a thin sheet of beaten gold.
* **Function:** Two holes near the centre suggest that the discs might have been sewn onto a garment or belt. They may have been status or symbolic objects. Gold is often associated with the sun in primitive cultures.
* **Technique:** The design was applied by the repoussé technique.
* **Decoration:** A repeating pattern of ridges, chevrons and dots was made around the perimeter with a cross shape in the centre.

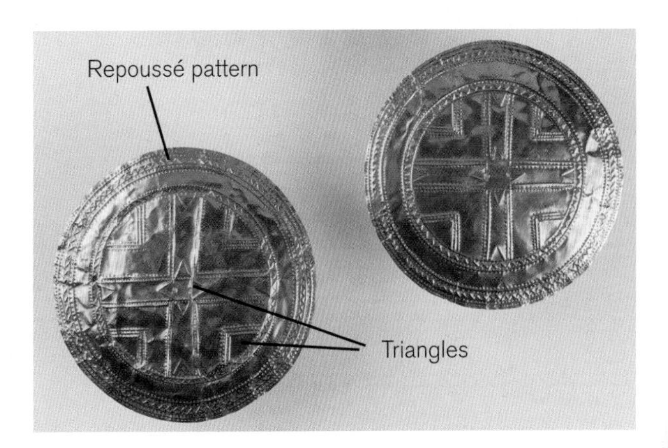

Fig. 1.24 Tedavent Sun Discs from Co. Monaghan

Designs made by incision: cutting into the surface

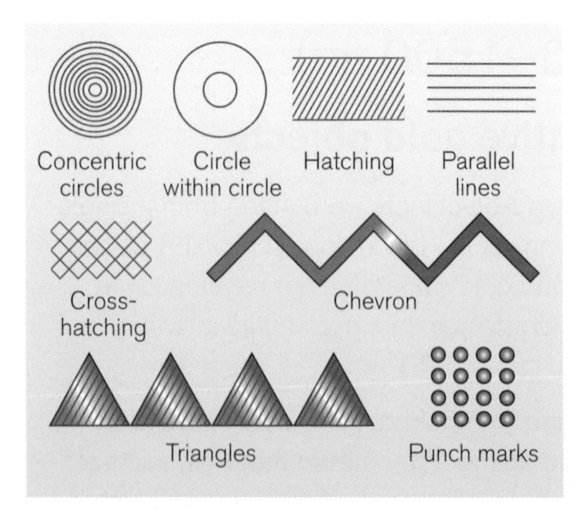

Some combinations of designs

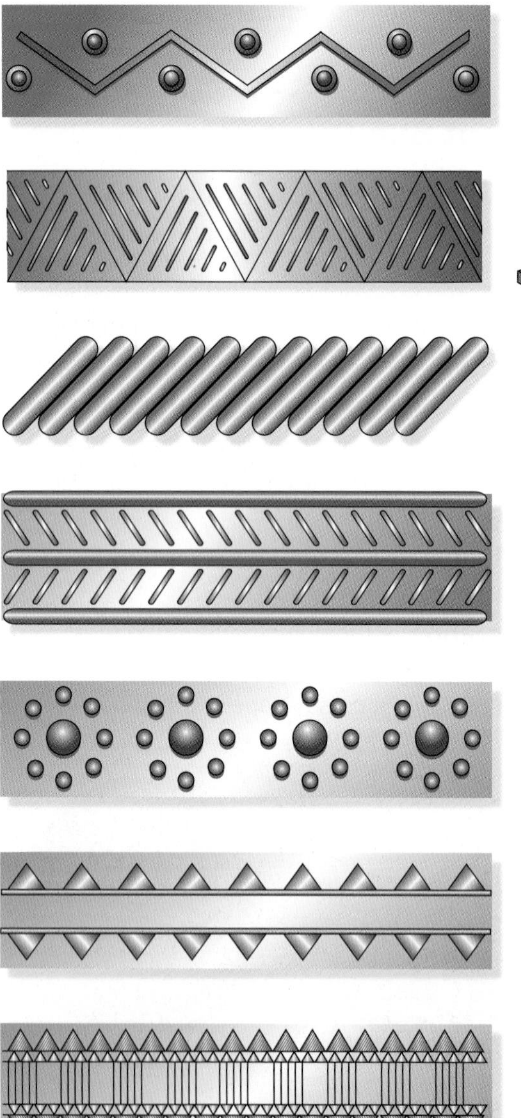

Designs made by the repoussé technique: designs raised on the surface

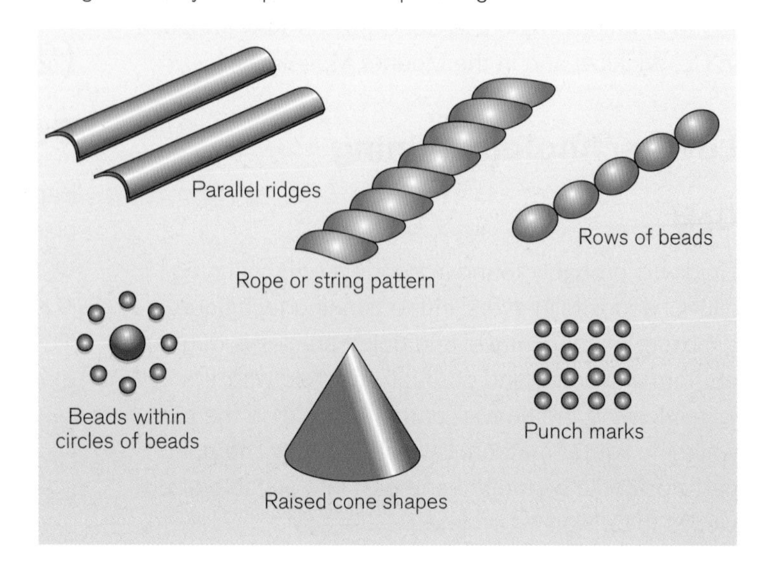

Some combinations of designs

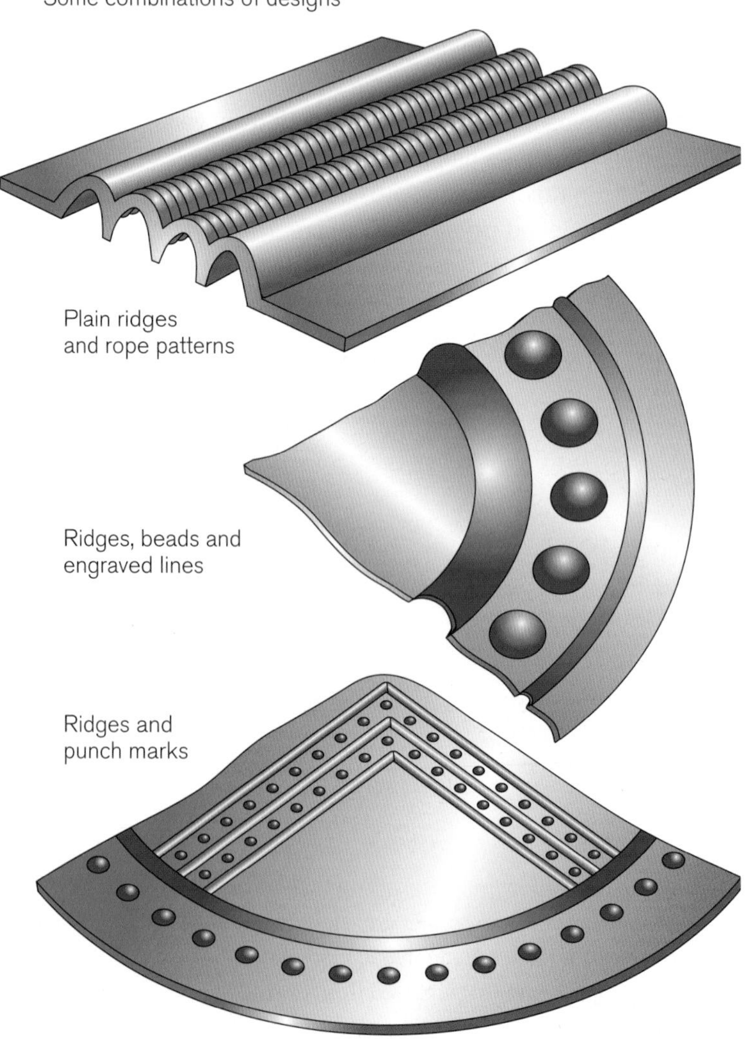

Fig. 1.25 Bronze Age designs

Triangles are formed at the centre and the ends of the arms. Triangles also appear between the arms of the cross, echoing the shape (Fig. 1.26).

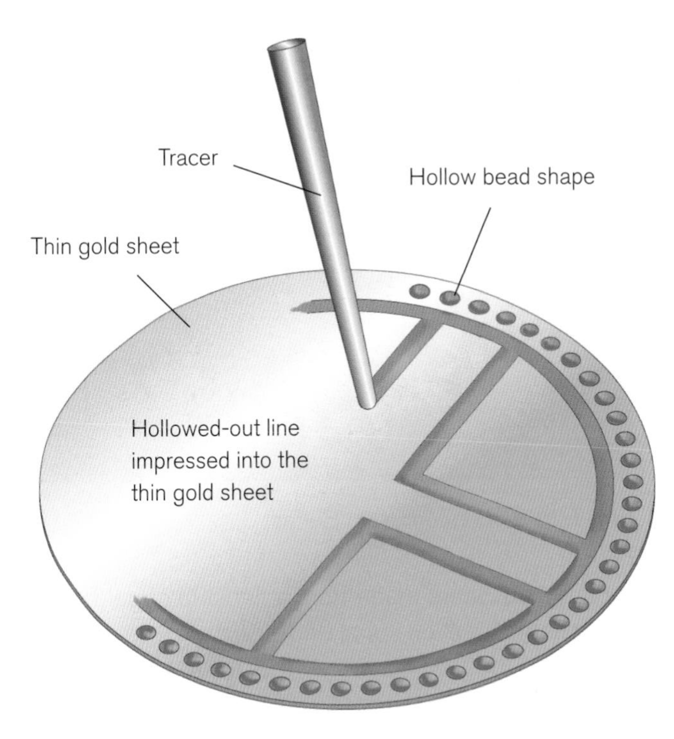

Fig. 1.26 The repoussé technique

To apply **repoussé** design, gold sheet would have been laid face down on a firm surface. (In more recent times, a leather sandbag or a bowl of mastic would have been used by goldsmiths.) A pattern could then be created on the surface using tracers (chisel-like tools with a variety of shapes cut into the tip, which were pressed or hammered into the surface) to produce a design. With the work completed, the sheet of gold was turned face up to reveal the design projecting from the surface. The work required careful craftsmanship, as a careless stroke could tear the thin gold sheet and the work would have to be started again.

NOTE! This cruciform design from 2,000 years before Christ is simply a result of the geometric pattern and has no Christian religious symbolism.

Lunula

The lunula is the most commonly found gold artefact from the Early Bronze Age. They are dated after 1800 BC.

* **Form:** The word lunula comes from the Latin *luna*, which means 'moon', because of its crescent moon shape.
* **Function:** A lunula was a neck collar that was probably worn as a status or magical item.
* **Technique:** A piece of gold was hammered flat into a thin sheet and the shape was cut from this. The lugs at the narrow end were then twisted at right angles to create a kind of catch. The decoration was incised into the surface.

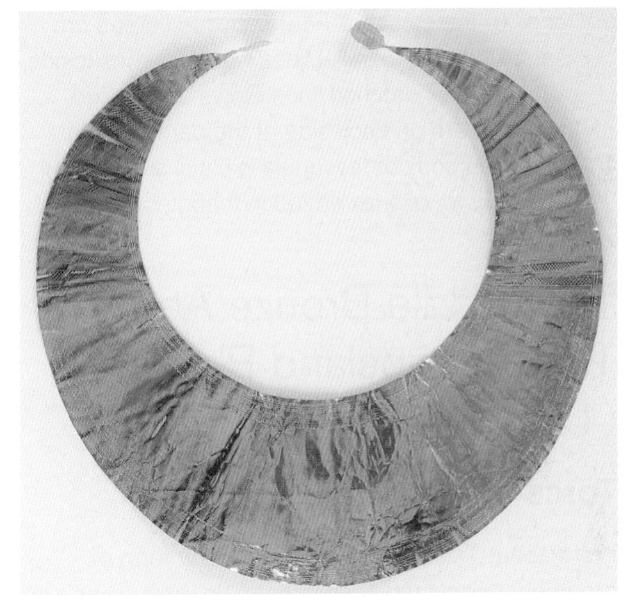

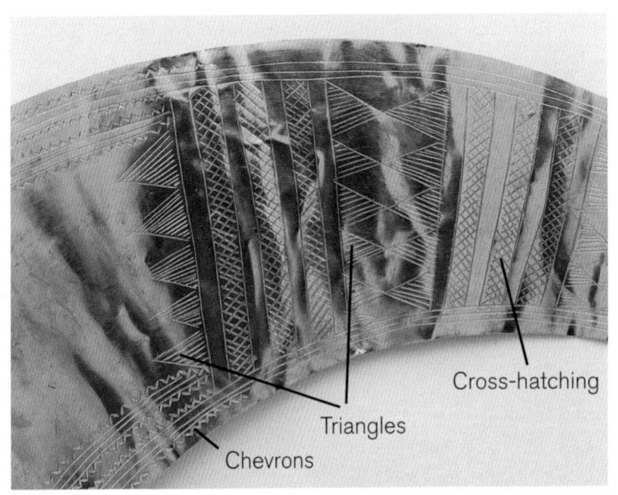

Fig. 1.27 A lunula and a close-up of an area of incised decoration

Lunulae were made of gold hammered into a thin sheet and cut into a crescent moon shape. They often had a plain surface but were frequently decorated with incised lines.

Incision: Decoration was incised (cut into the surface) with a scriber (a sharp, pointed, pencil-shaped bronze tool).

* **Decoration:** A lunula from Ross in Co. Westmeath (Fig. 1.27) has a repeating pattern of lines, triangles and chevrons incised into the surface. The pattern is concentrated in the narrow ends of the crescent. Four patterned areas on each side have parallel lines with chevrons inside, separated by hatched lines. Rows of hatched triangles are on each side of the parallel lines. The main body of the lunula is plain, surrounded by two rows of lines edged in triangles.

The Middle Bronze Age: The Bishopsland Phase (1500–1200 BC)

Torcs

From about 1400 BC, a completely new form of ornament largely replaced sheet gold work. These new objects, called torcs, were made by twisting gold into a variety of decorative forms.

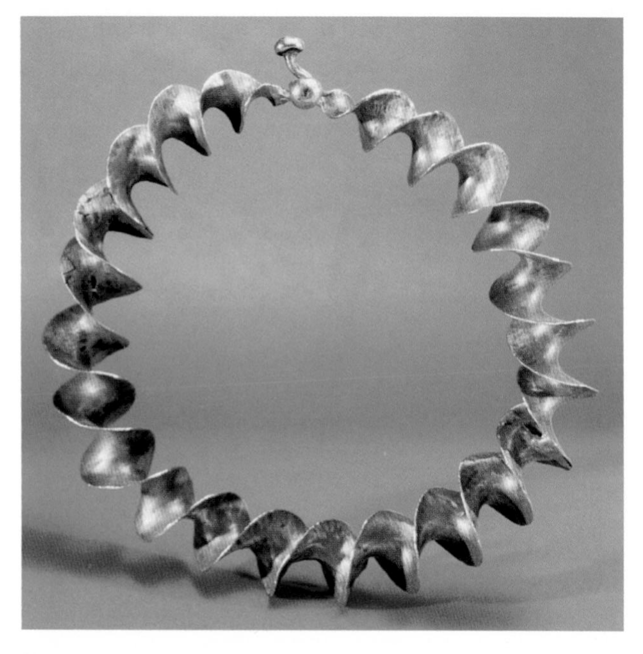

Fig. 1.28 Ribbon torc from Belfast

Ribbon torcs were made from a flat strip of gold, then twisted into an even spiral (Fig. 1.28).

Bar torcs and flanged torcs

* **Form:** Torcs come in a variety of shapes and forms.
* **Function:** Torcs were made to fit the neck, waist, arms and as earrings. They may have been purely decorative or a sign of status.
* **Technique:** By varying the size of the flanges, the length of the bar and the degree of twist that was applied, craftsmen could make a great variety of these flanged torcs. Hammering the ends of the torc into the required shape created

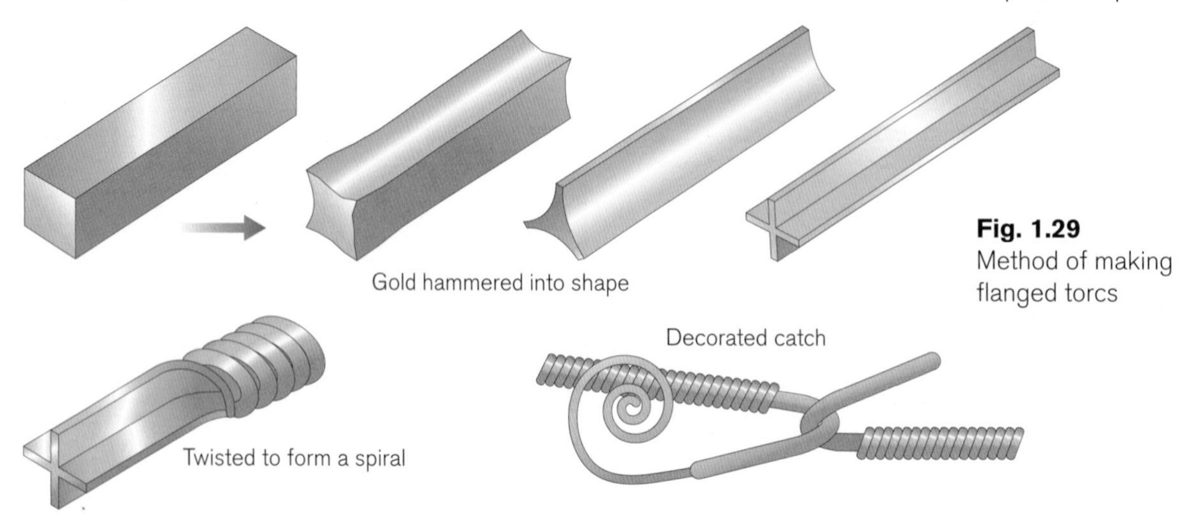

Fig. 1.29 Method of making flanged torcs

Torcs are made by twisting round, square or triangular sectioned rods of gold into a spiral shape. A variation of the basic bar torc was made by hammering flanges out from the angles of square or triangular sectioned bars before twisting.

catches, which could be simple hooks or more elaborate spirals (Fig. 1.29). All torcs were made from one piece of gold.

* **Decoration:** The twisted forms are the decoration as well as the structure of the torcs. Some have decorated terminals.

The Derrinboy Armbands

Some sheet metalwork was still being made during this time.

* **Form:** Rectangles of gold sheet were decorated with repoussé and curved to form a cylindrical band.
* **Function:** These bands could have been worn on the upper arm or at the wrist, probably as a sign of rank or status.
* **Technique:** Rectangles cut from a thin gold sheet were decorated with repoussé and heated so that they could be curved to form a band.
* **Decoration:** Boldly patterned in alternate smooth and string-patterned rows of repoussé, there is an area of finer string-patterned ridges arranged vertically around the opening of the band (Fig. 1.30).

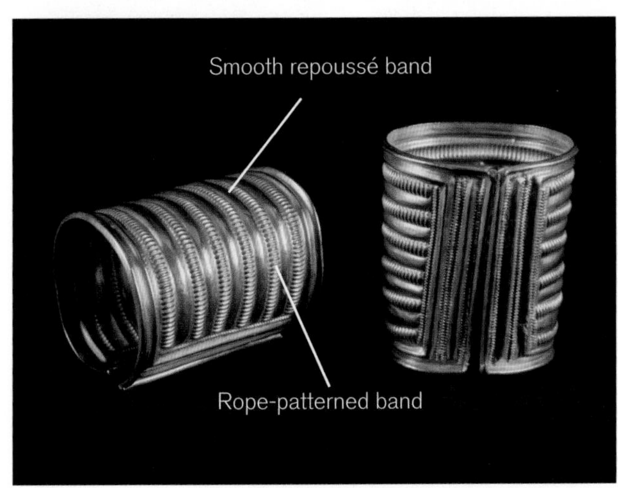

Fig. 1.30 The Derrinboy Armbands

The Late Bronze Age (Dowris Phase): The Golden Age (1200–500 BC)

After 800 BC there was a huge upsurge in metalwork production in Ireland. New types of bronze tools and weapons and gold ornaments have turned up in buried hoards found all over the country, but particularly in the counties surrounding the lower Shannon River. This was Ireland's first Golden Age. More gold objects have been found in Ireland from this time than in any other Western European country.

Fibula

The fibula may have been a type of dress fastener adapted from Northern European models, though some of the larger ones would have been too heavy to be practical and were probably only for ceremonial use.

The Clones Fibula from Co. Monaghan

* **Form:** Made from a kilogram of solid gold, the Clones Fibula has large open-cup ends joined by a bow or handle.
* **Function:** Fibulae are often described as dress fasteners, where the button-like ends could have been put through holes in a cloak or tunic. However, some of the shapes you can see in the photograph (Fig. 1.31) could not be used in this way. They may have been status or trading items. What do you think?
* **Technique:** The bow was cast and the end plates or terminals hammered into a hollow shape and decorated by incision. The work is very skilful and beautifully finished.

A **fibula** is made up of a gold bow or handle with a flat or cup-shaped disc at each end. The basic form would have been cast and the cups or discs at the end of the bow could be hammered out into the required shape. Fibulae come in a variety of forms, both decorated and undecorated (Fig. 1.31).

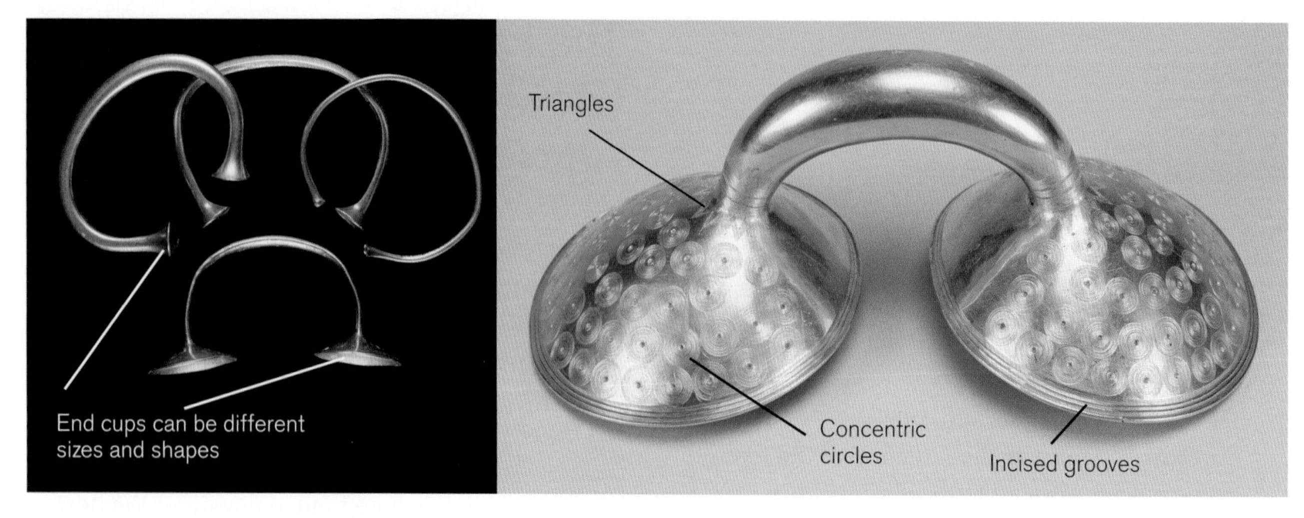

Fig. 1.31 A selection of fibulae

Fig. 1.32 The Clones Fibula

* **Decoration:** The terminals are decorated with irregular rows of small concentric circles with a little hollow at each centre. A special tool may have been used to make these patterns. The circles are arranged freehand across the surface, some with edges touching. The pattern of circles ends in the area below the bow, which might have been difficult to reach with the tool that made the circles. Three ridges surround the outer edge of each terminal. The area where the bow joins the cup is decorated with incised triangles and bands of lines. There are also triangles on top of the bow.

Gorget

Gorgets are perhaps the most beautifully made objects from the Bronze Age. There are several examples in the National Museum, the most perfect of which is the Gleninsheen Gorget (Fig. 1.33), which was found in a rock crevice near the tomb of the same name near Ballyvaughan in the Burren in Co. Clare.

* **Form:** A U-shaped gold collar with a gold disc connected to each end.
* **Function:** Gorgets would have been worn at the neck. They would have been a high-status item.

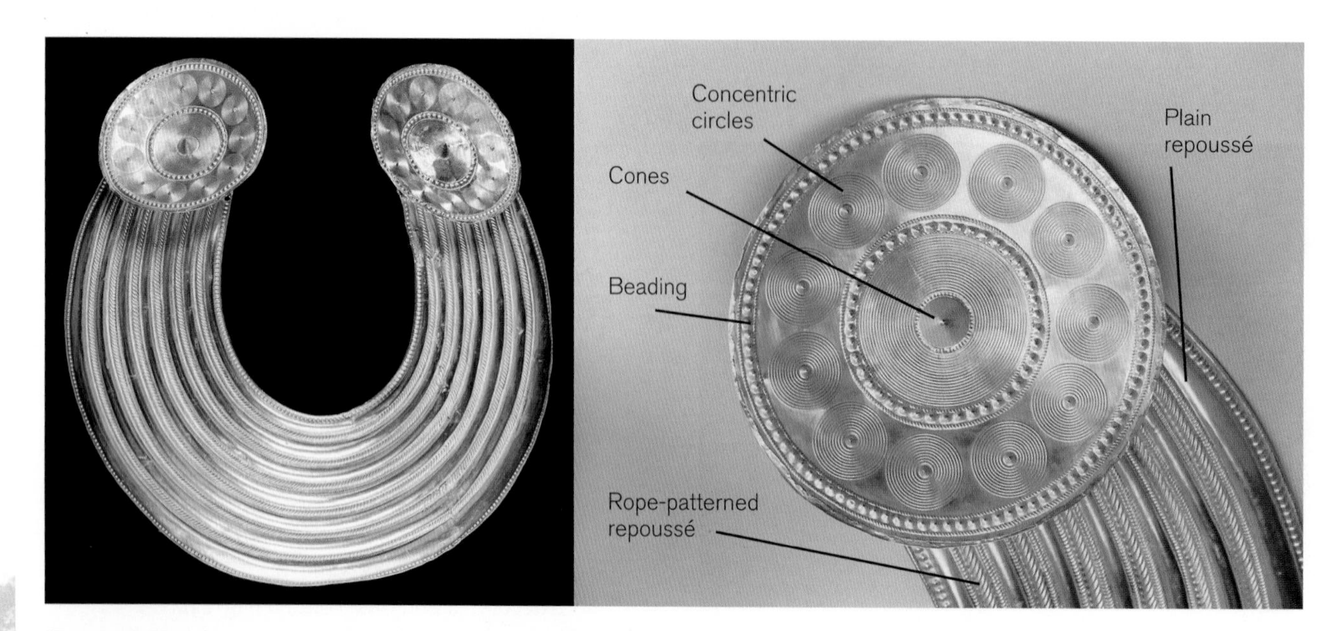

Fig. 1.33 The Gleninsheen Gorget with a close-up of an end disc

Gorget: A gold U-shaped collar with a gold disc attached at each end.

* **Technique:** Gorgets were constructed from a number of parts. The outer and inner edge of the collar were finished with a strip of gold wrapped around it to create a smooth finish. The discs were made from two layers, with the edges of the larger back disc wrapped over the edge of the upper disc again to create a more finished edge. The discs were connected to the collar by stitching with gold wire or in some cases by a hinge-like arrangement. All the parts are made of flat gold sheet decorated by the repoussé technique and incision – all very precise and skilful craftsmanship.
* **Decoration:** The U-shaped body of the Gleninsheen Gorget collar has rows of repoussé decoration, which are alternately plain and rope-patterned. A row of beading forms an outer and inner decoration. The six areas of rope pattern are each made up of three rows of rope design: a small one on each side of a larger one. The discs at each end are patterned in rows of beads and concentric circles, with a smooth cone at the centre of each. Similar designs appear on sunflower pins and little gold boxes from the same period. The alternately smooth and textured patterns of the surface of the collar catch the light beautifully, creating an impression of movement and dancing light.

Lock rings

* **Form:** Structurally, lock rings are the most advanced work of the Bronze Age goldsmiths in Ireland.
* **Function:** Lock rings seem to be a uniquely Irish invention. They may have been used as hair ornaments.

Lock rings take the form of two cones made of fine gold wire connected at their outer edges, with an open-sided tube set in a centre opening.

Fig. 1.34 The Gorteenareagh Lock Rings

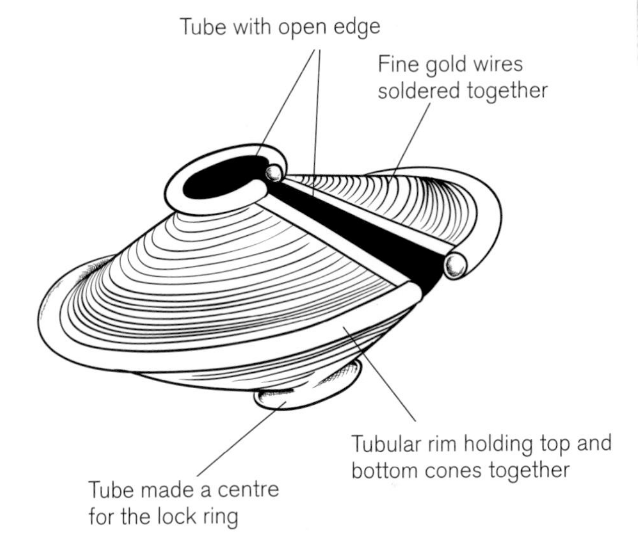

Fig. 1.35 The construction of the Gorteenareagh Lock Rings

Fig. 1.36 Late Bronze Age objects

Fig. 1.37
This bronze cauldron was found at Castlederg, Co. Tyrone. It is 56cm in diameter. It is from the Dowris phase of the Late Bronze Age.

* **Technique:** Fine gold wires were soldered together into a double cone shape. The two cones were held together at the outer edge by a tube of fine gold sheet. Another tube made of sheet gold was fitted through the centres of the cones. It was split at one side so that a plait of hair could be slipped through the space in the cone and the split in the tube. The split in the tube could then be turned out of line with the opening in the cones to hold the hair in place (Fig. 1.34).
* **Decoration:** The glittering effect created by the fine gold wire was the decorative element.

NOTE! The art of the metalworker reached a very high standard of craftsmanship in the Late Bronze Age, both in gold and bronze work. Clay moulds made of a number of parts were now used to cast more complicated objects. Bronze was beaten into sheets and joined with rivets to create large cauldrons and other vessels. Sophistication in design and workmanship is a hallmark of late Bronze Age metalwork (Fig. 1.35).

Review

* Note the changes from Stone Age to Bronze Age designs. Why, do you think, are the two styles so different?
* Decorated gold objects were the high point of Bronze Age design. Can you describe some of the techniques used to make these decorated items?
* The purpose for some of the gold objects from the Bronze Age is not clear. Can you offer some ideas for how they might have been used?

EXAM QUESTIONS

Ordinary Level (2016)

The Gleninsheen Gorget (see Fig. 1.33) is an example of Irish metalwork from the Bronze Age. Answer (a), (b) and (c).

(a) What was its function?

(b) Describe and discuss its form and decoration.

(c) Name and briefly describe and discuss **one** other artefact from the Bronze Age.

Illustrate your answer.

Higher Level (2016)

'By developing skills of working in gold, Bronze Age artists and craft workers ushered in a new period of cultural development in Ireland.'

Discuss this statement with reference to **two** named artefacts from this period. In your answer, describe and discuss form, function, materials used and decorative techniques.

and

Briefly describe and discuss where and how Bronze Age people in Ireland acquired the metals needed for their artefacts.

Illustrate your answer.

FURTHER RESEARCH

www.museum.ie

www.shee-eire.com

www.askaboutireland.ie

www.irisharchaeology.ie

3. The Iron Age: The Celts in Ireland (500 BC to 400 AD)

The Celts

The Celts were a group of tribes that populated much of Europe in the 700 years before the birth of Christ and for a few centuries after. They were known to the Greeks and the Romans as the Keltoi. They were renowned as warriors, horsemen and craft workers, skilled in the production of a wide range of goods and weapons in gold, bronze and iron (see Fig. 1.36).

By the end of this chapter, I will...

* Know a definition of La Tène design.
* Be able to draw and describe the Turoe Stone, the Broighter Collar, the Loughnashade Trumpet and the Petrie Crown.
* Know how design developed from the early to Ultimate La Tène.
* Understand how craft techniques developed.

Fig. 1.38 *The Dying Gaul of Pergamon*. This Celtic warrior is naked for battle except for a torc around his neck. His weapons and trumpet lie around him on the ground.

Iron technology

The Celts developed iron technology, which improved farming and military equipment and allowed them to expand their influence east and west. Some hints of their art and technology reached Ireland in the 6th century BC but did not seem to take root.

Fig. 1.39 Celtic design motifs. These were the basic forms that the La Tène designers elaborated on.

The La Tène style: By the 5th century BC, a new style of Celtic art had developed. It combined influences from classical Greek and Roman art, the Etruscans, the Scythians and Oriental art with the Celtic style. This style is called La Tène after a site on the shores of Lake Neuchâtel in Switzerland where the diagnostic examples were found (Fig. 1.39). This new style combined leafy palmate forms with vines, tendrils, lotus flowers, spirals, S scrolls, lyre and trumpet shapes into a flowing, sinuous, abstract style that the Celts used to decorate ornaments and weapons. The migrations and invasions of the Celtic people throughout Europe in the 5th and 4th centuries BC helped to spread the style.

Fig. 1.40 Scabbard plate design

La Tène art was evident in Ireland by the 3rd century BC, first in the form of imports. Gold collars found in Co. Roscommon, scabbard plates found in north-east Ulster (Fig. 1.40) and a sword hilt in the shape of a human figure found in the sea at Ballyshannon (Fig. 1.41) were all probably imported from Europe.

The Celts in Ireland

When the Celts arrived in Ireland and how they got here is still open to debate. In the early 20th century it was always assumed that the Celts invaded Ireland, but this is not so certain anymore. Significant sites like hill forts and places of burial seem to have been in continuous use from the Bronze Age into the Iron Age, so Celtic influence may have arrived by trading, migration and assimilation, with larger numbers arriving as the Romans invaded Gaul and Britain. By the 1st century BC, Ireland had a Celtic culture of some depth and substance. A Celtic language was spoken and there was a unified social and political system throughout the country. It was a tribal society based on family ties, with wealth built on cattle ownership.

Changes in style

Stone Age art was drawn freehand, without a ruler or compass. Bronze Age design was created mechanically using a straight edge and compass. Both of these styles were abstract (they did not represent objects in the real world).

Iron Age design combines mechanical and freehand elements and has abstract and stylised representational images. There does not appear to be any continuity in design from one age to another, though there are some common elements.

Insular La Tène: The style of art used by the first native craftsmen in Ireland is called Insular La Tène. It is a modified version of the European style. It consists of S scrolls, leaf and vine forms, trumpet ends and spirals. Some of its characteristics are peculiar to the islands off the west coast of Europe, which gives the style the name 'insular'. The patterns on the Turoe Stone and the Broighter Collar are in this style.

Fig. 1.41
The Ballyshannon Sword Hilt, probably an import

Iron Age structures (architecture)

Much of our knowledge of Stone Age and Bronze Age structures is based on the tombs and burial sites of the time. Little is known about the burial rites of the Iron Age people in Ireland, but habitation sites and ring forts in earth and stone are relatively common throughout the country. Some forts were built for defence, some were ritual sites and smaller ones were just homesteads. The circular enclosure with houses and animal pens inside continued to be used in Ireland after the Norman invasion, when the rest of Europe had long since developed towns and cities.

Dun Aengus

Dun Aengus is an enormous promontory fort that backs onto 100m cliffs on Inis Mór in the Aran Islands (Fig. 1.42).

* **Form:** It has three walls curving around it. The inner wall is 5m tall and up to 6m thick in places. It encloses an area approximately 130m x 100m. Inside, flights of stairs lead up to defensive ramparts. A second wall encloses an area outside the main structure, which in turn is surrounded by a field of chevaux-de-frise (upright stones set as a defence against cavalry attacks). A third wall surrounds a large area up to 200m from the inner wall.
* **Function:** There are some clear defensive features, but archaeological work has shown evidence of domestic buildings and areas where metalworking was carried out, so it was probably a chieftain's residence and it could have been a centre for ceremonies.
* **Technique:** The whole structure is built in uncut dry stone. No mortar was used to join the stones together. The main wall has a batter (it slopes back from the base to the top), creating a more stable structure. The buttresses that now support the walls were added in the 19th century to stabilise the structure when it was being restored. The building was begun in the Bronze Age, the main wall was enlarged during the Iron Age and it continued in use into medieval times.

Fig. 1.42 Dun Aengus, on Inis Mór in the Aran Islands, was in use from the late Bronze Age into the Iron Age

Stone carving

The first objects we can confidently claim to be of Irish manufacture in the La Tène style are a number of large boulders that have been dressed and carved with abstract patterns. The stones at Castlestrange, Co. Roscommon, Killycluggin, Co. Cavan, and Derrykeighan, Co. Antrim, have a linear pattern carved into the surface. The Turoe Stone in Co. Galway has a pattern sculpted in low relief.

Turoe Stone

The Turoe Stone has been dated to about 50 BC.

* **Form:** This 4-ton boulder, which is 1.68m tall, is pink feldspar Galway granite (Fig. 1.43).
* **Function:** The purpose of these decorated stones is not known. They may have been boundary markers or ceremonial objects.
* **Technique:** The stone was carved with iron chisels. The background was cut away to a depth of about 3mm, leaving a pattern standing out in low relief.
* **Decoration:** The pattern on the Turoe Stone (Fig. 1.44) takes the form of semi-abstract leaf and vine shapes, trumpet ends and spirals all flowing in a casual symmetry. The design has four segments. Two semi-circular areas of design take up most of the stone's surface, and between these are two smaller triangular segments of pattern, which connect over the top of the stone. A triskele (a motif of three curved limbs that spring from the same point and turn in the same direction) appears in one of the triangular segments. The flowing pattern takes up the domed top of the stone. Some of the spaces between the raised pattern can also be read as part of the design, showing the Celtic love of the play between positive and negative spaces. A brick or step pattern forms a band below the decorated dome and separates it from the plain base.

Fig. 1.43 The Turoe Stone. In this photograph, we are looking at the right-hand part of the schematic drawing.

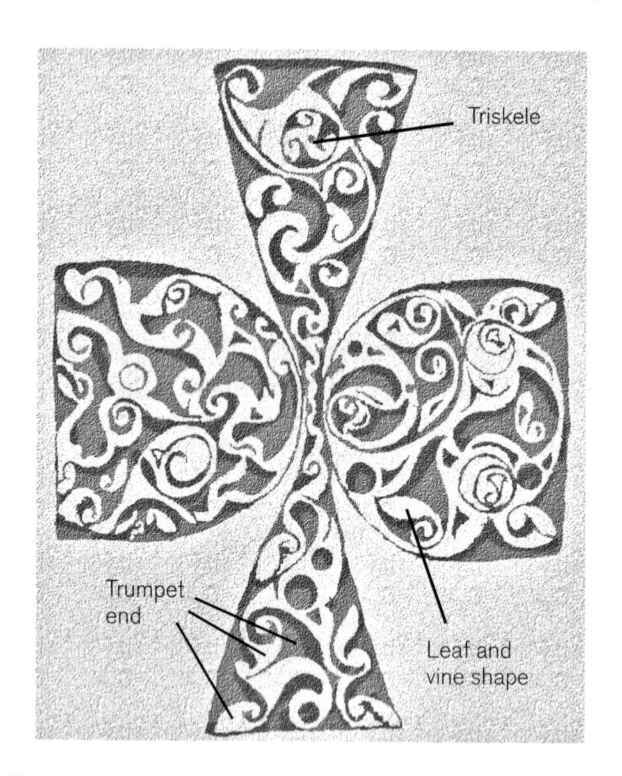

Fig. 1.44 A schematic drawing of the Turoe Stone

Some stone figure carvings may also be from the Iron Age, but it is difficult to date them accurately. The Triple Head from Corleck, Co. Cavan (Fig. 1.45), is generally accepted as Celtic, as is the Tandragee

Fig. 1.45 (left) The Triple Head from Corleck. The three faces rise slightly up the head.
Fig. 1.46 (right) The Tandragee Idol

Idol from Co. Armagh (Fig. 1.46). Other figures and heads once assigned to the Iron Age are now thought to be from a later date.

Metalwork

Iron

The arrival of iron technology in Ireland improved and simplified the production of tools and weapons (Fig. 1.47). Iron was readily available in the environment in the form of clay ironstone nodules, bog iron and other, less easily worked sources. It was not melted and cast, but heated until the impurities were burned off or melted away and then it was hammer forged and shaped.

The smith would have had similar tools and skills as any village

Fig. 1.47

Three iron swords from the Iron Age

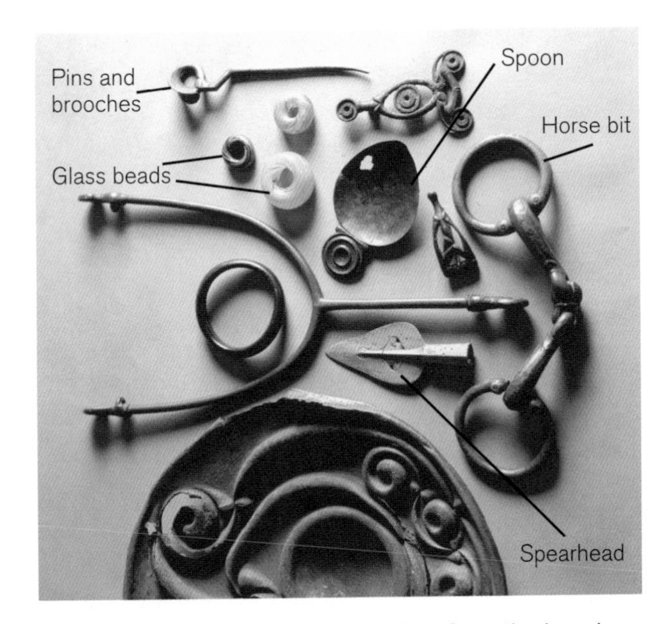

Fig. 1.48 Decorative bronze and glass from the Iron Age

blacksmith would have had up to the middle of the 20th century. All metalworkers were highly valued members of society, equal in status with physicians. Metalworkers' skills were associated with magical powers.

Bronze

Much of the decorative work from the Iron Age was made of bronze. Horse trappings, tools and utensils, brooches, armbands and rings were all beautifully crafted (Fig. 1.48). The 'lost wax' method of casting in bronze allowed complicated pieces, like horse bits, to be made. (Models made of wax were enveloped in a clay mould, which was fired. The wax melted out and the hollow space was then filled with molten bronze, which created an exact copy of the model.) Sheet bronze was turned and hammered to produce vessels and decorative items.

Gold

The finest decorative pieces were produced in gold. The ancient techniques of hammering and cutting to shape were still used. Casting was improved and chasing replaced repoussé for relief work.

The Broighter Hoard

Not many gold finds can be dated to the Iron Age, but the quality of some pieces makes up for the lack of quantity. The Broighter Hoard (Fig. 1.49) was turned up by a ploughman in Co. Derry and includes some of the finest examples of the goldsmith's art. The collection consists of a model boat and a bowl made of thin sheet gold, two chains, two twisted bracelets and a gold collar.

The Broighter Collar (c. 50 BC)

* **Form:** Two tubes are the main element of the piece. They are made from sheet gold with a foliage pattern chased onto the surface. Buffer terminals (they look like railway buffers) form a catch at one end. A T-shaped bar is used as the lock that holds the two terminals together. Another terminal, now missing, would have joined the other ends of the tubes together.

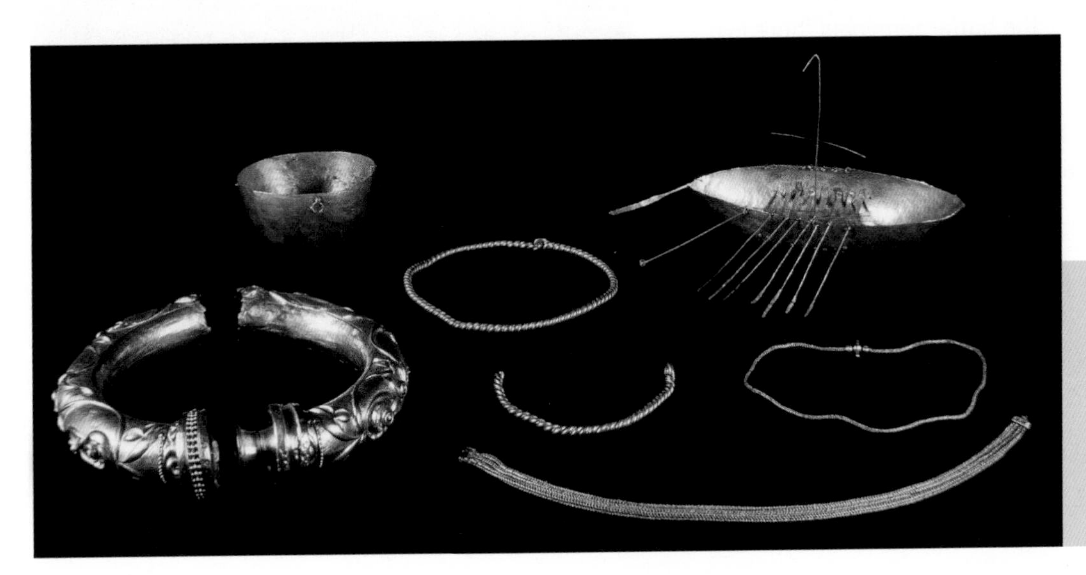

Fig. 1.49 The Broighter Hoard

* **Function:** The sculpture of the dying Gaul (see Fig. 1.38) shows a warrior wearing a neck collar. Elaborate collars like the Broighter example were high-status items worn by important people on important occasions.
* **Technique:** The collar is the most accomplished piece of Irish manufacture in the Insular La Tène style. The design would have been applied to a flat gold sheet that was raised by chasing. The flat areas between the raised patterns were incised with compass arcs. The patterned gold sheets were then heated and rolled into tubes, which were soldered shut and then filled with hot mastic (a wax-like substance) so that the tubes could be curved without tearing or crushing them. The cast buffer terminals are riveted onto the ends of the tubes. A row of beading has been raised along the edge to disguise the rivet heads.

Chasing is a metalwork technique that brings a design into relief by pressing back the surrounding area by hammering. In some ways, it is like a reverse of the repoussé technique.

* **Decoration:** The pattern is symmetrical. Based on interconnecting S scrolls, it combines a variety of plant-based forms ending in spiral bosses, which were made separately and pinned on (Fig. 1.50). The background area between the pattern elements has been incised with compass arcs to create a contrast with the smooth surface of the raised design. On the buffer terminals there is a raised pattern of lentoids and hollowed bosses with a little gold bead soldered in the centre where it meets the tubes. One of the terminals has rows of beading.

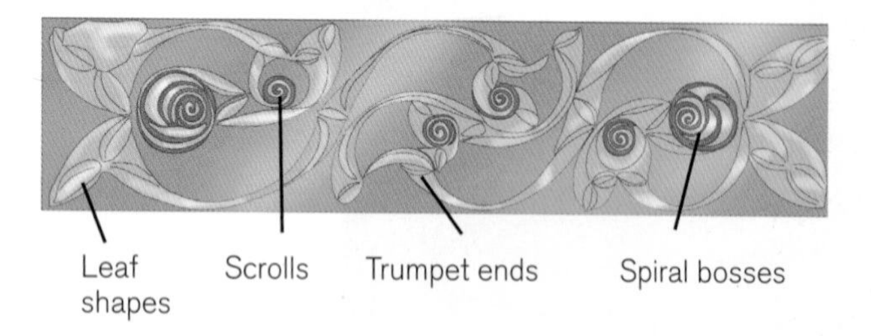

Fig. 1.50 Schematic drawing of a section of the Broighter Collar

Ultimate La Tène Style: Later in the Iron Age there was a change in the style of design. The patterns became lighter and more symmetrical. The vegetal designs of the Insular style gave way to the more geometric forms of the Ultimate La Tène, which continued into the Christian era. The following objects are in this style.

The gold chains and twisted bracelets from the Broighter Hoard are probably imports of Roman origin. The gold boat is a model of an ocean-going craft, probably a hide-covered boat driven by oars and a square sail. It is an interesting indication of how Celtic people travelled around the coast of Europe.

The Loughnashade Trumpet

The Loughnashade Trumpet (Fig. 1.51) was found in Co. Antrim. It is from the 1st century AD.

* **Form:** The trumpet is made of two tubes of sheet bronze joined by a knob in the middle. It has a decorative plate on the open end.
* **Function:** The trumpet was probably used at ceremonial occasions and for war.
* **Technique:** The tubes are expertly made. The edges are rolled together and riveted onto an internal strip of bronze. The plate at the open end has a four-part pattern raised by the repoussé technique.

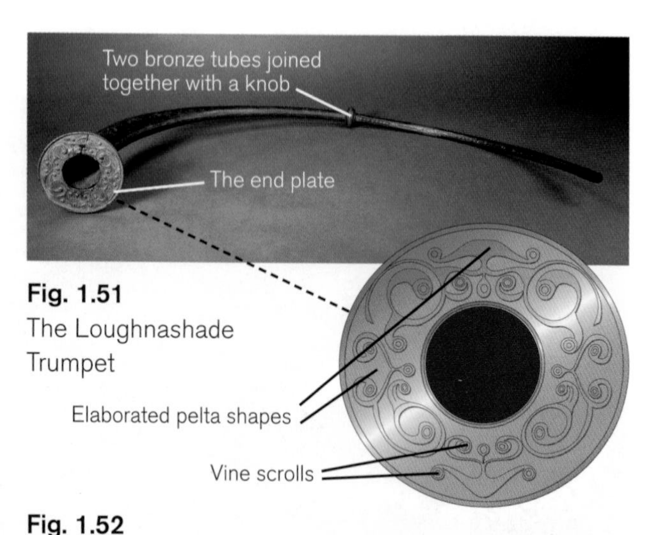

Fig. 1.51
The Loughnashade Trumpet

Fig. 1.52
The pattern on the end plate of the Loughnashade Trumpet

* **Decoration:** The decoration is based on the Roman pelta motif combined with spirals and plant forms. It is almost perfectly symmetrical. The design is lighter and more linear than earlier work, with broader areas in relief at the ends of the curves (Fig. 1.52).

The Petrie Crown

The Petrie Crown (Fig. 1.53) is an object of unknown origin from the collection of the 19th-century antiquarian George Petrie.

* **Form:** The crown consists of an openwork band with a cone and two discs fixed to it.
* **Function:** The top and bottom edges of the band are perforated, which would have allowed it to be sewn onto fabric or leather, or fixed to wood or metal. It is not known how long the band was intended to be or how many horns or discs were originally fixed to it, so it is difficult to imagine its original function.
* **Technique:** The raised outlines of the design were created by cutting back the surrounding metal. The cut-out openings in the band create the impression of a series of connected semi-circles. The concave discs that are mounted on this band would have been hammered into shape. Each disc has a boss slightly off centre, one of which still has a red enamelled bead in its hollow middle. Enamelled beads were probably fixed in the eye sockets of some of the bird heads. This is the first example of enamel work in Ireland. The cone-shaped attachment is made of sheet bronze formed into a tapering cylinder.
* **Decoration:** All the parts are decorated with spirals ending in crested bird heads. The deceptively simple designs on the discs combine palmate, lotus bud and triskele motifs created by slim trumpet curves (Fig. 1.54). The artist made use of both positive and negative shapes to create the design, a tendency that becomes even more common in the Christian period. The bird heads found on the band, discs and horn are among the earliest zoomorphs found in Irish art.

Fig. 1.53 The Petrie Crown

> **Zoomorphs:** This word comes from Greek words for 'animal' and 'change'. It describes the way animal forms are stretched and changed in Celtic designs, sometimes to a point where they are hard to read.

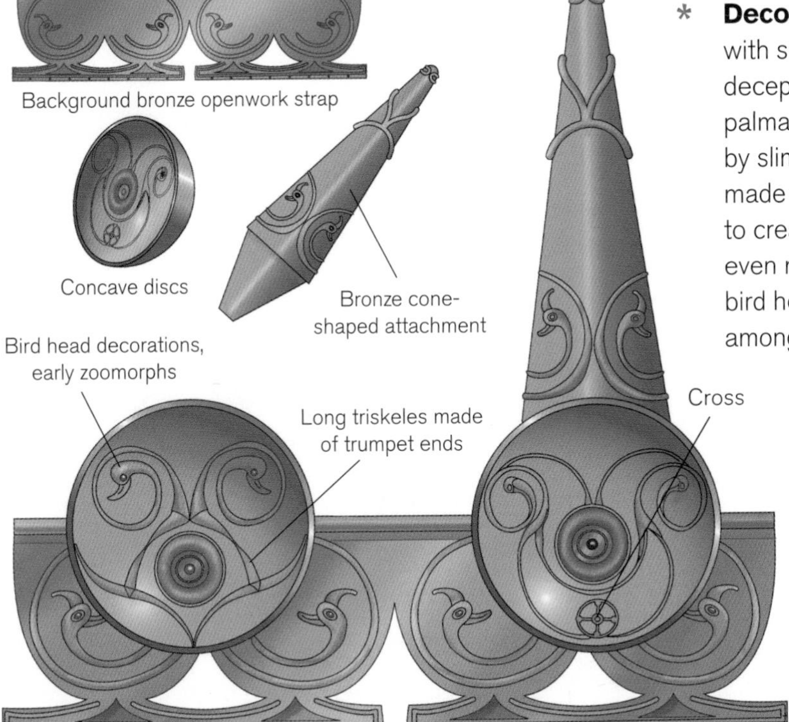

Fig. 1.54 The construction of and patterns on the Petrie Crown

There is a little cross in a circle on the right-hand disc. This may be a Christian symbol, which would date the crown to at least the 4th century AD, at the beginning of Christian influence. Otherwise it may simply be an abstract pattern that just so happens to look like a cross. What do you think?

The Cork Horns

The Cork Horns (Fig. 1.55) are probably some kind of ceremonial headgear. They are closest in design to the Petrie Crown, though not as elaborately decorated.

Fig. 1.55
The Cork Horns

Review

* Why did Iron Age technology bring changes to Irish society?
* La Tène design is a combination of influences. Can you identify some of these influences?
* Can you find some positive and negative shapes in the Turoe Stone or the Petrie Crown?
* Iron, bronze and gold were all used in making Iron Age/La Tène objects. Can you name some objects made of each metal?
* What was Ultimate La Tène design like? How was it different from the earlier style?
* What is a zoomorph? Where might you find one from the Iron Age?

NOTE! The work left to us from this time displays the elements of design and pattern that formed the basis for the decorative art that followed in the Christian Celtic period. Plant forms (vegetal decoration), animal forms (zoomorphs), simplified human figures and geometric patterns were brought together to create a style of art that was flexible, harmonious, imaginative, ambiguous and, above all, beautiful.

EXAM QUESTIONS

Ordinary Level (2016)

The Turoe Stone (see Fig. 1.43) is an example of stone carving from the Iron Age.

Answer (a), (b) and (c).

(a) What is its function?

(b) Describe and discuss its form and decoration.

(c) Name and briefly describe and discuss **one** other example of pre-Christian stone carving.

Illustrate your answer.

Higher Level (2015)

'The Petrie Crown (see Fig. 1.53) is an example of a remarkable change in style that took place during the Iron Age.'

Discuss this statement, referring to the function, form and style of the Petrie Crown and to the materials and techniques used in its production and decoration.

and

Name and describe **one** example of decorative stone carving from this period.

Illustrate your answer.

FURTHER RESEARCH

www.archaeology.ie

www.askaboutireland.ie

www.irisharchaeology.ie

www.museum.ie

Chapter 2

The 5th and 6th Centuries: Early Christian Ireland

Political and social background

Early medieval Ireland had a society based on kinship. The *tuath*, or tribe, was the social unit, which expanded into small kingdoms through alliances or tribute. It was a society without towns or coinage. Trade was by barter (exchanging goods or services of equal value). There is evidence of the import of wine, oils and other luxury goods from areas within the old Roman Empire and from farther afield.

By the end of this chapter, I will...

* Know what an early monastery looked like and what construction methods were used.
* Be able to draw and describe the Reask Pillar, some letters from the Cathach and the Ballinderry Brooch.
* Have definitions for vellum, codex, majuscule, diminuendo and penannular brooch.
* Note the significant changes for craft workers brought about by the introduction of Christianity.

The Roman Empire was in decline in Britain by the 3rd century and the legions left in the year 406 AD. Irish raiders were able to set up colonies in northern and southern Wales on the edge of the Empire and they took over large areas of west Scotland in Argyll. This contact with the outside world had effects on lifestyle and art in Ireland.

The arrival of Christianity in Ireland

The Christian message seems to have arrived in Ireland in a number of ways. Traders and raiders moving in and out of Ireland would have met Christians on mainland Europe and in Britain, and this influence may have penetrated back into Ireland. Anchorite monks and hermits looking for places of isolation along the coast of Europe settled on the islands off the Irish coast (Fig. 2.1). The heroic self-denial and endurance of these hermits would have appealed to an Irish society brought up on tales of the valour and strength of the old Celtic heroes and gods.

Palladius and St Patrick

In the year 431 AD, Pope Julius I sent Bishop Palladius 'to the believers in Christ in Ireland'. The bishop brought books and religious objects in the Roman style with him, as well as craftsmen to make more. Following this initiative from Rome, St Patrick and others succeeded in converting the country to Christianity without martyrs or much conflict with the pagan priesthood. In later centuries the role of Palladius was played down in favour of the cult of St Patrick, which was promoted by the archdiocese of Armagh to reinforce their position as the senior paruchia (united group of monasteries and diocese) in Ireland.

Church organisation

Initially the Christians of Ireland were organised under the European model, with the bishop controlling a diocese of parishes in a geographical area, but this did not suit the rural make-up of Irish Celtic society.

NOTE! A system of monastic federations evolved in Ireland based on kinship or allegiance to the founding saint of one of the great monasteries.

The abbot of the leading house of each monastic federation was called the comharba (successor to the founder) and was generally a kinsman of the founder – in some cases, sons succeeded fathers. Some of these comharba would have been laymen or in minor orders.

Monasticism in Ireland

The founders of monasteries were revered as saints and their burial places and relics became centres of pilgrimage over the years. Some saints were associated with many sites and holy wells, particularly Patrick and Brigid, while others had a more local following.

During the 6th century, Irish monastic sites became great centres of learning and strict spiritual practice. Students came from Britain and Europe, where the church was in disarray and scholarship was at a low ebb. In the following centuries, Irish monks travelled throughout Britain and Europe spreading the word of Christ and founding new monasteries. Columba used Iona as an outpost for the conversion of Scotland, which became a political colony of Ireland at the same time. Up till this time, 'scot' had been the Roman word for Irish man.

Fig. 2.1 The monastery of St Molaise on Inishmurray Island, off the Donegal coast

Layout of the early monasteries

Early monasteries were laid out following the local building style: an enclosing bank or wall surrounded an area, with the church or oratory at the centre of the bigger sites and towards the south-east in smaller enclosures. The cemetery was located near the church and the monastic buildings. The area around the perimeter of the enclosure would have been for domestic dwellings and craftwork (Fig. 2.2).

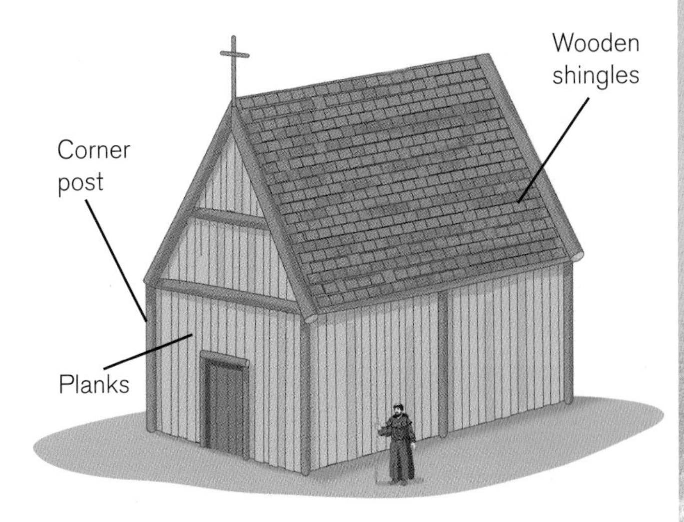

Fig. 2.2 A church constructed from wood

Most of the early monasteries were made of wood or wattle and daub (Fig. 2.3), but they were built over or used as burial grounds in the following years, so little can be discovered about them. In the West of Ireland and on some coastal islands, monasteries were built in stone and the remains are much more clear.

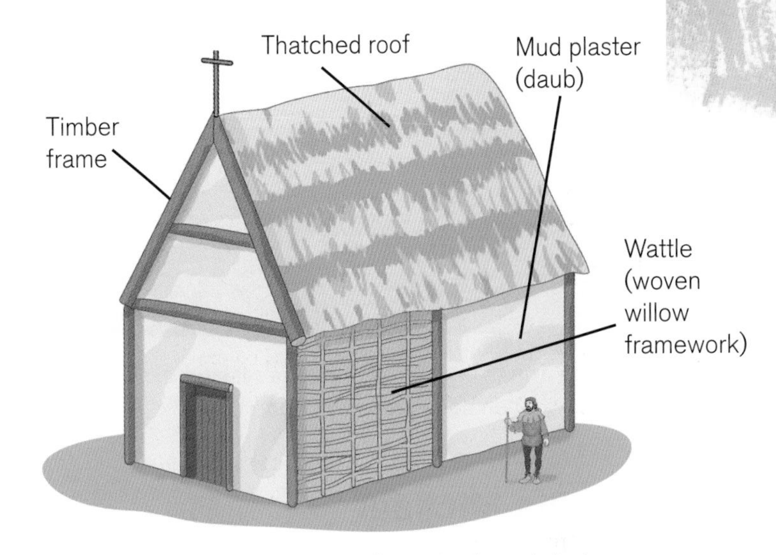

Fig. 2.3 A church constructed from wattle and daub

The style of early buildings

We have some idea of how these early buildings may have looked from written accounts in the annals and from images created in other crafts, the painting of the temple on the temptation of Christ page in the Book of Kells (see Fig 4.33) and a number of house-shaped shrines (see Fig 3.22). The capstone of Muiredach's Cross at Monasterboice, Co. Louth, is also house shaped (Fig. 2.4). The little 12th-century stone church on St Macdara's Island in Co. Galway copies the detail of the wooden construction of an earlier church, right down to the carvings in the shape of shingles on the roof (Fig. 2.5). The sheer plainness of these early churches reflects the austerity and self-denial of the early Christian monks in Ireland.

Churches had a simple rectangular plan and varied from being almost square to being twice the length of the width, which was more common. A small window in the east gable and the western doorway would have allowed little natural light to penetrate.

Fig. 2.4 The capstone of Muiredach's Cross, Monasterboice, Co. Louth, shows decorative shingles and decorated roof timbers and ridge board

There has been much debate about the age of the simplest stone churches. There is little mention of stone buildings in the texts before the 9th century. Carbon dating has produced a timescale of 640 to 790 AD for some of the corbelled buildings on the Dingle peninsula, which puts them close to the beginning of the development of stone churches in Ireland.

Fig. 2.5 The church on St Macdara's Island, Co. Galway, copies wooden construction in stone

Skellig Michael

* **Form:** The well-preserved monastic settlement on Skellig Michael off the Kerry coast consists of a group of corbelled buildings and stone enclosures.
* **Function:** The settlement on the Skelligs would not have been a typical monastery, clinging as it does to the crags of an island 180m above the Atlantic, but it does give us an idea of the scale and complexity of early monasteries (Fig. 2.6).
* **Technique:** All the walls, steps and buildings on the island are constructed in the dry stone walling technique – no mortar was used to join the stones together. Corbelling was an ancient method of construction dating back to the Stone Age (it was used at Newgrange). It allows the builders to create a dome of stone by laying each circular or rectangular course of stone a little inside the one below, creating an inward curve that continues until the walls meet at the top. There are both dome-shaped and rectangular corbelled buildings on Skellig Michael. Some are as large as 9m in diameter and 4.5m tall.
* **Decoration:** There are some simply decorated crosses in the graveyard, but all the buildings are plain.

Fig. 2.6 (above and left) Some of the corbelled buildings and a simple cross in the enclosure of the monastery on Skellig Michael

Gallarus Oratory

* **Form:** The Gallarus Oratory on the Dingle peninsula (Fig. 2.7) is the best-preserved and most complete of the group of corbelled rectangular oratories on the mainland.
* **Function:** The oratory is the church of a small monastery.
* **Technique:** It is a dry stone construction using carefully selected stones that are larger at the corners and at the base, and smaller and lighter towards the top and centre, where a cave-in was more likely. The stones were laid down sloping out from the centre of the wall and trimmed to an even surface on the outside to shed the rain and wind. The side walls form one continuous surface from ground to ridge and are supported by inward-leaning gables. The doorway has inclined jambs (the opening is narrower at the top than at the bottom) and a plain lintel. The tiny east window has a round top cut from two stones, so it is not a true arch.
* **Decoration:** It is a plain, undecorated building.

Fig. 2.7 Gallarus Oratory, Dingle peninsula, Co. Kerry. The thickness of the walls can be noted in the west doorway.

Stone carving

As we have seen in relation to the construction of monasteries, stone was not the material of choice during the 5th and 6th centuries. The development of carved stone monuments evolved over several hundred years. Because of gaps in the progression of design and technique, it is difficult to work out the reasons for the form and variety of the monuments that remain.

The carved pillar

Ogham stones

Dating from the 4th and 5th centuries AD, ogham stones, which are found mainly along the southern end of the country from Wexford to Kerry, were the earliest form of vertical stone monument from the Christian period (Fig. 2.8). A few examples are found in Britain in areas that once supported Irish colonies, but they are mainly of Irish origin. Ogham was a form of Latin script simplified down to marks across a line or around the corner edge of a stone.

Fig. 2.8
Ogham stone from Traigh an Fhiona on the Dingle peninsula, Co. Kerry. The inscription is in old Irish and reads: CUNAMAQQI CORBBI MAQQS. It is hard to translate ogham, but it might be 'Cuna (grand) son of Corbbi'.

Cross-inscribed pillars

Upright pillars and slabs with crosses inscribed into their surfaces are found at some of the earliest monastic sites. The decoration is usually a simple linear pattern carved into the surface of untrimmed stones. It can include Latin and Irish inscriptions with Greek, Latin or Maltese crosses, sometimes inside a circle. The Chi-Rho monogram (a symbol for Christ), swastikas, simple knots, fretwork, spirals and curves can also appear as part of the design repertoire. Most of these elements, except the Christian symbols, were in the La Tène style already in use during the Iron Age in Ireland (Fig. 2.9).

Cross-inscribed pillars are often found close to early churches. Tradition suggests that some of them mark the grave of the founding saint, which would have become a focus for pilgrimage in the following centuries. Most of these monuments are found in the western part of the country, from Kerry to Donegal.

Reask Pillar

The cross-inscribed pillar in the walled monastic enclosure at Reask on the Dingle peninsula in Co. Kerry dates back to the 7th century (Fig. 2.10).

* **Form:** An untrimmed, upright stone pillar with carved decoration.

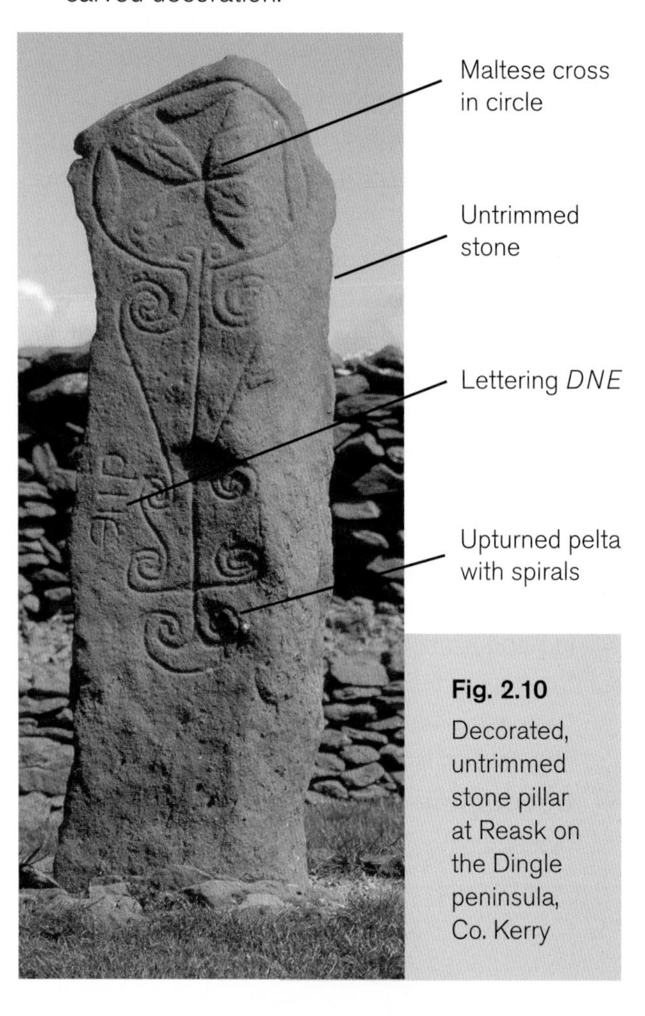

Fig. 2.10 Decorated, untrimmed stone pillar at Reask on the Dingle peninsula, Co. Kerry

Fig. 2.9

Cross-inscribed pillar from Kilshannig graveyard, Co. Kerry

Cross-inscribed pillar from Mount Brandon, Co. Kerry

Engraved slab from Inishkea, north Co. Mayo

* **Function:** It may mark the grave of the founder of the monastery or it might simply be a focus point for prayer.
* **Technique:** Using iron tools, the cross at the top of the slab is carved in shallow relief. The rest of the design is a thin carved line. The stone is not dressed and the shape is not changed from its natural uneven surface.
* **Decoration:** A Maltese cross surrounded by a circle takes up the top of the slab. A pattern of spirals extends down from the circle, ending in a pelta shape. The letters *D N E* are inscribed on the left of the shaft. They probably stand for the Latin word *domine*, meaning 'Lord'. The word 'Lord' may refer to 'the Lord our God' or it might mean 'the Lord Abbot'. All the design elements on this pillar relate to late La Tène design. The delicate line contrasts with the crude surface of the stone on which it was carved.

Manuscripts (book painting)

The importance of books in an Irish monastery

The books of the Bible were central to the practice of Christianity. A monk in an early Christian monastery needed a copy of the Bible and other texts for the daily readings and singing that were the centre of his life. Before the invention of printing in the 15th century, all books had to be copied by hand – not only Bibles, but books of prayers and services, texts on Latin grammar and all kinds of scholarship that were needed for the education of the clergy and nobility. Latin was the language of educated people throughout Europe.

NOTE! Books were very precious, not simply because of the time and effort that went into making them, but also as sources of knowledge and the word of God. Carelessly copied texts would be regarded as an insult to God, whose words were being transcribed. Monks offered their work as a prayer, so they tried to make it as perfect and beautiful as they could.

Making books

Books not only had to be written by hand, but every part had to be produced from raw materials. There was no source of ready-made pages, inks or pens. The scribe had to make everything from what was available locally or what could be imported. Pages had to be made and assembled into book form.

Vellum is calf skin that has been prepared for writing. In Ireland, vellum was the preferred material to make pages from.

Inks and pigments

Black and dark inks were made in a variety of ways. Carbon inks made from burnt wood or animal fat remained black but were prone to flaking off the page. Iron gall ink was made by mixing iron sulphate with crushed oak galls and gum to bind them together. This mixture was carried in a solution of water, wine or vinegar. There were also disadvantages to this type of ink: the iron etched into the vellum and the gall sometimes faded to brown shades.

The earliest books that have survived used very little colour, just a little red, orange or yellow dotting around the capital letters at the beginning of new sections.

A **codex** is groups of pages sewn together into book form. The codex became more popular than the scroll, as it was easier to refer to and to store.

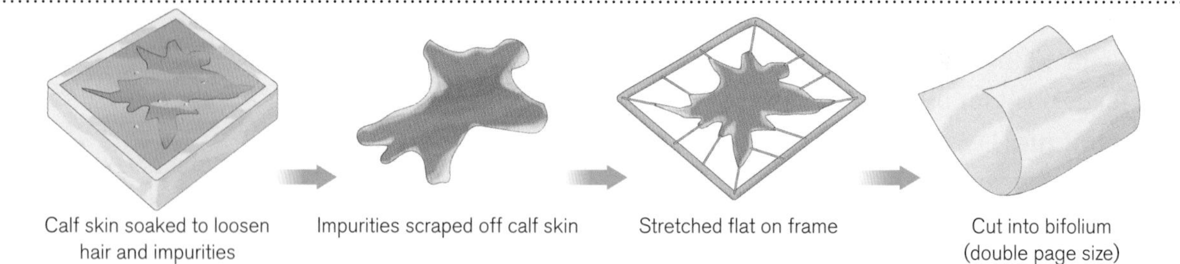

Fig. 2.11 Making vellum. The skin was placed in a bath of water and lime, or excrement, for some days to loosen hairs. Timing was an important element because if the skins were left in the bath too long, they could become prone to bacterial attack. The Book of Kells has suffered a little from this problem. After this preparation, skins were taken to be cleaned and scraped free of hair and impurities with a blade. Following this preliminary cleaning, the skin was rubbed smooth with a pumice stone. The hide was then stretched flat and dried before it was cut into pages. The vellum could then be sewn into rolls or made into a codex.

The Cathach

* **Form:** A vellum manuscript in the form of a codex measuring 27cm x 19cm. Fifty-eight damaged pages remain from an original 110 folios.
* **Function:** A psalter is a book of psalms. These are sacred poems from the Old Testament of the Bible that were sung or chanted as part of monks' daily practice.
* **Technique:** The vellum was made in the way described above. A dark ink was used, applied with a quill or reed pen. Red letters (rubrics) were used to write a short introduction (in old Irish) before each psalm. Orange dots were used to outline some of the decorated capitals at the beginning of each psalm.
* **Decoration:** The Cathach is written in a clear majuscule script with enlarged capitals introducing each psalm. The lettering is in a peculiarly Irish style. A little spring spiral, an animal head and a cross are all added to the tail of the Q and a row of pen flourishes decorates the inside. The letter *M* that opens the psalm on folio 21a in the Cathach is decorated with spirals and trumpet ends (Fig. 2.14).

Majuscule: A style of rounded capital letter written between two ruled lines with very few short ascenders or descenders above or below these lines (Fig. 2.12).

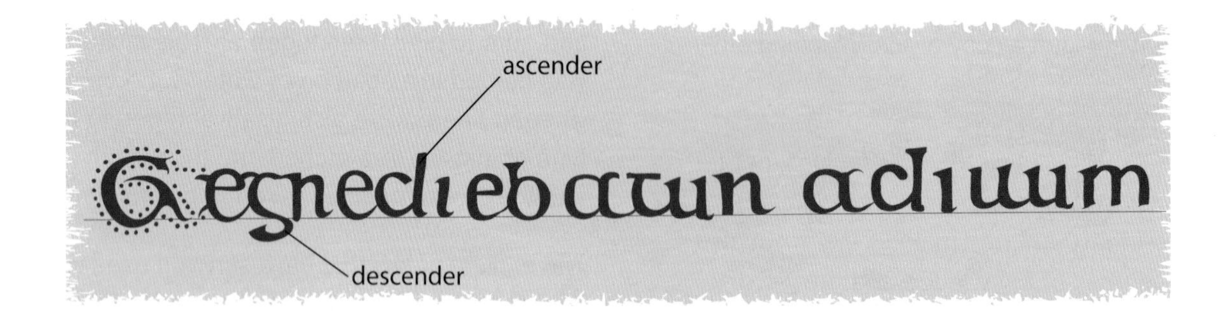

Fig. 2.12 Part of a line from the opening of St Mark's Gospel in the Book of Durrow showing the Insular majuscule style of lettering. It reads 'Et egrediebatur ad iuum' ('and they went out to him'). Parallel lines were lightly scored into the page as a guide for the scribe. The parts of letters above the line are called ascenders and parts below the line are called descenders. Some letters in this style are shaped differently so that they fit between the lines. For example, the letter *t* finishes at the cross stroke and the letter *r* looks like an *n*.

NOTE! The decoration used by the scribes seems to follow from the La Tène style (trumpet ends, spirals and a few animal and plant forms) along with the Christian cross and fish symbols.

The **diminuendo effect** is where the initial letter takes up four lines and the following letters gradually reduce in size until they are back to the general text size. This is a characteristic feature of Irish script that is not seen in Roman models.

The opening letter *Q* of Psalm 91, which begins 'qui habitat' (Fig. 2.13), shows a range of the designs used in this manuscript.

Historical background

The Cathach is probably the oldest surviving Irish manuscript. It was written in the late 6th century and is the second oldest psalter written in Latin in the world. Traditionally this book is from the hand of St Columba (Colmcille, 'Dove of the Church'), c. 521–597. He was the founder of the Columban order of monks who continued the tradition of manuscript writing and missionary work begun by their first abbot.

The name Cathach, an Irish word meaning 'battler', was given to the book by the O'Donnells, clansmen of Columba, who carried it with them into battle, invoking the protection of the saint.

This is reputed to be the book that Columba transcribed in haste without the permission of his master, Finnian, bringing about a court case that

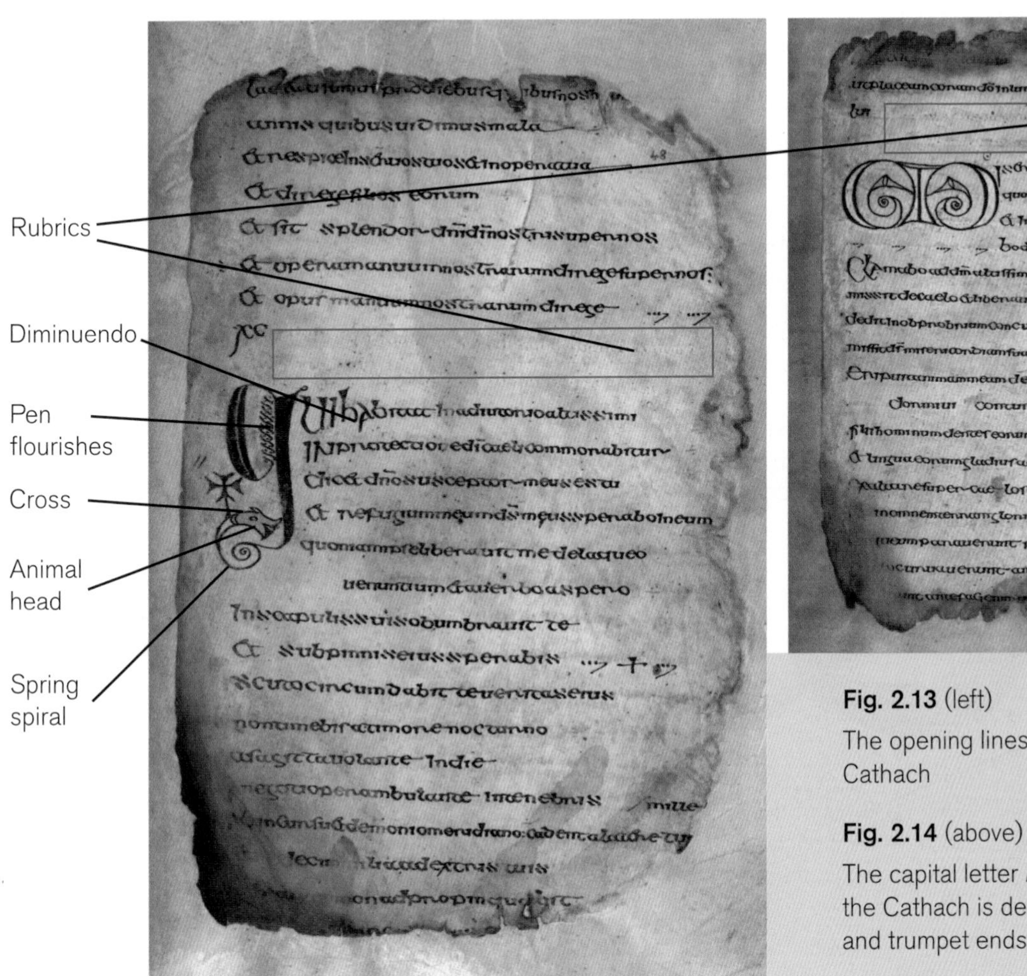

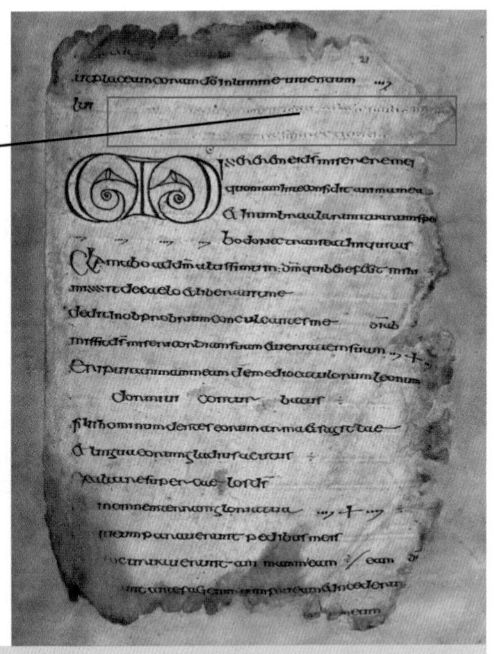

Fig. 2.13 (left)
The opening lines of Psalm 91 in the Cathach

Fig. 2.14 (above)
The capital letter *M* on folio 21a of the Cathach is decorated with spirals and trumpet ends

ruled 'to every cow its calf, to every book its copy'. Columba's clansmen disputed the court case and fought the Battle of Cuil Dremhne for ownership of the book. The story goes that Columba was so horrified by the death and destruction of the battle that he banished himself on permanent pilgrimage and exile from home. This *peregrinatio* (wandering) involved a life of prayer and self-denial while spreading the word of God to the heathen. His travels took him first to Iona, an island off the coast of Scotland where he founded a monastery that was to become the chief house of the Columban paruchia (family of monasteries) for the next 200 years. The missionary work then continued through Scotland to Northumbria in northern England.

The simple decoration employed in the Cathach is echoed in contemporary stone and metalwork. The small repertoire of designs and patterns forms the basis for the amazingly elaborate work produced by the following generations of craftsmen.

Metalwork

Roman designs found their way into Ireland through contacts with Britain and Gaul. A new range of objects appears at this time, including hand pins, penannular brooches, latchets and hanging bowls.

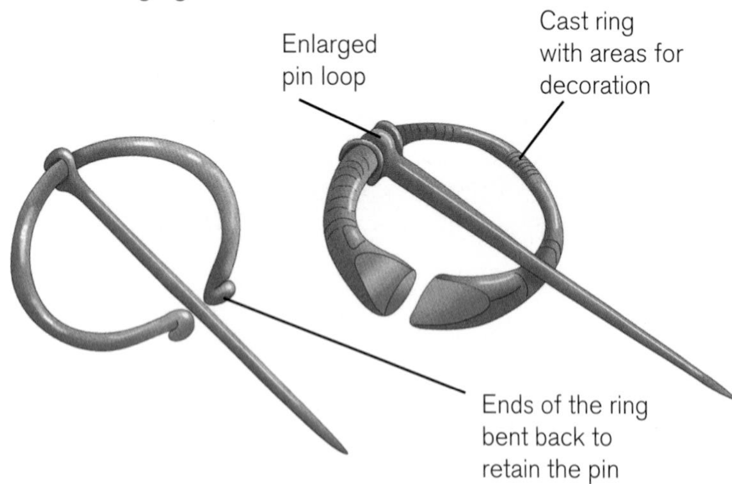

Fig. 2.15 Simple penannular brooches

Penannular brooches take the form of a broken circle with a pin attached to the ring. The earliest brooches were simple wire dress fasteners. The ends beside the opening in the ring were bent back to retain the pin, which was connected to it by a loop. Later, brooches were cast in bronze or silver (Fig. 2.15). As time went by, the loop on the pin and the decorated areas beside the opening of the ring were enlarged to incorporate more elaborate designs.

The Ballinderry Brooch (c. 600 AD)

* **Form:** A cast bronze ring with enlarged areas next to the opening. A pin with an enlarged loop and a bronze spiral are attached to the ring.
* **Function:** The brooch was used to fasten a cloak or tunic.
* **Technique:** The ring and pin were cast in bronze. There is millefiori glass decoration on the ends of the ring and on the pin head.
* **Decoration:** A range of textures and patterns on the cast bronze brooch form a zoomorph on each end of the ring. These animal heads are almost abstract. Viewed from above, their bulbous noses face the ring. Protruding eyes are met by the shield-shaped areas of enamel that form the tops of their heads, while small rounded ears border the opening.

The brooch, which was found at Ballinderry Crannog, is a beautiful example of the developing style (Fig. 2.16). Later brooches became even more elaborate and new techniques emerged through trade with Europe. Gold wire filigree is found in a few small pieces dating back to the 6th century. A small bird-shaped button was found in Lagore Crannog, where millefiori glass was also discovered in an enameller's workshop.

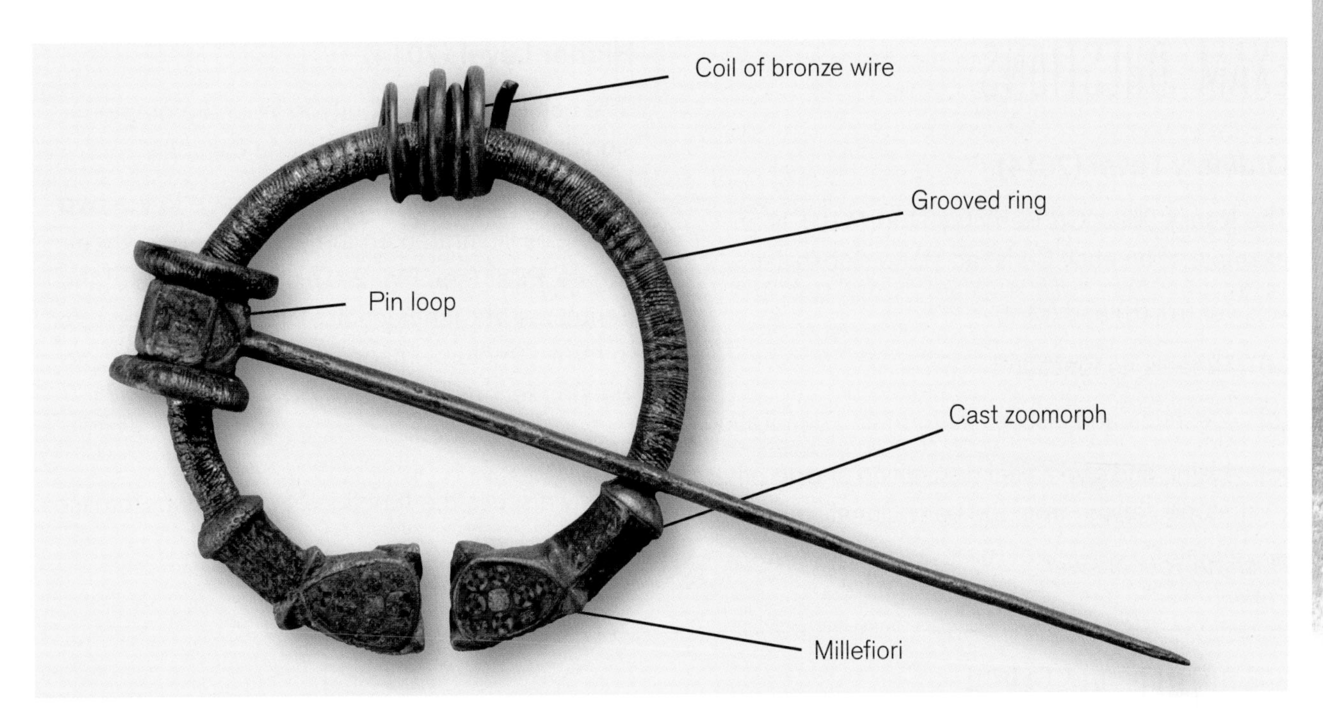

Fig. 2.16 The Ballinderry Brooch

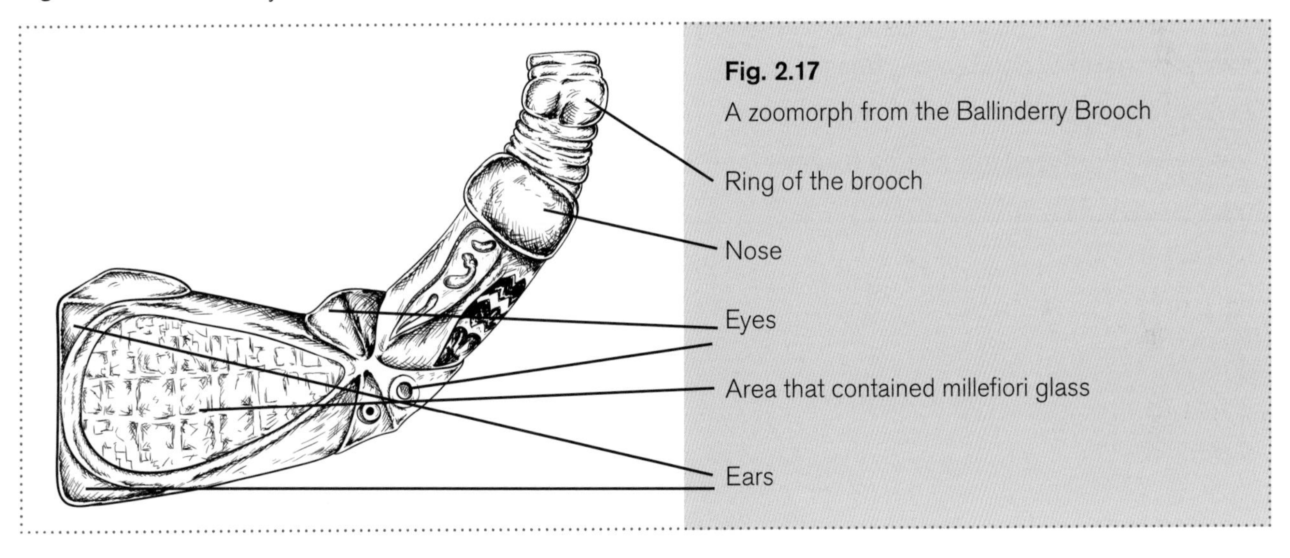

Fig. 2.17
A zoomorph from the Ballinderry Brooch

Chapter review

* The Christian mission to Ireland brought new influences and ideas. Can you identify some of these new elements in the crafts of the period?
* Judging from the buildings of the time, can you imagine the lifestyle of the early monks?
* What, do you think, was the purpose of the cross-inscribed pillars in early monasteries?
* Can you describe how vellum and inks were made?
* Can you identify some zoomorphs from 5th- and 6th-century craftwork?

NOTE! During the 5th and 6th centuries, technical skills and the variety of designs gradually increased to the point where all the elements needed for the explosion of creativity that happened in the 7th and 8th centuries were gathered together in the workshops of the larger monasteries.

EXAM QUESTIONS

Ordinary Level (2014)

The Reask Pillar, Co. Kerry (see Fig. 2.10), is an example of an early Christian stone slab/pillar.

Answer (a), (b) and (c).

(a) What is its function?

(b) Describe and discuss its form and decoration.

(c) Name and give a brief description of **one** other stone carving from the early Christian period.

Illustrate your answer.

Higher Level (2014)

'The coming of Christianity to Ireland prompted significant development in stone carving.'

Discuss this statement with reference to the **two** examples illustrated on the accompanying sheet (Reask Pillar (see Fig. 2.10) and the Cross of the Scriptures at Clonmacnoise). In your answer, refer to form, structure, imagery, decoration and stone-working techniques.

and

Briefly discuss the function of stone slabs/crosses.

Illustrate your answer.

FURTHER RESEARCH

www.irishtimes.com – A History of Ireland in 100 Objects

www.megalithicireland.com – Reask

www.ria.ie – Cathach Psalter, St Columba

www.sacredsites.com – Skellig Michael

Chapter 3

The 7th and 8th Centuries: Ireland's Golden Age

Political and social background

Europe became more stable through the establishment of strong kingdoms in the areas that are now France and Germany. Much of Europe was converted to Christianity, and the papacy had a stronger influence. Clergy from France converted southern Britain to Christianity.

Political and monastic dynasties in Ireland were also strengthened. The Uí Néill, kings of Tara, controlled the Midlands and a good part of Northern Ireland. They made an alliance with the Dál Riata, who were kings of Antrim and Argyll, which extended their influence into Scotland. The Uí Néill were in conflict with the Eóghanachta of Munster for 400 years.

The monasteries

Monasteries became more important in Ireland. They had become centres of learning and places of refuge for pilgrims, the sick, widows and orphans. Kells, Armagh, Glendalough, Clonmacnoise and other large monasteries grew in size and population and took on a new economic importance in the community. The simple austerity of the early monasteries was replaced by wealth and power, which even led to conflicts between monasteries.

By the end of this chapter, I will...

* Know about new influences on design from Britain and Europe.
* Be able to draw and describe the Fahan Mura Slab and the Carndonagh Cross.
* Learn how to draw and describe two pages from the Book of Durrow.
* Understand metalworking techniques.
* Know how to draw and describe the Tara Brooch and the Ardagh Chalice and some of their decoration, as well as another piece of metalwork.
* Be able to compare the design of human and animal figures in the different crafts.
* Be able to note the continuity and changes in each craft from earlier 5th- and 6th-century work and to later 9th- and 10th-century examples.

In 790 AD a war was fought between the monks of Clonmacnoise and the monks of Durrow.

Influences on design

Over a number of centuries, influences from outside mixed with native Irish design and evolved into a style that was used in all the crafts during the 7th and 8th centuries.

* Spirals and pelta shapes had their origins in Celtic design, which had already been in use for 800 years at this time.
* Interlace, which is of Coptic (the Christian church of North Africa and the eastern Mediterranean) origin, probably came to Ireland via the Mediterranean countries and Rome in particular, which had a strong input from the Middle East in early medieval times.
* Animal ornament of Germanic origin would have been introduced through Anglo-Saxon influences in Northumbria, which had close Irish connections.

Iconography (the symbolism of the images)

Though it is difficult to be certain about the meanings or significance that the artists of the early Middle Ages intended to put into their work 1,300 years ago, a certain amount is understood today. In this book, the meanings are given with the work as it is examined. This may lead to some repetition, but hopefully less confusion.

Structures (architecture)

Very little architecture survives that can be dated with any certainty to the 7th and 8th centuries. A few stone churches that would originally have had wooden roofs may date from this time. These

Fig. 3.1 Church with antae, Scattery Island, Co. Clare. The roofline was altered in later times.

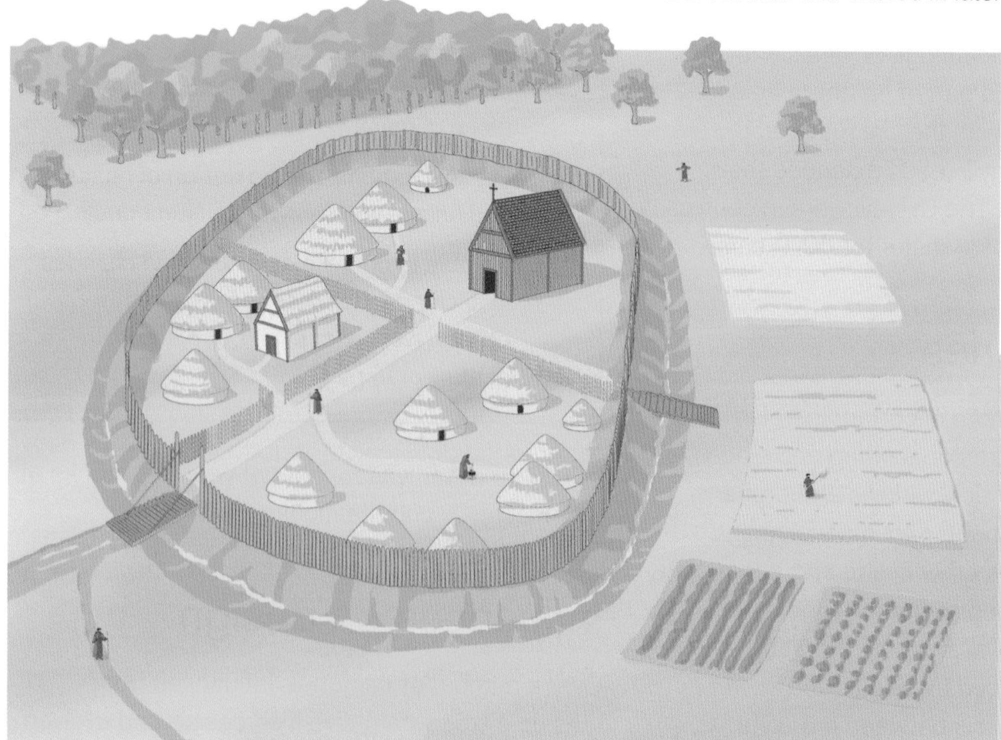

Fig. 3.2
A monastic enclosure with a wooden fence and church. Huts were built of wattle and daub with thatched roofs.

churches have antae (projections of the side walls beyond the surface of the gables), which may be an imitation, in stone, of corner posts from wooden buildings (Fig. 3.1).

Monasteries seem to have been laid out in the same way as they were in the 6th century, with a surrounding bank of earth or stone enclosing small stone or wooden buildings. This kind of enclosure could easily be expanded, adding more small buildings and moving the bank farther out to enclose a wider area (Fig. 3.2).

Stone carving

Cross-decorated slabs, simple crosses and grave slabs became more common in monasteries in the 7th and 8th centuries.

The Fahan Mura Slab

Fahan Mura in Donegal is the site of the monastery founded by St Columba for his disciple Mura, dating to the end of the 7th century AD.

- **Form:** A fully trimmed and dressed upright slab of stone with a low triangular top, the Fahan Mura Slab is 2.10m tall with low relief decoration related to Pictish slabs found in Scotland (Fig. 3.3). There are little stubs projecting from the sides of the slab, which some commentators regard as the beginnings of the arms that appear on later crosses.
- **Function:** This and other crosses may have been a focus point for prayer, a marker for the boundary of sanctuary, a memorial to a saint or perhaps all three.
- **Technique:** Carved in low relief using iron tools, the details are hard to see except in good light. The shallowness of the decoration has led some commentators to believe that the pattern may originally have been painted.
- **Decoration:** A pattern of outlined ribbon interlace is formed into a cross shape on both faces. On the west face, simple human figures stand at the left and right of the cross shaft. Each of these figures has an undeciphered inscription on their tunic.

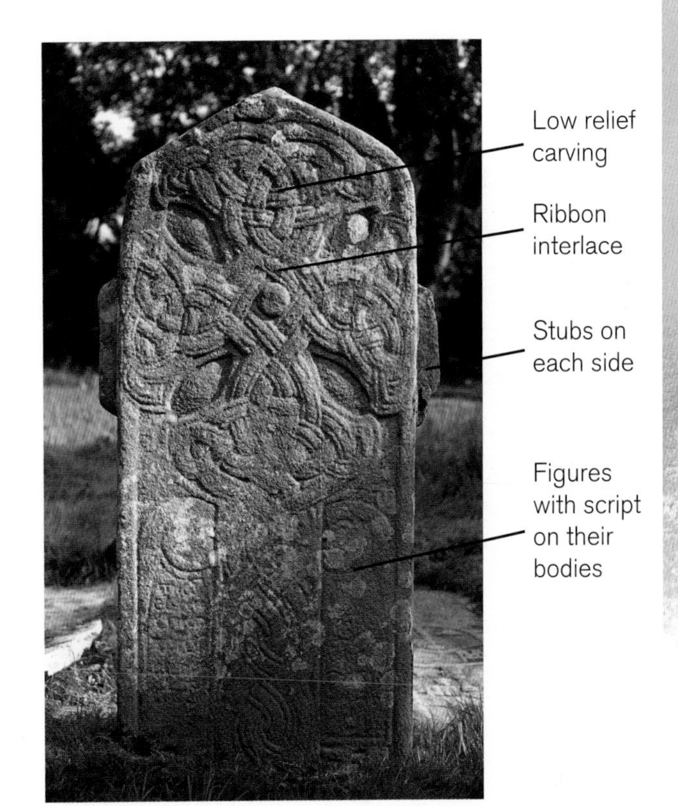

Fig. 3.3 The west face of the Fahan Mura Slab

NOTE! This decorated slab marks a further development in the art of stone carving in Ireland. It is a far more sophisticated piece of craftsmanship than we have seen before in stone. The accuracy of the design and the refinement of the low relief carving mark an important development in the evolution of Irish stone carving.

The Carndonagh Cross

The cross at Carndonagh in Co. Donegal (Fig. 3.4) was previously regarded as the transitional piece between stone slabs and pillars and the fully

Fig. 3.4 East face of the Carndonagh Cross, Co. Donegal

formed Celtic high cross. Scholars now believe that this cross is more likely to be contemporary with the early wheel-head crosses, but in a different style tradition. Like the slab at Fahan Mura, the Carndonagh Cross design may relate to the monastic connections between Donegal and Scotland.

* **Form:** The unevenly shaped cross stands 2.53m tall, without a wheel head.
* **Function:** Like other crosses, this may have been a memorial to a saint, a focus for pilgrims, a visual aid to help teach Bible stories, a marker of the sacred area surrounding the monastery or a focus for prayer. It could have been any or all of these things.
* **Technique:** Lightly carved with iron tools in low relief, it may have been painted originally.
* **Decoration:** The design in ribbon interlace on both faces of the cross echoes the designs found on Pictish cross slabs in Scotland. The ribbon interlace on the east face forms a cross on the upper part of the stone, with a little group of birds forming a triskele pattern in the crook of each arm. On the shaft there is a crucifixion scene and other groups of figures that are not clearly identified. There are small pillars beside the cross carved with figures representing David playing the harp, Jonah and the whale, and ecclesiastics with bell and crosier, all of which are themes that occur on other crosses.

The figures and patterns on the Carndonagh Cross are simple and linear. Detail could have been added by painting, creating an effect like the St Matthew figure page in the Book of Durrow (see Fig. 3.8).

Decorated grave slabs

Stone markers laid flat on the ground were the traditional style of gravestone from the 7th to the 10th centuries AD at the important monastic sites. The monastery at Clonmacnoise in Co. Offaly preserves a particularly good collection in a variety of sizes and patterns. Small slabs with a Greek cross inside a square seem to be the earliest type. A simple inscription, giving only a name, is all that accompanies the linear cross design. Larger, more elaborately carved slabs asking a prayer for the departed are probably from the 9th and 10th centuries, the period of the Viking invasions (Fig. 3.5). These slabs were decorated with accurately carved crosses with fret and spiral patterns at the centre and terminals. The designs executed on the grave slabs often resemble patterns in metalwork and book illumination.

Fig. 3.5

Two grave slabs. On the left is a decorated cross in a square frame, Durrow, Co. Offaly. On the right is a decorated cross with ring and terminals, Durrow, Co. Offaly. The inscription reads 'OR DO AIGIDIU'.

Manuscripts (book painting)

The Insular style

When new Irish monasteries were set up in Britain and Europe, they would originally have been stocked with books made in Ireland, and Irish monks probably trained the scribes in these monasteries. Influences from British and Continental traditions in art also found their way back into Ireland with migrating monks. Books in the Insular style survived in many European monasteries. Scholars can't be certain where every book was actually written, but there is a strong element of the Irish Celtic tradition in all of them.

Not many books survive from the 7th century. There are some from the monastery of St Columbanus at Bobbio in northern Italy, but we are very lucky to have an outstanding example in this country.

The Book of Durrow

* **Form:** The Book of Durrow is the earliest example (late 7th to early 8th century) of a fully decorated manuscript in the Insular style. It is a copy of the Four Gospels with some preliminary texts. The pages are 245mm x 145mm. There are 248 folios (leaves) of vellum, most of which have writing on both sides.
* The text is a copy of the Latin Vulgate version of the New Testament, which St Jerome compiled for Pope Damasus in the late 4th century AD in an effort to create a correct and standard translation of the books of the Bible.
* **Function:** This is a book of the New Testament, the Four Gospels of the Bible. A manuscript this richly decorated was meant for display rather than everyday use.

Technique

Making the book

The Book of Durrow was written on vellum pages.

The process for making vellum was described earlier (see Fig. 2.11). To assemble the pages into a codex, the vellum would have been cut into bifolia (a bifolium is a strip of vellum that is doubled over to create two pages), which were collected into groups called gatherings. These gatherings were then sewn together to form the codex or book.

Writing tools

Pens were made from the tail feathers of a goose or swan, but they could also be made from cut reeds. Brushes could be made from a variety of hairs tied into a goose quill ferrule. The hair of a marten could have been used for the finest brushes. Straight edges, a compass and dividers would have been needed for ruling out the pages and laying out designs.

Colours

Colours for the Book of Durrow were made in a variety of ways.

Orange-red was made from red lead. This is white lead that is heated, pulverised, washed, put back in an oven and stirred for two to three days until it reaches the correct intensity of colour. The resulting pigment was quite toxic.

Yellow could be made from ox gall, but it often discoloured to brown. A purer, brighter yellow was made from orpiment (from the Latin *auripigmentum*, which means 'gold pigment'). It is yellow arsenic sulphate, which had to be imported from parts of Europe or Asia, and is both toxic and foul smelling. It reacts chemically with lead or copper-based colours.

Green was most commonly made from verdigris, which is copper acetate, created by the action of ascetic acid and heat on copper. Sheets of copper smeared with honey and ground salt were placed in a hollowed-out section of oak that was filled with vinegar or hot urine, capped with wood and buried in dung for four weeks. Pigment could be scraped from the copper plates at intervals after this time. Verdigris could be unstable and has eaten through the vellum in parts of the Book of Durrow.

Decoration

There are 12 fully decorated pages and many more with decorated capitals. The script is in the Irish majuscule style, written in long lines across the page. Books of a similar type written in Lindisfarne and other Northumbrian monasteries with Irish connections were generally written in two columns. Smaller pocket gospels were also written in columns.

The decoration scheme

The Book of Durrow opens with some decorated pages. The first (folio 1v) is a carpet page with a design in the shape of a double-armed cross (Fig. 3.6). In the Coptic tradition of the eastern

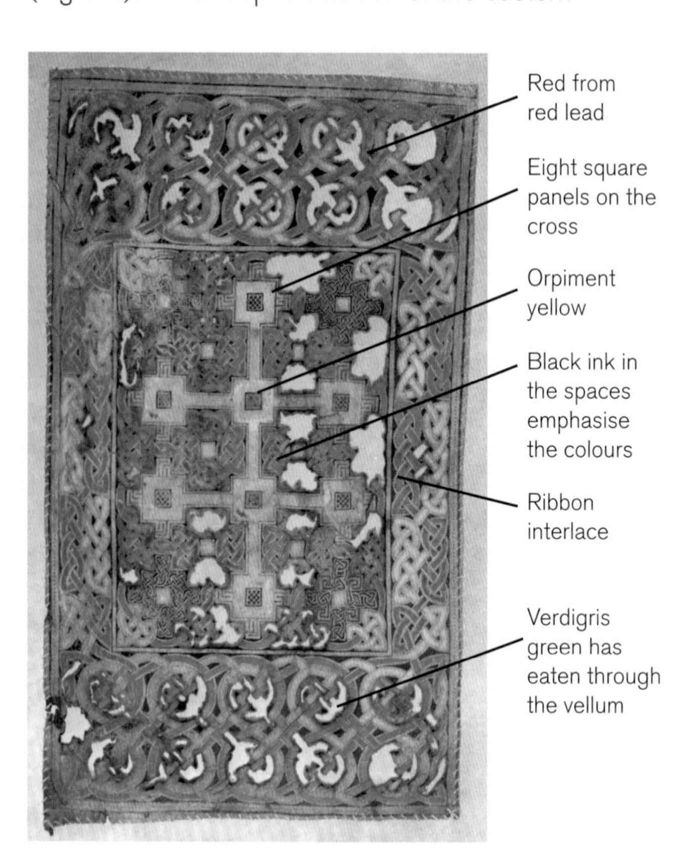

Fig. 3.6 The Book of Durrow, folio 1v, the double-armed cross carpet page

Mediterranean, double-armed metal crosses were used to house a fragment of the True Cross. The design may invoke the protection that such a relic would bring. The cross design includes eight squares, which may refer to the eighth day of Christ's passion (the resurrection). These symbols would announce the core message of the Bible, Christ's death and resurrection, for the sake of his faithful followers and mankind in general.

The Four Evangelists

Folio 2r is the second decorated page. It consists of a cross surrounded by the symbols of the Four Evangelists. These are framed in a pattern of squares in red, yellow and green that is quite faded and damaged (Fig. 3.7). The origins of the images of the Four Evangelists are based on the Bible, from Ezekiel 1:5–10 in the Old Testament and from the apocalyptic vision of St John 4:6–8. The creatures of these visions became associated with the Four Evangelists through the writing of St Irenaeus in the 2nd century, who compared them to the four regions of the cosmos and the four winds, which together symbolised the spread across the world of the message of the gospels. St Gregory, writing in the 4th century, identified the visionary figures as four stages of Christ's life: he was born as a man, put to death as a sacrificial calf, resurrected with the power of a lion and ascended into heaven like an eagle. St Jerome identified the man with Matthew, the lion with Mark, the ox with Luke and the eagle with John. In the Book of Durrow, the symbols are assigned by an older arrangement, where the lion is John and the eagle is Mark. On the Four Evangelists page, the artist has arranged the figures so that if you read them clockwise, you get the older order, and if you read them anti-clockwise, you get the more correct version of St Jerome.

The Four Gospels

The books of the Four Gospels begin on folio 21v. Each begins with an evangelist symbol page, followed by a carpet page (except in the case of St Matthew's Gospel, where the carpet page was misplaced at some point over the centuries; the book was quite jumbled up before it was restored in 1954). The first page of each gospel has a decorated capital letter. The opening lines are usually larger than the general text and are surrounded by red dotting.

Fig. 3.7 The Book of Durrow, folio 2r, the Four Evangelists page

NOTE! In a complete Bible manuscript, each gospel would begin with three decorated pages: an evangelist's symbol, a carpet page and an initial capital letter page.

The man symbol

The man symbol at the beginning of St Matthew's

Fig. 3.8 The Book of Durrow, folio 21v, the man symbol for St Matthew

Gospel is shaped like a contemporary Irish bell. The face is accurately drawn in fine line. There is no sign of arms or details of clothing (Fig. 3.8). The check pattern looks like millefiori glass decoration created in 7th- and 8th-century metalwork, and the overall shape of the figure is like those on the Carndonagh and Moone crosses. An area of plain vellum around the figure creates a well-designed balance with the heavily patterned areas. A border of ribbon interlace in shades of yellow and green surrounds the page. The area between the ribbons has been darkened for dramatic effect and a triangle of plain vellum breaks each dark triangular space into three parts, probably a reference to the Holy Trinity, which is picked up again on the Chi-Rho page.

The Chi-Rho

Folio 23r is the Chi-Rho page (Fig. 3.9). The Chi-Rho is a special decoration where the name of Christ is mentioned for the first time in the gospel. The letters *X* and *P* are the Greek letters Chi-Rho, which became a monogram for Christ. They are beautifully decorated with fine spring spirals and trumpets and surrounded inside and out

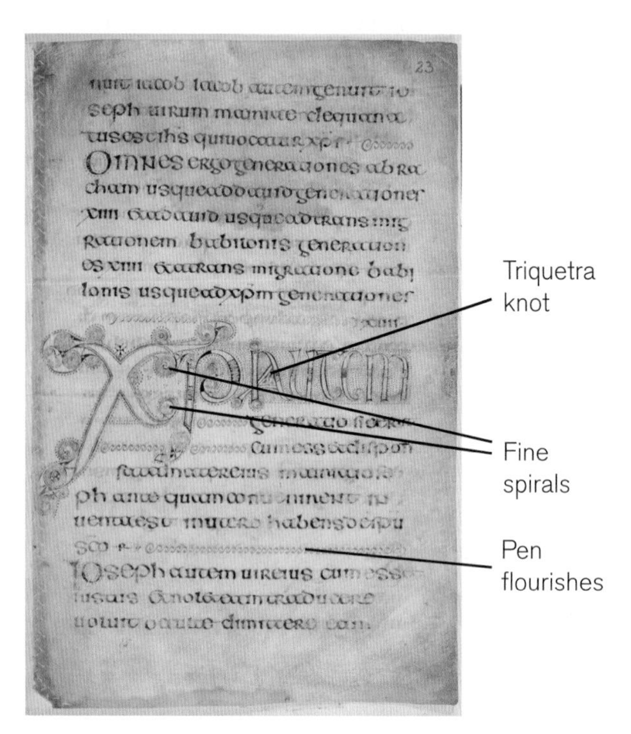

Fig. 3.9 The Book of Durrow, folio 23r, the Chi-Rho page

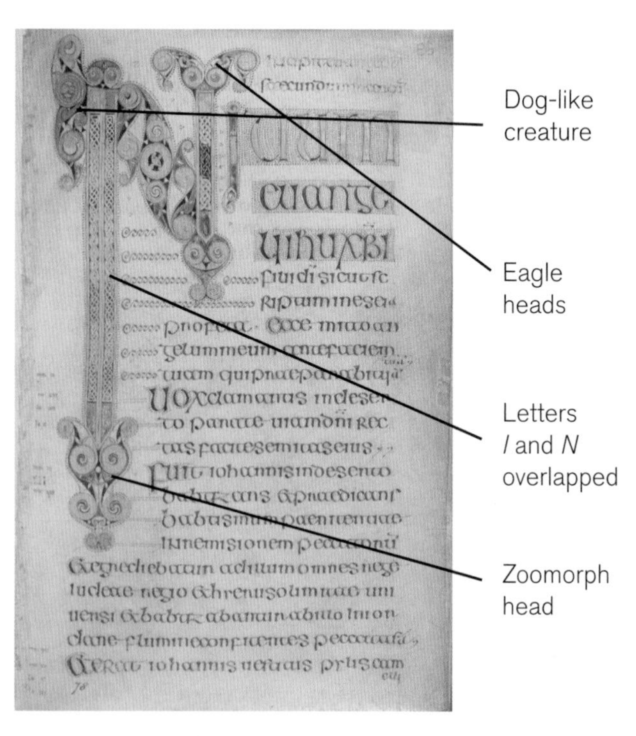

Fig. 3.10 The Book of Durrow, folio 86r, the Initium page from the beginning of St Mark's Gospel

by a field of red dotting, except for the space between the *X* and the *P*, which has little triangles of dots. The centre of the *A* has a triquetra knot, a symbol of the Trinity. The little cross at the top of the *X* is similar to the one on the tail of the *Q* at the beginning of Psalm 91 in the Cathach. The enlarged letter size at the beginning of each passage is a development of the diminuendo effect we saw in the Cathach. The most elaborately decorated letters are the opening lines at the beginning of each gospel.

Initial letter pages

The Initium page (folio 86r) from the beginning of St Mark's Gospel is the best preserved of the initial pages (Fig. 3.10). The letter *I* takes up three-quarters of the height of the page, with a sharp diminuendo to the *N*, *I* and *T*. The first three lines are surrounded with red dotting. The spirals and trumpet scrolls that decorate the ends of the *I* and *N* become zoomorphs on closer inspection.

Interlace and number symbolism

In some cultures, interlace patterns are considered to be a protection from evil. Intricate patterns, particularly ones with animal heads, were thought to be capable of confusing and intimidating evil spirits. This may be a reason for including such patterns at the beginning of the manuscript and at the start of each gospel.

Number symbolism is a common theme in early medieval Christian art. It was designed to aid the contemplation of the reader and to help them find new layers of meaning in the texts. A four-part design could imply the Four Gospels, the Four Evangelists, the four cardinal virtues, the four rivers of paradise, the four rings that carried the Arc of the Covenant, the four qualities of Christ and other meanings depending on the context of the design.

Animal interlace

The page of interlaced animals on folio 192v at the beginning of St John's Gospel is one of the highlights of the Book of Durrow and is full of number symbolism (Fig. 3.11). The circle in the middle of the page has a cross at its centre, which is surrounded by a three-part interlace pattern in red, yellow and green. Three discs with a black and white step pattern, which make cross patterns, punctuate the rim of the circle. These discs look like the glass studs with wire grilles that are found on the Ardagh Chalice and the Derrynaflan Paten. The emphasis on three-part patterns within the circle is a reference to the Trinity; the panels of three biting dogs to left and right might also have this underlying meaning. The panels of elongated animals in the top and bottom sections are alike, but they are not mirror images of each other. It can be interesting to unravel an animal interlace and see how the leg, tail or jaw can be extended

Fig. 3.11 The Book of Durrow, folio 192v, animal interlace carpet page at the beginning of St John's Gospel

to loop around other limbs or back on itself to fit the artist's pattern. The inner rows of eight animals refer to the eighth day of the passion of Christ, the resurrection. The top and bottom patterns have 10 animals in each panel, a reference to St Augustine's perfect number, 10, which symbolised unity. There are a total of 42 animals on the page, which may be a reference to the 42 generations of the ancestors of Christ.

Origins of the book

There has been much discussion in the past as to the origin of the Book of Durrow. Its associations with the Columban monastery at Durrow can be verified as early as 877 AD and in 916 AD, when it was enshrined in a metal case that is now lost, but the book does seem to be older than these dates. It was probably written in the late 7th or early 8th century.

The book we see today is in remarkably good condition considering the ups and downs of its 1,300 years of existence. It was knocked about during its enshrining in a metal cumdach (book shrine) in 916 and its value as a miraculous object led its keepers in the 17th century to dip it in water that they used to cure sick cattle, which caused some staining and loss of colour. It has been in the care of Trinity College Library in Dublin since the late 17th century and was completely restored and rebound in 1954.

Fig. 3.12 The Lindisfarne Gospels, cross carpet page

Insular manuscripts in Europe

A number of 8th-century Gospel books survive. A manuscript from Durham Cathedral Library, the Lindisfarne and Lichfield Gospels are all in England. Gospel books from Echternach in Luxembourg, Maihingen in Germany and the Abbey Library of St Gall in Switzerland are all written in the Irish style of script. They all have portraits of the evangelists, carpet pages, decorated initials, animal interlace and a wide range of colours. These books give us a wider picture of the style and quality of Irish manuscripts (Fig. 3.12).

Metalwork

The metalwork in the 7th and 8th centuries is of a very high quality. It is easily the most elegant and technically refined work of any country in Europe during the early Middle Ages. It might help to examine some of the techniques before we look at the objects themselves.

Metalwork techniques

* **Enamelling:** A variety of techniques were used in enamalling.
    - **Cloisonné:** Areas of design were surrounded with silver, gold or bronze wire and filled with enamel.
    - **Champlevé:** An old Celtic technique in which areas of a surface were carved away or beaten hollow and the spaces created were filled with enamel.

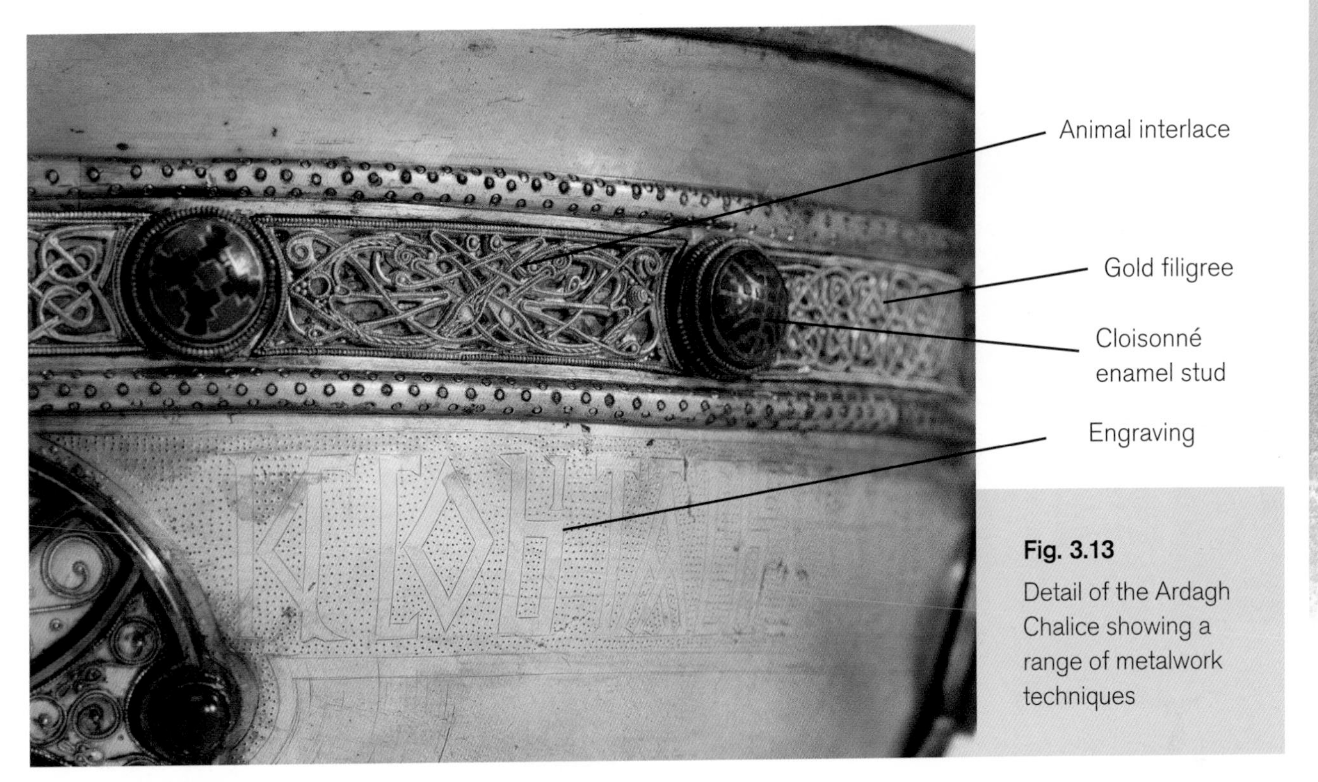

Fig. 3.13
Detail of the Ardagh Chalice showing a range of metalwork techniques

- **Millefiori:** Rods of coloured glass were heated and drawn together in a molten state and stretched into long, thin rods from which fine sections could be cut off and applied to enamel surfaces. The sections can look like flowers, hence the name millefiori, which means 'thousand flowers'.
- **Studs:** Studs were cast in clay moulds. Some had wire grilles fitted into the mould and were then filled with coloured glass enamel. Other studs were cast with hollow spaces, which could then be filled with a second colour.

* **Filigree:** Consisted of thin gold wires that were twisted together into a fine rope. Sometimes wires of different sizes were twisted together to create a more glittering effect. The filigree was bent into shape and soldered to a gold foil background that could then be fixed in its place (Fig. 3.13).
* **Chip carving:** Chip carving was a technique of carving metal in high relief, creating sharp outlines and deep shadows.
* **Casting:** A variety of methods and techniques were used in casting. Clay and bone moulds were used to create both plain and decorated objects. The lost wax technique was used for more complicated objects. Chip carving was sometimes imitated in cast designs.
* **Engraving:** Engraving involved cutting a design into a metal surface with a sharp point. Sometimes two metals were laid one on top of the other so that the colour below would be revealed when the upper metal was engraved.
* **Die stamping:** Die stamping involved stamping a thin sheet of metal, usually gold or silver, with a design that had been carved into a block of wood or cast into metal.
* **Turning:** A sheet of metal was pressed onto a former, rotating on a lathe, and gradually shaped into a bowl or cone shape, as required. The lathe was also used to polish beaten metalwork.
* **Amber:** Amber, which is fossilised resin, was cut to shape and used like enamel studs as a contrast to areas of filigree or chip carving. The amber could be heated and lightly moulded into shape.

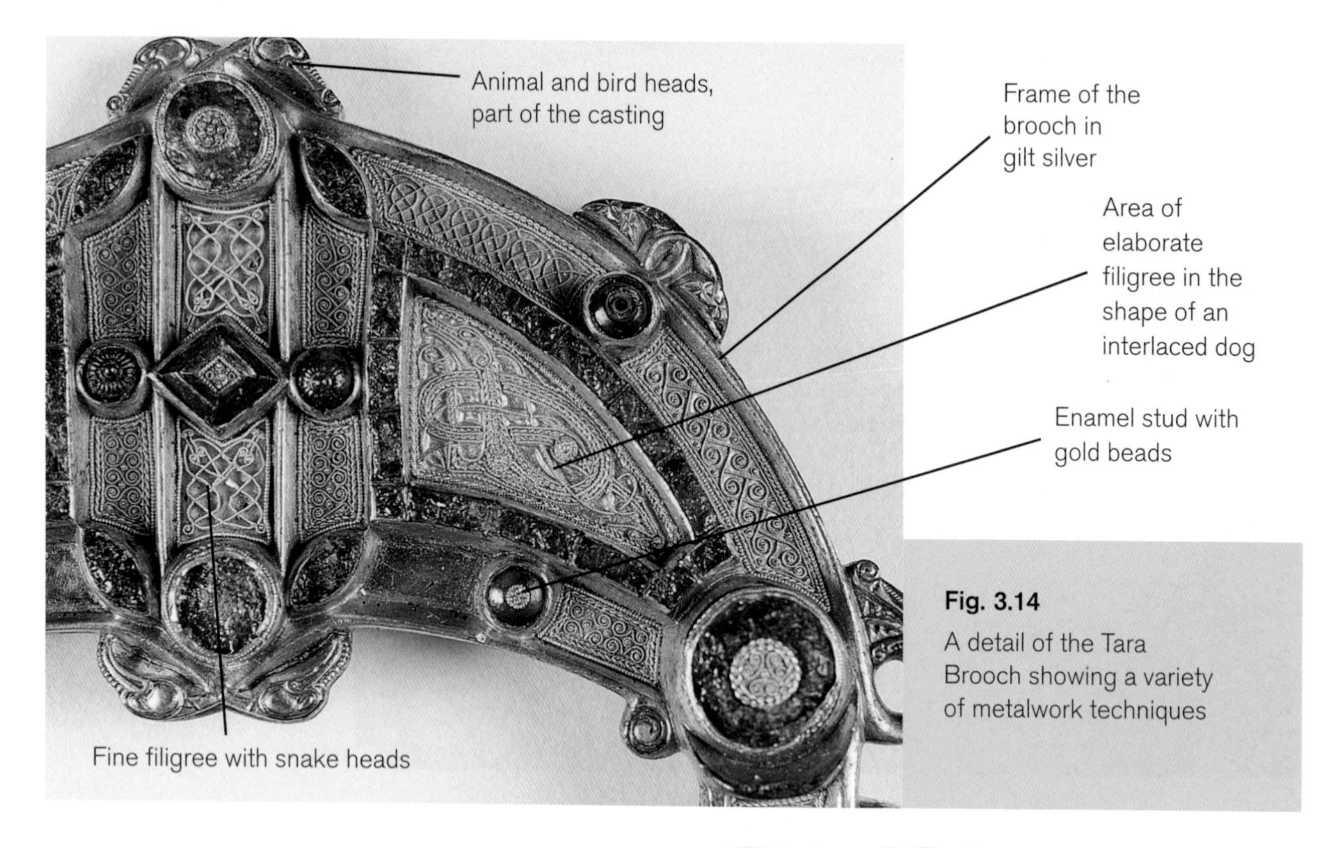

Fig. 3.14
A detail of the Tara Brooch showing a variety of metalwork techniques

* **Trichinopoly:** Trichinopoly is a type of wire mesh made in copper, silver or gold. It is formed into a chain on the Tara Brooch (Fig. 3.14) and is used to cover the rim on the Derrynaflan Paten.
* **Gilding:** There were two methods of gilding bronze or silver.
  - Gold leaf was attached mechanically. This was not often done.
  - In fire-gilding, gold was dissolved in mercury and applied to the surface, which was heated. The mercury evaporated, leaving a thin layer of gold.

Elaboration of design

At the beginning of this chapter we noted three sources for the origins of Christian Celtic design. In the following metalwork objects we will see how these basic elements were elaborated and distorted to create designs of the most extraordinary quality. There is nothing second-hand or copied in these designs. The elements were used with flair and originality to create a unique and subtly balanced art.

Pseudo-penannular brooches had larger decorated areas covering up to half of the ring. They look like penannular brooches, but the circle has been closed.

Many penannular and pseudo-penannular brooches ranging in size from 7cm to 13cm in diameter are known from the 7th and 8th centuries. Of these, the Tara Brooch is the finest (Fig. 3.15).

The Tara Brooch

The Tara Brooch was found in 1850 beside the sea at Bettystown in Co. Meath, near the mouth of the River Boyne. Though some sections are damaged, enough remains to give a clear impression of the quality of the craftsmanship and design that went into its manufacture. The chain attached to one side suggests that it was connected to a matching brooch, one worn on each side of the chest, with the chain connecting them.

* **Form:** The body of the 8th-century brooch, which is 8.7cm in diameter, was cast in silver, creating a raised framework. The front face of the brooch is divided into panels of filigree, separated by amber and enamel studs. There is a large area of decoration on the head of the pin.
* **Function:** Brooches were fasteners for cloaks or tunics. There were laws controlling the size and quality of brooches that could be worn by people from different levels of society. Brooches may have been part of clerical garb. They are shown on some of the figures carved on high crosses.
* **Technique:** The main body and the pin of the brooch are cast, creating frames to hold the decorative parts. Filigree is used in most of the panels on the front, separated by enamel studs. The reverse side of the brooch (Fig. 3.16) has sections cast in high relief, with zoomorphs and spiral patterns separated by enamel studs. Every part of the brooch that has not been decorated separately has been gilded. There are two silvered copper plates with fine spiral patterns engraved into them on the widest part of the ring on the back of the brooch. A cast double head connects the frame to a trichinopoly chain, which may have connected to a matching brooch.

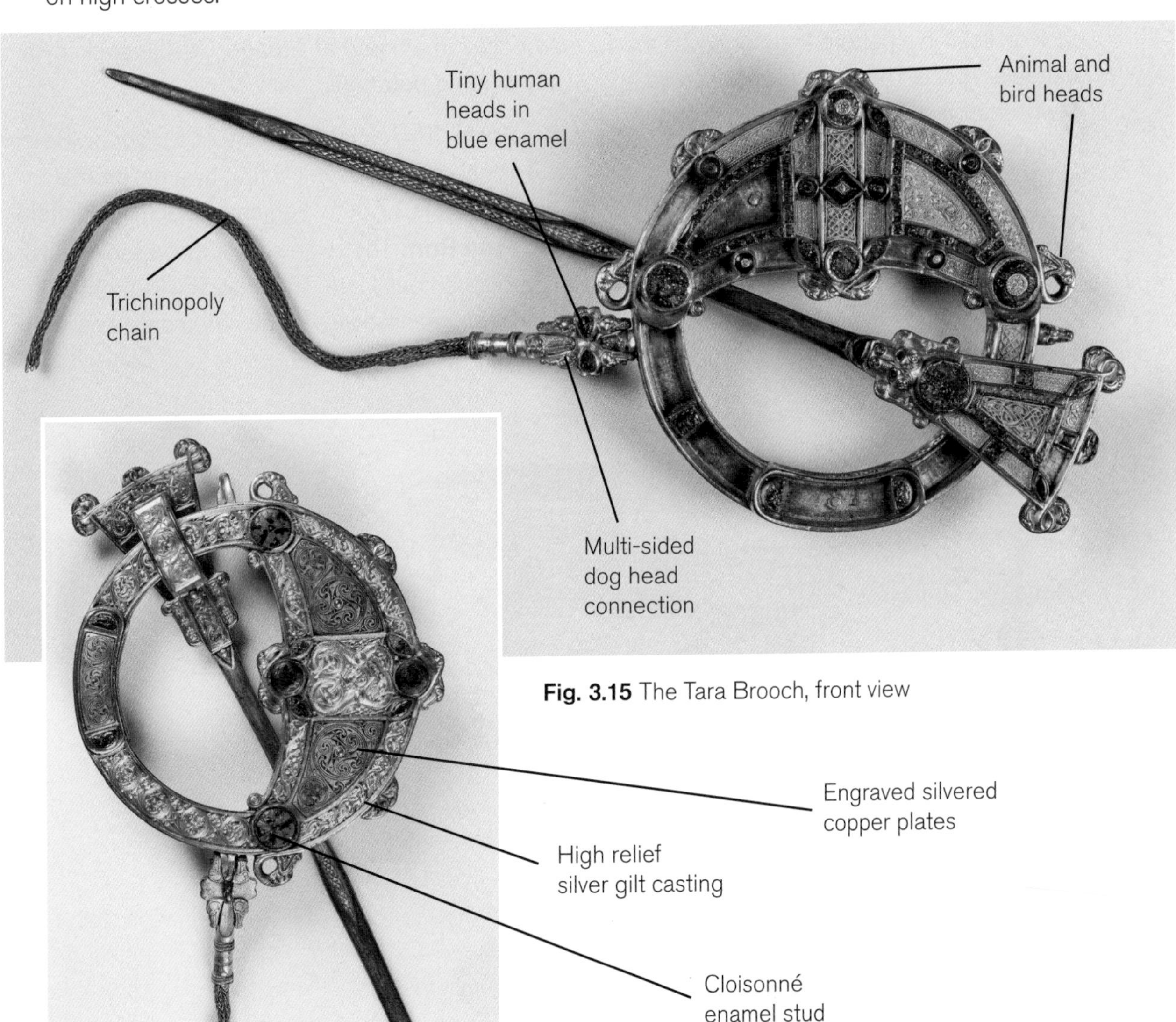

Fig. 3.15 The Tara Brooch, front view

Fig. 3.16 The Tara Brooch, back view

* **Decoration:** Fantastic animals seem to be the theme of the Tara Brooch. Stylised animals appear in the filigree sections, in cast areas, on the back, at several places on the perimeter, on the pin, and on the chain connection.
  - The trichinopoly chain is attached to the rim by an intriguing series of animal heads with interlocked jaws. This link also contains two tiny human faces made of moulded blue glass.
  - Most of the filigree is very fine and is wrought into spiral and interlace patterns. In the panel that remains at the centre left of the brooch there is an amazing dog design. His body, which is made up of a range of different-textured filigree strands, turns back on itself in a pattern that tightly fits the triangular space. The dog, which is upside down when viewed from the front, would have been right way up for the wearer looking down at it. There is another animal like him on the head of the pin.
  - One could read the pattern at the centre of the front of the Tara Brooch as a cross and the animal patterns could have a Christian meaning.

Communion vessels

The large chalice and paten that survive from the 8th century are in a style not common in Europe. The closest comparable pieces are of an earlier date and are from Syria. This does not necessarily mean that there were direct connections between Ireland and Syria, but it does point to differences in religious practice between Ireland and the rest of Europe.

The Ardagh Chalice

Many of the techniques we have seen used in the Tara Brooch were also used in making the Ardagh Chalice (c. 750 AD) (Fig. 3.17). It was found in 1868 with a small bronze chalice and three large brooches in a hoard at Ardagh, Co. Limerick, by a boy digging potatoes.

* **Form:** The chalice is made of a silver bowl connected to a conical foot by a gilt bronze collar. It is 17.8cm high and 19.5cm in diameter.
* **Function:** The large size of the vessel points to ceremonial use. The chalice was probably a *calyx ministerialis* (large ceremonial chalice),

Fig. 3.17 The Ardagh Chalice, front view

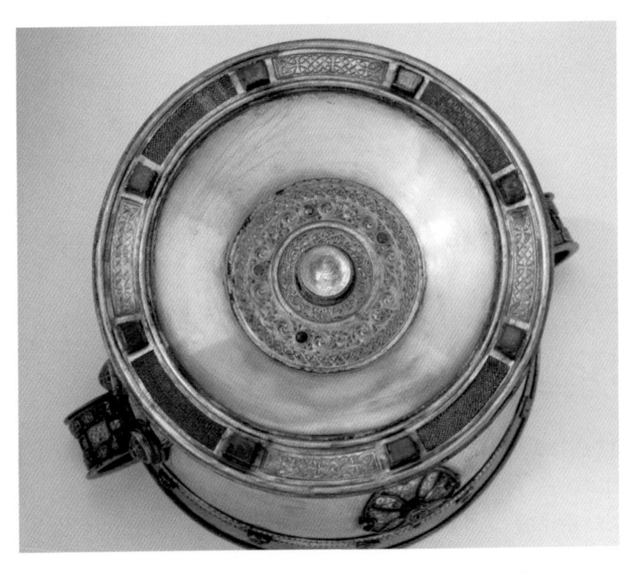

Fig. 3.18 The Ardagh Chalice, underside of the foot

which would have been used to distribute wine to the congregation and was probably brought to the altar in an offertory procession.

* **Technique:** The silver bowl and foot were made from sheet silver turned on a lathe. Gold filigree is soldered onto fine gold sheet and fixed into framed areas. Glass enamel studs with cloisonné decoration separate filigree areas. The stem that joins the bowl to the base was cast.
* **Decoration:** The decoration of the chalice is a masterpiece of subtlety and refinement, with an almost perfect balance between areas of sumptuous decoration and the plain silver of the bowl and foot.
  - A band of decoration just below the rim is made up of panels of gold filigree punctuated with 12 glass studs. The filigree is a mixture of animal and abstract panels. The names of the apostles are lightly engraved in a field of dots just below this band, and are probably symbolised in the 12 studs.
  - The handles and the plaques that attached them to the bowl are decorated with gold filigree, red and blue enamel, and glass studs inlaid with silver wire.
  - Two medallions in the shape of a Greek cross in a circle are placed centrally on each side of the bowl of the chalice. They are also decorated with filigree and glass studs.
  - The collar joining the bowl to the base is cast, in imitation of high relief chip carving, in spiral and interlace patterns.
  - A rim around the upper surface of the conical foot is decorated with filigree panels punctuated by squares of blue glass.
  - Underneath, at the centre of the foot, is a large glass crystal (which hides the bolt connecting the foot to the bowl). This is surrounded by three bands of decoration. The inner band, an animal interlace, is in gold filigree; the middle band has chip carved spiral decoration punctuated by small glass studs with gold granulations; and the outer band has an abstract interlace pattern in the chip carved style (Fig. 3.18).

The Derrynaflan Paten

This paten is the only one of its kind to come to light so far. It was found in 1980 at the monastery of Derrynaflan in Co. Tipperary. It was buried under a bronze cauldron with a chalice and other objects, which we will see more of later. The discovery of this paten shows that work of the quality of the Ardagh Chalice and Tara Brooch was not a rarity in Ireland in the 8th century. It adds to our understanding of the richness and quality of the craftwork of the period.

* **Form:** The paten is 35cm in diameter and made of over 300 components.
* **Function:** The large paten would have been used for distributing communion bread to the congregation and it would have been carried in procession. There are instructions in the Stowe Missal for the ceremonial breaking of bread, laying it out in the form of a wheeled cross on the paten, with different sections assigned to different parts of the congregation.

* **Technique:** The beaten silver dish has a gilt bronze rim, which is decorated with gold filigree panels and cloisonné enamel studs (Fig. 3.19). The rim is riveted onto the silver dish. A ring of trichinopoly wire, in copper and silver, frames the decorated upper rim and conceals the joint between it and the side panels. Die-stamped gold foil panels decorate the sides of the rim and the foot.
* **Design:** The design of the filigree panels relates closely to those on the Ardagh Chalice, as do the enamel studs. The quality of the decorative elements is very high.
  - Animal, human and abstract designs are used in the filigree (Fig. 3.20).
  - There are 24 glass studs around the upper rim of the paten. The number is probably a reference to the 24 elders of the Apocalypse who were seated around the throne of God. These studs are in two groups: 12 larger and 12 smaller, perhaps a reference to the apostles. The 12 smaller studs are set in little cups containing fine filigree. These studs hide the rivets that join the components of the paten together. All the studs are more patterned and colourful than any we have seen before.
  - The die-stamped gold panels on the side of the rim are decorated with interlace and scroll patterns. The panels on the foot are similar but not as finely made.

Shrines and relics

The fashion for pilgrimage was strong throughout Europe. Relics and shrines to saints became an essential part of any large monastery. Shrines in a variety of shapes – house-shaped, book shrines and a variety of other types and shapes – were made to display the relics of the saints.

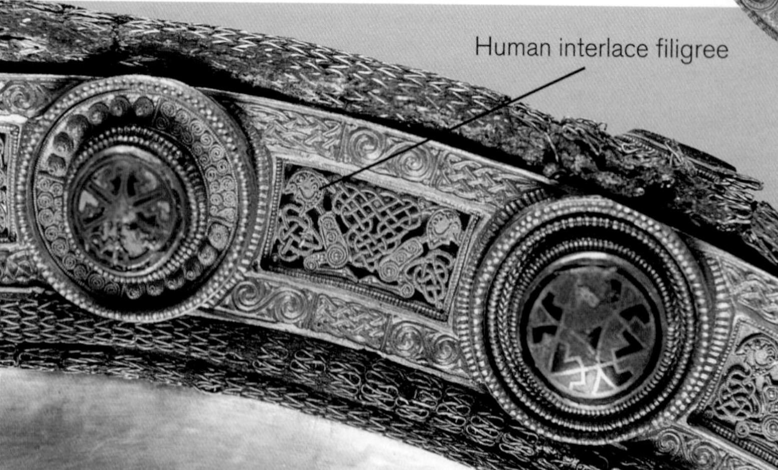

Fig. 3.19
The Derrynaflan Paten, viewed from above

Fig. 3.20
The Derrynaflan Paten, a section of the rim showing human interlace filigree and enamel studs

Fig. 3.21 The Athlone (Rinnegan) Crucifixion Plaque

The Rinnegan or Athlone Crucifixion Plaque

* **Form:** An 8th-century gilt bronze decoration that was probably once attached to a wooden book box. Holes around the perimeter would have allowed it to be pinned to the wood.
* **Function:** Probably a decoration on a book box or shrine box.
* **Technique:** A gilt bronze plaque, cast in low relief, with the areas between the figures cut away (Fig. 3.21).
* **Decoration:** The figures in the crucifixion scene are similar to ones we have seen on the Carndonagh Cross and in the Book of Durrow. An angel sits on each of Christ's shoulders and the sponge and spear bearers are at his sides. The figures are decorated with spirals based on triskeles and bands of interlace.

The Emly Shrine

* **Form:** It is house or tomb shaped, made of yew wood and decorated with silver, gold, enamels and gilt bronze (Fig. 3.22).
* **Function:** A portable reliquary.
* **Technique:** A wooden box with silver set into the surface, framed with gilt bronze binding strips. Champlevé enamelled plaques are fixed to the top and sides.
* **Decoration:** The whole surface is covered in a step pattern of silver inlay, which creates a pattern of silver crosses against the dark wood. The circular medallions fixed to the box have a simple pattern in green and yellow champlevé enamel. The decoration at the top of the shrine takes the form of a ridgepole that you might find on a wooden house or church. It has an animal head at each end, again in green and yellow enamel.

Fig. 3.22 The Emly Shrine, a house-shaped shrine

The Tully Lough Cross

- * **Form:** An 8th- or 9th-century wooden cross almost 2m tall, with metal decoration (Fig. 3.23).
- * **Function:** An Irish altar cross that could be carried in procession.
- * **Technique:** The sheet metal parts on the surface of the cross are nailed onto an oak core. The edges are finished in tubular binding strips with animal head cast terminals. Originally the decorated areas were gilt and the flat areas were tinned, which would have created a much more glittering effect than the exposed bronze plates and castings that we see today. The central pyramid-shaped boss originally had amber studs in the settings at the centre and corners.
- * **Decoration:** The front of the cross is more decorative than the back. It is divided into areas of interlace and figure panels interspersed with cast bosses and areas of plain metal. The two openwork figure panels are almost identical. A kilted figure with an open-mouthed animal on each side may represent Christ between two beasts or Daniel in the lions' den. All the bosses have chip-carved designs using a range of La Tène motifs.

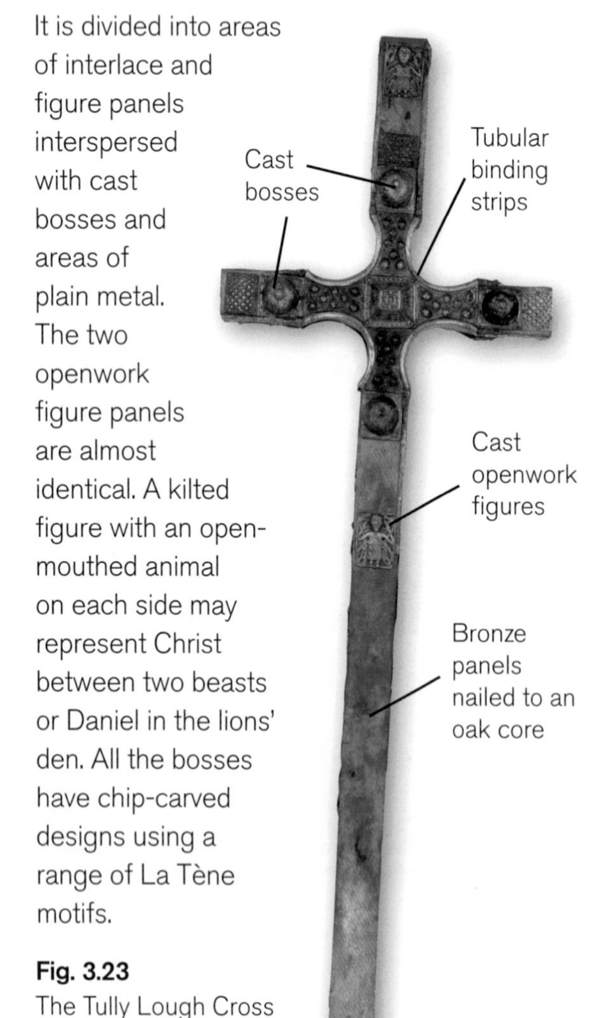

Fig. 3.23
The Tully Lough Cross

The human figure

During the 7th and 8th centuries the human figure was more symbolic than realistic. The figures on the Carndonagh Cross, in the Book of Durrow and on the Tully Lough Cross all have large oval heads with large almond-shaped eyes, small noses and simple, straight mouths. Their bodies and limbs are small and simply treated. The figure of St Mark from the Book of Durrow and some of the minor figures on the Carndonagh Cross are not even given arms. Feet generally face the same direction and are shown in side view. Figures in the filigree sections of the Derrynaflan Paten are more animated but just as stylised and unrealistic (Fig. 3.24).

Fig. 3.24 Human figures in 7th- and 8th-century Irish art

Human interlace panel from the Derrynaflan Paten

Christ figure from the Carndonagh Cross

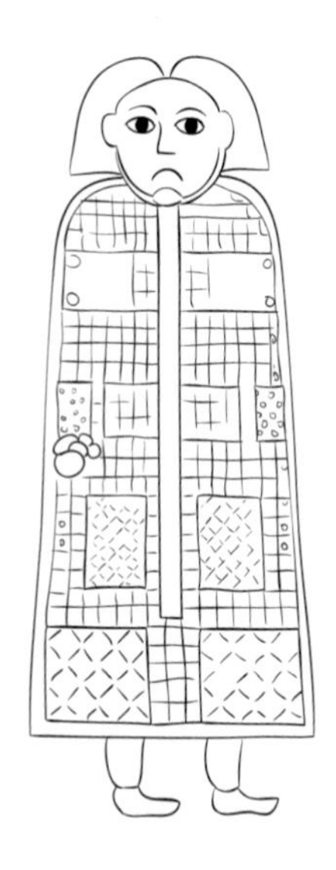

Man symbol for St Matthew in the Book of Durrow

Animal figures

Animals are used in a variety of ways as part of designs. Simple birds appear on the Carndonagh Cross. Bird heads appear on the outline of the Tara Brooch and on the Initium page in the Book of Durrow, where we also find a kind of dragon head made of spirals at the bottom end of the letter *I* (Fig. 3.25). This relates back to the terminals on the Ballinderry Brooch. Still on the Initium page, we find a dog-shaped animal clinging to the top left corner of the *I*. He has relatives on the animal interlace page in the Book of Durrow (folio 192v), which are interlaced together in a variety of patterns. The limbs, tongues, tails and crests of these creatures can be extended to any length and intertwined with each other or themselves. Creatures also appear in the areas of interlace, such as the dog in the triangular space on the Tara Brooch and other creatures on the Derrynaflan Paten. All these animals are used for their decorative qualities rather than having any meaning or symbolism.

Chapter review

* The 7th and 8th centuries were a high point in Irish art and learning. Why, do you think, did so much time, effort and expense go into craftwork at this time?
* Messages and symbols were an important part of the designs for all the crafts. What, in your opinion, was the point of these signs and symbols?
* How would you describe human and animal figures from 7th- and 8th-century Irish art? Use examples to help your description.
* What, do you think, are the most remarkable features of the metalwork on the Tara Brooch and the Ardagh Chalice?

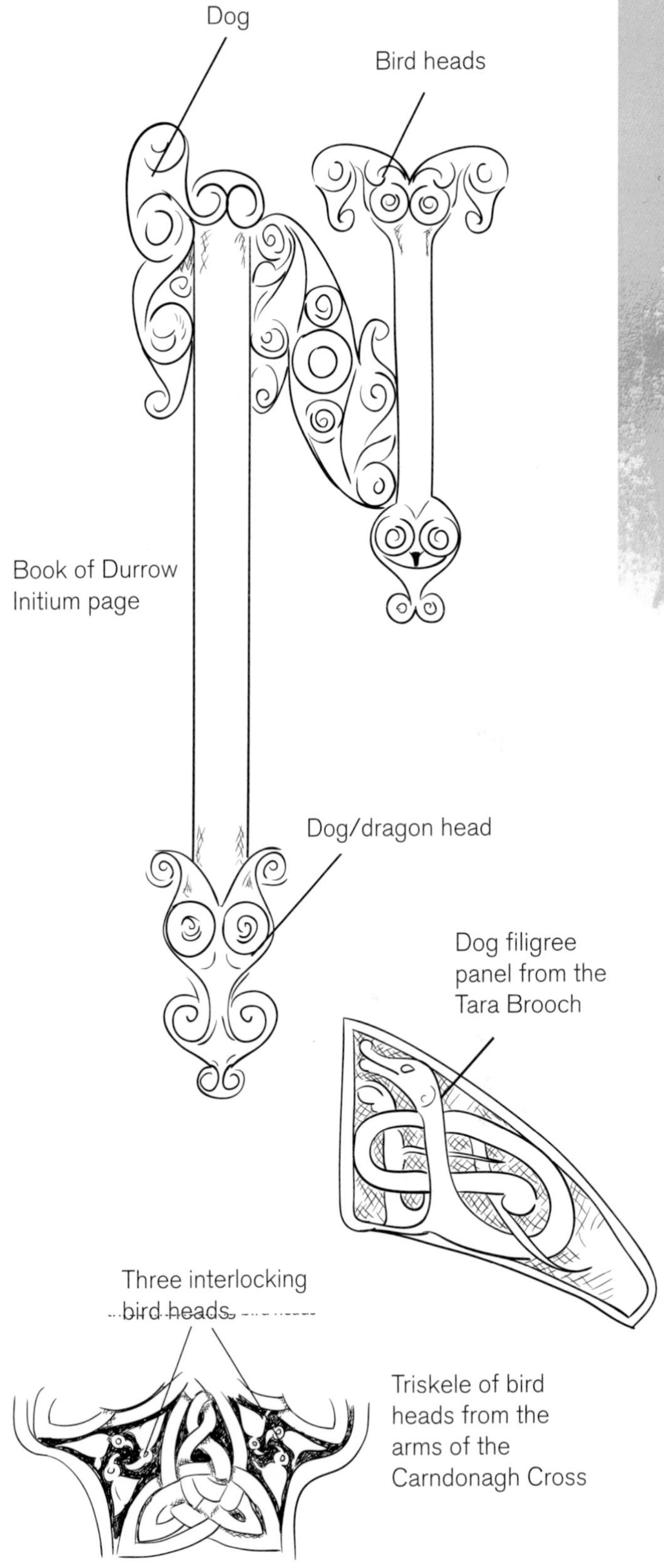

Fig. 3.25 Animal figures in 7th- and 8th-century Irish art

EXAM QUESTIONS

Ordinary Level (2016)

The Ardagh Chalice (see Fig. 3.17) is an example of Irish Christian metalwork.

Answer (a), (b) and (c).

(a) What was its function?

(b) Describe and discuss how it was made and decorated.

(c) Name and briefly describe **one** other metal artefact from this period.

Illustrate your answer.

Higher Level (2015)

'The skills of early medieval metalworkers have left us with a legacy of unique treasures.'

Discuss this statement with reference to the artefact illustrated on the accompanying sheet (the Tara Brooch with a detail of the decoration on the front of the ring; see Fig. 3.14). In your answer, name the artefact and refer to its function and form, and to the materials and techniques used in its production and decoration.

and

Name and describe **one** other early medieval artefact that was made using similar techniques.

Illustrate your answer.

FURTHER RESEARCH

www.3dicons.ie – Fahan Cross

www.arthistoryleavingcert.com – Early Christian Ireland Manuscripts

www.megalithicireland.com – Carndonagh High Cross

www.museum.ie – The Treasury Exhibit

Chapter 4

The 9th and 10th Centuries: The Viking Invasions in Ireland

Political and social background

Viking raids on Irish monasteries began in the year 795 AD, when several islands off the north and west coast were plundered. The island of Iona, where the chief monastery of the Columban order was located, was raided in that year and again in 802 and 804, when 68 people were killed. By 807, the Columbans had moved their headquarters to Kells in Co. Meath, which was away from the coast and immediate danger of Viking attack. In the first 40 years of the 9th century, most raids were on the northern coast, but in 842 they overwintered in a defended ship harbour in Dublin and established a settlement there. In the following years they established settlements at Arklow, Wicklow, Wexford, Waterford, Cork and Limerick. To an extent they were absorbed into the Irish tribal system, though periods of warfare and raiding were common until the end of the century.

The Vikings caused a good deal of destruction raiding monasteries, which were the centres of population and wealth in Ireland. Pieces of Irish art have been found in graves in Norway, including parts of book covers and reliquaries that were cut up to make jewellery. The Vikings took slaves, which they traded for silver in the Middle East. They traded and raided all over Western Europe, from Russia to the Mediterranean, gathering great wealth, some of which came back to Ireland.

By the end of this chapter, I will...

* Know the effect of the Vikings on Irish art.
* Be able to draw and describe a round tower.
* Know the origins of the wheel-head high cross.
* Be able to draw and describe at least two high crosses. I should know two panels from each and understand subjects, style and techniques.
* Be able to draw and describe at least three pages from the Book of Kells: one each from the Goldsmith, the Illustrator and the Portraitist. I should know the subjects, style and techniques involved.
* Know about the changes of style in metalwork and be able to draw and describe the Derrynaflan Chalice.

NOTE! There was also a positive side to the Vikings. They established the first towns and introduced coinage. They paid tribute to the local Irish kings, often in the form of silver, which became more readily available to Irish craftsmen. Precious metals were not easy to obtain up to this time in Ireland and were used in tiny amounts to gild bronze. Only the most important pieces used pure precious metals.

The monasteries

In spite of the Viking raids, Irish monasteries grew as centres of learning and pilgrimage, so expansion and reorganisation became necessary. A cross slab or a tomb shrine often marked the grave of the founding saint. Sometimes an oratory (a house of prayer) was placed over the tomb of the founder, as at Clonmacnoise (Fig. 4.1) and Glendalough.

Structures (architecture)

Stone churches

In the 9th and 10th centuries, stone churches became more common. There are a number of examples at Clonmacnoise in Co. Offaly. Temple Ciaran, only 3.8m x 2.8m internally, may have been an oratory to house the remains of the saint. The cathedral, which originally measured 18.8m by 10.7m, was the largest stone church in Ireland until Norman times (Fig. 4.2). It was built between 908 and 909 AD. Most of these simple rectangular churches have antae, which are projections of the side walls beyond the gables. Some art historians consider these antae to be a copy in stone of corner posts from wooden buildings. The roofs of these early stone churches were steeply pitched in the style of the wooden buildings that they copied, though many gables were lowered during later medieval reconstructions.

Fig. 4.1
An aerial view of Clonmacnoise. The round tower and the cathedral can be seen on the left. The monastery covered a much wider area in the 10th century.

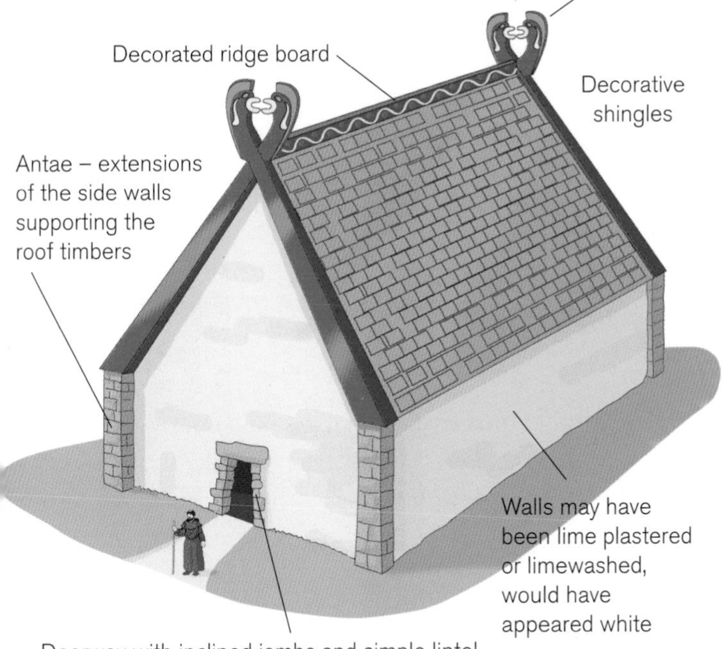

Zoomorphic heads on roof timbers. May have been painted (see temptation page in Book of Kells [Fig. 4.33]).

Decorated ridge board

Decorative shingles

Antae – extensions of the side walls supporting the roof timbers

Walls may have been lime plastered or limewashed, would have appeared white

Doorway with inclined jambs and simple lintel

Fig. 4.2 A conjectural reconstruction of the cathedral at Clonmacnoise

A few 10th-century churches have the chancel at the east end separated by a round-headed arch from the nave. These churches have a mixture of ancient and more up-to-date features. The antae are gone, replaced by corbels to carry the roof timbers. Trinity and Reefert churches at Glendalough, Co. Wicklow (Fig. 4.3), which are of this type, have small flat-headed doorways and small windows with arches cut from a single stone, which harkens back to the earliest churches.

Fig. 4.3 Reefert Church at Glendalough. Note the arch separating the nave and chancel, and the simple flat-headed doorway.

NOTE! Irish buildings were designed in a conservative style and were very small compared to contemporary European churches. This was probably a result of the different, rural, social structure and the style of monasticism practised here. Adherence to the ancient rules of the founding saints created problems when the Irish church came in close contact with the revitalised monastic orders of Europe.

Round towers

From early in the 10th century AD, round towers became part of the range of buildings found in Irish monasteries. An entry in the Annals of the Four Masters for the year 960 AD is the first written reference to a round tower: 'The Belfry at Slane was burned by the foreigners [the Dublin Vikings] with its full of relics and distinguished persons, together with Caeineachair, lector at Slane, and the crosier of the patron saint, and a bell, the best of bells.' Obviously the belfry was built before this date, which gives us an approximate starting point (Fig. 4.4).

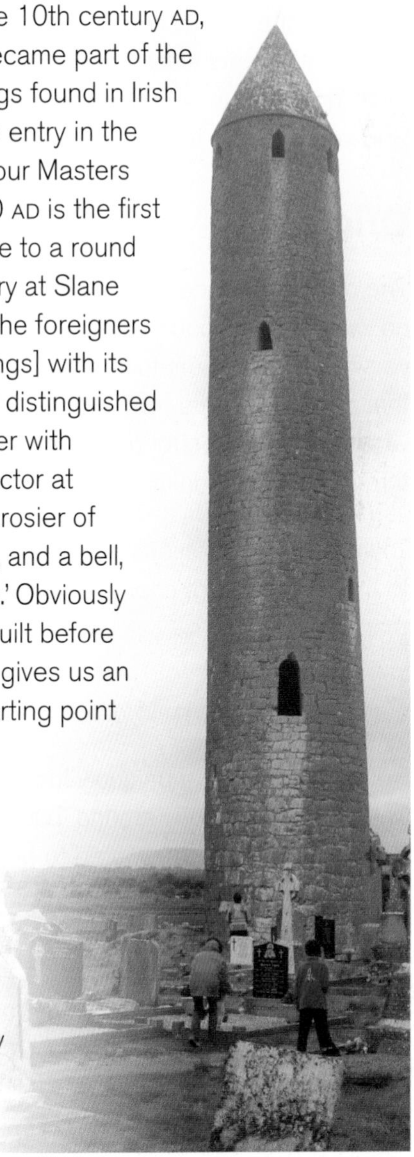

Fig. 4.4
Round tower at Kilmacduagh, Co. Galway. Note the very high doorway on this tower.

The Irish word for a round tower is *cloicteach*, literally 'bell house', which describes its primary function of calling the monks to prayer from their various duties around the monastery and surrounding fields. From the entry in the annals on the previous page we can see that towers were also used as the treasury to keep the relics and valuables of the monastery safe and as a place of sanctuary in times of trouble, but that sanctuary was not always respected.

Round towers would have been outstanding buildings in a society that normally built small-scale, low-profile buildings. They would have been important landmarks and status symbols pointing out places of pilgrimage and learning, distinguishing monastic sites from secular settlements. Remains of over 60 towers exist today, and there is evidence of far greater numbers having been built during the 250 years before the Norman invasions.

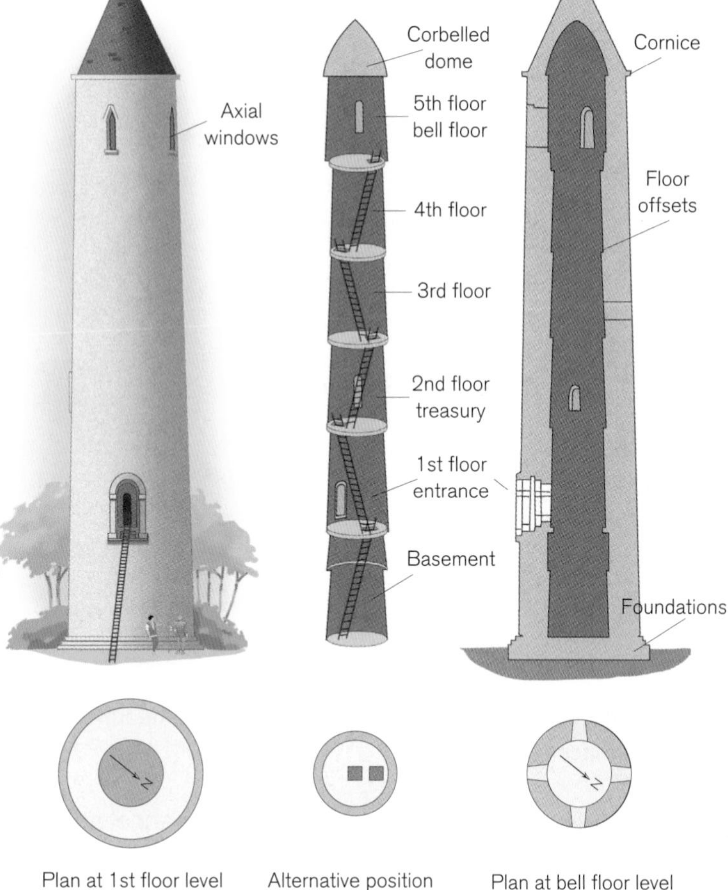

Fig. 4.5 The structure of a round tower

Origins

The origins of round towers are not clear. There is no evidence of wooden predecessors or simpler versions – they seem to begin as a fully formed idea that may have come from Britain or the Rhineland, where there were strong contacts with Ireland through pilgrim monks.

Towers in these regions would have been attached to the west front of churches, which were larger than Irish buildings.

Construction

Round towers are a uniquely Irish construction. They were frequently around 100 feet tall (the number 100 was considered to be a perfect number in medieval times). In proportion, towers were often twice the height of the circumference of the base. This not only led to an elegant shape, but also a stable structure. Construction followed the ancient tradition of building on a circular plan, though churches were the exception, as they were built on a rectangular plan.

Towers generally had quite shallow foundations less than 1m deep, constructed of large stones built in layers gradually stepping inwards to the diameter of the base of the tower (Fig. 4.5). The cylinder of the tower was built of an outer and inner skin of carefully selected or cut stone. The space between was filled with rough stone and lime mortar. It was this infill of stone and mortar, which turned to concrete when it set, that gave the towers their structural strength. When construction reached about 1m in height, a wooden scaffold was built to allow work to continue at a higher level. The scaffold was connected to the tower by put lock holes, which would have received wooden beams to build the scaffold on. Put lock holes can be found on the exterior of many towers, showing where the scaffold was connected to the rising walls.

Stone carving

The Celtic high cross

The earliest written mention of a high cross is in the Annals of the Four Masters for the year 951 AD, but crosses are clearly older than this. There are written accounts of crosses made of wood and stone from Northumbria in Britain, an area with strong Irish connections dating back to 750 AD. The Tully Lough Cross (see Fig. 3.23), now on display in the National Museum in Dublin, is a rare survivor of these wood and metal crosses, which may have been part of the inspiration for the shape and design of high crosses.

Numbers

Remains of over 200 high crosses exist in Ireland, but this may represent only part of the number that once existed. Several crosses are found at some sites, though the same Bible scenes are not often repeated at the same monastery. Not all crosses have figure scenes or decoration. There may be as many as 16 large plain crosses and over 40 with geometric ornament or an inscription but no figure scenes. Most of the crosses were erected in the 9th and 10th centuries, when the Columban order, which was based in Iona and Kells, created an impetus for cross construction.

The shape of the high cross: The ringed cross (the jewelled cross)

The reason for the shape of the Irish high cross seems to originate in the large jewelled cross that was erected on the hill called Golgotha (where Christ was believed to have been crucified) in Jerusalem by the Emperor Constantine to celebrate the finding of the True Cross by his mother, St Helena, in the 4th century AD. Images in early mosaics, manuscripts, sculptures and wall hangings show the cross on a stepped base, which represents Golgotha.

The cap on the top of crosses is thought to represent the church that Constantine built over

House-shaped cap represents the chapel Constantine built over the Holy Sepulchre.
The ring represents the wreath of victory (Christ's victory over death). The circle also represents eternity and the universe.
Shaft
Base
The whole image represents the cross erected in Jerusalem to celebrate the finding of the True Cross

Fig. 4.6 The parts of a high cross

NOTE! A wreath or circle surrounding the crossing of the shaft and the arms represents Christ's victory over death. It also represents eternity or the universe. Multiple layers of meaning attach to many parts of and scenes on Irish high crosses; this was a common element in medieval art and writing.

the Holy Sepulchre. It can be seen as a symbol of resurrection and eternity (Fig. 4.6).

The function of the high cross

The high cross standing in a monastic enclosure in Ireland represented the True Cross: the symbol of resurrection, which was the centre of Christian belief. It was also a reminder of the relics and holy places that a pilgrim might see on a visit to Jerusalem, the holiest place in the Christian tradition. Respect for the symbolism of the high cross made them important as markers of the boundaries of sanctuary in the monastery.

Sermons in stone

Crosses were used to illustrate Bible stories for the illiterate public. They were also a focus for prayer and repentance – most of the crosses with Bible scenes were designed to be read from the bottom up, starting from the eye level of a penitent kneeling in prayer. Scenes on Muiredach's Cross at Monasterboice in Co. Louth echo the penitential litanies that the monks would have chanted.

Prefiguration: A term used to note an image or idea that was imagined in earlier times. Scenes on high crosses from the books of the Old Testament in the Bible are understood to predict events that came about hundreds of years later in the life of Christ in the New Testament.

The crosses

The Ahenny Crosses

The Ahenny group of crosses is situated in a river valley north of Carrrick-on-Suir, Co. Tipperary, on the border with Kilkenny. They are located at Kilkieran, Killamery, Kilree and Ahenny itself. They seem to be a manifestation of the jewelled cross (see the previous page) in Ireland.

The shaft and arms are covered with patterns of curves, knotting, fretwork and spirals, which have close relationships with contemporary metalwork. A raised border of what looks like woven wire translated into stone surrounds the cross and ring, like the border on the Derrynaflan Paten that hides the edges of the metal plates. Stone bosses appear in high relief at the centre of the cross, and where the ring passes through the arms and shaft, they look like the studs that are used in metalwork construction to hide the rivets that join metal plates together.

This group of crosses was once thought to belong to the 8th century, but now they are placed in the early 9th century, along with the majority of high crosses.

The North Cross at Ahenny

* **Form:** An early 9th-century wheel-head cross, it stands 3.13m tall on its stepped base (Fig. 4.7).
* **Function:** It seems to commemorate the jewelled cross erected at Jerusalem, and marks the sacred area surrounding the monastery.

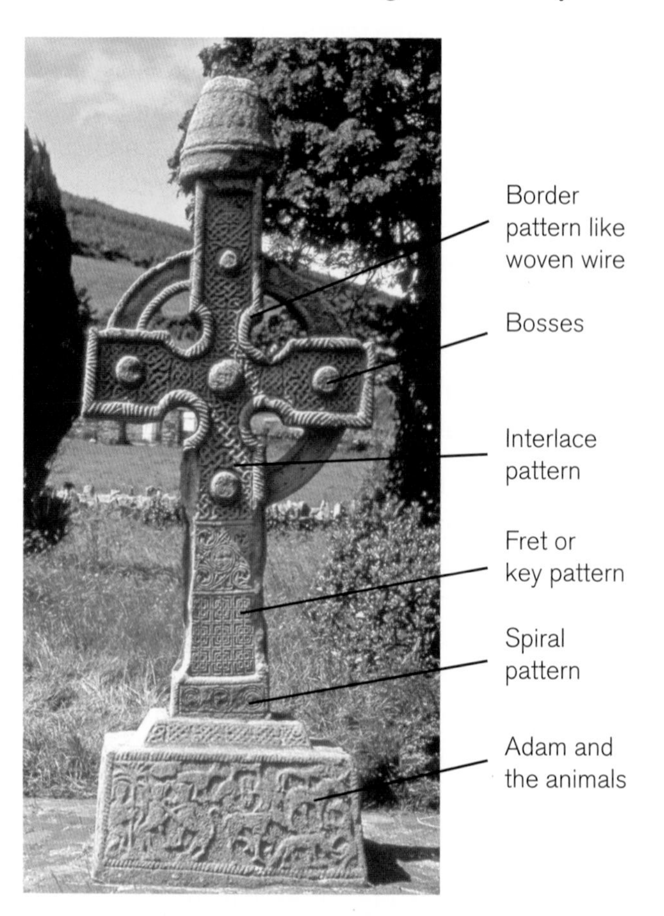

Fig. 4.7 The North Cross at Ahenny, Co. Tipperary, east face

Fig. 4.8

The North Cross at Ahenny, west side of the base. The figure in the centre facing forward is thought to represent Christ. The three figures facing him on each side may represent the apostles. Note the different styles of crosiers that they carry.

* **Technique:** The cross is carved from one piece of stone set in a base. There is fine detail cut with iron chisels.
* **Decoration:** The cross itself is completely encrusted in abstract pattern, including one panel of human interlace on the west face of the shaft. On the other hand, the base is decorated with human and animal figure scenes, which Peter Harbison, in his great survey of Irish high crosses, suggests can be read as lessons in the power and gifts of God and the victory of good over evil.
  - On the west face of the base is a group of seven figures with crosiers, representing Christ's mission to the apostles (Fig. 4.8).
  - On the east face a man sits under a palm tree facing a group of animals (Adam being given dominion over the animals).
  - On the north side, David charges into battle on a chariot, while on the south side David carries Goliath's head in a procession, with Goliath's headless body tied to a horse.
  - The style of figure carving is simple and non-classical, more in the Celtic tradition of symbolism in preference to realism. The low relief panels on the base of the North Cross are worn and difficult to see clearly except in good light.

The South Cross at Ahenny

The panels on the base of the South Cross (3.9m tall) are even more difficult to make out. Each face on the base is divided into two panels, with animal and human figure scenes (Fig. 4.9). One of the scenes on the eastern side may represent Daniel in the lions' den, but the meaning of the other panels is difficult to work out.

There are patterns of circles and spirals on the shafts of both the North and South Crosses, which are linked in style to the carpet page (folio 3v) in the Book of Durrow.

Fig. 4.9

The South Cross at Ahenny, east face. The spiral pattern on the lower part of the shaft has similarities with the pattern on folio 3v in the Book of Durrow.

The granite crosses

Most of the Irish high crosses are carved in sandstone, but in the area around Kildare there are a number of crosses carved in granite. This hard, granular stone presents a problem for the sculptor, as fine lines and small details are not possible and a smooth finish is hard to achieve. Despite these difficulties, interesting, even beautiful crosses were created in a design style that relates back to the Celtic traditions rather than the more classical style that we will see on the Scripture crosses from the Midlands.

The Cross of Moone

The monastery at Moone was probably a Colomban house. The cross on this site is unique in style and layout.

* **Form:** Over 7m tall, it is the second tallest cross in Ireland. Its height is emphasised by the narrow shaft and small wheel head. It is carved from three blocks of granite (Fig. 4.10).
* **Function:** This is another illustrated cross. The theme of the Cross of Moone seems to be the help that God gives his faithful followers, which is illustrated in scenes from the Old and New Testaments. A medieval monk looking at the scenes on this cross would have deciphered layers of meaning in all the scenes. Events recorded in the Old Testament were often understood as a prefiguration of events in the life of Christ and his followers.
* **Technique:** The stone carver was limited in the detail he could achieve by the hard granite he was carving.
* **Decoration:** Most of the upper part of the cross (the shaft, arms and head) is carved with patterns. A figure of Christ in Majesty appears on the crossing on the east side and animals appear in panels on the west side of the shaft. The tall base, which is almost square in plan, has figure scenes on every side, set in panels.

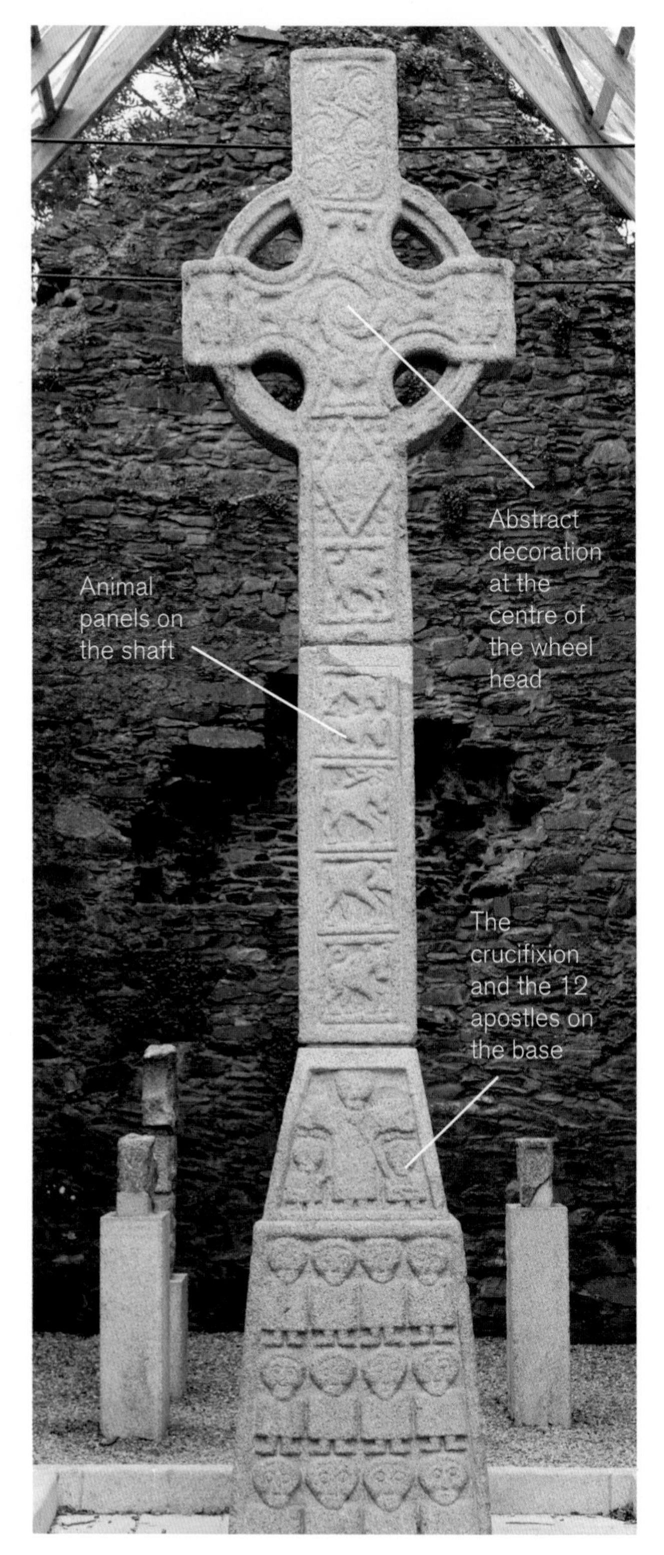

Fig. 4.10 The Cross of Moone, west face

The scenes on the base of the cross

The east side can be read from top to bottom (Fig. 4.11). In the first scene, Adam and Eve stand under a stylised tree with the serpent (Satan) coiling around the trunk. This represents man's original fall from grace.

Below this is the sacrifice of Isaac from the Book of Genesis in the Old Testament. The scene shows Isaac bent over the sacrificial altar. Abraham leans forward from an interesting-looking chair to strike the fatal blow. The ram that takes Isaac's place as the sacrifice is squeezed into the top left-hand corner. The scene of the father about to sacrifice his son is regarded as a prefiguration of the crucifixion.

At the bottom of this side is the scene of Daniel in the lions' pit, with seven lions, rather than the more common Daniel in the lions' den, with four lions. The pit scene comes from an apocryphal part of the Book of Daniel in the Old Testament. It can be read as God saving his faithful follower and as another prefiguration for the sacrifice of the crucifixion. It could also be understood as a symbol of redemption.

The south side is typical of the tight composition of the figure panels (Fig. 4.12). In the top panel, the three children (Hebrews) in the fiery furnace, from the Book of Daniel, are protected by an angel. The children under the arch that represents the furnace are carved in relief by removing small areas of stone between their heads and bodies. The little angel above them is squeezed into a small space, making him look more like a butterfly.

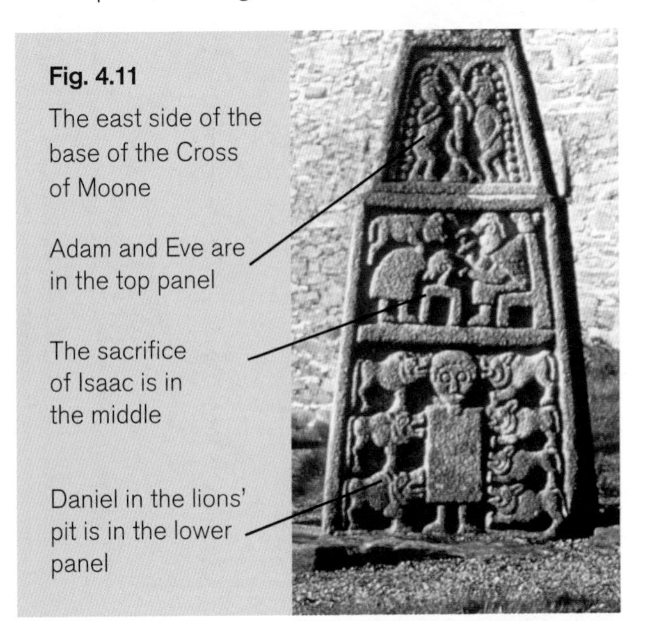
Adam and Eve are in the top panel
The sacrifice of Isaac is in the middle
Daniel in the lions' pit is in the lower panel

Fig. 4.11 The east side of the base of the Cross of Moone

The three Hebrews in the fiery furnace are in the top panel
The flight into Egypt is in the middle
The miracle of the loaves and fishes is in the lower panel

Fig. 4.12 The south face of the base of the Cross of Moone

The flight into Egypt scene shows Mary against rather than on the donkey. The Christ child's head, next to her, has no body and seems to share hers. The much larger figure of Joseph takes up all the space on the right. The miracle of the loaves and fishes scene below is reduced to its simplest form: five circles represent the loaves, two chubby fish fill the top of the panel and two skinny fish are squeezed in at each side.

The west side has the crucifixion scene arranged in its most frequently used form in Ireland: the sponge and spear bearers beneath the arms of the Christ figure. The 12 apostles fill the remainder of the base. Their simple rectangular bodies with large heads and prominent noses form three rows, with no individual details.

The north side of the base of the Cross of Moone seems to be dedicated to St Paul and St Anthony, who appear in two scenes above a seven-headed monster (probably a figure from the Apocalypse).

The simple human figures and animals on this cross bear a resemblance to the figures in the Book of Durrow. It has been suggested that the Cross of Moone was originally painted, so the relationship to the Book of Durrow may have been even closer.

The Scripture crosses of the Midlands

Although the crosses we have just looked at have Scripture scenes like the ones below, they are very different in style and detail. The crosses found in the Midlands, from Clonmacnoise to Monasterboice, have similarities in style, technique and subject matter, though each should be considered separately as a unique work of art and symbolism.

Origins of the designs

The iconography of the Scripture crosses is not simple to work out. The images and subjects relate to designs found on Roman sarcophagi (box tombs) from about the 4th century AD. These tombs were often reused for later burials, so an Irish pilgrim or cleric on church business in Rome who went to see the relics of saints or famous churchmen would have seen many of these sarcophagi (Fig. 4.13).

The images that appear in early Byzantine art also share themes and styles with scenes found on Irish crosses. This similarity may be due to common influences from Rome and an emphasis on the same messages being spread throughout the early Christian world.

Images may also have come second hand through Britain or the Carolingian Empire, which had contacts with Ireland. There are accounts of written descriptions of the relics and sites of Rome being circulated, so drawings might have been available as well.

Fig. 4.13

The 12 Apostles sarcophagus from the basilica of Sant'Apollinare in Classe, near Ravenna, Italy. Note that the grouping of the figures in the end panel is similar to panels on high crosses.

Fig. 4.14

An ivory book cover. The image is of St Luke writing his gospel.

NOTE! However it evolved, a style based on classical art was in use in Ireland in the 9th and 10th centuries. While the subjects and layout were often based on Roman designs, the details were based on local observations. For example, hairstyles and clothing were in the Irish style, not the classical togas seen on the sarcophagi.

The crosses at Kells

There is an important group of crosses at Kells, Co. Meath, which was the senior monastery in the Colomban tradition in the years that followed the Viking raids on Iona in the early 9th century. Kells would have been a centre of power and influence in the Irish church, active in the spread of new ideas and art forms.

The Cross of Saints Patrick and Columba

* **Form:** The Cross of Saints Patrick and Columba is 3.30m tall. It is a wheel-head cross carved from one block of sandstone set in a base.
* **Function:** This cross may have been erected to commemorate the founding of the monastery at Kells around 804 AD. The inscription 'Patricii et Columbae crux', unusually written in Latin, may indicate an agreement between the paruchia (group of allied churches and monasteries) of St Patrick, based at Armagh, and the paruchia of St Columba, then centred on Iona.
* **Technique:** The cross was carved in relief with iron chisels from a single block of sandstone.
* **Decoration:** This cross is unusual among Irish crosses because it is not divided into panels – figure scenes and areas of decoration meet without borders. The figures in the Bible scenes are more vigorous and animated than on other crosses. Some areas of the cross have different subjects side by side.

Fig. 4.15 The Cross of Saints Patrick and Columba, Kells, east face

- On the east face (Fig. 4.15), just above an area of interlaced circles at the bottom of the cross, a scene depicts Adam and Eve covering their nakedness, with Cain killing Abel beside them. Above this, the children in the furnace are shown with devils forking firewood on top of them, just under the feet of Daniel in the lions' den.
- On the left-hand arm of the cross there is a carving of the sacrifice of Isaac. On the right, a raven brings bread to St Paul and St Anthony (a prefiguration of the Eucharist). The top of the cross has a figure scene, the meaning of which is disputed. Françoise Henry reads it as the miracle of the loaves and fishes, while Peter Harbison interprets the scene as David playing his harp for Saul to banish evil.

- The west face of the shaft has a crucifixion scene above an area of human interlace. At the centre of the cross is a Christ in Glory or Last Judgement scene.
- The sides of the cross have areas of pattern and some figures that are difficult to interpret.
- The base has horses and riders and chariots on the west face, and there is a man hunting animals on the east.
- If this cross can be interpreted as the earliest one at Kells, its unusual style could be attributed to influences from Iona and the Scottish style of carving.

The Broken Cross and the Market Cross

These crosses seem to have been moved from their original orientation. The panels include some scenes not found on other crosses, deeply carved into designs that fit closely into their panels.

Together with the unfinished cross, which we will look at later, these crosses at Kells may have been the models that the designs of the Scripture crosses in the rest of the country were based on.

The Cross of the Scriptures at Clonmacnoise

Fig. 4.16
The Cross of the Scriptures at Clonmacnoise, west face. It is located in front of the west door of the cathedral.

* **Form:** One of the most beautiful and complete of the high crosses, dating from the first half of the 10th century (Fig. 4.16). It stands 3.9m tall in the interpretive centre specially built to protect the crosses at Clonmacnoise. Modern copies now stand in the original locations.
* **Function:** The theme of this cross is the passion, death and resurrection of Christ. The Old Testament scenes on the lower panels of the east face of the shaft can be interpreted as a prefiguration of the resurrection, which is illustrated in two panels on the base and lower shaft of the west side, which would have been the focus of a person kneeling in prayer before the cross.
* **Technique:** The sculpted panels are carved in high relief, with some of the figures almost projecting free from the surface. The designs are neatly composed and carried out in greater detail than we have seen on previous crosses. The ring at the head of the cross passes over the shaft and arms, which is different from other crosses, where the ring is set back from the surface of the shaft and arms.
* **Decoration:** There is a crucifixion at the crossing on the west face and a Last Judgement scene in the same position on the east. Scenes from the Bible fill most of the other panels. Men on horses and chariots and animals seem to follow in procession round the base.

The crosses at Monasterboice, Co. Louth

Mainistir Buite is on the site of the monastery founded by the 5th-century monk, Buite. He prophesied the importance of St Columba; tradition says that Columba was born on the day in 521 AD on which Buite died. This made Monasterboice an important place of pilgrimage, connected to Kells, which may explain similarities in the style between the crosses at Kells and Monasterboice.

Muiredach's Cross

Another local tradition stated that Muiredach's Cross was sent from Rome. This may relate to the themes and messages that are on the cross and even to the origins of the designs, which some scholars say are based on images from early Christian tombs in Rome.

* **Form:** The cross stands 5.2m tall and is one solid piece of stone except for the cap and base. Artistically and technically, it is the finest high cross in Ireland (Fig. 4.17).
* **Function:** Like other crosses with figure scenes, this cross would have been used to instruct pilgrims and as a focus for the monks' prayers.
* **Meaning:** Because of the layers of meaning associated with each scene, a number of messages can be taken from this cross. Christ the King can be seen in the mocking scene, the crucifixion and the Last Judgement. In fact, the entire west face could be interpreted in this way. The importance of the Eucharist can be noted in a number of scenes and the passion, death and resurrection of Christ are also emphasised.
* **Technique:** The quality of the carving on Muiredach's Cross is unsurpassed on any other Irish cross. There is a crispness of detail and depth of modelling rarely found elsewhere. Features of hairstyles, clothes and weapons can be seen on the larger figures, which are carved almost in the round.

Fig. 4.17 Muiredach's Cross at Monasterboice, east face

Design

The east face

The Old Testament scenes on the east face are crowded into panels of multiple subjects or large groups. The lowest panel shows Adam and Eve, and Cain killing Abel. The scene above this depicts David killing Goliath, while Moses strikes the rock in the next scene, providing water for the large group of Israelites included in the panel. The uppermost scene on this side of the shaft shows the adoration of the Magi, in which four kings, representing people from the four corners of the earth, come to adore the infant Christ in the arms of his seated mother.

Across the arms of the cross is a Last Judgement scene (Fig. 4.18), with Christ at the centre holding a staff and sceptre. An eagle is above his head.

At Christ's right hand is David playing his harp. An angel writes the judgements in a book and the good souls face Christ. On Christ's left hand is a flute player and behind him is the Devil with his

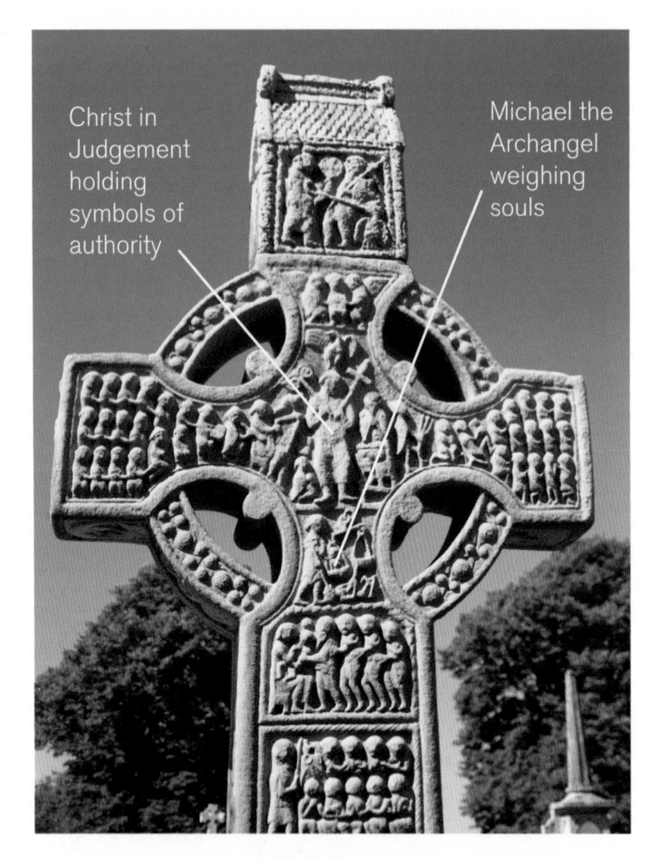
Christ in
Judgement
holding
symbols of
authority
Michael the
Archangel
weighing
souls

Fig. 4.18 The Last Judgement Scene on the east face of Muiredach's Cross at Monasterboice

trident, driving the souls who turned their backs on Christ into hell. Below Christ's feet is a small panel in which St Michael the Archangel weighs souls and the Devil tries to upset the balance. This scene is common in Romanesque art, which developed in Europe in the following centuries.

The west face

On the bottom of the west face of the shaft is an inscription written in old Irish: 'OR DO MUIREDACH LAS NDERNAD – – – – RO', meaning 'a prayer for Muiredach, who had (the cross) made'. This inscription, which gives the cross its name, appears in a small panel behind two cats that are playing with mice. The inscription does not help to clarify a date for the cross, as there were several abbots called Muiredach and the cross cannot be associated with any one in particular.

Above the inscription is a mocking of Christ scene, in which soldiers, who look like Vikings, have dressed Christ in an elaborate cloak fixed with a penannular brooch, like the Tara Brooch, to mock

Fig. 4.19 (left)
The lower panels on the west face of Muiredach's Cross at Monasterboice

Fig. 4.20 (right)
Muirdach's Cross at Monasterboice, west face

Note the brooch on Christ's cloak and the clothes and hairstyles of the soldiers
Cats holding mice lie in front of the inscription

him as king of the Jews. These figures are quite realistic. The proportions are almost accurate; the figures show movement and a variety of body angles in their poses. The long hair and big moustaches on the soldiers contrast with the short monastic haircut on the Christ figure (Fig. 4.19).

The next panel is interpreted by Harbison as the raised Christ, hovering above the world with St Peter and St Paul. In the uppermost panel on this side of the shaft, Christ gives the keys to the kingdom of heaven to St Peter and the book of the New Testament to St Paul.

The crucifixion is at the centre of the west face of the cross (Fig. 4.20). It shows Stephaton offering the sponge to Christ and Longinus piercing his left side with a lance. An angel hovers above each shoulder. Patterns and bosses surround the scene.

At the end of the arms there are figure scenes that may represent the denial of St Peter on the left-hand side and the resurrection on the right. The scene above the ring is the ascension of Christ.

The narrow sides and base

The north and south sides of the cross are decorated with interlace patterns on the shaft and figure scenes on the ends of the arms and at the top of the cross. The base is divided into panels that contain figure and animal scenes on the upper row and interlaced patterns along the bottom. On the underside of the arms of the cross – the parts that have been the least weathered – there is a pair of animals on the south side and the hand of God on the north. Snakes entwining around heads are carved on the underside of the ring (Fig. 4.21).

The Tall Cross

Near the round tower at Monasterboice stands the Tall Cross (Fig. 4.22). Over 7m tall, it is the tallest cross in Ireland. Because of its great height, the Tall Cross has the largest number of figure scenes found on any cross. Scenes appear on all faces, illustrating the life of David and God's help for his faithful followers on the east face, and scenes

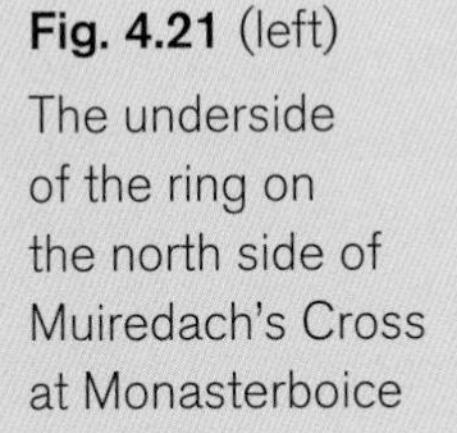

Fig. 4.21 (left)
The underside of the ring on the north side of Muiredach's Cross at Monasterboice

Fig. 4.22 (right)
The Tall Cross at Monasterboice

from the life of Christ on the west. The figure style is more animated but less detailed and deeply carved than Muiredach's Cross.

The construction of high crosses

We can get some idea of how crosses were made from the unfinished cross at Kells, Co. Meath. The basic blocks from which the cross was to be built would have been roughed out at the quarry. The mortises and tenons that were to connect the parts together would have been cut to fit each other. All the parts were then transported to the site where the cross was to be erected.

At the site, the stonemason would have marked out the areas for decoration and checked the shape of the stone for accuracy with a square and compass. The measurements of mouldings and panels seem to correspond with inches and feet used in the imperial system, which was based on the Roman measuring system.

Fig. 4.23 The unfinished cross at Kells

Blocking out

Different depths of carving were allowed for during the blocking-out process. This can be seen on the unfinished cross at Kells (Fig. 4.23), where panels are left projecting above the surrounding area to accommodate higher relief. All the surfaces were first trimmed flat so that drawings could be transferred onto them, providing guidelines for the carver. When all the preliminary work was complete, the parts would have been assembled in their final position before the panels were cut into so that edges and joints could be carefully matched, giving continuity to the design (Fig. 4.24).

Tools

The sculptors would have used iron chisels similar to the tools used by modern sculptors, but this is only an assumption, since tools from this time have not been found to date. In the 9th and 10th centuries crosses have a greater depth of carving, which may be accounted for by improved iron technology brought by the Vikings. On Muiredach's Cross, drill marks can still be seen in the areas under the arms and ring that have been the least weathered. The drill would have been used to bore down to the deepest areas of the design, followed by a chisel, which would have formed the details of the design (Fig. 4.25).

We know from later history that medieval masons had pattern books of abstract designs and figure scenes that they could choose from when they were carving decorations on churches. Irish masons may have had similar records to help them. In any case, there are close relationships between some of the designs and patterns found on Irish high crosses, which indicates that designers were at least aware of the work on other crosses.

Fig. 4.24
The construction of a high cross

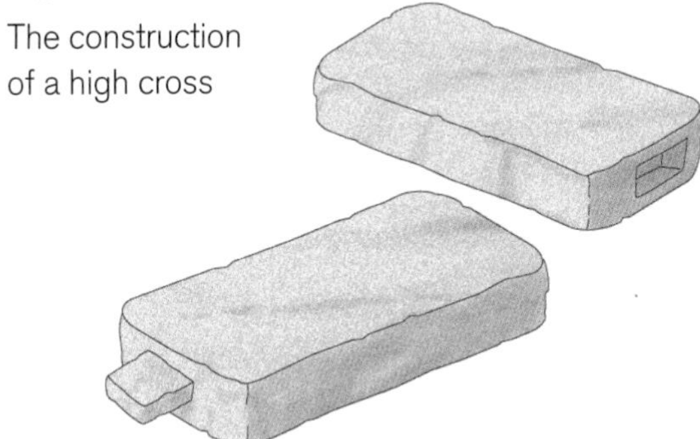

Blocks roughed out at the quarry.
Mortices and tenons cut to make joints.

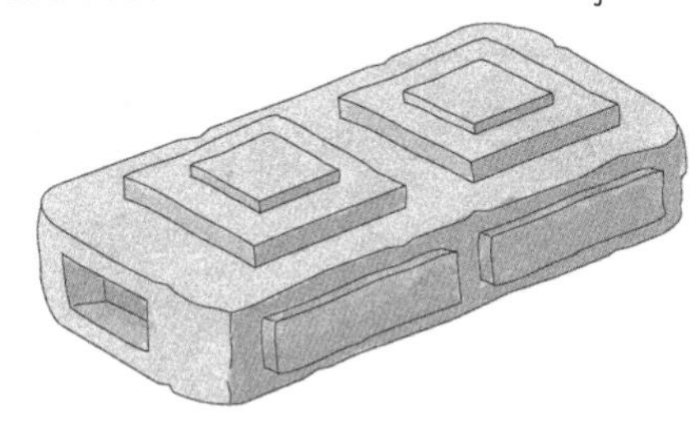

Panels blocked out on site. Different thicknesses allowed for different depths of carving.

Cross erected on site.
Carvers begin carving designs.

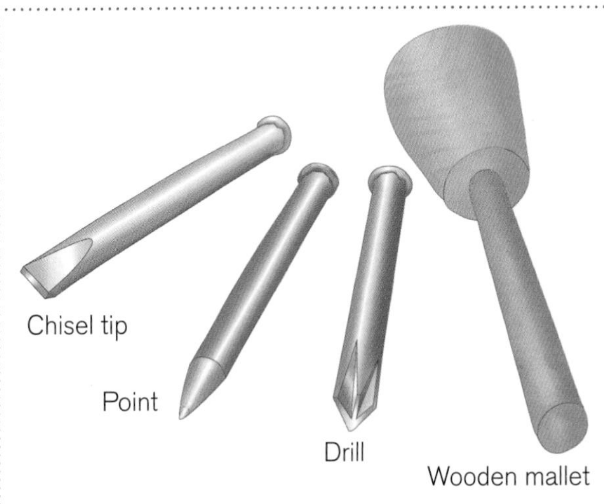

Fig. 4.25 Stone carving tools

Manuscripts

We have already seen how simple the buildings in an Irish monastery were and how few comforts were available for the monks. The beautifully decorated and elaborately laid out books of the 9th and 10th centuries seem to contrast with this simple life, but they are also an expression of Irish monks' attempt to lead a spiritual and intellectual life free from worldliness. Beautiful Bibles had a value beyond the everyday – they were an expression of the commitment of the community to spiritual ideals.

Colours

The range of colours in the Book of Kells includes the yellow, red and green that we have seen in the Book of Durrow, but some more exotic and expensive pigments were also used.

Blues were obtained from indigo (a plant imported from the Orient), woad (a Northern European plant) and lapis lazuli, a mineral from northern Afghanistan that is ultramarine blue (ultramarine means 'from across the sea'). Lapis lazuli was a very precious and expensive pigment usually reserved for the most important areas in a design.

Kermes red was obtained by crushing the bodies and eggs of the *Kermes vermillio* insect, which lives on the kermes oak. Vermillion is red mercuric sulphide, which probably came from Spain.

Folium comes from marsh plants grown around the Mediterranean. It produces a range of purple and plum colours.

White lead was used both as a colour and as a ground for over-painting. It was much used in spite of its toxicity.

Most of the organic pigments were extracted in ammonium (urine) and fixed in an insoluble mineral salt (aluminium hydroxide).

Writing tools

The scribes and artists who produced manuscripts used a variety of equipment. Pens were made from the tail feathers of the goose or swan; brushes were of varying fineness and the hair of the marten was suitable for the finest-quality brushes; and knives were used to scrape away mistakes.

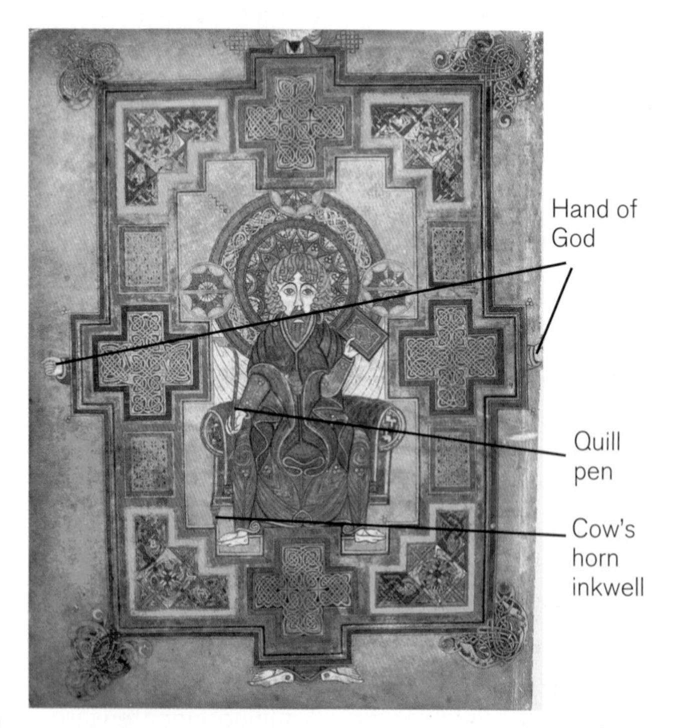

Fig. 4.26 Folio 291v: portrait of St John from the Book of Kells by the artist called the Portraitist

To create the decorated pages, artists would have needed a ruler, a compass and probably templates to lay out the designs and patterns. Cow horns were used as inkwells. The portrait of St John in the Book of Kells (folio 291v) shows the scribe with a pen in his right hand and a book in his left, with the inkwell sitting just above his right foot (Fig. 4.26).

Making and storing books

We can now see that the work of scribes and artists entailed a lot more than simply writing text or painting designs. They had to work with foul-smelling and poisonous materials and spend long hours preparing colours and pages. Even with all this work complete, the book still had to be bound together by sewing groups of pages along the spine and attaching them to wooden boards that formed the covers. A layer of decorated leather was sometimes used to create a final cover.

The most precious books, or books associated with the saints, were sometimes enclosed in decorated metal plates fixed to a wooden box. These book shrines prevented further use of the books, but they sometimes did physical damage to them. However, they also helped to preserve them for posterity. Books for everyday use were generally kept in leather satchels, which were used for carrying the books and storing them. These satchels could be hung up on hooks in the scriptorium or library. There are records in the annals of books being stored in round towers.

The Book of Kells

Origins

Scholars now generally agree that the Book of Kells was written at the chief monastery of the Columban order on the island of Iona and then brought to Kells when Iona became unsafe due to Viking raids. The book could have taken decades to write, so it may have been started on Iona and continued in Kells. These monasteries were regarded as one unit, under the authority of one abbot, in the early part of the 9th century. The book was probably written in the years around 800 AD, but it was never fully completed. Two pages are blank and a few have decorative elements that were begun but left unfinished.

* **Form:** The Book of Kells is the most elaborately decorated manuscript codex in the Insular style to have survived the ravages of time. The text is very similar to that of the Book of Durrow. The Four Gospels and related preliminary writings could have been copied from a common exemplar, even though Kells was written 100 years after Durrow. Both books were transcribed in Columban monasteries, which may account for the closeness of the texts.
* **The book today:** The Book of Kells now measures 330mm x 255mm. It was cut down for rebinding in 1830, damaging the design of a number of pages. It was badly rebound again in 1895 before it was restored in 1953. The decoration suffered damage from wetting the pages to flatten them at each rebinding. The book still preserves some of the most amazing work of the illuminator's skill from any time. Three hundred and forty folios remain, but it is estimated that about 30 have been lost, including some fully decorated pages.
* **Function:** The Book of Kells is a display Bible, made for use on special occasions.
* **Technique:** Calf vellum was used to make the pages for the Book of Kells (see Fig. 2.11). Skins of newborn or intrauterine calves were preferred to produce the finest vellum – only one bifolium could be made from each skin of this size. Stronger vellum for the fully decorated pages was obtained from two- or three-month-old calves, producing two bifolia from each skin, though decorated pages were often on single leaves, which could be worked on separately and sewn into the book later. It has been estimated that the hides of up to 185 calves could have been needed for the complete book; this suggests a monastery of great wealth, capable of affording these resources. We have already seen how pens, brushes and colours were made.

The contents of the book

The text begins with the canon tables, Breves Causae and Argumenta, which are supporting texts and commentary on the Bible.

The Four Gospels follow. In the original plan, each gospel began with a Four Evangelists page, a portrait of the evangelist and an initial page.

* Matthew's Gospel has six fully decorated pages.
* Mark's Gospel has only three fully decorated pages remaining – his portrait is missing.
* Luke's Gospel is missing the Four Evangelists and portrait pages, but it does have the beautiful *Quoniam* page, two other fully decorated pages and some decorated capitals.
* The three opening pages from John's Gospel survive, but no other fully decorated pages. This is the most damaged part of the book.

The Four Evangelists page from St Matthew's Gospel

Folio 27v (Fig. 4.27), the Four Evangelists page from the beginning of St Matthew's Gospel, is richly coloured and patterned in the style of enamelled jewellery. Translucent layers of colour are built up to create rich blues and purples, balanced with the bright orpiment yellow. The central cross form is emphasised by the arcs on the outside of the frame. There is human, animal, bird and snake interlace in the border. Panels of spirals and black and white maze and interlace patterns in very fine lines are used to separate the coloured sections.

The man symbol for Matthew seems to be skipping lightly forward in his gorgeous robes and wings, holding a processional cross.

Mark's lion symbol is shown in a leaping pose. He has a curling tongue and mane and fabulously decorated wings.

The ox or calf symbol of St Luke has four wings, the flight feathers entwining with his legs on one side and with the second wing on the other. The three white circles with crosses inside them on his haunch are a reference to the Eucharist.

The eagle symbol of St John has a halo with three crosses, a device that recurs a number of times and appears to be a reference to the Trinity. The beautiful tail of this eagle connects to the body in a sweeping S curve.

The portrait of St John

The painting of St John on folio 291v (see Fig. 4.26) portrays the author as a scribe, with his quill pen in his right hand, a book held aloft in his left and an ink horn down by his right foot. The stylised figure of John has an elaborate halo and the folds in his garments are arranged in a symmetrical way. The patterns in the border seem to be mirror images of their opposite number until you take a closer look to discover differences in pattern and colour. The crosses at the top, bottom and sides of the border emphasise the head, hands and feet that protrude beyond the frame, a reference to God the Father, who is behind everything, unseen. Alternatively, the crosses could be a reference to the fact that John was the only evangelist present at the crucifixion of Christ.

The *Quoniam* page

The opening word of St Luke's Gospel, '*Quoniam*' (Fig. 4.28), is given a full page to itself. The letters *Q*, *U*, *O* are overlapped into one shape framed in purple. The remaining letters, *N*, *I*, *A*, *M*, are surrounded by little groups of figures. The group to the left and inside the *A* seem to be overindulging in drink, while two at the bottom have their heads in the mouths of lions, which are formed from the ends of the letter *M*. This group of figures is sometimes thought to

Fig. 4.27 Folio 27v: the Four Evangelists page from Matthew's Gospel in the Book of Kells by the artist called the Portraitist

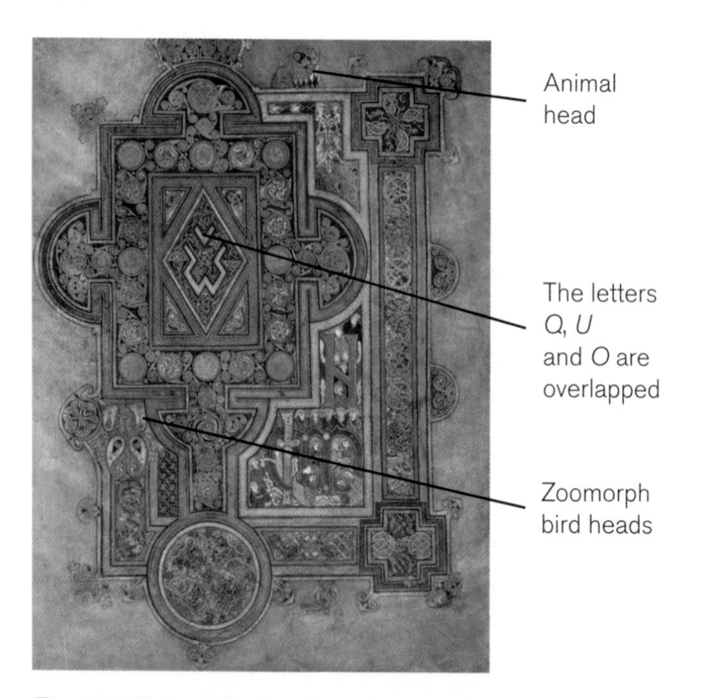

Fig. 4.28 Folio 188r: the *Quoniam* page from the opening of Luke's Gospel in the Book of Kells by the artist called the Portraitist

represent the Last Judgement or the punishments of hell.

Above the lettering is another group of figures forming an interlace pattern. Interlace patterns of a very high quality can be seen inside the circle at the bottom of the letter Q and in the panels that make a frame around the right and bottom sides, ending in a large dragon head that shares teeth and outline with lion and eagle heads – the work of an artist with an amazing sense of design. On the Tara Brooch there is a link connecting the chain to the frame that is designed in a similar way.

Turn in the path

Some decoration is used to mark the ends of passages, to highlight words in the texts or to point out a 'turn in the path' or 'head under wing' – where a line is finished in the line above, using up space left at the end of the previous verse

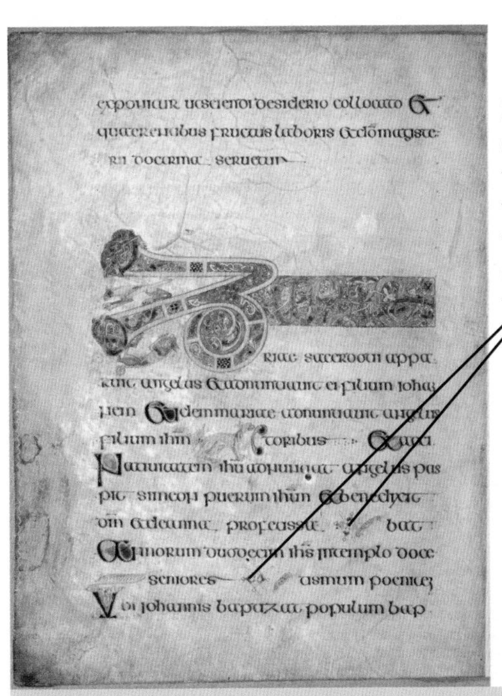

Fig. 4.29 Folio 19v: a page from the Breves Causae illustrates 'a turn in the path'. The word at the end of the third line from the bottom, 'doce', is finished 'bat' on the line above. The last line is also finished on the line above. A little decoration separates each ending from the rest of the line.

(Fig. 4.29). This was a strategy used by scribes to save precious vellum. All the copyists in the Book of Kells seem to have used this device.

Scribes and artists

A book as large as the Book of Kells and as elaborately decorated would have taken many years to produce and could have been worked on by many hands over the years. Scribes and artists trained in the same scriptorium would have learned similar styles and techniques, so the work is not always easy to identify. More than one artist may have worked on individual pages, making it even more difficult to separate styles.

The scribes

Scholars have identified a number of different scribes (Fig. 4.30). Françoise Henry, in her study on the Book of Kells, identified three, which she designated A, B and C. Other commentators think that different artists were involved in the work of C and so they have added a fourth scribe, D.

* Scribe A is regarded as the most conservative. He wrote 18 or19 lines to the page in a clear majuscule script. The decoration is controlled and may have been added by another hand. His work appears at the beginning of the book, in the preliminaries, and at the end of St Luke's and St John's Gospels.
* Scribe B has quite a different style. He used coloured inks and ended his pages in a line of minuscule script. This scribe added the rubrics (instructions and comments on the text, written in red) and other pieces throughout the text. He may have had the task of filling in gaps and finishing off incomplete sections of the book. The number of lines he writes to the page varies.
* Scribes C and D copied most of the Gospels of St Matthew, St Mark and St Luke. Their work seems to combine both script and decoration. Their style is very similar and some scholars treat all their work as having been done by the same hand.

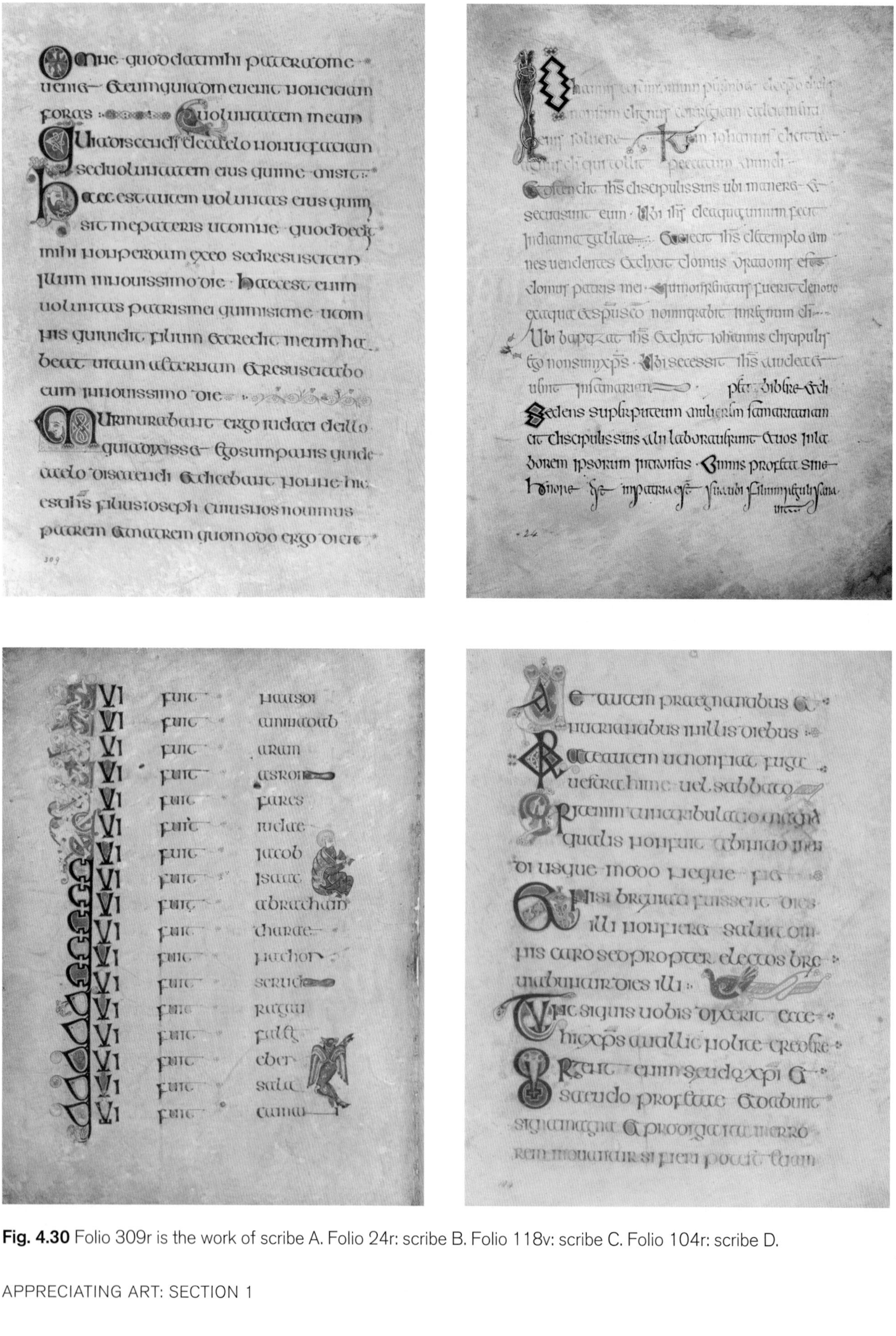

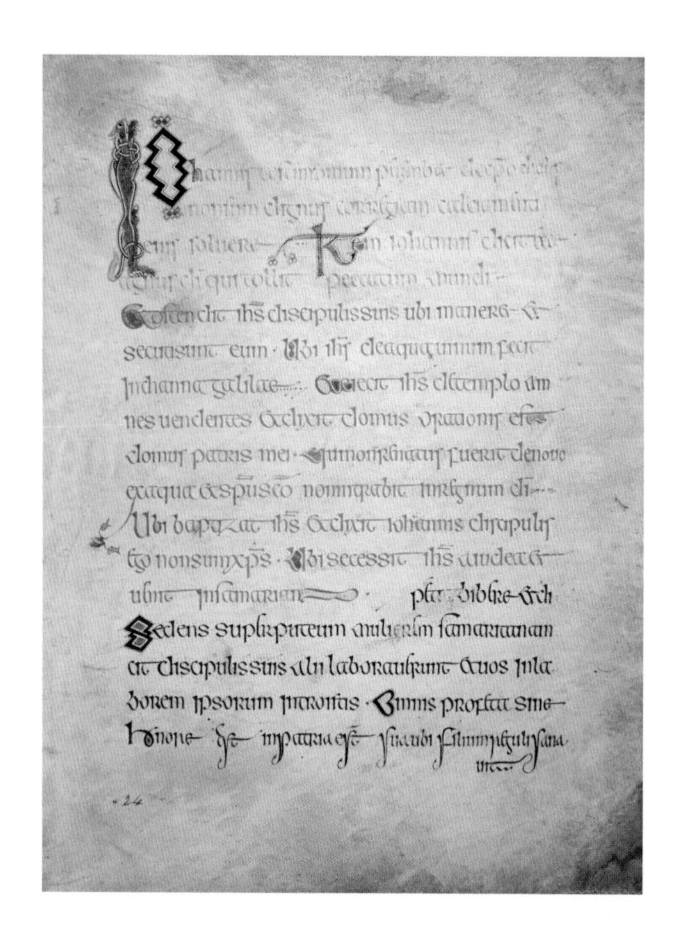

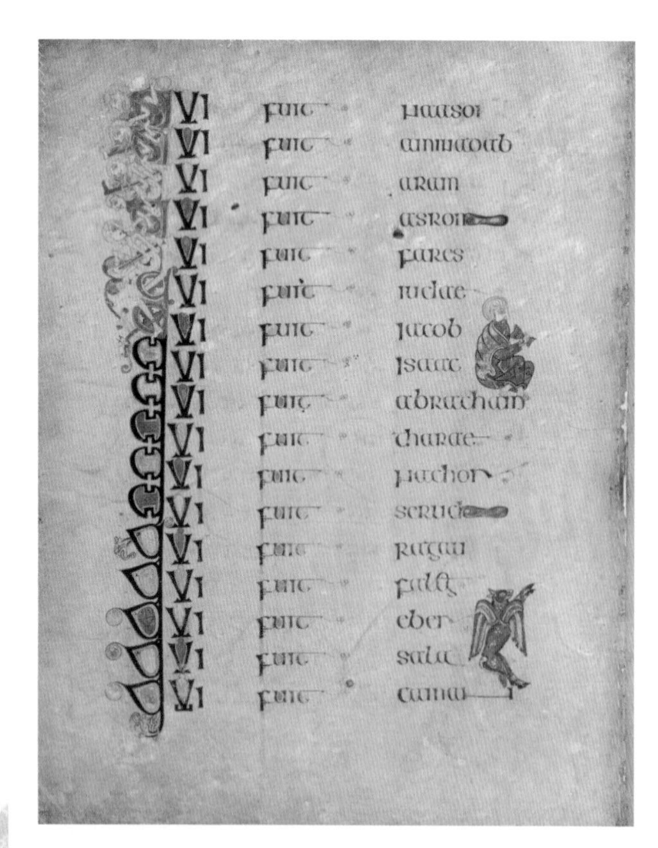

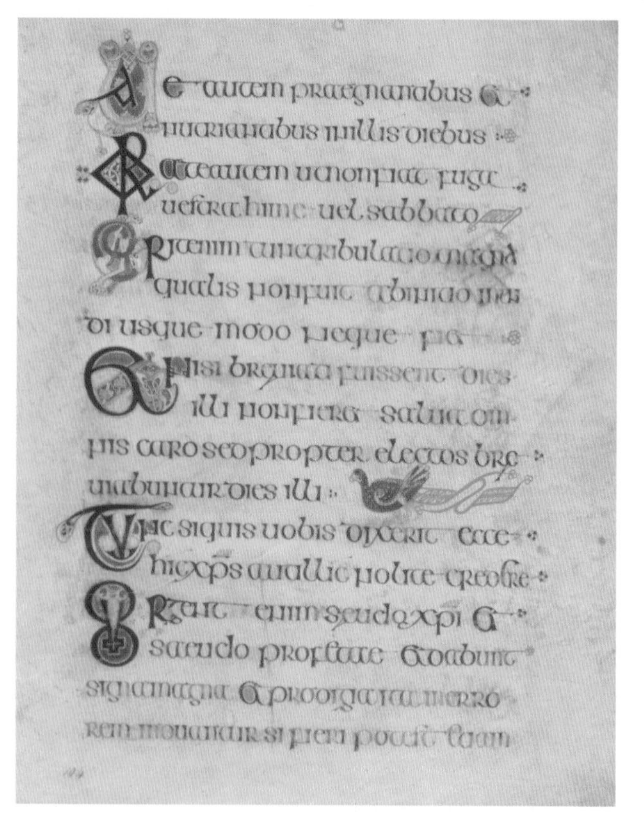

Fig. 4.30 Folio 309r is the work of scribe A. Folio 24r: scribe B. Folio 118v: scribe C. Folio 104r: scribe D.

The quality of the lettering is very high, but it is sometimes difficult for the modern reader because the conventions of word spaces and punctuation were not yet in use in the 9th century. Some of the more elaborately decorated capitals and the opening pages can be difficult to decipher. Most of the monks reading the book would have known the texts by heart, so they would have known which letters to expect.

The artists

The artists may not have been separate people from the scribes, but so much time would have been needed to complete the decorated pages that it would seem logical that some monks would be dedicated to this work alone. Françoise Henry identifies three main artists from the different styles she found on the fully decorated pages.

The Goldsmith

She calls the first artist the Goldsmith because his work looks like metalwork in gold and silver. He is credited with the eight circles carpet page, the Chi-Rho page, the opening words of the Gospels of St Matthew, St Mark and St John and with some other smaller pieces of decoration.

It is interesting to compare the Chi-Rho page in the Book of Kells (Fig. 4.31) with the same page in the Book of Durrow (see Fig. 3.9). In both cases the letters are decorated with spirals and trumpet curves, but in Kells the Goldsmith elaborates on everything. There is an almost endless variety of circles, spirals, triskeles and trumpet ends, twisting and turning together like the wheels of an old-fashioned clock mechanism. Between all these moving parts are panels and spaces filled with interlace, and men, birds, lions and snakes are interwoven in the most intricate patterns.

The colour scheme is subtler than some of the other pages. Delicate blues and violets make a counterpoint to smaller areas of bright red and yellow that outline the letters.

This page is also heavy with Christian symbols: the cross in yellow and red at the foot of the letter *P*, the presence of angels to the left of the down stroke on the *X*, the God the Father figure appearing at the top of the *X*, the cats and mice with the Eucharist bread and the otter with the fish (another symbol of Christ) on either side of the cross at the bottom of the design. Three-part patterns occur regularly, referring to the Trinity, while four-part patterns could refer to the gospels or the stages of Christ's life, or they might have other meanings.

The Portraitist

The Portraitist is the name given to the artist who painted the images of Christ, St Matthew, St John

Fig. 4.31

Folio 34r: the Chi-Rho page from the Book of Kells. This is one of the pages decorated by the artist known as the Goldsmith. Spend a little time looking for the angels, animals and people hiding in the decoration.

Fig. 4.32

Folio 7v: the Virgin and Child page from the Book of Kells

Fig. 4.33

Folio 200v: the temptation of Christ page from the Book of Kells. This is a page decorated by the artist known as the Illustrator.

and the symbols page for St Matthew's Gospel. We already looked at the Four Evangelists page (see Fig. 4.27) and the portrait of St John (see Fig. 4.26), which demonstrate a use of colour and space quite different from the Goldsmith's work. There was less interest in tiny detail and areas of open vellum were left to contrast with the painted areas.

The Illustrator

The Illustrator is thought to be the artist behind the paintings of the temptation, the arrest of Christ and the Virgin and Child as well as the evangelists' symbols before St John's Gospel. He may also have had a part in some other pages.

The Virgin and Child page

The first page completely devoted to decoration is folio 7v, a portrait of the Virgin and Child surrounded by angels (Fig. 4.32). This page comes before a beautifully decorated page of lettering about the birth of Christ. Mary wears a wine-coloured cloak fastened with a kite brooch. She sits on a throne of gold with a step pattern creating crosses of various shapes on the side. There is a lion's head terminal on the back of the chair. The Christ child is larger than the newborn baby mentioned in the text. He tenderly holds his mother's hand and she enfolds him in her arms. The four angels at each side of the throne are usually identified as the archangels Michael, Gabriel, Raphael and Uriel, who will appear a number of times throughout the book, witnessing important events in the life of Christ. Three of the angels carry a flabella and one carries a flowering bough. The flabella was a fan used in the Coptic church to keep flies away from the chalice during the celebration of the Eucharist. It became a symbol of purity in the early Christian church.

The small rectangle enclosing six figures looking to the right seems to have been a convention for linking two pages together – they look across to the text on the birth of Christ on the opposite page. The three crosses in Mary's halo and three arcs filled with interlace on the inside of the frame probably refer to the Trinity.

This painting is the earliest surviving image of the Virgin and Child from a Western manuscript, though there are written accounts of panel paintings and icons of this scene, now lost, which may have been models for its composition.

The temptation of Christ page, folio 200v (Fig. 4.33), shows Christ at the top of the temple, which can be interpreted as the church, the body of Christ. To his right is a group of figures, which may represent his faithful followers, whom he protects from the Devil. One of the group holds up a small shield, the shield of truth from Psalm 19:5, which the Devil quotes in the temptation story. The Devil, at Christ's left side, holds up a snare to trap the unwary. Four angels accompany Christ, as they do in the other scenes from his life. The beautifully decorated temple with the lion head finials on the roof may give some idea of how an Irish wooden church looked in the 9th century. The figure in the doorway may represent Christ the judge. The two groups of 13 torsos at the bottom of the page could represent the apostles and the prophets, who were the foundation of the church, or if the rectangle in the middle of the group can be seen as an empty table, they could be clergy fasting to see off the 'Evil One'. The panels of snake interlace inside the crosses and at the bottom and sides of the border can be understood as representing the presence of evil in this scene.

The Fadden More Psalter

Discovered in a bog in Co. Tipperary on 20 July 2006, this appears to be a complete book of psalms contained in a leather satchel. Damaged

Fig. 4.34

A restored page from the Faddan More Psalter

when it was found and suffering the effects of spending 1,000 years in a bog, it is still the most significant discovery in a long time. It is a large-format codex of 52 or 54 folios (104 or 108 pages) written in Irish majuscule with decorated pages. Surviving parts of the book are now on display in the National Museum (Fig. 4.34).

Metalwork

Metalwork continued largely in the same style as the century before, but it is less colourful. Enamel was not used as frequently and the fine, detailed filigree work of the 8th century was transformed into looser, simpler designs. Precious materials like silver, gold and amber were more widely used. Craftsmen were still highly skilled and work was well constructed and carefully finished, but there was a loss of creative ingenuity and designs and patterns were repeated more frequently.

NOTE! By the 10th century, a Viking influence was evident. An Irish version of the Viking Jellinge style appeared alongside Irish motifs. Brooches took on new shapes and forms, probably in response to a Viking preference for larger pieces cast in solid silver.

A brooch from Roscrea

* **Form:** A pseudo-penannular brooch cast in silver (Fig. 4.35).
* **Function:** A cloak or tunic fastener and status symbol.
* **Technique:** It is cast in silver and decorated with gold filigree and amber.
* **Design:** This brooch is a good example of this new style. The design is much broader and simpler than the Tara Brooch. The pin and ring are boldly outlined in a crest of semi-circles filled with amber. A band of simple animal interlace inside this border surrounds panels of loose spirals in filigree. The overall effect is simpler and bolder than the Tara Brooch, but it does not have the subtlety of design and ingenious craftsmanship of the older brooch.

New brooch types were also introduced during this time. Large silver kite brooches, bossed penannular brooches and thistle brooches (Fig. 4.36) became more common in the 10th century. The laws that dictated the size and value of brooches that could be worn by people from different layers of society were still very much in evidence at this time.

The Derrynaflan Chalice

The Derrynaflan Chalice (Fig. 4.37), found in the same hoard as the Derrynaflan Paten that we looked at earlier, is the finest piece of 9th-century metalwork yet discovered.

* **Form:** It is 19.2cm high and 21cm in diameter. It is made of silver and decorated with gold filigree and amber studs.
* **Function:** A large decorated chalice for use on special occasions.
* **Technique:** The bowl and foot are turned silver sheet with a cast stem joining them. Filigree sections decorating the rim, foot and stem are separated by amber studs.
* **Decoration:** The decoration is laid out in a similar way to the Ardagh Chalice. There is a band of filigree and amber studs just below the rim; the handles have large decorated escutcheons; and the collar between the bowl and the foot has bands of filigree and amber studs, which are also used on the decorative rim around the foot.
  - Bird and animal shapes are the main elements in the filigree decoration (Fig. 4.38), though the designs are simpler than those on the Ardagh Chalice. The artist

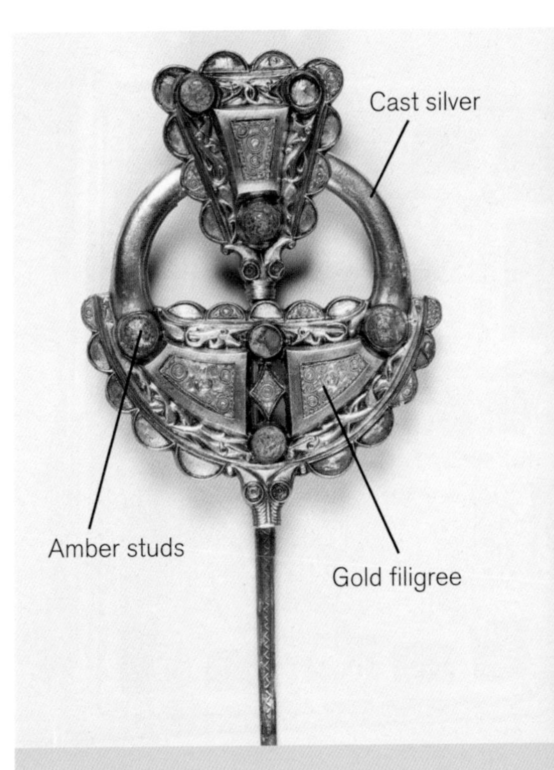

Fig. 4.35 (above)

A brooch from Roscrea, Co. Tipperary. It is a pseudo-penannular brooch in cast silver with gold filigree decoration and amber studs.

Fig. 4.36 (right top and bottom)

Two thistle brooches, two bossed penannular brooches (left) and a kite brooch (right). Cast silver brooches became more common during the period of the Viking invasions.

Fig. 4.37 The Derrynaflan Chalice

Fig. 4.38 A filigree animal from under the rim of the Derrynaflan Chalice

relies for his effect on the contrast between the warm tones of the gold and amber decoration and the cooler silver colour of the bowl and foot.

Other metalwork

The manufacture of other kinds of metal artefacts continued in the 9th and 10th centuries, including crosiers, book boxes and shrines (Fig. 4.39). Though none survive in very good condition, they indicate the range of objects that were made at the time. Skills and techniques had not greatly fallen away since the 8th century, but the taste for intricate design seems to have changed in favour of bolder work, maybe more suited to the taste of Vikings, who were important trading partners.

The human figure

The way the human figure was represented changed in the 9th and 10th centuries. The figures on the crosses from Tipperary and Kildare were carved very simply, with oval heads, rectangular bodies and simple or no limbs, similar to figures on earlier crosses and books. They were symbols of humans rather than an attempt at realism.

The Midlands crosses are quite different. The figures are strongly three-dimensional and quite well proportioned. Details of hair and clothing can be seen and some attempt at individual characters has been made (Fig. 4.40).

In the Book of Kells, the human figures are somewhere between the two. Facial features are simplified and stylised, but are close to correct proportions. Pattern and shape are more important than realism in the representation of bodies and clothes.

Fig. 4.39

The Soiscel Molaise Book Shrine from Dernish Island, Co. Fermanagh, early 11th century. Areas of gilding and filigree decorate the cast book box. The Four Evangelists surround the arms of a ringed cross.

Chapter review

* Do you believe that the Vikings put an end to the idea of Ireland as an island of saints and scholars?
* Were there any positive sides to the Viking invasions?
* There seems to have been a number of uses for round towers. What do you think they were?
* Can you imagine what work in a 9th-century scriptorium might have been like?
* Based on the evidence you have seen in images and craftwork, do you think 9th-century monks had a deep faith in God?
* What are the characteristics of a high cross?
* What do you like best about the Book of Kells?

Fig. 4.40

Human figures from stone and book decoration in 9th- and 10th-century Irish art

Adam and Eve from the west face of the North Cross at Castledermot, Co. Kildare. The figures are simple and symbolic. The circles around the frame are the apples on the Tree of Knowledge.

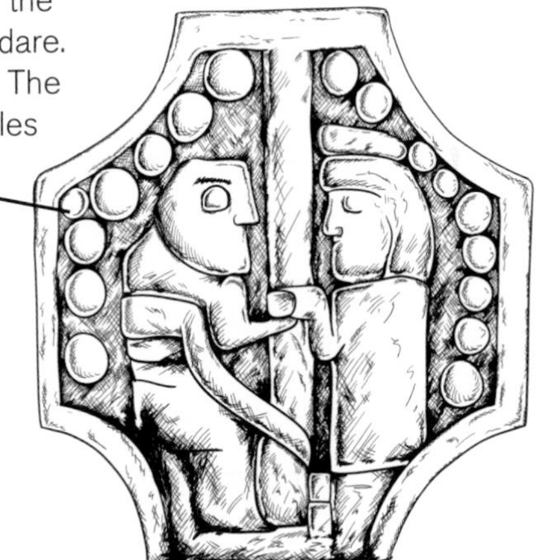

Adam and Eve from Muiredach's Cross at Monasterboice, lowest panel on the east face. The figures are almost three-dimensional and are animated.

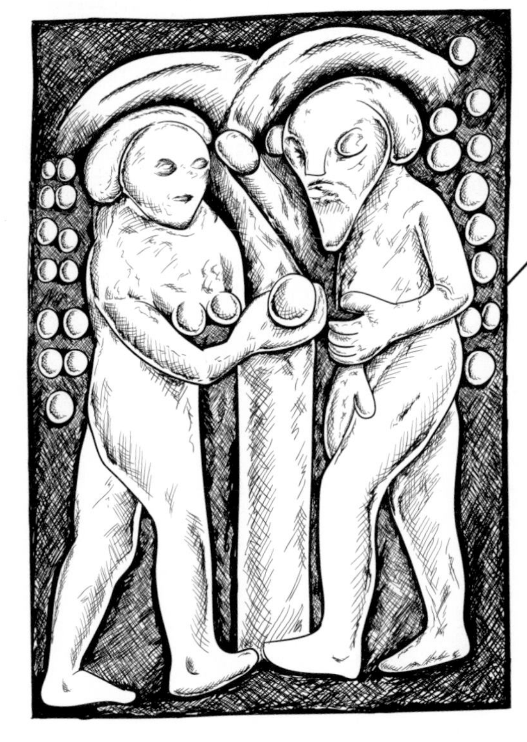

An angel from the top-right corner of the Virgin and Child page in the Book of Kells. Details of hair and clothing are represented, but in a linear and patterned way and are not fully realistic.

EXAM QUESTIONS

Ordinary Level (2015)

The Cross of the Scriptures at Clonmacnoise, Co. Offaly, is illustrated on the accompanying sheet (Fig 4.16).

Answer (a), (b) and (c).

(a) What is its function?

(b) Describe and discuss how it was made and decorated.

(c) Sketch, describe and discuss **one** other High Cross you have studied.

Illustrate your answer.

Higher Level (2016)

'The style of carving on the Cross of Moone, Co. Kildare, contrasts significantly with the style of carving on the Cross of Muiredach, Monasterboice, Co. Louth.'

Discuss this statement with reference to the illustration on the accompanying sheet (the west face of the Cross of Moone with a detail of the 12 Apostles panel, see Fig. 4.10, and the west face of Muiredach's Cross with a detail of the mocking of Christ panel, see Fig. 4.19). In your answer, refer to form, structure, imagery, decoration and stone-working techniques.

and

Briefly describe and discuss the functions of Irish high crosses.

Illustrate your answer.

FURTHER RESEARCH

www.3dicons.ie

www.irishhighcrosses.com

www.museum.ie

www.sacred-destinations.com – Clonmacnoise

www.visual-arts-cork.com – Celtic Metalwork Art

Chapter 5

The 11th and 12th Centuries: The Irish Romanesque Period (Hiberno-Romanesque)

Go to page 99 for a list of extra content available on **www.gillexplore.ie**.

By the end of this chapter, I will...

* Know some of the social and religious change that happened in the 10th century.
* Be able to draw and describe Cormac's Chapel at Cashel and the doorway at Clonfert Cathedral.
* Be able to draw and describe at least one high cross.
* Know one decorated capital from the Psalter of Cormac.
* Be able to draw and describe the Cross of Cong and at least one other piece of metalwork.
* Be able to trace the important developments of monasteries' stone carving, book painting and metalwork from the 5th to the 12th centuries.
* Have opinions that I can support on this final phase of Christian Celtic design.

Political and social background

The 11th and 12th centuries were a time of great religious and social change in Ireland. These changes brought new styles and forms of art, which were incorporated into the existing repertoire of Irish design. The style has become known as Hiberno-Romanesque. It is a particularly Irish version of the Romanesque style, which mixes old Celtic elements and Scandinavian designs with some aspects of the more formal European style. In Ireland, Romanesque was more a style of decoration rather than a significant structural advance in architecture.

Church reform

There was pressure from Britain and Rome to reform the Irish church and bring it in line with the structure practised in the rest of Europe. Bishops were supposed to be the authority in a region, with abbots, clergy and laypeople living in obedience to them. In the Irish tradition, abbots were the leaders of groups of affiliated monasteries. In 1101, Muirchertach Ua Briain (King of Munster) called a synod at Cashel to set out the boundaries of the dioceses in Ireland. He made a gift of the site at Cashel (Fig. 5.1) to the church to be the archdiocese for the south of Ireland. Armagh was the archdiocese for the north.

Pilgrimage

Pilgrimage was at its peak in Europe in these centuries. Rome and the shrine of St James the Apostle at Compostella in northern Spain were the main centres of pilgrimage in Europe, but every church tried to have its own relics to encourage local pilgrimage. Much of the surviving metalwork from the 11th and 12th centuries is in the form of shrines. These were mainly metal covers made to house the remains of an article associated with a saint. Bones, bells, books, crosiers and other relics were enclosed in cases of decorated and precious metals often paid for by the local royalty.

Patronage

Inscriptions on shrines, crosses and doorways offer praise and blessings on the kings who paid for their construction and the clergy who commissioned them. The craftsmen who carried out the work were sometimes mentioned, which shows how well appreciated craft workers were in Ireland. The annals often record the presentation of gold or silver on the occasion of a visit by a king to a church or monastery, and the purpose of the gift, such as to enshrine relics or to build a church, is usually noted.

Politics

Irish society went through a complete structural change in these centuries. It changed from a local tribal system into the feudal system, which was the norm in the rest of Europe. Local kings now looked on their land as a way of producing tax revenues from the peasants and gathering men for an army when it was needed. In return, the king offered leadership and protection to his subjects. This new feudal system created the need for symbols of power and authority, and God, through the church, was the ultimate authority. It is interesting to note that by the middle of the 12th century, many of the ring forts had been abandoned and people were living in closer communities around the fort of the king or near the church.

There was a lot of manoeuvring for power among local kings. Diarmait Mac Murchada, the King of Leinster from 1132 to 1171, was a patron to many churches. He brought Augustinian priors in to reform the abbeys of his kingdom and he gave lands to Cistercian monks at the edge of his territories with the subordinate kingdom of the O'Tuathails. He made Lorcan O'Tuathail, who was the abbot of Glendalough, the Archbishop of Dublin and married his half-sister to confirm the family bonds. Diarmait later abducted Derbforgaill,

Fig. 5.1

Aerial view of Cashel. Cormac's Chapel and the round tower, with an older church, were on the site before the 13th-century cathedral was built right up against them.

wife of Tigernán O'Ruairc, King of Breifne, and for this and other misdemeanours he was exiled in 1166. He returned in 1169 with Strongbow and his Anglo-Norman mercenary army to retake his kingdom and unwittingly change the course of Irish history.

Architecture

Cormac's Chapel

Built between 1127 and 1134 under the patronage of Cormac Mac Carthaig, King of Desmond, Cormac's Chapel was constructed on the site donated by Muirchertach Ó Briain in 1101.

* **Form:** Cormac's Chapel is a building unique in Ireland in its architectural completeness (Fig. 5.2). It is a simple nave and chancel church with two square towers, one on each side of the east end of the nave. There is a Romanesque doorway in both the north and south walls, with arcades (rows of arches) and string courses on all sides of the exterior. It is 15m long and 5m wide internally and the towers are 18m tall.
* **Function:** Clearly a church, it may be a memorial chapel for the Mac Carthaig kings.
* **Technique:** The church is built in finely cut ashlar (stone cut accurately into rectangular blocks). The nave is roofed with a barrel vault and the chancel is rib vaulted. The whole structure – roof, walls and decorations – is in stone.
* **Decoration:**
  - The north wall is the most richly decorated. There is a door with a gable pediment over it. Rosettes and heads form part of the design along with chevrons in the English style. This wall originally faced onto a

Fig. 5.2 (left)
Cormac's Chapel, Cashel, Co. Tipperary, viewed from the east

Fig. 5.3 (above)
The north doorway at Cashel

Fig. 5.4 Interior of Cormac's Chapel, Cashel. Traces of paint can be seen on the arches and the ceiling.

courtyard in front of the old church and the round tower. This courtyard was built over during the construction of the 13th-century cathedral, which is tight up against the chapel.

- The south wall has three stages of arcading and a colonnade (row of columns) on top, like the one on the north wall. The decoration on the doorway is sawtooth chevron. Chevron is also used to decorate the arches at ground level.
- The string courses, which run horizontally along the building and the arcades, continue around all the elements, creating a unity of design not normally seen in Irish churches of this time.
- The interior of the building, which was restored in the 1990s, reveals the remains of colourful murals and painted stonework. Some scenes on the chancel vault have been deciphered as the adoration of the Magi, the Magi before Herod and a shepherd scene (Fig. 5.3). The architectural features are again finely detailed, with arcades and pillars supporting the ribs of the barrel vault in the nave and the groin vaulting in the chancel. The chancel arch is decorated with human heads and heads appear again on all sides of the vault in the chancel (Fig. 5.4).
- The style of the decoration on Cormac's Chapel seems to owe so much to the contemporary Anglo-Norman style that it has been suggested that English craftsmen carried out the work. There are other influences present here as well: the arcading corresponds with some French examples and the overall appearance from east of the building is Germanic. This may be explained by the presence of Benedictine monks who were brought from the Schottenkirche of St James at Regensberg in Bavaria to run the church. The Schottenkirche (Irish church) in Regensberg had long-standing Irish connections.

Romanesque decoration

The decorated north doorway at Cashel seems to have impressed some influential people, as there are eight other doorways with pediments, mainly around the Midlands. The latest and most elaborate of these is at Clonfert Cathedral in Co. Galway.

Clonfert Cathedral

* **Form:** Clonfert Cathedral is more typical of the Irish Romanesque style. It is a simple nave

and chancel building with antae, much altered over the years.

* **Function:** This was the cathedral church for the diocese of Clonfert.
* **Technique:** The building has been altered many times over the generations. The finely carved Romanesque doorway was inserted in the 1170s.
* **Decoration:**
  - The decorated area surrounding the west door is 8m tall. It consists of a doorway with six orders of Romanesque arches, with a pediment on top (Fig. 5.5). The inside arch of grey limestone was added in the later Middle Ages and is not part of the rich brown sandstone of the original design that we are studying. The pillars on each side of the doorway are decorated in matching pairs, with lightly carved patterns of geometric and vegetal designs. The capitals have animal heads and human faces, again in matching pairs.
  - The arch rings are more deeply carved and come in a variety of designs. The inner row is decorated with plant forms.
  - The second row has animal heads holding a roll moulding in their jaws (Fig. 5.6).
  - The third row is made of square crosses connected to a roll moulding at the outer edge.
  - Flat discs are carved on both faces of the fourth arch, alternately pierced or decorated with spirals, serpents and flowers.
  - The fifth row has an open-ended cable moulding surrounding bosses on both faces, enclosing a roll moulding on the outer edge.

Fig. 5.5 (left)

The west door at Clonfert Cathedral, Co. Galway. The decorated arches and gable pediment make one of the largest Romanesque assemblies in Ireland.

Fig. 5.6 (above)

Detail of the pillars, capitals and arches at the Clonfert Cathedral doorway

- The sixth row is made of semi-spherical bosses decorated with interlace.
- The outer ring, which separates the arches from the pediment, has an interlace pattern in the Urnes style.
- The pediment is surrounded at its outer edges by a double cable moulding. There is a finial at the top, which has a human head on each side. The lower part of the pediment has a row of five arches with a head placed in each. Above this is a pattern of triangles decorated with plant forms. There are 10 heads set in the hollow spaces between the decorated triangles.

The carved doorway at Clonfert has some parallels in England and France. It may have been built at the time of the synod that was held there in 1179.

There are Romanesque features at over 100 sites around the country, ranging from simple chancel arches to elaborately carved doorways. Most of these features are added to smaller, plain buildings.

The Cross of Cong

* **Form:** The cross is 76cm tall. The surface is covered in a network of ornament (Fig. 5.7).
* **Function:** It was made to display a fragment of the True Cross taken from a larger fragment that was brought to Ireland from Rome in 1119 AD.
* **Technique:** Like the Tully Lough Cross that we saw earlier, it is made of bronze plaques and mounted on an oak core. The cross is outlined by a tubular silver edging, punctuated with glass studs on the front and enamel discs on the back. Rows of mounts, which once held glass or enamel studs, divide the front of the cross into panels. Silver and niello inlay are used on the mounting.
* **Decoration:** The centre of the cross has a semi-conical mount holding a rock crystal. The fragment of the True Cross was displayed behind this transparent crystal. Each panel on the front is filled with gilt bronze animal interlace in the Urnes style. Four skilfully cast gilt bronze openwork plaques, again in the Urnes style, make up the back of the cross. A pair of animal heads with blue glass eyes forms the mounting that joins the shaft to the cross. The animals, clamping the cross and their jaws, have scaly heads with mustachios and eyebrows of niello and silver.

Eleventh- and 12th-century metalwork is quite different in style from the 8th-century work, which is considered to be the high point of Irish metalwork. This later work relied for its impact on bolder designs and colour effects, though pieces like the Cross of Cong are beautifully balanced and subtle in their design.

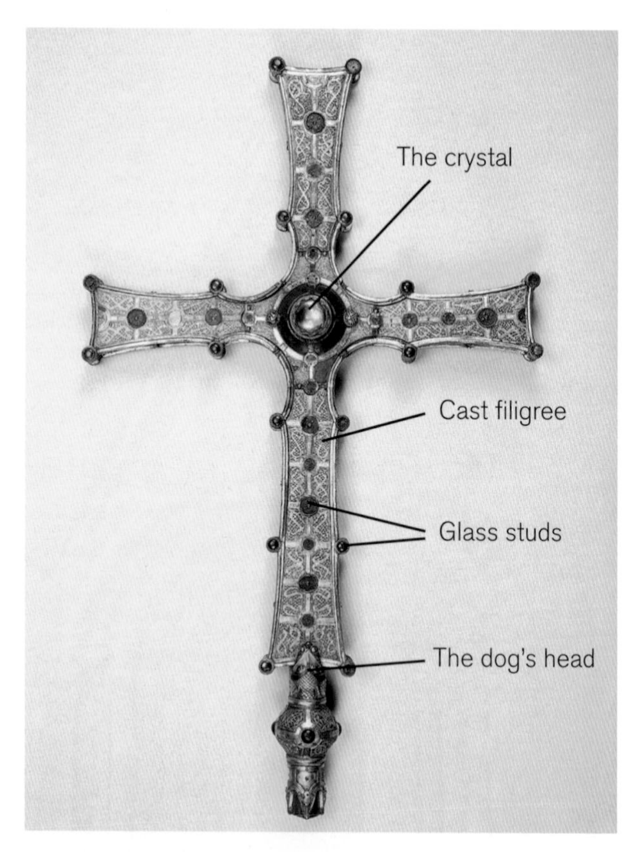

Fig. 5.7 The Cross of Cong was made to hold a fragment of the True Cross

Chapter review

* What were the effects of religious and social change on the arts in the Romanesque period?
* What were the main features of Romanesque architectural decoration?
* What changes do you notice in the design of high crosses in the Romanesque period?
* How do the decorated capitals of Romanesque manuscripts compare with the Book of Kells?
* A lot of Romanesque metalwork takes the form of reliquaries. Do you know why this is so?

EXAM QUESTIONS

Higher Level (2015)

'The simple design of stone churches in early Christian Ireland developed into a more complex Irish Romanesque style due to many influences from abroad.'

Discuss this statement, comparing the structure and design of **one** named early Christian Irish church with **one** named Irish Romanesque church.

and

Name an Irish monastic site that you have studied and describe its significant features.

Illustrate your answer.

FURTHER RESEARCH

www.3dicons.ie – Nuns' Church

www.bl.uk – Psalter of Cormac

www.megalithicireland.com – Drumcliff High Cross

www.megalithicireland.com – Dysert O'Dea High Cross

www.museum.ie

www.sacred-destinations.com – Rock of Cashel

Go to **www.gillexplore.ie** for extra content on Romanesque art, including the monasteries, architecture, high crosses, manuscripts and metalwork.

Chapter 6

Irish Georgian Architecture

Political and social background

The term 'Georgian' refers to a variety of styles in architecture and the decorative arts based on classical ideals of design and proportion.

The name 'Georgian' comes from the successive Kings George of England, from George I, who became king in 1714, to George IV, who died in 1830. The style is characterised by good craftsmanship in a classical system of design and proportion.

By the end of this chapter, I will...

* Know the social and political background to the Georgian period in Ireland.
* Understand what Palladianism means.
* Know suitable terminology for the details on architecture.
* Be familiar with the work of E. L. Pearce: Castletown House and Parliament House.
* Have examples of the work of R. Cassels and D. Ducart.
* Understand about stucco and the work of the Lafranchini brothers, West and Stapleton.
* Know about townhouses, the Wide Streets Commission and city squares.
* Appreciate the Neo-Classical style.
* Know the work of W. Chambers (the Casino at Marino).
* Know the work of T. Cooley and T. Ivory.
* Be familiar with the work of J. Gandon (the Custom House and the Four Courts).
* Know about E. Smyth, sculptor.

Export trade

Following the Battle of the Boyne in 1690, there was a period of peace and prosperity in Ireland where the landlords became wealthy. There was a strong export trade in wool, linen and agricultural produce, particularly salt beef, pork and butter. Trading and export centres in the towns and ports of Ireland often have well-built streets of Georgian buildings and market houses.

The Dublin Society

Organisations were set up for the improvement of infrastructure, agriculture, industry and the arts. The Dublin Society, founded in 1731, sponsored research and awarded prizes to encourage industry and crafts. They set up a school to train craft workers, architects and artists. The Wide Streets Commission, set up in 1757, regulated planning and street design in Dublin City, which was going through a phase of unprecedented expansion.

Fig. 6.1

The Irish House of Commons, a painting by Francis Wheatley (1780). This is the only record of what the interior of the Irish House of Commons looked like. The painting shows Grattan's famous speech on the repeal of Poynings' Law. The public gallery is full of spectators.

Grattan's parliament

There was a parliament in Dublin run by the Protestant Anglo-Irish gentry, which gained independence from Westminster for a short period. This came in 1782 following a motion proposed by Henry Grattan (Fig. 6.1). This relative independence was short lived because following the Irish rebellion of 1798, the Act of Union was passed in 1800, which created the United Kingdom of Britain and Ireland with one parliament in Westminster, putting an end to 'Grattan's Parliament'.

The Grand Tour

This was the age of the 'Grand Tour', when people of wealth and education visited the sights of Europe, with particular attention given to classical and Renaissance arts and architecture. The sights of Rome and Florence and the works of art being revealed at Pompeii influenced and inspired returning tourists to attempt classical design in their own public and private buildings.

Palladianism

Andrea Palladio (1508–80) had an enormous influence on architecture through his books, *I Quattro Libri dell'Architettura*, which were published in 1570 and translated into *The Four Books of Architecture* in England in 1715–20. These books contained drawings of plans and elevations of Palladio's buildings and advice on proportions, building materials, the 'correct' classical orders, porticos, columns and other useful details (Fig 6.2).

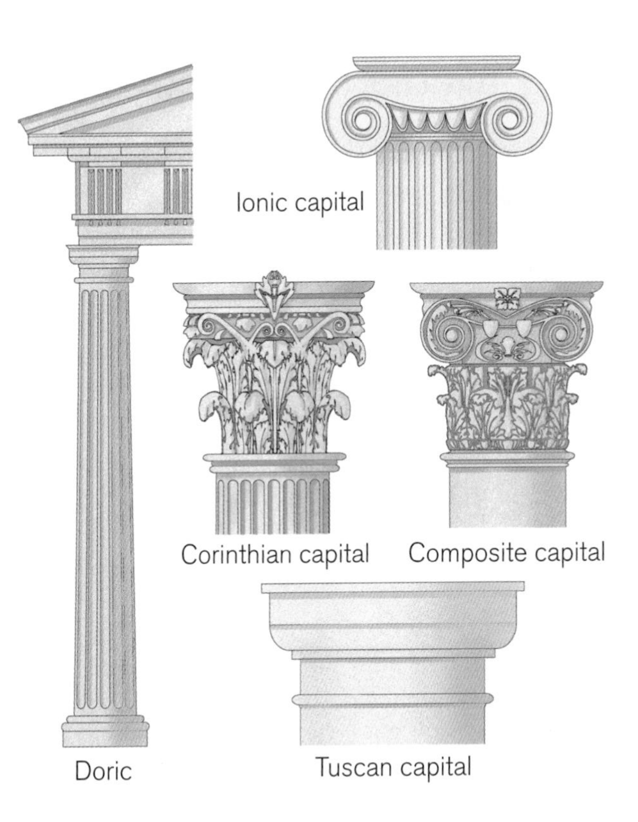

Fig. 6.2 The classical orders

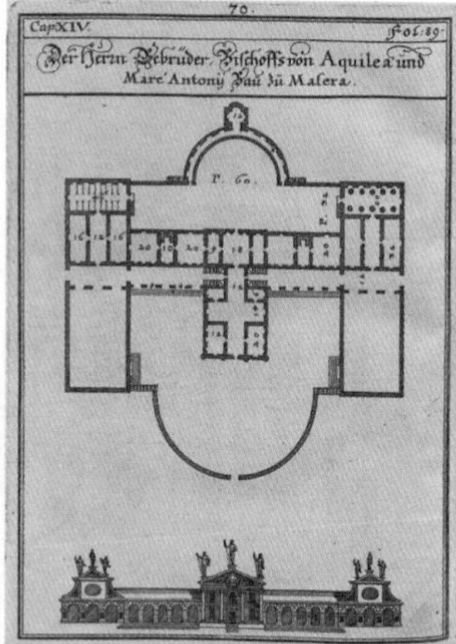

Fig. 6.3 The Villa Barbaro, Maser, Italy, 1558, by Andrea Palladio. The photograph of the house shows some changes from Palladio's design in his *Four Books of Architecture*, which was an important source of ideas for Georgian architects.

Palladio designed houses for wealthy Venetians in the countryside of the Vento region. These houses combined elegant living space for the owner with outbuildings for animals and farm work. This arrangement proved popular with Irish and English country gentlemen, who built a great number of houses, both large and small, in the style (Fig. 6.3).

The Palladian style in Ireland

Palladian buildings in Ireland were often truer to Palladian ideals than English examples. This may be because some of the architects came directly from Europe and were not influenced by the English version of the style. Irish interiors were often more elaborate, with Rococo plasterwork in high relief.

Sir Edward Lovett Pearce (1699–1733)

Born in Co. Meath, Pearce went to England to study architecture after the death of his father in 1715 with his father's cousin, the famous English Baroque architect Sir John Vanbrugh, who was working on the design of Blenheim Palace at the time. After a spell in the army, Pearce travelled

Layout of a Palladian-style house

The central block was often square in plan, with a temple front of columns and a triangular pediment forming a portico over the formal entrance, generally of three floors.

The basement was often of rusticated stone, containing the kitchen, services and minor rooms.

The ground floor, referred to as the *piano nobile* ('noble floor'), would have been reached by a flight of steps leading to the entrance. Inside were the main reception rooms and master bedroom. This floor had the tallest windows and the most spacious rooms.

The top floor had lower ceilings and contained bedrooms and rooms of less importance. The windows were often square on this level (Fig. 6.4).

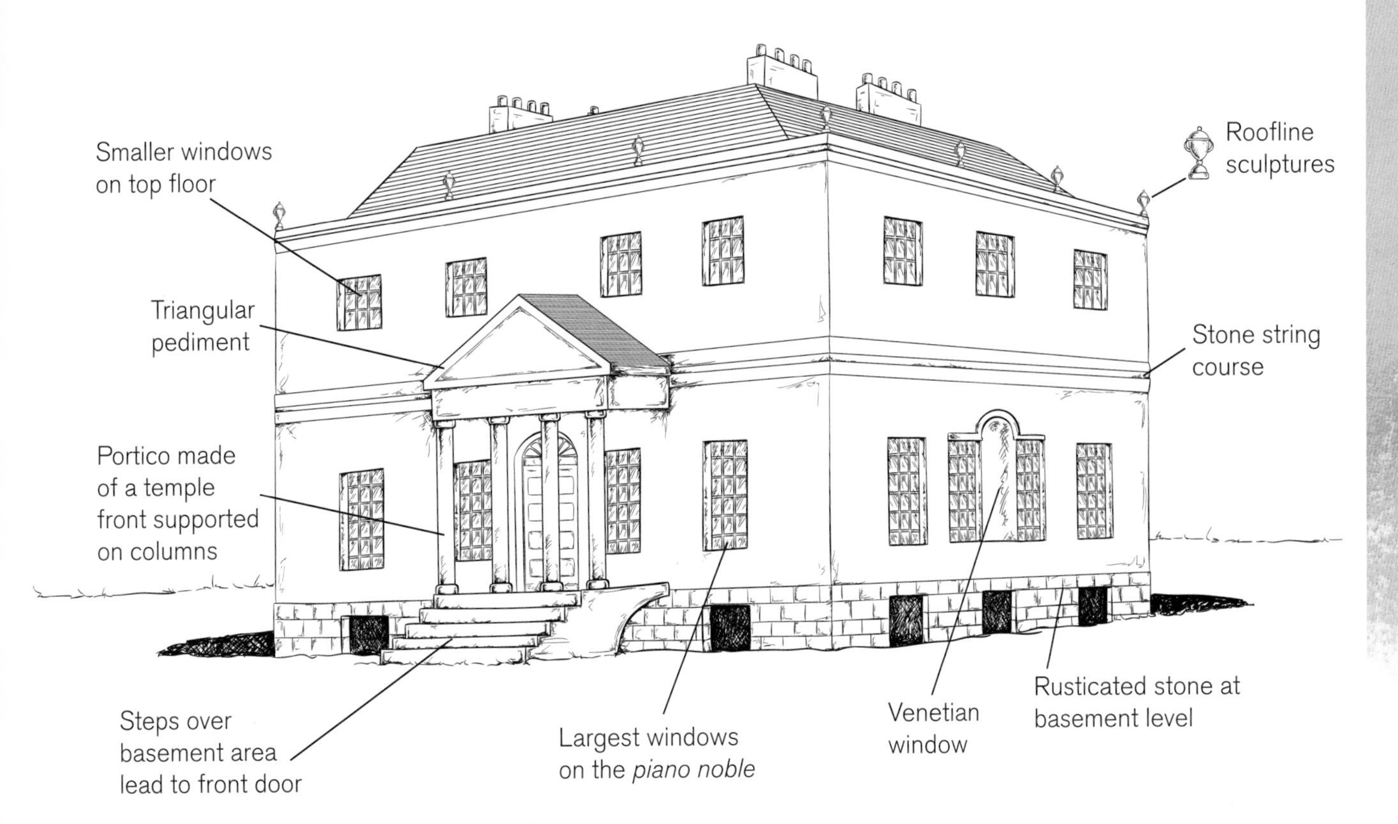

Fig. 6.4 Elements of a Georgian country house

to France and Italy for three years, studying architecture. He had a copy of Palladio's *Quattro Libri*, which he annotated with his own sketches and observations on the buildings he saw. He met Alessandro Galilei, the designer of Castletown House, in Florence.

Pearce was one of the most influential architects of his day and is credited with bringing the Palladian style to Ireland. Castletown House, Drumcondra House (All Hallows College), Bellamont Forest and Cashel Palace were among the large country houses that he worked on. The Parliament House (Bank of Ireland) in College Green, Dublin, was his greatest and most influential public building.

Pearce spent only seven years working in Ireland, but in that time he changed the direction of Irish architecture. He died in 1733 at the age of 34 with some of his work unfinished. Richard Cassels, who had been his assistant on a number of projects, took over the practice and became the leading architect in the country working in the Palladian style.

Castletown House, Co. Kildare

Castletown House (Fig. 6.5) is the earliest and largest of about two dozen large country houses that were built in Ireland between 1716 and 1745. It was built for William Conolly, who had risen from humble beginnings to become one of the richest and most powerful men in Ireland. He made a vast fortune from land deals and rose to political prominence as the Speaker of the Irish House of Commons.

The Italian architect Alessandro Galilei was commissioned to design the house. He came to Ireland in 1719. He spent less than a year on the job, producing drawings of the front elevation and probably the plan, and then he departed, leaving others to carry out the work, which was begun in 1722. Sir Edward Lovett Pearce took over the project in 1724 upon his return from his Grand Tour in Europe. He designed the quadrant Ionic colonnades that join Galilei's central block, built in pale limestone, to the two end pavilions, which are in a warm brown limestone.

Castletown is the first large country house in Ireland to have been designed by a professional architect using classical proportions.

Exterior

The central block is in the style of an Italian town palazzo, 13 bays wide. The building is four storeys tall. A set of broad steps reaches the main entrance across the open area in front of the basement. The tallest windows are on the ground floor. The first floor windows each have a pediment, alternately curved and triangular. The windows on the top floor are square. A balustrade at roof level helps to conceal the hipped roof. A matching balustrade runs along the top of the colonnades and continues along the roof level of the wings, creating unity in the whole composition.

Interior

There is a double-height entrance hall, which was designed by Pearce (Fig. 6.6). He used Ionic columns around the walls and to support a balcony that connects to the central corridor on the first floor. The columns in the hall match the colonnades outside. This balconied hall, with its black and white stone floor tiles, was frequently copied in other Irish houses and is the only part of Castletown that survives unchanged from Speaker Connolly's time.

Many of the features of Castletown's interior date from the late 1850s, when Tom Conolly, grandnephew of the speaker, inherited the estate. He married Lady Louisa Lennox in 1758; she was the daughter of the Duke of Richmond and a granddaughter of Charles II of England. Louisa was only 15 at the time of her marriage, but she took over the management and decoration of the house with some enthusiasm. She ordered the beautiful cantilevered stairway built in Portland stone and the plasterwork on the walls of the stairwell, which was carried out by Philip and Paul Lafranchini, the Swiss-Italian stuccadores. The plasterwork consists of floral swags, cherubs and family portraits in a high relief Rococo style. In the 1760s, Louisa, with her sister and friends, decorated the walls of one of the ground floor rooms with mezzotints and engravings, creating the only 'print room' still surviving in Ireland.

In the 1870s, the Long Gallery was completely redecorated (Fig. 6.7). The room, which is more than 24m x 7m, is on the rear of the first floor. The walls are decorated with paintings in the

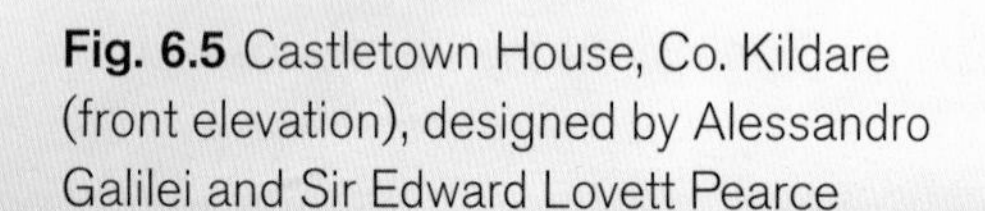
Fig. 6.5 Castletown House, Co. Kildare (front elevation), designed by Alessandro Galilei and Sir Edward Lovett Pearce

Fig. 6.6 (left) Castletown House entrance hall, designed by Sir Edward Lovett Pearce

Fig. 6.7 (right) The Long Gallery at Castletown House. The large room had a carefully balanced decoration scheme.

Pompeian style by Thomas Ryder. The room has eight windows overlooking the gardens; Conolly's Folly (1740) can be seen in the distance. The wall opposite the windows has two doors with a niche between them, which contains a statue of Diana the Huntress. Above the doors is a large semi-circular (lunette) oil painting, a version of Guido Reni's *Aurora*. Other oil paintings are incorporated into the decoration scheme, including portraits of Tom and Lady Louisa Conolly over the fireplaces at each end of the room. All the elements of the room design – including paintings, niches, sculptures, mirrors and even the coloured glass chandeliers specially ordered from Venice – were carefully balanced in a symmetrical arrangement of all the parts. The Conollys used this enormous room as their family living room, where they could have family meals, play games or music and entertain close friends. Several activities could go on at the same time without interfering with each other.

Bellamont Forest, Co. Cavan

Begun in 1730, Bellamont Forest (Fig 6.8) is a smaller villa that Pearce designed for Charles

Fig. 6.8 Bellamont Forest, Co. Cavan

Coote. Compared to Castletown, it is a very plain structure, almost square in plan.

Exterior

The building is constructed of locally fired red brick, with details picked out in cut limestone. The entrance front has a portico that consists of a pediment supported on Doric columns approached by broad steps. The windows on the ground floor are also pedimented. Pearce used stone to outline the *piano nobile*. A string course that runs around the building at portico level and corner stones create a kind of frame to emphasise the most important rooms of the house. The basement is of rusticated stone, with deep joints and a roughened surface. The upper floor has square windows. The Venetian windows on the side elevations were often copied by later architects.

Interior

The colonnaded lobby on the top (bedroom) floor, which is lit from above by a lantern window, was also frequently copied. There is some good high relief plasterwork in the interior.

Parliament House (Bank of Ireland)

Parliament House (Fig. 6.9) is considered to be the most important early Palladian public building in Britain or Ireland. It was the first structure designed to hold two houses of Parliament: it contained chambers for the Commons and the Lords of the Irish Parliament.

Interior

The House of Commons was at the centre of Pearce's design. A large octagonal space covered by a dome, it was damaged by fire in 1792 and removed when the building was converted to a bank in the early 19th century. The House of Lords, which is set off to the east side of the Commons, retains many of its original features (Fig. 6.10). In plan it is quite like a church with an

Fig. 6.9 The Irish Parliament (now the Bank of Ireland), designed by Sir Edward Lovett Pearce. The three fronts and the forecourt can be seen clearly in this print.

Fig. 6.10
The interior of the House of Lords. This chamber has many of its original features.

apse at the eastern end. It still retains its original plasterwork and a carved oak fireplace. The decoration includes large tapestries of the Battle of the Boyne and the Siege of Derry by Jan van Beaver and a Waterford Crystal chandelier made of over 1,000 pieces of glass.

Exterior

Pearce's design for the entrance incorporates three temple fronts. The ends facing the street combine round-headed arches with pediments overhead. The central portico supports a pediment on four Ionic columns, with roofline figure sculptures representing Commerce, Fidelity and Hibernia. An Ionic colonnade connects these three temple fronts; in plan, it is like a letter *E*. The central portico is set back from the ends, creating a piazza forecourt where parliamentarians could make a formal entrance arriving in their horse-drawn carriages.

The Parliament House would have been the most impressive building in Dublin of its day. It influenced the design of other public architecture in Britain and Ireland.

Later additions

The building in its present form includes a Corinthian temple front entrance on the east (Westmoreland Street) side, designed by James Gandon in 1782 as a separate entrance for the House of Lords. Gandon also designed the curved wall with niches that connects his entrance to Pearce's colonnade. Later, a portico and screen wall was built on the west side and pilasters were added to Gandon's wall to harmonise the whole composition.

Richard Cassels, Cassel or Castle (1690–1751)

Born in Hesse-Kassel in Germany of a Huguenot family with a background in architecture, Cassels trained originally as a military engineer but became interested in Palladian architecture when he was working in England in 1725. Sir Gustavus Hume brought him to Enniskillen in Co. Fermanagh in 1728 to design a house for him; he was also working with Pearce on the Parliament House that same year.

Cassels was an innovator in his plans for country houses. He designed an oval drawing room at the rear of Ballyhaise House in Co. Cavan and he put semi-circular bay windows on the side elevations of Belvedere House in Co. Westmeath. These features became popular in Ireland and England, but not until years later.

Russborough House near Blessington, Co. Wicklow

Russborough House (Fig. 6.11) is a high point in Irish Palladian country house design. It was begun in 1741 for Joseph Leeson, 1st Earl of Milltown, and built in local granite.

Exterior

The façade is over 200m long and includes a central block, six bays wide, connected by quadrant arcades to two pavilions, each seven bays wide. Walls continue beyond the pavilions to outbuildings at each end. There is a Baroque arch, topped with a cupola, at the centre of each wall to add interest and relief to the composition.

It is a perfect example of Palladio's idea of combining the master's house within the structures of a working farm. The buildings on the west side contained the stables. The kitchens and other out offices were on the east side. A lot of the original features have survived intact. Stone, statuary, inlaid floors, mantles and plasterwork are all original and in good condition.

The central block of Russborough is two storeys over basement. The entrance is reached by a stairway that is the full width of the frontispiece, which consists of four engaged Corinthian columns with floral swags between the capitals. These support a triangular pediment, which is applied to the wall. There is a semi-circular fanlight over the door. String courses at pediment and roof level create a horizontal emphasis. Cassels used urns as roofline sculptures on the main house as well as on the arcades and the wings.

Interior

The simplicity, even severity, of the exterior of Russborough is in contrast with the lavish Baroque and Rococo interior. There are seven interconnected reception rooms on the *piano nobile*, all 6m tall except for the dining room, with its coved ceilings (curved where the ceiling meets the wall). Dado rails in carved mahogany 1.2m high help to reduce the apparent height of the rooms. Carved mahogany is also used on the doors, stairs and banisters. The floor of the saloon is also mahogany with satinwood inlay (Fig. 6.12).

The Lafranchini brothers, whose work we noted at Castletown, decorated several of the ceilings. In the saloon, *The Loves of the Gods* are represented by cherubs and figure groups framed by plant forms and swags. The plasterwork at Russborough is considered to be the finest in the country.

Fig. 6.11 Russborough House, Co. Wicklow, designed in 1741 by Richard Cassels

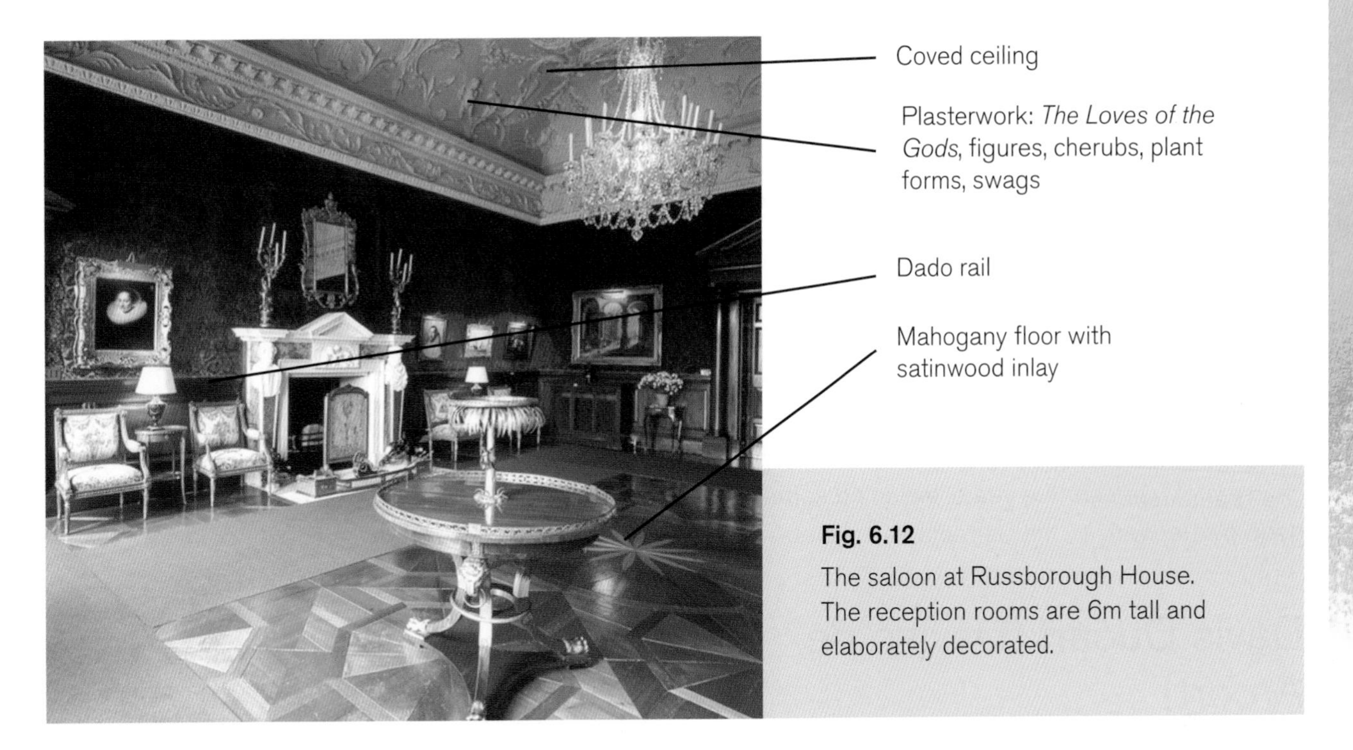

Fig. 6.12

The saloon at Russborough House. The reception rooms are 6m tall and elaborately decorated.

Leinster House

Originally built as a townhouse for the 22-year-old James Fitzgerald, the 20th Earl of Kildare and the 1st Duke of Leinster, in 1745, Leinster House is basically a Palladian country mansion relocated into the city (Fig. 6.13). The entrance front on Kildare Street is built in fine Ardbraccan limestone and the simpler Leinster Lawn front is built in granite. It is set back from the building line behind its own forecourt.

Exterior

The central block is three storeys tall and 11 bays wide. The entrance is emphasised by a three-bay breakfront, which runs the full height of the building. The ground floor of this section

Fig. 6.13

Leinster House (Kildare Street front), designed for the Duke of Leinster by Richard Cassels

is rusticated, and a plain moulding surrounds the doorway. At first-floor level a balustrade connects four Corinthian columns, which support a triangular pediment at roof level. The windows of the first floor have curved and triangular pediments, like those on the *piano nobile* at Castletown.

Interior

There is a double-height hall with a balcony, like the one at Castletown. A surprising amount of the original decoration survives, considering its changes of use over the years, including some good plasterwork by the Lafranchini brothers.

Davis Ducart (Daviso de Arcort)

A Sardinian architect and engineer, Ducart worked mainly in the South of Ireland in the 1760s. The Custom House, now the Hunt Museum, in Limerick is thought to be one of his earliest designs (Fig. 6.14). His style was a Franco-Italian version of Palladianism, which sometimes looked more modern than contemporary work.

The entrance front of the Custom House faces the river. It has a rusticated ground floor with three arches at the centre supporting the frontispiece, which has fluted pilasters supporting a simple entablature. He used a straight arcade as the connection to the end pavilions rather than the curved versions used by other architects in Ireland.

Ducart designed several buildings in Cork: the Mayoralty House, Lota and Kilshannig, which has beautiful plasterwork by the Lafranchini brothers in their later lighter style.

Stucco decoration

Eighteenth-century decorative plasterwork is more correctly referred to as stucco. Stuccowork was developed in ancient times and made into an art form during the Renaissance, Baroque and Rococo periods.

Stucco is a quick-setting, flexible material made of very fine sand, crushed white Carrara marble, gypsum, alabaster dust and other, sometimes secret, ingredients, which were mixed with water to create the stucco. It could be cast in moulds or applied freehand. When it was dry, the surface could be polished to a smooth finish.

Fig. 6.14
The Custom House, Limerick (riverfront), now the Hunt Museum, designed by Davis Ducart

The development of style

Decorative stucco was introduced during the building boom of the 18th century in Ireland, first in the compartmented style, which was a continuation of 17th-century design, where the ceiling was divided into decorated geometric shapes (see Fig. 6.10). In the 1740s the Lafranchini brothers introduced a Baroque style with human figures in high relief surrounded by Acanthus leaves, swags of flowers and putti. Their later work was more Rococo, lighter and with more movement. The human figure was less evident.

Sources for stucco designs

The classical scenes and decorations were probably borrowed from French and Italian engravings. It was the practice in the 18th century to use engravings as a reference for all kinds of decoration. Books of patterns and designs were produced so that architects and craftsmen could copy from them.

The Lafranchini brothers

Born in Ticino in the Italian-speaking part of Switzerland, Paulo (1695–1770) and Filippo (1702–79) were the most influential stuccodores (plaster modellers) to operate in Ireland. They worked in an Italian Baroque figurative and ornamental style on about 15 Irish houses. They are often associated with the buildings of Richard Cassels. At Carton House (Fig. 6.15) and Newman House they produced figures of classical gods and goddesses surrounded by swirling Acanthus cartouches and swags. Classical figures are used again at Riverstown House in Co. Cork, where personifications of the virtues decorate the walls.

Fig. 6.15

The stuccoed ceiling of the Gold Salon at Carton House by the Lanfranchini brothers

Fig. 6.16 (left)

Some of the plasterwork copied from Riverstown House at Áras an Uachtaráin

Fig. 6.17 (right)

Plaster portrait from Castletown House. The bust in classical drapery is surrounded in an oval frame decorated in leaf patterns.

Copies of the plasterwork at Riverstown were made for Áras an Uachtaráin in 1948 (Fig. 6.16).

There are figure scenes at Kilshannig House, also in Co. Cork, made in 1766. At Russborough House, a lighter style is more evident. Acanthus leaf and floral swags with occasional putti make up the rhythmic patterns that decorate the ceilings of the saloons (see Fig. 6.12). The walls in the stair hall at Castletown are also decorated in this lighter, lively, asymmetrical Rococo style (Fig. 6.17).

While Paulo went to work in England in the 1750s for a number of years, Filippo remained in Ireland into the 1770s.

Robert West (d. 1790)

West came from a family of stuccodores whose work was recorded from the early 17th century. He was also a master builder. West's best work is high relief birds and human heads emerging from curved

Fig. 6.18

An example of Robert West's plasterwork from his house at 20 Dominick Street, Dublin. West's high relief plasterwork can be almost freestanding.

plant forms. These almost freestanding birds appear at his own house, No. 20 Dominic Street (Fig. 6.18), and at No. 28 St Stephen's Green. The birds are surrounded by leaves, flowers, fruits and musical instruments. West or his studio also decorated some country houses, such as Dowth Hall, Co. Meath, and Dunsandle, Co. Galway.

Michael Stapleton (1740–1801)

Stapleton was a master builder and stuccodore. He was a pupil of West's and was able to do creative freehand plasterwork as well as copies of English designers like Adams. His stuccowork was in the Neo-Classical style. Stapleton's Neo-Classical designs look like lace or embroidery. Delicate white plant forms arranged in geometric patterns against a coloured background form the basis for most compositions. Figure scenes and classical devices like urns or musical instruments are used as centres of interest in the designs (Fig. 6.19).

Stapleton's masterpiece is considered to be Belvedere House in Great Denmark Street in Dublin, which he completed for the 2nd Earl of Belvedere in 1786. (The Jesuit order bought the building as a school in 1841 and it has been run ever since as Belvedere College; James Joyce was its most famous past pupil.) Stapleton was the architect and stuccodore for this project. He produced some of his most creative work for the stairs and the main reception rooms.

Mass-produced plasterwork

Commercially mass-produced moulds brought an end to the hand-crafted work we have just seen. Decorative mouldings could be obtained quickly and cheaply, which suited the needs of Irish developers in a market where prices were falling following the Act of Union in 1800.

Townhouses

At the beginning of the 18th century, Dublin was still a small walled medieval city with narrow

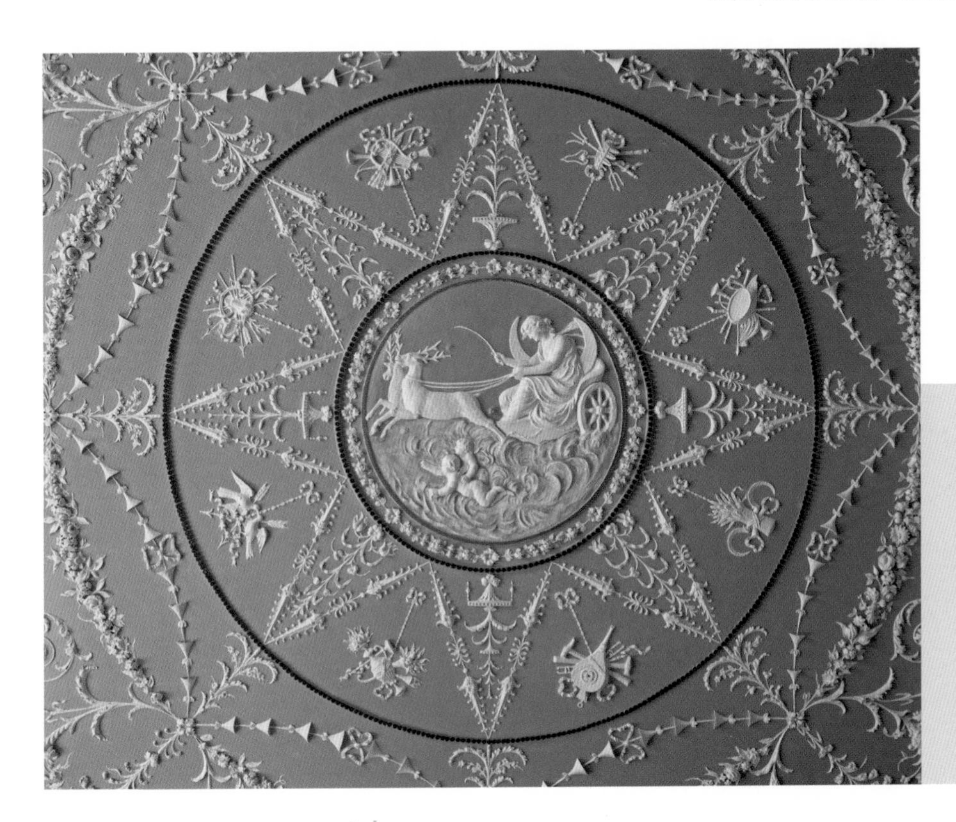

Fig. 6.19
In Michael Stapleton's Neo-Classical plasterwork, figure scenes and musical instruments are combined with plant forms in geometric patterns

streets and alleys. Houses were built of stone and wood. By the end of the century it was the second city of the British Empire, with elegant streets and squares and impressive public buildings. The city developed outwards from the area around Dublin Castle.

North of the Liffey

Much of the early development began north of the Liffey. Sir Humphrey Jervis developed lands around Capel and Jervis Streets. The Earl of Drogheda owned lands that were developed into Henry, Mary and Earl Streets. Luke Gardiner bought out many of the interests and became the main developer north of the Liffey from 1714 onwards.

South of the Liffey

On the south side, Sir Francis Aungier and the Earl of Meath were the early developers. Joshua Dawson, who was the Viscount Molesworth, planned Dawson, Molesworth, Nassau and Kildare Streets from 1710 on. The Fitzwilliam family (Lords Mountjoy) were the main developers on the south side after 1780.

Other towns

Other towns in Ireland have Georgian elements. For example, the redbrick terraces of Newtown Perry in Limerick, the Mall in Cork and parts of many towns contain Georgian streets or civic buildings.

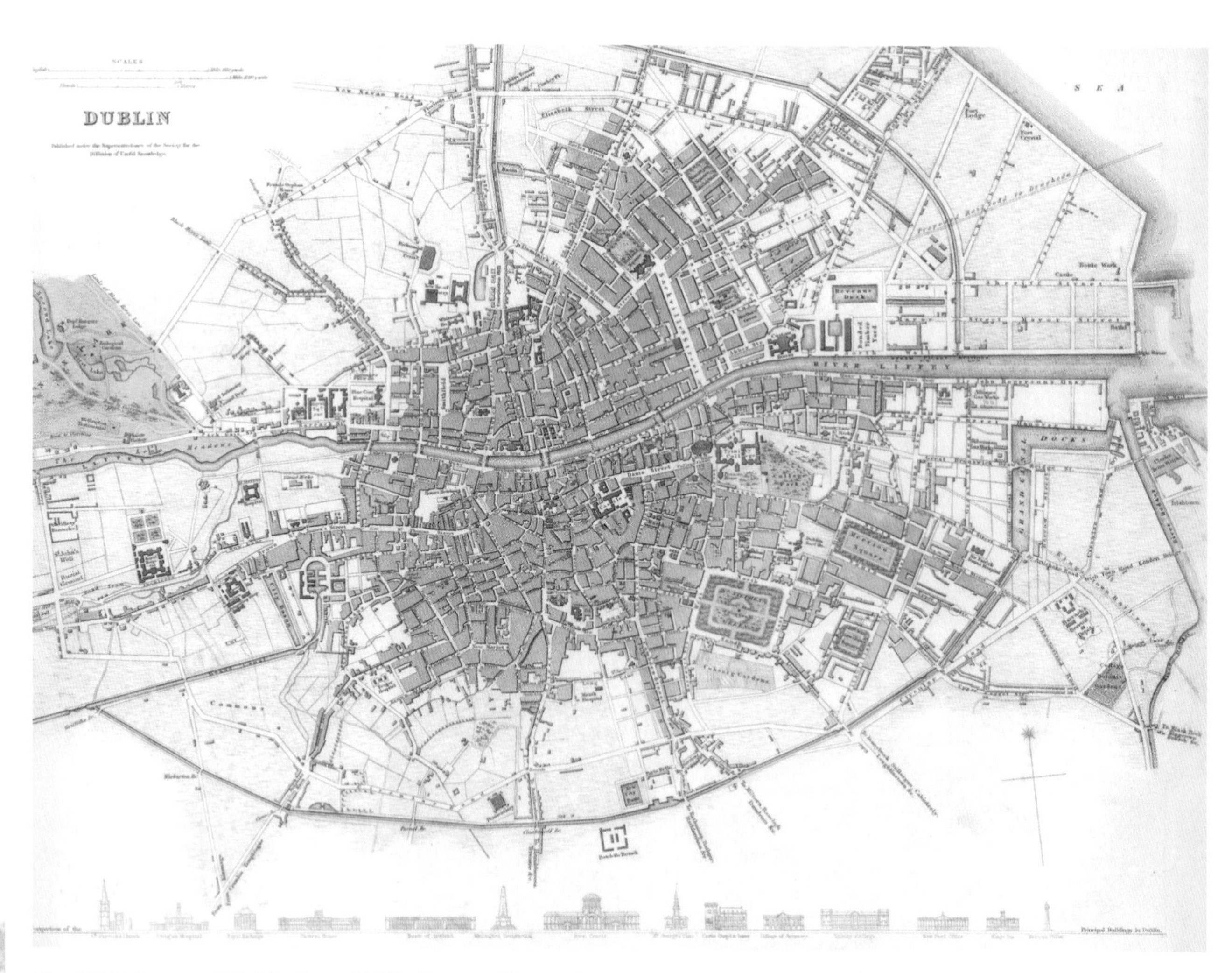

Fig. 6.20 A map of Dublin from 1836. The canals created a boundary for the growing city.

The Wide Streets Commission

The Wide Streets Commission was established to control planning and to create order and uniformity in the development of Dublin city. They had powers of compulsory purchase and to enforce regulations. The commission was made up of members of Parliament and the mayor, so they had considerable political clout. They cut through old parts of the city to create Parliament Street, which connected Dublin Castle to Capel Street Bridge and the north side of the city. Later they built another bridge (Carlisle Bridge, now O'Connell Bridge) further down the river, connecting Sackville (now O'Connell) Street with new developments at Westmoreland and D'Olier Streets. These streets were designed in the1790s with integrated shop fronts, a feature that did not appear in London until later.

The development of streets and squares

The earlier squares like Stephen's Green and Parnell Square were developed piecemeal, a few buildings at a time, but later squares like Mountjoy on the north side and Merrion and Fitzwilliam Squares on the south side were laid out in advance. Most streets and squares had a continuous building line, but there are streets that have houses that vary in height, width, size of windows and doors and the colour of the bricks. Some houses have basements and first floors in cut stone and a few of the larger houses were completely stone built. The North and South Circular Roads outlined the urban area, which was later redefined by the Royal and Grand Canals (Fig. 6.20).

The Georgian red brick terraced house

The Georgian red brick terraced house can vary in size, from being a single bay wide, which is rare, to five or even seven bays for some of the largest houses. The basements are at natural ground level. The streets were built on brick arches. The spaces beneath the arches were used as storage areas for the houses. Circular manholes on the pavements opened into chutes where coal, which was used to heat the houses, could be poured into the stores below. The streets were cobbled and the footpaths in the better parts of Dublin had granite kerbs. An open area between the street and the houses allowed light into the basement windows. This area was protected by a cast iron railing set in a low stone plinth at street level. Railings continued up the sides of the steps to the front door. The steps formed a bridge over the area. Cast iron was also used for balconies and for foot scrapers and other street furniture.

Fig. 6.21 Some examples of the range of styles used on Georgian doors

Exterior

The doorways provide one of the main decorative features of the Georgian street house. They come with a variety of fanlights and porticoes made up of classical elements (Fig. 6.21). Some houses have a small window on each side of the door to help light the hallway inside. The sash windows vary in size according to the importance of the rooms within. The tallest windows were on the first-floor reception rooms and the smallest were on the top-floor bedrooms (Fig. 6.22).

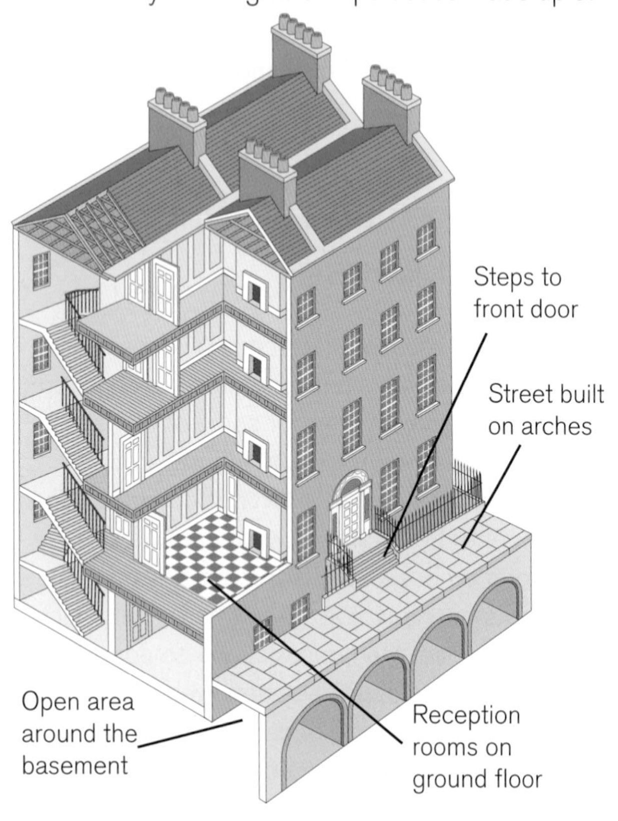

Fig. 6.22 Cutaway view of a Georgian terrace house

Interior

Most Georgian terrace houses were family residences, lived in by successful merchants and members of the professions. Some of the gentry used them as townhouses. They were most often four storeys over basement with two reception rooms on the ground and first floors, one at the front and one at the rear, with a stairway and passage running down one side (Fig. 6.23).

Arrangement of the rooms

The basement contained the kitchen and rooms for servants to work and live in. Ceilings were relatively low and there was little or no decoration. Ground-flour and first-floor rooms were taller and had decorative plasterwork. The quality and quantity of the stucco depended on the wealth of the owner and the skills and talents of the builder

Fig. 6.23 A three bay red brick Georgian terrace house with a cast iron balcony (left). The roof cannot be seen from street level. A Georgian-style bedroom (right).

or architect. The drawing room was normally more elaborately decorated; some of the finer houses have fully patterned ceilings surrounded with a frieze up to 30cm deep. Dining rooms were less elaborately decorated.

Craftsmanship

Fine joinery was a feature of Georgian houses. Panelled doors and shutters, decorative door frames and balustrades, well-made sash windows with thin glazing bars, and fine patterned framing on fanlights were all carried out to the highest standards.

The Neo-Classical style

There was a change of style in architecture in the late 18th century. Original Roman and Greek designs were preferred to the Renaissance interpretation of them through architects like Palladio. There was a movement away from Baroque and Rococo in favour of 'classical' design. New ideas came from buildings seen on the Grand Tour or from books of engravings that showed Roman ruins or reconstructions of them. Giambattista Piranesi (1720–84) produced several influential books of engravings, which exaggerated the size of Roman buildings. Another book of engravings, *The Antiquities of Athens*, which was published in 1762, led to a Greek Revival. The discoveries at Pompeii and Herculaneum helped create the Etruscan style, which influenced the Adam and Empire styles.

A patron of the arts

James Caulfield, Lord Charlemont, spent a number of years on the Grand Tour in Europe. His cultural interests led him to spend a lot of his time in Rome, where he was friendly with artists and architects. On his return to Dublin in 1755 he wanted to bring Italian style to his Irish properties, so he employed a friend he had made in Rome to make the designs for him.

Sir William Chambers (1723–96)

Chambers was the leading English architect of his day. He designed a townhouse and a garden temple for the country estate of Lord Charlemont, who renamed the estate at Donnycarney 'Marino' in memory of an Italian town he had visited on the Grand Tour. Marino House was demolished long ago, but the garden temple, the Casino at Marino, and his townhouse, Charlemont House in Parnell Square, now Dublin City Gallery The Hugh Lane (Fig. 6.24), still stand.

Charlemont House

Charlemont House, which was built in 1763, formed the centrepiece for the north side of Parnell Square (originally Ruthland Square). The house is connected to the red brick terraces on each side by quadrant walls, which are decorated with niches. The ground floor is of rusticated stone, while the two upper floors are finished in smooth cut stone. The entrance has a simple entablature supported on Ionic columns. It is a relatively simple exterior compared with the early Palladian townhouses of Dublin.

Fig. 6.24 Charlemont House, Dublin (now Dublin City Gallery The Hugh Lane) was designed for Lord Charlemont by Sir William Chambers

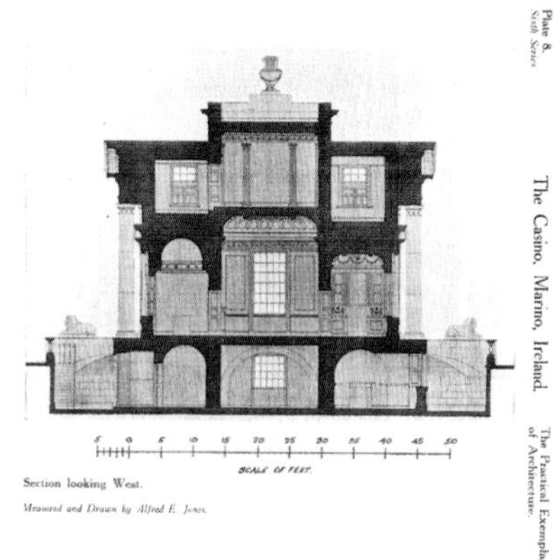

Fig. 6.25

The Casino at Marino, designed by Sir William Chambers for Lord Charlemont. The section drawing shows how much accommodation was created within the building.

The Casino at Marino

Casino means 'little house'. It was built during the 1760s. It is basically a garden ornament on a grand scale (Fig. 6.25). Chambers designed it as an architectural gem first; function was not of primary importance. The building is deceptively large – a second attic storey is almost hidden above the cornice. In plan it is a Greek cross inside a Doric colonnade.

Exterior

The Casino stands on a podium that is stepped on the north and south sides and has a balustrade on the east and west sides. The columns support an entablature decorated with ox skulls and concentric circles. The walls are rusticated to create a contrast with the smooth columns. A pediment creates a centrepiece on the north and south sides, and the attic storey decorated with swags and figure sculptures forms part of the centrepiece on the east and west sides.

Chambers never came to Ireland, so Simon Vierpyl, an English sculptor who had also befriended Lord Charlemont in Rome, supervised the work. Vierpyl was in charge of the stone carving and the exquisite detailing of the building, as well as having overall responsibility for the construction. All the functional parts are incorporated into the design – the urns on the roof are chimney pots and the pillars are hollow to bring rainwater from the roof into cisterns in the basement, where it could be used for household needs.

Interior

The glass in the windows is curved, which causes a reflection that prevents someone on the outside from seeing in. This provides some privacy and disguises the fact that partitions and stairs, which form part of the ingenious interior, cross some of the window spaces. The basement has a kitchen and workrooms for the servants. The ground floor has a formal entrance hall and three reception rooms, with geometric patterned floors in exotic woods and fine plasterwork by Cipriani, another of Lord Charlemont's friends from Rome. The highlight of the interior is the stateroom on the first floor, which is richly coloured, in contrast with the pure white interiors on the ground floor.

The Casino was built with the best materials and to the highest standards. It cost £20,000 at the time, which was a considerable fortune. The Casino was an influential building and aspects of its design appeared in several important buildings in following years.

Thomas Ivory (1732–86)

Born in Cork, Ivory worked as a carpenter before turning to architecture. He had picked up some Neo-Classical ideas from the drawings exhibited at the time of the Royal Exchange competition and put them to good use in his design for another competition to design a school for the Kings Hospital students.

The Blue Coat School

Now home to the Law Society of Ireland in Blackhall Place, Dublin, the Blue Coat School was so called because of the colour of the uniform of the Kings Hospital students (Fig. 6.26).

Exterior

The layout follows the plan of Palladian country mansions, with the main central block connected to two wings by curved walls with niches. The entire ground floor, including the quadrant walls, is rusticated except for the frontispieces on the wings. The central block is still generally Palladian, but the wings are treated differently, relying more on form than detail for their effect. Round-headed niches create hollow spaces at first-floor level, as do the large relieving arches over the central windows. Recesses with swags and oval niches also form part of the design. Balustrades at the windows and niches on the first floor support a string course that runs the full length of the building, tying all the elements together. The towers that are shown in the print were never built.

Fig. 6.26 *The Blue Coat School*, a print by Thomas Malton, National Gallery of Ireland, Dublin. The towers shown in the print were never built.

Ivory had a major influence on Irish architecture through his role as the first Master of the School of Architectural Drawing at the Royal Dublin Society. One of his pupils, James Hoban, designed the White House in Washington, DC.

James Gandon (1743–1823)

An Englishman and a student of Sir William Chambers, Gandon became the leading architect of the Neo-Classical period in Ireland. He was brought over to design a new Custom House in 1781, almost a mile downriver from the old building. This was part of the eastward development of the city away from the medieval centre around Dublin Castle.

The Custom House

The Custom House was built on previously undeveloped, marshy ground, which made for complicated and expensive construction. In plan the building is a square with long façades on the north and south sides connected to corner pavilions (Fig. 6.27).

Exterior

The riverfront, which faces south, is two storeys tall. The entrance is a temple front with a pediment supported on freestanding Doric columns reaching over two storeys. An attic storey helps to emphasise the slightly projecting central block. Arcades at ground level make a bridge between the central block and the end pavilions. Columns set in recesses create a feature on the end pavilions and on each side of the entrance. A cornice runs the full length of the building. Above this, balustrades connect the roofline of the pavilions to the attic storey. Enormous sculptures of coats of arms and urns on the rooflines of the pavilions continue the vertical emphasis created by the columns below, making a contrast with the horizontal nature of the building. The riverfront can be seen reflected in the surface of the Liffey, which also helps to increase the apparent height of the building. A tall columned drum supports the dome, which has a figure representing commerce on the top. Edward Smith was responsible for much of the sculpture on the Custom House.

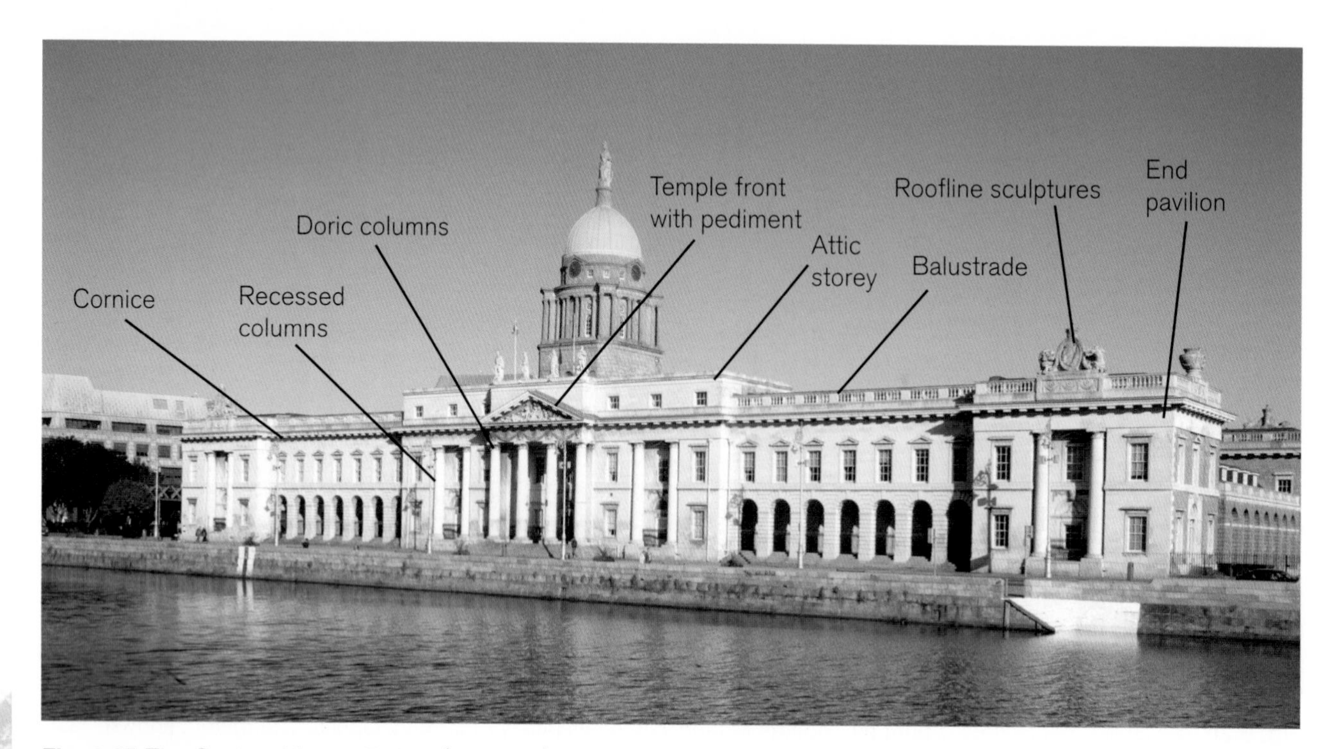

Fig. 6.27 The Custom House, Dublin (riverfront), designed by James Gandon in 1781

The Four Courts

Built in 1786, the Four Courts (Fig. 6.28) is considered by some to be one of the finest Neo-Classical buildings in Britain or Ireland.

Exterior

The building has a central block that is square in plan, supporting a large pillared drum with a saucer-shaped dome. Screen walls with triumphal arches at the centres connect the main building to the wings. Large carved crests are mounted on these arches, again sculpted by Smyth.

Interior

The ground floor has a large circular reception area with four courts leading diagonally off it. Originally the courts were only separated from the hall by pillars. Curtains were hung shortly after construction and then timber and glass screens were built. The partitions were built in masonry when the building was reconstructed following its burning in 1922, when all the interior decoration was lost.

Edward Smyth (1749–1812)

An Irish sculptor, Smyth was responsible for much of the carving on the Custom House and other buildings designed by Gandon. The riverine heads that decorate the keystones of the arches on the riverfront show Smyth's bold style to advantage. Carved in high relief and classically proportioned, they are based on Greek and Roman models. Fourteen heads represent the rivers of Ireland: the

Fig. 6.28 The Four Courts, Dublin (riverfront), designed by James Gandon in 1786

Fig. 6.29 Keystone from the Custom House representing the River Blackwater, carved by Edward Smyth

Foyle, the Erne, the Liffey, the Boyne, the Nore, the Blackwater (Fig. 6.29), the Atlantic, the Ban, the Shannon, the Lee, the Lagan, the Suir, the Barrow and the Slaney. The hair or headdress of each head carries symbols in the form of plants and animals to represent each river. The keystone over the main door represents the Liffey, the only female figure in the group.

Chapter review

* Can you work out what effect people taking the Grand Tour had on the design of Georgian buildings?
* What aspects of Palladio's designs did architects use in Ireland?
* What are the exterior and interior characteristics of Irish country mansions?
* What are the differences between Palladian and Neo-Classical design?
* What is stucco? How was it used in interior decoration?
* How were Georgian terrace houses decorated, both outside and inside?
* Can you describe the structure and decoration of one of Gandon's public buildings?

EXAM QUESTIONS

Ordinary Level (2016)

James Gandon (1743–1823) designed public and private buildings in Ireland.

Answer (a), (b) and (c).

(a) Name a building designed by James Gandon.

(b) Describe and discuss the architectural features and style of this building.

(c) Briefly describe and discuss one decorative feature of this building.

Illustrate your answer.

Higher Level (2016)

Select one of the following architects.

- Richard Castle (Cassels) (1690–1751)
- William Chambers (1723–96)

Describe and discuss the architectural features, both structural and decorative, of a named building by your chosen architect.

and

Name and briefly describe and discuss **one** other building by your chosen architect.

Illustrate your answer.

FURTHER RESEARCH

www.archiseek.com

www.buildingsofireland.ie

www.castletown.ie

www.iarc.ie

www.russborough.ie

Chapter 7

Irish Art in the 19th and 20th Centuries

Go to page 148 for a list of extra content available on **www.gillexplore.ie**.

The 19th century

The social and economic conditions in Ireland changed following the Act of Union and the loss of the Irish Parliament in 1800. Commissions for artists were hard to come by and many had to go abroad to make a living.

Art continued in the classical style. Accurate drawing and careful finish were still the norm well into the 19th century. Towards the end of the 1800s, influences from Europe led artists to question subjects, style and techniques.

By the end of this chapter, I will...

* Know about the changes in style, techniques and subjects during the 19th and 20th centuries.
* Be aware of the influence of the Celtic Revival in painting and at least one artist involved in it.
* Have seen samples of stained glass art.
* Know some artists involved in Cubism.
* Be familiar with some modern painters.
* Know some modern sculptors.

The Greek Revival led to the use of classical draperies and props in many works, even portraits. A number of public monuments were erected. These commissions were often decided by competition.

Nineteenth-century sculpture

There was a demand for religious sculptures following Catholic emancipation in 1829, but many of these were imported from Italy or produced in poor-quality workshops in Dublin, rather than given as commissions to artists.

John Henry Foley (1818–74)

Foley trained under John Smyth in the Dublin Society schools and then went to London, where he soon made a name for himself. He won public commissions in Ireland, England and India and did a variety of other work too, including portraits and subject sculptures.

A number of his outstanding works survive in Dublin, including life-size statues of Goldsmith, Burke and Grattan outside Trinity College. A seated figure of Benjamin Guinness can be seen in front of St Patrick's Cathedral (Fig. 7.1).

Fig. 7.1 Seated portrait sculpture of Benjamin Guinness outside St Patrick's Cathedral, Dublin, by John Henry Foley

Foley also worked on monuments outside Dublin, among them the bronzes of Lord Rosse in Birr, Co. Offaly, and Fr Matthew, the founder of the Irish temperance movement, which is a prominent landmark on Patrick's Street in Cork City.

Foley's most important work was in England. He designed the beautiful group of marble figures representing Asia and the bronze figure of Prince Albert for the prestigious Albert Memorial in London.

The O'Connell Monument

Subject

Located on O'Connell Street near the quays, the main figure of O'Connell faces the river (Fig. 7.2). Standing in a long cloak, hand on heart, he looks down to the passing people. Below his feet is the female figure personifying Erin. She holds the Act of Catholic Emancipation in her left hand and her right hand points up to him. She is the centrepiece of a frieze that runs all the way around the drum of the monument. The rest of the figures in the frieze represent all the

Fig. 7.2
The O'Connell Monument, 1866–74, by John Henry Foley, a large cylindrical monument on a four-sided base with bronze figures fixed to a stone structure, O'Connell Street, Dublin

professions and classes of Irish people freed by the act; the figures are all individual characters. Below the frieze, four seated angels, twice life size, face out from each corner of the monument.

Composition

The three layers of figures, set on a wide base, form a steep triangular shape, which leads the eye up to the figure of O'Connell at the top. The figures on the frieze are arranged in cleverly connected groups, varying in height and depth to avoid creating a monotonous row.

Style

The figures are in modern dress, but the composition and the draperies on the angels are classical.

Techniques and materials

The stone structure is in the tradition of architectural masonry. The large bronze figures were modelled in the round, except on the frieze, where background figures are in low relief.

Nineteenth-century painting

In the early part of the 19th century, style and technique continued much as they had in the 18th century. Most artists got their early training in Ireland and then went to England to continue their education and hopefully make a living. Artists painted in the Neo-Classical or Romantic styles, making careful, realistic drawings and finishing their paintings in blended brushstrokes. Subject matter was often sentimental, a trend that was also common in English literature of the time. Watercolour became more popular as paints and materials improved, not just for sketching, but for finished work as well.

The rule of thirds

The rule of thirds (Fig. 7.3) is a guideline for composing visual images. It is still used today, particularly in photography and film. The picture space is divided into nine equal spaces by two

The tower is visible beside this vertical line
The dominant figure is close to the crossing point of two thirds
The foreground fits in the bottom third
Foreground and middle ground features are on this vertical line

Fig. 7.3 The rule of thirds was developed to help artists compose their paintings. This example is a watercolour by George Petrie, *The Last Circuit of Pilgrims at Clonmacnoise*, 1838.

evenly spaced horizontal and vertical lines. Elements of the composition should then be placed along the lines or at the intersections. This arrangement is supposed to create more energy and interest than simply centring the subject.

Daniel Maclise (1816–1900)

Maclise was born in Cork and had his early training at the Cork School of Art. He financed his further education in London and Paris by selling portraits and landscapes. By the 1830s he was an established painter, working on large, detailed canvases and smaller subject pictures such as *The Falconer* (Fig. 7.4), which hangs in the Crawford Art Gallery in Cork. In the 1850s he painted part of the mural decorations in the House of Lords in London. *The Meeting of Wellington and Blücher on the Field at Waterloo* and *The Death of Nelson* are considered to be his finest works.

Maclise was a popular and successful artist in London. He drew illustrations for *Fraser's Magazine* and illustrated books for Dickens and other writers and moved in their social circles. He won medals at the Royal Academy for his drawing and painting early in his career and painted historical and literary subjects throughout his life.

Fig. 7.4 *The Falconer* by Daniel Maclise, Crawford Art Gallery, Cork

The Marriage of Aoife and Strongbow

Subject

The subject is the marriage of Aoife, daughter of Dermot MacMurrough, King of Leinster, to Strongbow (Fig. 7.5). Strongbow was the leader of the Normans who came to Ireland to help MacMurrough to regain his kingdom, but he went on to invade the country. It is a sentimental portrayal of the destruction of Celtic Ireland by the Normans. It is full of symbolism, like the old man in the left foreground playing the harp with the broken strings, a symbol of Ireland. A lot of effort went into the details of clothing, jewellery and weapons.

Composition

A circle of light and gesture links the figures in the lower centre, where Aoife joins hands with Strongbow. The dark figures of the Normans form a band across the middle third of the painting. The defeated Irish form two large triangular figure groups in the foreground (Fig. 7.6).

Style

The work is in the style of Italian Renaissance figure paintings, with accurate drawing of figures and details of costume and still life. The whole effect is theatrical, from the dramatic poses to the shallow stage the scene is set on.

Technique and materials

This is an accurate, smoothly finished oil painting in great detail. The brushwork is hardly visible.

Fig. 7.5 *The Marriage of Aoife and Strongbow*, 1854, by Daniel Maclise, 309cm x 505cm, National Gallery of Ireland, Dublin

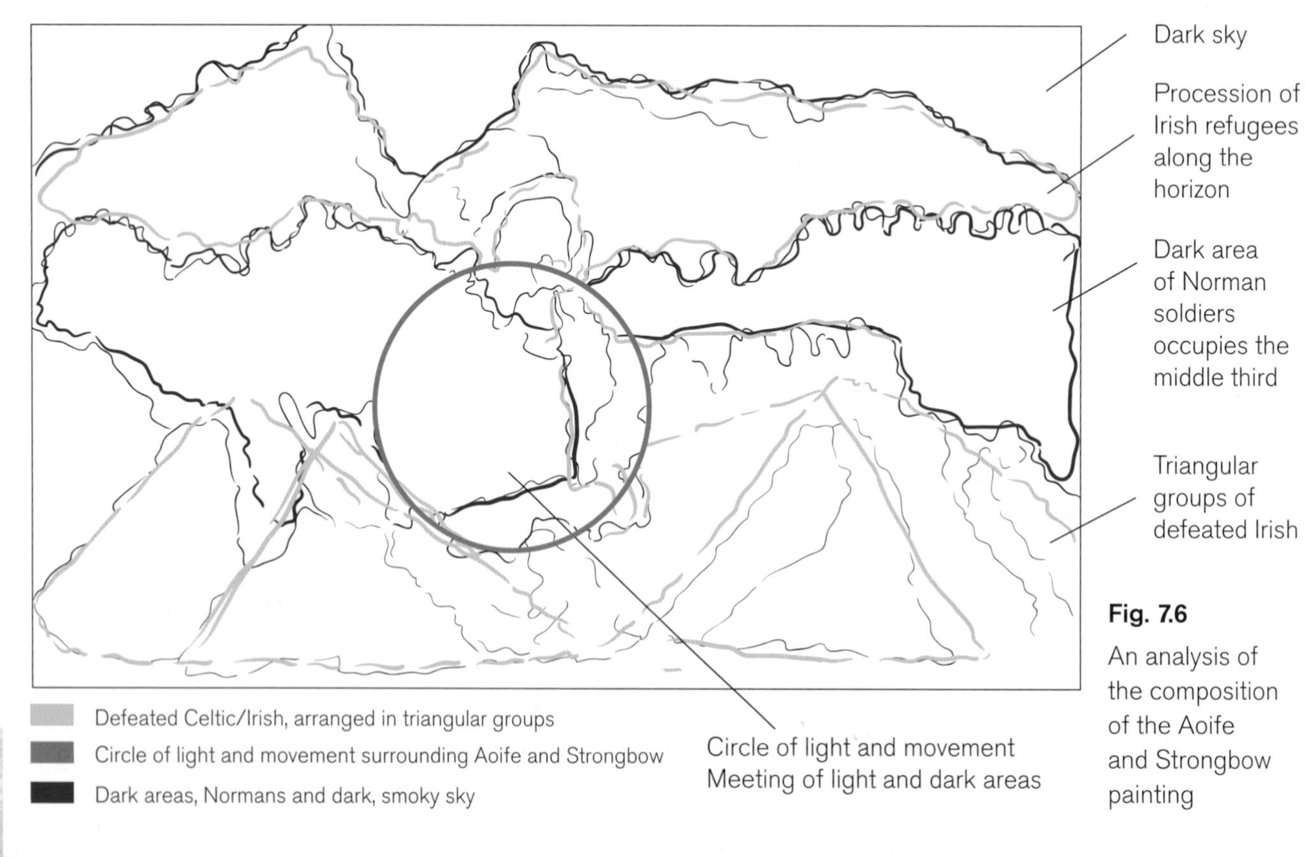

Fig. 7.6

An analysis of the composition of the Aoife and Strongbow painting

Form and volume are created with light and shadow rather than brush direction.

Influences

Maclise's training in London was in the style of Joshua Reynolds. On a trip to Paris in 1844, he was greatly influenced by the French and Italian Renaissance work he saw.

Continental influence

From about 1850 on, Irish artists began to find their way into European art academies, particularly Antwerp, and Paris, which had become an important centre for new developments and ideas in art.

A new approach to painting was developing in the French academies and in the artists' colonies that sprang up in the small towns around the Forest of Fontainebleau, south of Paris.

Impressionist colours

The Impressionists used a colour palette based on theories of light. They excluded earth colours and black, using colours close to spectrum colours: red, orange, yellow, green, blue, indigo and violet. Modern synthetic paints produced a better colour range. Newly invented tin tubes allowed artists to carry paint outdoors more easily.

NOTE! Subjects changed from formal classical or Romantic themes to scenes from the everyday lives of ordinary people and pieces of simple landscape.

Techniques also changed. Brushwork became looser and paint was applied thickly to allow artists to work more quickly and expressively, capturing changing light and colour as they worked outdoors. Paintings for exhibition were still finished in the studio, working from sketches made directly from life.

Roderic O'Conor (1860–1940)

Born in Roscommon into a land-owning family with an ancient history, O'Conor had independent means and did not need to make his living by his art, which left him free to experiment with the most advanced styles and ideas of his time. He became integrated with French art and did not often exhibit with other Irish artists.

His early art education was in the Dublin Metropolitan School of Art. He furthered his education in Antwerp and then worked under Carolus-Duran in Paris in the 1880s. He was aware of the Impressionists and admired Sisley in particular. He would have seen the work of Gauguin and Van Gogh in the Salon des Indépendants in 1889. O'Conor exhibited for many years at the Salon des Indépendants and the Salon d'Automne.

By 1892 O'Conor was working in Brittany in an advanced Post-Impressionist style. His *Field of Corn, Pont-Aven* (Fig. 7.7) owes a lot to the style of Van Gogh. Bold stripes of colour contour the landscape, emphasising its form, while the powerful colours radiate heat. He continued working in this 'striped' technique for the next 10 years while he lived in Brittany, painting landscapes, seascapes and Breton women in traditional costumes.

Paul Gauguin was the leading artist in the group of painters who lived around Pont-Aven. When he returned from his first Tahiti trip in 1894 he became friendly with O'Conor and they were close for a few years, though O'Conor maintained an independent style. He did not exhibit for the 10 years from 1893 to 1903.

Fig. 7.7 *Field of Corn, Pont-Aven* by Roderic O'Conor, Ulster Museum, Belfast

Fig. 7.8 *Iris*, 1913, by Roderic O'Conor, Tate Gallery, London

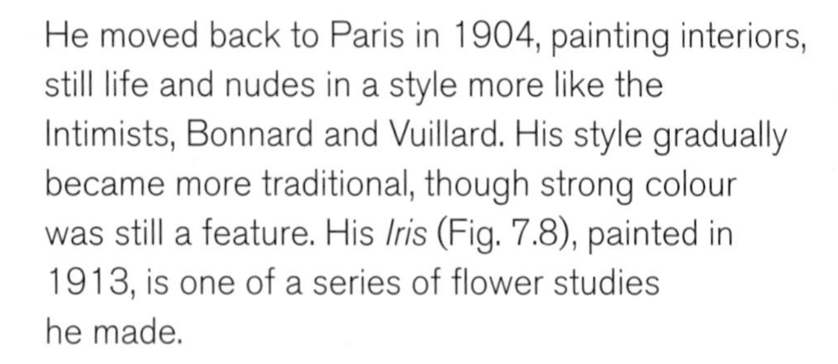

He moved back to Paris in 1904, painting interiors, still life and nudes in a style more like the Intimists, Bonnard and Vuillard. His style gradually became more traditional, though strong colour was still a feature. His *Iris* (Fig. 7.8), painted in 1913, is one of a series of flower studies he made.

O'Conor died in 1940 in Nueil-sur-Layon in the south of France. His studio remained closed for 15 years, until his wife died. A large body of his work was discovered in the studio, along with a collection of paintings by Impressionists and Post-Impressionists that he had purchased over the years.

Breton Girl

Subject

This is a portrait of a young woman in traditional costume (Fig. 7.9). The direct, guarded gaze of the young woman creates a strong impression.

Composition

The traditionally placed figure creates a triangular composition.

Style

O'Conor's boldly painted brushwork shows the influence of Van Gogh and anticipates the Fauves and Expressionists. His style was unique amongst the Pont-Aven group.

Technique and materials

This oil painting on canvas is strongly marked with broad brushstrokes that are thickly painted. The painting was made during the time O'Conor was working in his striped technique. Complementary colours are laid down side by side and the eye is allowed to mix them into areas of light and shadow.

Colour

The complementary reds and greens used to create tones make for a 'hot' colour scheme, which is found often in his work.

Fig. 7.9 *Breton Girl*, 1890s, by Roderic O'Conor, oil on canvas, private collection

Influences

When O'Conor moved to Paris in the 1880s he came in contact with the Impressionists and Post-Impressionists, and immediately adopted aspects of their style and techniques. Van Gogh in particular interested him and led to his striped technique, which he developed over his 10 years in Brittany. When he moved back to Paris in 1904 his style developed differently, to a more Intimist style.

Early 20th century

This next group of artists had most of their careers in the 20th century but continued to paint in the style that had begun in the 19th century. They often followed the educational path of the earlier artists, with an initial education in Dublin followed by time in France.

William Orpen (1878–1931)

Son of a Dublin solicitor, Orpen was a child prodigy – he went to the Metropolitan School of Art in Dublin when only 12 years old. He went on to the Slade School of Fine Art in London from 1897 to 1899, where he was greatly influenced by his teacher, Henry Tonks. Orpen was knowledgeable about art history and often included references to the work of the masters in his own paintings. Unlike many of his contemporaries he did not study abroad, although he did make trips to Europe, where he visited galleries and was familiar with the work of the Impressionists.

From 1899 he exhibited with the New English Art Club in London and with the Royal Hibernian Academy in Dublin. His early paintings are often interiors in dark tones in the Dutch style. Convex mirrors, like the one in the *Arnolfini Portrait* by Jan van Eyck, are sometimes used as a centrepiece

Fig. 7.10 *The Mirror* by William Orpen, National Gallery of Ireland, Dublin

in these paintings. *The Mirror* (Fig. 7.10) is one of these genre pieces.

Orpen taught part time at the Metropolitan School of Art in Dublin from 1902 to 1914, where he was highly influential on a generation of students. He spent his summers at Howth, where he painted scenes of the gravelly beach and the cliffs.

During the First World War he was an official war artist and was troubled for the rest of his life by the things he saw. Many of his paintings show no man's land under winter snow or blooming with spring flowers, but he did paint the wounded and dying and the terrible conditions they were in. There is a large collection of his war paintings at the Imperial War Museum in London.

Orpen made a very good living as a society portrait painter in London right to the end of his life.

Midday on the Beach

Subject

A mother and child lie on a rug in the shade of an umbrella (Fig. 7.11). The light and colour create an impression of heat.

Composition

The figures are placed in the bottom left corner of the format. A diagonal drawn from the top left corner to the bottom right would enclose them. This is balanced by the clothes and picnic hamper in the top right. The diagonal from bottom left to top right catches the mother's hand and legs and the child's face. This is quite a modern arrangement – it is a little unbalanced to create a more dramatic effect.

Style

This painting is Impressionistic both in composition and colour. Outlines are reduced and the effects of light are closely observed.

Colour

Orpen uses mainly spectrum colours in the Impressionist way in the shadow areas as well as in the brighter areas in this painting. His normal palette of colours was more traditional, using ochres, earth colours and black as well as spectrum colours.

Fig. 7.11
Midday on the Beach, 1910, by William Orpen, oil on canvas, 88.9mm x 116.8mm, private collection

Technique and materials

The oil paint is applied in dabs, freely painted direct from the brush, without blending. Outlines are reduced to a minimum, allowing changes of colour to create the forms. The brush marks are particularly clear in the highlights on the mother's dress.

Influences

Orpen's understanding of Impressionism can clearly be seen in this painting, though he generally painted in more earthy colours and a more traditional manner.

The influence of the literary movement and the Celtic Revival

By the early 20th century there was a search for a national Irish identity in literary circles. Plays, poetry and novels sought 'the real people of Ireland'. This subject soon found its way into art. Themes from mythology, the people and the landscape of Ireland were taken up by the younger generation of artists. The art of the past, particularly from the Christian Celtic period, became a popular reference for artists and craft workers.

New techniques from French art were combined with the older academic training in composition and drawing.

Jack Butler Yeats (1871–1957)

Son of the portrait painter John Butler Yeats and brother of the poet W. B. Yeats, Jack was born in London but spent much of his childhood in Co. Sligo with his grandparents.

He went to art school in London and spent his early career as an illustrator of magazines, papers and books. These illustrations were tightly composed, drawn in strong line. An impish sense of humour sometimes appears.

From the 1890s to the early 1900s Yeats painted watercolours of everyday characters and events in England, such as races, markets and street scenes. *The Man from Arranmore* (Fig. 7.12), made on a trip to the Aran Islands, is in this style.

In the early 1900s Yeats moved back to Ireland and began painting in oils. His subjects were still everyday scenes. *The Double Jockey Act* from 1916 is typical of the moments of tension and action that he liked to paint.

By the 1920s he had developed a more fluent painting style. *The Liffey Swim* (Fig. 7.13) won a silver medal in the Arts and Culture section of the Paris Olympics of 1924 (Arts and Culture are no longer part of the Olympics). The painting shows the strong brush marks and brighter colours of this stage of his development.

Yeats began to paint more from memory than direct observation in the 1930s. He was developing a style with bold brush marks, thick paint and strong colours, which combined to create a sense of movement and change. *In Memory of Boucicault and Bianconi* (1937) recalls a scene from Yeats's childhood in Sligo.

Yeats was a very private person. He did not allow anyone to watch him paint, he took no pupils and he gave no lectures, allowing his art to speak for him.

Grief

Subject

This painting may be based on one of Yeats's sketches, *Let There Be No More War*. There are buildings in the background suggesting a street. The central figure is a man on a white horse surrounded by armed soldiers. In the right foreground is a figure of a woman holding a blonde child, while to the left an old man reaches out his

Fig. 7.12 (left)
The Man from Arranmore, c. 1905, by Jack B. Yeats, National Gallery of Ireland, Dublin

Fig. 7.13 (above)
The Liffey Swim, 1923, by Jack B. Yeats, National Gallery of Ireland, Dublin

arms in despair. The painting seems to be an anti-war statement (Fig. 7.14).

Composition

Our eye is led to the figure on horseback through the dark triangular group of figures in the left foreground. The mother and child on the right complete a pyramid with the rider at its top. The violent reds and yellows are in the top left half of the picture, while the lower right is mainly blues.

Colour

Colours are used in the Expressionist way to show emotion: blues for sorrow and reds and strong yellows to show more violent emotions.

Style

Yeats's later work was Expressionist, where colour and brushwork are used to express ideas and emotions.

Technique and materials

The thin underpainting shows through in many areas, overlaid with strong marks loaded with oil paint. He used a variety of tools, not just brushes, to apply paint. One can see the big gestures the artist made with the paint.

Influences

The closest artist in style to Yeats was his friend, the Expressionist artist Oskar Kokoschka.

Stained glass art

An Túr Gloine (The Tower of Glass) was a co-operative stained glass studio set up in Dublin in 1910. The portrait painter Sarah Purser managed the studio, though she did not design many windows herself. Michael Healey (1873–1941), Catherine O'Brien (1881–1963) and Wilhelmina Geddes (1888–1955) were among the most important members of the group.

Fig. 7.14 *Grief*, 1951, by Jack B. Yeats, oil on canvas, 102cm x 153cm, National Gallery of Ireland, Dublin

A. E. Child, who had trained in the studios of William Morris, set up a stained glass department in the Metropolitan School of Art in Dublin. The craft was taught to a very high technical standard.

Harry Clarke (1889–1931)

Clarke's father, Joshua, had a church decorating and stained glass business in North Fredrick Street in Dublin. His secondary education was with the Jesuits in Belvedere College, which was close to his home. He left school at the age of 14 following his mother's death. He began an apprenticeship in his father's workshop and went to night classes at the Dublin Metropolitan School of Art under A. E. Child. He won a full scholarship in stained glass in the School of Art in 1910 and won a gold medal for stained glass at the Board of Education National Competition in London three years in a row from 1911.

Book illustrations

He began to get commissions for book illustrations early in his career. The first to be published was Hans Andersen's *Fairy Tales* for Harrap publishers of London, which was well received when it came out in 1916. The book had 40 full-page illustrations, 16 of which were in colour. He illustrated several books for Harraps. He made 96 drawings for a 1925 edition of Goethe's *Faust*. The *Walpurgis Night* page (Fig. 7.15) shows Clarke at his macabre best. A sniggering devil pushes a victim into the festering zoomorphic mass at the bottom right. An arc of hair connects to a scaly witch at the top of the composition grasping pieces of people who have led less than virtuous lives. The drama of the dense black background contrasts with the fine line and texture marks that Clarke used to describe fur, fabrics and fantasy. The drawing and some of the decoration are beautiful, which makes the weird subject even stranger.

Fig. 7.15 *Walpurgis Night* from Goethe's *Faust*, 1924, by Harry Clarke, published by Haarp in 1925

Clarke's style can be described as Symbolist, but it includes elements of Celtic art and Romanticism. His figures have a characteristic look: large eyes, long separated fingers and toes and elongated proportions.

Stained glass

His success in competitions led to the commission for nine windows for the Honan Chapel of Saint Finbarr at University College Cork, which he worked on between 1915 and 1918. An Túr Gloine got the commission for the other eight windows. A bequest from the Honan family allowed the church to be built to the highest standards in the Celtic Revival style.

Clarke designed some secular windows as well as church windows. The Eve of St Agnes window, now in the Dublin City Gallery The Hugh Lane, won a gold medal when it was exhibited at the Aonach Tailteann art exhibition in 1924. The Geneva Window (1930), commissioned by the government for the International Labour Court in Geneva as a gift of the Irish state, was ultimately rejected because some of the subjects and images were considered to be too controversial. It is now in the Wolfsonian art museum in Miami, Florida, in the US.

Clarke suffered from ill health all his life and for the last few years was seriously ill with tuberculosis. In spite of this, he worked extremely hard. He produced 130 windows, several illustrated books, graphic designs, fabric designs and decoration schemes for the family church decorating business and was also involved in organising and judging exhibitions.

Clarke was the outstanding stained glass artist of his day.

The St Gobnait window

Subject

The subject is St Gobnait, the patron saint of beekeepers (Fig. 7.16). She had a church on Inisheer in the Aran Islands in Co. Galway (where Clarke spent many summer holidays and sketching trips with family and friends). Scenes at the top and bottom of the window show the saint and her companions driving off thieves who came to rob her church. The main panel shows St Gobnait in profile, with a church in her left hand and a staff in her right. Thieves cower behind her robes and bees surround her.

Composition

Our attention is drawn to the pale profile of Gobnait, with her flowing red hair outlined by a dark halo with a green cross that echoes the semi-circular curve of the arch of the window. In the arch, another curve of bright stars and crosses surrounds the nuns in the top left. Yet another

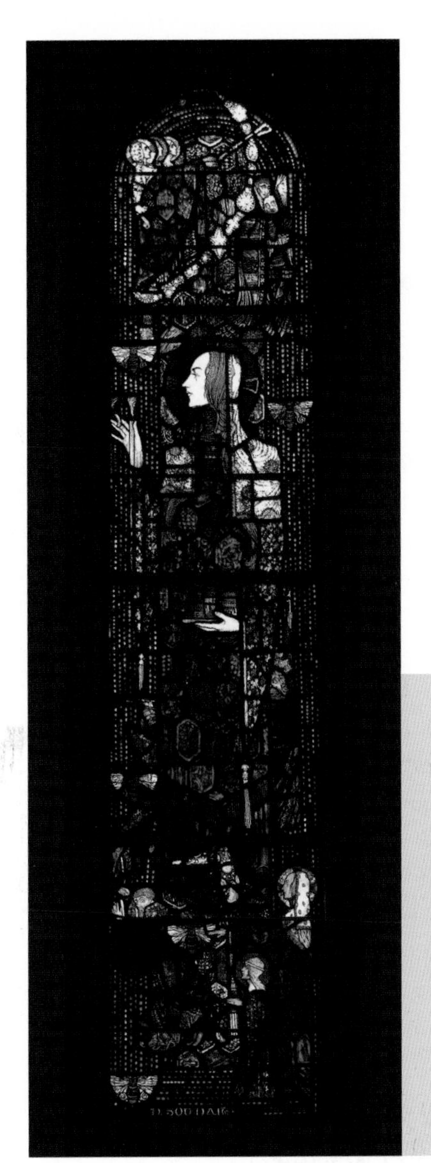

Fig. 7.16
The St Gobnait Window by Harry Clarke, a single stained glass lancet window, Honan Chapel, Cork

curve connects the faces of the nuns and thieves in the bottom section. The large patterned area of Gobnait's robe is almost abstract. We need the face and hands to identify her figure.

Colour

Clarke was famous for his careful choice of colour. He went to London several times a year to get the coloured glass he needed for each project. He even had special coloured glass made for him. In this window the royal blue of Gobnait's robe dominates, contrasted with the white veil she wears. Gem-like beads of red and blue form a screen behind the figures. He used green to separate areas of red, and bright areas like hands and faces are set against areas of darker glass.

Style

Clarke's style is described as Symbolist. One might compare it with the exotically robed figures of Gustav Klimt.

Technique and materials

Clarke was a very talented craftsman. He used acids to thin coloured glass and create a range of subtle tones. His painting of details and shading was very skilful. He used leading as strong line to emphasise areas of the composition. See how he creates honeycomb patterns in Gobnait's robes in this window (see the section on making stained glass on page 197).

Influences

Clarke saw an exhibition of international art in Dublin in 1905 and was impressed by the work of Aubrey Beardsley and the Pre-Raphaelites. He kept in touch with movements in art and craft through magazines and trips to London and Paris.

The Cubist influence

The movements in modern art that followed each other in quick succession in Europe in the early years of the 20th century went largely unnoticed in Ireland.

Evie Hone and Mainie Jellett met at art college in London and decided to go to Paris to learn what they could about the new styles of art that were developing there. They studied first with André Lhote and then with Albert Gleizes, and together they developed theories on Cubism.

They exhibited Cubist work in Dublin in 1923 and 1924, but the work was little understood. They went on to raise awareness of modern theories among the younger Irish artists.

The second generation of modern painters

Louis le Brocquy (1916–2012)

Le Brocquy was one of the leading figures in 20th-century Irish art. He was born in Dublin and studied chemistry in Trinity College. He spent a number of years working in the family business before he set out to study the Old Masters of art in the galleries of Europe.

He returned to Dublin at the beginning of the Second World War in 1940 working as a self-taught painter. He was a founder member of the Irish Living Art Exhibition in 1943. He had his first solo exhibition in London in 1947. In 1948 he married another Irish artist, Anne Madden, and they moved to the south of France.

His busy painting career can be divided into a number of series where he worked on similar subjects. The first was a series of 'Tinker' paintings in the late 1940s. The first part of the 1950s was his 'Grey Period'. He went on to a 'White Period' in the late 1950s, which evolved into a series of 'Heads', which continued on and off until 2006. There was a 'Procession' series in the 1980s and 1990s. A series of 'Human Images' from the 1990s into the new millennium and finally a 'Homage' series, where he worked from images of his favorite artists, including Velázquez, Goya, Cézanne and Manet.

During his 70-year career, Le Brocquy illustrated books, designed theatre sets and costumes and reintroduced tapestry as an art form. *Hosting the Tain* (1969) in the Irish Museum of Modern Art is one of his beautifully coloured tapestries.

His illustrations for Thomas Kinsella's translation of *The Tain* (Fig. 7.17) in 1969 have great strength and vigour. The controlled brush marks demonstrate Le Brocquy's ability to be sensitive to any medium he used.

His 'Heads' series of paintings was his longest-lasting and, some would say, most important body of work. He painted images of writers and artists, trying to reveal the spirit and imagination of his

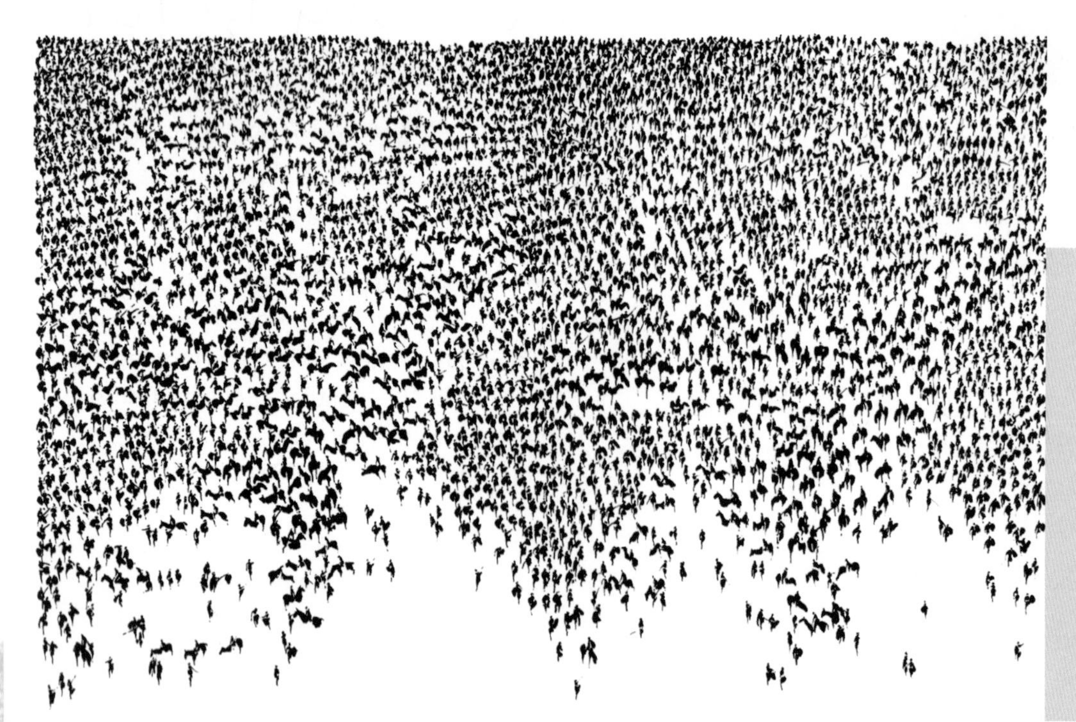

Fig. 7.17
Army Massing, 1969, by Louis le Brocquy, an illustration from Thomas Kinsella's translation of *The Tain*

Fig. 7.18 *A Family*, 1951, by Louis le Brocquy, National Gallery of Ireland, Dublin

chosen characters. W. B. Yeats and James Joyce were painted many times. Samuel Beckett, Francis Bacon and Seamus Heaney were among the acquaintances that he painted.

Le Brocquy is regarded as one of Ireland's greatest artists. His work has been shown all over the world and is in some of the great collections.

A Family

Subject

This painting of a family group represented Ireland at the Venice Biennale in 1956, where it won an important prize (Fig. 7.18). It was also shown at the *50 Years of Modern Art* exhibition at the World Fair in Brussels in 1958, in the company of work by Cézanne and Matisse.

Composition

The heavy structure in the upper middle of the painting divides the family in two. The alert, stony-faced man in the left foreground is cool in colour and has his back to the woman and child. The woman, who is in warmer tones, leans down to the child, who is looking up to her. One could make a commentary on family and relationships based on the painting.

Colour

Colour is reduced to a minimum – just shades of grey – to emphasise form.

Style

There are hints of Cubism in the simplified forms of the figures.

Technique and materials

The oil paint is applied in evenly marked brushstrokes on the canvas. The brushwork helps to describe form.

Image of W. B. Yeats

Subject

The painting depicts an image of W. B. Yeats's face (Fig. 7.19).

Fig. 7.19 *Image of W. B. Yeats* (detail), 1976, by Louis le Brocquy, Irish Museum of Modern Art, Dublin

Composition

The face dominates the 70cm x 70cm space. The unexpected colour and application of paint distort the image and yet add energy and interest to the emerging face.

Colour

Primary colours are used to create the structure and modelling of the face.

Style

Le Brocquy's painterly style is unique. He does not belong to any school or group.

Technique and materials

The face emerging from the almost white canvas is painted wet into wet. That is, paint is applied and smudged or moved with the brush on the wet surface, then more paint is added or moved while the surface is still wet. Oil paint is the ideal medium for this style of painting.

Abstraction based on landscape

Tony O'Malley (1913–2003)

Born in Callan, Co. Kilkenny, O'Malley drew and painted from an early age. He began a career as a bank official. In 1940 he became ill with tuberculosis and painted a lot during his convalescence. He went back to banking, but by 1958 he resigned and took up painting full time. He found it difficult to get his work noticed in Ireland so he went to live in St Ives in Cornwall, England, in 1960, where he had visited on holiday in the 1950s. There was a thriving artistic community in St Ives and he kept a studio there for 30 years.

In 1973 he married the artist Jane Harris, who had connections with Lanzarote and the Bahamas, where they spent part of the year until the 1990s, when they returned to Ireland.

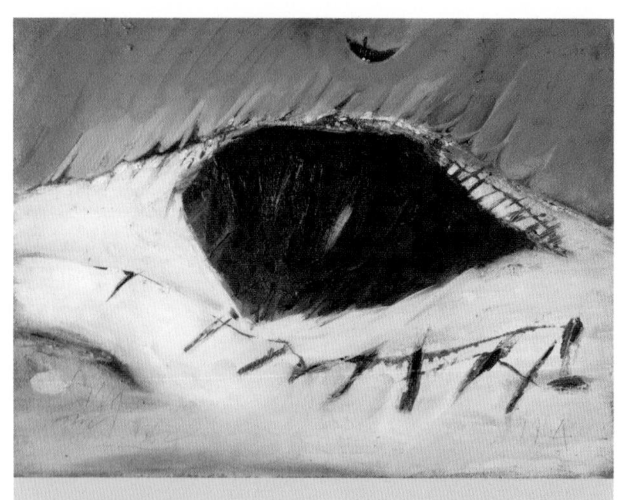

Fig. 7.20 *Hawk and Quarry in Winter, in Memory of Peter Lanyon*, 1964, by Tony O'Malley, oil on board, 53cm x 72cm, Crawford Art Gallery, Cork

Hawk and Quarry in Winter, in Memory of Peter Lanyon (Fig. 7.20) is an abstraction based on landscape, as many of his paintings are. The cool colours suggest winter. He said of his work, 'Abstraction does enable you to get under the surface, to get beyond appearance, and express the mind.'

O'Malley had a very successful career – his work is in collections all over the world. He was made a Saoi of Aosdána in 1990 and given an honorary doctorate by Trinity College in 1994.

Mid-Summer Window with Moths

Subject

This colourful abstraction is based on an observation of nature. The title suggests a time and place (Fig 7.21).

Composition

A square panel is almost divided in half by a dotted yellow motif. The painting could be explained in terms of nature and creatures, but this would

Fig. 7.21 *Mid-Summer Window with Moths*, 1992, by Tony O'Malley, oil on board, 125.8cm x 125.8cm, Dublin City Gallery the Hugh Lane

overlook the essentially abstract nature of the work.

Colour

Natural greens and browns are decorated with small areas of bright yellows and reds.

Technique and materials

O'Malley sometimes applied textures and scratches to the surface of his work. In this painting, brushwork and surface marks create a sense of movement and depth.

Twentieth-century sculpture

Figurative sculptors

Oisín Kelly (1915–81)

The son of a teacher in Dublin's inner city, Kelly was christened Austin but used the name Oisín. He studied languages at Trinity College Dublin and worked as a teacher for 20 years while he made sculptures in his free time.

He attended night classes in the National College of Art and spent nine months studying in Chelsea Polytechnic under Henry Moore in 1947–8.

Much of his early work was woodcarving and he was receiving church commissions from 1949 for his figures, which showed genuine religious feeling.

He was involved in the Irish Exhibition of Living Art and the Royal Hibernian Academy and he exhibited frequently.

In 1964 he became artist-in-residence at the Kilkenny Design Workshop and produced designs for fabrics, ceramics and metalwork. This was the beginning of his full-time art career.

The Children of Lir (Fig. 7.22) was the first of a number of public sculptures that he was commissioned to do. The *Working Men* that stand outside City Hall in Cork, the James Larkin figure on O'Connell Street in Dublin, the Roger Casement figure at Ballyheigue in Co. Kerry and the *Chariot of Life* group outside the Irish Life Centre in Dublin are just a few of the large sculptures he made.

Kelly also made smaller pieces for private sale and exhibition. He made dancers, animals and more abstract work. *The Marchers* (Fig. 7.23) is an example of his smaller work, which leans towards abstraction.

Bronze was not the only medium Kelly worked in. He also carved stone and wood and did work in cast iron, steel and cement. He always worked in sympathy with his materials.

The Children of Lir

Subject

This bronze sculpture (Fig. 7.22) is a memorial to the freedom fighters of 1916. It takes the form

Fig. 7.22

(left) *The Children of Lir*, 1966, by Oisín Kelly, bronze sculpture, Garden of Remembrance, Dublin

Fig. 7.23

(above) *The Marchers*, 1969, by Oisín Kelly, cast aluminium, 18cm x 78cm x 7cm, Irish Museum of Modern Art, Dublin.

of four children and four swans. It may refer to the fall of the old regime and the new state rising from it.

Composition

The four children spiral down in increasing degrees of collapse into the pool that the sculpture stands in. The swans rise from within the figure group, moving upward in a tighter spiral. One needs to walk around the sculpture to appreciate the complicated interplay of shapes and forms and the sense of movement that is achieved.

Style

Most of Kelly's work is figurative, but not realistic. Forms are simplified and movement is often suggested.

Technique and materials

This is a large sculpture cast in copper and bronze. The original work would have been modelled in clay and scaled up to the final size.

Modern approaches to sculpture

Alice Maher (1956–)

Born in Co. Tipperary, Maher graduated from the University of Limerick and the Crawford School of Art in Cork. She did an MA in Fine Art at the University of Ulster in Belfast and was awarded a Fulbright Scholarship to the San Francisco Art Institute in 1986. She represented Ireland at the São Paulo Biennial in 1994.

Maher combines painting, sculpture, photography, animation, digital media and installation in her practice, sometimes combining media in an unexpected way.

Part of Maher's practice is conventional drawings. Sometimes long strands of hair are loosely interwoven, like in *Andromeda* (1999) or the drawings of an adolescent girl doing a series of tasks in *The Thicket* (1991).

The Irish Museum of Modern Art, Dublin, hosted an exhibition, *Becoming*, in 2013, which reviewed her work so far.

Fig. 7.24 *Cassandra's Necklace*, 2013, video installation by Alice Maher (still from the video), Irish Museum of Modern Art, Dublin

Cassandra's Necklace (Fig. 7.24), a two-screen video installation, was specially commissioned. It is a collaborative work based on a script for a play by Anne Enright. Music was composed by Trevor Knight, it was filmed by Vivienne Dick and edited by Connie Farrell. It runs for 7.5 minutes.

The Cassandra in the title was the daughter of King Priam and Queen Hecuba of Troy. She was admired by the god Apollo, who gave her the gift of prophesy. Cassandra annoyed Apollo, so he cursed her that her prophesies would not be believed. The lambs' tongues worn round the neck of the actress in the video illustrate the stilled tongue of the prophetess, useless for speech because she will not be believed.

Maher's work is in collections around the world. The wide range of her practice gives her the freedom to express ideas in any number of ways.

Berry Dress

Subject

This appears to be a child's dress with berries attached (Fig. 7.25).

Composition

The little dress is displayed on a glass shelf above eye level so that the viewer can see inside. The pins that hold the berries in place stick through to the inside. This creates a contradiction between the purpose of a dress – to keep a child warm – and the injuries that might be inflicted by the pins.

Colour

The relationship between the vermillion red of the painted dress and the original red of the rosehip berries is changing over time as the berries wither.

Style

There is no particular style in a work like this. It is a conceptual piece, where the ideas or the thoughts provoked in the viewer are more important than the physical presence of the work.

Fig. 7.25 *Berry Dress*, 1994, by Alice Maher, Irish Museum of Modern Art, Dublin

Technique and materials

The dress shape is made of painted cotton. The rosehip berries are fixed with sewing pins. The whole construction is very delicate and will probably disintegrate over time, which is another calculated part of the work.

Meaning/ideas

This work has been interpreted as an illustration of the innocence and cruelty of childhood. Fairy tales like Snow White, Little Red Riding Hood and Sleeping Beauty have explored similar themes.

Traditional materials, modern approaches

Rowan Gillespie (1953–)

Gillespie was born in Dublin, spent his early years in Cyprus and was educated in England, where he went to the York School of Art and Kingston College of Art. He completed his art education in Statens Kunstole in Oslo, Norway. His greatest artistic influences are Henry Moore and Edvard Munch.

He returned to Dublin in 1977 and set up a studio and foundry in Blackrock, Co. Dublin. Gillespie is unusual in that he carries out the entire design, modelling and casting process by himself. He uses the lost wax process to produce his bronze sculptures.

Many of Gillespie's sculptures are site specific – that is, they are made to be placed in a particular location and are designed for that environment.

There is a companion piece to his *Famine* sculpture on the quayside in Ireland Park in Toronto, Canada. It represents the surviving emigrants arriving off the coffin ships hoping for a new start in life. This sculpture was unveiled by President Mary McAleese in 2007.

Gillespie produces smaller work for private sale and for some unusual locations. His *Aspiration* figure climbs up the wall of the Treasury Building and *Birdy* sits on the windowsill of 3 Crescent Hall in Mount Street, both in Dublin.

His *Proclamation* group (Fig. 7.26), located opposite Kilmainham Gaol in Dublin, commemorates the signatories of the Declaration of Independence and the 14 men who were executed following the 1916 Rising. The figures are more abstract than other work we have seen by him because they represent the idea of an imagined ideal world rather than the specific people who were shot. The bronzes are arranged in a circle. They are simplified down to leaf or flame shapes with a blindfolded head on top and no limbs or human features. The Declaration of Independence is placed in the centre of the circle on a bronze plaque. At the foot of each figure is

Fig. 7.26 *Proclamation*, 2007, by Rowan Gillespie, Dublin

a name and the death sentence passed by the British military tribunal. Each figure is pierced with a different pattern of holes, representing the bullet holes of the firing squad.

Gillespie has sculptures all over Ireland and in Europe, the US and Canada.

Famine

Subject

This is a memorial to the victims of the Irish Famine who had to emigrate from the Dublin quays (Fig. 7.27).

Composition

The figure group is strung out along the quay. Each seems isolated in their own misery. A man carries a limp child, while others carry small parcels of their possessions. A skinny dog follows.

Style

The figures are basically realistic, but their features and anatomy have been exaggerated for dramatic effect.

Technique and materials

The figures are cast in bronze by the lost wax method. The finish is rough – the bronze was not cleaned or polished after it came out of the mould. This crude treatment adds to the ragged and starved look of the people on their way to the ship that will hopefully take them to a new life.

Changes in the arts in the 19th and 20th centuries

During the 19th century, the arts became more important in society. There was a higher level of education and a growing middle class who wanted original art to decorate their homes.

Many of our national collections were started at this time. The National Gallery and the National Museum were both built in the 19th century.

Schools of art were set up in the main cities. Young Irish artists got a grounding there and then

Fig. 7.27
Famine, 1997, by Rowan Gillespie, bronze scultpure, Custom House Quay, Dublin

went on to England and later to the Continent to complete their studies. Many of these graduates found it difficult to make a living in Ireland and had to emigrate to further their careers.

Few Irish artists were in the forefront of developments in art. Roderic O'Conor in the late 19th and early 20th century and Jack Yeats, Evie Hone and Maine Jellett in the early 20th century were exceptions to the generally conservative position of most Irish artists and educators. It was not until the 1970s that the art schools modernised their approach to education and Irish artists became part of the international movement.

Many modern Irish artists have an international reputation and their work is in important collections worldwide.

Chapter review

* What changes came with Continental influence in Irish art?
* What was the effect of the Celtic Revival on art?
* Do you think Cubism was well received in Ireland? Which artists promoted it?
* Which modern painter appeals to you most? Work out reasons for your preference.
* Do you think public sculptures have a purpose? Build your ideas around examples you have studied.

EXAM QUESTIONS

Ordinary Level (2016)

Robert Ballagh (b. 1943) is one of Ireland's best-known contemporary artists.

Answer (a), (b) and (c).

(a) Name one work by Robert Ballagh that you have studied.

(b) Describe your chosen work under the following headings:

- Subject matter
- Compositions
- Use of colour

(c) Give some general information on Robert Ballagh.

Illustrate your answer.

Ordinary Level (2016)

Choose a work by one of the following artists:

- James Barry (1741–1806)
- Paul Henry (1876–1958)
- Harry Clarke (1889–1931)
- Seán Keating (1889–1977)
- Rowan Gillespie (b. 1953)
- Alice Maher (b. 1956)
- Dorothy Cross (b. 1956)

Answer (a), (b) and (c).

(a) Name your chosen work.

(b) Describe and discuss your chosen work under the following headings:

- Subject matter
- Composition/form
- Technique and use of materials

(c) Give some general information on your chosen artist.

Illustrate your answer.

Higher Level (2016)

'Walter Osborne (1859–1903), through his keen observation of the world around him, captured the atmosphere and light of everyday life.'

Discuss this statement with reference to *In a Dublin Park, Light and Shade* (see online). In your answer refer to subject matter, composition, style and technique.

and

Name and describe and discuss **one** other painting by Osborne.

Illustrate your answer.

Higher Level (2016)

'Alice Maher (b. 1956) creates artworks in a wide variety of media, often outside the tradition of fine art.'

Discuss this statement with references to *Berry Dress* (see Fig. 7.25). In your answer refer to subject matter, composition, form, style and media/materials used.

and

Name and briefly describe and discuss **one** other work by Alice Maher.

Illustrate your answer.

Higher Level (2016)

Select one of the following:

- John Henry Foley (1818–74)
- Paul Henry (1876–1958)
- William Orpen (1878–1931)
- Louis le Brocquy (1916–2012)

- John Burke (1946–2006)
- Dorothy Cross (b. 1956)
- Grace Weir (b. 1962)

Describe and discuss the work of your chosen artist, making detailed reference to **two** named works by that artist. In your answer refer to subject matter, style, media/materials, techniques and influences.

Illustrate your answer.

FURTHER RESEARCH

www.crawfordartgallery.ie

www.eilisoconnell.com

www.hughlane.ie

www.imma.ie

www.imma.ie – Alice Maher Becoming: Information for Second Level Teachers and Students

www.nationalgallery.ie

www.nmni.com/um – 19th- and 20th-Century Irish Art

www.publicart.ie

www.robertballagh.com

www.rowangillespie.com

www.visual-arts-cork.com

www.visual-arts-cork.com – Celtic Art Revival Movement

In addition to the artists featured in the book, you will find extra content on the following on **www.gillexplore.ie**:

John Hogan (1800–58)
James Arthur O'Connor (1792–1841)
Frederick William Burton (1816–1900)
Nathaniel Hone (1831–1917)
Walter Osborne (1859–1903)
William John Leech (1881–1968)
Paul Henry (1876–1958)
Seán Keating (1889–1977)
Evie Hone (1894–1955)
Mainie Jellett (1897–1944)
Norah McGuinness (1901–80)
Patrick Scott (1921–2014)
Gerard Dillon (1916–71)
Robert Ballagh (1943–)
John Behan (1938–)
Dorothy Cross (1956–)
Eilis O'Connell (1953–)
Michael Quane (1962–)

SECTION

Part 1: Medieval Art and Architecture

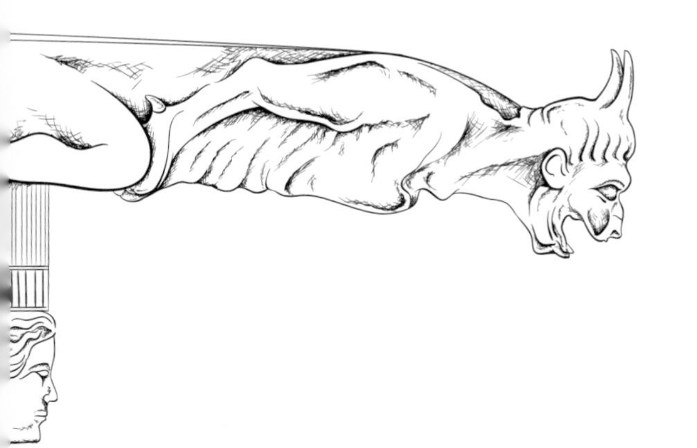

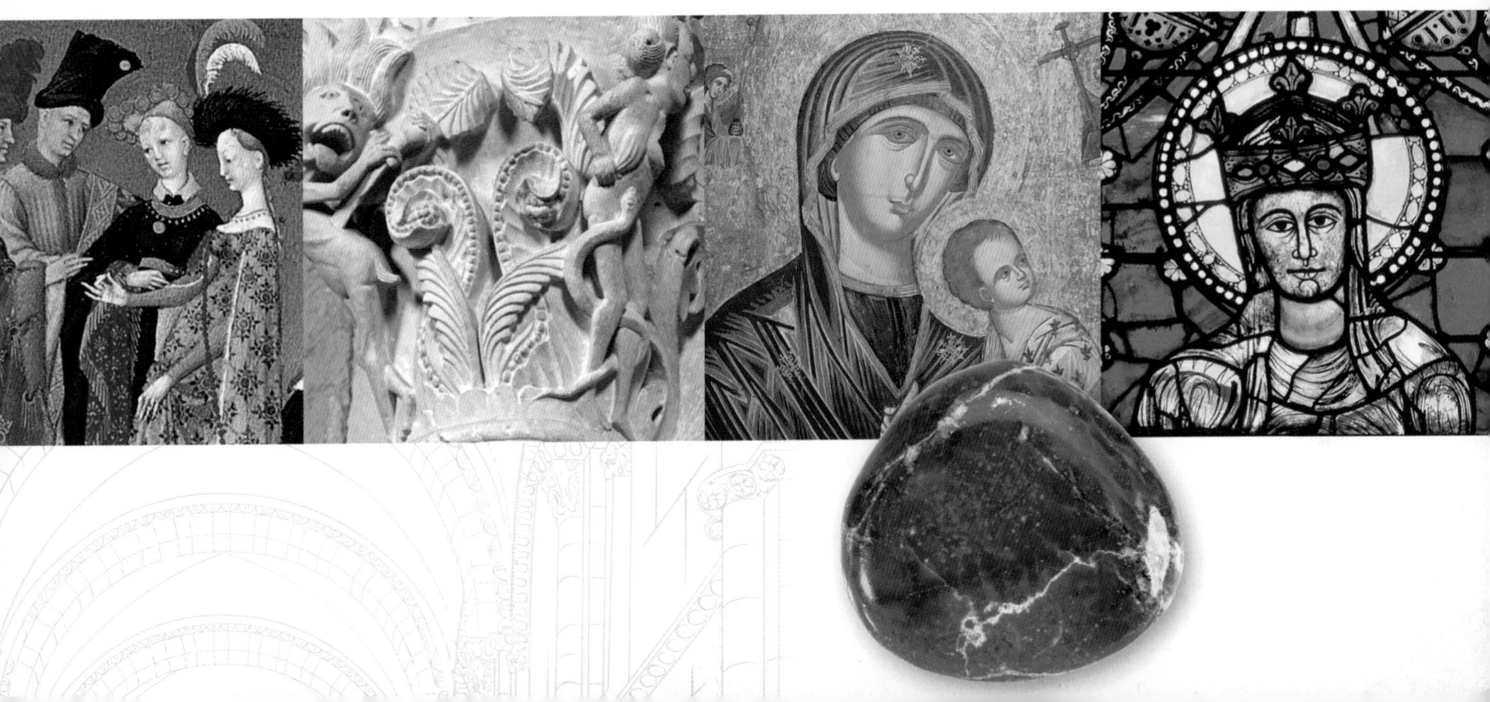

Chapter 8

Life in Medieval Europe

Emerging from the Dark Ages

After the fall of the Roman Empire, Europe was in a period of turmoil known as the Dark Ages. Invading tribes had ravaged the towns and the rich Roman lifestyle had disappeared. Gone too was their knowledge of science, technology, medicine and literature.

Europe was now divided into small tracts of land and rulers were constantly at war with each another.

By the end of this chapter, I will...

* Know one of the main reasons for the development of Romanesque art.
* Understand why economic conditions improved in Europe during the 11th century.
* Know the effect these improvements had on art and architecture.
* Be able to discuss how the pilgrimage route to Santiago de Compostela developed.
* Know how pilgrimages affected the building of churches.

A new beginning

By the 11th century, however, things were beginning to settle down. Fear that the world would end in the year 1000 had passed and the new millennium brought energy and a spirit of optimism.

In large areas such as France (which at this time was a collection of kingdoms and dukedoms with few politically stable areas), cities began to form again and trade increased. An improved economy helped population growth. Better farming meant better food and more work. Education also increased, which encouraged developments in art and architecture.

The feudal system

Society in Medieval Europe was organised in a pyramid-like structure known as the feudal system.

The king awarded land grants to important nobles, barons and bishops. In return, their knights served his army and could be called to battle at any time.

Small communities formed around the manor, with its castle, church, village and surrounding farmland. The lord of the manor owned the land and everything in it. He kept the peasants safe and leased them land to grow crops.

However, this rigid system prevented real progress and people had very little freedom.

The Christian Church

Christianity had spread across Europe throughout the Early Middle Ages, becoming stronger all the time. By the 11th century it was a well-organised, wealthy institution with huge power and influence.

The church was a strong and powerful force in medieval Europe because:

* It was outside of the feudal system, so clever men could rise to positions of power.
* The church guided everyone's life from birth to death, from the richest king to the lowest serf.
* Taxes and donations made the church extremely wealthy.
* The monasteries were strong and influential.
* Bishops and church leaders had leading roles in government.

Church influence

The magnificently lit churches must have had an extraordinary effect on people whose own dwellings were crude and dark.

The church promised an afterlife of comfort and happiness in return for prayer and penance. With life so hard and short, it is little wonder that people believed deeply in this.

NOTE! Death was considered the passage to the next life. This could be sudden and unexpected, so prayer, penance and pilgrimage were part of everyday life.

Monasteries

Monasteries were wealthy establishments set on large estates. Many monks had connections with the nobles, and the abbot was a powerful political figure.

The Benedictines (followers of St Benedict) had a high regard for art and music. They were one of the main influences on the development of Romanesque art.

Monasteries were places of prayer and good works. They housed travellers, nursed the sick and helped the poor. They also promoted learning, produced beautiful books and preserved ancient manuscripts. They made beautiful art objects for religious services and built fine churches for the glory of God.

Pilgrimages

The Christian practice of pilgrimages to holy places reached its height during the Middle Ages. The church encouraged the practice and millions of people set out on foot. The journey often took them several years.

Fig. 8.1 Relic of the True Cross. Relics were extremely valuable to churches or monasteries because they could charge pilgrims money to see them.

Fig. 8.2
Santiago de Compostela

Pilgrimages were often undertaken as a penance for sins. The long, hard journey was part of the penance and a test of a pilgrim's faith.

Relics

Many sites had holy relics. A relic is something from a saint (Fig. 8.1), such as a part of their body, like hair or a piece of bone, or an object they touched, like clothing. People believed in their curative powers and numerous miracles were associated with them.

The Crusades

Christian knights were called upon to join the Crusades. These were religious campaigns undertaken by the Christian Church to capture Jerusalem and stop the Western spread of Islam. As a result, a steady flow of important relics found their way west.

Santiago de Compostela

The most popular pilgrimages to Rome and Jerusalem became dangerous due to bandits and pirates, but fortunately the tomb of St James the Apostle was discovered in Santiago de Compostela on the westernmost tip of Spain. A new pilgrimage developed (Fig. 8.2) and it quickly became the most famous route in Europe. Pilgrims came in such huge numbers that churches were built along the routes and monasteries were established to cater for the ever-growing number of people.

Chapter review

* The buildings along the pilgrimage routes to Santiago de Compostela are a long-lasting legacy of the 11th and 12th centuries. Why was church building so important then?
* The strength and dominant position of the Roman Catholic Church was one of the main reasons for the development of Romanesque art. Why do you think it had such a strong influence?

FURTHER RESEARCH

cmsnew.pdst.ie – European Art History: Romanesque Architecture

www.khanacademy.org – Art of Medieval Europe: Latin (Western) Europe

Chapter 9

Romanesque Architecture

Romanesque and Gothic were the two major art movements of the medieval era.

The term 'Romanesque' means 'Roman like' and was first used in the mid-19th century, when it was linked to Roman architecture. Before that the art and architecture of the Middle Ages had been thought of as heavy and crude compared to the Renaissance. It is now considered to be one of the great phases of Western culture.

By the end of this chapter, I will...

* Understand how Cluny Abbey influenced the Romanesque style of architecture.
* Be able to discuss which architectural features catered for the needs of pilgrims.
* Know why experiments with stone vaulting continued.
* Know that sculptural decoration was linked to architecture.

Architecture was the main focus of the Romanesque period. Romanesque architects looked to Roman building for inspiration. They used round arches and barrel vaulting, but they also made changes to the Roman model to allow pilgrims to file past relics.

Romanesque churches

Fig. 9.1 Pisa Cathedral and Baptistery in Italy. The cathedral was begun in 1063, with construction on the Baptistery beginning in 1153. The famous leaning tower was constructed from 1173 to 1372.

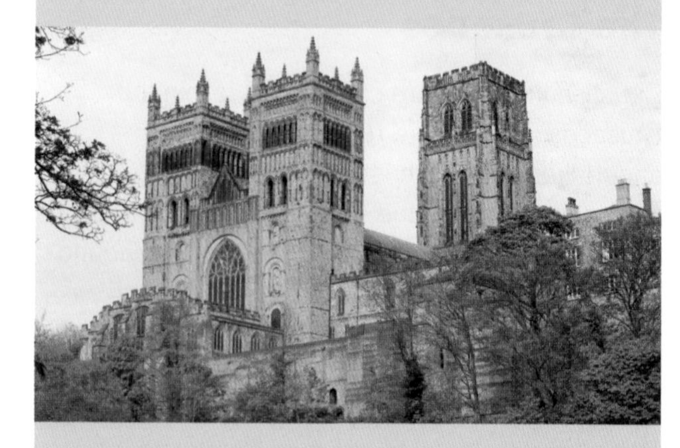

Fig. 9.2 Durham Cathedral in northern England. It is a masterpiece of Romanesque architecture. This superb example of Norman craftsmanship has survived with its original design almost intact.

Cluny Abbey

Cluny Abbey was the most important Romanesque building. It was famous for its great wealth and splendour (Fig. 9.3 and Fig. 9.4).

Architectural sculpture in Cluny

The Benedictine order in Cluny had an extremely high regard for art. Accounts describe the beautiful architectural ornamental carved capitals, arches and windows. Imagery on these was used to teach the doctrine of Christ.

No castle or palace of the time had anything like this luxury in art because the church forbade it. Wealth and splendour were only for the glory of God.

Fig. 9.3 Cluny, France. Today only the Clocher de l'eau Bénite (Holy Water Belfry) remains. The wonderful Abbey Church of Cluny and all its splendid art was demolished during the French Revolution of 1789.

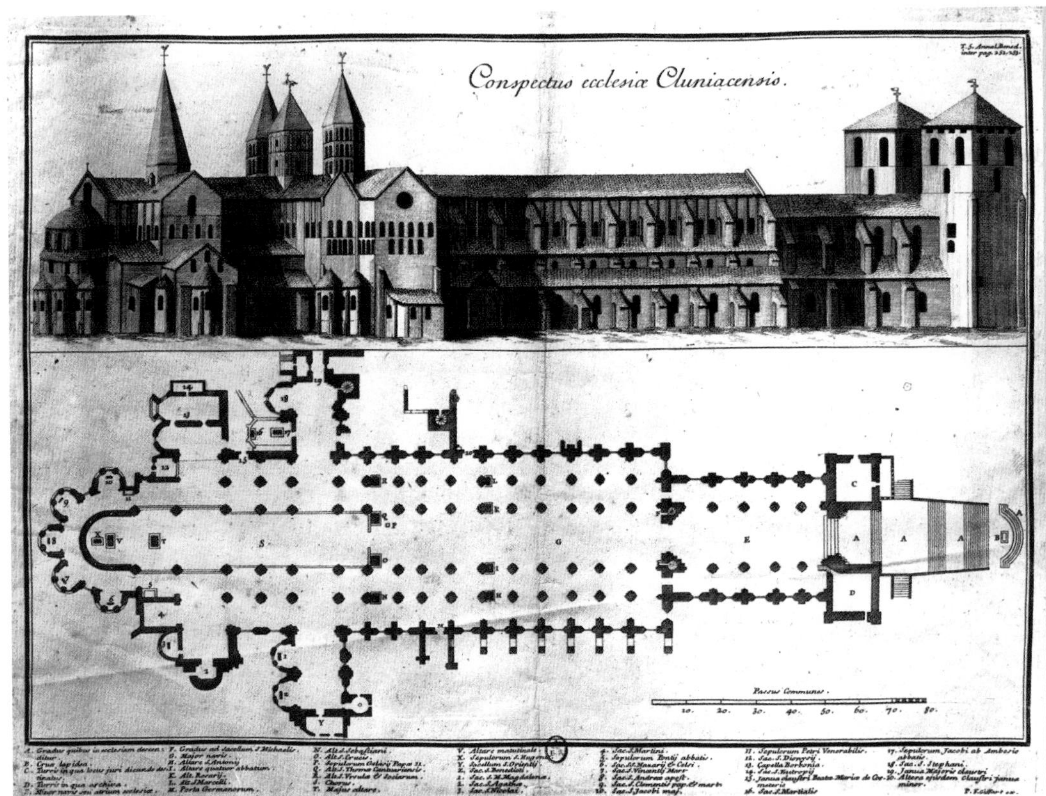

Fig. 9.4 Plan and elevation of Cluny Abbey. Rebuilt three times, Cluny III was the largest and most beautiful church in all of Christendom. Accounts describe the beautiful architectural sculptured ornament of carved capitals, arches and windows.

Fig. 9.5 Notre Dame of Paray-le-Monial is much smaller than Cluny but has many of the same architectural features

Romanesque pilgrimage churches

The great pilgrimages of the 11th and 12th centuries generated a massive building boom in churches. The churches on the four main pilgrimage routes in France were a similar style to Cluny (Fig. 9.5 and Fig. 9.6).

Structural and architectural features

Characteristics of a typical Romanesque pilgrimage church (Fig. 9.7):

* **Heavy construction:** A solid geometric appearance.

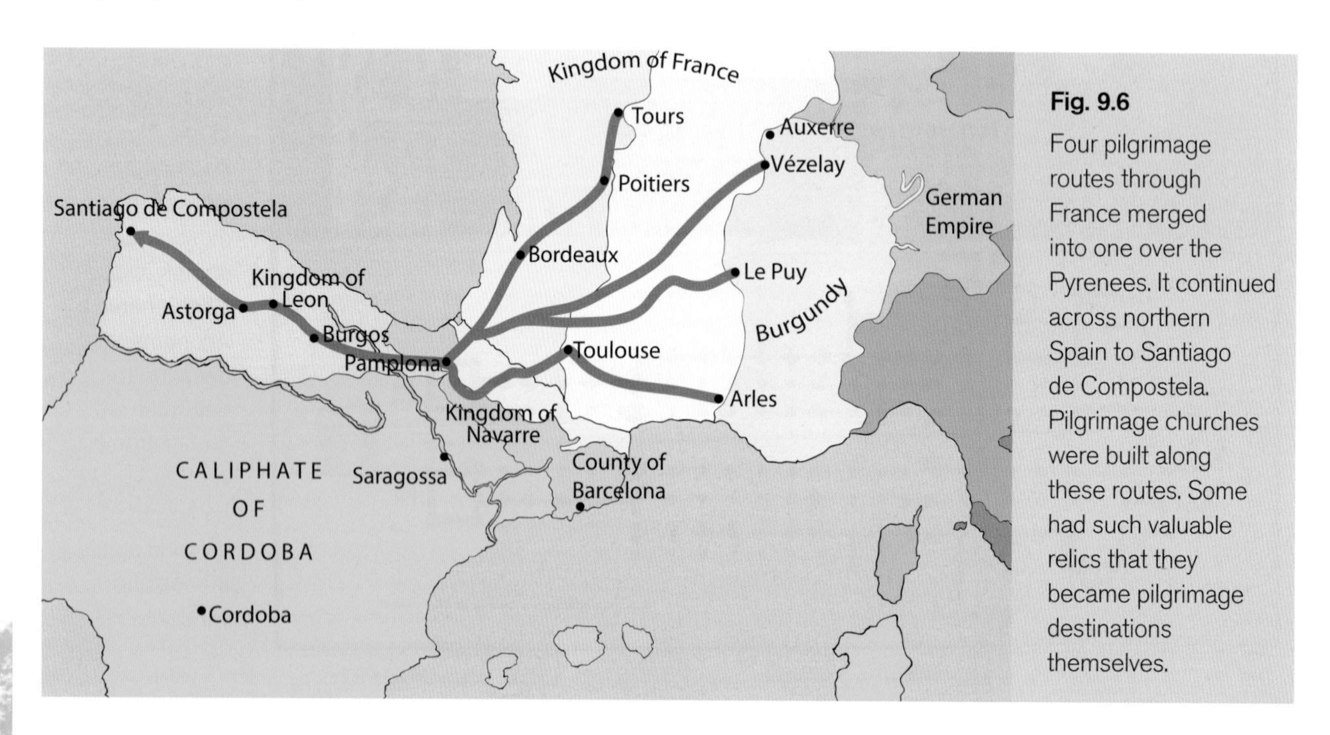

Fig. 9.6
Four pilgrimage routes through France merged into one over the Pyrenees. It continued across northern Spain to Santiago de Compostela. Pilgrimage churches were built along these routes. Some had such valuable relics that they became pilgrimage destinations themselves.

* **Round arches:** Roman-style arches on doors, windows and towers.
* **Stone roofs:** Stone vaulting to prevent fire.
* **Dark interiors:** Churches had high small windows because large openings would have weakened walls.
* **Based on a Roman basilica:** See Fig. 9.8.
* **Cruciform in shape:** Crosswise transepts were extensions to, or part of, a building lying across the main axis, creating a cruciform shape in the plan.
* **Strong, thick walls:** These held the weight of huge stone roofs.
* **Sturdy piers (columns):** These supported round arches.
* **Capitals:** The shape at the topmost part of the columns and piers.
* **Ambulatory:** A walkway around the altar to help pilgrims view relics.
* **Radiating chapels:** Smaller chapels extending from the ambulatory, each containing a minor relic (Fig. 9.10).
* **Central tower or cupola (dome):** This brought light to the centre at the crossing.
* **Cut stone blocks:** Also known as ashlar masonry.

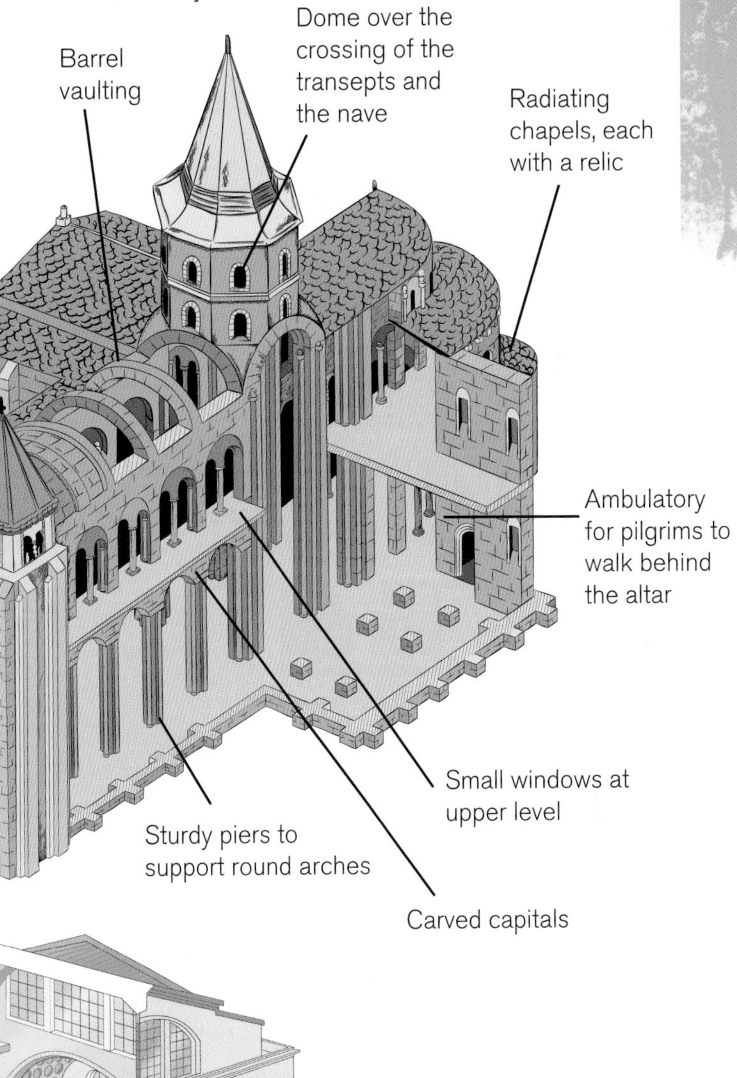

Fig. 9.7 A Romanesque church

Fig. 9.8
Early Christian churches were based on the Roman basilica, a general community building. Round Roman temples to the gods were considered too pagan.

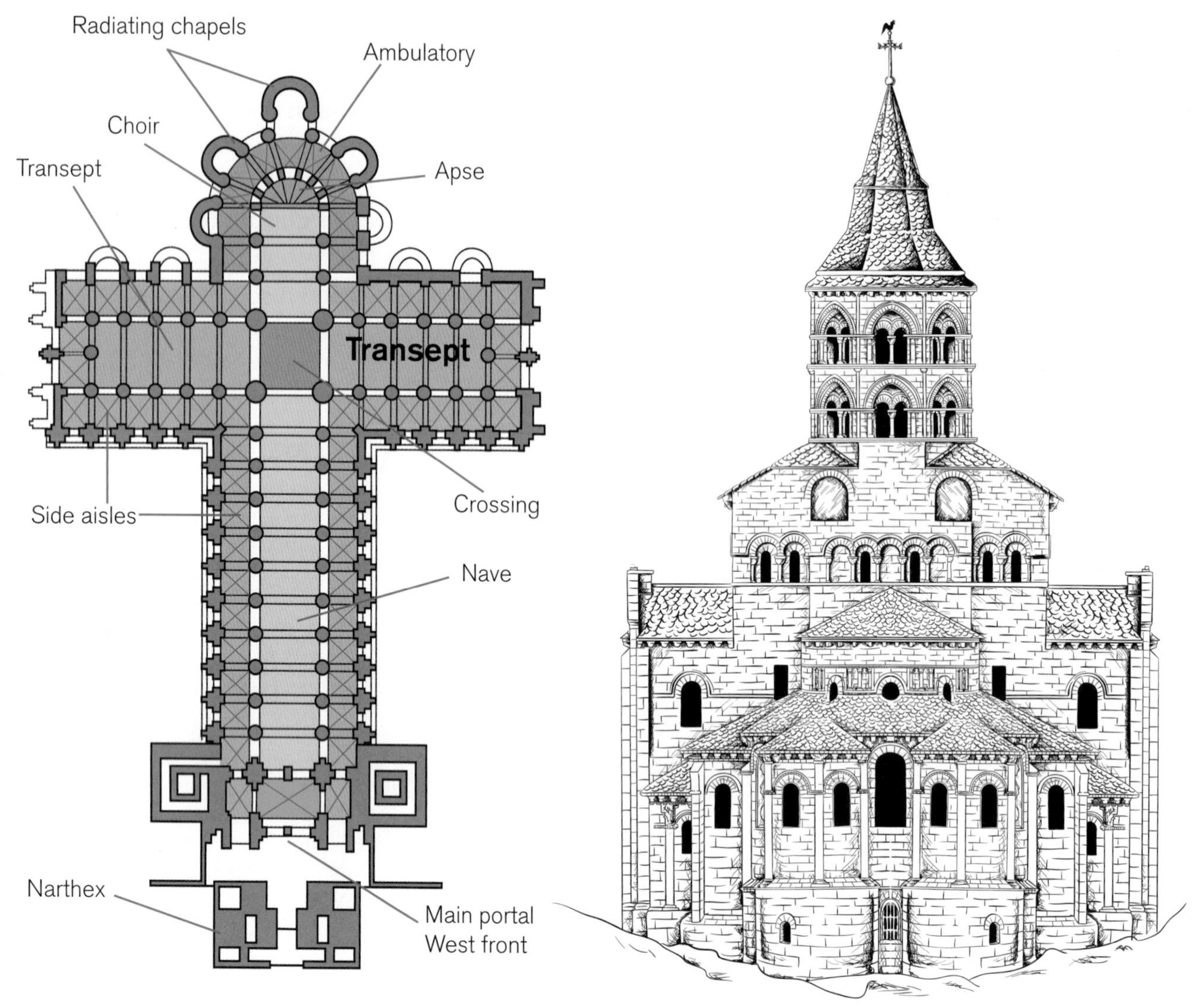

Fig. 9.9 Floor plan of a Romanesque pilgrimage church

Fig. 9.10 Radiating chapels at the back of a Romanesque church

Vaulting

Wooden roofs in churches were a constant fire hazard and there had been many catastrophes. Replacing them with stone was not an easy task. Masons studied the vaulting of old Roman buildings, but without plans they had to experiment.

> **Vault:** An architectural term for a roof based on the structural principle of the arch.

Problems and solutions

* **Barrel vaulting** came first, but problems with **outward thrust** soon developed.
* **Pointed barrel vaulting** was an improvement, but problems continued.
* **Groin vaulting** seemed to solve the issue, but problems re-emerged.

The problem of outward thrust

Heavy stone roofs pressed **down**, but they also pressed **out**. This meant that arches flattened, walls pushed outward and sometimes the roof collapsed (Fig. 9.11).

Fig. 9.11 Vaulting

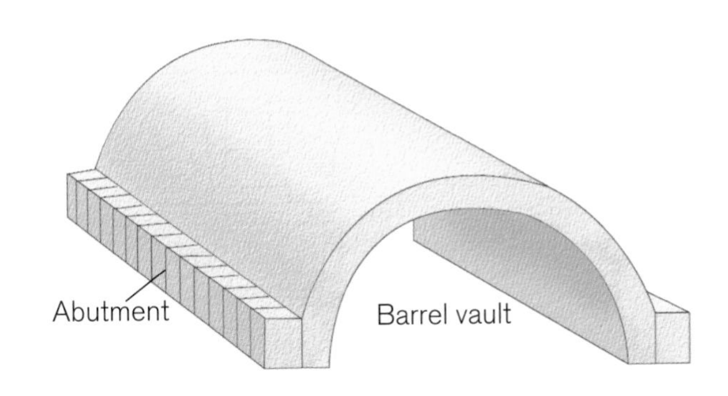

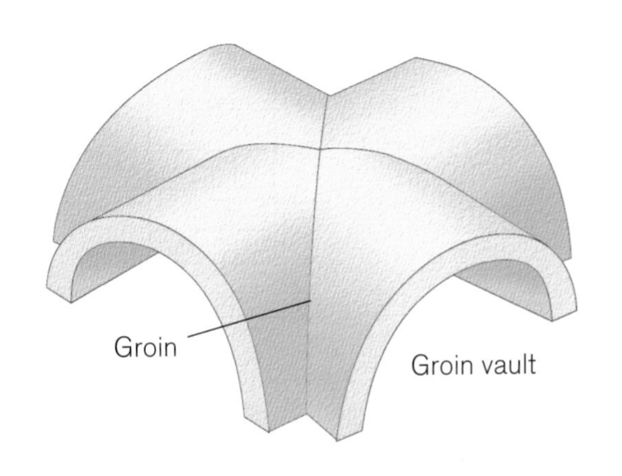

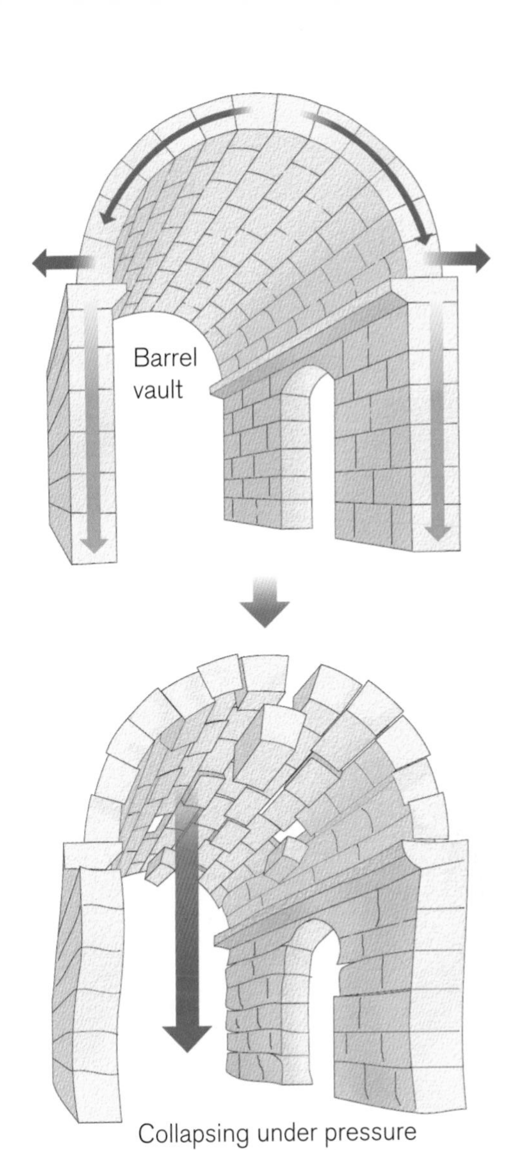

Decorative features

Sculptural decoration was firmly tied to architectural space. Decoration included:

* **Ornamental patterns, foliage and animal forms**.
* **Spiral motifs** used in both figurative and abstract sculpture. They were adapted into folds for drapery.
* **Blind arcades:** Rows of arches built on the walls that had no function – they were simply decorative.
* **Figurative narrative scenes:** Bible stories using a combination of the human figure and foliage.
* **Carved in relief:** Features stood out from the surface (not freestanding).
* **Symbolic meaning** and strict religious traditions were very important. For example, columns symbolise trees. The base represents roots on earth and the capital symbolises the crown reaching towards heaven.

Architectural spaces for sculpture

Some architectural spaces on the churches were filled with sculpture. This was placed on the tympanum over the doorway and on the capitals of the interior.

Tympanum: The surface enclosed by the arch and lintel of an arched doorway, frequently carved with relief sculptures.

Capital: The topmost member of a column, wider than the column and providing a broader support for the structures above.

Archivolt: Ornamental moulding or bands surrounding the arches that frame the tympanum.

Lintel: A horizontal piece of stone or timber placed across the top of an opening to support the wall above.

Trumeau: Central doorpost supporting a lintel.

Jamb: The side of a window-, door- or other wall-opening.

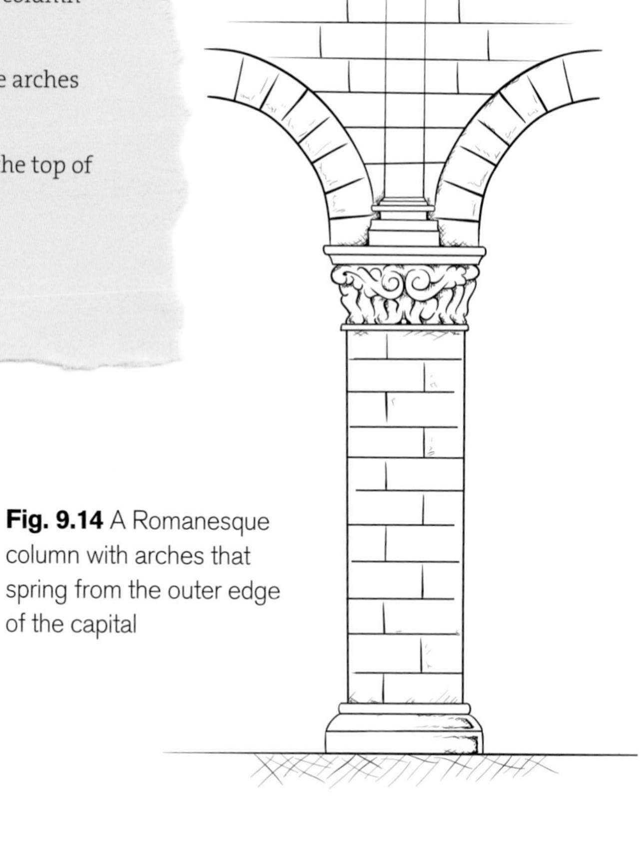

Fig. 9.14 A Romanesque column with arches that spring from the outer edge of the capital

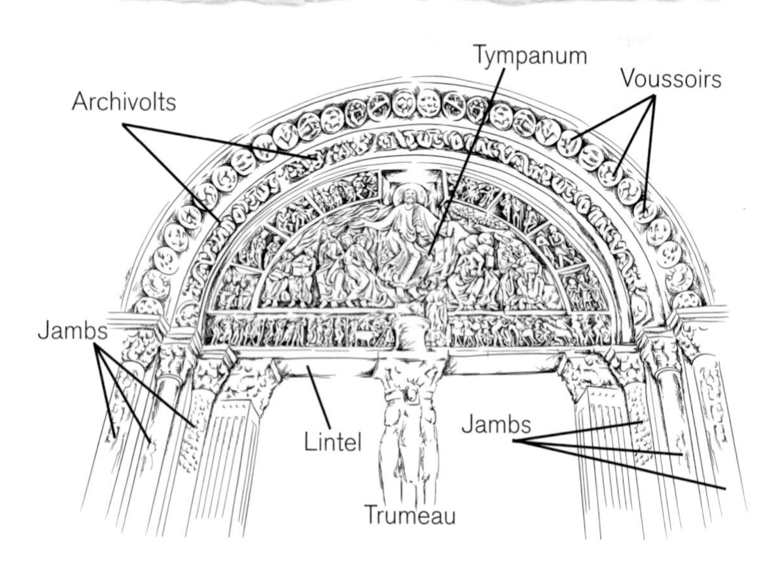

Fig. 9.12 A Romanesque portal (doorway)

Fig. 9.13 Window arch piers and blind arcade

St Foy de Conques

St Foy de Conques is a well-preserved example of a typical 12th-century pilgrimage church (Fig. 9.15). It has typical Romanesque architectural and decorative features, including:

* Heavy construction
* Barrel vaulting
* Thick walls
* Dark interior
* Radiating chapels

The monastery and church of St Foy was developed in stages over 300 years. Very little remains of the monastery. A larger church was built to replace the old 8th-century chapel after the arrival of the relics of St Foy made it a major pilgrimage route. The new church was completed by the end of the 10th century and it included five radiating chapels and the ambulatory. Galleries were also added over the aisle and the roof was raised to allow people to move about at a higher level.

Interior

Like most pilgrimage churches, the main feature of St Foy de Conques is a cruciform plan. Not only was this symbolic of the cross, but it also helped to regulate the flow of the crowds of pilgrims throughout the church. People could enter from the western portal and then circulate around the church towards the relics at the eastern end. An octagonal-shaped lantern tower over the crossing and high windows over the nave were the only light source for the interior.

Vaulting

The nave was roofed with very thick continuous barrel vaulting lined with arches.

Exterior

Conques has a solid geometric exterior appearance. There is no real ornamentation except for buttresses, which were needed to counteract the outward thrust of the walls. The towers on either side were added in the 19th century.

The tympanum

The only decoration is on the tympanum above the western entrance. This features a Last Judgement scene that depicts Christ in Majesty presiding over the judgement of the souls of the deceased.

Fig. 9.15 P. 2-14 (2.11) St Foy de Conques

Fig. 9.16
The Last Judgement sculpture in the tympanum at St Foy de Conques. This famous scene is full of activity and expression. Among the figures are real people of the time, like bishops and kings. Some of these are even found in hell. Traces of the original colour still exist.

St Lazare of Autun

The Cathedral of St Lazare in Autun is an important pilgrimage church (Fig. 9.17). It was built in the 12th century when its famous relic, the bones of Lazarus, drew pilgrims from all over Europe. It is best known for its splendid sculpture by Gislebertus.

St Magdalene in Vézelay

The Basilica Church of St Magdalene in Vézelay is the largest Romanesque church in France (Fig. 9.18). The Benedictine abbey acquired relics of Mary Magdalene in 1037 and it became a major stop on the Compostela route. It was rebuilt around 1150 having burned down, an incident in which 1,200 pilgrims lost their lives.

Exterior

The west front of Vézelay has suffered over the years. Originally built around 1150 in the Romanesque style, it was given a Gothic central gable and south tower in the 13th century. It was badly damaged during the French Revolution and was restored quite clumsily in the early 19th century.

Narthex: A single-storey porch attached to the front of a church. The main door of the church is inside the narthex (see Fig. 9.9).

The narthex

Inside the spacious narthex the main door has survived very well. The narthex contains three portals, each with a superb 12th-century tympanum of richly sculptured figures. (See details in Chapter 10.)

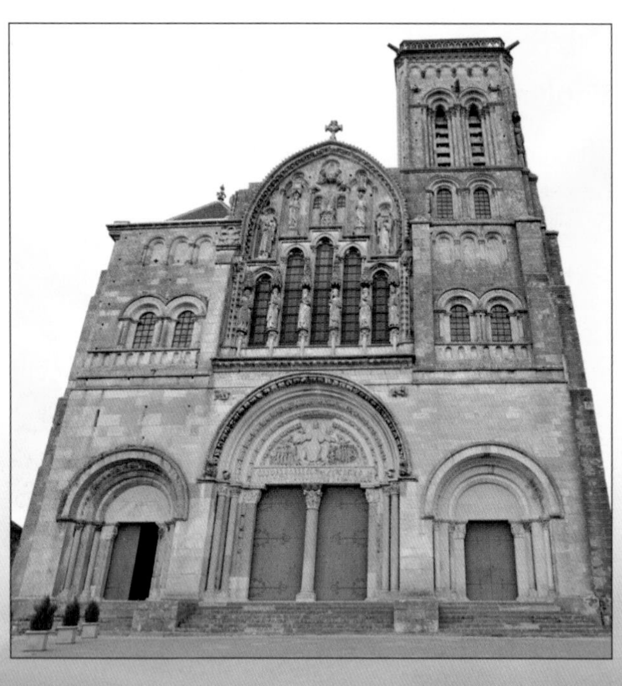

Fig. 9.18 St Magdalene in Vézelay

Fig. 9.17 The Cathedral of St Lazare of Autun. The interior shows the original Romanesque barrel vaulting and sculpture on the capitals.

Fig. 9.19 Interior of the Basilica Church of St Magdalene in Vézelay

Rhythm and light

The interior of Vézelay is a perfect gem of 12th-century architecture and a beautiful example of stately Romanesque design (Fig. 9.19 and Fig. 9.20). Signs of outward thrust can be seen in the flattened arches and outward-leaning piers, but buttressing added later on the exterior solved this problem.

The nave, constructed between 1120 and 1132, is one of the oldest parts of the church and is based on a simple basilica plan without transepts. It is roofed with a series of transverse arches and groin vaulting. Groin vaulting was used instead of barrel vaulting to counteract the problem of outward thrust and lighten the load on the walls. This allowed for larger windows and brought more light into the nave. Each of the semi-circular arches on the roof is supported by a decorated column attached to a solid pier.

The walls of the main aisle are separated on both sides by arcades of semi-circular arches. These arches are supported by columns, and the upper capitols are decorated with sculptured narrative biblical scenes. (See details in Chapter 10.)

One of Vézelay's most notable characteristics is the use of pink and white stone on all of the arches and pillars. The chequered effect creates a perfect balance of rhythm and light.

Sunlight

Another of Vézelay's most remarkable design features is its orientation in relation to the sun. The effects of this can be seen on two occasions in the year: on 21 June (summer solstice) at midday, nine pools of sunlight fall upon the exact centre of the nave. These form a path of light that leads directly to the altar. At the same time on 21 December (winter solstice), the same light pattern falls on the upper capitals of the northern (left) arcade.

Fig. 9.20 Capitals in the Basilica Church of St Magdalene in Vézelay

Chapter review

* Why, do you think, did Cluny Abbey have such a powerful influence on the Romanesque style of art and architecture?
* Romanesque churches were specifically designed to cater for the needs of pilgrims. Would you agree that the designs were sophisticated as well as functional? Why?

EXAM QUESTIONS

Ordinary Level (2014)

(a) Name, describe and discuss any Romanesque church that you have studied using the following headings:

- Overall plan
- Exterior features
- Interior features
- Decorative features

(b) Briefly discuss the main function of Romanesque sculpture.

Higher Level (2010)

'The Christian Church influenced the development of art and architecture during the Romanesque period.'

Discuss this statement, making detailed reference to the structure, layout and decoration of one named church from the period.

FURTHER RESEARCH

www.youtube.com –
Cluny Abbey, Professor Carol

www.sacred-destinations.com – Cluny Abbey

Chapter 10

Romanesque Sculpture

One of the most significant developments in Romanesque art was a return to stone carving. Beginning at Cluny, the practice soon spread to other pilgrimage churches.

By the end of this chapter, I will...

* Understand how architectural spaces influenced sculptural composition and design.
* Know that narrative scenes were used to teach illiterate people about religion.
* Know that Romanesque imagery was stylised, imaginative and grotesque.
* Be able to identify, draw and describe key examples of Romanesque sculpture.

Sculptural decoration

The two architectural spaces for sculpture were the tympanum and the capital.

Tympanum

Sculpture in the tympanum often featured the Last Judgement.

* Figures were distorted to fit the shape.
* Figures were either small and squat or thin and elongated.
* Facial expressions and gestures were exaggerated.
* The most important figures were the largest.

Fig. 10.1
Main portal (doorway) at the Cathedral of St Lazare in Autun. Pilgrims passing under dramatic Last Judgement scenes were faced with the most terrible images that imagination could conjure up.

Fig. 10.2 (above)
Roman Corinthian-style columns decorated with stylised leaf patterns. These inspired Romanesque capitals like those at Cluny

Fig. 10.3 (right)
Sculptured capital, Cluny

* Christ occupied the central position.
* Grotesque devils and scenes of hell warned pilgrims to repent of their sins.

Capitals

Sculpture on capitals combined a strong narrative element with abstract decoration. They included:

* Figures from Bible stories
* Grotesque imaginary creatures
* Stylised foliage
* Abstract patterns

NOTE! The purpose of medieval art was to teach. Stories and messages in sculpture helped illiterate people to learn the truths of their religious faith by 'reading' the pictures from the Bible.

Sculpture in Romanesque churches

Some of the most impressive Romanesque sculpture is on the tympanum and capitals of St

Fig. 10.4 The main portal inside the narthex (porch) of St Magdalene at Vézelay

Magdalene in Vézelay (Fig. 10.4) and St Lazare in Autun (Fig. 10.5).

St Mary Magdalene in Vézelay

Inside the narthex (the porch) are three portals. A tympanum over each of these features sculpture. The tympanum over the left door depicts the ascension of Christ, while various scenes from the nativity are depicted over the right door.

The central tympanum

The scene over the central door depicts the Pentecost or Christ's command to his apostles to preach the Good News (Fig. 10.5). The central figure of Christ in a mandorla (oval-shaped area representing a 'glory' of light surrounding a figure of the resurrected Christ) is the largest. He is calm and serene. His arms are thrown open to symbolise the glory of his resurrection. He sits with knees bent to one side in a beautifully pleated robe arranged in whirling spiral patterns.

Figures include:

* St Peter, who is identified by the key to the Kingdom of Heaven.
* The apostles of Jesus. Flames of the Holy Spirit fall on their heads, giving them the strength to teach the word of God.

Fig. 10.5 The central tympanum at St Magdalene in Vézelay

Fig. 10.6 (left)
P.3-6 (13.5) The Mystic Mill at St Magdalene in Vézelay

Fig. 10.7 (above)
Moses pours grain into a mill and St Paul the Apostle gathers the flour. The grain represents the law given to Moses and the mill symbolises Christ.

Fig. 10.8
The Last Judgement scene from the tympanum at Autun Cathedral. Souls rise from their coffins on the Day of Judgement. The Blessed look up to heaven but the Damned are driven, crouched and cowering from God, by an angel with a flaming sword.

* People of the world are arranged in the semi-circular surround. Some are pagans – they have animal heads or donkey ears.

Carved capitals in the nave

Vézelay's most famous capital is the Mystic Mill (Fig. 10.6 and Fig. 10.7). It is an interesting as well as beautiful work of art.

St Lazare in Autun

Tympanum: The Last Judgement

This is probably the most famous of all Romanesque sculptures. It was carved from separate blocks that were designed to fit together after mounting. It was carved in high relief and some figures are almost freestanding.

Depiction of the human figure

Figures were:

* Distorted to fit into the tympanum shape
* Thin and elongated with bent knees
* Highly expressive, with a definite character and showing real emotion
* Large and dominant – Christ the Judge is placed in the centre
* Smallest in the lintel – souls rising from the dead (Fig. 10.9)
* Grotesque demons in hell with animal hoofs

Fig. 10.9 A close up of The Last Judgement scene on the tympanum of St Lazare in Autun. The sculpture survived the French Revolution because it had been covered over. It was rediscovered in the 19th century, safe beneath a thick layer of plaster.

Details of figures on the tympanum

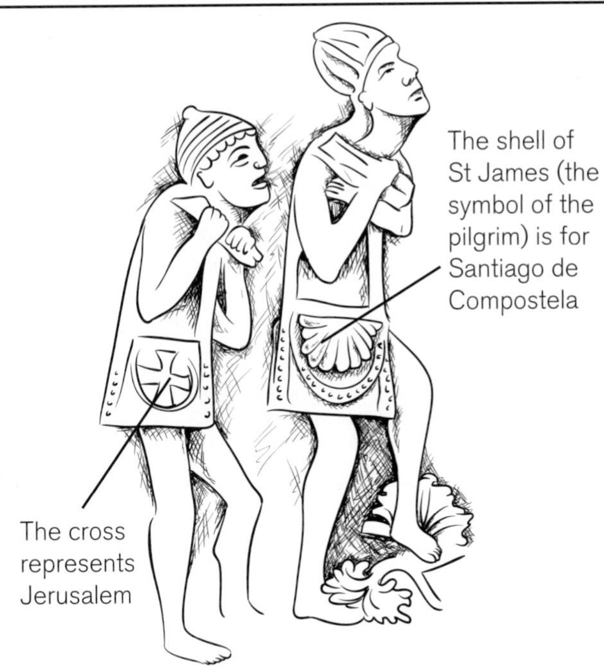
The shell of St James (the symbol of the pilgrim) is for Santiago de Compostela
The cross represents Jerusalem

Fig. 10.10 (above) Pilgrims on their way up to heaven. They are easily identified by the signs on their satchels.

A grotesque devil pulls the scales and another devil sits on it to make it heavier

A laughing demon pours condemned souls down a chute

Archangel Michael weighs the souls – terrified souls hide in his robes

Trembling souls are dragged up to be weighed

The gaping jaws of hell and fires below

Fig. 10.11 (right) The Weighing of Souls. This most gruesome of Romanesque images represents a struggle between good and evil. The Archangel Michael tries to lift them in the right direction, but grotesque devils pull the scales downwards.

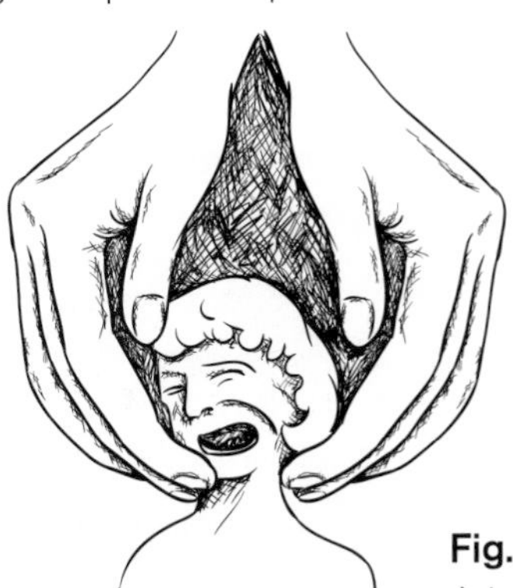

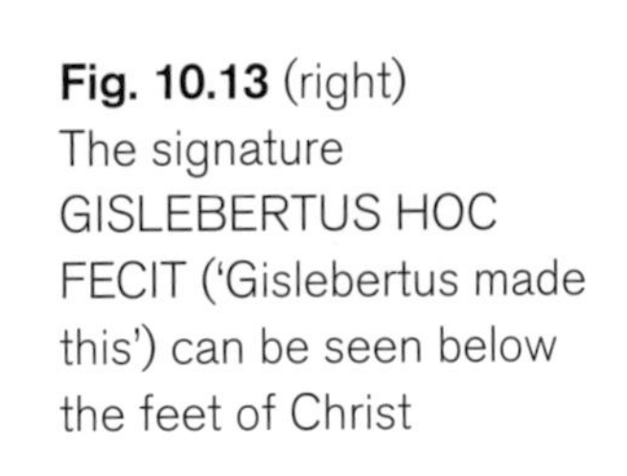

Fig. 10.12 (left) A tormented soul grabbed by giant hands

Fig. 10.13 (right) The signature GISLEBERTUS HOC FECIT ('Gislebertus made this') can be seen below the feet of Christ

GISLEBERTVS HOCFECIT

High relief: A carving that stands out from the surface to a greater (high relief) or lesser (low relief) extent.

The artist

Gislebertus was the artist at Autun. We know this because unusually for the time, he signed the work on the lintel. Like all good storytellers, he seemed to enjoy horror. His unique style features:

* Elongated figures with exaggerated expressions
* Dramatic imagery
* Full colour (originally)

Narrative scenes on the capitals

These are some of the most charming and touching works of Romanesque sculpture. The narrative elements are cleverly combined with ornamental foliage. The skilfully designed compositions fit perfectly in the awkward shapes of the capital.

The flight into Egypt

Having been warned in a dream that Herod wants to kill Jesus, the Holy Family leaves for Egypt on a donkey (Fig. 10.14). In traditional manner, Mary sits still and upright. Her lap forms a throne for the solemn figure of the Christ child. The donkey, however, is quite naturally portrayed and even has a hint of a smile.

NOTE! Romanesque art is quite stylised. Figures are elongated, dignified beings in swirling ornamental drapery. Portraying God or the saints in a natural way was considered disrespectful.

Fig. 10.14 The flight into Egypt

The suicide of Judas

Judas, full of remorse and despair, hangs himself. Gislebertus includes horrific details of the tongue hanging out and the head lolling grotesquely to one side (Fig. 10.15 and Fig. 10.16). His betrayal of Christ was inspired by the Devil and two hideous demons pull the rope on his neck. The three figures form a balanced triangular composition. This highlights the misery of the very human tragedy.

Fig. 10.15 The suicide of Judas

Fig. 10.16 The suicide of Judas

The dream of the Magi

The three kings, still wearing their crowns, share one bed. An ornate semi-circular cover unites the composition (Fig. 10.17 and Fig. 10.18).

The story is told in three simple gestures. The angel points to the star, gently touches a hand and a king opens one eye. It is a warning not to return to King Herod after Bethlehem.

Chapter review

* Architectural sculpture was part of the overall design of churches, but these are also powerful works of art. How do you think pilgrims were affected by this art?
* The imagery was stylised, imaginative and grotesque. Why do you think artists worked in this style?

Fig. 10.17 (left) The dream of the Magi

Fig. 10.18 (above) The dream of the Magi

EXAM QUESTIONS

Ordinary Level (2009)

Look at the example of Romanesque sculpture from the cathedral at Autun in Fig. 10.8.

Answer (a) and (b).

(a) Describe and discuss this piece of sculpture using the following headings:
- Subject matter
- Location

(b) Name and describe an example of Romanesque architecture that you have studied.

Use sketches to illustrate your answer.

Higher Level (2016)

'The artistic imagination and skills of Romanesque sculptors allowed images of life, death, judgement and the afterlife to be central to the churches and cathedrals of the time.'

Discuss this statement with reference to a named Romanesque church or cathedral you have studied.

and

Briefly describe and discuss the main architectural features of Romanesque architecture.

Illustrate your answer.

FURTHER RESEARCH

www.khanacademy.org – Last Judgement Tympanum, Cathedral of St Lazare, Autun

www.khanacademy.org – Pentecost and Mission to the Apostles Tympanum, Vézelay

www.sacred-destinations.com – Autun Cathedral

www.sacred-destinations.com – Vézelay Abbey

www.sacredsites.com – Vézelay

Chapter 11

The Gothic Period

Gothic architecture

Gothic architecture began in the Benedictine Abbey of St Denis near Paris. The church was associated with the French monarchy and nearly all the kings and queens of France were buried there.

The head of the abbey, the Abbot Suger, had a deep love of art and a vision of God as divine light. He set about restoring the abbey and wanted the brightest and most beautiful church soaring towards heaven.

By the end of this chapter, I will...

* Know that Gothic architecture represented Abbot Suger's vision of divine light.
* Be able to compare the features of Gothic and Romanesque architecture.
* Know how to name, draw and describe two Gothic cathedrals in France.
* Be familiar with the features of Early, High, Flamboyant and Rayonnant Gothic styles.

Height, light and colour

Abbot Suger found an architect to help with his ideas. Together they took elements of Romanesque architecture and combined them in an entirely new way.

Such grandeur and elegance had never been seen and the style of St Denis spread quickly around Paris. The 'French style' soon became widespread and magnificent Gothic cathedrals appeared in towns across Northern Europe (Fig. 11.1).

The 13th century was the age of the great cathedral. These were awe-inspiring structures with towers and spires that reached to incredible heights. The soaring vertical interiors and the colourful stained glass windows created a mysterious atmosphere of sacred light.

A cathedral had several important functions over a church in a town. It was:

* An impressive centre for religious services
* An important symbol of religious and civic pride
* A constant reminder of the presence of God and the power of the church
* The highest building for miles around
* A way of educating people in their religious faith

Fig. 11.1 Chartres Cathedral from a distance

New building techniques

New architectural features spread the weight and allowed buildings to be constructed to greater heights. They included:

* The pointed arch (Fig. 11.2).
* The rib vault (Fig. 11.3).
* The clustered column that supported the ribs spreading in different directions (Fig. 11.4).
* Buttresses on exterior walls.
* Flying buttresses – arches to support the walls on the higher areas. This allowed for more openings for large clerestory (upper level) windows (Fig. 11.5).
* Tall thin walls – skeletal stone rib structures were sufficient to support the vaulting system (Fig. 11.6).

Other characteristics included:

* **Stained glass windows:** Thinner walls allowed for large openings for windows.
* **Tracery:** Ornamental stonework of delicate, lacelike patterns that supported the glass in the windows.
* **An ambulatory with radiating chapels:** Like in Romanesque churches to facilitate pilgrims and accommodate relics.

Fig. 11.3 Rib vaulting

Fig. 11.2 Pointed arches

Fig. 11.4 Clustered column

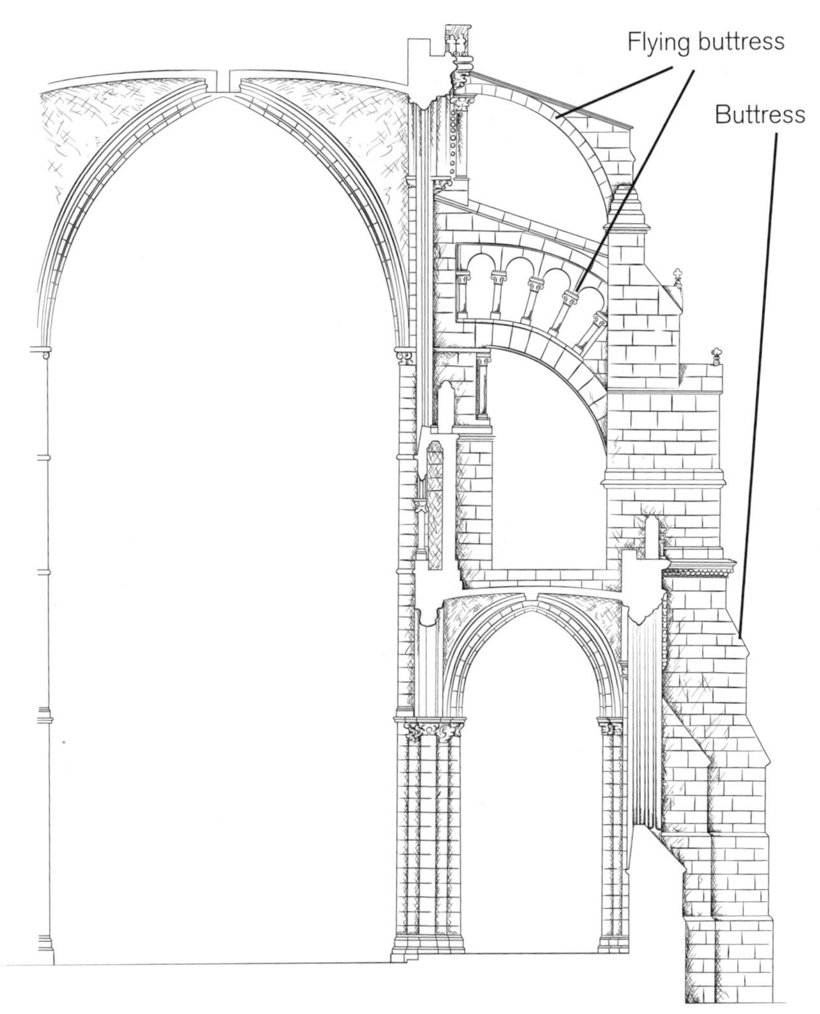

Fig. 11.5 Buttresses and flying buttresses. Flying buttresses were often very decorative and elaborately designed. They created a sense of movement around the exterior of the cathedrals.

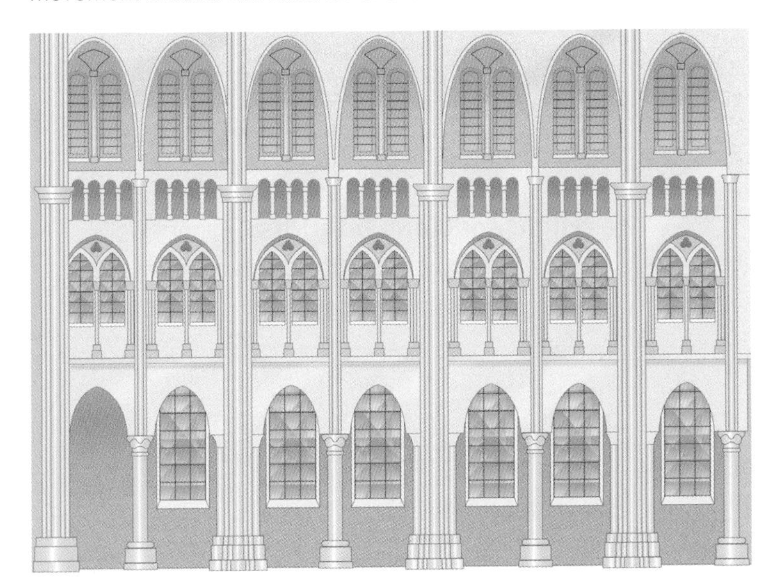

Fig. 11.6 Gothic wall with pointed lancet windows, triforium and high clerestory windows

Fig. 11.7 The Noah Window at Chartres Cathedral filled with stained glass

Fig. 11.8 Rose window showing Gothic tracery

Gothic architectural features compared to Romanesque

* **Great height:** Gothic cathedrals were built to far greater heights than Romanesque churches (Fig. 11.9).
* **Pointed arches:** These distributed weight efficiently and were stronger than round Romanesque arches.
* **Rib vaulting:** Also called crosswise vaulting, this was a far more effective system of supporting stone roofs than either barrel or groin vaulting.
* **Flying buttresses:** These absorbed the outward and downward pressure of the vault. This solved the Romanesque problem of outward thrust.
* **Slender pillars:** These were sufficient because pressure from the vaults was concentrated in small areas at the end of the ribs. Thick Romanesque columns were no longer needed.
* **Thinner walls:** Gothic cathedrals were skeletal-like structures, whereas Romanesque walls were very thick.

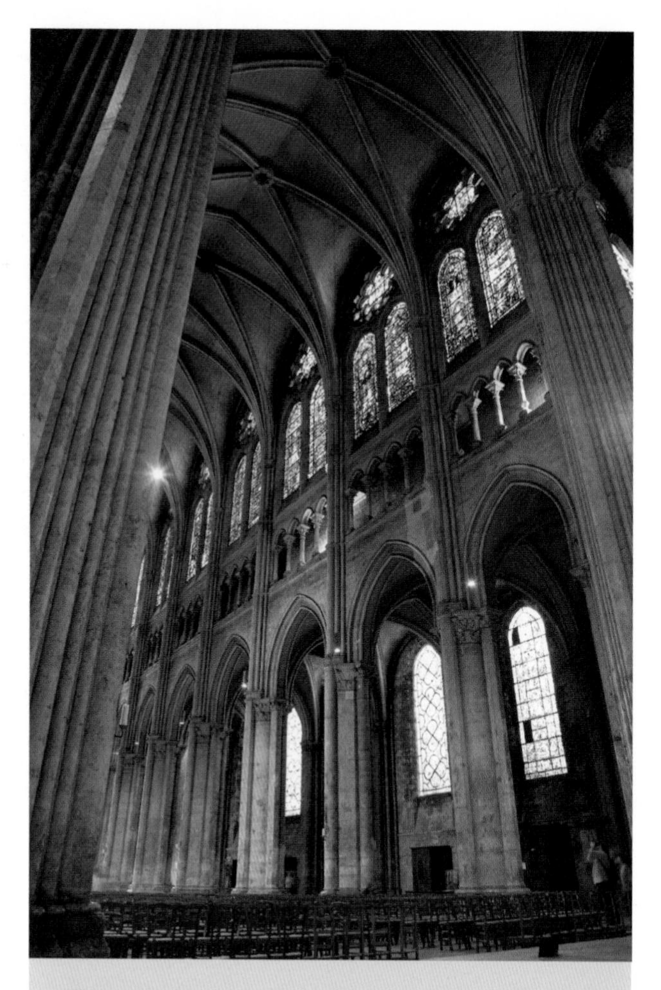

Fig. 11.9 Interior of Chartres Cathedral. Even today, Gothic cathedrals are highly impressive structures. Such height must have greatly impressed people in the 13th century, and the light pouring in must have made it seem like heaven on earth.

* **High, spacious interiors:** Thinner walls allowed for more windows and light. Thicker walls made Romanesque interiors smaller and darker.

The three phases of Gothic architecture

Gothic architecture developed over two centuries. Rivalry and competition led builders to construct higher, grander and ever more decorative designs.

Fig. 11.10

Notre Dame, Amiens, with decorative lighting on the façade. During the process of laser cleaning in the 1990s, traces of the original colour were identified on the west façade of Amiens Cathedral. Elaborate lighting techniques were developed to project colour directly. The stunning display that brings the figures to life can be seen on summer nights, at Christmas and the New Year.

The three distinct phases were:

* Early Gothic
* High Gothic
* Rayonnant and Flamboyant (Late Gothic styles)

Decorative features of Gothic cathedrals

The decorative features of Early Gothic architecture were quite simple compared to Romanesque. The figures and stories of the Romanesque capital completely disappeared.

Early and High Gothic architectural decoration included:

* Doorways with sculptural decoration
* Column statues on the jambs
* Stained glass windows

The Late Gothic styles were more ornate and decorative. Architectural features included:

* More complex rib vaulting (Fig. 11.11)
* More ornate flying buttresses
* More intricate window tracery and mouldings (Fig. 11.12)
* More decorative spires and pinnacles (Fig. 11.13 and Fig. 11.14)
* More elaborate sculpture on the portals (doorway and surrounds)

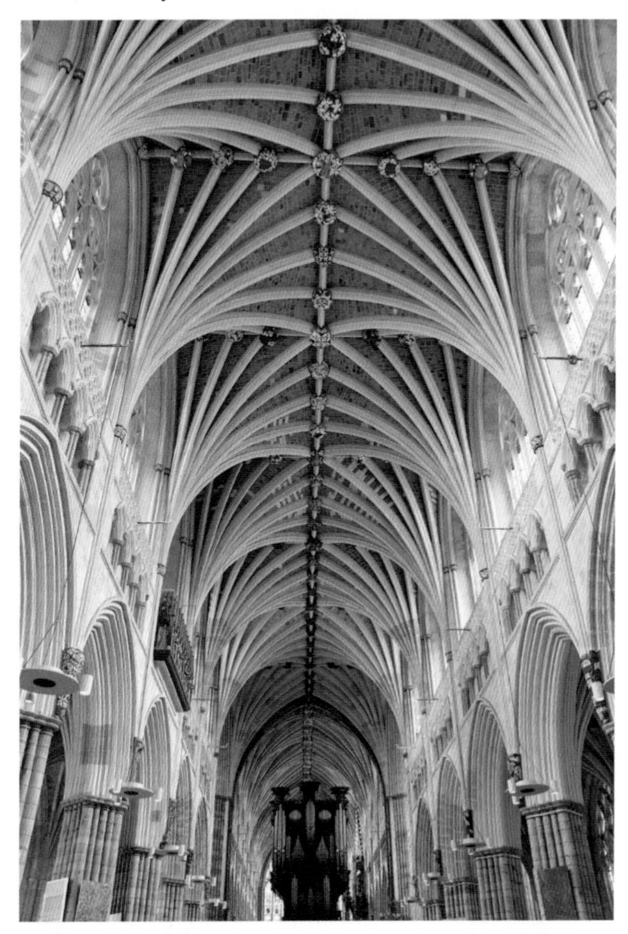

Fig. 11.11 Complex rib vaulting. Exeter Cathedral in England is famous for its 14th-century vaulted ceiling.

Fig. 11.12 Ornamental window tracery and window moulding at Rouen Cathedral

Fig. 11.14

Spires at Chartres Cathedral. The Flamboyant Gothic spire at Chartres north tower on the west front was erected in the early 16th century.

Fig. 11.13 Spires, towers and pinnacles in the Flamboyant Gothic style on the façade of Rouen Cathedral

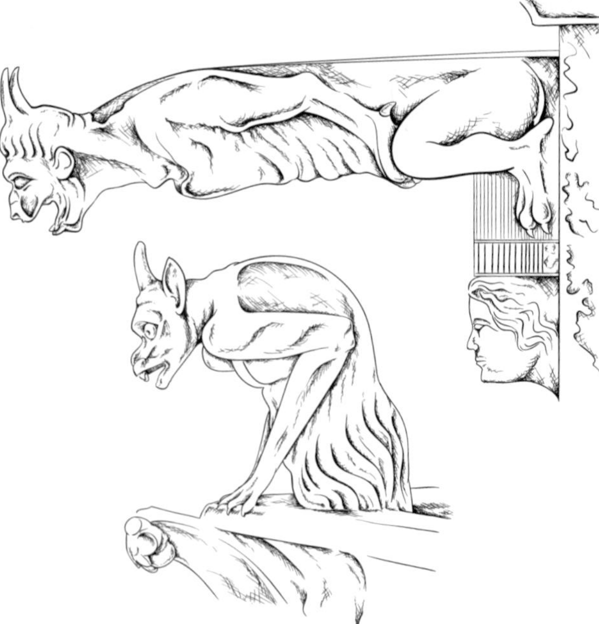

Fig. 11.15 Gothic gargoyles. One of the most notable decorative and functional features of Gothic cathedrals is the gargoyle. The grotesque little creatures project from the gutters of roofs and spires. Rainwater gushes through their open mouths and falls to the ground, well clear of the building.

Gothic cathedrals in France

The Royal Abbey of St Denis was demolished during the French Revolution. Only the church remains, although the interior was damaged (Fig. 11.16).

Fig. 11.16 The Basilica of St Denis, now in a northern suburb of Paris, is of unique importance because it was the first Gothic church

Notre Dame of Paris

Begun in 1163, the impressive new architectural features of Notre Dame Cathedral (Fig. 11.17) were intended to surpass others nearby. The construction was supported and encouraged by King Louis VII. The new features included:

* Tall towers (the spires were never built)
* Single-arch flying buttresses in the late Rayonnant Gothic style

The original glass and sculpture were almost all destroyed during the French Revolution. They were replaced with 19th-century copies. The famous Notre Dame gargoyles (Fig. 11.18) are also from the 19th century.

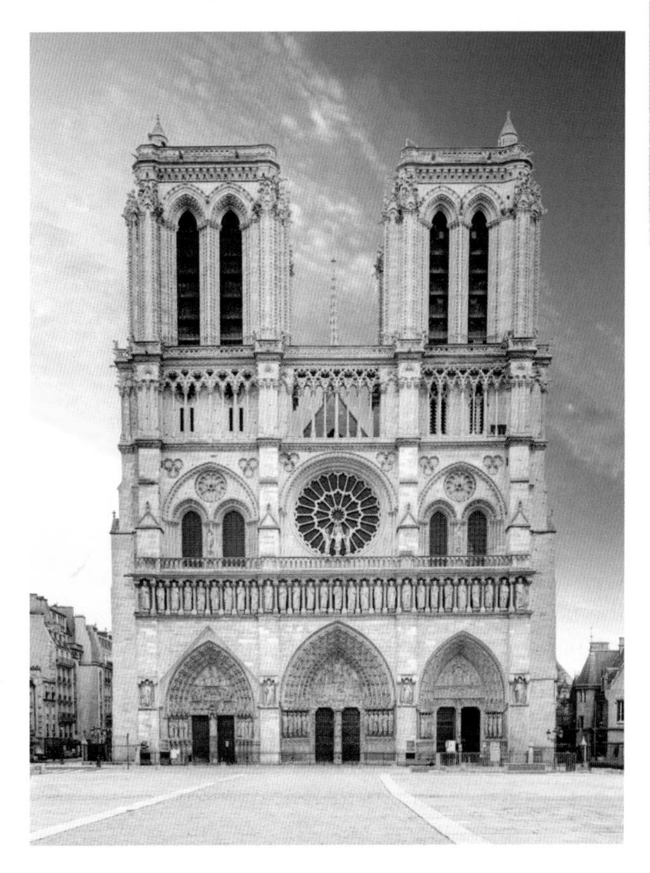

Fig. 11.17 Notre Dame Cathedral, Paris

Fig. 11.18 Gargoyle at Notre Dame Cathedral, Paris

Chartres Cathedral

Chartres Cathedral is the best-preserved example of the 13th-century High Gothic style (Fig. 11.19). It miraculously survived the French Revolution and its original 13th-century glass and sculpture are mostly intact.

Chartres Cathedral is dedicated to the Virgin Mary. Its sacred relic, the Sancta Camisia (Fig. 11.20), was said to be the gown worn by the Virgin during childbirth.

The cathedral was rebuilt after a fire in 1194 all but destroyed the cathedral. The precious relic was thought to have perished, but the Sancta Camisia was found safe in the crypt after three days. This was seen as a sign from the Virgin to build a new and even more magnificent cathedral.

Huge sums of money poured in from all over France. Rich and poor helped to build a new cathedral. It took eighty years – a relatively short period of time. It combined the older Gothic façade as well as the south tower, both of which survived the fire, and included the sculptures of the Royal Portal and its three stained glass windows (Fig. 11.21 and Fig. 11.22).

The mismatched towers are a particular feature of Chartres. The south spire is a 12th-century plain Transitional Gothic pyramid. The north is an early 16th-century Flamboyant Gothic spire on top of an older tower. This replaced the original, which was destroyed by lightning in 1506.

Interior

The plan is a Latin cross (Fig. 11.24) with three aisles, a short transept and an ambulatory. The round east end has five semi-circular radiating chapels.

The nave is over 36 metres in height and is the widest in France. Clustered columns soar dramatically upwards from plain bases to support the high pointed arches and rib vaulting of the ceiling (Fig. 11.26). Huge clerestory windows on the upper level allow light to pour in.

The nave is three-storied, with tall arcades, a triforium and a huge clerestory. The massive weight of this requires significant support from flying buttresses (Fig. 11.25).

Arcade: A series of arches carried by columns or piers.

Triforium: The space above the nave arcade, below the clerestory – sometimes used as a walkway.

Clerestory: The upper part of the nave of a large church, containing a series of windows.

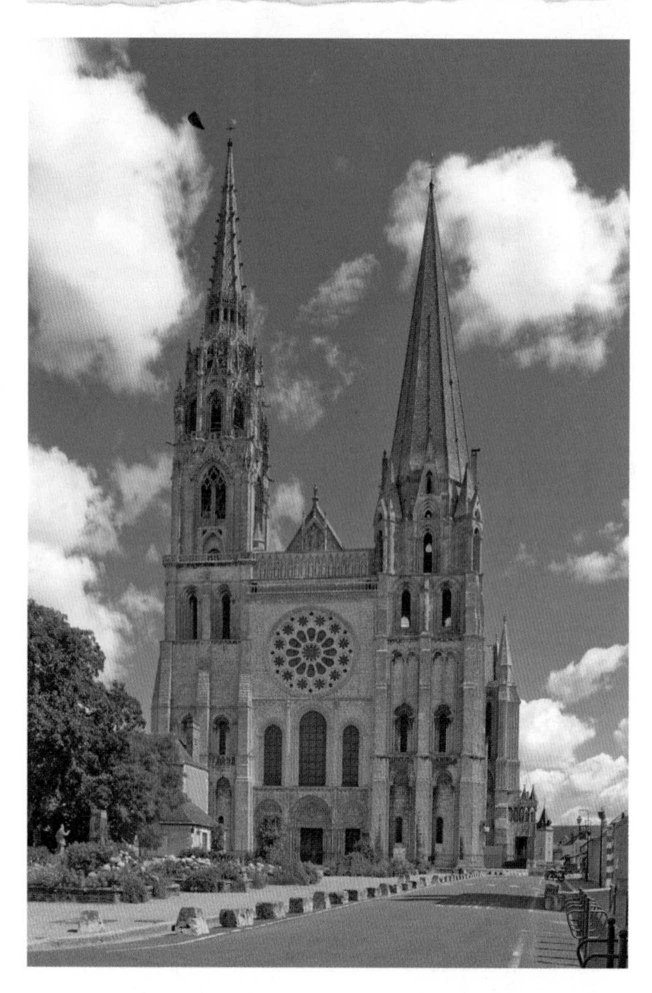

Fig. 11.19 Chartres Cathedral was rebuilt in the 13th century. Part of the original church that survived the fire of 1194 was incorporated into the new building.

Fig. 11.20 The Sancta Camisia relic at Chartres Cathedral

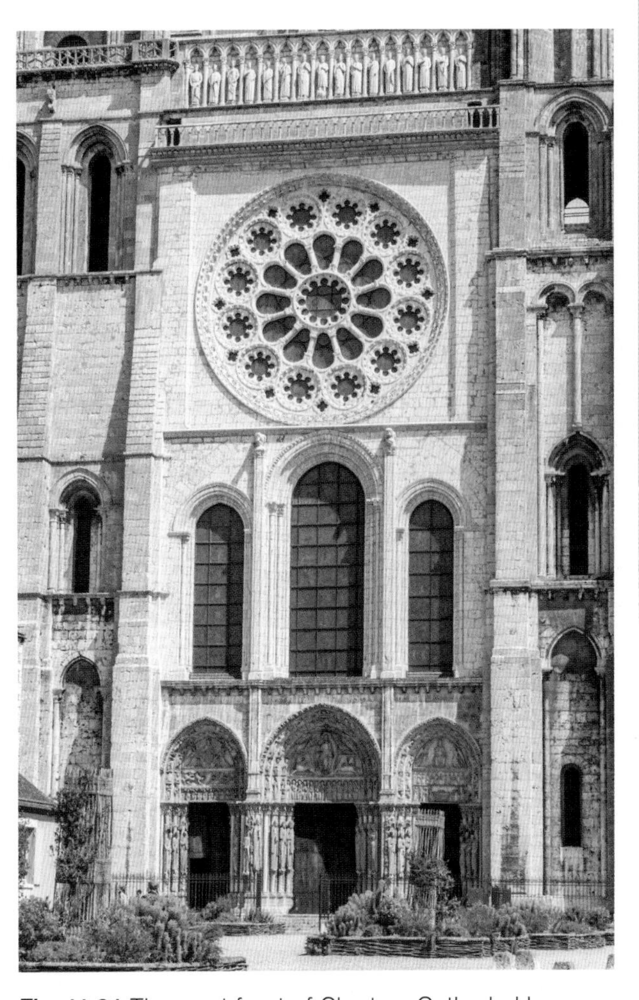

Fig. 11.21 The west front of Chartres Cathedral has a large circular rose window and three large lancet windows

Transepts

The west façade (Fig. 11.21) and both transepts have large rose windows. Each has a three-portal entrance making nine individual doors (Fig. 11.22).

Fig. 11.22
The Royal Portal (main entrance) of Chartres Cathedral. The three-portal layout is unique to Chartres. The column statues of kings and queens on the jambs are some of the most famous sculptures in Western art.

Fig. 11.23
Flying buttresses at Chartres Cathedral. There are three levels of flying buttresses along the exterior of the nave.

At the third level a flyer of arches stretch to just below the gutter of the upper nave

At the second level they are connected by small columns arranged like spokes of a wheel

At the first level they take the form of a simple arch

Fig. 11.24
Floor plan of Chartres Cathedral. The spacious nave is the widest in France.

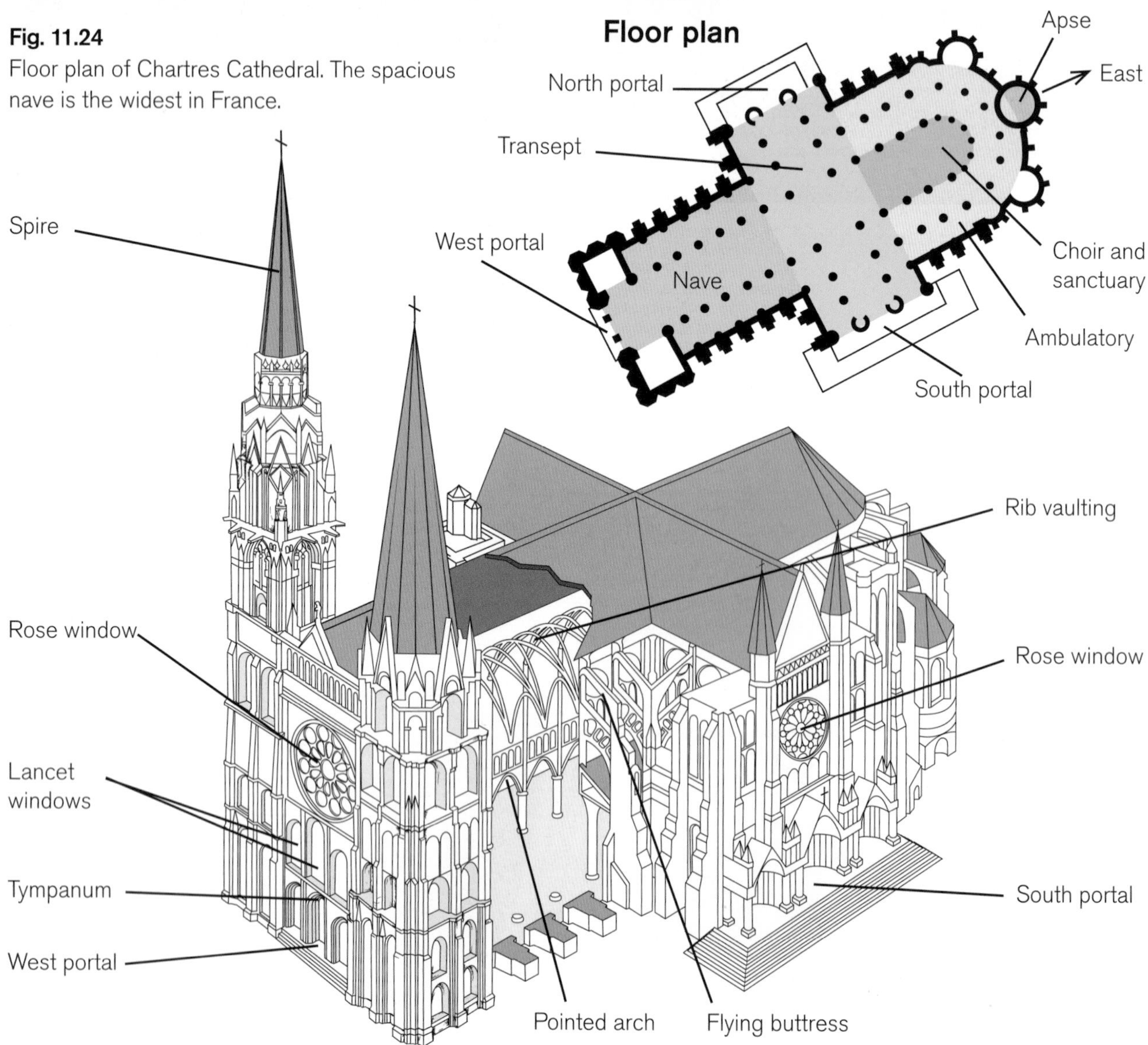

Fig. 11.25
Chartres Cathedral ceiling vaulting. Slender columns soar dramatically upwards to support the rib vaulting.

Flying buttresses

Chartres was one of the first large buildings to explore the full potential of flying buttresses (Fig. 11.23).

Interior features

* A **central aisle and transepts** form the shape of a cross with arms (Fig. 11.24).
* **Clustered slender columns** support the vaults.
* **Rib vaulting** (Fig. 11.25).
* **Three large rose windows** (Fig. 11.26).
* An **ambulatory** separated by a 16th-century carved **choir screen**.
* **Radiating chapels**, among them the most precious relic of Chartres: the Sancta Camisia.

Fig. 11.26 Rose windows at the doorways of Chartres intensify the feeling of light and space

Reims Cathedral

Reims Cathedral was rebuilt in 1210 (Fig. 11.27). It is one of the most perfect examples of Late Gothic architecture. It suffered damage to the roof and glass during World War I.

New architectural techniques at Reims Cathedral

The cathedral includes several innovative Gothic architectural techniques, notably:

* Delicate bar tracery on its windows (very thin stonework resembling twisted iron bars)
* Flying buttresses
* Very thin walls

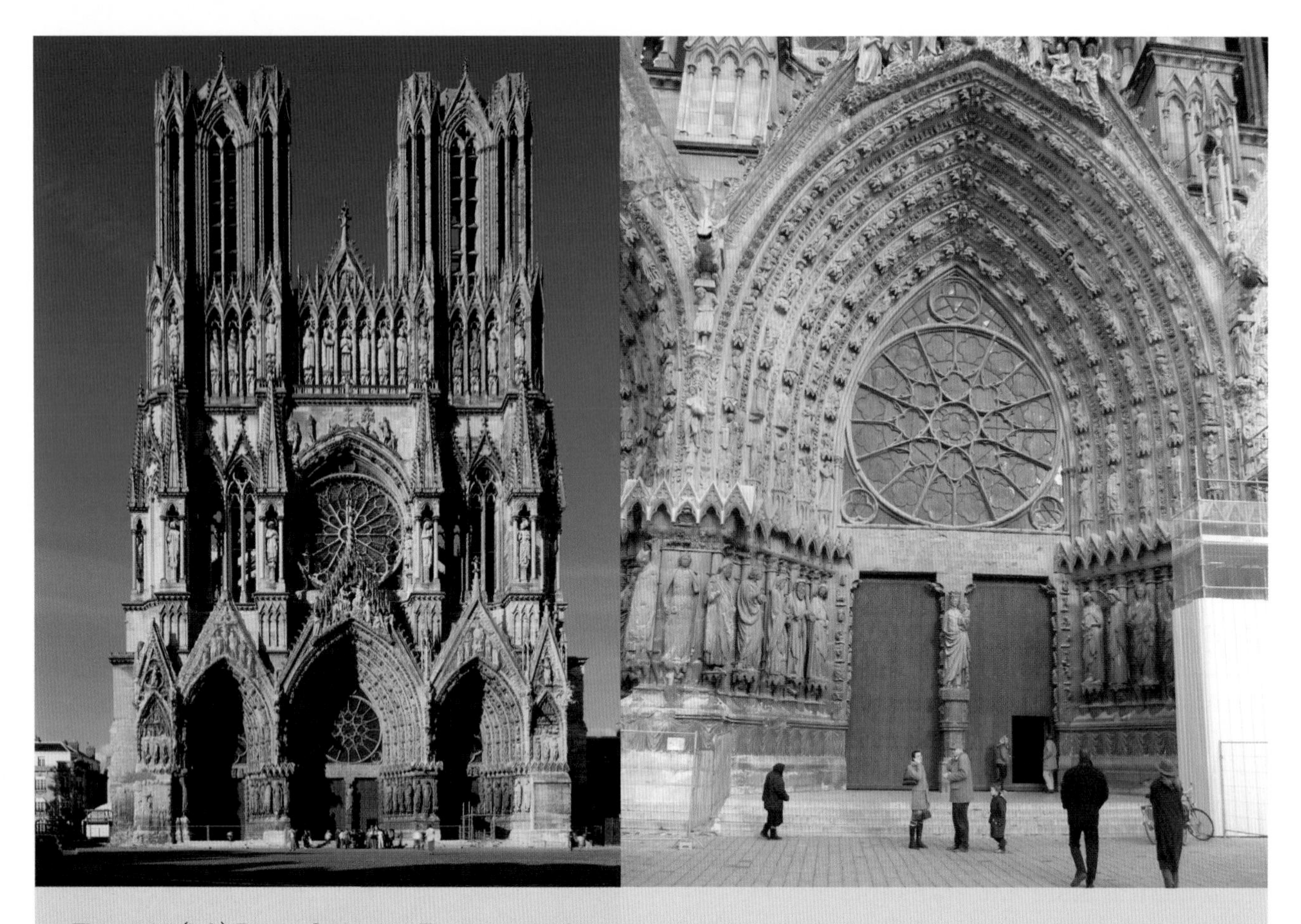

Fig. 11.27 (left) Reims Cathedral. The plan was for seven towers, but only the two on the western façade were completed. Its spires were never built.

Fig. 11.28 (right) Tympanum at Reims Cathedral. The central portal is dedicated to the Virgin, but instead of the traditional tympanum it is surmounted by a rose window framed by a triangular sculptured arch.

Coronations of kings

The cathedral is dedicated to the Virgin Mary and is famous for its association with royalty. All the kings of France were crowned here. Clovis, the first king of the Franks, is in a central position in the 'gallery of the kings'. Most of the sculpture survived war damage.

Rouen Cathedral

Rouen Cathedral (Fig. 11.29) is a mixture of different Gothic styles. It was rebuilt in the High Gothic style after a fire in 1200 destroyed most of the original Early Gothic structure.

Different styles

The parts of that 12th-century building that survived the fire can still be seen today: the nave, the left portal and one of the towers. The façade was completely changed in the 15th century to the lacy stonework and ornamental pinnacles of the late Flamboyant Gothic style (Fig. 11.30).

Gothic cathedrals in France and beyond

Important cathedrals in France include Amiens, Beauvais, Laon and Strasbourg. There are also a number of very fine cathedrals in Germany, England, Italy and Spain.

Fig. 11.29 Cathedral of Notre Dame de Rouen

Fig. 11.30 Ornamental tracery on the façade of Rouen Cathedral

Chapter review

* Gothic architecture was the latest in building technology of its time, but also represents one man's vision of the divine. What was this vision?
* Can you identify the architectural features of the Early, High, Flamboyant and Rayonnant Gothic styles?

Fig. 11.31 *Rouen Cathedral in Full Sunlight: Harmony in Blue and Gold* (1894) by Claude Monet. The French Impressionist artist painted more than 20 versions of the cathedral façade in different weather conditions and times of the day.

EXAM QUESTIONS

Ordinary Level (2013)

Answer (a), (b) and (c).

(a) Name a Gothic cathedral you have studied.

(b) Describe and discuss your chosen building.

(c) Describe and discuss the sculpture on your chosen building.

Illustrate your answer.

Higher Level (2015)

'The creators of Gothic churches and cathedrals used architecture, sculpture and stained glass to communicate ideas about the power of the church as well as about the story of Christianity.'

Discuss the statement with reference to a named Gothic church or cathedral.

and

Briefly describe and discuss the treatment of the human figure in a named Gothic sculpture.

Illustrate your answer.

Higher Level (2011)

Discuss the ways in which the main architectural and decorative features of Romanesque churches differ from those of Gothic cathedrals. In your answer, name one Romanesque church and one Gothic cathedral, making detailed reference to scale, structure, layout and decoration.

and

Name and discuss briefly **one** example of Gothic sculpture that you have studied.

Illustrate your answer.

FURTHER RESEARCH

www.khanacademy.org – Gothic Architecture: An Introduction

www.khanacademy.org – Birth of the Gothic, Abbot Suger and the Ambulatory in the Basilica of St Denis

www.khanacademy.org – Cathedral of Notre Dame de Chartres (parts 1–3)

Chapter 12

The Gothic Image

Books of stone

The purpose of Gothic art was didactic – in other words, it had a teaching role. People learned with their eyes from the sculpture in the church porch and the glass on the windows. This included the history of the world from creation, the arts, sciences, Bible stories and the doctrine of their religion. Only the more learned intellectuals could understand some of the complex lessons and symbolism, but ordinary people could 'read' the stories of their beloved saints.

The vivid and terrifying Romanesque visions of death and damnation had disappeared and the new Gothic imagery offered a message of hope, comfort and salvation.

Didactic: Intended for teaching purposes, particularly to convey a moral lesson.

By the end of this chapter, I will...

* Understand how changes in religious teaching affected sculpture.
* Know that column statues are a unique feature of Gothic doorways.
* Know that the human figure was stylised, but facial features became more natural.
* Be able to discuss how Late Gothic sculpture became more natural, lifelike and almost freestanding.
* Understand why Claus Sluter was considered to be one the greatest sculptors of the medieval era.
* Be able to write about how impressive *The Well of Moses* must have been when it was fully intact.

Gothic sculpture

Gothic sculpture was closely linked to architecture and was used mainly to decorate the exteriors of cathedrals.

Early Gothic sculpture

In the Early Gothic period, sculptures of saints and other religious figures were portrayed on the doorways of cathedrals. This was a transitional period and the figures were similar in style in many ways to those found on Romanesque churches.

The figures, for example, on the Royal Portal of Chartres Cathedral (Fig. 12.4), were stiff, straight, elongated and quite simple forms. During the early 13th century, sculptures became softer and more naturalistic. The figures at Reims Cathedral (Fig. 12.14) have individual facial expressions, natural poses and gestures. Their flowing drapery and classical poses suggest that the sculptors were observing antique Roman statues.

High Gothic sculpture

As naturalism developed during the High and Late Gothic periods of the late 13th-century, statues like St Modeste (Fig. 12.9) on the north portal at Chartres began to look more 'real'.

The International Style

By the 14th century, Gothic sculpture had become more refined and elegant. The elaborate drapery and curved poses of sculptures like the Virgin of Notre Dame (Fig. 12.16) were now part of a movement spreading throughout Europe. This dainty and mannered 'International style' was also found in painting and manuscript illumination.

Northern naturalism

Naturalism was more popular in countries of Northern Europe. The figures in Naumburg Cathedral in Germany (Fig. 12.17) show amazingly detailed clothing as well as very 'real' facial features.

Naturalism is seen at its most vigorous and dramatic in the work of the Late Gothic sculptor, Claus Sluter (Fig. 12.18).

The Virgin Mary

Devotion to the Virgin Mary was widespread. Many Gothic cathedrals are called Notre Dame (Our Lady) and are dedicated to the Virgin. She was also an important figure in art (Fig. 12.1).

Fig. 12.1 Coronation of the Virgin by Christ, Notre Dame de Reims Cathedral

The human figure

One of the most original and unique features of Gothic sculpture is the column statue or jamb figure. They were carved out of the same block as the columns on the jambs of doorways (Fig. 12.2

Fig. 12.2
Column statues at Chartres. The tall linear statues show similarities to the Romanesque but have more expressive facial features.

and Fig. 12.3). These tall, slender figures stood on ornamental pedestals. Their finely pleated drapery lines are a reference to classical columns.

Fig. 12.3 The Annunciation, Reims Cathedral

Plinth: The pedestal that supports a statue.

Sculpture on the cathedrals

Chartres Cathedral

Sculpture at Chartres progressed from 12th-century Early Gothic on the west front portal to 13th-century High Gothic on the north and south transept portals.

The west front – Early Gothic (12th century)

The west front is one of the few surviving parts of the original Early Gothic church (see Fig. 11.22).

Fig. 12.5 Christ in Majesty on the tympanum of the Royal Portal at Chartres Cathedral. The theme is one of hope and salvation, with Christ in Majesty welcoming the visitor with a raised hand.

The human figure

Nobody knows exactly what the jamb figures on the Royal Portal represent (see Fig. 11.23). The carving on the central doorway is more accomplished and was probably the work of the master sculptor. The work on the side door is cruder – it was probably done by assistants.

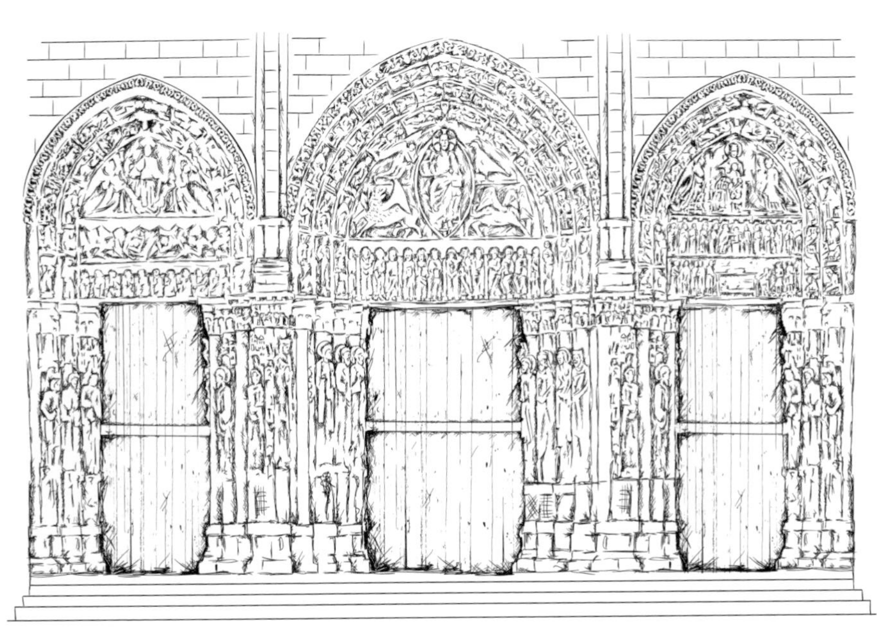

Fig. 12.4
The Royal Portal at Chartres Cathedral gets its name from the column statues of the Old Testament kings and queens on either side of the doorway. They show the transition in style from Romanesque to Gothic.

Fig. 12.6
Column statues at Chartres Cathedral. The figures on the jambs form the upper part of ornamental columns.

In a similar manner to Romanesque sculpture, little emphasis is placed on depicting the real human body, and drapery and pedestals are stylised. However, the faces are more lifelike and have natural, gentle expressions (Fig. 12.6).

The north portal – High Gothic (13th century)

Blanche of Castille was a strong and powerful figure in medieval France. She funded the decoration of the north portal. Not surprisingly, it is dedicated to the Virgin Mary and features many women (Fig. 12.7).

The human figure

The sculpture on the north portal is more advanced, and there are some individual characters, including Abraham (Fig. 12.8) and St Modeste (Fig. 12.9).

Just as he is about to sacrifice his son Isaac, an angel calls Abraham. He turns to look over the head of the next figure – this natural gesture makes him a much more lifelike character.

The St Modeste figure is typical of the refinement of the High Gothic period. She has a very lifelike pose and a naturally shaped body. She is almost freestanding. The change can be seen in

Fig. 12.7 The north portal, Chartres Cathedral

Clockwise from top left:

Fig. 12.8 Abraham and Isaac, the north portal, Chartres Cathedral

Fig. 12.9 St Modeste, the north portal, Chartres Cathedral

Fig. 12.10 St Anne on the central trumeau of the north portal at Chartres Cathedral. The mother of the Virgin Mary holds her as a baby.

comparison to the figure of St Anne on the central trumeau (Fig. 12.10). In a very natural gesture, St Modeste gracefully lifts her mantle, raises her hand and gently inclines her head to one side.

The south portal – High Gothic (13th century)

Theme of the south portal sculpture

The south portal is dedicated to Jesus Christ, his apostles and his church (Fig. 12.11).

The human figure

The figure of Christ on the central trumeau is completely different to the harsh Romanesque judge of sinners. This Christ has a gentle facial expression and his gestures shows him to be a more caring figure. He is a teacher (with a book) and he holds the other hand in a blessing for mankind (Fig. 12.12).

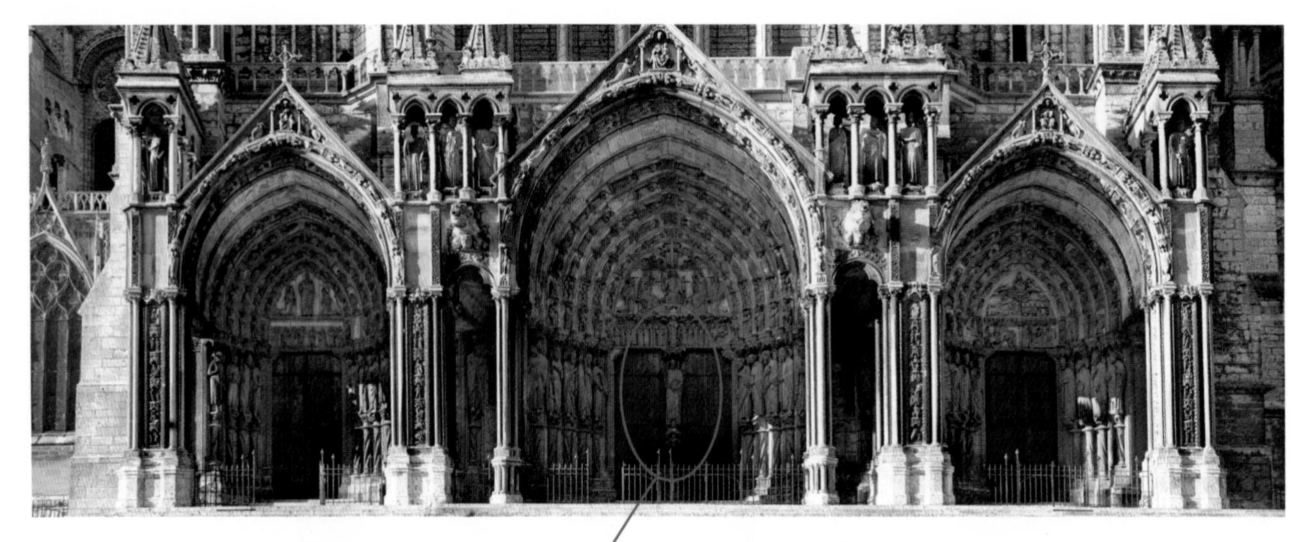

Fig. 12.11 The south portal at Chartres Cathedral

Jesus Christ as teacher

Cruciform nimbus (halo) behind his head

Lifelike human gestures and expression; peaceful and calm appearance

Right hand is lifted in blessing

Christ as the teacher holds a book in his hand

Clothing falls in naturalistic folds

Gentle, refined imagery

He is the shepherd who gave his life for mankind

He welcomes the visitor

Fig. 12.12 Jesus Christ blessing on the central trumeau of the south portal at Chartres Cathedral

Reims Cathedral

Reims is one of the most important High Gothic cathedrals of 13th-century France (Fig. 12.13). The west front is laden with elegant architectural sculpture. A rose window instead of sculpture in the tympanum is an unusual feature of the three doorways.

The human figure

The figures are almost freestanding. They have become very realistic in gesture and facial expressions (Fig. 12.14 and Fig. 12.15).

Fig. 12.13 Tympanum at Reims Cathedral. The Coronation of the Virgin is the most important image on the cathedral.

Fig. 12.14 (left)
Virgin Mary and St Elizabeth, Reims Cathedral. Mary with her cousin Elizabeth shows the influence of Roman statuary.

Fig. 12.15 (right)
The Smiling Angel of Reims. The graceful smiling Angel Gabriel has an elongated body and contrapposto pose. It is the emblem for the city.

Late Gothic sculpture

The 14th century brought many changes in art. The church and the feudal system had less influence. Wealthy individuals now commissioned art.

Curved poses

The most noticeable change in sculpture was the portrayal of religious figures in a more real and human way. Curved poses became fashionable (Fig. 12.16).

The Naumburg master

Artists who learned their craft in France often travelled to other countries. One such talented sculptor is known only as the Naumburg master because of his work in St Peter and Paul's Cathedral in Naumburg, Germany.

Ekkehard and Uta

Twelve statues represent the founders of the church. The most famous are Count Ekkehard and

Fig. 12.16 The Virgin of Notre Dame. The exaggerated S curve posture is typical of the 14th-century Late Gothic style and her garments fall gracefully from her outstretched hip. She is a very real mother smiling tenderly at her baby.

Fig. 12.17 Ekkehard and Uta, Naumburg Cathedral, Germany. The figures have amazingly detailed clothing, faces and hands and a real human quality. Uta seems to feel the cold and pulls her heavy ermine cloak to her face. Uta is said to have influenced Walt Disney in the creation of some of his own cartoon queens.

his wife, Uta (Fig. 12.17). They are completely real looking. The figures were originally painted and still have some bright colours.

Claus Sluter

Claus Sluter was a creative and powerful sculptor in the late Middle Ages. He was one of the first artist to create realistic, lifelike characters.

He moved to France from the Netherlands to work for the Dukes of Burgundy in the magnificent monastery of Chartreuse de Champmol outside Dijon. The monastery and the works of art suffered great destruction during the French Revolution.

The Well of Moses

The Well of Moses (1396–1404) was Claus Sluter's most celebrated sculpture. Some of the drama from this large sculptural composition has been lost because a great cross that once stood on top of the fountain was destroyed (Fig. 12.18). A single kneeling figure of Mary Magdalene was at the foot of this cross.

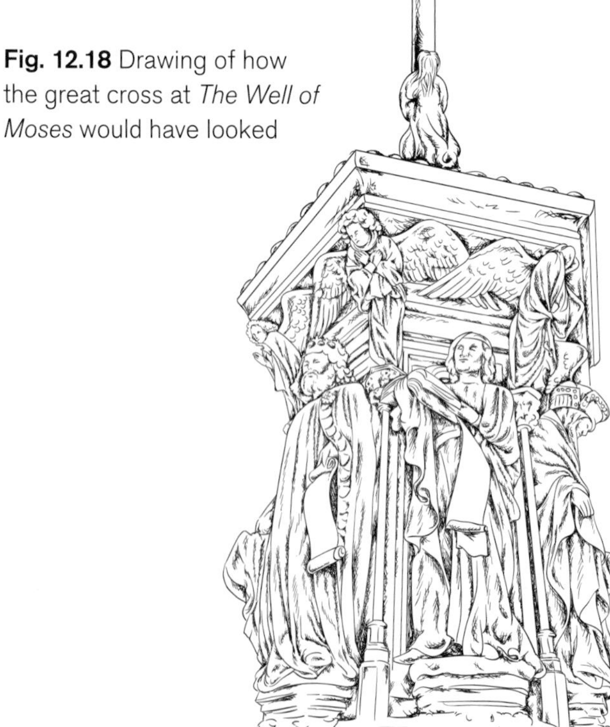

Fig. 12.18 Drawing of how the great cross at *The Well of Moses* would have looked

Theme

The original name, *Fons Vitae*, meant 'fountain of everlasting life'. This symbolised the blood of Christ flowing over the grieving angels and Old Testament prophets and bringing redemption to all those who drank from the well.

The figures are Moses, David, Jeremiah, Zachariah, Daniel and Isaiah. A weeping angel hovers over each one. These were called 'pleurants' (weepers).

Composition

Old Testament prophets frequently appeared in Gothic sculpture, but Claus Sluter's group composition was quite unique for its time. The six life-sized prophets (Fig. 12.19) around the base of the fountain were designed to be seen at eye level, and the hexagonal shape of the base meant the viewer would have to walk around the structure to see them.

The composition unfortunately lacks its full impact due to the missing crucifixion scene. The cross and figure were set well above eye level and the viewer had to look high up to contemplate Christ's agony. It also gave the work its full meaning as the 'fountain of life'.

Style

Claus Sluter was extremely innovative in style and was one of the first to show real individual characters in sculpture. Each one of the figures has a distinct personality and an individual expression, almost like actors on a stage.

The work clearly shows the transition from the stylised International Gothic style to the earthly naturalism of the Early Renaissance style. This is seen best in the exquisite detail on the faces of the angels and prophets. The naturally flowing drapery, rich skin and hair textures are some of Sluter's most admired artistic qualities.

Materials

Sluter and his assistants worked with limestone, which they crafted into the figures, pillar and crucifixion scene. After they were carved, the figures were handed over to artists who carefully decorated them in colour and partly gilded them. Traces of this colour and gilding can still be seen.

Stylised: Depicted or treated in a particular, non-realistic style.

Gilded: Covered in a thin layer of gold leaf.

Fig. 12.19 *The Well of Moses* by Claus Sluter

Chapter review

* Gothic sculpture developed from Romanesque sculpture. Can you identify some of the most important new features?
* If you were to make a drawing of how *The Well of Moses* looked originally, what colours would you use for the figures and where would you place the cross?

EXAM QUESTIONS

Higher Level (2014)

Name and discuss the sculpture in Fig. 12.19, making reference to the sculptor, theme, composition, style and the period in which it was produced.

and

Name a cathedral from this period and briefly describe and discuss its main architectural features.

Illustrate your answer.

Higher Level (2013)

'The façade of a Gothic cathedral must have made a powerful impression on approaching worshippers.'

Discuss this statement with reference to **one** named Gothic cathedral you have studied. In your discussion, refer to architectural features and sculptural decoration.

and

Briefly describe the role of stained glass in a Gothic cathedral (see Chapter 13).

Illustrate your answer.

Higher Level (2009)

'During the Gothic period in Europe, the range and style of religious sculpture developed significantly.'

Discuss this statement in relation to **two** named examples of Gothic sculpture you have studied. Emphasise the treatment of the human figure in your answer.

and

Name a Gothic church you have studied and discuss briefly the relationship between its architecture and sculpture.

Use sketches to illustrate your answer.

FURTHER RESEARCH

www.khanacademy.org – Sluter, Well of Moses

www.wga.hu – Well of Moses by Claus Sluter

wellofmoses.weebly.com

Chapter 13

Gothic Stained Glass

The art of stained glass

The art of stained glass reached new heights during the Gothic period. The magnificent coloured sunlight scattered a mosaic of transparent rubies, emerald and gold on all who walked below.

Abbot Suger believed that beauty brought people closer to God. He wanted the stained glass in St Denis to 'shine with the wonderful light'.

By the end of this chapter, I will...

* Be able to discuss how stained glass was used to tell a story.
* Be able to name the various shapes of stained glass windows.
* Know how to describe, draw, label and annotate important examples of stained glass windows.
* Understand the technique used in making a stained glass window.

Making a stained glass window

The same basic method for making stained glass windows has been in use since medieval times.

Step 1: The artist makes a coloured design on a small scale. A full-size drawing, called a cartoon, which emphasises the leading (see Step 3), is made on paper. In medieval times a whitewashed board or table was used for the cartoon. Pieces of glass (white or coloured) are cut to shape and laid on the cartoon.

Step 2: Black or dark brown enamel paint is used to paint details and textures. The glass is then fired in a muffle kiln to fix the painting.

Step 3: Leading in a variety of cross-sections is very flexible.

Step 4: The painted glass is laid back on the cartoon and the leading is fitted around it and cut to size.

Step 5: In larger windows, iron bars are set in the frames and wired onto the leading to provide additional strength and support against wind pressure.

Step 6: The joints in the leading are soldered.

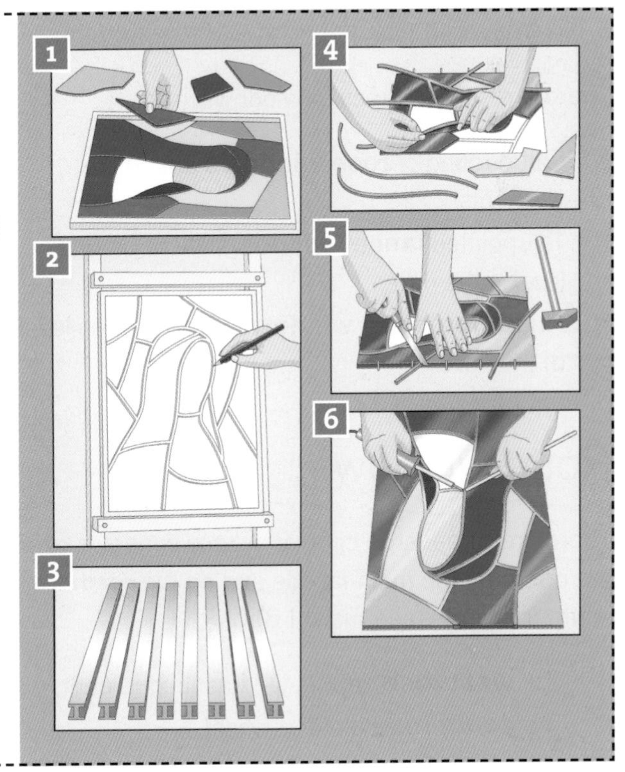

Stories in the glass

The Abbot Suger was the first to use stained glass for teaching purposes, but the glass at St Denis has been mostly destroyed.

Stained glass at Chartres

Chartres Cathedral has one of the most complete collections of medieval stained glass in the world. Amazingly, it survived the French Revolution and World War I intact. In 1939 it was removed and stored for safety and was later cleaned and replaced.

Stained glass was extremely expensive, but Chartres had many wealthy donors. Like sculpture, it was intended to be educational; each window had a story to tell. Scenes from the life of Christ and his mother, as well as the saints and the miracles associated with them, were all represented.

The narratives were told in detail, episode by episode, in the coloured glass panels. These stories are more easily followed in the tall ground-level windows. They read from the bottom up and from left to right (see Fig. 11.6 and Fig. 11.7).

There are several types of windows:

* Large round or **rose windows** are on the transepts.
* Tall, pointed **lancet windows** are at ground level in the nave.
* Huge **clerestory windows** are at the top level of the nave.

Rose windows

There are three large circular or rose windows over the doors on the main façade and on the north and south transepts (see Fig. 11.8).

* The **west rose** depicts the Last Judgement.
* The **south rose** glorifies Christ.
* The **north rose** is dedicated to the glorification of the Virgin. This and its five lancet windows below were a gift from Queen Blanche of Castille.

The Blue Virgin window

The four central panels of the Blue Virgin window (Fig. 13.2) survived the fire of 1194 and were set into a new 13th-century lancet window. The panels are square, but an ornamental frame in the pattern of the glass creates the impression of a long, narrow rectangular-shaped window.

Subject

Mary is crowned and enthroned as Queen of Heaven and Earth. Her lap forms a throne for her son, who lifts his hand in blessing. He holds an open book showing the prophecy of his birth.

The panel just above her head represents the Kingdom of Heaven, with the white dove of the Holy Spirit. The angels on either side and below hold up her throne.

Colour

The Virgin and Child are set against a rich ruby-red background. Mary's halo and clothing are a luminous blue. A deeper blue in the background of the new panels creates an overall image of a blue window. Appropriately, this blue has become known in stained glass terms as 'Chartres blue'.

Composition

The window can be divided into two parts. The four square panels of the Virgin dominate the upper half. These are surrounded by panels with angels. The lower half features six panels showing scenes from the marriage feast at Cana and the three temptations of Christ.

These scenes have quite a quite different pattern and include medallions on each of their four corners.

Fig. 13.1 The Blue Virgin, or Notre Dame de la Belle Verrière, is the most famous window at Chartres Cathedral.

Fig. 13.2 The Blue Virgin of Chartres Cathedral. These panels survived the fire of 1194.

Fig. 13.3 Plan of the Blue Virgin window at Chartres Cathedral

Fourteenth-century stained glass

Sainte-Chapelle

Sainte-Chapelle in the centre of Paris is a small but perfect example of the Rayonnant style of Gothic architecture (Fig. 13.4).

King Louis IX (St Louis) was a renowned patron of the arts. He paid a fortune for important relics, including the Crown of Thorns, so he wanted Sainte-Chapelle to be perfect.

There are two churches, one above the other. The lower chapel was the parish church for the palace. The upper chapel was for the relics.

The glass

The wall of glass at Sainte-Chapelle (Fig. 13.5) creates a purplish haze, giving the chapel its famous magical atmosphere. However, this is actually a result of poor craftsmanship. It is important to separate the small panes of blue and red so that the colours do not blend, but pressure to produce at Sainte-Chapelle meant standards slipped. As a result, the narrative scenes are impossible to make out.

Destruction during the Revolution

Sainte-Chapelle suffered great damage during the French Revolution. The sculpture was hacked off the tympanum and the spire was pulled down, but the glass survived.

Chapter review

* Stained glass was not a new art, but the great Gothic cathedrals brought it to new level. Do you think it was the 'heavenly' light that Abbot Suger hoped would lift people's souls closer to God?
* Do you think that the average person of the time could read stories in the glass more easily than now? Why is that?

Fig. 13.4 (left) Church of Sainte-Chapelle, Paris. The exterior of Sainte-Chapelle has typical characteristics of the Late Gothic Rayonnant style, like deep buttresses surmounted by ornate pinnacles. The spire was replaced in the 19th century.

Fig. 13.5 (right) Stained glass windows in Sainte-Chapelle, Paris. The tall, narrow lancet windows create the most amazing atmosphere in a haze of purplish light.

EXAM QUESTIONS

Ordinary Level (2015)

The Gothic church of Sainte-Chapelle, Paris, celebrated for its stained glass windows, is shown in Fig. 13.4 and Fig. 13.5.

Answer (a) and (b).

(a) Describe and discuss the exterior and interior of this church.

(b) Briefly describe and discuss how a stained glass window is made.

Illustrate your answer.

Higher Level (2013)

'The façade of a Gothic cathedral must have made a powerful impression on approaching worshippers.'

Discuss this statement with reference to **one** named Gothic cathedral you have studied. In your discussion, refer to architectural features and sculptural decoration.

and

Briefly describe the role of stained glass in a Gothic cathedral.

Illustrate your answer.

FURTHER RESEARCH

www.sacred-destinations.com – Chartres Cathedral

www.khanacademy.org – Cathedral of Notre Dame de Chartres (parts 1–3)

www.medievalart.org.uk – Chartres Cathedral Stained Glass – Bay 30a, Notre Dame de la Belle Verrière

Chapter 14

The International Style

French Gothic art spread to the rest of Europe and became known as the 'International Style'. The works were often small: artists moved from place to place seeking work and patronage from princes of the church and state, so they had to carry their materials with them. Also, smaller work was made for private devotion and as a focus for prayer in the private chambers of the wealthy.

By the end of this chapter, I will...

* Know the main characteristics of the International Style.
* Understand why the *Wilton Diptych* is such a precious work of art.
* Know why *Les Très Riches Heures Du Duc De Berry* is regarded as one the finest examples of painting in the International Style.
* Be able to describe, draw and discuss particular pages from this book.
* Know the materials and techniques used to create these paintings.

Typical characteristics of the International Style:

* Delicate and refined
* Decorative patterns and rich colours
* Raised areas of gold leaf-patterned surfaces (gilding)
* Highly realistic floral and landscape details
* Elongated, elegant figures in curved poses wearing exceptionally fine clothing
* Delicate facial features, blonde hair and sweet, gentle expressions and gestures

Diptych: Two panels hinged together.

Triptych: Three panels hinged together.

Polyptych: Many panels hinged together.

Wilton Diptych

The *Wilton Diptych* (Fig. 14.1) is one of the most beautiful examples of the International Style. This small painting shows a blend of subtle colouring, graceful line and sharpness of detail that is typical of the style.

Two wooden panels are hinged together and close like a book to protect the painting and to make it portable. The size of each panel is 53cm x 37cm (smaller than an A2 page).

The artist is unknown but was likely to have been French or English.

Subject

When closed, the outer panels of the diptych show a white stag, the emblem of Richard II, and a shield with the coat of arms of Edward the Confessor. The

Fig. 14.1
Wilton Diptych, 1395–9, egg tempera on oak panel, National Gallery, London

inner panels depict King Richard II being presented to the Virgin and Child by his patrons, making it both a religious/devotional painting and a royal portrait.

Style and composition

The importance of line and composition is emphasised by the painting's refined style. This is seen in the delicate floral motifs and gentle expressions and gestures. The elongated figures of the Virgin and angels stand in elegant curved poses, with robes falling into soft folds, and all have long, tapering fingers.

The Virgin is surrounded by angels in foreshortened poses such as the kneeling angel on the left side, and the panels connect very subtly through the glances and gestures. Even though they are in separate worlds the figures turn toward each other. Mary holds her son's foot to show where the nails will be driven, but Christ pulls away from her to lean towards the king and offer his blessing. The young king in turn opens his hands to receive it and stares intently at the child. This portrays Richard's belief in his divine right to rule.

Materials and techniques

The panels are painted using egg tempera, applied in thin glazes onto an oak panel. The background and other details are decorated with gold tooling.

Colour

The panel on the right depicts the Virgin dressed in brilliant blue robes. This colour was made from very expensive lapis lazuli (see Fig. 15.9). She stands in a heavenly meadow strewn with flowers and surrounded by angels. They are dressed in the same blue and the tall, elegant wings have blue tips. The Christ child wears cloth of gold (the most expensive cloth of all).

On the opposite panel, the young king's magnificent cloak is coloured with gold and vermilion red, another very expensive pigment.

The roses in the angels' hair have faded. They were once a richer pink and the green of the grass is now darker.

Egg tempera: A mix of pigment, egg yolk and gum arabic.

Gilding: Applying gold leaf over a surface.

Glazes: Thin layers of transparent paint applied on top of one another to build depth and modify the colours in a painting.

Gold leaf: Gold beaten into thin sheets and used to cover surfaces.

Gold tooling: Embossing a decorative design through a sheet of gold leaf. The surface beneath may be 'tooled' over cut wood to form a pattern.

Pigment: Dry colourants made from a variety of natural materials that were ground into a fine powder.

Les Très Riches Heures Du Duc De Berry (The Very Rich Hours of the Duke of Berry)

Books were all handwritten and some were illustrated by artists. These are called illuminated (painted) manuscripts. A Books of Hours contained appropriate prayers for specific hours of the day, days of the week, months and seasons.

Les Très Riches Heures Du Duc De Berry is one of the most beautiful examples of the International Style (Fig. 14.2, Fig. 14.3 and Fig. 14.4).

Artists Jean and Paul de Limbourg from the Netherlands painted it for Jean Duc du Berry. The duke was brother to the King of France and extremely wealthy. He was a strong patron of the arts. He and the artists all died of the plague before the book was completed.

Subject

This is a book of prayer, but the imagery also features the duke and his beautiful castles, possessions and courtiers. The calendar pages are the most famous, featuring 12 full-page miniature paintings.

Fig. 14.2 *Les Très Riches Heures Du Duc De Berry*, 1412–16, illumination on parchment, Musée Condé, Chantilly – January. The scene shows a feast with elegant courtiers in colourful clothing. The duke wears a brilliant blue velvet robe and fur hat. His prized gold tableware is on the table and his small pet dogs are eating the scraps.

Size

Bound with red leather, the book is quite large at 29cm x 21cm (the size of an A3 sketchbook).

Materials

The manuscript is painted on parchment (sheep or goat skin, vellum being calf skin). The paint pigment was mixed with water and thickened with gum arabic to make sure it would stick to the vellum. Colours included black, white, pink, violet, three shades of red and two shades each of blue, green and yellow.

Fig. 14.3 *Les Très Riches Heures Du Duc De Berry*, 1412–16, illumination on parchment, Musée Condé, Chantilly – February. Snow covers the land and peasants go about their chores. It gives a real picture of medieval life. The farm has a sheep pen, beehives, barrels, bales of straw and even hooded crows pecking at the straw on the ground. Inside the farmer's house, a woman warms herself at the fire. She turns from the crude peasants lifting their garments – one is male, the other is female.

Fig. 14.4 *Les Très Riches Heures Du Duc De Berry*, 1412–16, illumination on parchment, Musée Condé, Chantilly – April. It is early spring and green is the dominant colour. Blossoms grow on the fruit trees in the walled garden and ladies pick flowers. In the foreground, a couple exchange rings. This is the duke's granddaughter and the engagement means an alliance between two families who were previously at war.

Gum arabic: A natural gum made from the hardened sap of the acasia tree.

Style

The paintings are highly realistic and are filled with the finest detail.

Chapter review

* The International Style was a sophisticated style that developed among the royalty and higher nobility. Which characteristics do you think appealed most to the nobility? Why do you think that?

EXAM QUESTIONS

Ordinary Level (2010)

The *Wilton Diptych* (Fig. 14.1) is an example of the International Gothic style of painting.

Answer (a) and (b).

(a) Describe this painting using the following headings:

- Subject matter
- Composition
- Use of colour

(b) Give some general information about the International Gothic style.

Use sketches to illustrate your answer.

FURTHER RESEARCH

www.nationalgallery.org.uk – The Wilton Diptych

www.history.ac.uk – The Wilton Diptych

www.khanacademy.org – Wilton Diptych

Chapter 15

Fourteenth-Century Painting in Italy

This period is sometimes called the Proto Renaissance. The term refers to painting and sculpture created in Italy between 1280 and 1400. This is an interim period between Gothic and the Renaissance. It can also be called the Trecento, which is Italian for 300 and is short for *mille trecento*, 1300.

By the end of this chapter, I will...

* Know that Cimabue and Giotto changed from the Italian Byzantine style to realism.
* Be able to discuss what was new and innovative in Giotto's style.
* Be able to draw and annotate three works by Giotto.
* Know how to describe and discuss at least three works by Giotto in detail.
* Know the steps of the fresco technique.
* Be able to write about how Giotto influenced Masaccio.

Cimabue and Giotto

Cimabue was a painter and a mosaic artist in the 13th century. He came from Florence but worked in Rome for the pope and in Assisi for the Franciscans. He was one of the last to work in the Italian Byzantine style and the first to bring realism to Western art. He was very famous in his time but is now better known for his student, Giotto di Bondone.

Byzantine art

Byzantine art refers to art from Byzantium (it became Constantinople and is now Istanbul), which was originally part of the eastern Roman Empire. The art was the accepted manner of religious painting in Italy. Realism was avoided because it was associated with pagan Rome.

Fig 15.1 The most famous Byzantine painting, the Hodegetria icon, was widely copied. St Luke the Apostle was believed to have painted the Virgin Mary from life.

Characteristics of the Byzantine style:

* A solemn, flat, stylised appearance
* Rich gold background
* Unreal figures

Stylised: Depicted or treated in a particular non-realistic style.

St Francis of Assisi

St Francis of Assisi preferred realistic art because it explained the scriptures to ordinary people. The Franciscans persuaded the pope to employ artists who worked in a real and lifelike manner.

Cimabue painted frescoes in the little church of Assisi. The figures had correct proportions and shading, but unfortunately it is now in a very poor state of repair.

Giotto di Bondone (c.1267–1337)

Giotto di Bondone was apprenticed to Cimabue in Florence and he soon surpassed his master. As a successful artist, he worked for the richest and most influential people in Florence and beyond.

Giotto's innovations

Giotto's figures were lifelike and natural and were set against realistic backgrounds. His innovations included:

* Correct proportions
* Foreshortening
* Light and shade
* Facial expression and gesture to show human emotion

Giotto's life

The most famous story about Giotto was by biographer Giorgio Vasari. His wrote that Cimabue found the boy on a hillside drawing sheep on a slate and brought him back to Florence as his apprentice.

Giotto's career

Giotto worked in Florence but he also travelled to northern Italy. He painted a very famous series of frescoes in Padua.

Influences

Giotto's influence by Roman frescoes and the sculptures of the Pisano brothers, who worked in Pisa, can be seen in the Arena Chapel frescoes. Giotto's work was greatly admired, but after his death realism fell out of favour again. It was to be 100 years before Masaccio revived the great master's style.

Works

Madonna Enthroned

Images of the Madonna were objects of devotion, like relics, and popular as altarpieces.

A comparison between Giotto's version of *Madonna Enthroned*, or *Madonna Ognissanti (All Saints)* (Fig. 15.2), with Cimabue's *Madonna Enthroned with Angels* shows the changes in style. Compared with Cimabue's more traditional imagery (Fig. 15.3), Giotto's work shows real space and depth. The figure is lifelike and he uses perspective.

Fig. 15.2 *Ognissanti Madonna (Madonna Enthroned)*, c. 1310, by Giotto, tempera on wood, Uffizi Gallery, Florence

Fig. 15.3 *Madonna Enthroned with Angels* by Cimabue, Uffizi Gallery, Florence

Altarpieces: Large devotional works of art placed on, above or behind the altars of churches. They were later replaced with tabernacles to hold the Blessed Sacrament in Roman Catholic churches.

Arena Chapel

This was the family chapel of the wealthy Enrico Scrovegni. He was a great admirer of the Franciscans. He employed Giotto to cover the walls with scenes from the life of Mary and Jesus (Fig. 15.4). The paintings are set out like a comic book strip. Architectural detail is painted around the scenes to resemble marble.

The Lament for Christ

Subject

Giotto depicts the scene from the Bible where Jesus is taken down from the cross and presented to his mother, Mary (Fig. 15.5).

Dramatic foreshortening, individual gestures and facial expressions give the characters real human emotion. Surrounded by the other distraught mourners, Mary cradles her son. Angels above

Fig. 15.4 Arena Chapel, Padua

wring their hands and cry out in grief. Two mourners have their backs to the viewer.

Composition

The composition brings the eye to Mary and the lifeless figure of Christ. The background shows a real space with a diagonal jagged rock and leafless tree.

Fig. 15.5 *The Lament for Christ* (also known as *The Deposition*) by Giotto di Bondone, Arena Chapel, Padua

The Kiss of Judas

Subject

Giotto depicts the scene from the Bible in which Jesus is betrayed by Judas (Fig. 15.6). It is a powerful image of good and evil.

Composition

The huge semi-circle of the cloak is central to the composition. It focuses attention on the faces: one serene and dignified, the other evil and repellent.

Fig. 15.6 *The Kiss of Judas* by Giotto di Bondone, Arena Chapel, Padua

Joachim and Anne at the Golden Gate

The gestures of greeting in *Joachim and Anne at the Golden Gate* (Fig. 15.7) could not be more different from *The Kiss of Judas*. Joachim and Anne embrace with great tenderness after she tells him she is to bear a child.

Fig. 15.7 *Joachim and Anne at the Golden Gate* by Giotto di Bondone, Arena Chapel, Padua

The Flight into Egypt

This fresco shows a problem with the blue paint Giotto used: the blue of Mary's mantle and the sky has disappeared. Giotto used azurite rather than the more expensive lapis lazuli to make blue. This was not compatible with lime in the wet plaster and was applied dry, or *a secco*.

Fig. 15.8 *The Flight into Egypt* by Giotto di Bondone, Arena Chapel, Padua. The colour has flaked off during the years because lapis lazuli was too expensive, so Giotto used azurite, which could only be applied to dry plaster.

Fig. 15.9 Lapis lazuli. 'Lapis' means stone in Latin and 'azul' means blue in Arabic. This deep blue gemstone is ground down to make ultramarine ('from beyond the seas'), which is one of the most important colours in art. The stone is found only in the rough mountains of Afghanistan, making it so expensive that artists usually quoted prices for blue separately.

Fresco painting

1. The bare masonry was covered in a layer of plaster.
2. A composition was sketched in *sinopia* (red chalk).
3. The painter applied enough smooth plaster for one day's work (*a giornata*).
4. Azurite blue was sometimes added *a secco*, or on dry plaster, at the end.

Chapter review

* Giotto was one of the first artists to paint in a more naturalistic way. Why do you think other artists did not follow his direction?
* Giotto's techniques for conveying emotion were particularly effective. Try acting out some of these gestures in class.

EXAM QUESTIONS

Ordinary Level (2012)

The Kiss of Judas by Giotto (c.1266–1337) is shown in Fig. 15.6.

Answer (a) and (b).

(a) Describe and discuss this work using the following headings:

- Subject matter and composition
- Colour
- Perspective

(b) Name and briefly discuss **one** other artist from this period.

Illustrate your answer.

Higher Level (2014)

'Giotto (c.1267–1337) created an illusion of depth on a flat surface and portrayed dramatic events as if they were happening on a stage.'

Discuss this statement with reference to a named work by Giotto, commenting on subject matter, composition, style and the techniques used in his work.

and

Name and briefly discuss **one** other work by this artist.

Illustrate your answer.

FURTHER RESEARCH

www.khanacademy.org –
Giotto, The Ognissanti Madonna

www.khanacademy.org –
Giotto, Arena (Scrovegni) Chapel (parts 1–4)

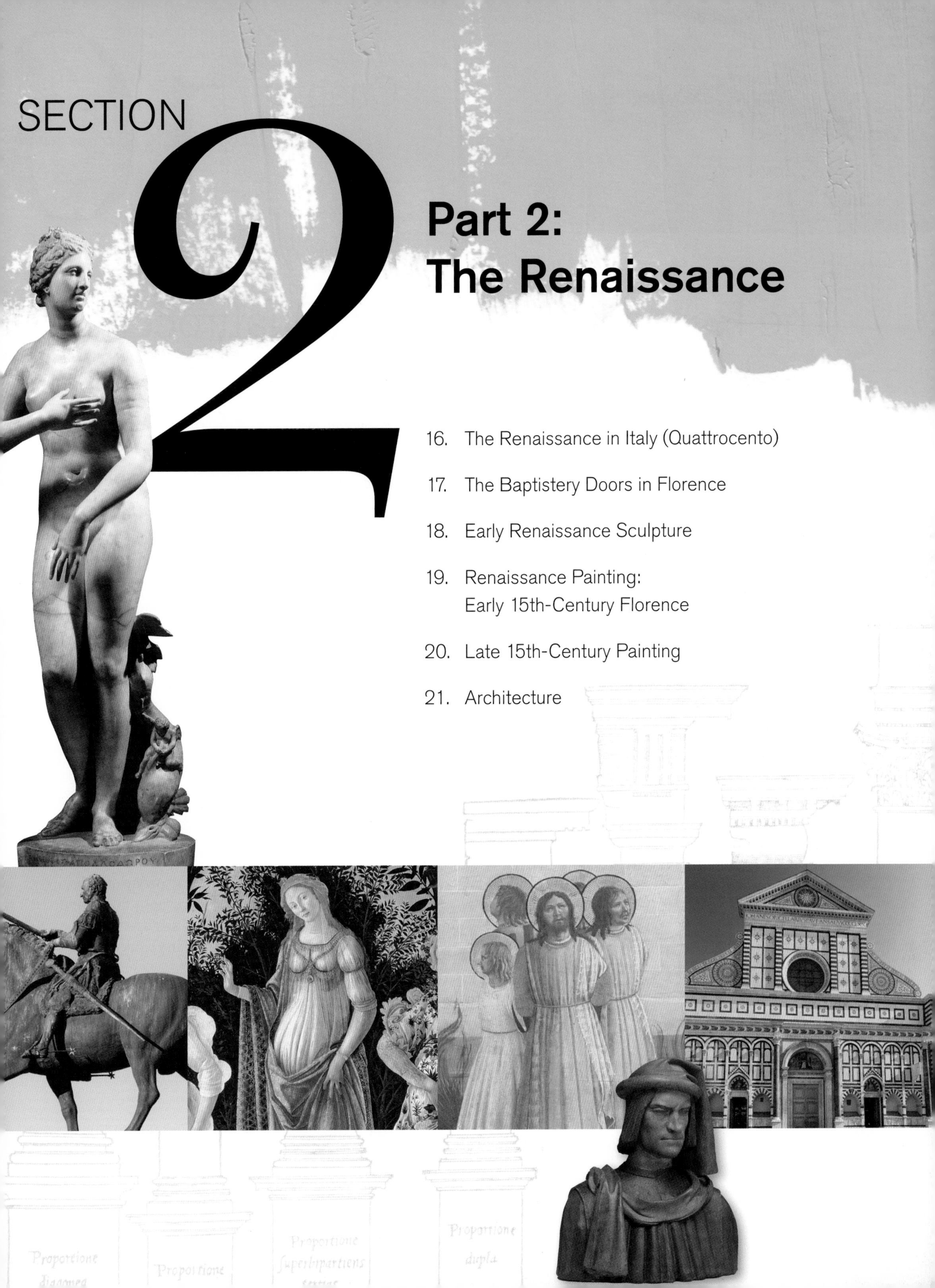

SECTION 2

Part 2: The Renaissance

Chapter 16

The Renaissance in Italy (Quattrocento)

The Renaissance was an extraordinary period of art and culture that spread throughout Europe in the 15th and 16th centuries. It was inspired by ancient Greek and Roman literature and art. The period is also called the Quattrocento, which means 400 and refers to Italy in the 1400s or 15th century (Fig. 16.1).

By the end of this chapter, I will...

* Know the influence of classical culture on Renaissance art.
* Understand the influence of humanism on art.
* Be familiar with the way in which artists worked with patrons.

NOTE! The word 'Renaissance' is French and means 'rebirth'. A French historian first used the term in the mid-19th century.

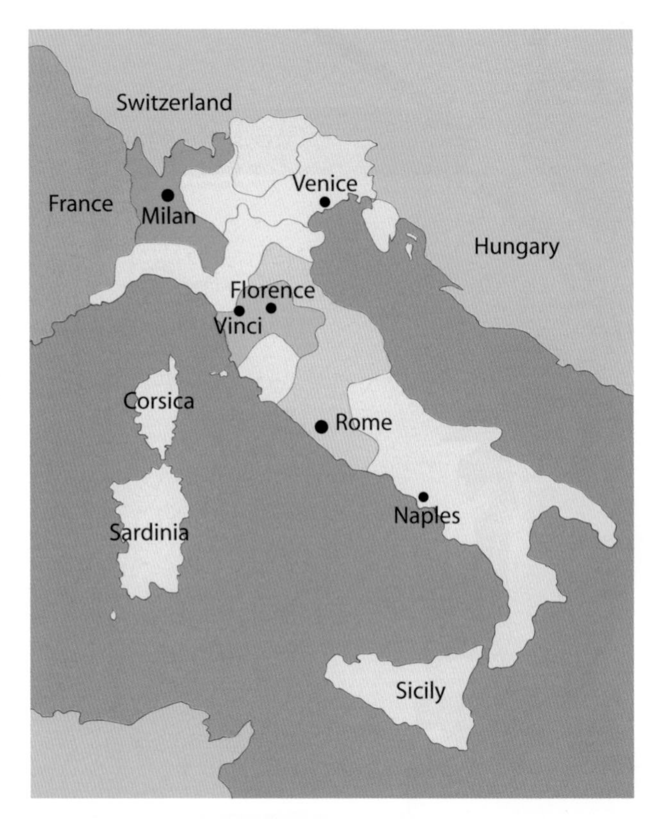

Fig. 16.1 Renaissance Italy. The Italian peninsula was a series of independent states ruled over by dukes and princes. They employed many artists and spent huge amounts of money on fine buildings and works of art.

Renaissance humanism

Renaissance art was driven primarily by the new ideas of humanism. This was a cultural and intellectual movement based on the rediscovery and re-evaluation of classical civilisation (Greece and Rome). It promoted the study of original texts in literature and surviving works of art from these ancient times.

Humanists believed that:

* Humanity and life on earth were also important.
* The individual has beauty, worth and dignity.
* The human ability to learn and create were God-given gifts.
* There was harmony between the philosophy of Greece and Rome and Christian belief.

Florence: The birthplace of the Renaissance

These new ideas began in Florence (Fig. 16.2). This small city-state was a thriving centre of trade and culture with a high standard of living. There were many wealthy people there who believed in humanism and the dignity of man.

Artists

In the Early Renaissance, the term 'artist' did not really exist. Painters and sculptors were considered merely craftsmen and they had to work hard to get good commissions. Sometimes they entered competitions, but the most important thing was to have a patron.

Patronage

There were many private patrons in Renaissance Florence. Religion was an integral part of life and wealthy families commissioned religious works of art for churches and private chapels. They decided on the subject matter, style and all the important details of the work.

Patrons of art were:

* Wealthy private citizens
* Religious orders
* The guilds of Florence
* Rulers and princes of the Italian states

The guilds of Florence

These associations of master craftsmen were extremely powerful and virtually controlled the city's government.

Many members of the guilds had humanist values. They wanted the classical style (the style of Greece and Rome) to be used for the sculpture and buildings of the city.

The Medici: Rulers of Florence and patrons of art

The Medici family made their fortune in banking for the pope. Cosimo il Vecchio (Cosimo the Old) became ruler of Florence in 1424. He was followed by his son Piero and his grandson Lorenzo, better known as Lorenzo the Magnificent (Fig. 16.3).

The Medici were tough, but Florence prospered and the arts flourished. They were patrons to artists like Donatello, Botticelli and Michelangelo. Florence became the cultural inspiration for other Italian states.

Fig. 16.2 City of Florence, Italy

Fig. 16.3 *Lorenzo de' Medici*, probably after a model by Andrea del Verrocchio and Orsino Benintendi, painted terracotta, National Gallery of Art, Washington, DC

The artist as genius

As the Renaissance progressed, the status of the artist changed. They were more respected and their ideas were considered to be important. It became a status symbol for wealthy patrons to have a famous artist working for them.

Chapter review

* Many patrons of art in Florence were humanists as well as deeply religious. How do you think these ideas inspired the great works of Renaissance art?

NOTE! Patrons of art made all the decisions. As a craftsman, the artist's skills were important but his own ideas were rarely considered.

FURTHER RESEARCH

www.visitflorence.com – What to See in Florence

www.themedicifamily.com – Lorenzo de Medici

www.theflorentine.net – Guilded in Florence

Fig. 16.4

Procession of the Magi, 1459–60, by Benozzo Gozzoli, fresco at Medici Chapel, Medici Palace, Florence. The subject is the arrival of the kings to Bethlehem, but it also shows the wealth and power of the Medici in their magnificent costumes. Cosimo, dressed in black, rides a mule to show his humility. His son Piero rides a white horse with an ornate bridle. Following in the crowd behind are sons Lorenzo and Giuliano.

Chapter 17

The Baptistery Doors in Florence

Florence Cathedral

A new cathedral in Florence was under construction for most of the 14th century. The city welcomed the 15th century with a competition to design new doors for the baptistery. It became the most famous competition in art history.

The cathedral and baptistery of Florence were traditionally the responsibility of the Calimala (wool and cloth merchants' guild).

The baptistery was restored in 1200 and the green and white marble cladding we see today was added. In 1329 the Calimala commissioned Andrea Pisano to design new doors for one of the three entrances.

By the end of this chapter, I will...

* Know why the competition for the baptistery doors became so famous.
* Be able to describe, draw and discuss the layout and design of the baptistery doors by Andrea Pisano and the two new doors by Lorenzo Ghiberti.
* Be able to compare the themes, style and technique of Ghiberti's early panels with those on his later 'Gates of Paradise'.

Fig. 17.1
Florence Cathedral and Baptistery

The first baptistery doors (Andrea Pisano)

The first baptistery doors by Andrea Pisano:

* Were cast entirely in bronze
* Had 28 scenes in quatrefoil shapes based on the life of St John the Baptist
* Were partially gilded (the figures were covered in thin gold leaf)

Quatrefoil: A shape commonly used in medieval architecture of four arcs linked together.

Fig. 17.2 Baptistery of St John the Baptist, south door, by Andrea Pisano, Florence. Fourteen scenes each on the left and right doors illustrate the life of John the Baptist on one side and his death on the other.

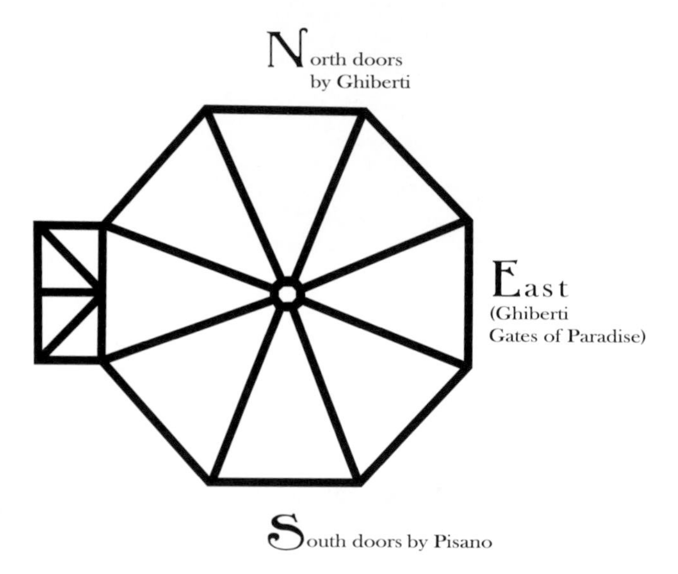

Fig. 17.3 Plan of the baptistery showing the position of the doors

The competition for the second baptistery doors

In 1400 the Calimala instigated a competition to design new doors for the east façade.

The rules required contestants to:

* Submit a model panel featuring the biblical scene of the sacrifice of Isaac as a relief sculpture in gilded bronze
* Follow precise specified details
* Maintain the quatrefoil framing shape.
* Match Andrea Pisano's original doors on the south

Seven artists competed, but it quickly came down to two intense young rivals: Filippo Brunelleschi and Lorenzo Ghiberti (Fig. 17.4). Ghiberti's bronze panel was in one piece. Brunelleschi's was cast in several pieces and then bolted together.

Ghiberti was awarded the commission because of his superior technical skills. Brunelleschi was bitterly disappointed and left immediately for Rome.

Fig. 17.4
Models of the sacrifice of Isaac by Brunelleschi (left) and Ghiberti (right) hanging side by side in the National Museum of Bargello, Florence

Lorenzo Ghiberti

Lorenzo Ghiberti was born near Florence and trained as a goldsmith. He got his first commission at the age of 20 and worked on the baptistery doors all his life.

He spent an intense period studying new ways to compose pictorial space and lifelike figures. He worked as a sculptor, painter, stained glass artist and architect at different stages throughout his life.

Influences

* Leon Battista Alberti influenced Ghiberti's ideas on humanism.
* Donatello was one of Ghiberti's assistants. He went on to become the most prominent sculptor in Florence. He influenced Ghiberti's later work.

The second doors of St John the Baptist

Ghiberti made considerable artistic progress in the new doors. The panels are fuller and more adventurous than Pisano's earlier work.

The scenes show classical influence. The figures are correctly proportioned and have more lifelike gestures (Fig. 17.6).

Fig. 17.5 Baptistery of St Giovanni, north door, by Lorenzo Ghiberti. These doors originally faced the cathedral but were later replaced by the 'Gates of Paradise'.

He used the new art of perspective developed by his rival, Brunelleschi. The second doors:

* Were cast entirely in bronze and partially gilded
* Had 28 scenes based on the life of Christ, set in a quatrefoil shape
* Took 27 years to complete

Fig. 17.6 The flagellation of Christ panel by Lorenzo Ghiberti on the north door of the Baptistery of St Giovanni, Florence. Note the classical influence: Jesus has a gently curved contrapposto pose and is set against an architectural background of classical Corinthian columns.

Contrapposto: This word means 'opposite' in Italian. It was first developed by classical Greek sculptors to create movement. The weight on one leg causes the shoulder and hip lines to slant in opposite directions.

The third baptistery doors (Lorenzo Ghiberti)

Once in place, the doors were such a success that the Calimala commissioned another set. These were for the third door of the Baptistery. By now, Ghiberti was a master craftsman and could make his own decisions. He changed the framing system and created an entirely new design scheme (Fig. 17.7). The new doors had:

* Five fully gilded panels on each side
* A more unified appearance
* Old Testament scenes that were clearer and had several episodes of a story within one panel
* High and low relief to show perspective and real space
* Figures that were correctly proportioned, with lifelike gestures and movement
* Figures in high relief, sometimes almost three-dimensional

Fig. 17.7 A copy of the east doors, or 'Gates of Paradise', by Lorenzo Ghiberti on the Baptistery of St Giovanni, Florence. The original gold panels have been fully restored and are on display in the Museum of the Cathedral.

Jacob and Esau

The panel depicting Jacob and Esau is one of Ghiberti's most masterful and shows many aspects of Renaissance art (Fig. 17.8).

The artist was no longer satisfied with simply representing the figures in typical traditional poses with symbols to identify them. Instead, real figures are depicted in convincingly real space.

Composition

The complex story is clearly told in six parts on the single panel, beginning with Rebecca giving birth attended by the women. It is organised into a horizontal composition (left to right). Single-point perspective leads the eye to the central architectural arch and the various groups of figures. The perspective helps to distinguish one fragment of the narrative from the next.
The receding tiles of the floor illustrate Ghiberti's knowledge of the new art perspective. The arches and pilasters are inspired by Roman architecture.

Fig. 17.8 The Jacob and Esau panel by Lorenzo Ghiberti from the east doors of the Baptistery of St Giovanni, Florence. Esau was so hungry after work in the fields that he gave up his inheritance to his brother Jacob in exchange for food. In his blindness, Isaac mistakenly blesses his younger son, watched by his wife, Rebecca, who set up the deceit.

The human figure

The soft folds of the drapery enhance the natural movement of the body. The elegant women in the foreground are almost freestanding. Their dress and contrapposto poses show the classical influence.

Art takes priority

Ghiberti's Golden Doors are also known as the 'Gates of Paradise'. Legend has it that Michelangelo called them that because of their beauty.

The Calimala were so impressed by their splendour that they moved the second doors with the scenes of the life of Christ to the north façade and placed the new doors with the Old Testament scenes opposite the main cathedral door. This was a groundbreaking decision because it valued art over subject matter.

Chapter review

* Tradition was broken in a radical way when the art on the 'Gates of Paradise' was given priority over subject matter. What made this art so unique?

EXAM QUESTIONS

Higher Level (2015)

'The "Gates of Paradise" in Florence (Fig. 17.7) demonstrate Lorenzo Ghiberti's (c.1378–1455) great skill as a sculptor.'

Discuss this statement with reference to **one** named panel from the doors. In your answer, refer to subject matter, composition, perspective and the treatment of the human figure.

and

Briefly describe and discuss **one** other named sculpture from the Early Renaissance period.

Illustrate your answer.

FURTHER RESEARCH

www.youtube.com – Florence's Gates of Paradise documentary, LDM News, 2012

www.khanacademy.org – Brunelleschi and Ghiberti, the Sacrifice of Isaac

Chapter 18

Early Renaissance Sculpture

Ghiberti was considered the most important sculptor of the early 15th century, but this completely changed when the young Donato di Bardi, better known as Donatello, began to produce his extraordinary work.

By the end of this chapter, I will...

* Understand how the Orsanmichele statues impacted traditional sculpture.
* Know that Donatello showed a new sensitivity to the portrayal of the human figure.
* Be able to discuss how Donatello created the illusion of space and perspective in sculpture.
* Know that Donatello influenced other artists.
* Be able to describe and analyse key works by Renaissance sculptors.
* Know how to draw and annotate key works by Renaissance sculptors.

Donatello (1386–1466)

Donatello was the first to break from the traditional role of sculpture as architectural decoration. For the first time since antiquity, he introduced the:

* Freestanding human figure
* Life-sized nude figure
* Equestrian statue

He was a master in both marble and bronze and created numerous works in Florence, Siena and Padua.

Influences on Donatello

Lorenzo Ghiberti

Donatello trained in Ghiberti's studio and worked on the baptistery doors. Ghiberti was only eight years older but he learned valuable skills in bronze working. This was extremely important in the development of his career.

Nanni di Banco

Donatello also spent time in the sculptural workshop of the cathedral working with Nanni di Banco. They made studies of the human figure by drawing from live models and they developed freestanding sculpture.

Filippo Brunelleschi

He learned the rules of proportion and perspective from Brunelleschi. The two artists travelled to Rome together to study antiquities.

NOTE! The most important influence on Donatello was his studies of the classical sculpture of Rome. This helped him develop his own unique style of art.

Public sculpture in Florence

In the early 15th century, the Signoria (city governors) of Florence asked each of the guilds to produce statues of their patron saints for the new Church of Orsanmichele in the city centre (Fig. 18.1).

Orsanmichele was associated with miracles of the Virgin Mary and this radically new and very public sculpture was placed in niches on the outside walls.

Fig. 18.1 The Church of Orsanmichele, Florence

The huge freestanding statues were just above street level and the people of Florence were delighted with the lifelike figures.

The statues of Orsanmichele

St John the Baptist by Lorenzo Ghiberti

The Calimala (wool and cloth merchants' guild) chose Ghiberti as the sculptor of their patron saint, St John the Baptist (Fig. 18.2). This was the first full bronze statue. Only major guilds could afford such expense.

Fig. 18.2 *St John the Baptist*, 1413, by Ghiberti, Orsanmichele, Florence. Ghiberti's St John the Baptist is in the Late Gothic style. The beautiful drapery falls in elegant folds, but the figure has no real human presence.

The Four Crowned Saints by Nanni di Banco

The Stonemasons' Guild commissioned the only group sculpture on Orsanmichele. It is made of marble (Fig. 18.3).

St Mark by Donatello

The Linen Workers' Guild commissioned Donatello to sculpt St Mark in marble (Fig. 18.4).

St George by Donatello

The Armourers' Guild also chose Donatello to sculpt their patron saint, St George, in marble (Fig. 18.5).

Fame in Donatello's own lifetime

Donatello lived a long life and achieved great fame in his own lifetime. In his biography, Giorgio Vasari said

Clockwise from top:

Fig. 18.3 *The Four Crowned Saints*, 1415, by Nanni di Banco, Orsanmichele, Florence. These four Christian sculptors were executed because they refused to carve an image of a Roman god. Architects, sculptors and stonecutters are depicted on the pedestal below.

Fig. 18.4 *St Mark*, 1412, by Donatello, Orsanmichele, Florence. In contrast to Ghiberti's *St John the Baptist*, Donatello's *St Mark* is oozing with life and energy. He stands in a contrapposto pose staring out on the street with furrowed brow and deep-set eyes.

Fig. 18.5 *St George*, 1416, by Donatello, Orsanmichele, Florence. St George is full of strength and courage. He originally had a real sword and metal helmet, but the warrior knight in classical armour still stands firm, feet resolutely apart, tense and determined. In the words of Vasari, 'Life itself seems to be stirring within the stone.'

Fig. 18.6 *St George and the Dragon.* A panel on the pedestal is the first example of single-point linear perspective in relief sculpture. In a clever illusion of space, St George fighting the dragon is set against a landscape fading into the background.

of the sculptor, 'He possessed invention, design, skill, judgement and all the other qualities that one may reasonably expect to find in an inspired genius.'

Donatello's influence

Donatello's work was a huge influence on many artists, both in his own lifetime and later. He influenced Ghiberti, Masaccio and Michelangelo.

Donatello's works

David

David by Donatello (Fig. 18.7) is one of the most important sculptures of the Early Renaissance. It was the first life-sized freestanding nude figure since classical times.

Subject

The story of the heroic shepherd boy who killed the giant Goliath comes from the Bible. He is described as a perfect, beautiful youth. Donatello captured this youthful beauty perfectly. The gentle S shape of the body echoes classical statues, but the slim youth is quite different to the powerful nudes of ancient Greece.

Composition

David stands with his left foot on the severed head of Goliath. The full composition rests on a laurel wreath, a symbol of victory.

The casual contrapposto stance is graceful and the right hip is thrust slightly outward. However, with the left hand on the left hip, holding an oversized sword, it is also very sensual and effeminate (feminine looking).

The statue stood in the courtyard of the Palazzo Medici and probably symbolised the family's struggle against powerful enemies.

The human figure

Portraying David, a heroic biblical figure, in this way showed his inner strength and power, but it also showed the beauty and sensuality of the human form.

The Feast of Herod

This was Donatello's first relief in bronze (Fig. 18.8). It is organised by the rigorous application of the rules of perspective.

Fig. 18.7 *David*, 1408–9, by Donatello, bronze, Florence. The bronze surface is polished to a different finish for various areas. The skin is highly polished in a blue-black shine, but the hat and hair have a rougher finish.

Fig. 18.8 *The Feast of Herod*, 1427, by Donatello, bronze panel, Siena. This is one of six panels on the baptismal font in the baptistery in Siena.

Subject

The story from the life of St John the Baptist is told in several episodes. The setting is the banqueting hall for King Herod's birthday feast after he asked the beautiful Salome to dance for him. She agreed, but only if he gave her the head of John the Baptist on a platter. The highly emotional scene shows the king recoiling in horror from the ghastly sight.

Composition and perspective

The scenes move inwards through a complex set of spaces in classical arches to the musicians' gallery and to the prison cell. The execution itself can be seen at the very back.

The human figure

* The figures are grouped together on either side of the table. They stand out clearly, even though they are modelled in very low relief, called *rilievo schiacciato*, or flattened relief.
* Our attention is drawn to the energetic pose of the kneeling figure in the foreground. This brings us to the platter in his hands with the severed head of the saint.
* Each person in the scene reacts individually in gestures of shock.
* Salome, in flowing gown, continues to dance, unmoved, as her mother tries to explain the deed to Herod.

Mary Magdalene

This haunting image of Mary Magdalene is one of Donatello's later works (Fig. 18.9). The figure is carved from poplar wood. Her long, bony fingers are held together in prayer, but they do not touch.

Bones protrude from her gaunt cheeks and her flesh is eaten up from fasting.

Colour

The statue was once painted and gilded, but now only traces of the sad blue eyes stare out from hollow sockets, and partially opened lips show broken white teeth.

She appears to be covered in rags, but this is in fact her own long, yellowed hair, which is matted and twisted around her body.

Composition

The slender figure is extremely tall (nearly two metres high). The very long torso and thin bony legs might convey an impression of unsteadiness, but *Mary Magdalene* is a vibrant work of art with the energy and power to touch our deepest emotions.

Fig. 18.9 *Mary Magdalene*, 1457, by Donatello, painted wood, Florence. The harrowing figure is slightly bent over in a pitiful gesture of grace. In a timeless way, she is a reminder of tragedy and all human suffering and pain.

Gattamelata

Donatello worked in the city of Padua for over 10 years and created the *Gattamelata* (Fig. 18.10), or 'honeyed cat'. The subject was Erasmo of Narni, a powerful Venetian nobleman and *condottiere* (mercenary). Gattamelata was his nickname.

Material

Bronze was a difficult medium, and casting such a large equestrian figure to stand securely on three legs caused a sensation in its time.

The *Gattamelata* has definite similarities with the famous statue of the Emperor Marcus Aurelius in Rome, but Donatello's personal style makes this a more expressive piece of work.

Composition

It stands on a 25-foot-high pedestal. The statue itself is life-sized and majestic.

The figure in military armour is perfectly proportioned to his horse, which appears to be trotting. The horse is powerfully built with well-defined muscles, showing Donatello's studies of equine anatomy and his skills at naturalism.

Chapter review

* The radical changes in sculpture in 15th-century Florence took place long before anything like it in painting and architecture. It was the main influence on artists that followed and therefore key to Renaissance art. Why, do you think, did these changes take place in sculpture and not painting?

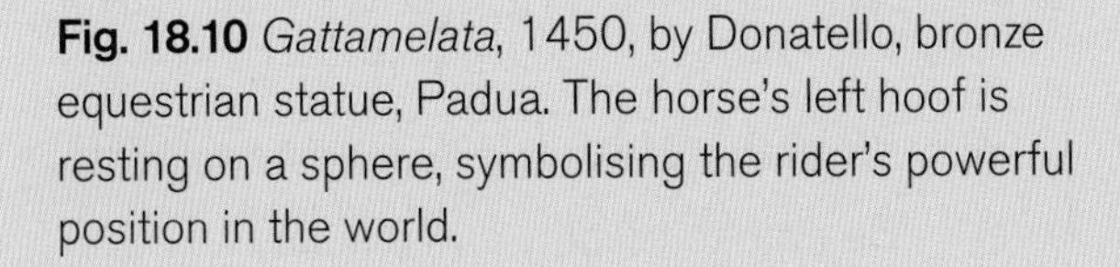

Fig. 18.10 *Gattamelata*, 1450, by Donatello, bronze equestrian statue, Padua. The horse's left hoof is resting on a sphere, symbolising the rider's powerful position in the world.

EXAM QUESTIONS

Ordinary Level (2011 – adapted)

Describe and discuss Mary Magdalene by Donatello (1386–1466) under the following headings:

- Subject matter
- Composition and style
- Medium
- Use of colour/light

Give some general information about the artist.

Illustrate your answer.

Higher Level (2016)

'Donatello (1386–1466) was an artistic innovator who created dramatic works of art.'

Discuss this statement with reference to *Mary Magdalene* (Fig. 18.9). In your answer, refer to subject matter, composition, treatment of the human figure and the period in which this work was produced.

and

Name and briefly describe and discuss **one** other work by Donatello.

Illustrate your answer.

FURTHER RESEARCH

www.museumsinflorence.com – Orsanmichele

www.museumsinflorence.com – Museum of the Cathedral

www.italianrenaissance.org – Donatello's Gattamelata

Chapter 19

Renaissance Painting: Early 15th-Century Florence

The city-state of Florence was one of the most powerful and prosperous in Europe. Its wealth provided the perfect intellectual conditions for humanist ideas. Humanist scholars believed in the dignity and importance of man.

By the end of this chapter, I will...

* Know that Masaccio learned from Giotto.
* Be able to identify and discuss Masaccio's innovations.
* Know that artists used perspective in distinctly different ways.
* Be able to draw and annotate examples of Masaccio's and Uccello's work.
* Know how to describe and discuss *The Tribute Money* by Masaccio and one more example of his work.
* Know *The Battle of San Romano* by Uccello and compare it with *The Hunt in the Forest.* (Use the www.ashmolean.org website at the end of the chapter as a guide.)

Cosimo il Vecchio

Florence was a republic, but Cosimo de Medici was the ruler. However, he was still a private citizen and lived quite simply although he was one of the wealthiest men of his time.

As a humanist, he believed that rulers should be patrons of art. He was deeply religious and spent a fortune on the construction, restoration and decoration of churches and monasteries.

San Marco in Florence and Fra Angelico

Cosimo paid for the restoration of the Dominican monastery of San Marco. He chose one of the monks, Fra Giovanni, better known as Fra Angelico (which means 'angelic'), as his artist.

Fra Angelico (1395–1455)

Fra Angelico acquired the reputation of an 'inspired saint', but he was a highly professional artist and ran a very efficient workshop. His was influenced by Brunelleschi, Masaccio and other contemporary artists, but his work reflects the quietness and discipline of religious life.

The San Marco frescoes

He painted a series of frescoes in the monks' cells of San Marco in a simple, restrained style. *The Annunciation* (Fig. 19.1) is one of the most captivating of these.

Fig. 19.1 *The Annunciation* by Fra Angelico, a fresco in a cell at San Marco, Florence. The figures are lifelike yet serene. The perspective in the arches suggests the influence of Masaccio.

The main altarpiece of the chapel at San Marco

Cosimo de Medici commissioned a grand altarpiece for the church of San Marco of the Virgin and Child with saints. The story of the saints was told in nine small pictures in the predella. One of these is in the National Gallery of Ireland in Dublin (Fig. 19.2).

Predella: The painting placed beneath the main scene at the bottom of an altarpiece.

The Attempted Martyrdom of Saints Cosmas and Damien

The scene shows an attempt to execute the saints and their brothers by fire. Behind them is the proconsul of Syria, who ordered their deaths. Divine intervention caused the flames to spread outwards and forced the executioners to flee.

Fig. 19.2
The Attempted Martyrdom of Saints Cosmas and Damien by Fra Angelico, National Gallery of Ireland, Dublin. Fra Angelico carefully planned the composition. Even in such a small work, the perspective lines create a clever illusion of depth.

The Brancacci Chapel

The rich and powerful Brancacci family commissioned the decoration for their small family chapel in Santa Maria del Carmine in 1423 (Fig. 19.3).

They engaged Masolino da Panicale, a well-established painter, and his young assistant, Masaccio. Masolino left to work elsewhere and Masaccio worked alone on the lower panels until his early death at the age of 27.

Masaccio (1401–28)

Masaccio was a highly innovative artist who created some of the most monumental works of the Early Renaissance. His classical, restrained style inspired many artists in his own time and in the period that followed.

Influences on Masaccio

Masaccio learned from Brunelleschi's studies of perspective and Donatello's freestanding figures, but Giotto was the biggest influence on Masaccio.

Masaccio studied Giotto's frescoes in Florence and imitated their naturalism by creating:

* Real three-dimensional space
* Solid, realistic sculptural figures
* Expressive gestures and lifelike facial expressions

Paintings in the Brancacci Chapel

Adam and Eve

Masolino and Masaccio both painted Adam and Eve. Facing each other across the chapel, these scenes are strikingly different.

Masolino's is the elegant Late Gothic style, but the fresh realism of Masaccio's Early Renaissance style is special and new.

Masaccio's figures have a dignity and beauty in spite of their despair. Eve's gestures echo those of the classical statue *Venus Pudica* (Fig. 19.6), so called because of the way she covers her nakedness with her hands.

Fig. 19.3
The Brancacci Chapel, 1425–26. The paintings are based on the life of St Peter, who was the first pope and the mediator between God and man.

Fig. 19.4 (left)
The Temptation of Adam, 1426–7, by Masolino, Brancacci Chapel, Florence

Fig. 19.5 (right)
Expulsion from the Garden of Eden by Masaccio. The outline around Adam's head shows *a giornata*, or one day's work in fresco (see the section on fresco technique on page 212). The blue azurite has faded – only the grey blue primer undercolour remains.

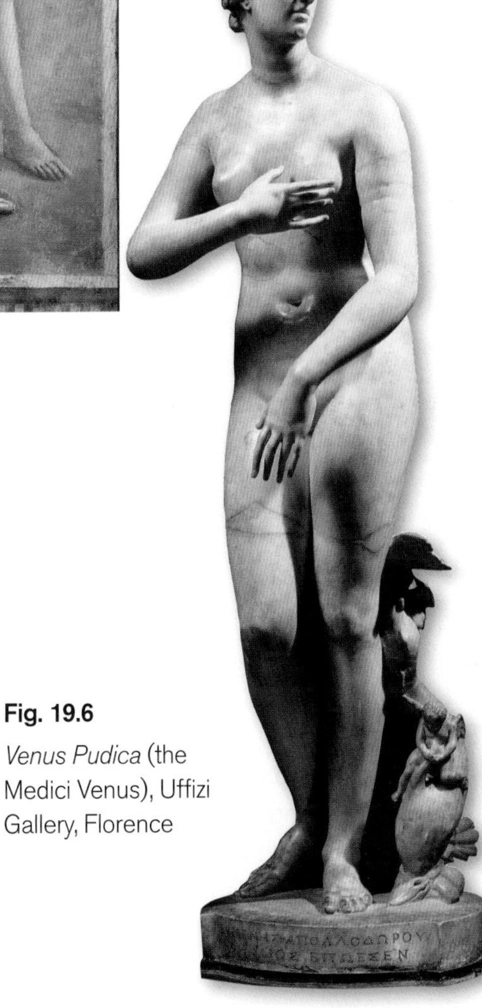

Fig. 19.6
Venus Pudica (the Medici Venus), Uffizi Gallery, Florence

A comparison of the two works

The Temptation of Adam by Masolino (Fig. 19.4):

* The figures have long, slender bodies and gentle facial expressions.
* The couple are standing quietly in the garden.
* A serpent in the form of a woman hovers above them.

Expulsion from the Garden of Eden by Masaccio (Fig. 19.5):

* This is a simple but dramatic scene.
* The expressive gestures and facial expressions show the characters' emotion.

Fig. 19.7 *The Tribute Money* by Masaccio, Brancacci Chapel, Florence

* The couple stumble forward, looking awkwardly naked.
* Eve lifts her head to cry out in anguish. Adam covers his face and weeps bitter tears of shame and regret.

The Tribute Money

The most famous painting of the great fresco cycle is *The Tribute Money* (Fig. 19.7). The huge scene relates to the yearly tax payment for the temple in Jerusalem. There has been much speculation about why this event was chosen as the subject, but it was probably a reminder of the duty to pay taxes.

Subject

According to the Gospel of St Matthew, Jesus and his disciples arrived at the gates of the city of Capernaum and the tax collector asked Peter, 'Does your master not pay the half shekel?' Peter was reluctant to pay, but Jesus said, 'Go to the lake and cast a hook; take the first fish that bites, open its mouth and there you will find a shekel. Take it and give to them for me and for you.'

Three-part composition

Masaccio painted this story in three parts.

* Part 1: Christ is the focal point. He points towards Peter hesitating.
* Part 2: Peter is crouched at the lakeside taking money from the fish's mouth.
* Part 3: Peter gives the coin to the tax collector.

Links in the composition

Peter's pose, with one knee bent and an arm outstretched, is an exact replica of Christ's. On the two occasions when Peter is confronted by the tax collector, the poses mirror each other. This has the effect of locking the main characters together within the composition.

Detail

A fire in the chapel many years ago blackened the frescoes, but after restoration in the 1980s, details on the faces and distant farmhouses became clearer.

Perspective

The architecture frames the figures on the right and the crisp lines of perspective lead the eye directly to

Fig. 19.8 Perspective in *The Tribute Money*

the figure of Christ. The vanishing point is his head. Landscape and trees recede into the distance, creating a sense of depth that is enhanced by the use of atmospheric perspective (Fig. 19.8).

Treatment of the human figure

The figures are strong and sculptural with carefully modelled features. They show the clear influence of classicism and are similar to the semi-circle of figures in Nanni di Banco's *Four Crowned Saints* (see Fig. 18.3), in the same Greek tunics.

Chiaroscuro: The treatment of light and shade in drawing and painting (Italian for 'light-dark').

Fig. 19.9 The Brancacci Chapel – light and shade (*chiaroscuro*). The artist followed the direction of the natural light from the chapel window on the figures. Shadows form dark sculptural pockets on the garments and the dramatic *chiaroscuro* greatly enhances the painting.

The Trinity

Masaccio's *The Trinity* (Fig. 19.10) is considered to be the first painting to have used mathematical perspective. It is likely that he had help from Brunelleschi.

Perspective

All the lines of perspective converge to a single vanishing point at eye level. To construct them, Masaccio first drew a rough sketch of the scene (Fig. 19.11). This was covered by plaster, but he put a nail in the wall to mark the central point. He drew strings out from this and pressed them into the plaster. These marks can still be seen.

Composition

The painting creates the image of real space with a small chapel and the three people of the Trinity. It was painted from a low viewpoint, so we are looking up at Christ. From here we can see the squares on the barrel-vaulted ceiling, but we cannot see the step on which the donors kneel.

The figures

A huge figure of God the Father supports the arms of the cross. He solemnly presents his son, Christ.

Fig. 19.10 *The Trinity*, 1428, by Masaccio, St Maria Novella, Florence

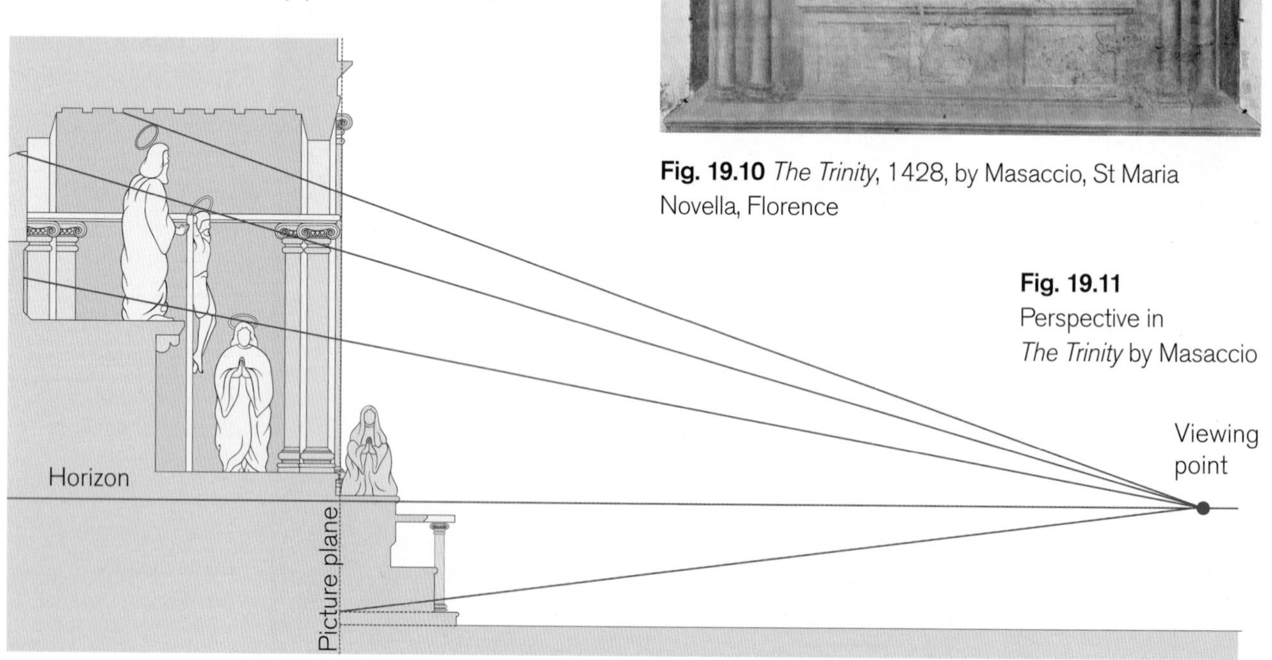

Fig. 19.11 Perspective in *The Trinity* by Masaccio

Perspective: A way to create a convincing impression of three-dimensional space on a two-dimensional surface.

One-point linear perspective: All lines appear to converge on a single 'vanishing point' on the horizon. It makes objects on a flat surface look three-dimensional and realistic.

Mary and John stand at the base. The Holy Spirit is represented as a dove, just above Christ's halo. Below our line of vision, a tilted sarcophagus shows a skeleton and the words of an ancient warning in Latin: 'I WAS WHAT YOU ARE AND WHAT I AM YOU SHALL BE'.

Damage to the fresco

The Trinity was covered with a tabernacle that was removed during the 19th century. The fresco was taken down at the time, causing considerable damage. It has now been replaced and is located close to its original position.

Paulo Uccello (1397–1475)

Paulo Uccello was once highly regarded, but his popularity declined due to his eccentric, solitary nature and his obsession with perspective. Vasari wrote that when Uccello's wife pleaded with him to come to bed, he refused and said only, 'Oh what a lovely thing is this perspective!'

The Battle of San Romano

This 182cm x 320cm panel depicts a victory for the Florentines at San Romano against the combined forces of Lucca, Siena and Milan in 1432 (Fig. 19.12).

Fig. 19.12 *The Battle of San Romano* by Paulo Uccello, National Gallery, London. The artist's profound fascination with weapons of war can be seen in the amazing detail of soldiers, shields, lances, crossbows, trumpets, horses and even the rivets in the armour and the nails in the horseshoes.

The Medici and *The Battle of San Romano*

The three panels depict the three stages of the battle: dawn, midday and dusk. They originally belonged to the Salimbeni family in Florence, but Lorenzo de Medici had them forcibly removed and brought them to hang together in the Medici Palace.

Niccolò da Tolentino

The mercenary leader Niccolò da Tolentino was a friend of the Medici, but there is also a symbolic significance. The bright orange fruit on the trees was *mala medica*, or 'medicinal apple', and the name Medici means 'doctors'. This was the Medici symbol.

Today one is in Paris, another is in Florence and the third is in London's National Gallery.

Subject

The Battle of San Romano is a colourful painting that depicts the scene at dawn after the Sienese ambushed the Florentines. Greatly outnumbered, the forces of Florence held the enemy at bay for eight hours until reinforcements arrived and then saw them off without difficulty.

Composition

The composition is brilliantly structured using one-point linear perspective, seen in:

* The lances held by the riders
* The foreshortening of shapes, especially the figure of the fallen soldier
* Broken lances that are scattered on the ground
* The posture and proportions of the horses

Style

The painting is certainly more ornamental than historical because the battle was no more than a skirmish.

The artist was probably aiming for a high degree of realism, but the effect is much more ornamental. The figures appear to be cut from stiff cardboard and the horses look like wooden toys.

Materials

The Battle of San Romano was painted with egg tempera, walnut oil and linseed oil on eight horizontal panels of poplar wood.

Some areas were covered with gold and silver leaf, but these were lost in early restorations. The gold on the bridle decorations has remained bright, but the silver leaf on the soldier's armour has oxidised to a dull grey or black. The burnished silver would originally have been quite dazzling.

Ceremonial costume

General Niccolò da Tolentino, the leader of the forces, wears his magnificent parade outfit and colourful headgear. He is seated on a lovely white charger in an ornate bridle. The young page carrying his ceremonial helmet alongside seems completely unaffected by the commotion.

Other works by Uccello

Very few other works by Uccello are still in existence.

Chapter review

* The painterly techniques of linear perspective, shading and other methods of realism began with Masaccio's innovations and Brunelleschi's experiments with the accurate depiction of space. Why, do you think, did perspective become such an important aspect of Renaissance art?

EXAM QUESTIONS

Ordinary Level (2014)

The Trinity by Masaccio (1401–c.1428) is shown in Fig. 19.10. Answer (a) and (b).

(a) Describe and discuss this work using the following headings:

- Composition/perspective
- Colour
- Subject matter

(b) Name and briefly discuss one other work by Masaccio.

Illustrate your answer.

Higher Level (2012)

Masaccio's (1401–28) grasp of perspective and three-dimensional modelling is seen in *The Tribute Money* (see Fig. 19.7).

Discuss Masaccio's work with detailed reference to *The Tribute Money*, the period in which it was produced, its subject matter, composition, materials and the techniques used in its production.

and

Name and briefly discuss **one** other artist from this period.

Illustrate your answer.

Higher Level (2008)

'The art of perspective was developed during the Early Renaissance in Florence.'

Discuss this statement, making detailed reference to a named work of art by Paolo Uccello (1397–1475).

and

Discuss briefly another work by Uccello **or** a work by any artist of the Early Renaissance that clearly shows the use of perspective.

Illustrate your answer.

FURTHER RESEARCH

www.ashmolean.org – The Hunt in the Forest

www.khanacademy.org – Masaccio, The Tribute Money in the Brancacci Chapel

www.khanacademy.org – Masaccio, Holy Trinity

www.khanacademy.org – Uccello, The Battle of San Romano

www.khanacademy.org – Early Renaissance in Italy, Painting in Florence and Rome

Chapter 20

Late 15th-Century Painting

By the end of this chapter, I will...

* Know the influence of Renaissance humanism on artists.
* Understand the importance of mathematics in Piero della Franceso's painting.
* Be able to draw, describe and discuss Botticelli's *Primavera* and *The Birth of Venus*.
* Know two important examples of Piero della Francesca's work.
* Be able to compare Botticelli's mythological paintings with his religious work.

Florence

Lorenzo the Magnificent

Twenty-one-year-old Lorenzo de Medici took over as ruler of Florence with his younger brother, Giuliano, after their father's death. He ruled alone after his brother was murdered.

The Golden Age

Lorenzo was both ruler and scholar. A distinguished poet, he was also passionately interested in classical antiquity and during his time the arts flourished. The Florentine Renaissance surpassed all previous achievements in a 'Golden Age', and the people of Florence rewarded him by granting him the title 'Lorenzo the Magnificent'.

Sandro Botticelli (1445–1510)

Alessandro Filipepi was brought up in the backstreets of Florence. His brother gave him the nickname Botticelli, which means 'little barrel', and the name stuck.

Influences on Botticelli

His most recognised characteristic – a wistfully delicate feminine beauty – came from his master, Fra Filippo Lippi. It can also be seen in Lippi's *Madonna and Child* (Fig. 20.1).

Fra Filippo worked for the Medici. Piero de Medici was impressed by his young apprentice, Botticelli, and brought him into the Medici household. He quickly became friends with his sons, Lorenzo and Giuliano, and learned humanist ideas.

Classical inspiration

Botticelli created an entirely new genre of art based on classical poetry. His most famous works relate to commissions from rich patrons that were linked to Florentine customs of marriage. This was the most important family ceremony of the time, and paintings depicting themes of love symbolised

Fig. 20.1 (left) *Madonna and Child* by Fra Filippo Lippi, Uffizi Gallery, Florence

Fig. 20.2 (right) *The Adoration of the Magi* by Botticelli was commissioned to impress the Medici family. It includes their portraits gathered around the Holy Family. Botticelli included his own self-portrait in the crowd.

the occasion. The works were displayed in a chamber specially prepared for the newly married couple in the family palace of the groom.

Mythological figures had been used in earlier Renaissance secular art, but in the humanist and deeply intellectual atmosphere of Medici Florence, mythological themes developed in an entirely new way. They were inspired partly by classical literature and sculpture, and partly by the Renaissance desire to portray the most perfect and highly idealised human figure.

The greatest examples of this new style of secular painting are Botticelli's *Primavera* (Fig. 20.3) and *The Birth of Venus* (Fig. 20.4). The panels were painted for the home of Lorenzo di Pierfrancesco de Medici, a younger cousin of the family.

These paintings were inspired by the mythological poetry of Florentine poet Boccaccio but are not based on any particular myth. They are instead more symbolic of the various aspects of love.

Genre: A style or category of art, defined by its content or subject matter.

Primavera, for example, symbolises the early beginnings of love and its fruition in marriage, while in *The Birth of Venus*, the birth of love in the world is depicted.

These paintings also depict some of the most sensuously beautiful nudes and semi-nudes painted during the Renaissance.

Primavera

Subject

Classical mythology is used to symbolise the ideals of love and feminine virtues. Venus, ancient goddess of beauty and fertility, is surrounded by the allegorical figures of virtues and gods. All the women are pregnant as they celebrate the arrival of spring.

> **Allegorical figures:** Characters that stand for an abstract idea or a symbolic meaning.

Composition

The painting reads from right to left. A group of three figures swings in from the right, towards the centre, where Venus is framed in an arc of blue sky among the trees. She looks like a Madonna from a religious painting. To her right, the elegant figures of the Three Graces, in their delicate translucent gowns, dance in a never-ending circle. Mercury's upward-reaching arm leads the eye up and around the composition to the little Cupid at the top centre.

Colours

The silvery greys and reds are carefully balanced around Venus to highlight the goddess.

Over the head of Venus, Cupid, her blindfolded son, shoots his arrow. It is aimed at the Three Graces dancing in an endless circle of life.
Flowers representing fertility fall from her mouth
The leaves are laurel (Lorenzo means 'laurel' in Italian, a reminder of the Medici patronage)
Mercury, the messenger of the Gods, holds up his staff and removes a cloud that hides the truth. Mercury is a likeness of Giuliano, Lorenzo da Medici's murdered younger brother.
She transforms into Flora, scattering blossoms before her
Zephyr, the wind, pursues Chloris, the wood nymph

Fig. 20.3 *Primavera (Allegory of Spring)* by Botticelli, Uffizi Gallery, Florence

Fig. 20.4
The Birth of Venus by Botticelli, Uffizi Gallery, Florence. Venus is the perfect image of grace and elegance in the pose of *Venus Pudica* (see Fig. 19.6). Her face is considered one of the most beautiful in art.

The human figure

The pose of the Three Graces follows classical sculpture. All the women are pregnant. The figures are elongated and stylised and their flowing garments suggest movement.

The Birth of Venus

Botticelli took his radical style to a new extreme with *The Birth of Venus* (Fig. 20.4), painted as a wedding present for Lorenzo di Pierfrancesco. Inspired by the Medici collection of classical sculptures, the painting refers to the creative power of love.

Designed to hang above the marriage bed, this painting was unlike any of its time. The nude figure was so controversial that it was kept behind closed doors for years afterwards.

Truth is beauty

In humanist thinking, Venus was the personification of beauty, and to the ancient Greek philosopher Plato, truth was beauty. Neo-Platonists combined this thinking with Christianity (Fig. 20.5). To them, Venus was the soul purified by baptism.

Idealised feminine beauty

Despite her awkward feet and unnatural neck and shoulder line, Botticelli's Venus represents the ideal of feminine beauty. Her elongated figure adds to her air of elegance and mystery.

Subject

The birth of Venus at sea comes from a well-known legend. She is about to step from her shell after the gods Zephyr (the wind) and Aurora (the dawn) have blown her ashore. Hora the nymph reaches out to cover her with a cloak.

Composition

The central figure in the composition, Venus, is still and serene. All around her there is motion: hair blowing, roses with golden centres floating, waves gently breaking and clothing billowing in the breeze.

Colours

Until recently, the painting was covered in several layers of varnish. This darkened to a dull yellow over the years, but cleaning has restored Botticelli's delicate colours. We can now see the porcelain-like, almost translucent quality of Venus' skin, rich golden hair and the blue-green ocean. Her pale skin has the faintest pink blushes in the areas of the cheeks, nose and mouth.

Line

Botticelli painted almost entirely with line. He used very little light and shade, but included decorative features on surfaces, like the little Vs on the waves of the sea.

Materials

The Birth of Venus is thought to have been the first large-scale canvas created in Renaissance Florence. It is like a fresco in its freshness and brightness. This was achieved by mixing a little oil with egg tempera to make the paint more transparent. The picture was built up slowly in layers and it hardened to a compact, enamel-like surface.

Botticelli's technique can be seen at its most refined in the flesh tones. He applied these colours with tiny brush strokes using a crosshatching technique to achieve perfect smoothness.

Botticelli the artist

Some Renaissance painters and their works were pushed aside and almost forgotten by the fame of the great artists who followed. Botticelli's name in particular had all but disappeared until he was rediscovered in the 19th century.

Savanarola

The artist became a follower of the Dominican monk Savonarola, who preached fiery public sermons against the paganism of the city. The Florentines responded in a frenzy of religious intensity and Botticelli destroyed many of his early paintings. From 1494, he concentrated only on religious subjects and fell out of favour with his patrons. He died in 1510, neglected and forgotten.

Fig. 20.5 *The Madonna of the Pomegranate*, c. 1487, by Botticelli, Uffizi Gallery, Florence. The Madonna has the same perfect oval face and expression of melancholic purity as Venus.

Urbino

The small hill town of Urbino attracted many artists and scholars from all over Italy and beyond. Federico da Montefeltro, the Duke of Urbino, was its ruler. He had a great love of art and engaged many poets, musicians, architects and artists at court.

Federico da Montefeltro, Renaissance man

Federico was deeply religious and lived a quiet life, but he had a great interest in philosophy, Latin, Greek and mathematics. His chosen painter was Piero della Francesca, who shared these intellectual interests. Piero's interest in mathematics can be seen in his paintings.

Fig. 20.6 *Portraits of the Duke and Duchess of Urbino* by Piero della Francesca, Uffizi Gallery, Florence. The art of portraiture was quite new, but in keeping with classical influence the faces are depicted in profile. This imitates the medals of ancient Rome. However, the left side of the duke's face was disfigured in a jousting tournament. He lost his right eye and part of his nose.

Portraits of the Duke and Duchess of Urbino

Piero painted a double portrait of his patron with his wife, Battista Sforza of Milan (Fig. 20.6).

The intelligent dignity of the great ruler is clearly portrayed, even though it is completely truthful and shows the duke literally warts and all. Battista was highly regarded for her intelligence and Piero has depicted her nobility with the detail of her fine clothing. The portrait may have been painted after her death at age 25, shortly after the birth of her ninth child and only surviving son. The duke greatly mourned her loss, but in this portrait they remain together in a poignant, never-ending partnership.

Influences

The figures dominate the composition, but Piero was the first artist to attempt a landscape in the background. This indicates the influence of Northern artists, who were admired for their use of atmospheric perspective (see Chapter 24).

Piero della Francesca (1416–92)

Piero della Francesca was not that well known in his lifetime and was forgotten about for many years. Most of his work was created in his hometown of Sansepolcro, in nearby Arezzo or in Urbino.

Influences

He absorbed the influence of his contemporaries in Florence. He knew Brunelleschi and Masaccio, but he was also interested in Leon Battista Alberti's new theories (see page 254).

Painting style and mathematics

Most of Piero's paintings are religious. His style is harmonious and graceful, with no frivolous detail. There is a remote, strange but calm quality about his work.

The artist and his patron, Federico da Montefeltro, also shared a deep interest in mathematics. This greatly influenced his painting. The pattern-like quality of his work suggests compositions were carefully and geometrically planned.

Colour

Piero's colours tended to be quite light. He often painted large areas in white or off-white.

Fig. 20.7 *The Baptism of Christ*, 1448–50, by Piero della Francesca, National Gallery, London. The pale blue sky is mirrored in the water and not a ripple disturbs the stillness. The still, serene figures are bathed in a gentle light from above.

The paintings

The Baptism of Christ

The Baptism of Christ (Fig. 20.7) is one of Piero's early works. It hangs in London's National Gallery but it was originally part of an altarpiece painted for the church where Piero himself was baptised.

Subject

St John the Baptist baptises Jesus. Above them, the perfectly horizontal wings of the white dove represent the Holy Spirit.

Composition

The painting is centred on the vertical. Christ stands solemn and majestic in the direct centre. Above his head, the Holy Spirit hovers exactly above the line of the baptismal water. The dark leaves of the tree form a perfect curve over the figures and unite the composition.

Colours

Delicate pastel colours against a dark landscape combine with the perfect geometric composition to create a deeply spiritual atmosphere.

Fig. 20.8
The Flagellation of Christ, 1455–60, by Piero della Francesca, Galleria Nazionale delle Marche, Urbino. The floor tiles are dramatically foreshortened but the pattern is highly accurate. The detail can clearly be worked out by projecting the perspective.

The human figure

The figures have a still, static quality. The limbs in particular are solid, almost like tree trunks. Christ is in a contrapposto pose and is still and composed, like a Greek god.

The Flagellation of Christ

This picture is very small – only 58.4cm x 81.5cm (smaller than A1 size) – but it is a highly impressive masterpiece (Fig. 20.8).

Subject

The scene features the passion of Christ, when he is tied to a pillar and whipped before Pontius Pilate. The three figures on the right have never been fully identified, so the real subject remains a mystery.

Composition

The composition is in two parts. The scenes and the figures are separated by the central line of ornate columns. Piero, however, was an accomplished mathematician and has used perfect one-point perspective. Both scenes are carefully bisected to make sure all the lines converge directly above Christ.

Fig. 20.9 Expanded drawing of the pattern in the paving tiles and the space. It shows how the perspective lines were organised.

Colour

Each scene has its own source of light. The crystal-clear morning light produces a quiet atmosphere and the pale colours make the torture of Christ all the more brutal. This contrasts sharply with the red and especially the fashionable blue and gold damask of the splendid costumes on the figures on the right.

Piero's influence

One of the painters influenced by Piero was Perugino. His pupil was Raphael, the great master of the High Renaissance who grew up in the court of Urbino.

Mantua

The Gonzaga family of Mantua were progressive rulers and founded a school of classical studies. They were artistic patrons with humanist ideas.

Andrea Mantegna (1431–1506)

Ludovico Gonzaga (Fig. 20.10) invited Andrea Mantegna as a court artist in 1460. It proved to be the turning point in his career. He worked for three Gonzaga rulers in succession. He was a famous and respected artist until his death in 1506.

Influences

Mantegna had a passionate interest in classical antiquity. Donatello's influence can be seen in his solid, expressive and realistic human figures.

Paintings

His most celebrated work is the superb series of frescoes in the Palazzo Ducale in Mantua that include portraits of Duke Ludovico Gonzaga and his family.

Fig. 20.10
Fresco of Ludovico Gonzaga and His Family, 1465–74, by Andrea Mantegna, Palazzo Ducale, Mantua, Italy

St Sebastian

This painting – a work of religious devotion – shows all the characteristics of Mantegna's style: his love of precise detail, his fascination with antiquity and his skill with perspective (Fig. 20.11).

Subject

Devotion to St Sebastian was very popular during the 15th century because he was the protector against the plague.

Composition

The column and the Roman arch divide the composition in two. The perspective is emphasised by an upward-looking viewpoint.

Style

Traditionally St Sebastian is shown tied to a post and shot with arrows, but miraculously still alive. Mantegna's painting keeps with the tradition but introduces the new element of humanism.

The Lamentation of Christ

Mantegna's mastery of perspective is possibly best displayed in the amazingly foreshortened figure of the dead Christ (Fig. 20.12).

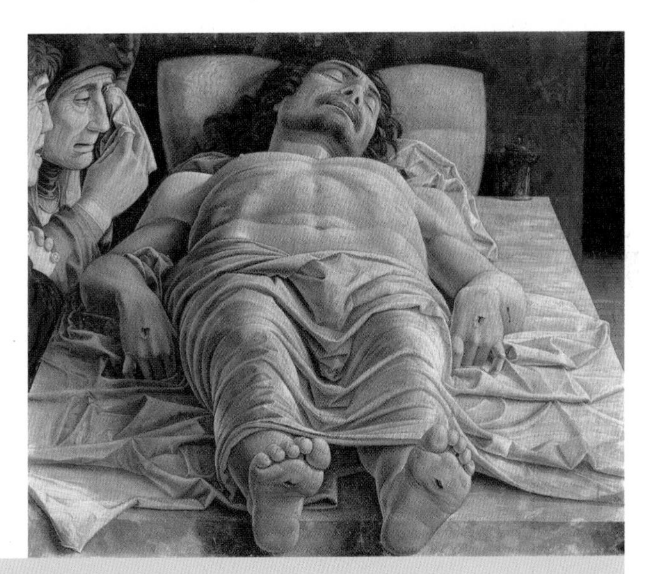

Fig. 20.11 *St Sebastian*, 1481, by Andrea Mantegna, Louvre, Paris. A mixture of architectural styles and symbols blends the ancient and Christian worlds. The coldness of the body creates the impression of an antique statue. The large stone foot next to the saint's feet symbolises the triumph of Christianity over paganism.

Fig. 20.12 *The Lamentation of Christ*, 1480, by Andrea Mantegna, Pinacoteca di Brera, Milan. The illusionist technique means that the dead figure appears to follow the viewer around the room. The painting was shown at the head of the artist's own coffin when he died, which may have been what he intended.

Chapter review

* Botticelli's most famous works were hidden away for many years. Why, do you think, were *Primavera* and *The Birth of Venus* so controversial?
* There are several theories on the meaning of *The Flagellation of Christ*. Why, do you think, is it so mysterious? What do *you* think it means?

EXAM QUESTIONS

Ordinary Level (2011)

Primavera by Botticelli (1444–1510) (Fig. 20.3) is illustrated on the accompanying sheet. Answer (a) and (b).

(a) Describe and discuss this work using the following headings:

- Subject matter
- Composition
- Medium
- Use of colour

(b) Name and briefly describe one other work by Botticelli.

Illustrate your answer.

Higher Level (2014)

'Mythology and symbolism were the main concerns of the painter Sandro Botticelli (c.1445–1510).'

Discuss this statement with reference to *The Birth of Venus* (Fig. 20.4). Refer in your answer to composition, subject matter, treatment of the human figure and the period in which the work was produced.

and

Name and briefly discuss **one** other work by this artist.

Illustrate your answer.

Higher Level (2010)

Describe and discuss *The Flagellation of Christ* by Piero della Francesca (1420–92) (Fig. 20.8). Make reference to the period in which it was produced, composition, style and the use of light and colour in the painting.

and

Name and discuss briefly **one** other work by this artist.

Illustrate your answer.

FURTHER RESEARCH

www.khanacademy.org – Piero della Francesca's Flagellation of Christ

Chapter 21

Architecture

Renaissance architecture was inspired by classical Rome. Architects visited Rome as part of their training to study ancient buildings and ruins like the Coliseum and Pantheon. They were also influenced by the writings of Vitruvius, a Roman architect and military engineer. His methods of mathematical proportion and measurement were based on the human scale.

Classical elements were incorporated into Renaissance buildings. Architects also tried to create buildings that would appeal to both emotion and reason.

Architects of the Renaissance

The key figures in Renaissance architecture were Filippo Brunelleschi and Leon Battista Alberti.

Brunelleschi (1377–1446)

Filippo Brunelleschi was the first Renaissance architect. He trained as a goldsmith in his native city of Florence before turning to architecture and the study of ancient buildings in Rome. He also studied mechanics and had a keen interest in mathematics. His best-known work is of the dome of the Florence Cathedral (Santa Maria del Fiore) (Fig. 21.1).

By the end of this chapter, I will...

* Understand the influence of classical antiquity on Renaissance architecture.
* Know how Brunelleschi's design for the dome of St Maria del Fiore in Florence worked.

The dome of Santa Maria del Fiore

The new Cathedral of St Maria del Fiore in Florence had been under construction for more than a century. It included a massive drum for a dome, but no one knew how to design a dome for such a wide span. In 1418, the governors of the city announced a competition to design the dome.

Designing the dome

Brunelleschi had left Florence after his design for the baptistery doors was rejected 18 years before (see page 218), but he was determined to win this new competition. He enlisted the help of two of the most innovative sculptors of the day, Donatello and Nanni di Banco. They produced a model that was so technically brilliant that the judges immediately awarded the commission to Brunelleschi.

Brunelleschi's design

Brunelleschi's design was unique. Other designs included wooden scaffolding, but there was no wooden beam long enough to span the width.

Brunelleschi's highly innovative double shell self-supporting cupola solved the problem. His system also included:

* Scaffolding that started at the top of the drum rather than the ground
* An access walkway and steps between the walls
* Massive stone ribs to bind the inner and outer shells together
* A series of stone chains buried within the masonry (Fig. 21.3) to stiffen each of the eight faces and prevent the dome from buckling under its own weight
* A herringbone brickwork technique copied from the Pantheon in Rome (Fig. 21.4)
* A circular interior on the octagonal walls (Fig. 21.5)

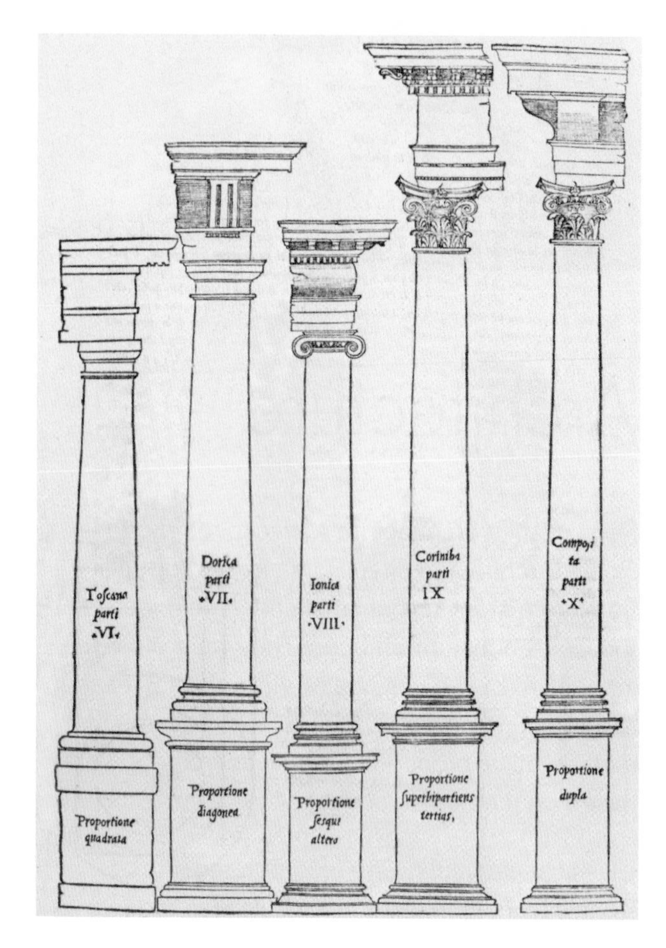

Fig. 21.2 Classical orders of architecture. Greek temples were built with very strict rules (orders). There were three basic types of column: Doric, Ionic or Corinthian.

Fig. 21.1 Cathedral of Santa Maria del Fiore, 1420–36, Florence. Like 'a great umbrella over the city', the vast curved silhouette of Brunelleschi's dome stands out huge and magnificent against the sky as the landmark of Florence. The white ribs surge upwards towards the lantern and make a striking contrast with the russet tiles of the dome. This two-colour effect was a characteristic of Renaissance architecture.

Brunelleschi's technology

The inward-facing circular vault had to be self-supporting. For this, Brunelleschi used:

* Specially invented machinery
* His expertise in mathematics and geometry
* His knowledge of mechanics, combined with his studies of classical buildings in Rome

Cupola: A rounded dome forming a roof or ceiling.

Fig. 21.3 Stone chains within the eight faces of the cupola. A series of chains were set in the walls for strength, with four stone chains and one of wood encircling the dome at regular intervals upwards.

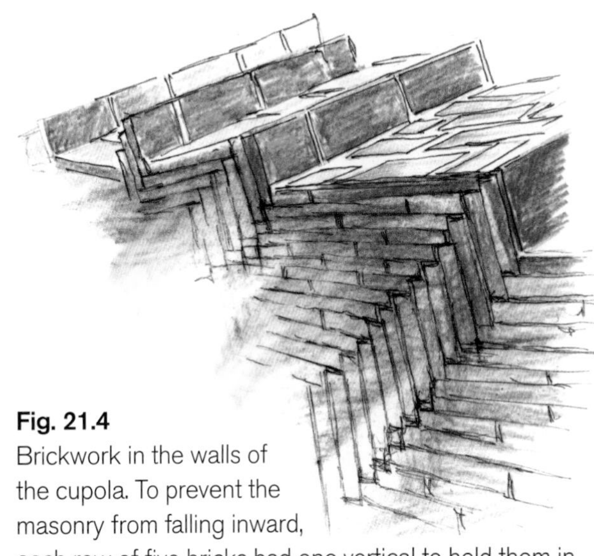

Fig. 21.4
Brickwork in the walls of the cupola. To prevent the masonry from falling inward, each row of five bricks had one vertical to hold them in position on either side. This gave the brickwork a zigzag or herringbone-like pattern. Each ring of bricks was supported by the one below.

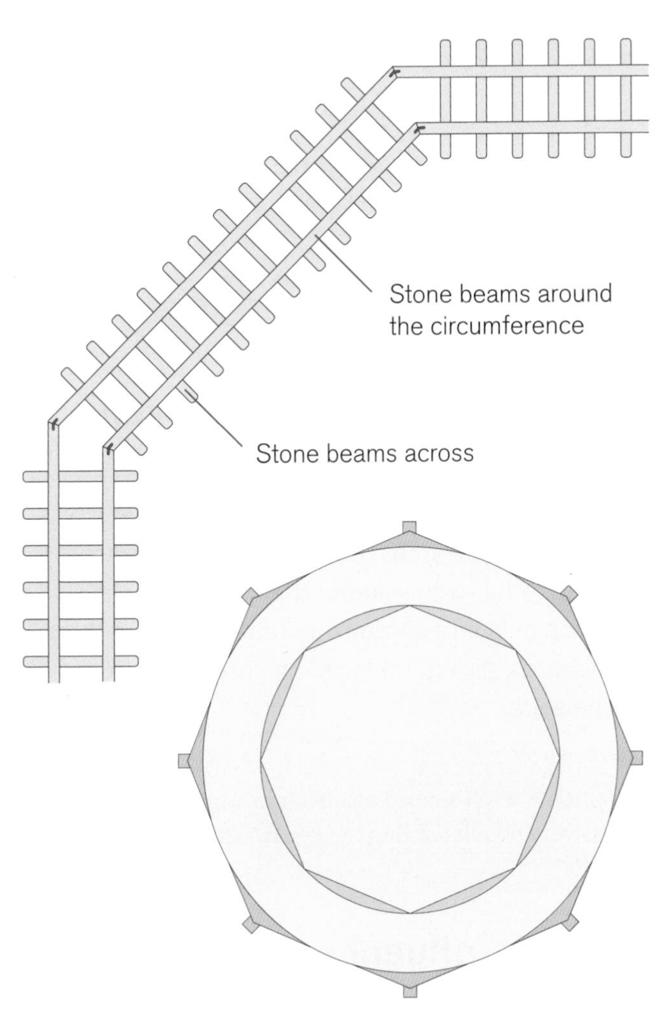

Fig. 21.5 A circle within the walls. The inner wall of the dome was constructed as a circular vault. The thickness of the walls was then cut away to form an octagonal.

The lantern

After the completion of the dome, Brunelleschi won first place in another competition to design the lantern for the top of the dome.

The lantern design:

* Pulled the composition of the dome together
* Combined new architectural elements with classical features
* Used white to convey a sense of weightlessness
* Shaped the marble to pick up shadow and create variations in the pure white

Brunelleschi did not live to see the lantern on the dome. He died in 1446, the year construction began.

The Pazzi Chapel

Brunelleschi designed a private chapel in St Croce in Florence for the powerful Pazzi family. The Pazzi Chapel (Fig. 21.6) is a rectangular shape, but the domed roof creates a circular space and a central round arch unites the two sides of the portico.

The interior is decorated in the characteristic two-coloured stone. The classical ornaments include shells, cherubs and low relief medallions (Fig. 21.7).

Fig. 21.6 The Pazzi Chapel, 1429–61, by Filippo Brunelleschi

Fig. 21.7 Interior of the Pazzi Chapel, 1429–61, by Filippo Brunelleschi

Influence of Brunelleschi

Brunelleschi influenced many later architects, including Michelangelo.

Leone Battista Alberti (1406–72)

Alberti was a humanist writer and an influential architect. His new classical style became extremely popular in Italy. He wrote the first Renaissance books about art and architecture.

Church façades made up a large part of the work of Renaissance architects and sculptors. The design and style were sometimes completely different from the interior of the church.

The façade of St Maria Novella

Alberti's design (Fig. 21.8) was based on the combination of a Roman temple on top and a Roman triumphal arch. The two sections were joined together with volutes. The composition is based on a square divided into rectangles and then into squares, giving the façade a sense of rhythm and balance.

Volute: A scroll-shaped architectural ornament that was very popular during the Renaissance and later.

Alberti's influence

Alberti's theories were very influential in changing the status of artists.

Fig. 21.8 The façade of St Maria Novella, 1470, by Leone Battista Alberti, Florence

Chapter review

* Brunelleschi had to invent new building methods and structures, as well as many tools for the construction of the dome of St Maria del Fiore in Florence. Where, do you think, did his inspiration for all this come from?

EXAM QUESTIONS

Higher Level (2012)

Answer (a), (b) and (c).

(a) Choose and name a building by Filippo Brunelleschi (1377–1446).

(b) Discuss the work you have chosen in detail, making reference to the style, composition/design, materials, technique and the period in which it was produced.

(c) Name and briefly describe and discuss **one** other work by this architect.

Illustrate your answer.

FURTHER RESEARCH

www.youtube.com – How an Amateur Built the World's Biggest Dome (National Geographic)

www.khanacademy.org – Brunelleschi, Dome of the Cathedral of Florence

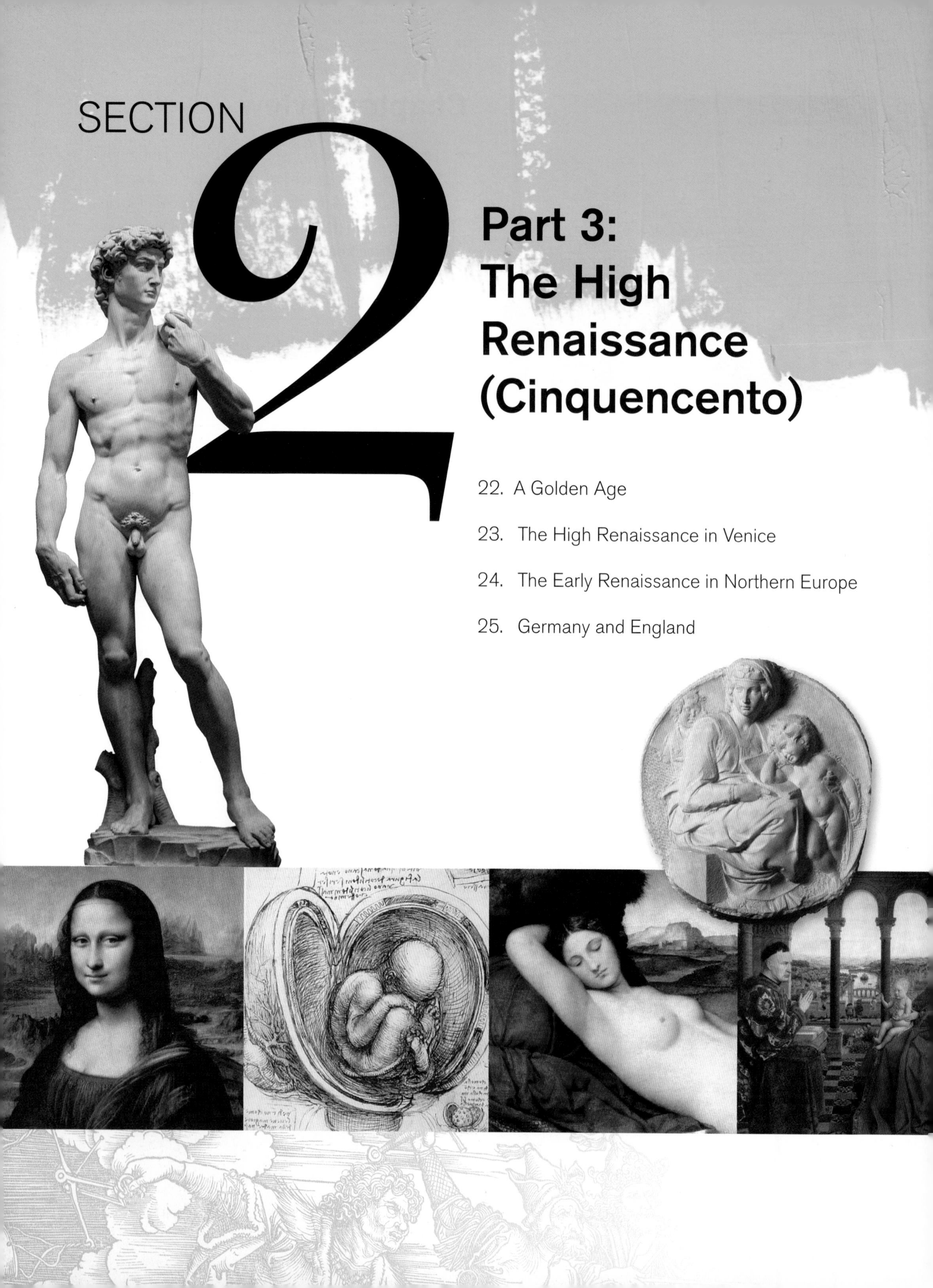

SECTION 2

Part 3: The High Renaissance (Cinquencento)

Chapter 22

A Golden Age

Rome and Florence

The High Renaissance is considered to have been a 'Golden Age' in its own time, but in the years leading up to the 16th century the great city of Rome was in a sorry state of neglect. The economy was weak and it had fallen badly into disrepair, but two popes sought to rectify this and return the ancient city to its former glory.

Between 1503 and 1521, Pope Julius II and Pope Leo X employed craftsmen and artists to build a new St Peter's Basilica, refurbish streets, build bridges, construct churches and create some of the world's most treasured works of art.

By the end of this chapter, I will...

* Be able to discuss how artists achieved an 'ideal beauty'.
* Be familiar with the developments in painterly techniques.
* Know how Leonardo da Vinci's work was a psychological study.
* Understand why Michelangelo's sculpture was so expressive.
* Be able to discuss how Raphael achieved balance and harmony in his compositions.

Status of the artist

During the High Renaissance, the status of the artist changed completely. No longer considered mere craftsmen, artists were now viewed as people of intellect and ideas. This change in status was largely due to the new Renaissance practice of writing about art and artists.

Renaissance writers

Renaissance thinkers absorbed the ideas of classical Greek philosophy. As a result, humanist ideas developed, which in turn inspired Renaissance theorists. Leon Battista Alberti, Leonardo da Vinci and Giorgio Vasari were among those who wrote about art and whose opinions were respected.

Ideals of the High Renaissance

High Renaissance painting and sculpture was based on the study of nature and the human figure. Artists were not just interested in clever realism – they also strove towards the ideal beauty of the human figure in Greek and Roman culture.

Humanism and artists

Humanism gave the art of the Renaissance its unique quality. Artists often worked with non-religious subjects, and even religious themes were not only glorifying God, but also Man.

NOTE! Artists during the High Renaissance achieved a high degree of realism, but the emphasis was much more on the humanist idea of ideal beauty, harmony and balance.

Innovations in painting and sculpture

Developments included:

* Correct proportions in the human figure
* More natural facial features and expressions
* A greater range of human movement
* More natural interaction between figures
* A striving towards 'ideal' beauty

Oil painting

Italian artists were now using oil paint in preference to tempera. This helped to make colours richer and to achieve a more naturalistic effect. Oil paint was applied either to a wood panel or to a cloth base, such as linen.

Artists of the High Renaissance

The three great artists of the High Renaissance in Florence and Rome were:

* Leonardo da Vinci
* Michelangelo
* Raphael Sanzio

These artists were very famous in their own time and patrons felt honoured to have them. This gave them much more freedom to explore their own ideas.

Leonardo da Vinci (1452–1519)

Leonardo da Vinci was the oldest and most famous of the great Renaissance masters. He was an artist of exceptional ability and his innovations in painting influenced Italian art for more than a century after his death.

He was the ultimate Renaissance man. In addition to being a painter, Leonardo was also a sculptor, architect, musician, scientist, inventor and writer. A good deal of his time and energy were devoted to scientific interests.

Fig. 22.1 *Baptism of Christ*, 1472–5, by Andrea del Verrocchio, oil on wood, Uffizi Gallery, Florence. Legend has it that when Verrocchio saw Leonardo's angel, he stopped painting and concentrated only on sculpture.

The son of a Florentine lawyer and a servant girl, Leonardo came from Vinci, a little town in the Tuscan hills. At school he showed a particular interest in nature but excelled at drawing. He was sent to Florence as an apprentice with the sculptor Andrea del Verrocchio, but he soon outstripped his master. His earliest known painting is of a beautiful young angel in Verrocchio's *Baptism of Christ* (Fig. 22.1). Leonardo worked in Florence for a time before leaving for Milan.

Milan

Ludovico Sforza of Milan was one of the wealthiest and most powerful princes of Renaissance Italy. Leonardo became his court artist. Leonardo organised elaborate festivals and designed buildings, drainage systems, weapons of war and of course his famous flying machine.

The Last Supper

During the rebuilding of the church of Sante Maria delle Grazie, Ludovico engaged Leonardo to paint the Last Supper on one of the walls in the nearby monastery.

Subject

The Last Supper was a traditional subject for artists. In previous paintings, Jesus and the apostles sit on one side of the table and Judas is alone sitting opposite them (Fig. 22.2).

Leonardo took an entirely different approach. He studied the Bible and imagined the moment of

Fig. 22.2 *The Last Supper*, 1480, by Domenico Ghirlandaio, fresco, Church of Ognissanti, Florence

Fig. 22.3 *The Last Supper*, 1498, by Leonardo da Vinci, fresco with oil, Convent of Santa Maria delle Grazie, Milan

Fig. 22.4 and **Fig. 22.5** (above left and right) Leonardo's picture tells the story in a silent but highly dramatic language of gestures and expressions

Fig. 22.6 (left) The figure of Jesus represents the vanishing point for all persective lines

chaos when Jesus announced, 'One of you will betray me.' In a superb psychological study of human emotion, the apostles reel in confusion and self-doubt and react with denial and disbelief (Fig. 22.3).

Composition

Leonardo used the golden ratio or 'divine proportion' in the design and architectural features of *The Last Supper.*

Golden ratio: A mathematical ratio used to work out aesthetically pleasing proportions in composition. It is also called the golden section or golden mean. By applying correct mathematics, exact proportions can be calculated in any number of geometric forms, including circles, triangles, pyramids, prisms and polygons.

To solve the problem of the long composition, he arranged the apostles in groups and connected them with gestures.

Peter, with a knife clutched in his hand, leans forward to John and whispers in his ear (Fig. 22.4). This action manages to isolate Judas from the group and pushes him out in a pose opposite to that of Jesus with Peter's knife at his back. One seems to say, 'Lord is it I?' and clasps his hands to his breast (Fig. 22.5).

Framed by the window, Jesus is serene and dignified. With hands placed calmly on the table, his pyramidal shape is in the exact centre of the composition.

Perspective

The picture was painted for the refectory (dining room). The sharp linear perspective creates an impression that the wall is receding back and the group is sitting at the top table in the room. The vanishing point is the face of Jesus. The strong diagonals draw the eye towards the calm figure in the midst of human energy and turbulence. He is alone in the knowledge of his suffering to come (Fig. 22.6).

The open windows in the background show the use of atmospheric perspective.

Experimentation with new fresco techniques

Leonardo was dissatisfied with fresco. It dried too fast and prevented him from using fine detail. He experimented by mixing oil with tempera and by working dry (*a secco*). This proved to be disastrous, as in less than 20 years the great painting began to disintegrate.

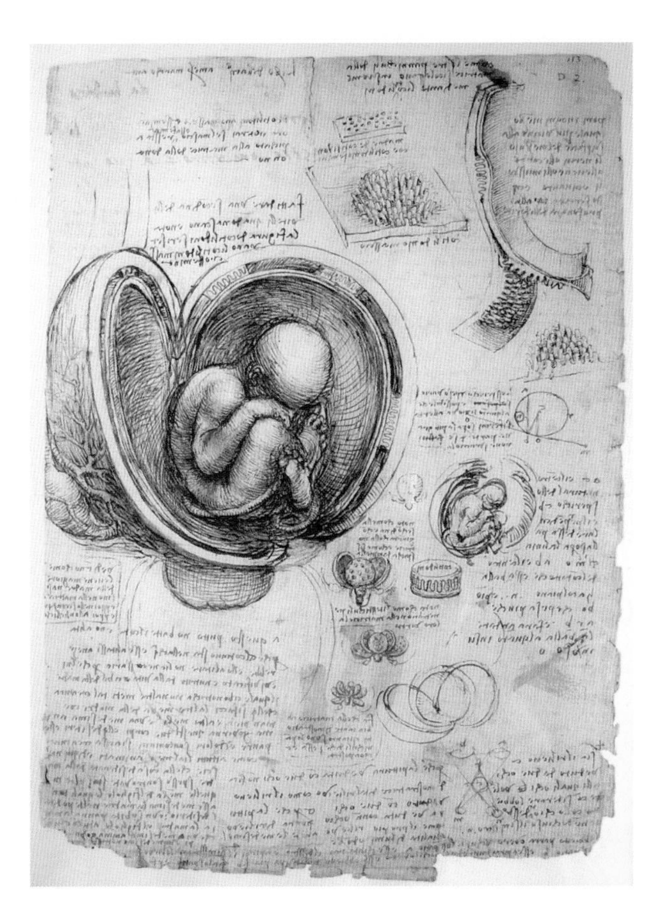

Fig. 22.7 The babe in the womb page from Leonardo da Vinci's notes, Royal Library, Windsor Castle, England

Leonardo's scientific interests

Leonardo's reflections on mathematics, geology, the human body and other scientific subjects were recorded in thousands of manuscript pages. He made numerous sketches of anatomy, which were very controversial at the time, but he discovered many features of the human body (Fig. 22.7).

Leonardo the artist

His many interests meant that Leonardo spent less time on painting. There are only 15 paintings and one fresco, but he made significant technical discoveries.

Techniques

Leonardo was a slow, meticulous painter; oil paint allowed him to paint in extremely fine detail.

He broke with the Florentine tradition of outlining the painted image and began by covering his canvas in brown tones. He built up the image in layers of very thin paint or glazes using small brushes. He also used his fingers to smooth and soften the edges while the paint was still wet. This was particularly effective on the edges of faces and helped to make smooth shadows.

Colour

He used only a small natural range and never intense or bold colours. He used just one colour in tonal studies and graded it from very light to dark – almost white to black.

Atmospheric perspective

He studied the effect of rain and dust on colour and distance and was one of the first artists to use atmospheric perspective in Italy.

Sfumato

He developed sfumato, a technique that became known as 'Leonardo's smoke'. This softened outlines and blended areas of light and shade together. It also created an illusionistic atmosphere.

Sfumato: A technique that allows tones and colours to blend gradually into one another, producing softened outlines or hazy forms.

The human figure

His stunningly realistic figures show Leonardo's love of nature and anatomy. He dissected bodies and studied the physical proportions of men, women and children. He also loved faces and watched people's expressions, but in his painting he sought to go beyond everyday realism and show the perfect – the 'ideal' human figure.

He depicted religious figures as real-life people and was the first artist to completely abandon halos around their heads in some of his paintings.

Paintings

The Virgin of the Rocks

Subject

This painting features the Virgin Mary tenderly watching over the infant Christ and John the Baptist. Next to them is a mysteriously smiling, pointing angel with curly hair and soft, dreamy eyes (Fig. 22.8).

The subject is based on a popular legend about St John the Baptist, but Leonardo has gone beyond the simple story with a deeper and more meaningful concept (idea). This is the very idea of Christianity. In a dark cave, four figures are illuminated by divine light – they shine from a light within in a blessed and mysterious truth.

Later in his life, Leonardo painted a second version. This is in the National Gallery in London.

Fig. 22.8 *The Virgin of the Rocks*, 1495–1508, Leonardo da Vinci, oil on panel, Louvre, Paris. The figures are treated with great tenderness, but Leonardo's love of mystery shows in the gestures, expressions and strange lighting.

Composition

The figures are grouped in a structured, ordered, pyramidal shape. Exquisitely detailed rocks, water and plants all studied from nature surround the figures.

Colours

Thick yellowed varnish has dulled Leonardo's colours, but dramatic, soft highlighting draws out the faces from the more subdued background.

Portraits

Portraiture was one of Leonardo's main subjects and he painted many women. Traditionally women were painted in profile, but Leonardo placed them in a three-quarter pose. This gave them a stronger presence and placed them in pyramidal compositions.

He used chiaroscuro (contrasting light and dark) on the clothing to great effect. Sfumato was particularly effective on faces.

Mona Lisa

Subject

Leonardo's most famous portrait is *Mona Lisa* (Fig. 22.9). It is thought to be Lisa Gherardini, wife of a Florentine cloth merchant named Francesco del Giocondo.

Composition

This is a half-length portrait from head to waist. She looks directly at the viewer, but her arms, torso and head are each subtly twisted in different directions. Her hands are joined in the foreground.

The landscape behind her seems to be assembled from many views and there are more than one possible horizon lines.

The scene looks forbidding and is in contrast to the warm, welcoming face of Mona Lisa.

Painterly techniques

The flexibility of oil paint allowed Leonardo to fully explore the soft folds of the drapery and the texture of skin. Her face, neck and hands glow with an inner light, which he created through the use of chiaroscuro.

The ground and hills behind the subject are painted in warm tones of reddish-brown. As the landscape recedes, the mountains become progressively more blue.

The use of sfumato adds to an atmosphere of mystery. The figure seems to dissolve into the background, with its winding rivers and strange rock formations.

Fig. 22.9 *Mona Lisa*, c. 1503–5, by Leonardo da Vinci, oil on wood panel, Louvre, Paris. Mona Lisa's mysterious, unfathomable smile has made her more famous than any of Leonardo's other works. It is possibly a visual representation of happiness suggested by the word *gioconda* ('happiness' in Italian).

Over the years the glazes have darkened and the very fine detail has become obscured.

The Virgin and Child with St Anne

Subject

The real meaning of the work is unclear. The Christ child plays with the sacrificial lamb and this symbolises the passion. Mary leans across her mother to pull him back but she is sitting on St Anne's lap. This may refer to the stream of life flowing through the three generations (Fig. 22.10).

Fig. 22.10 *The Virgin and Child with St Anne*, c. 1510, by Leonardo da Vinci, oil on wood, Louvre, Paris

Composition

The figures are tightly grouped together in a pyramidal composition. Grouping of figures was an important development and Leonardo's experiments greatly inspired later artists.

Painterly effects

Sfumato has softened the expressions and enveloped the figures and landscape in a strange bluish haze. This contributes to the mystical atmosphere but also unites the composition.

Later life

Leonardo had to leave Milan when the French invaded in 1499. He wandered between Florence and Rome but ended his days in Amboise, France, under the protection of King Francis I. He had tried to work in Rome but the pope had little time for an artist with such a reputation for slowness and unfinished work.

Michelangelo (1475–1564)

Michelangelo Buonarroti made his name in Florence when he was only 17 years old. As a young sculptor, he benefitted greatly from the patronage of Lorenzo the Magnificent and lived in the Palazzo Medici for a while. He moved between Rome and Florence during his long career, working on many architectural, painting and sculptural projects.

Style

Michelangelo had a personal vision and had the freedom to express it in his art. He also had a keen eye for light and shadow and understood its role in creating volume and shape, both in sculpture and painting.

The human figure

He believed that all beauty could be seen in the human body and he became an expert in its portrayal. He studied drawing from life and made hundreds of sketches. He studied anatomy and obtained special permission from the Catholic Church to work with human corpses.

Difficult poses were a challenge for the artist and his figures are often twisted and curved. He was not afraid to bend the rules of realistic anatomy and proportion to increase the power of expression.

Working methods

Despite difficulties and frustrations, Michelangelo worked with patrons because they had the money to facilitate his grand schemes. However, he always retained his independence.

His choice of marble blocks was key to his sculptural process. He spent months in the quarry at Carrara finding the perfect stone for a subject.

Sculpture

Michelangelo was an accomplished artist in painting, sculpture and architecture, but he considered himself a sculptor first and foremost.

As an infant, Michelangelo was cared for by a wet nurse whose husband was a stonecutter. His mother died when he was very young but he grew up absorbed by drawing and carving. He spent a short time in the studio of the artist Ghirlandaio and, at the age of 13, he moved to a school of sculpture set up by Lorenzo the Magnificent. The sculptor Bertoldo di Giovanni was his teacher and he studied from the collection of classical statues in the Medici gardens.

Influences

Michelangelo always said he was self-taught, but he learned drawing and fresco in Ghirlandaio's studio and developed opinions about art. Masaccio and Lorenzo Ghiberti were also an influence.

The Pietà

After the death of Lorenzo the Magnificent, Michelangelo could no longer rely on patronage in Florence, so he left for Rome, where he made studies of antique statues. His first major commission was *The Pietà*, made for an elderly cardinal who wanted a statue for his tomb.

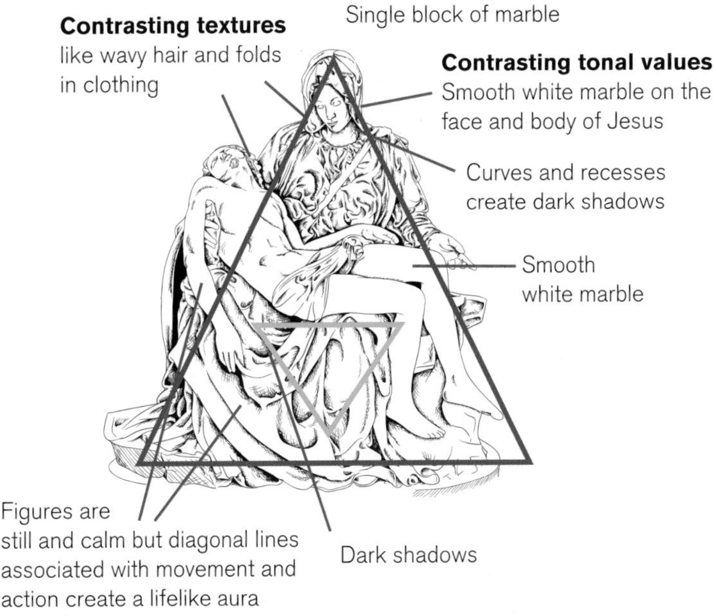

Fig. 22.11 (left) *The Pietà*, 1500, by Michelangelo, marble, St Peter's Basilica, Rome. In his first masterpiece, the artist groups the figures in a pyramidal composition. This beautiful mixture of design elements makes it one of the most valued statues in modern history.

Fig. 22.12 (right) Pyramidal composition of *The Pietà*. Mary's head is the pinnacle of the triangle and her foot on the block and those of Jesus form the other points. Her face is an oval. The position of Jesus' body makes another less obvious triangle, inverted inside the main one.

Subject

The word *pietà* in Italian means 'pity'. In art, it refers to the Virgin grieving over the dead Christ. It was a subject more typical of the Northern Renaissance, but 23-year-old Michelangelo gave it an elegance never seen before in Italy (Fig. 22.11).

Style

The drama is treated in the restrained classical manner of Greek sculpture. The grieving mother is serene and accepting and the realistic figures have gone beyond the human to the divine. Mary's youthful, idealised beauty suggests spiritual purity.

Divine: Like a god.

Composition and line

The pyramidal composition shows the influence of Leonardo (Fig. 22.12). It creates a harmonious symmetry and draws the eye to the Virgin's face and downcast eyes. The lines in the work also give it its energy and life. The folds in Mary's clothing follow many directions, but Jesus' body has few distinct lines. This emphasises his lifelessness, but the sash across Mary's chest creates a subtle message that they are absolutely connected.

A technical solution

Stretching a grown man over the lap of a seated woman was a complicated problem. Michelangelo's solution was to build a support with elegant folds of cloth.

A signature in marble

When *The Pietà* was unveiled in 1500, some viewers could not accept that so young an artist could produce such an accomplished work. Michelangelo responded by carving his name on the sash – it was the only work he ever signed.

Later *pietàs*

Mother and child groups were a constant theme in Michelangelo's sculpture. Throughout his life, he returned again and again to the subject of the *pietà*. It was a reflection of his deep religious faith.

Florence

Michelangelo returned to Florence in 1500. The city was celebrating its re-establishment as a republic with a series of art commissions and the Signoria (governors) asked Michelangelo to make a large statue of David for the cathedral.

David

He was given a huge block of marble and from this he produced *David* (Fig. 22.13), a flawlessly beautiful young male with a calm, classical appearance. The figure was highly realistic but also idealised like a Greek god.

Subject

The Bible story of David, the young boy who killed the giant Goliath with one shot from his sling, was a popular one for Florence. It also symbolises the small city-state strong against its larger enemies.

Artists traditionally depicted the young hero after he had killed Goliath, but Michelangelo chose to show him preparing for battle. With stone in hand and sling casually thrown over his shoulder, this manly warrior has his gaze fixed on the distance and his brow is furrowed in concentration.

Composition

The extremely long and rectangular shape of the marble block may have determined the composition. A more active pose could have caused problems with balance.

The head and hands are too large for the body, but this may be explained by the fact that the statue was originally planned for high up on the cathedral.

Fig. 22.13 (left) *David*, 1501–4, by Michelangelo, marble, Galleria dell'Accademia, Florence. At over three times life size, this was the first time such a monumental freestanding statue had been seen since Roman times.

Fig. 22.14 (above) *Apollo Belvedere*, The Vatican, Rome

The upward-looking viewpoint would have caused distortions, so Michelangelo deliberately adjusted the proportions to counteract this.

David's pose and gesture echo that of Venus from Botticelli's *Birth of Venus* (see Fig. 20.4). Michelangelo spent time in the Medici household and would have known Botticelli.

Influences

The turn of the head in a contrapposto pose suggests that *Apollo Belvedere* (Fig. 22.14), discovered in Rome in the late 1400s, may have been an influence. Influences can also be seen in the pose and furrowed brow of Donatello's *St George* (see Fig. 18.5).

David, symbol of Florence

The Signoria were so impressed with *David* that they placed the symbolic figure in the main square of the city, the Piazza del Signoria. It was removed for safety in the 19th century to a special room in the Accademia. Today, a copy has replaced it outside of the Palazzo Vecchio (town hall).

A tomb for Pope Julius

Shortly afterwards, the newly elected Pope Julius II summoned Michelangelo to Rome. He wanted a huge freestanding tomb that would occupy a prominent position in the new St Peter's.

The tomb started out as a very grand structure, but Michelangelo had to redesign it several times. Each time it got smaller and less impressive as Pope Julius changed his mind and money ran low. Michelangelo spent 40 years working on the tomb, on and off, becoming utterly frustrated with the task.

Moses

Pope Julius's tomb was eventually finished by Michelangelo's assistants and is now in the church of St Pietro in Vincoli in Rome. The only statue of note is Michelangelo's *Moses*.

Fig. 22.15 *Moses*, 1515, by Michelangelo, marble, tomb of Pope Julius II, St Pietro in Vincoli, Rome. There were to have been four prophets. Moses was the only one that was finished, but the figure has a unity and symmetry that works completely independently.

Subject

Moses is a powerful and majestic figure with a ferocious stare. Holding the tablets with God's commandments, his face expresses the supreme authority of lawgiver and messenger (Fig. 22.15).

Composition

Well over life size, this superhuman Moses is seated with his body facing forward and his head turned to the left. The left hand is intertwined in the mighty beard. With one leg pulled beneath, he looks strong, tense and ready for instant action.

Painting

Pope Julius and Michelangelo were both proud, obstinate men and their relationship was difficult. The new St Peter's was costing a fortune and eventually the pope had to divert funds from his tomb and abandon the project. When Michelangelo heard this, he left Rome in a fit of temper.

The Sistine Chapel ceiling

With considerable difficulty, Pope Julius managed to entice him back to Rome in 1508. He offered him the commission of painting the ceiling of the largest chapel in the Vatican, the Sistine Chapel (named after the pope's uncle, Sixtus IV) (Fig. 22.16).

Michelangelo protested that he was a sculptor and that painting was an inferior art, but he eventually agreed. The ceiling of the Sistine Chapel proved to be one of his greatest achievements.

Subject

The subject is from the Book of Genesis, the opening passages of the Bible. It begins with the creation of the world, Adam and Eve and the story of Noah – in other words, the stages of the human race from its beginning to its fall. All around are the prophets and sibyls who foretold the coming of Christ. In the corners are the *Ignudi*, or idealised nude youths.

Fig. 22.16 The ceiling of the Sistine Chapel, 1512, by Michelangelo, fresco, The Vatican, Rome. The panels are separated by painted architectural moulding and read from the creation scenes over the altar to the story of Noah. Michelangelo painted them in reverse order, beginning with Noah and finishing with God creating the sun, moon, Earth and darkness and light.

Composition

The ceiling is divided into nine narrative paintings in three groups of small and large panels. Around them are medallions and triangular spandrels. All the shapes are framed by illusionistic painted architecture.

Style

Midway through the project, the scaffolding was removed and Michelangelo studied the work from the ground. He then changed his style and painted larger figures that make the scenes in the second part of the ceiling much stronger.

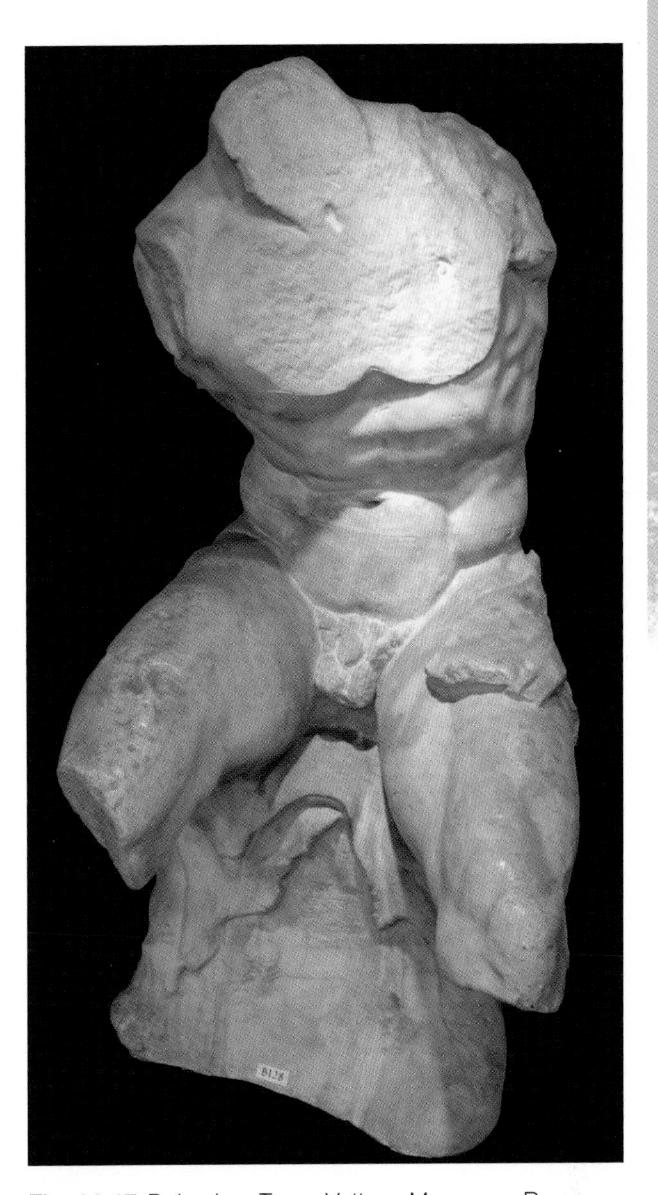

Fig. 22.17 *Belvedere Torso*, Vatican Museums, Rome

The human figure

The artist's deep understanding of the human form can be seen in the huge numbers of figures in complex poses. These were influenced by classical sculptures such as *The Laocoön and His Sons* (Fig. 22.18) and Adam resembles a fragment of the *Belvedere Torso* (Fig. 22.17).

Fig. 22.18 *The Laocoön and His Sons.* Michelangelo was present when this most famous of ancient sculptures was excavated in Rome in 1506. It was placed on public display in the Vatican, where it still can be seen today.

Colours

The soft grey tones of the imitation marble architecture and the translucent blue of the sky contrast with some extremely vivid colours.

The original golden yellows, pinks and deep blues contrasting with pale peaches and salmon were restored when the ceiling was cleaned in the late 1980s.

These strong colours were important because they could be seen better in the natural lighting of the time. They also made the complicated scenes easier to follow from the ground, some 18m below.

The light source for shading comes from the direction of the altar.

Creating an image

Michelangelo created an entirely new image of God in the Creation scenes. A stern, bearded God the Father reaches upwards to create light before wheeling around to form the planets with a mere gesture (Fig. 22.19).

Fig. 22.19 *The Creation of Light*, 1512, by Michelangelo, fresco, ceiling of the Sistine Chapel, The Vatican, Rome

The Creation of Adam

The Creation of Adam is the most famous scene (Fig. 22.20). God surges across the empty sky, with his great billowing cloak filled with 11 angels, and reaches out to the reclining figure of Adam. Adam is depicted as a young, muscular, idealised male. A spark of life passes through their outstretched fingers. Adam's hand is limp and accepting as it rests on his bent knee. This contrasts with the energy and determination of God's pointed finger.

Fig. 22.20 (above) *The Creation of Adam*, 1512, by Michelangelo, fresco, ceiling of the Sistine Chapel, The Vatican, Rome

Michelangelo's techniques

Michelangelo worked entirely alone and in a great burst of energy. Using the traditional fresco technique, he completed the huge task in just four years.

The Last Judgement

Twenty years later, Pope Paul III invited Michelangelo back to the Sistine Chapel to paint a large fresco over the altar.

Michelangelo's *The Last Judgement* (Fig. 22.21) was a break with tradition. It was placed on an eastern instead of western wall and combined classical mythology with traditional Christian imagery. Christ can be compared to Apollo, god of the sun.

Fig. 22.21 *The Last Judgement*, 1436–41, by Michelangelo, fresco on the altar wall, Sistine Chapel, The Vatican, Rome. St Bartholomew clutches the knife with which he was skinned alive and holds the skin, on which Michelangelo imprinted his own features.

Composition

The huge scene has no frame. The composition is symmetrical and organised, but there is no landscape or perspective.

The human figure

Over 300 figures are depicted in an amazing variety of contorted and energetic poses. All the figures were originally nude.

The swirling mass of humanity floats around the large and powerful figure of Christ. He steps forward with a great sweeping gesture to say to those on his right, 'Come, you who are blessed by my Father, inherit the kingdom prepared for you', and to those on his left, 'Depart from me, you cursed, into the eternal fire prepared for the devil.'

Style

Michelangelo changed from the traditional depiction of this scene; the distorted, elongated figures are more in the style of Mannerism.

Mannerism: An overly stylised 'manner' of painting from the late Italian Renaissance. Artists Portormo and Bronzino portrayed the human body in complex, witty compositions and unnatural, vibrant colours.

Colours

A deep blue sky dominates *The Last Judgment* and the bright golden yellow of the light behind Christ radiates out from the centre.

Influences

Raphael was strongly influenced by Michelangelo, and Mannerism developed directly from the work of Michelangelo.

Architecture

Fig. 22.22 The dome of St Peter's Basilica, Rome

St Peter's Basilica

Pope Julius II's grandiose tomb was never to be, but in 1506 he ordered the old Basilica of St Peter to be demolished. The building of the new St Peter's continued for almost 150 years.

Several architects were involved and the design was altered many times. Michelangelo became chief architect at 81 years of age and as was typical, he poured all his energy into the project. He redesigned the basilica to a square and centralised the entire space with a huge semi-circular dome.

Only the drum was built when he died and the design of the dome was changed to an egg shape for structural reasons (Fig. 22.22). However, Michelangelo's double Corinthian columns on the drum were already in place. These give the structure its strong upward movement.

Raphael (1483–1520)

Raphael Sanzio was a highly accomplished artist, but his easy personality and ability to get the job done without fuss greatly helped his success. He had neither Leonardo's cleverness nor Michaelangelo's powerful drive, but he absorbed the influence of these older artists and brought their techniques together in his own classical, serene and long-lasting style.

Characteristics of Raphael's work were:

* Perfectly balanced and harmonious compositions
* Noble and ideal figures that move in a calm and dignified manner
* Humanistic ideals of the High Renaissance in which the beautiful and perfect man lives in harmony with the world

Early life

Raphael's father was a man of culture at the court of Urbino. He introduced the boy to painting, artistic ideas and humanist philosophy.

When his father died he worked as an assistant to the artist Perugino. He gained extensive professional knowledge there.

He arrived in Rome in 1504 and almost immediately came to the attention of Pope Julius II.

The young artist's talents were also recognised by his successor, Leo X. Unfortunately, Raphael's career was cut short as he died on his 37th birthday.

Influences

Perugino

Raphael quickly mastered Perugino's sweet and gentle style. In fact, their painting styles are so similar that it can be difficult to tell the artists' work apart (Fig. 22.23 and Fig. 22.24).

Images of the Madonna

Raphael adopted Leonardo's pyramidal compositions and painterly techniques. From Michelangelo, he learned to study antiquities and he included lively figures in contrapposto poses.

He is, however, probably best known for his many images of the Madonna.

Fig. 22.23 (left)
Marriage of Our Lady, 1500–4, by Perugino, oil on wood, Musée des Beaux-Arts, Caen

Fig. 22.24 (right)
Marriage of Our Lady, 1504, by Raphael, oil on roundheaded panel, 170cm x 117cm, Pinacoteca di Brera, Milan

Fig. 22.25 *The Madonna of the Goldfinch*, 1507, by Raphael, oil on wood, 107cm x 77cm, Uffizi Gallery, Florence. The group of figures form a pyramidal composition, but each retains its own individuality and shape.

The Madonna of the Goldfinch

In *The Madonna of the Goldfinch* (Fig. 22.25), the child Jesus stretches out in a gentle, almost languid manner. The young St John offers him a goldfinch, a symbol of the passion.

The Madonna della Seggiola

The Madonna della Seggiola (*The Madonna of the Chair*) (Fig. 22.26) is the most loved of all Raphael's Madonnas.

The tondo, or circular shape, was very popular during the Renaissance but it was a difficult composition.

Composition

Raphael cleverly adapted the figures. The Virgin protectively cradling the infant Christ follows the curve so that they become more closely entwined. The interlocking arms and legs emphasise the circular composition and the baby becomes the centre of the picture. The elbow is the pivotal point.

Colour

The artist used an unusual combination of strong red, blue, orange and bright green.

The Stanze Raphael

The frescoes in the Stanze Raphael are the artist's most celebrated work. These rooms were once part of Pope Julius II's own residence in the Vatican.

Michelangelo was painting in the Sistine Chapel, and much to his annoyance the pope allowed Raphael to study the ceiling before it was complete.

The School of Athens

Raphael's most famous painting is in the Stanza della Segnatura, so called because important papal documents were signed there. It was also the pope's personal library.

Subject

The School of Athens (Fig. 22.28) represents the ancient Greek philosophers Plato and Aristotle and other ancient scientists in an imaginary setting. The architecture links the new St Peter's to ancient Rome.

Theme

The theme is the Renaissance humanist idea of harmony between Christian and ancient Greek philosophy. It also refers to the books in the pope's library on philosophy, law and poetry.

Fig. 22.26 *The Madonna della Seggiola* (*The Madonna of the Chair*) by Raphael, Pitti Palace, Florence

Fig. 22.27 *The Pitti Tondo* by Michelangelo. This round low relief sculpture may have influenced Raphael's *Madonna della Seggiola* (see Fig. 22.26).

The groups are engaged in lively debate.

* Euclid, surrounded by students, works out a problem in geometry with a pair of compasses on a slate.
* The Greek astronomer Ptolemy holds the earth, and the Persian astronomer Zoroaster holds a sphere of the stars on his fingertips.
* Socrates makes a point on the fingers of his left hand. Men of all ages listen attentively and one calls urgently for pen and paper.
* A young man laden with parchment rushes in. His orange cloak looks like a rolled document.
* Pythagoras is so wrapped up in his theorems that he does not notice the figure at his elbow stealing his ideas.
* There are no women in the scene.

Composition

The architecture provides much of the grandeur in *The School of Athens*. Influences from classical architecture can be seen here, in particular the Baths of Caracalla and the Pantheon in Rome.

The characters in the 'drama' are divided across the two sides and the eye of the viewer is led up the steps between them.

The two main characters, Plato and Aristotle, are set against the daylight under the domed area at the vanishing point of the composition.

Leonardo's influence

The composition is drawn from aspects of Leonardo's *Last Supper*:

* Figures are divided into separate but connected groups.
* Gestures are used to convey the narrative.
* One-point perspective is used in the architecture.

Colour

The bright pinks, blues and salmon colours echo those of Michelangelo in the Sistine Chapel.

Fig. 22.28
The School of Athens, 1510–12, by Raphael, fresco, Stanze Raphael, The Vatican, Rome. Raphael depicts the great philosophers and mathemeticians of ancient Greece as colleagues in a great academy.

Fig. 22.29 (right) and **Fig. 22.30** (below left)
The groupings and poses of the figures interacting in philosophical debate were unlike anything seen in earlier painting

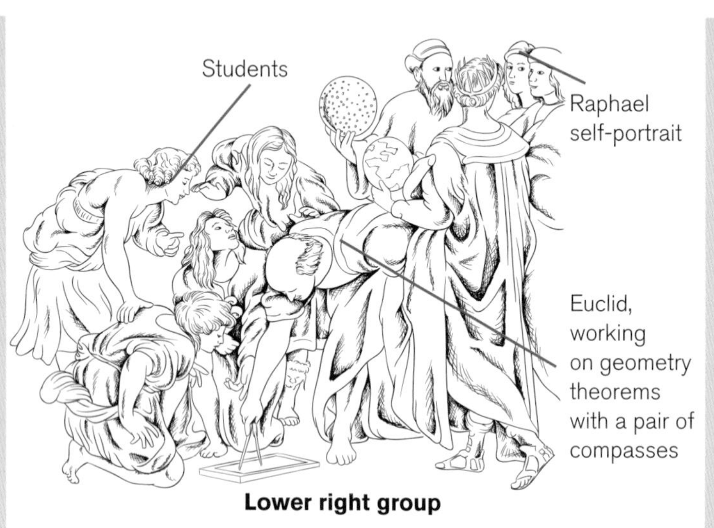

Fig. 22.31 (below)
The perspective lines converge at the centre with the philosopher Plato. This figure probably represents Leonardo da Vinci. The finger of his right hand points towards the heavens and in the other he holds his theories on the origin of the world. Next to him, his younger pupil, Aristotle, also holds a book and describes the Earth with an elegant hand gesture.

Heraclitus has Michelangelo's features and is modelled on figures from the Sistine ceiling

Pythagoras engrossed in mathematical theories

Lower left group

Fig. 22.32 *Portrait of Leo X*, 1518–19, by Raphael, oil on wood, 154cm x 119cm, Uffizi Gallery, Florence

The human figure

Michelangelo's influence can also be seen in the twisted and contrapposto poses.

Portraits

Raphael's portraits are some of his most compelling works. His psychological insight into his sitters' characters marked a new departure.

Portrait of Leo X

Portrait of Leo X is one of the most significant portraits (Fig. 22.32). The 'narrative'-style portrait is a realistic depiction of a strong and dignified leader.

The pope was Lorenzo the Magnificent's son, Giovanni, and like most papal portraits, it is a political statement.

Composition

Leo is the central figure. His face and body dominate the pyramidal composition.

The group portrait also features Cardinals Luigi de' Rossi and Giulio de' Medici, who were related to the pope.

Symbolism

Leo X loved books and has just glanced up from the examination of a beautifully illuminated manuscript with the aid of a magnifying glass. The finely carved bell on the table also indicates his status as one of Rome's great art collectors.

Colour

The delicately brocaded white cassock and lush velvet cape are depicted with the greatest care. The deep red tones of the clothing add richness and enhance this image of power and splendour.

Influences

Raphael's art was particularly influential on artists to come.

Chapter review

* The Early Renaissance was centred largely on Florence and was mostly paid for by rich patrons like the Medici family. The High Renaissance was centred on Rome and paid for by the popes. How, do you think, did this affect the different character of these cities?
* The change in the status of the artist from craftsman to an intellectual meant that artists like Leonardo, Michelangelo and Raphael were considered geniuses. How, do you think, did this affect the work of later artists?

EXAM QUESTIONS

Ordinary Level (2015)

The Last Supper is a fresco by Leonardo da Vinci (1452–1519). Answer (a) and (b).

(a) Describe and discuss this work under the following headings:

- Composition and use of perspective
- Technique and use of colour
- Treatment of the human figure

(b) Give some general information on Leonardo da Vinci.

Illustrate your answer.

Ordinary Level (2010)

Michelangelo (1475–1564) was a great artist of the High Renaissance. Answer (a) and (b).

(a) Name and describe one of his artworks under the following headings:

- Subject matter
- Composition
- Materials and technique

(b) Give some general information about Michelangelo.

Use sketches to illustrate your answer.

Higher Level (2016)

'Raphael (1483–1520) was a master of harmony, balance and subtle light and shade.'

Discuss this statement with reference to *Madonna of the Goldfinch* (Fig. 22.25). In your answer, refer to subject matter, composition, treatment of the human figure and the period in which this work was produced.

and

Name and briefly describe and discuss **one** other work by Raphael.

Illustrate your answer.

Higher Level (2015)

'Leonardo da Vinci's (1452–1519) study of science and nature as well as his acute powers of observation led him to create some of the greatest works of the Renaissance.'

Discuss this statement with reference to the painting *The Virgin of the Rocks* (Fig. 22.8). In your answer, refer to the name of the work, subject matter, composition, technique and the period in which the work was produced.

and

Briefly describe and discuss **one** other named work by this artist.

Illustrate your answer.

FURTHER RESEARCH

www.youtube.com – National Gallery Podcast: Restoring Leonardo's The Virgin of the Rocks

www.youtube.com – National Gallery Podcast: Leonardo – From the Louvre to London

www.italian-renaissance-art.com – The Last Judgment: Images of a Masterpiece

www.khanacademy.org – Last Judgment – Essay by Dr Esperanca Camara

www.khanacademy.org – High Renaissance: Florence and Rome

Chapter 23

The High Renaissance in Venice

Venice, 'Queen of the Adriatic', was the most splendid city in Italy in the 16th century. Built on canals and lagoons, it shimmered and glistened in a soft, radiant light.

By the end of this chapter, I will...

* Know that colour and light define Venetian painting.
* Understand why the Venetian artists painted with oil paints on canvas.
* Be able to describe and discuss examples of Venetian art.
* Know how to discuss the key characteristics of Titian's style.
* Be able to draw, describe and discuss two important works by Titian.

Painting in Venice

Colour and light are the main characteristics associated with Venetian painting. This was due mainly to the artists' use of oil paint on canvas.

Gesso: White chalk powder mixed with a thin base of animal glue. Artists put it on canvas or wood to give the surface more texture and to prevent the paint from sinking into the fibres.

Drawing and colour

The painting techniques of Venice and Florence can be compared in two words: drawing and colour.

In Florence, drawing was the most important thing. Paint was added only when this was perfect. In Venice, colour was an end in and of itself.

Giovanni Bellini (c. 1430–1516)

Giovanni Bellini (c. 1430–1516) revolutionised Venetian painting. He ran a large workshop in Venice and influenced his students Giorgione and Titian.

Giorgione (1477–1510)

Little is known of the life of Giorgione (which means 'big Giorgio'). He died at an early age but his mysterious, dreamlike painting brought the new word 'poesie', or visual poetry, to Renaissance art. These mysterious pictures are halfway between dream and reality.

The Tempest

The meaning of *The Tempest* (Fig. 23.1) has been greatly debated, but the strange landscape remains a mystery.

Fig. 23.1 *The Tempest*, c. 1505, by Giorgione, oil on canvas, 82cm x 73cm, Gallerie dell'Accademia, Venice

Light

A vibrant brightness comes from a single flash of lightning just before a storm.

Colours

The blue-green sky and other vibrant greens and the use of sfumato create a feeling of impending doom.

Sleeping Venus

Sleeping Venus (Fig. 23.2) is a picture of poetic beauty. Bathed in afternoon sunlight, the goddess of love sleeps in the peace of the countryside.

Concert Champêtre

Concert Champêtre (Pastoral Concert) (Fig. 23.3) may have been finished by Titian.

Fig. 23.2 *Sleeping Venus*, c. 1510, by Giorgione, oil on canvas, 108cm x 175cm, Gemäldegalerie Alte Meister, Dresden

Fig. 23.3
Pastoral Concert (*Fête Champêtre* or *Concert Champêtre*), 1508–9, by Giorgione or Titian, oil on canvas, 110cm x 138cm, Louvre, Paris

Titian (1485–1576)

Tiziano Vecellio, or Titian, was the greatest artist of 16th-century Venice.

Titian began his career in Bellini's workshop and later worked with Giorgione. He was so affected by Giorgione's style that for a while it was difficult to tell the two artists' work apart, but his own style changed and developed over the years. He painted altarpieces, portraits, mythological subjects and landscapes with figures.

Techniques and style

Titian was a most expressive artist and was the first to fully explore the possibilities of oil painting. He painted directly onto the canvas with rich, vibrant colours, often changing as he went along. He used soft, fluffy brushwork and had a distinctive smooth, velvety-textured style.

Fig. 23.4 *Assumption of the Virgin*, 1516–18, by Titian, oil on wood, 690cm x 360cm, Santa Maria Gloriosa dei Frari, Venice

Paintings

Assumption of the Virgin

Titian's huge painting *Assumption of the Virgin*

(Fig. 23.4) is set over the high altar in the church of Santa Maria Gloriosa dei Frari. It established Titian's reputation in Venice.

Composition

The innovative composition shows Mary as she is assumed 'body and soul' into heavenly glory. Its three sections are linked by colour:

* In the lowest section the disciples react with amazement.
* In the middle section the Virgin Mary soars upward, surrounded by angels.
* The top section represents heaven, where God awaits.

Colour

The disciples in red form a pyramidal shape with Mary's vibrant red gown. This draws the eye to God's red robe above.

The human figure

Titian's figures are bursting with energy and life. The twisting and complex poses give the work enormous emotional power and drama.

Bacchus and Ariadne

The scene is based on a theme from classical poetry, but the real idea is love at first sight. It depicts a dramatic moment when Bacchus, the wine god, sees Princess Ariadne, daughter of the King of Crete. He leaps from his chariot, drawn by two cheetahs (Fig. 23.5).

Colour

Intense blue ultramarine and red vermillion are complemented by the beautiful gold-orange sash on the woman with the cymbals.

The human figure

The noisy group shows clear references to classical sculpture. Ariadne's graceful pose is like a dancer. The leaping figure of Bacchus is the most dramatic.

Composition

Bacchus is the cental figure in the triangle. The focal point is the dramatic look between him and Ariadne.

Fig. 23.5

Bacchus and Ariadne, 1520–2, by Titian, oil on canvas, 175cm x 190cm, National Gallery, London

Fig. 23.6
Venus of Urbino, 1538, by Titian, oil on canvas, 119cm x 165cm, Uffizi Gallery, Florence

Venus of Urbino

Venus of Urbino (Fig. 23.6) is a similar composition to Giorgione's *Sleeping Venus*. It was probably a marriage gift and contains many symbolic references.

The little dog is a symbol of faithfulness, but the picture suggests that the perfect Renaissance woman would be like Venus: a goddess of love who is sensual, beautiful and aware of her charms.

Symbolic: Representing or relating to something else.

Fig. 23.7 *Ecce Homo*, 1558–60, by Titian, oil on canvas, 73.4cm x 56cm, National Gallery of Ireland, Dublin

Ecce Homo

One of the most moving and deeply spiritual examples of Titian's religious paintings is *Ecce Homo* ('behold the man'). This 'Man of Sorrow' was painted when Titian was almost 80 years old.

The soft painterly tones enhance this deeply moving image of a gentle Christ, bound, tortured, beaten and crowned with thorns. The bright yellow glow places the face in shadow and the eyes are downcast. This divine halo suggests that the human body is easily damaged or destroyed, but the spirit cannot be reached.

Chapter review

* Venice's location made it less susceptible to outside influences, but perhaps the greatest contribution to its distinctive artistic style was the unique quality of the natural light there. Do you think this gave Venetian painting its unique character or was it the use of oil paint on canvas?

EXAM QUESTIONS

Higher Level (2008)

Describe and discuss *Assumption of the Virgin* by Titian (1488–1576) (Fig. 23.4), making reference to style, composition and colour.

and

Name and briefly discuss **one** other work by Titian or a work by another Venetian artist of the period.

Illustrate your answer.

FURTHER RESEARCH

www.khanacademy.org – Venice

www.nationalgallery.org.uk – Bacchus and Ariadne

Chapter 24

The Early Renaissance in Northern Europe

Northern Renaissance painting in Flanders

Flanders was part of a large area of northern France and Belgium in the 15th century. It was centred on the cities of Ghent and Bruges. The area was wealthy, and although religious it was not dominated by the church. Italian humanist ideas had little influence there.

By the end of this chapter, I will...

* Know that the Northern Renaissance had quite a different character to the Renaissance in Italy.
* Understand that illusionism and symbolism were important elements in painting.
* Know that the painting features precise details.
* Be able to describe how oil painting affected technique and colours.

Renaissance painting in Flanders was remarkable for its keenly observed nature, realistic space, landscape backgrounds and delicately precise brushwork. The style was based on the new technique of oil painting.

NOTE! The Northern Renaissance and the Italian Renaissance in Florence took place at the same time, but they had quite different characteristics.

Characteristics of Flemish paintings

* Paintings were 'illusionist' and showed highly realistic depictions of space.
* Detailed landscapes were often glimpsed through open windows or doors.
* Landscapes included atmospheric perspective.
* The paintings featured precise detailed depictions of objects like flowers, jewels, fabric, shiny metal, glass or floor tiles.
* Figures had solemn faces and stood in awkward poses.
* Symbolism featured very strongly.

Illusionism: The use of artistic techniques like perspective, foreshortening or shading to deceive the eye and create a convincing impression of reality.

Atmospheric perspective (also called aerial perspective): The technique of representing objects receding into the distance becoming hazy or blurry.

Oil painting

Oil paint:

* Was made with finely ground dry paint pigment mixed with linseed or nut oil
* Dried slowly, which allowed for better transition between colours
* Allowed for details to be added to a still-wet surface or when the paint was dry
* Produced deep, rich colours
* Could be applied in varying thickness
* Had a smooth, shiny surface that dried to a hard enamel finish

Jan Van Eyck (1390–1441)

Jan Van Eyck was the foremost artist of the Northern Renaissance. He worked with his brother Hubert in their native city of Ghent at the same time that Masaccio was working in Florence.

He was artist for Philip the Good, Duke of Burgundy. The duke regarded him highly as an artist but also valued his intellectual and scientific achievements.

NOTE! Jan Van Eyck did not invent oil painting, but he took it to a completely new level by applying several very thin layers. In this way, he achieved a startling new realism and a highly luminous, permanent finish.

Portraits

Van Eyck was chiefly a portrait painter and his innovative use of the three-quarter pose of face was quite unique. His work was in high demand with wealthy merchants and businesspeople.

The Arnolfini Portrait

The portrait of Giovanni Arnolfini and his wife (Fig. 24.1) is considered to be one of the greatest paintings ever. This small portrait was the first to show real people in full length in a real-life event. It lifted portraiture to a new and more important position. It is famous for its realism, symbolism and attention to detail.

Fig. 24.1 *The Arnolfini Portrait*, 1434, by Jan Van Eyck, oil on oak panel, 82cm x 60cm, National Gallery, London

Subject matter and symbols

This formal picture shows a solemn couple holding hands in the bedroom of their home. They are Giovanni Arnolfini, a successful merchant from Lucca in Italy, and his fiancée, Giovanna Cenami, who lived in Bruges. This painting celebrates their marriage contract.

Their clothing is painted in precise detail. Details such as the soft white fur lining on her gown and

One candle burning represents the presence of Christ but also the taking of an oath.
The crystal beads and the spotless mirror indicate Mary's purity.
The fruit on the window could refer to man's innocence in the Garden of Eden or that the couple could afford to buy it.
The shoes on the floor show it is a holy place for a sacred ceremony.
Children of the marriage are suggested by a carving of St Margaret (patron saint of childbirth) on the back of a wooden chair. This overlooks the marriage bed.
The bride stands in a way that suggests pregnancy.
The dog could represent faithfulness in marriage or that the couple could afford to keep a pet.

Fig. 24.2 Symbolic references in *The Arnolfini Portrait*

her veil of fine and expensive lace show them to be very wealthy.

The room is middle class, prosperous and shows the couple's deep religious faith. It also has many symbolic references (Fig. 24.2).

Colour

Colour is significant in the painting.

* **Black and purple:** Giovanni Arnolfini wears a black beaver hat, tunic and stockings, as suits a dignified man. Over this he wears a fur-trimmed coat of purple, a colour associated with Christ.
* **Blue and green:** Giovanna wears a blue dress that signifies the sky. Over this she wears a fashionable green gown. This colour would be considered most suitable for a society portrait and marriage picture. Green also symbolises spring, youth and fertility.
* **Red:** The vivid red draperies represent passion.

Fig. 24.3 Mirror detail of *The Arnolfini Portrait*, 1434, by Jan Van Eyck, National Gallery, London

Fig. 24.4

Madonna of Chancellor Rolin, 1435, by Jan Van Eyck, oil on wood, 66cm x 62cm, Louvre, Paris

Technique

Van Eyck's technique of thin, translucent glazes over the highlights allowed light to shine through and created an intensity of tone and colour. It allowed the artist to paint minute details in striking realism.

Illusionism

Ten tiny scenes around the mirror show Christ's passion, but the mirror itself (Fig. 24.3) is a remarkable piece of illusionism. It is a miniature picture of the complete room with figures, floor, ceiling, sky and the garden outside all fitting in the curved shape of the convex glass.

The backs of the couple are clearly depicted and in between we can see the painter working at his easel. Another figure is coming through the door behind him.

The artist as witness

The inclusion of the artist in the mirror suggests he was a witness at the ceremony. To emphasise this, he has signed his name on the wall in the formal decorative handwriting associated with legal documents. The wording says 'Johannes Van Eyck Fuit Hic 1434' (which means 'Jan Van Eyck was here 1434').

The Madonna of Chancellor Rolin

The Chancellor of Burgundy (similar to a prime minister) in *The Madonna of Chancellor Rolin* (Fig.

24.4) was the trusted aide of Duke Philip the Good for over 40 years. Kneeling in prayer, he raises his eyes from his Book of Hours to see the Queen of Heaven in the room.

Composition

The figures are arranged in a strict symmetrical composition. The series of arches separate the divine world from the earthly world. Van Eyck has skilfully used linear perspective on the floor tiles and atmospheric perspective in the landscape seen through the window.

Rogier van der Weyden (1400–64)

Rogier van der Weyden was one of the top Flemish painters in the 15th century. He worked in Florence and Brussels. He is best known for his colourful altarpieces on biblical subjects.

The Descent from the Cross

The Descent from the Cross (Fig. 24.5), also known as *The Deposition*, was one of the most influential works of the Northern Renaissance. Rogier van der Weyden's large masterpiece shows the moment that Christ's body was removed from the cross. The painting was intended as an altarpiece.

Composition

The scene is illusionist and looks as if it is set in a box. The composition is based on rhyming bodies. Christ's slim lifeless body falls into in a curved shape. Overcome with grief, Mary collapses into the same pose. This mirror imaging and the hands hanging loosely side by side indicates their shared suffering. It also creates a link between the two main groups.

The artist had difficulty fitting nine figures and the cross into the restricted space, so he adjusted the poses. The man in red is quite contorted and the

Fig. 24.5
The Descent from the Cross, c. 1435, by Rogier van der Weyden, oil on oak panel, 220cm x 262cm, Prado Museum, Madrid

Virgin's left leg is stretched so that her mantle can hide the base of the cross.

Symbolism

The skull on the floor represents Golgotha, 'the Place of Skulls', where Jesus was crucified.

The human figure

The painting is highly regarded for its calm, sculptural figures. They all have very realistic facial features and show deep emotions. The Virgin Mary's sorrow is especially obvious, but only two of the group are openly weeping. There are no dramatic gestures and there is very little interaction between the figures. The real secret lies in the painting's power to connect with the viewer and draw out feelings of sympathy and emotion.

Materials and colour

The surface of the wooden panel was covered with gold. The artist used strong primary colours like red as well as the finest lapis lazuli to make blue. Fabrics such as sable, silk, gold thread embroidery, linen, leather and rope are painted in very fine detail.

Chapter review

* Jan Van Eyck perfected the skills of oil painting and brought a new realism to painting. What makes his work so real compared to some other paintings?
* Why do think *The Arnolfini Portrait* is one of the most famous works in the history of art and is considered an image of true marriage?

EXAM QUESTIONS

Ordinary Level (2016)

Answer (a) and (b).

(a) Describe and discuss *The Arnolfini Portrait* by Van Eyck (died 1441) (Fig. 24.1) under the following headings:

- Composition
- Colour and style
- Subject matter/theme

(b) Name and briefly describe and discuss **one** other work by the artist.

Illustrate your answer.

Higher Level (2013)

'Early Flemish painters made significant advances in pictorial realism and natural representation.'

Discuss this statement with reference to *The Deposition* by Rogier van der Weyden (c.1399–1464) (Fig. 24.5). Refer in your answer to subject matter, composition and the treatment of the human figure.

and

Name and briefly describe **one** other painting by a Northern European artist from this period.

Illustrate your answer.

FURTHER RESEARCH

www.louvre.fr/en – The Virgin of Chancellor Rolin

Germany and England

The Renaissance spreads

Northern Europe was never comfortable with the pomp and majesty of the Roman church. Religious devotion was much more austere in this part of Europe.

By the end of this chapter, I will...

* Know how humanist ideas in Germany and England differed from Italy.
* Be familiar with Dürer's range of artistic activities.
* Know how Dürer's self-portraits convey a message.
* Understand why Dürer's work developed printmaking as an independent art form.
* Know that Holbein became court artist to Henry VIII.
* Know why Holbein is best known for his portraits.
* Be able to identify the meaning of *The Ambassadors*.

The Renaissance in Germany

The German writer Desiderius Erasmus was a very different style of humanist scholar than the Italians. His ideas spread rapidly due to the new technology of the printing press.

Albrecht Dürer (1471–1528)

Albrecht Dürer was the most gifted and versatile artist of the German Renaissance. He grew up in Nuremberg and was apprenticed to his father, a goldsmith. The young artist learned the basics of drawing and learned woodcutting from his godfather, a printer and publisher.

His art includes:

* Altarpieces and other religious works
* Numerous portraits and self-portraits
* Keenly observed drawings of nature and animals

Printmaking

Dürer brought printmaking to a new level and established it as an independent art form.

Influenced by the art of Italy

Dürer was very impressed with the art of Italy. He visited the country twice and saw some of the great works of the Italian Renaissance firsthand.

Fig. 25.1 *Self-Portrait in a Fur-Collared Robe*, 1500, by Albrecht Dürer, oil on lime panel, 67.1cm x 48.7cm, Alte Pinakothek, Munich

Self-portraits

Dürer produced a series of self-portraits between the ages of 22 and 28.

Self-Portrait in a Fur-Collared Robe

The artist depicts himself full face, with flowing hair, staring coldly out at the viewer (Fig. 25.1). The head-and-shoulders image is clearly an imitation of the head of Christ.

Composition and colour

The picture is almost completely symmetrical. The pyramidal composition shows the influence of the Florentine Renaissance. Its dark mood is achieved through the use of brown tones set against the plain black background. Chiaroscuro and dark shadows add to the solemn atmosphere.

Symbolism

This is a statement of faith and a reminder that artistic skills are a God-given talent. The monogram of Dürer's initials, AD, refer in this case to AD, or anno Domini – the year of our Lord.

Woodcuts

Like Erasmus, Dürer used the new printing technology. Responding to a wave of apocalyptic (end of the world) feeling that was circulating in the 16th century, he produced a series of 15 woodcuts from the Apocalypse based on the

Fig. 25.2 *The Four Horsemen of the Apocalypse*, 1497–8, by Albrecht Dürer, woodcut, 399mm x 286mm, Kupferstichkabinett, Staatliche Kunsthalle Karlsruhe, Germany

revelations of St John. They were terrifying visions of the horrors of Doomsday.

The Four Horsemen of the Apocalypse

The most famous of these woodcuts is *The Four Horsemen of the Apocalypse* (Fig. 25.2). The riders represent the Conqueror, War, Famine and Death and bring plague, war, hunger and death to mankind.

An avenging angel in the sky urges them on as they trample all beneath their hooves and Hades, a hideous Leviathan (Hell), swallows everything that Death has passed in his enormous jaws.

England

The influence of Italian art was not strongly felt in England at this time. Northern artists were in great demand and one of the most gifted was Hans Holbein.

Hans Holbein (1497–1543)

Hans Holbein the younger was a key figure in German Renaissance art. His arrival in 1526 brought the Renaissance from Continental Europe to Britain.

His work was in great demand, but his career was unfortunately short lived. He died in the great London plague at the age of 46.

The Ambassadors

The huge panel painting of *The Ambassadors* (Fig. 25.3) was commissioned by Jean de Dinteville to hang in his family chateau in France. He and his

Fig. 25.3
The Ambassadors, 1533, by Hans Holbein, oil on oak, 207cm x 209cm, National Gallery, London

friend Georges de Selve, the Bishop of Lavaur, were ambassadors from the French court for the coronation of Anne Boleyn.

Composition

The painting takes the form of a rich man's cabinet. In Renaissance times this was designed to hold secrets and no one could open it unless they understood the tricks of its construction. The two men leaning on their elbows are like human doors on either side of the cabinet.

Symbolism

The two ambassadors visited England at a politically difficult time, when religious division was splitting Europe apart. The painting is a kind of test with hidden clues. The objects symbolise the turmoil of their world.

The instruments for astronomy and telling time by the sun are all incorrectly set. This suggests chaos in the world.

The musical instrument, a lute, has a broken string. This is a traditional sign for disharmony.

The strange shape that floats between the men is the final clue to its true meaning. The anamorphic image of a human skull makes the painting a *momento mori*, or a reminder of death. It indicates that despite all man's worldly achievements, we all must die and only God can judge.

Anamorphosis: An image that is distorted in a particular way. It can only be recognised when seen from a certain angle or by reflection in a curved surface.

Fig. 25.4 *Portrait of Sir Thomas More*, 1527, by Hans Holbein, National Portrait Gallery, London

Portrait of Sir Thomas More

Holbein painted Sir Thomas More (Fig. 25.4), a lawyer, author and statesman as well as a leading humanist scholar.

He was Lord Chancellor for Henry VIII but was executed for treason. He had refused to recognise the king as head of the Church of England after he split with the Church of Rome to marry Anne Boleyn.

Chapter review

* Holbein's most famous painting is *The Ambassadors.* It is filled with hidden clues as to its meaning. Why, do you think, was the artist asked to produce a painting like this?

EXAM QUESTIONS

Ordinary Level (2015)

Look at *Self-Portrait in a Fur-Collared Robe* by Albrecht Dürer (1471–1528) (Fig. 25.1).

Answer (a) and (b).

(a) Describe and discuss this painting under the following headings:

- Composition and technique
- Light and use of colour
- Treatment of the human figure

(a) Sketch and briefly describe and discuss **one** other work by Albrecht Dürer.

Illustrate your answer.

Ordinary Level (2011)

Answer (a) and (b).

(a) Describe and discuss *The Ambassadors* by Hans Holbein (1497/8–1543) (Fig. 25.3) using the following headings:

- Subject matter
- Composition and style
- Medium
- Use of colour/light

(b) Give some general information about the artist.

Use sketches to illustrate your answer.

Higher Level (2015 – adapted)

Answer (a), (b) and (c)

(a) Choose and name a painting by Hans Holbein the Younger (c. 1497–1543).

(b) Discuss the work you have chosen in detail, making reference to the artist, subject matter, style, composition, materials, technique, and the period in which the work was produced.

(c) Name and briefly describe and discuss one other work by this artist.

Illustrate your answer.

FURTHER RESEARCH

www.nationalgallery.org.uk – The Arnolfini Portrait

www.nationalgallery.org.uk – The Ambassadors

www.khanacademy.org – Van Eyck, The Arnolfini Portrait

www.wga.hu – Albrecht Dürer

www.wga.hu – Jan Van Eyck

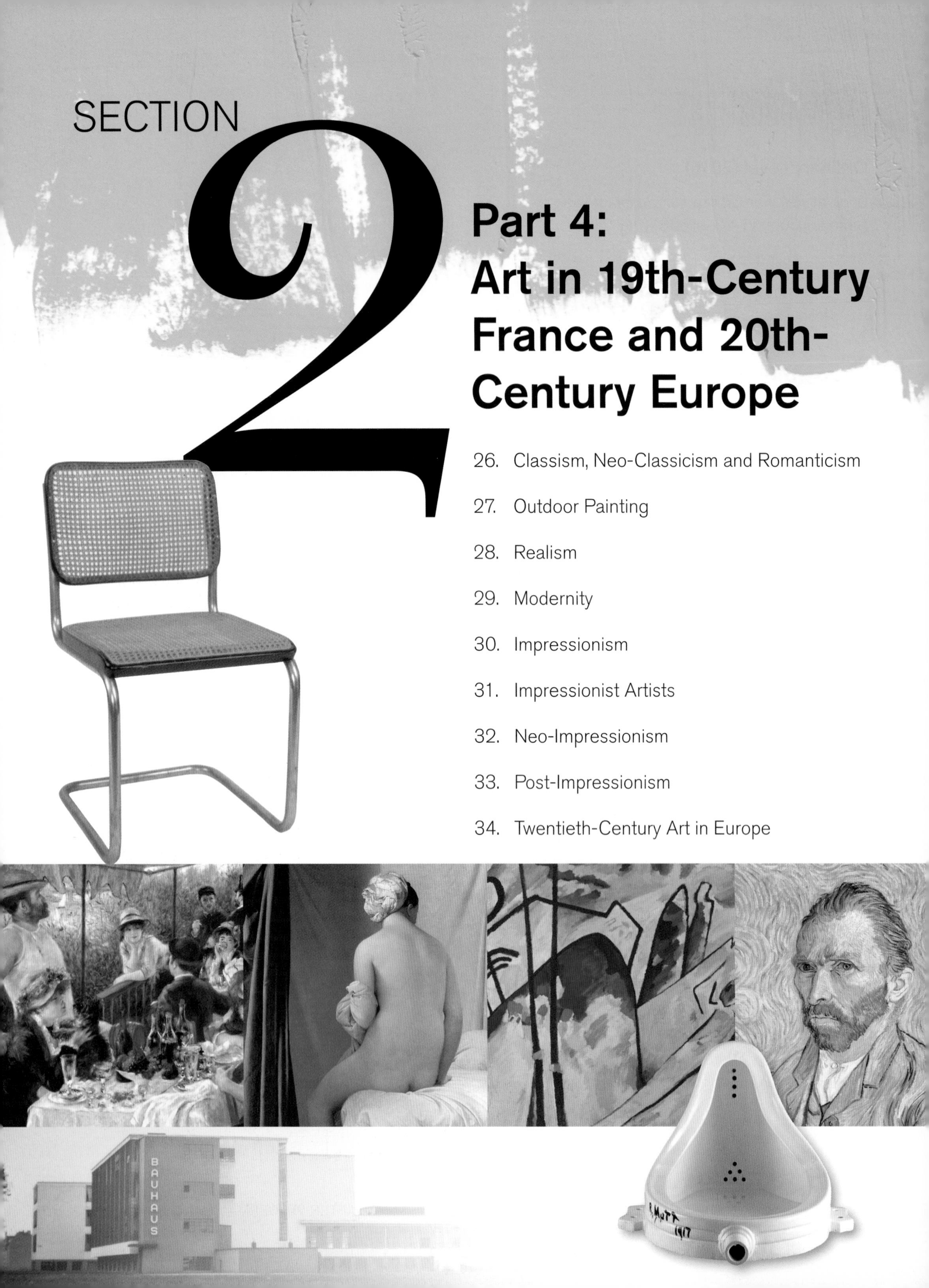

SECTION 2

Part 4: Art in 19th-Century France and 20th-Century Europe

Chapter 26

Classism, Neo-Classicism and Romanticism

Painting in mid-19th-century France marks the beginning of a more modern approach to art. The country had gone through revolution and major political upheaval. The Industrial Revolution in the 1850s brought even more social division.

A rich new middle class was the art-buying public. They depended on 'experts' to help them make a good buy. For that, they turned to the Academy.

By the end of this chapter, I will...

* Know why political events had an effect on art styles in France.
* Know why classicism was favoured by the Academy of Art.
* Understand how the Neo-Classical and Romantic styles evolved as reactions to what went before.
* Be able to identify the characteristics of each of these styles.
* Know how to identify, describe and analyse at least one work by each of the following artists: Jacques-Louis David, Jean-Auguste-Dominique Ingres, Théodore Géricault and Eugène Delacroix.

The Royal Academy

The Royal Academies of literature, painting and sculpture, music, dance and architecture were founded under Louis XIV in the 17th century. After the French Revolution, some of these institutions were grouped together to form The Académie des Beaux-Arts or Academy of Fine Art.

The Salon

To become a member of the Royal Academy of Painting and Sculpture, artists originally had to exhibit in the Salon Carré (Square Room) in the King's Palace of the Louvre. This very popular exhibition retained the title of 'Salon', but by the mid-18th century it had moved to a more spacious venue and a jury was appointed to select work and award prizes. Another committee decided where to hang them. The position of the painting was very important for success with buyers and patrons, as it was one of the year's biggest public events in Paris. People queued for hours to see the works.

Academic artistic training

Students entered the studio of a recognised master and studied in the Academic system. Over time, this system became more and more rigid.

Art was organised like a science and students spent many years on repetitive drawing exercises before moving to the 'higher' art of painting. There were strict rules and expectations regarding composition, perspective and even the surface, which had to be smooth and polished, like enamel.

Subject ranking

Subjects were ranked in three levels of importance.

Level 1:

* **History painting:** Factual events from ancient history, mythology or religion that often included instructive or moralising themes.

Level 2:

* **Literature:** Subjects from classic or contemporary writing.
* **Portraiture:** Of significant people.

Level 3:

* **Landscape:** Backgrounds for historical scenes.
* **Genre scenes:** Depictions of ordinary people that reflected noble attitudes or virtue.

History painting: Painting that is defined by subject matter. The word 'history' relates to the Italian word *istoria*, meaning 'narrative' or 'story'.

Classicism

The Royal Academy favoured the classical style developed by artist Nicholas Poussin well into the late 19th century.

Nicholas Poussin (1594–1665)

Nicolas Poussin was a 17th-century French artist. He spent most of his career in Rome and was greatly inspired by classical Italian art and ancient Greek sculpture. His work was mostly history painting of drama and action. He was highly influenced by Raphael.

Neo-Classicism

Neo-Classicism became the predominant artistic style during the French Revolution. This new (neo)

Fig. 26.1
The Rape of the Sabine Women I, 1634–5, by Nicholas Poussin, oil on canvas, 154.6cm x 209.9cm, Metropolitan Museum of Art, New York. This dramatic interpretation of an old story shows Romulus, ruler of the newly founded city of Rome, making a signal to his soldiers with his cloak to carry off the Sabine women as their wives. The Sabine men are taken by surprise and have had to flee.

NOTE! Revolutionaries saw themselves almost as Greeks and Romans reborn. They rejected the art of the Rococo because it was associated with royalty and aristocracy.

Rococo: An 18th-century artistic movement and style associated with the reign of Louis XV in France. It was typified by ornate S curves and C scrolls. It was based on motifs taken from natural sources like rocks, shells and plants.

form of classicism was more severe and stripped down. It stressed science and logic over tradition and religion and was politically inspired. Neo-Classicists favoured:

* Clear, well-drawn figures and restrained colours in painting
* Severe horizontal and vertical compositions

Jacques-Louis David (1748–1825)

The name most associated with Neo-Classical painting is Jacques-Louis David. He greatly admired Poussin but developed a starker, highly finished and morally educational style.

The Oath of the Horatii

He presented *The Oath of the Horatii* (Fig. 26.2) in Rome in 1785 and then at the Paris Salon. This huge canvas, with its life-sized figures, created a sensation and became the model for Neo-Classicism throughout Europe.

Subject

The picture was based on a legendary struggle for dominance between Rome and the city of Alba in the 7th century. Both cities agreed to settle their struggle with a fight between three representatives from each side. The Horatii brothers of Rome were pitted against the Curatii family of Alba and the only survivor was one of the Horatii. Rome was therefore victorious.

Composition

The action centres on the threatening image of the glittering blades. The poses and architecture are strictly geometrical. This is emphasised by the harsh, slanting light. The starkly athletic young men stand firm and resolute, with arms outstretched.

Fig. 26.2
The Oath of the Horatii, 1784, by Jacques-Louis David, oil on canvas, 330cm x 425cm, Louvre, Paris. David tells the story with dramatic and frightening intensity. The Horatii brothers take the oath and accept their weapons from their father, but the women of the family turn from the spectacle in resigned suffering.

Their straight-line poses contrast with the softly modelled and curved women.

Painter to the king

David was painter to King Louis XVI and was elected to the Royal Academy. He became involved in the politics of the French Revolution and even voted for the execution of the king. He welcomed the new regime and considered it to be a chance to recreate Republican Rome.

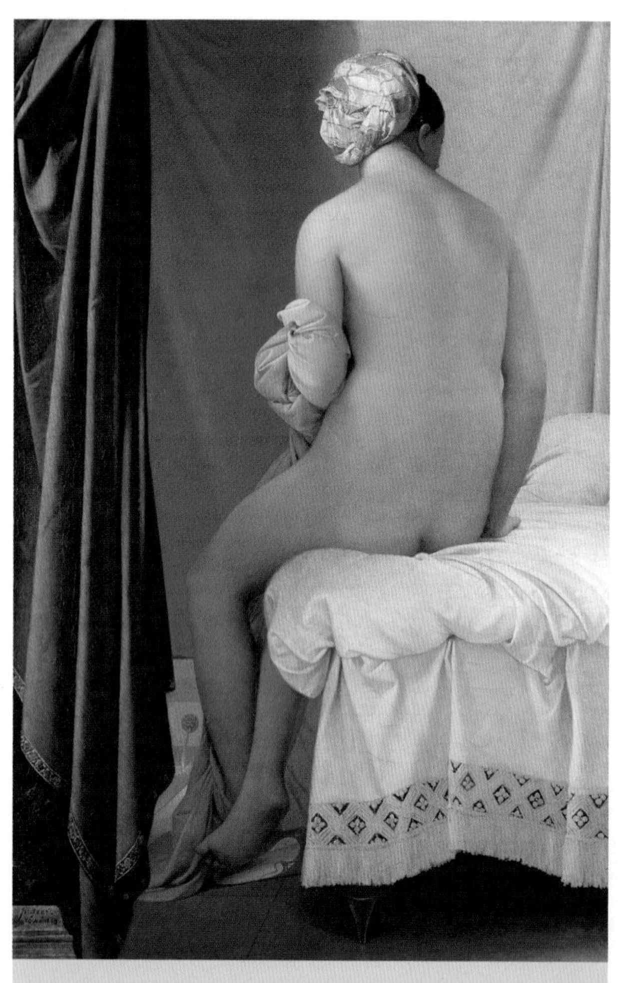

Fig. 26.3 *The Valpinçon Bather*, 1808, by Jean-Auguste-Dominique Ingres, oil on canvas, 146cm x 97cm, Louvre, Paris. Painting the back view was considered highly unusual, but the small setting draws the viewer into the tranquil, almost poetic mood. The subtle light and hidden face add to the mystery.

Jean-Auguste-Dominique Ingres (1780–1825)

David's style passed on to his student Jean-Auguste-Dominique Ingres in particular, who continued the Neo-Classical style. He adored Italian art and favoured the traditional method of Academic study from the nude, but he often distorted proportions for the sake of beauty.

The Valpinçon Bather

Ingres enjoyed painting women and *The Valpinçon Bather* (Fig. 26.3) is regarded as one of his finest works. However, it was not well received in its day.

Romanticism

Romanticism developed in the late 18th and early 19th centuries and emphasised imagination and emotions. It began with literature in England. The term 'romantic' originally meant 'romance-like' or resembling the fanciful character of medieval romances.

NOTE! Romanticism was a reaction to the cold, restrained Neo-Classical style of art, but the movement had no one definite style, technique or subject.

Romanticism encouraged:

* Imagination and a direct appeal to the emotions
* The exploration of complex concepts such as liberty, survival, hope, heroism and despair

Romantic themes

Romantic artists looked for alternative themes to Neo-Classical ones. Some of these were landscapes, images of nature, animals and natural disasters.

Théodore Géricault (1791–1824)

The artist Jean-Louis André Théodore Géricault had a personal fascination with violence and murder. His most famous painting, *The Raft of the Medusa* (Fig. 26.4), reflects this. It was based on an event that took place after the restoration of the monarchy, when all officers of the previous regime were replaced by political appointments.

The Raft of the Medusa

The story of the wreck of the frigate *Medusa* scandalised the public and acutely embarrassed the new government, but Géricault's strikingly original painting created a sensation. It won a gold medal at the Salon of 1819.

Subject

The ship ran aground in 1816 on a sandbank in West Africa. The captain and crew took all the lifeboats and abandoned 149 soldiers. The captain had no experience of commanding a ship at sea, and his incompetence and cowardice led to disaster.

The men constructed a raft from masts of the ship. Standing waist deep in seawater, they drifted for 13 days without food or water. They had resorted to murder and cannibalism before the raft was found by accident. Only 10 survived.

Composition

The composition forms a powerful X shape in two pyramidal shapes. The huge painting, with its life-sized figures, almost invites the viewer to step onto the raft with them.

Colour and lighting

The sombre, dramatic colours are typical of the Romantic movement. The ochre, burnt sienna, umber and deep browns contrast with the deep blue of the stormy sea and the flesh tones of the mass of bodies. The dramatic light and dark tones of grey-green storm clouds in the light sky are in sharp contrast to the green and black darkness of the sea, and it highlights the deathly pallor of the piled-up bodies.

The human figure

Géricault visited hospitals and made detailed sketches of the sick and dying, as well as corpses in the morgue.

Fig. 26.4
The Raft of the Medusa, 1818–19, by Théodore Géricault, oil on canvas, 491cm x 716cm, Louvre, Paris. Géricault chose the moment of despair as the survivors gather up the last of their strength to form a human pyramid but fail to attract the attention of the distant ship.

Eugène Delacroix (1798–1863)

The principal artist associated with Romanticism in France is Eugène Delacroix. He was profoundly influenced by Théodore Géricault and watched him working on *The Raft of the Medusa*.

Delacroix's pictures are stimulating and emotional. He used vivid colours, chose imaginative subjects and worked with quite loose brushstrokes. In a famous quote he wrote, 'Without daring and even extreme daring, there is no beauty.'

Early career

His formal Academic training followed Jacques-Louis David's technique and he developed his skills by copying works of the Old Masters at the Louvre. He greatly admired Venetian painting and was also influenced by English artists after he spent time in England.

Liberty Leading the People

Delacroix's first modern political composition was *Liberty Leading the People* (Fig. 26.5). It was inspired by the July Revolution of 1830 in Paris. The vibrant, rebellious, bare-breasted woman leading the people is the symbolic moral and political figure of Liberty. She wears the red hat of the revolution and runs forward with a musket with bayonet attached in one hand and the French flag raised with the other.

Theme

The theme is that this revolution is for all classes in society.

* A child in the foreground suggests it serves the next generation.
* A man in an apron and working shirt waving a sword represents factory workers.
* A younger-looking man wearing a fine black coat, top hat and an open-collared white shirt with a cravat looks more affluent. He may represent the artist himself.

Fig. 26.5
Liberty Leading the People, 1830, by Eugène Delacroix, oil on canvas, 260cm x 325cm, Louvre, Paris. This painting is the defining image of French Romanticism and one of the most enduring modern images of revolution.

Fig. 26.6
The Women of Algiers in Their Apartment, 1834, by Eugène Delacroix, oil on canvas, 180cm x 229cm, Louvre, Paris. The dark background accentuates the brightly coloured textiles and the beautiful women sitting in the gentle half-light. The vibrant colours and dark flesh tones contribute to the warm, sensuous mood.

Composition

The peak of the pyramid-shaped composition is the monumental figure of Liberty with the fighters spread at her feet. This technique brings order to what might otherwise look like chaos in a hectic and crowded canvas.

Colour

The red, white and blue of the tricolour is echoed throughout and brings unity to the work.

The government's reaction

The picture was not well received at the Salon in 1831. It was bought by the state but kept from view until 1848, when a new revolution swept away the government.

Influence from Morocco

A trip to Morocco in 1832 was one of the most important journeys of Delacroix's career. It greatly inspired him to experiment with colour. He filled several notebooks with drawings and visited a harem. Upon returning to France he produced a large canvas, *The Women of Algiers in Their Apartment*, for the 1834 Salon (Fig. 26.6). Painted in small but free brushstrokes and thick paint, the picture conveys the calmness and serenity of the women's private apartment.

Influence on later artists

Delacroix's colour theories influenced later artists, including Renoir, Seurat, Cézanne and Van Gogh.

Chapter review

* The fixed dogma of the 'noble and 'ideal' classical style that dominated the Academy was first challenged by Eugène Delacroix. Why do you think that his paintings of imagination, colour and emotion were acceptable to the Academy in the mid-19th century?

EXAM QUESTIONS

Ordinary Level (2016 – adapted)

(a) Describe and discuss *The Oath of the Horatii* by Jacques-Louis David (1748–1825) under the following headings:

- Subject matter
- Composition
- Style and use of colour

(b) Name and briefly describe and discuss one other work by your chosen artist.

Illustrate your answer.

Higher Level (2013 and 2011)

Describe in detail the main characteristics of **one** of the following:

- Neo-Classicism
- Romanticism

and

Describe and briefly discuss **one** named work by an artist whose work is typical of the style or movement you have chosen.

Illustrate your answer.

FURTHER RESEARCH

www.wga.hu – paintings by Jacques-Louis David, Jean-Auguste-Dominique Ingres, Théodore Géricault and Eugène Delacroix

www.metmuseum.org – Neoclassicism essay

www.khanacademy.org – Neo-Classicism, an introduction

www.khanacademy.org – Géricault, Raft of the Medusa

www.khanacademy.org – Delacroix, Liberty Leading the People

Chapter 27

Outdoor Painting

Landscape painting began with the Romantic movement in England. Artists traditionally sketched out of doors, but large paintings were done in the studio. This influenced French landscape painting.

By the end of this chapter, I will...

* Know that English landscape painting influenced the development of *plein air* painting in France.
* Be able to discuss why it was easier to paint directly from nature than in earlier times.
* Know why artists wanted to work *en plein air.*
* Know how landscape painting became an important subject in its own right.
* Know who the Barbizon painters were.
* Be able to describe and discuss Camille Corot's landscapes.
* Understand why this artist was so influential on younger artists.

England

The two English painters most associated with landscape painting in the early 19th century are John Constable and William Turner. These artists were very different, both in personality and in their approach to nature. Turner travelled a great deal and painted dramatic seascapes and landscapes. Constable preferred to paint the calm, rural countryside of Suffolk.

John Constable (1776–1837)

John Constable had considerable success in Paris when he exhibited *The Hay Wain* (Fig. 27.1) at the Salon of 1824. Eugène Delacroix was particularly affected by this large work and went on to imitate its shifting light, flickering brushwork and broken colour.

Constable sketched outdoors directly from nature but always completed his paintings in the studio. His work also had quite moral overtones.

Joseph Mallord William Turner (1775–1851)

William Turner was called 'the painter of light' because of his brilliant colours and his interest in skies (Fig. 27.2). He travelled continuously in Europe, particularly in Italy, France, Germany and Switzerland, making drawings and watercolours.

NOTE! *Plein air* is French for 'open air'. The term is used to describe the practice of painting a subject outdoors directly from nature.

Fig. 27.1
The Hay Wain, 1821, by John Constable, oil on canvas, 130.2cm x 185.4cm, National Gallery, London

Fig. 27.2
Shipwreck Off Hastings, c. 1828, by William Turner, watercolour on paper, 185mm x 285mm, National Gallery of Ireland, Dublin

New technology for artists

One of the main reasons for the popularity of landscape painting was the development of new and more convenient materials. Solid blocks of watercolour paint and folding portable easels made working outdoors more accessible, but life changed for artists in 1842 when Winsor & Newton began selling oil paint in collapsible tin tubes.

Landscape painting in France

English tourists began arriving in France in the early 19th century and among these were many watercolour artists. These artists were particularly attracted to the Channel coastline because of the amazing quality of light there. French artists were subsequently encouraged to sketch directly from nature (*en plein air*) and gradually centres of *plein air* painting began to emerge in various parts of the country.

The Barbizon school and Realism

The Barbizon group of painters was the first to specialise only in landscape. They settled outside of Paris in the village of Barbizon during the 1830s. The village was on the edge of the Forest of Fontainebleau. The peasants, the forest and the open fields near the village were an endless source of inspiration.

Characteristics

* The Barbizon artists tried to capture the real light and colours of the countryside.
* They were interested in *plein air* painting.
* They focused on rural life, its seasons and above all, its changing light and colour.
* The work was finished in studio, where the painter tended to add 'meaning' or emotion to the work.

The artists

Theodore Rousseau was the driving force behind Barbizon. Better-known artists like Jean-François Millet and Camille Corot soon joined him.

Camille Corot (1796–1875)

Gentle landscapes

Corot's work often included classical or literary figures. This was in line with the Salon tradition, but the landscape still has a gentle, silvery-toned mood (Fig. 27.3).

Influence on younger painters

Corot is a transitional figure. He was highly influential on younger painters and constantly praised nature. He also urged his followers to hold fast to their first impression.

Fig. 27.3 *The Wood Gatherer*, 1865–70, by Camille Corot, oil on canvas, 45.7cm x 64.1cm, National Gallery, London

Chapter review

* Camille Corot was highly influential within the Barbizon group of painters. He encouraged younger painters to study nature out of doors, but he remained quite conservative. Why, do you think, was he so influential on these artists, who had much more radical ideas than him?

FURTHER RESEARCH

www.khanacademy.org –
Constable and the English Landscape

www.youtube.com –
Barbizon: The Cradle of Impressionism

Realism

The Realist movement in French art flourished from about 1840 until the late 19th century. The style spread to almost all genres, including history painting, portraits and landscapes.

By the end of this chapter, I will...

* Be able to identify the main characteristics of the style of Realism.
* Know why Gustave Courbet set out to shock.
* Be able to describe and discuss in detail one work by Courbet.
* Know why Jean-François Millet chose to paint peasants in the fields.
* Understand why Millet's painting was regarded as crude.
* Be able to describe and discuss in detail one work by Millet.

Gustave Courbet (1819–1877)

The established leader of the Realist movement was Gustave Courbet. He was a farmer's son from Ornans in south-eastern France near the Swiss border. He was a larger-than-life character and was often at the centre of controversy. He had a reputation as an arrogant, beer-swilling peasant, but beneath it all he was an intelligent and sensitive man.

Courbet's career

As a young artist, Courbet copied the works of the Old Masters in the Louvre. He was interested in Dutch and Spanish painting and he studied these on his travels abroad. He painted scenes from his own farming background and his work reflected his staunch socialism. His works included portraits, still life, nudes and landscapes, but he avoided every subject that was previously thought suitable for fine art.

The 'Temple of Realism'

Courbet was one of the first to challenge the Academic system. He and a group of intellectuals often met in a Paris café called the Brasserie Andler. They renamed this the 'Temple of Realism'. The group rejected the Academic standards of painting. They preferred to depict typical everyday people and situations with truth and accuracy.

'Truth, not prettiness'

Courbet said he wanted 'truth, not prettiness' and was determined to portray the world as he saw it. His aim was to shock society with straightforward images of contemporary rural society. He painted realistic depictions of farmers, gravediggers, woodsmen and poachers in paintings that glorified the hard work.

Exhibiting at the Salon

He found it very difficult to get these paintings shown at the Salon, but in 1848 another short-lived revolution in Paris brought Louis Napoleon to power as President of the French Republic. That year the Salon opened without a selection committee. Courbet won a gold medal, which meant he was exempt from the selection process for life and could now present Realist scenes from his beloved hometown of Ornans at the Salon.

A Burial at Ornans

A Burial at Ornans (Fig. 28.1) was the first of Courbet's great masterpieces. The huge painting was shown at the 1850 Salon exhibition. The painting had nearly 60 life-sized figures. Traditionally, this would have been reserved for grand and noble subjects. Workers and peasants were considered suitable only for smaller genre scenes.

This funeral at Ornans was for Courbet's uncle, but the artist wanted to make this his 'statement of principle' and remind us all of the true nature of death. Actors would have traditionally been used for the figures, but Courbet depicted the actual townspeople, relatives and friends who were at the burial.

Composition

The frieze-like composition of mourners follows a horizontal structure in line with the hills in the background. No heads reach above this line.

Lighting and colours

The dark greens and dull greys create an austere tone. Courbet deliberately kept all light out of the painting and chose a cloudy, dark evening sky.

Realism

A Burial at Ornans was utterly shocking and considered a 'glorification of vulgarity', but Courbet said it was 'the burial of Romanticism'. It marked the beginning of Realism.

Courbet's paintings continued to offend the Academic notions of dignity and grandeur. The Universal Exhibition of 1855 was a huge international event in Paris, but the jury refused his work. Courbet responded with a one-man show in his own pavilion close to the site of the official exhibition. This was advertised under a single heading: 'Realism'. The venture was a flop, but it was the turning point of his career.

Fig. 28.1 *A Burial at Ornans*, 1849–50, by Gustave Courbet, oil on canvas, 315cm x 668cm, Musée d'Orsay, Paris. The painting was originally called *A Painting of Human Figures, the Story of a Burial at Ornans.*

Fig. 28.2 *The Meeting* or *Bonjour Monsieur Courbet*, 1854, by Gustave Courbet, oil on canvas, 129cm x 149cm, Musée Fabre, Montpellier. This direct, anti-bourgeois gesture went against the image of the 'respectable' artist.

Bonjour Monsieur Courbet

In 1854 Courbet paid a visit to Montpellier in the south to stay with one of his rich patrons, the art collector Alfred Bruyas.

In his work *Bonjour Monsieur Courbet* (Fig. 28.2), he represents himself with no graceful poses, but as a simple artist. Dressed casually in his shirtsleeves with a stick and painting equipment strapped to his back, the painter holds his head high. The poses were based on a well-known popular print called *The Wandering Jew.* In the 19th century this would have been associated with an outsider, and that is exactly what Courbet would have identified with.

Influence on modern movements

The modern movements that followed Realism were highly influenced by Courbet's philosophy, but he had no direct followers in France.

Jean-François Millet (1814–75)

Jean-François Millet depicted rural French life with insight and compassion. He grew up on a farm near Cherbourg in Normandy and wrote, 'I have never seen anything but fields since I was born. I simply try to say what I saw and felt.'

Barbizon

Millet moved to the village of Barbizon in 1849 and worked there for the rest of his life. He painted country scenery, but his real love was the peasants at work. He depicted the huge Barbizon harvest fields in his paintings *The Gleaners* and *The Angelus.* These distinctive and personal scenes show peasants working in the fields in a low-key, almost melancholy but deeply emotional atmosphere.

The Gleaners

The Gleaners (Fig. 28.3) was shown at the Salon in the summer of 1857 and was given a hostile, conservative response. Gleaning was one of the lowest jobs in society. It was traditionally given to women, who had to go to the fields at sunset and quickly pick up the ears of corn one by one.

The three figures in the foreground are the central focus of the picture. This position was reserved for heroes in Academic works, but Millet's silhouetted figures have an air of quiet nobility and their labour is presented as worthwhile and beautiful.

The Angelus

Subject

The Angelus (Fig. 28.4) shows a hard-working couple at work in the fields as they take a short break and bow their heads. This was based on a childhood memory and was not intended as a

Fig. 28.3
The Gleaners, 1857, by Jean-François Millet, oil on canvas, 83.5cm x 110cm, Musée d'Orsay, Paris. The painting depicts the three phases of this backbreaking, repetitive task as the figures bend, pick up and straighten again.

religious message. The small canvas shows the couple set against the huge empty field. This gives them a monumental quality, and the reflected light emphasises their posture and gestures.

Fig. 28.4 *The Angelus*, 1858, by Jean-François Millet, oil on canvas, 55.5cm x 66cm, Musée d'Orsay, Paris. Millet said, 'I remembered that my grandmother, hearing the church bell ringing while we were working in the fields, always made us stop work to say the Angelus prayer for the poor departed.'

Influence on later artists

Millet's painting had a profound impact on his artistic contemporaries and younger artists like Degas, Seurat, Pissarro, Gauguin and especially Van Gogh.

Realism and its influence

Édouard Manet and the Impressionists greatly admired Realism and Courbet's stand against worn-out artistic practices.

Chapter review

* Realism challenged the Academic system and Gustave Courbet was seen as a dangerous rebel. Why was he so shocking?
* Younger artists were highly influenced by Courbet's philosophy, but he had no direct followers. Why do you think that was?
* Jean-François Millet created empathy with both the landscape and the people working in the fields. How did he achieve this?

EXAM QUESTIONS

Higher Level (2015 – adapted)

Answer (a), (b) and (c).

(a) Discuss the development of Realism.

(b) Describe the main characteristics of this movement.

(c) Describe and discuss **one** named work by a named artist whose work is typical of Realism.

Illustrate your answer.

Higher Level (2014)

'Portraying everyday country life was a recurring theme in the work of the Realist painter Gustave Courbet (1819–77).'

Discuss this statement with reference to *Bonjour Monsieur Courbet* (Fig. 28.2), illustrated on the accompanying sheet, and refer to subject matter, composition, style and the treatment of the human figure.

and

Briefly describe and discuss how Impressionist artists were influenced by Realism.

Illustrate your answer.

FURTHER RESEARCH

www.theartstory.org/movement-realism.htm

www.khanacademy.org – Courbet, Burial at Ornans 1850

www.khanacademy.org – Bonjour Monsieur Courbet

www.khanacademy.org – Millet, The Gleaners 1857

www.jeanmillet.org

Chapter 29

Modernity

Édouard Manet (1832–33)

Édouard Manet was highly influenced by Gustave Courbet's energy and independent spirit, but his subjects held no interest for him. Manet dreamed of a different kind of art revolution.

By the end of this chapter, I will...

* Undestand why Manet was so anxious to succeed with the official Salon.
* Know why contemporary subjects were important for Manet.
* Be able to discuss how Manet's style went against the tradition of Academic art.
* Know how Manet's work related to the Impressionist artists.

A modern revolution

Manet's ambition was to work in a truly modern style as an established Academic artist. He had the highest regard for the Paris Salon and his goal was to gain recognition there. This ambition never changed throughout his life.

He admired 17th-century Dutch and Spanish painting. He was also greatly inspired by Italian Renaissance art, particularly Venetian art. He had a clear vision of how to modernise these grand traditions but in a specifically French way. Unfortunately, his ideas did not fit with the accepted manner of Academic thinking and he suffered official rejection and even ridicule. This deeply troubled him and caused him great upset all his life.

A well-to-do background

Édouard Manet was the son of a wealthy lawyer. He was born into a prosperous upper-middle-class family with aristocratic connections. He trained in the studio of respected painter Thomas Couture for six years and developed a high regard for the art of the past. Manet respected and admired his teacher, but the Academic system of instruction frustrated him. He said, 'I paint what I see, and not what others choose to see.'

Manet's style and technique

After he left Couture's studio, his art took a very different direction and he developed his own style.

* He preferred painting directly from reality rather than with imaginary elements.
* His drawing line was firm and strong and he liked dark colours.
* He avoided the method of building up colours into a thick glaze over under-painting.
* He worked directly and often applied wet paint on wet, which meant paintings were completed much more quickly.

* Instead of mixing colours on his palette, he often placed colours side by side. This allowed the eye to mix them.
* His brushstrokes were loose and parts of the canvas were often sparsely covered.
* He used strongly contrasting tones and many different colours to suggest tone.
* The Academic method of lighting from one side was too false for him. He preferred to work with natural light like sunlight.
* He chose stark contrasts of light and dark rather than the traditional grading of tone. As a result, his figures tended to 'flatten out' rather than have the smooth, rounded Academic finish.
* His paintings appear simple but they were, in fact, quite difficult to produce.

Influence of photography

The influence of the new art of photography can be seen in Manet's paintings. The picture frame cuts off some figures as if they are captured in a random photo. The frontal or 'flat lighting' popular in studio photography bleaches out the flesh tones of the sitter, creating a contrast between light and dark, thus reducing the grades of tone.

Modern subjects

Manet was anxious to depict modern life. He chose everyday scenes of fashionable people in Paris, but his subjects also included beggars, street singers and scenes in the cafés.

Early works

Spanish influence

Manet's early works drew heavily on elements of 17th-century Spanish artists like Velázquez. In 1861, *The Spanish Singer* (Fig. 29.1) earned him an honourable mention at the Salon. The artist's success was short lived, though, and from then on he had very little luck with the Salon.

Salon des Refusés

The Salon jury of 1863 rejected more than two-thirds of the paintings submitted for exhibition. Manet's work was among these. The artists and their friends protested, and this reached Emperor Napoleon III. Under pressure from the Emperor, the Salon committee instigated the now famous Salon des Refusés, or Salon for the Refused. More than 1,000 visitors a day came to see the paintings, but very few took them seriously.

Fig. 29.1 *The Spanish Singer*, 1860, by Édouard Manet, oil on canvas, 147.3cm x 114.3cm, Metropolitan Museum of Art, New York. The figure is depicted in vivid, realistic colours with strong and vigorous brushstrokes. A brightly lit area behind the guitarist's hands gives it life and movement.

Le Déjeuner sur l'herbe

Manet's painting created a particular furore. *Le Déjeuner sur l'herbe* (Fig. 29.2) made him an immediate celebrity, but critics accused him of only trying to shock.

Subject

The painting shows two fully clothed men having a picnic in the woods with a nude woman. It refers to *Fête Champêtre* (see Fig. 23.3), a painting by Venetian artist Giorgione in the Louvre. The model for the painting is Victorine Meurant. She posed regularly for Manet and was well known in artistic circles. She is looking directly at the viewer, which makes her far more sensual than the idealised goddesses in older paintings. The fruit spilling from the basket nearby and her discarded clothing greatly contribute to this.

Composition and meaning

Manet deliberately included some visual contradictions that confused the public and critics alike:

* A nude woman at a picnic with clothed men is a very strange depiction of modern life.
* The bather is out of scale and the background lacks depth and perspective.
* The woodland scene is painted with loose brushstrokes and thin washes of colour, but the figures and trees in the foreground are more real and finished.
* The hand of the reclining man connects with both the bather and the nude figure. He wears indoor clothes in an outdoors scene.
* The 'live' model is clearly painted from life while the bather suggests a figure from a painting.

Lighting

The foreground is lit from behind the viewer, but the background is lit from above like sunlight. This means the nude figure only makes sense in a studio and not outdoors.

The scandal of *Olympia*

The next controversy for Manet involved his painting *Olympia* (Fig. 29.3). Manet painted this in 1863, but after his previous experience he was slow to submit it for the Salon. However, his friends persuaded him and amazingly the jury of 1865 accepted it. (They were probably more lenient following the Salon des Refusés.)

Fig. 29.2
Le Déjeuner sur l'herbe, 1863, Édouard Manet, oil on canvas, 208cm x 265cm, Musée d'Orsay, Paris. The painting, originally called *Le Bain* (*The Bath*), and its meaning continue to intrigue spectators to this day.

Once the exhibition opened, however, Manet's worst fears were more than confirmed. The reception by the public was one of real hatred. The critics savaged it and the reaction was so intense that the jury ordered it to be moved to the top corner of the wall.

Subject

Olympia is a very large painting of a reclining nude woman attended by a black servant who presents her with a gift of flowers, presumably a gift from a lover. A black cat gazes out mysteriously.

Olympia was a name used to describe prostitutes in Paris and this shocked spectators. Respectable gentlemen certainly did not want to be reminded of the hidden but well-known reality of their lives.

Composition

Olympia was based on one of Titian's most famous works, *Venus of Urbino* (see Fig. 23.6). Victorine Meurant was again the model and the comparisons with the Renaissance work were clear and intended. The pose is generally the same and both women are propped up with a pillow. The backgrounds include a vertical that, in Titian's painting, falls directly in line with the woman's left hand, but Manet has moved it slightly to the right.

Instead of carefully constructed perspective and smooth shading, Manet flattened the picture into two simplified planes of light and dark. The white skin blends with the bed covers and contrasts with the darkness of the background.

Style

Manet's Olympia is no idealised beauty. Instead, she is a very real woman who raises her head in confidence.

The harsh lighting and off-white skin went against the traditions of Academic art, but he believed that these old-fashioned principles had no part in the art of modern France.

This very modern young woman wears a neck ribbon and bracelet, a ribbon in her hair and one satin slipper. These are all symbols of wealth and sensuality. They also emphasise her nakedness. The dog (a symbol of fidelity in marriage) has been replaced with a black cat, which suggests immorality.

Vigorous brushstrokes are clearly visible on the surface of the canvas, which suggests that it was painted quickly.

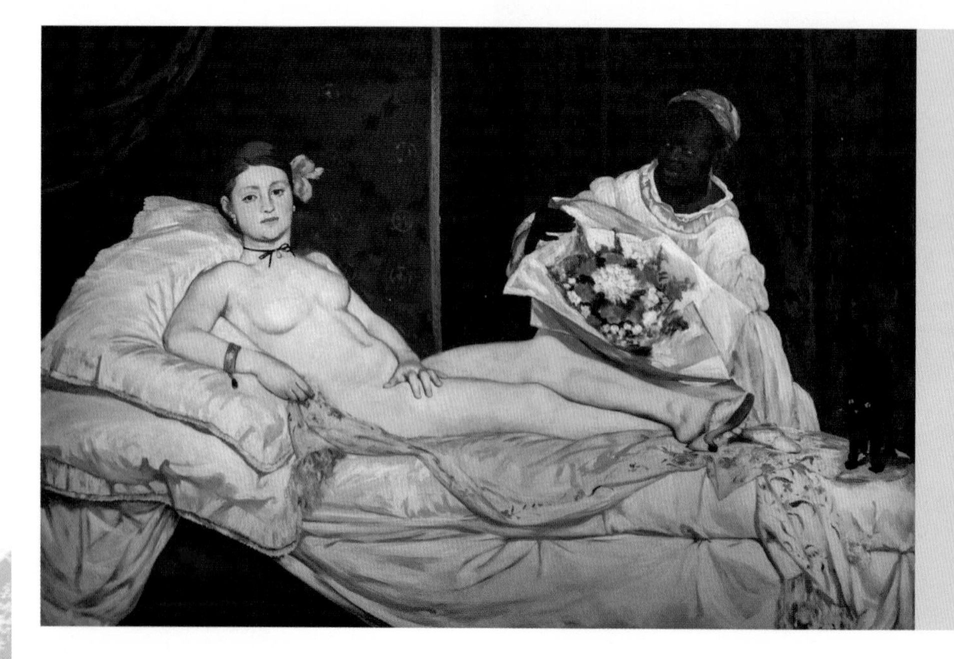

Fig. 29.3
Olympia, 1863, by Édouard Manet, oil on canvas, 131cm x 190cm, Musée d'Orsay, Paris. Manet considered *Olympia* to be his masterpiece and kept it until his death. Afterwards, Claude Monet organised a fund to purchase it and offered it to the French state. It is considered one of the finest works of 19th-century French painting.

NOTE! It was scandalous for any woman, not to mention this type of woman, to stare at the viewer so directly.

What the critics said

Viewers weren't sure whether *Olympia* was an attempt to make fun of other paintings. Manet was referred to in one article as 'a brute that paints green women with dish brushes' and all the critics agreed that the painting had a 'childish ignorance of drawing'. Manet was shattered by this criticism and never repeated this type of powerful imagery or bold colours. Even so, his work continued to cause controversy.

The Academy in 19th-century France

Édouard Manet had never intended to lead a revolt against the traditions of French art, but by the late 19th century the Academy had become very rigid. It had such a strong influence on public opinion that going against it was extremely difficult for any young artist.

Nudes

One of the most popular Academic subjects related to the myths of ancient Greece and Rome. This often involved nude figures.

Strict rules applied to the depiction of nude women. Nymphs or figures from ancient history were perfectly acceptable if they were idealised with little or no real detail. But female shapes were full and rounded and even the most graceful of poses could often be quite tempting and attractive.

In 1863, when Manet's *Le Déjeuner sur l'herbe* caused such uproar, *The Birth of Venus* by Alexandre Cabanel (Fig. 29.4) was the hit of the Salon exhibition.

The painting had everything that visitors to the Salon expected. Venus is completely lacking in character, but the idealised, sexually passive figure is perfection itself. The smooth brushwork and polished surface make this the perfect Academic work.

Fig. 29.4
The Birth of Venus, 1863, by Alexandre Cabanel, oil on canvas, 130cm x 225cm, Musée d'Orsay, Paris

A man of 'agreeable character and correct appearance'

People naturally assumed that Manet was a rough, almost revolutionary type. In fact, he was a man of elegance and charm. He had a cutting wit, but his friends all spoke of his goodness and generosity of spirit. Even the critics wrote about his 'agreeable character and correct appearance'.

Music in the Tuileries

Manet inherited considerable wealth when his father died in 1862. This allowed him great independence and when *Music in the Tuileries* (Fig. 29.5) was first shown in March 1863, he funded the private exhibition himself.

Subject

Concerts were held twice weekly in the gardens of the Tuileries Palace. It became a centre for the fashionable people of Paris to meet and be seen. In a direct statement about contemporary life, Manet included his brother Eugène in the centre and his own portrait on the extreme left.

Style

Some of the figures are fully finished, while others are treated very loosely.

Composition, colour and rhythm

There is no sign of a band or orchestra in *Music in the Tuileries*, but the painting has a decided rhythm. Three blots of red, from the woman on the right to the child's sash and the military uniform on the left, link across the painting in a triangular shape. The seated women's blue bonnets, the hat on the extreme right edge and the patch of blue sky form another movement. The black vertical lines of the trees against the whites obviously refer to the keys of the piano.

Association with the Impressionists

Manet had a wide circle of friends and supporters. They met in the Café Guerbois, near his studio, to have lively discussions about art.

Fig. 29.5
Music in the Tuileries, 1862, by Édouard Manet, oil on canvas, 76cm x 119cm, Dublin City Gallery The Hugh Lane. This 'snapshot' of modern life and the figures cut off on the edge of the canvas show the influence of the new art of photography.

Influence of Impressionism

Younger artists were very inspired by him. The artist Berthe Morisot and Édouard were close friends, and she married his brother, Eugène Manet. She modelled for several of his works and encouraged Manet to try painting out of doors. As a result, his tones became lighter and he began to use colour in shadow instead of grey or black, and to observe the effect of light on water.

He was happy to play the part of modern master to the younger artists, but in 1874, when they put on an independent show, he declined to take part.

NOTE! Although Manet became the leader of the emerging Impressionist group, he steadfastly refused to join in their independent exhibitions. His goal remained what it had been from the beginning: to achieve success at the Salon.

A medal of honour at last

In 1881 Manet won a second-class medal at the Salon and the following autumn he was made a Chevalier of the Legion of Honour. Unfortunately, success came too late because by then he was a very sick man. His leg was amputated due to gangrene and he never recovered. He died in April 1883, aged 51. After his death, his work was exhibited at the École des Beaux-Arts. Five years later his works were shown at the International Exhibition in Paris and were greatly admired.

A Bar at the Folies-Bergère

Manet's last great painting was *A Bar at the Folies-Bergère* (Fig. 29.6). His leg was so bad that he had to sit all the time while working on it.

Subject

The painting shows the charm of life in Montmartre. Like so much of Manet's work, the painting's meaning is somewhere between reality and illusion. A young woman in a neat blue dress stands alone at the bar with hands placed firmly on the marble countertop. She has a detached, melancholy look and a locket around her neck suggests a gift of love, a long way from this job. Loosely painted figures can be seen in the mirror, but the only solid realities are the bottles, a bowl of oranges and the flowers.

Composition

The mirrors create a deliberate sense of dislocation and the girl's reflection does not match with her figure. It suggests that Paris is a hall of mirrors where she floats helplessly, clinging to her bar.

Lighting

The Folies-Bergère was the most famous and modern of Paris's café-concert halls. It attracted

Fig. 29.6 *A Bar at the Folies-Bergère*, 1881–2, by Édouard Manet, oil on canvas, 96cm x 130cm, Courtauld Gallery, London. Manet persuaded a barmaid he knew from the nightclub to pose in his studio for the picture. It captures all the coolness, cruelty and glamour of modern life.

a wide audience that included prostitutes and men of all classes on the lookout for casual relationships. It also had very new and modern electric lights. Manet has suggested this with the bright light shining directly on the girl as well as the chandeliers in the mirrors.

Influences

The painting was probably influenced by the use of the mirror as a device in *Las Meninas* by the 17th-century painter Diego Velázquez (Fig. 29.7). Manet greatly admired Velázquez.

Fig. 29.7 *Las Meninas*, 1656–7, by Diego Velázquez, oil on canvas, 318cm x 276cm, Museo del Prado, Madrid

Chapter review

* Manet supported and encouraged the Impressionist artists, but he never exhibited with them. Why do you think he did not?
* Manet sought official recognition until the end. Why, do you think, did he have such regard for the Paris Salon?

EXAM QUESTIONS

Ordinary Level (2008)

Look again at *A Bar at the Folies-Bergère* by Édouard Manet (1832–83) (Fig. 29.6).

Answer (a) and (b).

(a) Describe this painting under the following headings:

- Subject matter
- Composition
- Colour and brushwork

(b) Name and describe **one** other work by Manet.

Use sketches to illustrate your answer.

Higher Level (2011)

Discuss the contribution that Édouard Manet (1832–83) made to the development of 19th-century painting. Make detailed reference to his painting *Le Déjeuner sur l'herbe* (Fig. 29.2).

and

Name and briefly discuss **one** other work by Édouard Manet.

Illustrate your answer.

FURTHER RESEARCH

www.hughlane.ie – About Us

www.khanacademy.org – Manet, Le Déjeuner sur l'herbe

www.khanacademy.org – Manet, A Bar at the Folies-Bergère

Chapter 30

Impressionism

On 15 April 1874, a group of young artists mounted their own independent exhibition. They called themselves The Anonymous Society of Painters, Sculptors and Engravers. These artists had grown tired of having their work rejected by the Salon and had made a decision to present it directly to the public. Among the 30 artists in this group were Claude Monet, Edgar Degas, Paul Cézanne, Pierre-Auguste Renoir, Camille Pissarro, Alfred Sisley and Berthe Morisot. Society was shocked by their paintings and the work was ridiculed and rejected. The artists, now better known as the Impressionists, had seven more exhibitions, during which time buyers gradually accepted the new style.

By the end of this chapter, I will...

- Know how Impressionism began.
- Be able to describe how Impressionism reacted against Academic art.
- Be familiar with the characteristics of Impressionist art.
- Understand why the first Impressionist exhibition took place.
- Know why the public rejected the Impressionists' work.
- Be able to discuss why Impressionism eventually succeeded.

The first independent exhibition

The first exhibition was held in the studio of the photographer Nadar in the centre of Paris. Visitors found the paintings with their short, slapdash brushstrokes impossible to understand. They wondered why the artists didn't take the time to finish their works. Critics wrote that the artists couldn't draw, that their colours were vulgar and their compositions were strange.

Impressionism – the term

One art critic, Louis Leroy, saw the painting entitled *Impression: Sunrise* by Claude Monet

Fig. 30.1 *Impression: Sunrise*, 1872, by Claude Monet, 48cm x 63cm, Musée Marmottan Monet, Paris

(Fig. 30.1). In a sarcastic article for his newspaper, he described the work as 'an impression' of nature, nothing more. He wrote, 'Wallpaper in its preliminary state is more finished!' 'Who,' he wondered, 'were these "Impressionists"?'

The 'Impressionists'

These 'Impressionists' were merely a group of friends who had a shared approach to painting and had established a particular style. The artists were quite a diverse group, but what they had in common was a spirit of independence and their reaction against the Academic system. They met regularly in the Café Guerbois in Paris to discuss their art. Édouard Manet was a significant influence on them.

Subjects and style

Their paintings were mostly simple scenes of landscapes, cityscapes and everyday life. These were quickly painted directly from nature, out of doors and with loose brushstrokes. The artists felt that this better captured the life, character and play of light on the subject.

A break with tradition

The artists broke almost all Academic rules and their painting was considered to be a dangerous protest against the establishment. Quick outdoor sketching with loose brushstrokes had always been part of the Academic process as preparation for more finished work in the studio, but Impressionist painters presented these as finished works.

Innovations of Impressionist painting

Impressionism went on to become one of the most famous movements in the history of French painting. The main characteristics were:

* **Working out of doors,** *en plein air*: Painting subjects including figures directly from nature, out of doors.
* **Using colour in place of black or grey:** Artists became aware that shadows are not grey or brown, but coloured. They avoided black and mixed complementary colours to achieve dark tones. They examined the effects of bright sunshine or light on water and snow. They noticed that the blue of the sky reflecting on surfaces made blue and purple shadows.
* **Observing the effects of light:** Artists noticed how subjects change colours when placed in different lights. They used slabs of unmixed primary colours and small strokes to simulate reflected light. They created 'optical mixing' by placing small brushstrokes of vivid colours together on the canvas and allowed colour to mix in the eye of the viewer.
* **Working with loose brushstrokes:** The artists used short, thick brushstrokes to capture the essence of the subject rather than its details. Loose brushstrokes better captured a feeling of movement or quivering light.
* **Painting with flat brushes – the '*tache*':** Impressionist paintings have become known for the *tache*. This means 'patch' and refers to a stroke with a new type of brush that was flat rather than round.
* **Applying thick wet paint on the surface:** Wet paint was often placed onto wet paint to produce a soft-edged effect and a mingling of colour.
* **The influence of photography:** Impressionist art was influenced by the rise of photography in the late 19th century. This is seen in objects cut away at the frame.
* **Japanese prints:** Japanese woodblock prints influenced Impressionist art. The simple, everyday subjects were presented in an appealingly decorative manner.

Colour theory

Another innovation of Impressionism was the use of colour theory. In 1666, Isaac Newton discovered that light shone through a glass prism divided into its component spectrum colours: red, orange, yellow, green, blue, indigo and violet (the colours of the rainbow). These are the colours of light.

Artists experimented with colour wheels made up of the spectrum colours, noting that colours on the opposite sides of the wheel (complementary colours) created strong contrasts when placed side by side. They developed theories on harmony and contrast in colour.

Impressionist exhibitions

The Impressionists had eight exhibitions in Paris and one in New York.

Support from Durand-Ruel

The art collector Paul Durand-Ruel was crucial to the eventual success of the movement. He supported the artists from the beginning and bought their work when he could. It was he who encouraged them to mount an independent exhibition.

The Anonymous Society of Artists

Their first exhibition made huge losses for the artists. The next one two years later was no better. The group began to exhibit under the title 'Impressionists', but Edgar Degas detested this. Disagreements continued over the next few years and after Manet's death the artists disbanded.

New York exhibition

Durand-Ruel took charge of business arrangements. He organised a huge Impressionist exhibition in New York in 1886 and American buyers paid high prices for the paintings.

The Hugh Lane Collection

The Irish art collector Sir Hugh Lane bought several paintings from the gallery of Paul Durand-Ruel in Paris. He brought some of them to Dublin. His collection included *Music in the Tuileries* and *Eva Gonzalès* by Édouard Manet and *The Umbrellas* by Renoir.

A unique shared agreement with the National Gallery in London and Dublin City Gallery The Hugh Lane involves eight of his paintings. Four of these alternate between Dublin and London for six years at a time.

Chapter review

* Impressionist painting caused deep outrage in French society when it was first seen. What made it so shocking?
* Impressionism can be considered to be the first distinctly modern movement in painting. How does it differ from Academic paintings?
* As the work of the Impressionist artists became acceptable, the style grew popular with buyers. What role do you think the art collector Durand-Ruel had in that?

FURTHER RESEARCH

www.impressionism.org

www.youtube.com – Paul Durrand-Ruel: The man who invented Impressionism

www.khanacademy.org – Realism, Impressionism and Post-Impressionism

Chapter 31

Impressionist Artists

Of all the Impressionist artists, only Claude Monet, Edgar Degas, Pierre-Auguste Renoir, Camille Pissarro, Berthe Morisot, Alfred Sisley and Paul Cézanne became associated with the Impressionist movement. These eight artists each had their own unique style. Their careers took very different paths, but they all had a modern approach to art.

By the end of this chapter, I will...

* Know the individual characteristics of each Impressionist artist's work.
* Understand what the artists had in common.
* Know why Claude Monet was the leader of the group.
* Be able to analyse a typical Impressionist painting.
* Know how Claude Monet broke new ground with his later work.

Claude Monet (1840–1926)

Claude Monet was the key figure of Impressionist art. He devoted his life to painting out of doors and was fascinated by natural light and its effects. His subjects included leisure activities in and around Paris, the Normandy coastline and scenes from his own gardens. His early career was marked by extreme poverty. He only achieved prosperity in the 1880s.

Early influences

Oscar Claude Monet grew up in Normandy in the busy port of Le Havre on the Channel coast. He started painting while he was still in his teens with the landscape artist Eugène Boudin.

Boudin persuaded Monet to accompany him on painting trips out of doors, or *en plein air*, and taught him to use oil paints. Outdoor landscape painting was still quite new in France, but the young artist was completely captivated. From then on his life's direction was set.

Monet famously recounted the life-changing event of painting *en plein air* with Eugène Boudin. He said, 'It was as if a veil had been torn from my eyes. I understood what painting could be.'

Paris

In 1860, Monet left home to study in Paris. He met artist Camille Pissarro, who was 10 years older but also interested in landscape painting. Pissarro introduced him to the Barbizon painters and the artist Camille Corot.

He enrolled in Charles Gleyre's studio and met fellow students Frédéric Bazille, Alfred Sisley and Auguste

Renoir. At the local café they met other young artists, including Paul Cézanne and Edgar Degas. These friendships proved to be extremely significant for Monet and for the future Impressionists.

Meeting with Édouard Manet

Monet submitted two seascapes of his home coastal area for the Salon of 1865. These were not only accepted, but were well received.

That year the work was placed in alphabetical order. By chance, Monet's two small paintings were hanging next to the huge and notorious *Olympia* by Édouard Manet. Much to Manet's displeasure, the critics confused both names but the two artists became good friends.

Manet had a reservation at the Café Guerbois in Paris every Friday evening. Monet and the other artists joined in the lively discussions that centred on Manet's engaging personality and witty and intellectual conversation.

Financial difficulties

Monet wanted celebrity like Manet and began to work with figures in the landscape. His father, however, disapproved of his career direction and lifestyle and refused to continue paying him an allowance or to pay his debts. In preparation for the Salon of 1867, Monet borrowed money from his friend Frédéric Bazille.

Women in the Garden

Women in the Garden (Fig. 31.1) was painted entirely out of doors in the garden of the house he was renting in the Paris suburbs. He dug a trench so that the canvas, more than 2.4m tall, could be lowered on a pulley when he needed to reach the top parts.

Subject

The painting features four life-sized women in

Fig. 31.1 *Women in the Garden*, 1866, by Claude Monet, oil on canvas, 255cm x 205cm, Musée d'Orsay, Paris

contemporary fashionable dresses. Camille Doncieux posed for all of these. She was only 18 when she first modelled for Monet, but her family disowned her when she began living with the impoverished artist.

Colour and shadow

The painting shows the clear influence of Manet in the simplified treatment of the faces and dark blobs of colour. Monet went even further than Manet and used only the smallest amount of black. Clearly defined purple-blue shadows are one of the picture's most dominant features, and dappled light is carried around the composition on figures and the foliage.

Composition

The painting is divided into quarters by the branches of the small tree. The deeper tones of the leaves form the top half, while the figures are concentrated in the lower left.

Rejection

To Monet's utter shock and devastation, the Salon of 1867 rejected *Women in the Garden*. The jury criticised the work for its lack of subject and narrative. They said it was unfinished and regarded the visible brushstrokes as a sign of carelessness.

Monet was deeply depressed; he realised that the success he dreamed of was not going to come easy. Life became very difficult and, after the birth of his son, he and Camille lived in miserable poverty.

Monet's style

After the failure of *Women in the Garden*, Monet abandoned figure painting and returned to painting landscape. By the 1860s he had developed his own unique style:

* He observed the effect of light, particularly on water.
* He avoided lines and used fast brushstrokes, dots and patches of broken colour.
* He used wet paint on wet, producing softer edges and blurred boundaries.
* He became ever more attentive to light and colour as he matured.
* He came close to abstraction in the end as form dissolved into swirling shapes of colour and light.

Japonism

Monet had quite a collection of Japanese woodblock prints. These were a significant influence on his work. The flat planes of bright colour and irregular shapes offered an alternative approach to traditional landscape painting.

Monet and Impressionism

The real beginning of the Impressionist style began in 1869, when Monet painted directly from nature with his friends Auguste Renoir and Camille Pissarro. He painted in summer with Renoir at La Grenouillère (the Frog Pond), a leisure area on the banks of the Seine just outside of Paris, and with Pissarro in both summer and winter. Painting snow taught the artists to see the blues and purples in shadows rather than grey or black. To capture fleeting moments in time, they worked quickly and painted directly onto the canvas with short, loose brushstrokes.

Fig. 31.2 *Bathers at La Grenouillère*, 1869, by Claude Monet, oil on canvas, 73cm x 92cm, National Gallery, London. This is one of a number of painted sketches produced in a very fresh and direct manner.

Monet and Renoir's work from this time was almost identical, but Monet was the more adventurous of the two. He devised a floating studio, painting both the boat itself and scenes from it.

Bathers at La Grenouillère

In *Bathers at La Grenouillère* (Fig. 31.2), the whole scene is constructed from detached brushstrokes. These emphasise the patterns of light on water. Broad areas of colour indicate the jetties, tree trunks, bathing sheds and the boats moored in the shadows. Glittering white brushstrokes indicate sunshine, while dots in the background represent bathers in the river.

Argenteuil

One of the more prosperous periods of Monet's life was spent in Argenteuil near Paris. He was enthralled with the loveliness of the countryside and for a brief period his work was selling well. The family had recently returned from London after a period of exile during the Franco-Prussian War of 1870–1. In London, Camille Pissarro had introduced him to art dealer Paul Durand-Ruel. He was immediately impressed and bought Monet's work after he returned to Paris and opened his business.

Regatta at Argenteuil

The River Seine at Argenteuil was Monet's favourite subject. He produced over 70 pictures of the river, boats, bridges and boat races at Argenteuil, including *Regatta at Argenteuil* (Fig. 31.3).

Subject

Regattas were popular here because the river widened into a clear, wide stretch of water. Monet used the opportunity to make an impressive study of shimmering reflections.

Composition

The composition is based on horizontal lines broken by the triangular shapes of the sails and the landscape. The reflections are spread evenly across the blue water. The eye is drawn first to the tallest sail in the centre and then outwards in a harmonious and pleasing design.

Colour

The scene is one of glowing colour. The background colours of rust reds, oranges and greens are all reflected with the sails in the blue water. This makes the creamy white triangles against the blue sky all the more striking.

Fig. 31.3 *Regatta at Argenteuil*, 1872, by Claude Monet, oil on canvas, 48cm x 75cm, Musée d'Orsay, Paris

Style

The subject is very simplified. Long brushstrokes and slabs of pure colour suggest the shimmering effects on the water.

The first independent exhibition

Durand-Ruel's business ran into difficulty after a few years. This badly affected Monet and the other artists, but with the art dealer's encouragement, they took the brave step of mounting an independent exhibition in 1874. The reviews were extremely harsh and the critics selected Monet's painting *Impression: Sunrise* (see Fig. 30.1) in particular for severe criticism. The title of this painting gave the movement its famous name.

Giverny

Monet's fortunes improved in the 1880s. His wife, Camille, had died when their second son was just a year old, but he married again, to Alice Hoschedé. He bought a house and lived with Alice, his two sons and her six children in the little village of Giverny in Normandy. He spent 43 years there, painting almost until his death in 1926 at the age of 86.

Monet's garden at Giverny

Monet loved plants and flowers. He collected rare species and created a beautiful garden where he painted continuously.

Later he bought a piece of land across the road and diverted a section of the small local river to create a magnificent water garden. A large water lily pond was crossed over by a Japanese-style bridge. The inspiration for this came from his many Japanese prints (Fig. 31.4).

During the last 30 years of his life, he spent a great deal of his time here and produced some of his famous water lily paintings.

Waterlily Pond: Green Harmony

Monet painted the pond in different light conditions and vantage points. Sometimes he painted the bridge from a small boat he kept moored for painting.

Subject

Waterlily Pond: Green Harmony (Fig. 31.5) features the Japanese footbridge and the surrounding plants. Water lilies are in flower and weeping willows can be seen in the background, but the main subject of the painting is the reflections in the water.

Composition

Monet compressed the composition into a square shape. The edges of the bridge are covered by plants, but its graceful curves form a natural division across the centre.

Colour

The surface is a rich carpet of colour, with brushstrokes of yellow, pink and lavender woven in with the shimmering green of the plants. The flowers are just blobs of white tinged with yellow and pink, but the colours reflect brilliant sunshine.

Style

The painting shows Monet's characteristic short brushstrokes and patches of pure paint, or *taches*, applied with the square brush. He used a palette knife to create the textures of the water and plant reflections. He also used a dry brushing technique on the bridge, where he dragged a loaded brush across the dry surface, building up layers of paint. This created very rich textures that pick up light.

Light

The bright light suggests morning, but there is only the slightest suggestion of sky. He has closed off the background and all sides of the scene.

Fig. 31.4 (left) *The Bridge with Wisteria* by Utagawa Hiroshige, Galerie Janette Ostier, Paris

Fig. 31.5 (right) *Waterlily Pond: Green Harmony*, 1899, by Claude Monet, oil on canvas, 89cm x 93.5cm, Musée d'Orsay, Paris. Monet depicts his garden of flowering plants. The water is visible through the leaves and flowers and it shows reflections of the sky, willows and reeds around the pond.

Monet in later life

Monet had little contact with the Impressionist group in later life. He had no interest in working with other artists and felt he was the only one to hold true to the modern ideals. He was extremely conscious of maintaining his status as the leader of modern French art.

Change of style

He further developed his style by painting the same object at different times of day. He captured nature's moods in a remarkable series of deeply personal landscape paintings.

He had a case specially designed to carry several canvases. He focused on a sequence of moments in time – as the light changed, he put one away and worked on another. His paintings became a complex relationship between the scene and his own reaction to time and colour.

Grainstacks series

Subject

Monet painted the huge grainstacks that stood 4.5m to 6m tall in the fields near Giverny, silhouetted against the sky (Fig. 31.6 and Fig. 31.7).

Composition

The compositions are simple and strongly geometric. The background of trees and distant hills is reduced to parallel bands extending across the entire canvas.

Fig. 31.6 (left) *Stacks of Wheat (Sunset, Snow Effect)*, 1891, by Claude Monet, oil on canvas, 65cm x 100cm, Art Institute of Chicago. These huge stacks of wheat or oats are known as *meules* in French.

Fig. 31.7 (right) *Stacks of Wheat (End of Day, Autumn)*, 1890–1, by Claude Monet, oil on canvas, 65.8cm x 101cm, Art Institute of Chicago

Colour

He sometimes increased the light by adding pink, red or orange for evening or summer sunlight and even moved the direction of shadows. They are works of art in and of themselves rather than realistic depictions of nature.

The reaction

People were perplexed by his new work and had difficulty with the subject matter at first. Monet intended that the series would be seen as one unit; viewers found this concept hard to understand, but the exhibition of the series in May 1891 in the Durand-Ruel gallery in Paris was an enormous success.

Rouen Cathedral series

Monet's series reflect values that were dear to him and his native French culture. The Rouen Cathedral series (Fig. 31.8 and Fig. 31.9) struck a chord in the public mind. His choice of a Gothic cathedral was distinctly French.

He rented a room opposite that gave him the best view of the sun moving over the cathedral façade. He painted over 30 close-up views in a variety of colours and moods. Highly textured brushstrokes convey the atmosphere of sculpted grey stone dissolving in gold and shadows of deep purple and red.

Colour

Sometimes he saw yellow, orange, pink, green, blue and white playing off the façade as the sun moved across the sky or was suddenly lost behind clouds. In one painting, with mist swirling at street level, the building seems to be floating away.

Changing light

In the early morning, the sun lit up the sky behind the cathedral, making a dark silhouette. In the early afternoon it rose gradually until the façade glistened in full sunshine. As shadows crept up the façade, only the upper reaches picked up the last rays of the setting sun.

Last works

Monet's last works were huge wall paintings based on his water lily garden. The giant canvases were painted during the war of 1914–18 and he had to construct a new studio to fit them. These paintings were left to the state after his death in 1926. In accordance with his wishes, they are displayed in oval rooms built specially for them in the Orangerie museum in Paris.

Fig. 31.8 (left) *Rouen Cathedral in Full Sunlight*, 1893, by Claude Monet, oil on canvas, 107cm x 73cm, Musée d'Orsay, Paris

Fig. 31.9 (right) *Morning Sun, Harmony in Blue*, 1893, by Claude Monet, 91cm x 63cm, Musée d'Orsay, Paris

Camille Pissarro (1830–1903)

Camille Jacob Pissarro spent his childhood in the Virgin Islands but was educated in France. He worked for a time with his parents but eventually returned to Paris to study painting. In Paris he met Claude Monet and introduced him to the Barbizon painters.

His early submissions to the Salon were quite successful, but this ended when he began to work in the Impressionist style. He was in his sixties before he had real artistic success. He suffered a good deal of financial hardship trying to provide for his large family.

Pissarro was about 10 years older than the other artists and they regarded him as their teacher. He constantly advised and encouraged them, but he also learned from them. He had an easygoing, friendly manner and got on with everybody – even Degas! He organised the Impressionist exhibitions and was the only one to exhibit in all eight of the shows.

Varied painting styles

Pissarro absorbed the Impressionist ideas of light and colour in nature, but he never forgot the importance of solid structure in painting. He explored several styles during his career, including Realism and Neo-Impressionism. In his early

Fig. 31.10
The Versailles Road at Louveciennes (Snow), 1869, by Camille Pissarro, oil on canvas, 38cm x 46cm, Walters Art Museum, Baltimore. Loose brushwork creates the effect of snow and thick blotches of pink, lilac and violet blend with the white.

career he was highly influenced by the Barbizon painters. He particularly admired Camille Corot. His subjects included landscape, cityscape, portrait, still life and peasant scenes.

Working with the Impressionists

In the mid-1860s, Pissarro settled in Louveciennes on the River Seine. He lived on the road to Versailles and was the first Impressionist artist to paint snow. He painted with Claude Monet in summer and winter (Fig. 31.10 and Fig. 31.11).

London

The war of 1870 forced the Pissarro family to move to safety in London. He had the good fortune to meet the Parisian art dealer Paul Durand-Ruel there, who had also left France. Durand-Ruel became one of Pissarro's most loyal supporters.

Fig. 31.11 *Route de Versailles, Louveciennes*, 1870, by Camille Pissarro, oil on canvas, 32.5cm x 41.1cm, Clark Art Institute, Williamstown, MA. Straight roads lined with trees disappearing at a sharp angle into the distance are a common theme in Pissarro's work.

Return to Louveciennes

After the war Pissarro returned to Louveciennes to find that the Prussians had commandeered the

Fig. 31.12
Red Roofs, Corner of a Village, Winter, 1877, by Camille Pissarro, oil on canvas, 54.5 cm x 65.6cm, Musée d'Orsay, Paris

house. They had used his paintings as a walkway for the soldiers and a huge number of his works were ruined.

Impasto: A technique of laying on paint thickly so that it stands out from a surface.

Red Roofs, Corner of a Village, Winter

Red Roofs, Corner of a Village, Winter (Fig. 31.12) shows a corner of the village through a pattern of bare branches. The trees create a feeling of winter in spite of the bright colours.

Colour and light

The painting is built up with small, thick brushstrokes in a wide range of colours. The orange-reds and browns are spread across the surface, on the fields, the plants and on the hillside. The thick impasto strokes catch the light to create a vibrant intensity and give a feeling of movement.

Composition

The depth in the picture is achieved simply by decreasing the size of the objects.

Neo-Impressionism

Dissatisfaction about his own ability led Pissarro in the direction of Neo-Impressionism. He became involved with two young artists, Paul Signac and Georges Seurat, and exhibited with them in the last Impressionist exhibition of 1886. However, he found the method too laborious after a while and abandoned it.

Success at last

Pissarro returned to the Impressionist style as his work began to sell. He was at last in a position to offer his wife and seven children security. He bought the house he had been renting at Eragny and painted some of his finest works in the countryside near his home.

Fig. 31.13
The Church and Farm of Eragny, 1895, by Camille Pissarro, oil on canvas, 60cm x 73.4cm, Musée d'Orsay, Paris

The Church and Farm of Eragny

The Church and Farm of Eragny (Fig. 31.13) is a freely painted but beautiful study of diffused sunlight. The colours are warmer than in his earlier works, but the artist has remained faithful to the realistic origins of Impressionism. The strength of the composition can be seen in the structure of the building.

Street scenes

In later life Pissarro could no longer work out of doors, but he rented hotel rooms and painted some splendid street scenes. He died in 1903 at the age of 73.

Auguste Renoir (1841–1919)

Pierre-Auguste Renoir came from Limoges. He had been working as a painter on porcelain, painting figures and scenes. When he began his studies in Gleyre's studio in 1862, he met Camille Pissarro, Claude Monet, Alfred Sisley and Frédéric Bazille. Monet persuaded him to travel to Fontainebleau and they painted together *en plein air* with Camille Corot at Barbizon.

Influences and early career

Monet and Renoir remained very close friends. Over the summer of 1869 they both painted at Bougival, on the River Seine near Paris. Renoir's *La Grenouillère* (Fig. 31.14) is remarkably similar to Monet's.

Together, Monet and Renoir:

* Observed that the colour of an object is affected by the light and reflections of surrounding objects
* Discovered that shadows are not brown or black, but coloured
* Became fascinated with flickering light and shimmering colour in outdoor scenes

Like Monet, Renoir was skilled at capturing the effect of dappled light, but he placed more emphasis on figures in his paintings. These were executed in a soft-edged and even blurred style.

Fig. 31.14
La Grenouillère, 1869, by Auguste Renoir, oil on canvas, 66cm x 81cm, Nationalmuseum, Stockholm. This painting is very similar to Monet's (Fig. 31.2) but there is more emphasis on the figures and their activity.

Subjects

His early works featured groups in cafés, dance halls, boats or riverside scenes. He painted people enjoying themselves and his images of pretty children and smiling, happy women had instant appeal. He said, 'Why shouldn't art be pretty? There are enough unpleasant things in the world.'

Dance at Le Moulin de la Galette

Dance at Le Moulin de la Galette (Fig. 31.15) is a masterpiece of Impressionist painting and shows Renoir's skill at capturing dappled light. It is one of the artist's largest works and was displayed on a wall of its own at the third Impressionist exhibition in 1877. It was painted directly at the scene and fully completed over one summer. Several of his friends posed for him, and it was the first time that such a large painting with so many figures had been painted entirely *en plein air*.

Subject

Public dances were very popular in the 1870s and this snapshot of real life depicts a fleeting moment of movement, noise and light. These modern, ordinary working-class Parisians are dressed in the latest style enjoying a Sunday afternoon at Le Moulin de la Galette in Montmartre. The bar had an outdoor dance floor and served galettes (a kind of waffle).

Composition

At first glance, the composition appears to be chaotic. The foreground and the background merge and the overlapping figures seem to blend into one another. However, the dappled sunlight filtering through the leaves falls on the figures and ground alike and unites the picture.

Style

The painting shows the typically loose brushstrokes of the Impressionist style. Renoir's characteristically blurred outlines help to capture the carefree mood.

Fig. 31.15
Dance at Le Moulin de la Galette, 1876, by Auguste Renoir, oil on canvas, 131cm x 175cm, Musée d'Orsay, Paris

Colour and light

Soft patches of pink and purple light contrast with vibrant shades of blue, red and green in the clothing. In true Impressionist style, there is no black in the painting. The light moves with the figures in little flares as they move and dance.

Financial success

Renoir found success quite soon with portrait commissions. By the late 1870s, Durand-Ruel had found regular buyers for his work.

Aline Charigot

Around 1890, Aline Charigot began modelling for the artist in his studio. The couple went on to have three sons and married in 1890 when Renoir was 49.

Luncheon of the Boating Party

The figures in *Luncheon of the Boating Party* (Fig. 31.16) are more clearly defined than Renoir's earlier work. The colours are stronger and the forms are more solid.

Subject

The painting shows a group of friends enjoying lunch on a sunny afternoon on the balcony in the Maison Fournaise. The restaurant was on a little island on the Seine. Aline is the woman on the left with the dog. Depicting modern life was an important feature of Impressionist painting and a newly built railway bridge can be glimpsed in the distance.

Composition

The composition is cleverly linked by an interchange of glances between the figures (Fig. 31.17). On the lower right, the seated man looks up to the man

Fig. 31.16 (above) *Luncheon of the Boating Party*, 1881, by Auguste Renoir, oil on canvas, 130cm x 173cm, Phillips Collection, Washington

Fig. 31.17 (right) *Luncheon of the Boating Party*, sketch

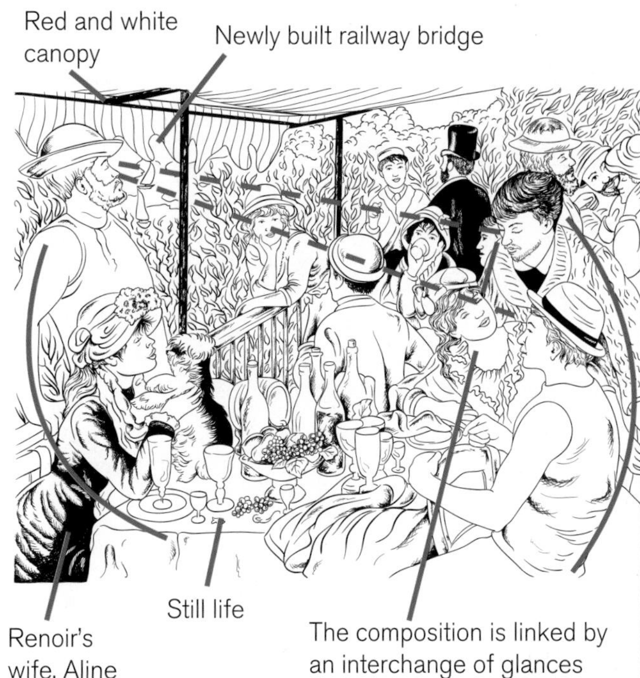

leaning on the rail. His glance directs the viewer along the railing past the woman leaning on her elbow and over to the face and white jacket of the man in the foreground. His jacket merges into the white singlet and the circle is complete.

Renoir skilfully used colours, shapes, space and texture to create this scene. The bottles, glasses and grapes make a bright still life on the tables. The red and white striped canopy encloses the scene to create an indoor feeling of intimacy.

Light

This is a brightly lit outdoor scene. Some of the dappled sunlight has found its way onto the figures.

Beyond Impressionism

Renoir felt that his work needed more structure after a visit to Italy, so he completely changed his style. He was particularly impressed by Raphael and admired the clarity of form and masterful compositions. Influenced by this, he entered what he called his 'harsh style'.

The Umbrellas

The Umbrellas (Fig. 31.18) was clearly created in two distinct stages, with an interval of about four years. The change of style can be seen both in the women's fashion and in the painting method.

Subject

The painting shows a busy street scene in Paris. The figure hidden from view in the centre seems to be lowering her umbrella, so perhaps the rain has just stopped.

Change in fashion and painting style

Renoir always painted his figures in the latest fashions. The women on the right are wearing the fashions of the 1880s, but by 1885 hats had gone out of style and the woman on the left wears a more up-to-date, simple dress.

Renoir's painting style also changed. The figures on the right are painted in the bright colours and

Fig. 31.18 *The Umbrellas*, 1881–6, by Auguste Renoir, oil on canvas, 180.3cm x 114.9cm, Dublin City Gallery The Hugh Lane

soft, feathery Impressionist style. The two figures on the left have a more 'finished' look and are more subdued in colour.

Composition

The umbrellas were carefully planned in an abstract geometric pattern. This three-dimensional rhythm of blues and greys is spread across the top of the painting. The little girl's hoop and the hatbox held by the woman on the left provide a balance of curves in the foreground. The cut-off figures at either side have a random 'snapshot' look and show the influence of photography.

Later works

Around 1888, Renoir was painting in what he called the 'pearly' method. Female nude figures or semi-nudes were painted in half tones of pink and white. Working in sunlight, he returned to his earlier free brushwork style.

A world-renowned artist

Renoir was afflicted by arthritis in later life. He moved to the south of France but continued to paint even when the brush had to be placed in his hand by the nurse.

When the Louvre acquired some of his work in 1919, he travelled to Paris. He was wheeled around the gallery as an honoured world-renowned artist. He died shortly after.

Edgar Degas (1834–1917)

Edgar Degas was one of the founders of the Impressionist movement, but he preferred to call himself a Realist or Independent. He was interested in depicting modern subjects and tried to capture fleeting moments of life, but he had no interest in landscape or *plein air* painting. He never used quick brushstrokes. Instead, his painting was slow and deliberate and he always worked in the controlled conditions of his studio. His work is defined by meticulous compositions, precise drawing and clever use of light.

Degas's working methods

* He made numerous sketches of everyday life.
* The figure was his primary subject.
* He would scrutinise the model and make studies.
* He carefully planned and built up his compositions in parts.

* He would move these about and experiment until he was satisfied.
* He made bold colour experiments.
* There was often a psychological element in his work.
* His painting crossed over many artistic styles.

Subjects

Degas liked modern subjects, including the ballet, racehorses, the circus and cafés. His outstanding figure drawings included ballet dancers and women ironing, trying on hats and, quite controversially, women in private bathroom scenes washing.

Early life

Degas was born in Paris. His father, Auguste De Gas, a well-to-do banker, was supportive of his son's artistic talents. He was French but had connections with the family bank in Naples. The name De Gas was considered to be aristocratic, but he always used Degas.

Academic training and influences

Rigorous Academic training provided Degas with a solid foundation. He always considered drawing and line to be the most important aspects of painting, and he greatly admired Ingres. He made several long trips to Italy and was impressed by the paintings and frescoes of the Italian Renaissance.

Portraits

His early works included highly accomplished portraits of family and friends. His aim was to capture not only appearances, but also personality traits.

The Bellelli Family

Part of his family lived in Italy, and during his studies he stayed with his father's sister in Florence. On his return to Paris he painted *The Bellelli Family* (Fig. 31.19) submitted for the Paris Salon of 1867.

Subject

Degas was apparently very close to his Aunt Laure. She confided her unhappiness with life and her husband to him. The disturbingly frank family portrait suggests this tension and disharmony.

Laure Bellelli stands severely upright, her face set and her head held high. On the wall, one of Degas's own drawings depicts her father (and his grandfather), Hilaire De Gas. This old man watches over the group and his daughter faces in the same direction. Despite the married name, it presents the image of a De Gas family picture that subtly includes another member – the artist himself.

Composition

The huge size, simple composition and sober, cool colours create a sense of melancholy. Laure Bellelli has one hand on her daughter's shoulder and the other on the table for balance. The dark triangular shape holds the composition together.

Baron Gennaro Bellelli sits apart. He does not engage with the family and even turns from the viewer. He appears to be barricaded behind his armchair, and the mirror on the wall forms a separate frame.

Colour

The most striking feature is the black and white of the little girls' dresses. Set against the muted blue background, they complete the triangular composition. Laure Bellelli's father had just died, which explains the black clothing. Her shape suggests pregnancy, but there is an empty baby cradle in the background. A son

Fig. 31.19
The Bellelli Family, 1858–67, by Edgar Degas, oil on canvas, 200cm x 250cm, Musée d'Orsay, Paris

born to the family did not survive – the white candle on the mantelpiece may well be symbolic of this.

The painting

The portrait remained rolled up in Degas's studio until the end of his life. It was discovered, covered in dust, after his death in 1918.

Impressionist period

Degas's paintings were accepted in the Salon, but he was generally unhappy with the hanging of his work. He was not getting the attention he would have liked, so he eventually joined the Impressionists.

Degas met Édouard Manet in the 1860s. They had similar backgrounds and got on well. Manet's influence led him to seek out more contemporary themes.

He enjoyed the discussions in Café Guerbois with the other artists, but he was a shy and awkward man. His aloof manner and sharp tongue meant he had few close friends and apparently no love affairs. His colleagues accepted his cantankerous personality and constant complaining because of his spectacular talent, but he constantly tried to move them away from Impressionism. He wanted them to join him in more 'realist' studies. By this he meant subjects related to contemporary life and actual experiences.

Degas's style and techniques

Inspired by Japanese prints, Degas included some unusual visual angles and cropped the edges of his compositions. This also reflected his lifelong fascination with photography.

He experimented with a wide range of media, including oil, watercolour, chalk, pastel, pencil, etching and photography. Pastel gave him the opportunity to use the drawing line he so enjoyed, and he built up the texture in layers, sometimes combining them with oil paint. He experimented in rich surface effects and sometimes mixed pastel so heavily with liquid fixative that it became a sort of paste.

Horse racing

Horse racing had become very fashionable for the middle classes in Paris. Encouraged by Manet, Degas went to the racetrack and made hundreds of sketches.

Race Horses in Front of the Tribunes

The nervous action of a horse in the background in *Race Horses in Front of the Tribunes* (Fig. 31.20) is the only indication that a race is about to begin. The composition relies on strong diagonal lines to bring the eye to this. The flat colours show the influence of Japanese prints and the cropped edges imitate the effect of a photograph. The contrasts of light, especially the long shadows of the horses, reinforce the perspective lines.

Dancers

Female dancers (Fig. 31.21) became Degas's favourite theme. He made many pastel drawings on paper, which suited him after his eyesight deteriorated very badly. He dampened the surface of the paper and sometimes stuck on pieces of paper at the end or sides.

He was a frequent visitor to the ballet at the Paris Opera House. He observed the dancers' movements, gestures and poses in the rehearsal room and the young girls came to pose for him in his studio.

The Dance Class

The ballet master Jules Perrot had been a famous dancer in his youth. He had been retired from dancing for many years when Degas made some superb life studies of him. He used these drawings for several paintings. *The Dance Class* (Fig. 31.22) was shown at the first Impressionist exhibition of 1874.

Fig. 31.20
Race Horses in Front of the Tribunes (also known as *The Parade*), 1866–8, by Edgar Degas, oil on paper on canvas, 46cm x 61cm, Musée d'Orsay, Paris

Subject

The dancers relax in the foreground and gather in groups. The focus, however, is on the ballet master leaning on his cane and giving advice to the ballerina.

There are some typical Degas characteristics in this painting. The dancer on the piano scratches her back and almost hides another who twists her earring as she reads.

Composition

Degas presents the scene from a slightly raised viewpoint. The lines of the floorboards accentuate the sharply receding linear perspective. Heightened perspective adds to the illusion of space by exaggerating the small size of the figures opposite.

This large, empty space running diagonally across the studio is key to the composition:

* It draws immediate attention to the ballet master.
* It links the two groups.
* It creates a strong contrast with the busy figures.

Heightened perspective: The higher up in the ground area of the picture (up to the horizon) that the base of an object is located, the further away it seems from the viewpoint and the greater its height perspective.

NOTE! *The Dance Class* conveys a charming image of dancers relaxing, but it is in fact a highly complex composition.

Influences

Influenced by photography, Degas has cropped the edges. The dancer on the right is half in and half out of the painting and the frame cuts off the girl on the piano.

Colour and light

The light source comes from the tall windows on the right. Their reflection in the mirror creates a second source of light. The blue and yellow sashes are bright against the white dresses and the sober green background. The composition relies entirely on three small amounts of red to bring the eye quickly around from the dancer in the foreground to the girl beyond the mirror and the girl against the far wall.

Symbolic detail

Degas draws attention to the floor, which is so important in a dance studio. The ballet master uses it to beat out the time with his cane and it is the most essential work tool for the dancers. The inclusion of the watering can is a reminder that the floor must be kept moist to prevent the dancers from slipping. The cello silhouetted against the window is reflected in the mirror and is a reminder that music is the life-blood of dance (Fig. 31.23).

Absinthe

The Impressionist artists often met at Café de la Nouvelle Athènes, which was a well-known meeting place for intellectual bohemians in Paris. It is also the setting for *The Absinthe Drinker* (Fig. 31.24), one of Degas's most compelling works.

Absinthe had become popular in France in the 1850s and was commonly known as 'the queen of poisons' or '*la fée verte*' ('the green fairy'). It was later prohibited, but at that time this highly toxic, addictive liquor was extremely harmful. Degas's picture is a comment on this.

The Absinthe Drinker

Subject

A couple sit in a café but they are in no way engaged with each other. The woman's shoulders are slumped and her legs are splayed out. Her

Fig. 31.21

Two Ballet Dancers in a Dressing Room, c. 1880, by Edgar Degas, pastel on paper, 48.5cm x 64cm, National Gallery of Ireland, Dublin. This pastel drawing depicts two young dancers adjusting their costumes. It shows Degas's skilled drawing line and expressive colour. The high viewpoint and the angle of the sideboard indicate the influence of photography and Japanese prints.

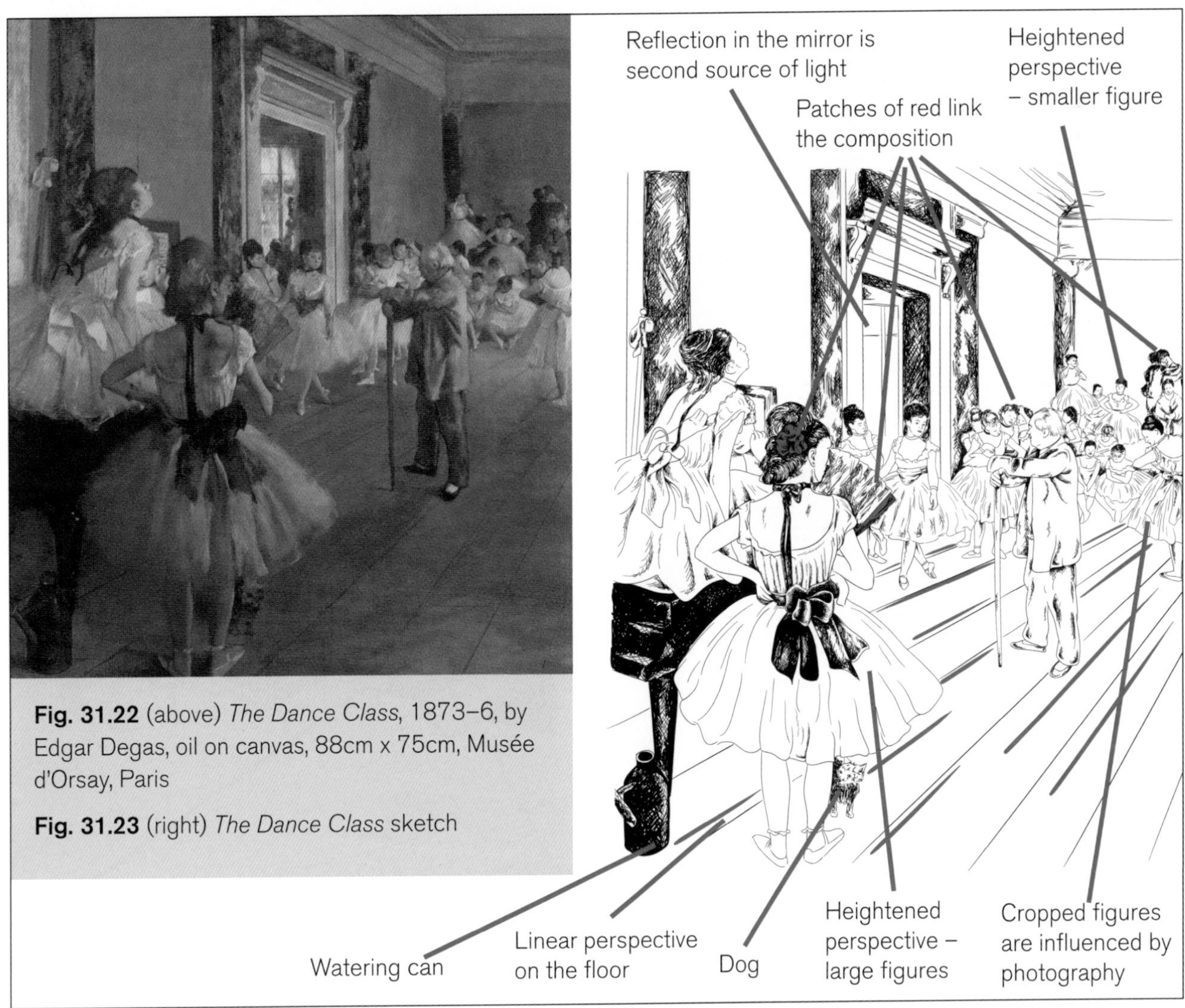

Fig. 31.22 (above) *The Dance Class*, 1873–6, by Edgar Degas, oil on canvas, 88cm x 75cm, Musée d'Orsay, Paris

Fig. 31.23 (right) *The Dance Class* sketch

> NOTE! This scene was carefully set up in the studio. Degas used the well-known actress Ellen Andrée and an artist friend, Marcellin Desboutin, as models.

eyes are downcast and she has an expression of hopelessness. The drink in front of her is absinthe, which can be identified by its light green colour and the water jug on the table.

Lighting

The morning is suggested by the grey light coming through the lace curtain windows and reflected in the mirror.

Composition

The strange composition is a major element in the painting's psychological impact. The figures are placed to the right of centre and the white marble café tables come forward in a zigzag pattern.

Degas has cropped the frame and cut off the man's pipe and hands. This makes it look like a photo taken from a nearby table.

On the foreground table there is a match container and a newspaper on a baton. Degas has signed the painting along this baton and the matchstick holder is like a small pot of paint.

This all gives the impression that the artist himself has been sitting there. The folded newspaper

Fig. 31.24 (above) *The Absinthe Drinker*, 1876, by Edgar Degas, oil on canvas, 92cm x 68cm, Musée d'Orsay, Paris

Fig. 31.25 (right) *The Absinthe Drinker* sketch

forms a bridge to the next table and draws the viewer in. We soon realise that we are, in effect, sitting here, staring straight at the couple.

Colour

Sombre colours underline the mood of the painting. Blacks are pitched against creamy whites and combined with pale yellows and translucent greens. The overwhelming feeling is one of gloom (Fig. 31.25).

Berthe Morisot (1841–1895)

Berthe Morisot was one of the founders of the Impressionist movement. She suffered criticism of her painting, but she also had to battle against the prejudice of being a woman.

Early influences

Morisot came from an upper-class family. She grew up in the town of Bourges, where she and her sister, Edma, were given art lessons. In 1855 the family moved to Paris, which gave them the opportunity to study painting. However, the girls' painting teacher warned their mother that professional painters were not suitable company for young ladies.

Painting career

When Edma married she gave up painting, but Berthe continued to paint even after marriage. Her background meant she had no need to earn a living from her art, but she was never taken seriously as a professional artist; this hurt her more deeply than anything else.

Édouard Manet was a considerable influence on her and she married his brother, Eugène.

Morisot and Impressionism

She had success with the Salon until 1873, when she became involved with the Impressionists. In spite of Manet's attempts to dissuade her, she exhibited in their first exhibition in 1874 and was ridiculed along with the other artists.

Style and technique

* Most of Morisot's work is small.
* She painted in oil and watercolour. She also used various drawing media, including pastel.
* She painted in the loose Impressionist style using small, fast brushstrokes.
* Her colours were typically limited but were cleverly used to create a sense of space and depth.
* She included a good deal of white that she sometimes mixed with other colours to great effect.
* Around 1880 she began painting on unprimed canvases and her brushwork became even looser.
* Later she began to use long, sinuous drawing lines and often left the outer edges of the paintings unfinished.

Subjects

Women were quite restricted in what subjects they could paint. They could not visit cafés or work with nude figures, so Morisot concentrated instead on family scenes, domestic interiors and gardens. Her portraits convey the comfort and intimacy of family life.

The Cradle

The Cradle (Fig. 31.26) was shown at the Impressionist exhibition in 1874. The model was the artist's sister, Edma, and her baby daughter, Blanche.

Fig. 31.26 *The Cradle*, 1872, by Berthe Morisot, oil on canvas, 56cm x 46cm, Musée d'Orsay, Paris

Subject

This is a tender portrayal of a mother watching her child sleep.

Composition

Soft diagonals form harmonious rhythms in this small painting. The curtain on the cradle falls in a sweeping wave across the painting. The mother's gesture is mirrored by the baby's arm in a connecting line between them. Her left hand resting on the little bed completes the triangle.

Colour

The cradle is bathed in a golden yellow light and the atmosphere is calm and quiet. There is no black, but the dark of the mother's dress, neckband and background wall are a balance for the soft yellow and pinky whites of the cradle.

Sale of the painting

This is considered to be one of Morisot's finest paintings, but it received very little notice at the exhibition. It remained in Edma's and her daughter's family until it was sold to the Louvre in 1930.

Summer's Day

Berthe Morisot's pictures reflect her upbringing and class. Her subjects are mostly bourgeois (upper middle class) women.

Subject

Summer's Day (Fig. 31.27) is a modern-day depiction of two women dressed in the latest Parisian style. The models pose in a rowing boat on the lake in the Bois de Boulogne, the large wooded park on the edge of Paris near where Morisot lived.

Style, techniques and composition

The painting shows many typical Impressionist techniques.

* It is painted *en plein air.*
* The composition is sliced diagonally across the foreground.
* It is off centre and the figures are cropped at the edges, showing the influence of photography.
* It is painted in quick, loose brushwork.
* The sketchy textured 'impression' is an effort to capture a fleeting moment in time.
* The tiny horse-drawn carriage moving swiftly along the far shore reinforces this image.
* The paint has been applied quickly, wet on wet, creating a soft, blurring effect.
* The shimmering whites darkening to blues and lime green convey the atmosphere of bright summer light reflecting on the water.

Fig. 31.27 *Summer's Day*, 1879, by Berthe Morisot, oil on canvas, 45.7cm x 75.2cm, Dublin City Gallery The Hugh Lane (and National Gallery, London)

Morisot's daughter

Morisot became very close to Renoir. They had a shared interest in painting women and children and during her last illness she asked him to look after Julie. Berthe Morisot died at age 54, four years after her husband, Eugène. Julie was 16.

Alfred Sisley (1839–99)

Alfred Sisley met with the other artists in Gleyre's studio. He was quite a docile student, and without Monet he might never have challenged the system. He tends to get overlooked in the history of Impressionism, but some of his works are quite powerful and dramatic.

Sisley was born in Paris of wealthy English parents. He spent some time in London, where he saw and admired works by Constable and Turner.

Impressionist years

His style did not greatly appeal to the public, so Sisley's only real source of encouragement was his group of friends. He worked with the Impressionists in all the well-known places like Bougival, Argenteuil and Louveciennes. He painted from a very limited number of subjects, but his landscapes are 'pure' Impressionism in style, with no social or political aspect. He exhibited with the Impressionists but did not attract the same scornful criticism.

He settled in Louveciennes and painted in the neighbouring district of Marly-le-Roi, along the River Seine. His paintings of villages overrun by floods convey a peaceful image of nature rather than scenes of distress. Many consider these to be his finest paintings (Fig. 31.28).

Working out of doors in winter (Fig. 31.29) caused severe rheumatism. He died from cancer in 1899.

Fig. 31.28 (above) *Boat in the Flood at Port Marly*, 1876, by Alfred Sisley, oil on canvas, 61cm x 50.5cm, Musée d'Orsay, Paris

Fig. 31.29 (right) *Snow at Louveciennes*, 1874, by Alfred Sisley, oil on canvas, 61cm x 50cm, Musée d'Orsay, Paris

Chapter review

* The French Impressionists were quite different artists, both in subject matter and characteristics. Why, do you think, did they become so famous as a group?
* The artists were regarded with deep suspicion and were even considered to be dangerous revolutionaries after their first exhibition. These paintings were colourful, cheerful in mood and easy to understand, so why, do you think, did they cause such a reaction?

EXAM QUESTIONS

Ordinary Level (2011)

Look again at *The Dance Class* by Edgar Degas (1834–1917) (Fig. 31.22). Answer (a) and (b).

(a) Describe and discuss this work using the following headings:

- Subject matter
- Composition and style
- Medium
- Use of colour

(b) Name and describe **one** other work by Degas.

Use sketches to illustrate your answer.

Ordinary Level (2010)

The Impressionists painted scenes of everyday life. Answer (a) and (b).

(a) Name and describe **one** Impressionist painting under the following headings:

- Name of the artist
- Subject matter and composition
- Use of colour and light

(b) Give some general information about the Impressionist movement.

Use sketches to illustrate your answer.

Higher Level (2016)

'In her paintings, Berthe Morisot (1841–95) sought to capture the optical effects of light and to convey moments in time.'

Discuss this statement with reference to *Summer's Day* (Fig. 31.27). In your answer, refer to style, subject matter, composition, technique and use of colour.

and

Name and briefly describe and discuss **one** work by another named Impressionist artist.

Illustrate your answer.

Higher Level (2012)

'Claude Monet (1840–1926) and Auguste Renoir (1841–1919) embraced the general principles of Impressionism while developing their own individual style.'

Discuss this statement, referring to the characteristics of Impressionism and to **one** named painting by each artist.

and

Name another Impressionist artist and briefly describe **one** named work by him/her.

Illustrate your answer.

FURTHER RESEARCH

www.impressionism.org

www.musee-orangerie.fr – Water Lilies Virtual Visit

www.khanacademy.org – Realism, Impressionism and Post Impressionism

Chapter 32

Neo-Impressionism

Georges Seurat challenged Impressionism with a new and 'scientific' method of painting. It was immediately recognised as a new direction for modern art.

By the end of this chapter, I will...

* Know how Scientific Impressionism was influenced by scientific colour theory.
* Understand how painting techniques reflected science.
* Be familiar with the basic theory of colour.
* Know how Georges Seurat hoped to achieve classic grandeur in his paintings.
* Know why the Neo-Impressionist movement did not last.

Georges Seurat (1859–91)

Georges Seurat was the leader of a new movement in painting. After his studies he moved into his own studio and began experimenting with colour theory.

Impressionism vs. Neo-Impressionism

* The Impressionists were interested in capturing fleeting moments. Seurat wanted solidity, clarity and timeless grandeur.
* The Impressionists liked to paint quickly *en plein air*. Seurat worked in his studio from sketches. He planned his paintings in meticulous detail and worked slowly.
* The Impressionists observed the effects of light on colour and painted what they saw. Seurat and the Neo-Impressionists applied formal scientific principles to painting light and colour.

Bathing at Asnières

Bathers at Asnières (Fig. 32.1) was Seurat's first major painting. He submitted the huge canvas for the Salon of 1884 and, not surprisingly, it was rejected.

Subject

Asnières is an industrial suburb north-west of Paris on the River Seine. The painting shows a group of young workmen swimming and relaxing on the riverbank. Factories are seen in the background and smoke spews from one of the six tall chimneys.

A ferry is crossing the river and the red, white and blue of the tricolour flag is clearly visible on its stern. The boatman, wearing a straw hat, stands up to push his paddle while the passengers, a lady and gentleman, indicated by her white sunshade and his top hat, sit and relax.

Fig. 32.1
Bathers at Asnières, 1883–4, by Georges Seurat, oil on canvas, 201cm x 300cm, National Gallery, London

Composition

A series of diagonals take the eye from left to right across the picture. They bring the focus directly to the bright red hat and pale skin of the boy standing in the water.

Style

The paint is dabbed on. The artist had not yet developed the pointillist technique, but he later reworked areas of this picture using dots of contrasting colour. This creates a vibrant, luminous effect.

Colour

The grass is made up of green, yellow and grey. The young man's swimming shorts contain orange, pink, blue and the odd streak of black.

Scientific Impressionism

Seurat's next painting, *A Sunday Afternoon on the Island of La Grande Jatte* (Fig. 32.2), was exhibited at the last Impressionist show in 1886. The huge painting stunned the Parisian art world and attracted the attention, ridicule and sarcasm of the press. One art critic, Félix Fénéon, was impressed by 'Scientific Impressionism' and used the term 'Neo-Impressionism'. He wrote a pamphlet called 'The Impressionists in 1886' that set the stage for a battle between the Neo-Impressionists and Impressionists.

The end of Impressionism

When Pissarro insisted that Seurat and his follower, Paul Signac, should be included in the exhibition, Monet, Renoir and Sisley refused to exhibit. This marked the end of Impressionism.

Seurat's techniques

Seurat studied writings on colour theory by French chemist Eugène Chevreul and American physicist Ogden Rood.

His new painting techniques were:

* **Divisionism:** Separation of colour.
* **Pointillism:** The application of small strokes or dots (points) of colour to the canvas.

* **Optical mixing:** From a distance, colours blend together in the spectator's eye. For example, small dots of blue and red side by side become purple in an optical illusion.

The main advantage of these techniques is vibrancy of colour.

A Sunday Afternoon on the Island of La Grande Jatte

A Sunday Afternoon on the Island of La Grande Jatte (Fig. 32.2) is crowded with respectable, well-to-do Parisian people in fashionable dress enjoying their leisure. It took the artist two years to complete. He would sketch all morning on the Île de la Grande Jatte, an island on the Seine, and paint later in the studio.

Style

Seurat wanted to create a modern painting like a frieze of Ancient Greece. The people are arranged in groups and face only sideways or straight ahead. This gives them a statuesque and monumental quality. They look dreamlike and frozen in time.

Composition

The picture is carefully proportioned and balanced. The river on the left, full of yachts and rowing boats, balances the large figures on the right. Areas of light and shade take the eye back, and the receding diagonal line of the water creates an illusion of space.

Light and colour

Seurat's colours were spectacularly bright. Natural colours mingle with complementary colours like red with green and orange with blue.

Seurat's two paintings

A Sunday Afternoon on the Island of La Grande Jatte makes more sense when it is looked at in combination with *Bathers at Asnières*. The first depicts working-class men relaxing on a riverbank, and the second shows members of the bourgeois on the opposite side.

Influences

Scientific Impressionism played an important part in the development of colour in painting and it brought serious attention to composition, both in line and colour.

Paul Signac (1863–1935)

Paul Signac was a younger, largely self-taught painter. He was strongly influenced by Impressionism but was open to new ideas when he met Seurat. He became enthusiastically involved in Neo-Impressionism and wrote articles of art criticism. His paintings are mainly landscapes, seascapes and harbour scenes.

Lady on the Terrace

The artist's wife, Berthe, stands on the terrace at his home in St Tropez. The harbour and the mountains can be seen in the distance (Fig. 32.4). Receding bands of colour take the viewer's eye from the foreground right through to the far distance. The vertical forms of church spire and tree mirror the standing figures.

The end of the movement

The dot-by-dot technique was quite laborious. Pissarro soon lost interest and after the death of Seurat at the age of 31, the movement disappeared.

Fig. 32.2 (left)
A Sunday Afternoon on the Island of La Grande Jatte, 1884–6, by Georges Seurat, oil on canvas, 208cm x 308cm, Art Institute of Chicago

Fig. 32.3 (below)
A Sunday Afternoon on the Island of La Grande Jatte sketch

Chapter review

* Georges Seurat and the Neo-Impressionist artists developed theories of colour and light. Do you think it was a science or an art movement? Why do you think that?
* Scientific Impressionism caught the popular imagination and was highly regarded. Why, do you think, didn't it continue after Georges Seurat's death?

Fig. 32.4 *Lady on the Terrace*, 1898, by Paul Signac, oil on canvas, 73cm x 92cm, National Gallery of Ireland, Dublin

EXAM QUESTIONS

Higher Level (2015)

'Georges Seurat's (1859–91) study of the scientific theories of colour is apparent in his distinctive style of painting.'

Discuss this statement with reference to *A Sunday Afternoon on the Island of La Grande Jatte* (Fig. 32.2) and refer in your answer to subject matter, composition, style, technique and influences.

and

Briefly describe and discuss **one** other named work by this artist.

Illustrate your answer.

FURTHER RESEARCH

www.tate.org.uk – Neo-Impressionism

www.theartstory.org – Georges Seurat

www.khanacademy.org – Seurat, A Sunday on La Grande Jatte

Chapter 33

Post-Impressionism

Impressionism was gradually absorbed into the mainstream and, in turn, its limitations became frustrating for the next generation. Paul Cézanne, Vincent van Gogh and Paul Gauguin pushed the boundaries of the style in different creative directions. In doing so, they laid the foundations for 20th-century art. They became known as the Post-Impressionists, but they had little in common and worked alone. The term came from an exhibition in London entitled *Manet and the Post-Impressionists* in 1910.

By the end of this chapter, I will...

* Know how Post-Impressionist artists went beyond Impressionism.
* Have some general information on each Post-Impressionist artist.
* Be able to outline their individual techniques and styles.
* Be able to draw, describe and discuss at least two important works by each artist.
* Know how the Post-Impressionist artists influenced 20th-century art movements.

Paul Cézanne (1839–1906)

Paul Cézanne exhibited with the Impressionists but had a vision of art that went far beyond Impressionism. It was many years before his genius was appreciated, but he had a widespread influence on generations to come. He was reclusive, moody and difficult. It was always his dearest wish to exhibit at the official Salon, but harsh criticism and even ridicule had caused him to become suspicious and bitter.

Early career

Born in Aix, the capital of Provence in southern France, Paul Cézanne was the only son of a wealthy banker. His father was a domineering and authoritarian figure who fully expected his son to follow in his footsteps. Paul chose to study art instead and moved to Paris to continue his training. He enrolled at the Académie Suisse in 1861, where he met Claude Monet, but most importantly where he also met Camille Pissarro.

A pupil of Pissarro

Pissarro introduced the young artist to Manet, Degas and others at the Café Guerbois. Cézanne greatly admired Manet but was himself sensitive, shy and socially awkward. He had a heavy Provençal accent and a rude and blustering manner, so he rarely took active part in the discussions.

His early painting was quite clumsy and his real strength only appeared when he began working with Pissarro. For two years the two painted side by side out of doors and Cézanne became influenced by the older artist in a deep and profound way.

His painting became calmer as he abandoned the palette knife and began to use lighter, purer colour in smaller dabs of colour. He began to work more methodically and focus only on the careful and meticulous study of nature.

Rejection of Impressionism

Cézanne wanted to 'make of Impressionism something solid and durable, like the art of the museums'. He believed strong composition should be carefully balanced to work in harmony with the visual elements.

He rejected Impressionism because in his opinion:

* It was limited because of the artists' obsession with colour and light.
* The paintings lacked structure and would eventually be just a brightly coloured haze.

NOTE! Cézanne hoped to create a 'harmony parallel to nature'. His theory was that a painting of nature was quite a different entity to nature in reality. He believed it was the painter's job to translate nature onto the painted surface.

The Hanged Man's House

Cézanne's painting *The Hanged Man's House* (Fig. 33.1) is considered to be the most important work of his Impressionist period and a key work in his career. It was shown in the first Impressionist exhibition of 1874.

Subject

The landscape shows no human presence. The abandoned house is isolated, the walls are cracked

Fig. 33.1 *The Hanged Man's House, Auvers-sur-Oise*, 1873, by Paul Cézanne, oil on canvas, 56cm x 66cm, Musée d'Orsay, Paris

and trees partly block it. Steep roads make it look as if it is springing out of a hollow.

Composition

The composition has a firm overall structure and moves out from a central point. A diagonal track descends from left to right in the foreground and the dark roof of the house on the right draws the eye to the blue door.

Style

Pale colours and broken brushstrokes show Impressionist influence, but Cézanne's solid, structured approach can be seen in the dense and granular surface.

Post-Impressionist development

In the early 1880s, Cézanne made a clear break with Paris and Impressionism. He returned to his home in Aix-en-Provence and remained there until his death in 1906. His style continued to mature and develop as he learned more about his craft.

Cézanne's technique

Cézanne called his pictures 'constructions after nature'.

* He outlined forms such as tree trunks and fields in dark blue. He then applied several coats of paint to emphasise its three-dimensional nature.
* He translated nature into patterns, shapes and colours arranged on a flat canvas.
* He said, 'Treat nature by means of the cylinder, the sphere and the cone.'
* He built up the structure slowly and painstakingly with blocks of strong colour.
* Each brushstroke was carefully placed. Horizontal strokes were used for breadth and vertical ones suggested depth.
* He created depth without using the traditional method of perspective.
* The objects interlock in a dense and intensely coloured structure of brushstrokes.
* He often used multiple viewpoints in still life, such as objects seen from different positions at one time, or tabletops tilted upwards or at a slant.
* He distorted objects and compositions to prevent the composition from becoming rigid, but always maintained order.
* It took him months to finish a painting. He was rarely satisfied and signed only a few.

Cézanne's subjects

Portraits

Cézanne did not like working with a model and only painted people he knew well, like his wife. He was also comfortable with humble, respectful people like servants, gardeners and peasants. They would sit quietly, without moving, for hours while he worked.

Still life

Cézanne began painting still life subjects in his early career in an effort to capture solidity and composition. He often worked on the same motif over and over, but wax fruit and paper flowers suited him better because the real thing rotted long before he had finished the paintings. He produced over 200 still life paintings of apples, oranges, onions, bottles and ornaments.

Landscape and nature

He painted the landscape, sea, harbours and rocks of his home area and nearby Marseille. One of his favourite subjects was the Mont Sainte-Victoire; the mountain gradually came to dominate his painting. For him, it was a symbol of home and the landscapes of his native Provence. He painted it over and over until his death.

Still Life with Apples and Oranges

Still Life with Apples and Oranges (Fig. 33.2) is one of six late paintings that feature the same dishes and the same floral decorated jug.

Subject

The arrangement is a reminder of 17th-century Dutch still life, but Cézanne's complex construction of space is more innovative.

Composition

He has stripped the display down to the minimum of detail. The apples, cloth, dishes and backdrop are arranged on flat but uneven planes. It is set against a background of loudly patterned cloth, and the deep twists and folds are painted with dramatic energy.

Cézanne has ignored the laws of classical perspective, but the arrangement creates an

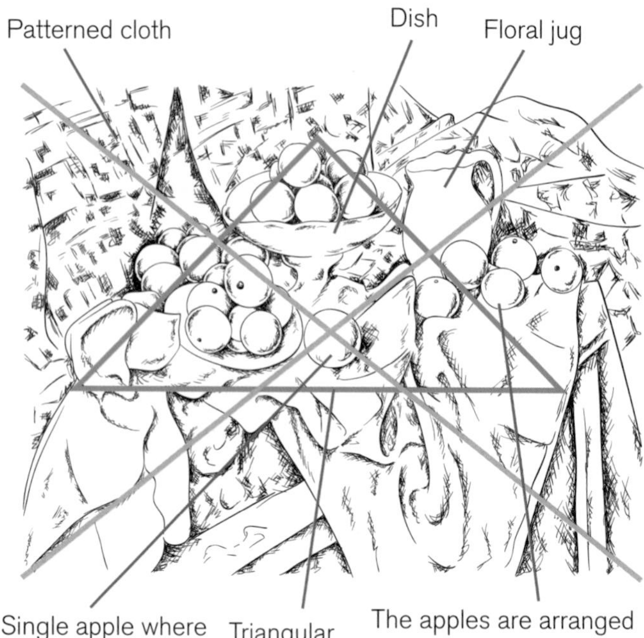

Fig. 33.2 (above) *Still Life with Apples and Oranges*, 1899, by Paul Cézanne, oil on canvas, 74cm x 93cm, Musée d'Orsay, Paris

Fig. 33.3 (right) *Still Life with Apples and Oranges* sketch

impression of depth. For him, the relationship of one object to another is more important than traditional single-point perspective. The focal point is the single apple at the front where the two diagonals cross.

The painting shows multiple viewpoints. The main objects are arranged in a pyramid shape. In a formal composition, the tabletop line would form the base of this, but the table is at another angle entirely. The table leg is vertical, but the plates are tilted and the jug and dish are leaning (Fig. 33.3).

Colour

The fruit that spills from the plate onto the folds of the white cloth is painted in vibrant reds and oranges.

The Card Players

Cézanne deliberately picked up on past traditions in painting. He made several pictures of card players. Scenes like this were often depicted in 17th-century Dutch and French art and usually featured drama, bad behaviour and drunkenness. In contrast, Cézanne's scenes are so quiet that they have been described as 'human still life'.

Subject

The models were workers on Cézanne's family estate and the man with the pipe is 'père Alexandre', the gardener. The scene shows a timeless tranquillity with no conversation or excitement (Fig. 33.4).

Composition

The bottle, with the light playing on it, forms the central line of the composition between the men's hands. The space is divided evenly in two, hinting at the opposing players in the game.

Colour

The white cards contrast with the deep red of the background, the yellows and greens of the jackets and the orange of the table.

Fig. 33.4 *The Card Players*, 1890–5, by Paul Cézanne, oil on canvas, 47.5cm x 57cm, Musée d'Orsay, Paris

The human figure

The card players have a three-dimensional reality, but like so many of Cézannes figures, they are painted like still life objects.

Montagne Sainte-Victoire

From the mid-1880s Cézanne began to focus on the landscape he knew from his childhood. This included the Montagne Sainte-Victoire, the peak of a low range of mountains near Aix. He painted more than 60 versions of what he called 'his' mountain. None of these are exactly alike and are seen from different viewpoints and weather conditions. He painted in both oil and watercolours.

In the early paintings he often used trees to frame the scene and included details such as roads, viaducts and houses. In his later paintings the mountain gradually loomed nearer and larger, with greater freedom of expression. He continued to emphasise solidity and structure, but in a less obvious way and without lines. He concentrated more on a strong pattern of dense, vibrant brushstrokes.

Montagne Sainte-Victoire with Large Pine

There are several versions of the same view about 13km west of Aix, over the valley of the River Arc. These early paintings include foreground trees and bushes, buildings and bridges, fields or quarries.

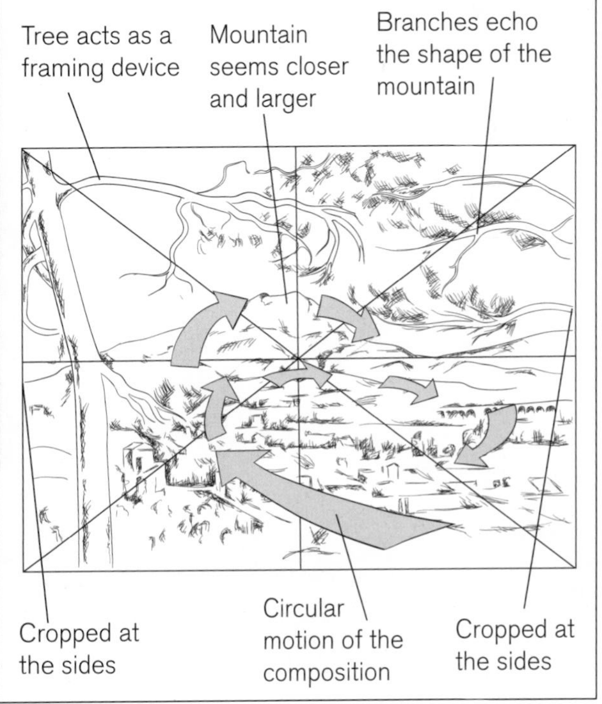

Fig. 33.5 (above) *Montagne Sainte-Victoire with Large Pine*, 1887, by Paul Cézanne, oil on canvas, 67cm x 92cm, Courtauld Gallery, London

Fig. 33.6 (right) *Montagne Sainte-Victoire with Large Pine* composition sketch

Subject

Montagne Sainte-Victoire with Large Pine (Fig. 33.5) could be described as an intellectual organisation of nature and landscape in a study of line, form and colour.

Composition

The view is cropped and only part of the pine tree is visible at the left and the top. The tree acts as a framing device, like a window, but the high viewpoint makes the distant mountain appear closer and larger.

The branches perfectly echo the outline of the mountain and draw the eye across the landscape into the valley. The view continues around the mountain, follows the lines of the viaduct and returns to the foreground in a circular motion (Fig. 33.6).

Style

The painting reflects the solidity of a traditional balanced and harmonious landscape, but the structured, parallel brushstrokes break up the surface in a very modern way.

Colour

Colour harmonies rather than perspective hold the painting together. Bold colours like orange and purple balance the vivid green. The solid mass of the mountain is worked in with the brighter blue tones of the sky.

Mont Sainte-Victoire

During his final years Cézanne made another series of the mountain from the hill above his new art studio (Fig. 33.7).

Composition

The composition is divided into three equal horizontal sections. The high viewpoint looks over the foreground of bushes and houses and across the plain. The mountain itself completely fills the upper part of the picture. Its peak is slightly to the right of centre.

Fig. 33.7

Mont Sainte-Victoire, 1902–4, by Paul Cézanne, oil on canvas, 73cm x 91.9cm, Philadelphia Museum of Art

Style

The brushstrokes are arranged in slabs of vibrant colour and fit together like a mosaic. The work has moved closer to abstraction, but the mountain never loses its form or sense of grandeur.

Colour

Patches of yellow ochre, emerald and vivid green suggest the rooftops and foliage of the expansive plain. Contrasting blues, violets and greys form the great bulk of the mountain and sky.

Portraits of Hortense

Cézanne painted nearly 30 portraits of his wife Hortense. The poses were always simple because she had to sit absolutely still for hours, something she had grown used to as his model in Paris. Unbeknownst to his father, she had been living with the artist and had given birth to his son, also named Paul. The couple married sometime after she moved to Aix with him. However, she found the city backward and rustic, and when Cézanne became increasingly difficult she moved back to Paris.

Fig. 33.8 *Madame Cézanne in a Red Armchair*, 1877, by Paul Cézanne, oil on canvas, 73cm x 56cm, Museum of Fine Arts, Boston

Madame Cézanne in a Red Armchair

Madame Cézanne in a Red Armchair (Fig. 33.8) is an early portrait.

Composition and style

It is painted in loose, fluid brushstrokes and is built up of small blocks of subtly varied colour locked together.

Colour

The blue, grey, green, violet and brown of the jacket bodice and the patterned wallpaper are echoed even in the flesh tones. Her stillness and monumentality are all the more remarkable for being set against the impressive red chair and voluminous striped skirt.

Recluse

After 1878, Cézanne became more and more reclusive. He lived quite comfortably on an allowance from home, but in 1886 he inherited a considerable amount of money and the family estate after his father died.

Exhibition in Paris

After 20 years, many in the Paris art world thought Cézanne was dead. Then, in 1895, the art dealer Ambroise Vollard organised an exhibition of his work. His reputation as a great artist grew quickly and he was discussed and promoted by a small circle of enthusiasts that included Renoir and Degas.

Painting to the last

In October 1906, at the age of 67 and suffering from diabetes, Cézanne was caught in a storm while painting. He collapsed and lay unnoticed in the rain for several hours before he was brought home in a labourer's cart. He died a week later, but one of his deepest wishes had been fulfilled: he had died painting. The next year, he was honoured with a large retrospective exhibition in Paris.

Influence

Paul Cézanne's influence was crucial to the modern movements and the 20th-century artists that followed. His influence continued directly into the 1930s and 1940s. To this day, his paintings continue to inspire artists.

Vincent van Gogh (1853–90)

Van Gogh's painting career was one of the shortest but most intense in the history of art. He died at 37 years old, only eight years after he began painting, having developed his unique style in just four years.

Early life

The son of a Dutch minister, Vincent was deeply affected by the poverty around him and set out to be a preacher. However, his personality was not suited to it and his licence to preach was withdrawn. This was a severe blow, but his despair drove him to paint. His art became his mission and he worked hard to master drawing and lithography. The peasants and the hardship of their lives became the subject of his painting.

Paris

Van Gogh went to Paris in 1885 and lived with his brother Theo for two years in Montmartre. Theo supported his older brother both financially and psychologically throughout his life.

Formal art training was far too rigid for him, but he saw the final Impressionist show and was introduced to some of the artists. He began to work with Pissarro, who taught him the methods and aims of both Impressionism and Divisionism. He tried working in the pointillism technique, but it was far too tedious.

Changes in colour

His connection with the French avant-garde brought about significant changes in Van Gogh's work, especially in his use of colour. He dropped the dark browns and greys, and adopted the bright, pure colours of the Impressionists and Neo-Impressionists. He soon developed his own personal and highly expressive style.

Avant-garde: A group of people who develop new and often surprising ideas that are ahead of their time.

Van Gogh's style

His choice of canvas was very important. He preferred to buy them ready made and then carefully prepare them by making his own primer with a mix of chalk, barium sulphate and lead white. He also liked to work on cardboard.

Colour

Van Gogh is probably best known for his bright colours. Over his short career he experimented more and more, and began to match them with emotion. He exaggerated what he considered important and dismissed the trivial or insignificant.

His favourite colours were chrome yellow, chrome orange, cadmium yellow, geranium, Prussian blue and emerald, but he still liked to use some black and dark brown.

Impasto

Energetic brushstrokes are the strongest characteristic of Van Gogh's style. He is most famous for very thick paint, or impasto, that created raised, almost three-dimensional surfaces.

Perspective frame

To help with perspective, Van Gogh got a handy, boxy kind of frame made. This helped him to view the scenes as if he were looking through a window. It also shortened the painting process and allowed him to achieve more.

Van Gogh's subjects

Van Gogh's subjects included portraits, self-portraits, interiors, landscapes and urban scenes.

Self-portraits

Between 1886 and 1889, he painted more than 30 self-portraits. For him this was not just a way to develop his skills as an artist; it was also a method of examining himself critically. These amazingly candid images reveal his psychological decline with humility and honesty.

He was influenced by the 17th-century Dutch artist Rembrandt, whose self-portraits span over 40 years. Van Gogh described these works as 'more than a view of nature, they are more like a revelation'. By linking himself to the great artists of the past, he showed his own desire to be taken seriously as an artist.

Arles

Vincent enjoying meeting other artists in Paris, but he found that city life was too much of a strain. He longed for the sunlight and dazzling colour of the south, and in 1888 he left for Provence. He settled in the little town of Arles.

The beauty of the landscape around Arles entranced him. He worked frenetically, spending all day in the open air and in all weathers. He weighted his easel onto the ground when the strong mistral wind blew, and on one occasion he even sat at his canvas all night because he wanted to paint the stars. He wore a crown of candles stuck in the brim of his hat so that he could see.

He worked with a new intensity and drive. His strokes broadened, his drawing grew more confident and his colours became stronger and brighter. He persuaded the artist Paul Gauguin to come and live with him in Arles for a while, and the two artists painted together. Gauguin painted a good deal from memory and Van Gogh began to do the same.

His paintings from the period in Arles are some of his most powerful and emotional. He rented a room in a house close to the railway station and lived there alone for a year. It was probably the closest he came to having a home and he made many paintings in the Yellow House. It is where he painted his room, his chair and his famous sunflowers.

Yellow was his favourite colour throughout his time in Arles, whether he was working outdoors or indoors.

Bedroom in Arles

Subject

Van Gogh painted his room in preparation for the arrival of his friend Gauguin. It remained one of his own personal favourites and he made two other copies of it.

The simple interior and bright colours of *Bedroom in Arles* (Fig. 33.9) were meant to convey notions of rest and sleep. He painted two of everything. There are two pictures on the wall, two pillows on the bed and two chairs, which are all to celebrate the end of his months of solitude.

Fig. 33.9
Bedroom in Arles, 1888, by Vincent van Gogh, oil on canvas, 72cm x 90cm, Vincent van Gogh Museum, Amsterdam

Composition

One of the most striking aspects of this work is the odd perspective. The rear wall appears strangely angled. It is not a complete mistake: this corner of the Yellow House was slightly skewed, but the artist has exaggerated the downward tilt.

Colour and style

The scene is painted in the simplest manner with pure colour and strongly outlined shapes. The bright colours are in harmonies of yellows, browns and pale blue. The paint is thickly applied.

Chairs

Van Gogh also painted two chairs. One was his and the other was for Gauguin.

In *Gauguin's Chair* (Fig. 33.10), the curved armchair is made of red-brown wood. It has an upholstered seat and has a burning candle and books resting on it. The scene is set in the evening and the chair rests on a colourful carpet with a green wall and lighted lamp in the background.

The predominant colour in *Vincent's Chair with His Pipe* (Fig. 33.11) is yellow, but the complementary colours of blue/orange and red/green balance this. The lighter colours suggest daylight. He distorted the perspective of the floor and chair to achieve a more harmonious composition.

Sunflowers

Highly excited at the prospect of his friend's arrival, Van Gogh painted a series of sunflowers.

He was forced to work indoors because of the wind and finished four pictures of sunflowers in six days. He had planned to paint 12, but when the weather improved he raced off on another idea. He signed two favourites and hung them in Gauguin's bedroom to welcome him.

The sunflower symbolised the Provençal summer sun's energy, which had religious associations and expressed his feelings of optimism.

Fig. 33.10 (left) *Gauguin's Chair,* 1888, by Vincent van Gogh, oil on canvas, 91cm x 72cm, Vincent van Gogh Museum, Amsterdam

Fig. 33.11 (right) *Vincent's Chair with His Pipe*, 1888, by Vincent van Gogh, oil on canvas, 92cm x 73cm, National Gallery, London

Vase with Fourteen Sunflowers

Subject

His final picture, *Vase with Fourteen Sunflowers* (Fig. 33.12), was the boldest of all. Breathing new life into the traditional subject of a vase of flowers, he depicts yellow flowers in a yellow jug against a yellow wall in a symphony of ochre, gold and corn colours. Using colour, line and texture, he expressed the entire lifespan of the flowers, from the young bright yellow to the wilting and dying faded ochre blossoms.

Composition

The composition is simple and direct. The curved line of the earthenware vase echoes the horizontal line of the background. The ground colour is balanced on the upper part of the vase and picked up by each of the blooms.

Style and colour

The flowers are built up with dabs of thick brushstrokes and the impasto technique suggests the texture of the seed-heads. The wide range of yellow was due in part to the newly developed pigments that made tones of new colours possible.

Disaster

Gauguin's time in Arles with Van Gogh was disastrous. Two more incompatible people could hardly have been found. Vincent was suffering from nervous exhaustion, and Gauguin was completely exasperated by him. Van Gogh had also been smoking and drinking heavily, so the disaster that followed was almost inevitable.

Fig. 33.12 *Vase with Fourteen Sunflowers*, 1888, by Vincent van Gogh, oil on canvas, 93cm x 73cm, National Gallery, London

On 23 December 1888, the two friends argued and Gauguin left the house to walk to the square. Van Gogh followed him but then returned to the house and cut off part of his left ear with a razor. He wrapped it in paper and went to find Gauguin in the local brothel. When one of the women answered the door, he handed it to her and asked her to treat it with great care.

Gauguin took the first train home in the morning and Van Gogh was taken to hospital. He signed himself into a mental asylum at St Remy, near Arles, and lived there for over a year.

The Starry Night

Shortly after he arrived in St Remy he wrote to Theo of his terrible need for religion. When he felt like this, he would paint the stars.

Subject

The Starry Night (Fig. 33.13) was painted from memory and may have been based on something he had seen earlier. The village was partly invented and the church spire suggests Van Gogh's native land, the Netherlands.

Composition

A flame-shaped cypress tree in the foreground balances the composition against the powerful night sky. The gently rising horizon line of the hills is set in the lower half and the village creates depth in the picture.

Colour and style

Huge stars that look more like great yellow fireballs contrast the cool, fluid, undulating blue and grey lines of the night sky. The crescent moon at the top right corner shines an even brighter yellow and orange.

The richly textured, sweeping impasto brushstrokes create rhythm, energy and emotion in a rich mix of ultramarine blue and yellow. The green-black tones of the dark tree silhouette contrast with the churning sky and the blue tones of the hills (Fig. 33.14).

Influences

The painting was a deliberate exercise in stylisation. Van Gogh told his brother in a letter: 'These are exaggerations from the point of view of arrangement, their lines are contorted like those of ancient woodcuts.'

Self-portraits

Van Gogh made two self-portraits not long after the 'ear incident'.

In *Self-Portrait with Bandaged Ear* (Fig. 33.15), he appears calm but the bandage on his mutilated ear is prominently displayed. The damage was inflicted

Fig. 33.13 (left)
The Starry Night, 1889, by Vincent van Gogh, oil on canvas, 74cm x 92cm, Museum of Modern Art, New York

Fig. 33.14 (below)
The Starry Night sketch

on his left ear but it looks like the right because of the mirror.

Wearing an overcoat and a hat, his head is turned to give a better view, but everything in the picture suggests the artist's horror at what he has done to himself. The act of self-mutilation has shocked and changed him.

Self-Portrait

Another self-portrait (Fig. 33.16) painted after he left St Remy later that year shows that Van Gogh's state of mind is obviously very agitated once again.

Subject and composition

In this head-and-shoulders view, the artist is wearing a suit and not his usual working jacket.

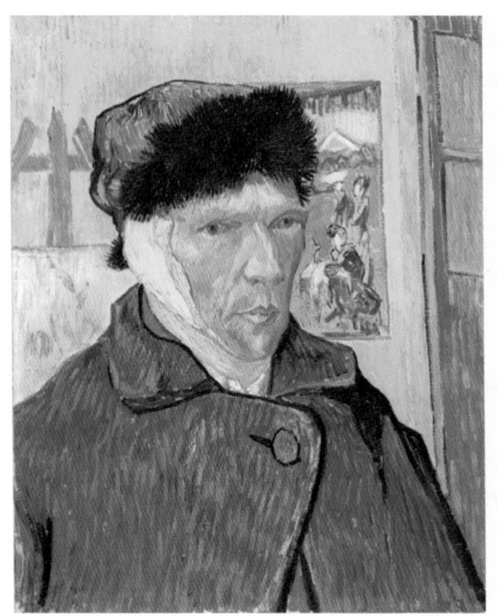

Fig. 33.15 (left)
Self-Portrait with Bandaged Ear, 1889, by Vincent van Gogh, oil on canvas, 60cm x 49cm, Courtauld Gallery, London

Fig. 33.16 (right)
Self-Portrait, 1889, by Vincent van Gogh, oil on canvas, 65cm x 54cm, Musée d'Orsay, Paris

Attention is focused on the face and particularly the piercing eyes, which are the most tightly drawn feature. They illustrate the mental anguish that lies behind the stern and passive expression. A fearful knot in the forehead completes this terrifying image.

Style

Pounding with energy, the swirling patterns ripple throughout the picture in a churning, turbulent motion. The colour and rhythmic brushstrokes connect the figure and background.

Colour

Cool blues and greens reflect the artist's emotional state. These normally calm colours change in mood when seen against the contrasting fiery orange of the hair and beard.

Death

Van Gogh spent a short time in Auvers with Dr Gachet. The doctor was an old friend of the Impressionists and he tried to help Van Gogh. The two men got on very well and for a time Vincent appeared calmer and seemed to be getting better.

His depression returned, however, and on 27 July 1890 he shot himself. He had been working at his easel, painting crows in a wheat field. He died two days later, attended by his brother Theo and Dr Gachet.

Van Gogh's influence

In his lifetime, Van Gogh sold only one painting. After his death, Theo and his son promoted his work and it became known and appreciated.

Paul Gauguin (1848–1903)

Paul Gauguin spent some time in Peru as a young child, but he returned to France with his mother after his father died.

He worked as a stockbroker but was haunted by his desire to paint. At the age of 34 he left his wife and family and exchanged his comfortable job for a life of poverty and suffering as an artist.

'Sunday painter'

For years he was an amateur 'Sunday painter', and spent many weekends in the country painting with Camille Corot. The turning point came in 1877, when he met Pissarro. He became involved with the Impressionists and spent his holidays working with Pissarro at Pontoise. Under Pissarro's influence, he began to use primary colours.

Exhibiting with the Impressionists

Pissarro persuaded the other members of the group to allow Gauguin to exhibit with the Impressionists. Monet and Renoir in particular disapproved of their shows being open to 'any dauber'.

Pont-Aven

In 1886 he made his first visit to Pont-Aven in Brittany, where he established an artists' colony. His eccentric dress, moodiness and self-centred personality were seen as signs of genius.

A new theory

In his early career, Gauguin worked out a new theory, known as Synthetism. It involved:

* Simplifying forms and eliminating details
* Using thick lines and large, flat areas of colour
* Getting rid of shadows and linear perspective
* Suggesting depth with planes of colour

Gauguin did not want to paint too closely from nature, but to draw it out, dream about it and paint from imagination.

Vision after the Sermon

Gauguin was inspired by the religious Breton women. His use of colour, form and line in *Vision after the Sermon* (Fig. 33.17) was quite new and unique. The inspiration for this style of non-naturalistic imagery came from Japanese woodblock prints.

Subject

The scene, taken from the Old Testament Book of Genesis, shows Jacob wrestling with an angel. The angel represents god or goodness itself and the struggle between good and evil.

Fig. 33.17
Vision after the Sermon (Jacob Wrestling with the Angel), 1888, by Paul Gauguin, oil on canvas, 73cm x 92cm, National Gallery of Scotland, Edinburgh

Composition

A tree splits the painting in half. It creates the divide between the Breton women and Jacob and frames the main subjects of the painting. The curve of the trunk follows the woman's head, while the branch curving off to the right leads directly to Jacob and the angel.

The artist has deliberately distorted the perspective so that it looks like two paintings. The Breton nuns in the background seem to be too large for the small cow next to them.

Colour and style

Harsh reds, blacks and whites characterise the work. The figures have exaggerated features and have been blocked in with strong contour lines and flat, solid colour. They have little or no tonal gradation or depth.

Tahiti

Following the disastrous period spent with Van Gogh in Arles, Gauguin began to think about establishing an artists' colony in the tropics, far from any taint of European civilisation. Eventually he settled on a plan to go to the South Sea island of Tahiti. A large auction of his work in Paris helped him raise the money to get there.

He spent the rest of his life in Tahiti, but it was not quite the paradise he had expected. His work did not sell in France and the project was a failure in

Fig. 33.18 *Tahitian Women*, 1891, by Paul Gauguin, oil on canvas, 69cm x 91cm, Musée d'Orsay, Paris

many ways. He was, however, always fascinated by the women's gentle beauty. He compared their behaviour and manner to the women of ancient Greece.

Tahitian Women

Soon after he arrived in 1891, Gauguin painted *Tahitian Women* (Fig. 33.18).

Subject

The impassive, almost melancholy mask-like faces are without expression. The painting tells its own story of Tahiti, both in the women and the background. One wears the traditional red wraparound skirt with white floral print, and her dark hair is tied with a yellow ribbon. She is turned away and is completely unoccupied. The other wears a Western-style dress and faces the viewer. She sits with her legs crossed under her skirt and is busy with her task of making a basket.

Composition

The proportions of the two figures have been distorted, but the poses fall into an easy rhythm of curves. Their solid forms against the lightly coloured sand dominate the space. The dark horizontal stripes of black sea and green lagoon spread out behind them. The woman on the left leans on her arm, which creates a straight hard edge to the left side of the painting.

Colour

Rich, simplified flat colours are separated by dark outlines.

Two Tahitian Women

Gauguin's life in Tahiti was difficult, but amazingly, none of this turbulence shows in his cool, timeless and mysterious paintings. His later works are softer and painted with paler colours. *Two Tahitian Women* (Fig. 33.19) depicts the beauty and serene virtues of the native women.

The women are bare breasted in the typical South Sea island manner. The painting captures Gauguin's idea of Tahiti as a mythical paradise of beautiful, mysterious women. They carry a basket of mango blossoms, like an offering of their innocence and purity of spirit. The painting portrays them without shame or embarrassment and follows the artistic tradition of comparing women's breasts to flowers or fruit.

Fig. 33.19 *Two Tahitian Women*, 1899, by Paul Gauguin, oil on canvas, 94cm x 72cm, Metropolitan Museum of Art, New York

Financial difficulties

In spite of his efforts to live in a completely natural way, Gauguin still needed money and he found it difficult to sell his paintings in France. His debts led him into trouble and he constantly fell foul of the colonial authorities. He suffered a broken leg in a fight with French sailors, which left him with a bad foot.

Fig. 33.20 *Where Do We Come From? What Are We? Where Are We Going?*, 1897, by Paul Gauguin, oil on canvas, 374.6cm x 139.1cm, Museum of Fine Arts, Boston

Where Do We Come From? What Are We? Where Are We Going?

In December 1897, in a burst of energy, he painted his largest ever work. *Where Do We Come From? What Are We? Where Are We Going?* (Fig. 33.20) was finished by June 1898. Gauguin wrote out its strange title in the top left corner but he never explained its precise meaning. It reads from right to left and depicts a life cycle from birth to death.

Death in prison

In a search for the perfect place, Gauguin left Tahiti and travelled to Hivaoa, one the Marquesas Islands. He refused to pay taxes to the French colonial authorities and when he wrote an article criticising the governor, he was imprisoned. Already very ill, unable to walk and suffering from ulcerated sores on his legs, he died from a heart attack in prison in May 1903.

Gauguin's legacy

Gauguin wrote a good deal about his art and his time in Tahiti. His writings and paintings were to influence 20th-century painting. Cézanne, however, remained unimpressed. He said, 'It's all nonsense. He's not a painter. All he's ever done is make Chinese pictures.'

Post-Impressionist influence on 20th-century art

Cézanne, Van Gogh and Gauguin's artistic innovations inspired a whole generation of 20th-century artists.

* Paul Gauguin was a major influence in the development of Fauvism.
* Paul Cézanne's art influenced the Cubists.
* Vincent van Gogh influenced German Expressionism.

Gauguin and Les Fauves

The first 20th-century movement in modern art, Les Fauves ('Wild Beasts') was a group of French painters with shared interests. Henri Matisse became its leader.

Gauguin's use of pattern and bright colour had a direct influence on this movement (see page 375).

Cézanne and Cubism

Cézanne's art directly influenced Spanish artist Pablo Picasso. He referred to Cézanne as 'the father of us all'. Cézannes's *The Bathers* was the direct inspiration for his *Les Demoiselles d'Avignon* (see Fig. 34.13).

Cézannes's ideas that nature can be depicted with the cylinder, sphere and cone and his use of multiple viewpoints directly inspired Cubism, one of the most influential artistic movements of the early 20th century. Georges Braque was the other founder of this movement. He admired Cézanne almost obsessively (see page 380).

Van Gogh and Expressionism

Vincent van Gogh's energetic brushwork, distortion of form and use of strong colours to convey emotion were a major influence on the development of Expressionism.

Expressionism

Expressionism emphasised an emotional response to subjects and events. The artists expressed themselves in a personal and individual way with the use of bold brushwork, distortion, exaggeration and imagination. Their colours and shapes were strong and vivid.

German Expressionism

Expressionism appeared mostly in Germany after 1910. Among the artists were the Germans Max Beckmann, Franz Marc and Ernst Ludwig Kirchner. The Norwegian Edvard Munch and Wassily Kandinsky from Russia were also related to this movement (see page 379).

Chapter review

* Post-Impressionism was both an extension of Impressionism and a rejection of that style's limitations. How did the artists go beyond Impressionism?
* The Post-Impressionist painters were three individual and reclusive artists. Why, do you think, was their work so influential?

EXAM QUESTIONS

Ordinary Level (2014)

Choose any work you have studied by Paul Cézanne (1839–1906). Answer (a) and (b).

(a) Name, describe and discuss your chosen work using the following headings:

- Composition
- Colour and style
- Subject matter/theme

(b) Give some general information on Cézanne.

Illustrate your answer.

Ordinary Level (2012)

Look again at *Self-Portrait with Bandaged Ear* by Vincent van Gogh (1853–90) (Fig. 33.15). Answer (a) and (b).

(a) Describe and discuss this work using the following headings:

- Subject matter
- Composition
- Colour and style

(b) Name and briefly describe and discuss **one** other painting by Van Gogh.

Illustrate your answer.

Ordinary Level (2011)

Look again at *Vision after the Sermon* by Paul Gauguin (1848–1903) (Fig. 33.17). Answer (a) and (b).

(a) Describe and discuss this painting using the following headings:

- Subject matter
- Composition and style
- Medium
- Use of colour

(b) Give some general information about Paul Gauguin.

Use sketches to illustrate your answer.

Higher Level (2014)

Describe and discuss the work of **one** named Post-Impressionist artist. In your answer, refer to **two** named works that are typical of your chosen artist's style and refer to the subject matter, composition and techniques used in each work.

and

Briefly describe and discuss how the work of your chosen artist influenced the development of art in the 20th century.

Illustrate your answer.

Higher Level (2010)

'Paul Cézanne (1839–1906) was a major innovator in the history of painting.'

Discuss this statement with reference to his painting *Mont Sainte-Victoire* (Fig. 33.7).

and

Name and discuss briefly **one** other named work by Cézanne.

Illustrate your answer.

FURTHER RESEARCH

courtauld.ac.uk – Montagne Sainte-Victoire with Large Pine

www.vangoghmuseum.nl – Vincent's Life and Work

www.abcgallery.com – Paul Gauguin

www.khanacademy.org – Post-Impressionism

Chapter 34

Twentieth-Century Art in Europe

Go to page 402 for a list of extra content available on **www.gillexplore.ie**.

The pioneering work of Cézanne, Van Gogh, Gauguin and the Neo-Impressionists was seen in exhibitions and galleries in Europe and America in the first few years of the 20th century.

To the young artists who saw the work, it provided a new starting point for them to explore new possibilities, free from the limits of Academic art.

The years leading up to the First World War saw an explosion of a new creative thinking unparalleled since the Renaissance. The foundations had been kicked from under illusionist painting (where an impression of three dimensions is created on a two-dimensional surface). The art and culture of the world outside Europe and from before the Renaissance was seen to be as important as the European painting tradition of the previous 300 years.

By the end of this chapter, I will...

* Know the reasons for the development of Fauvism and Expressionism.
* Have seen examples of the work of Expressionist artists.
* Understand the basic goals of Cubism and the work of two Cubist artists.
* Know the development of abstract art and Wassily Kandinsky's part in it.
* Have explored Surrealism and the Surrealist artists.
* Know about the Bauhaus.
* Know about the International Style of architecture and at least one architect.
* Have studied the work of Henry Moore.

Fauvism

The Fauves was a name given to a group of artists who first exhibited together in the Paris Salon d'Automne of 1905. The critic Louis Vauxcelles, seeing a small bronze sculpture in a Renaissance style in the same room as the brightly painted pictures, exclaimed, '*Ah, Donatello*

The Fauves: Not a long-lived or planned association. There was no formal group or written manifesto. It was simply a number of artists who had a feeling for colour as a way of expressing themselves separate from reality. Pure colours were used for emotional or decorative effects, as in the work of Van Gogh and Gauguin, or to describe space, as in Cézanne's work.

NOTE! For many critics, the work of the Fauves exhibited in 1905 marks the beginning of modern art.

Fig. 34.1
The Pool of London, 1906, by André Derain, 65.7cm x 99cm, Tate Gallery, London. Derain used colour to emphasise shape. It also creates space and drama. It is not meant to describe what he saw.

au milieu de fauves' ('Donatello among the wild beasts').

Henri Matisse (1869–1954), André Derain (1880–1954), Raoul Dufy (1877–1953), Maurice de Vlaminck (1876–1958) and later Georges Braque and Georges Rouault were among the major Fauves, but most went on to work in other styles later in their careers. Many of them began painting in a loose, Divisionist style but moved on to broader areas of colour in deliberately harsh contrasts.

Derain's *The Pool of London* (Fig. 34.1) is part of a series he painted along the Thames in London in powerful colours that are clearly divorced from reality. Fauve subjects were of the same type as those of the Impressionists: people and places of pictorial interest. They generally did not choose emotional or dramatic subject matter.

Henri Matisse (1869–1954)

One of the major artists of the 20th century and leader of the Fauves, Henri Matisse soon moved on to develop a personal style that relied on pure colour, flat shape and pattern. His *Portrait of Madame Matisse. The Green Line* was one of the most controversial exhibits at the 1905 Salon. It was heavily criticised for its colours and handling of paint.

Portrait of Madame Matisse. The Green Line

Subject

This is a portrait of the artist's wife (Fig. 34.2).

Composition

The placement of the head and shoulders is quite traditional, but the seemingly random break-up of background space into coloured areas is new.

Style

This is a painting in the Fauve style. Colour is used in an untraditional way, and the drawing and handling of paint seem rough.

Technique

The paint is applied in strong outlines and big brush marks, which also describe the angles of the face and give direction to the background.

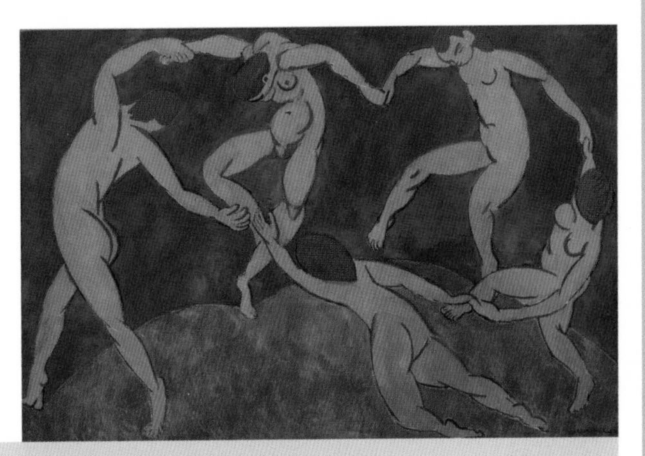

Fig. 34.2 (left)
Portrait of Madame Matisse. The Green Line, 1905, by Henri Matisse, oil on canvas, 40.5cm x 32.5cm, Statens Museum, Copenhagen. The bold painting and colouring and the tight composition turn a simple portrait into a powerful work of art.

Fig. 34.3 (above)
La Danse, 1910, by Henri Matisse, 258.5cm x 390cm, The Hermitage, St Petersburg. Great energy and movement are created by the simple figures.

Colour

This painting is an exercise in the use of colour for modelling. The warm tones of the face and dress contrast with the green background on the right-hand side and come forward in space from it, while the sharp yellow of the left side of the face also comes forward from the warm background on that side.

Matisse shows that he can make a warm colour project from a cool background and at the same time make a pale, cool colour project from a warm background. The green line down the middle of the face is the correct tone to connect the two different colours of the face.

La Danse

La Danse (Fig. 34.3) is reduced to areas of strong colour without brushwork or modelling. Sky, land and flesh are represented in single colours. The simplicity of line and shape was worked out in a series of preliminary sketches in which Matisse refined and simplified everything to a minimum.

This almost abstract style appears again in his later work, but during the 1920s he often used elements to express space and volume, though pattern and colour are still the most important parts.

Odalisque with Red Trousers

Subject

A model in Matisse's Nice studio represents the exotic world of North Africa that he had seen on visits to Algeria in 1906 and Morocco in 1912–13 (Fig. 34.4).

Composition

The figure seems to be almost falling out of the bottom left of the canvas. The strongly patterned

Fig. 34.4 *Odalisque with Red Trousers*, 1924, by Henri Matisse, oil on canvas, 50cm x 61cm, Musée de l'Orangerie, Paris. This is one of a series of odalisques painted following visits to North Africa.

screens behind her dominate the space. The few three-dimensional objects are squeezed into the top left corner.

Style

This work is in Matisse's mature style, where the human figure and strongly coloured patterns are his main subjects.

Technique

Matisse varies the way he applies paint: thinly and without much brush marking in the background areas and more thickly and with direction on the figure and three-dimensional parts. He uses outlines and brush drawing on details in the figure and patterns.

Colour

From his early Fauve work, Matisse was interested in the power of colour and pattern. He often uses the same colour in several areas of a painting to ask questions about three-dimensional space. In this painting, the red on the trousers, floor and the pattern on the screen have this effect.

Later years

In his later years Matisse suffered from very poor health and was bedridden much of the time, but he continued to work, cutting out shapes in paper that had been painted in strong colours with gouache. *The Creole Dancer* (Fig. 34.5) is an amazingly joyful work for an old man in poor health. 'The paper cut-out allows me to draw in the colour,' he claimed, enabling him to produce work of simplicity and vigour as he had done all his life.

Fig. 34.5 *The Creole Dancer*, 1950, by Henri Matisse, 210cm x 120cm, Musée Matisse, Nice. Matisse's later coloured paper cut-outs have an abstract quality in spite of the simplified figures.

Expressionism

These artists were influenced by early German art (Grünewald and Dürer) and primitive art. They had also seen the work of the Post-Impressionists, the Norwegian Edvard Munch and the contemporary Fauves and Cubists, which contributed to a forceful and direct style, a style of protest and rebellion.

The Expressionists experimented widely with media. Many of them painted, sculpted, drew, made prints and wrote plays and music, as well as writing artistic criticism. It was the expression of ideas and emotions that counted, not artistic skill or external appearances.

Expressionism: A term adopted to describe art that uses distortions and exaggerations in shape and/or colour to express the artist's emotions.

Die Brücke

Die Brücke (The Bridge) was founded in Dresden in 1905 by a group of architectural students at the Dresden technical school. Ernst Ludwig Kirchner was a founding member. Emil Nolde had a shorter association with the group. Part of their idea was to create a 'bridge' from the art of the past to modern art.

Ernst Ludwig Kirchner (1880–1938)

Kirchner was a founding member and leader of the group. He worked in Berlin from 1911 painting street scenes and nudes. In 1915 he had a nervous breakdown following his involvement in the First World War and moved to Switzerland, where he painted landscapes. He exhibited in Germany and abroad and had some success. The Nazis condemned his work as degenerate in 1937 and burned more than 600 of his paintings. Kirchner committed suicide the following year, depressed about the loss of his work and the political state of Germany.

Five Women on the Street

Subject

The five women are dark against the greenish yellow of the street lights (Fig. 34.6). Their spiky clothes and sharp outlines suggest something unpleasant is happening. They appear to be looking in a shop window while a car passes close to the kerb.

Composition

The figures are tightly hemmed into the picture space. They contact every side, creating a sense

Fig. 34.6 *Five Women on the Street*, 1913, by Ernst Ludwig Kirchner, oil on canvas, 90cm x 120cm, Museum Ludwig, Cologne. The harsh colours and jagged painting style express an unpleasant subject.

of tension and restraint. Conventional perspective is not used. The figures are almost flat against the background, while the car and shop window are shown at steep angles. The eye is drawn over and back across the faces. There is no comfortable place to rest the eye.

Style

This shows the Expressionist style, where brushwork and distortions of shape and colour were used to create a harsh commentary on German city life.

Technique

It is painted in a forceful, almost violent style. Strong brush marks and simplified drawing create a dramatic effect.

Colour

Kirchner worked with a limited palette here, which is in contrast to some of his other work. The yellows, greens and black help to create an unpleasant atmosphere.

Der Blaue Reiter

Der Blaue Reiter (*The Blue Rider*) was the title chosen for a yearbook that was being prepared by the Russian artist Wassily Kandinsky (who we will look at later) and the German Franz Marc during 1911 (Fig. 34.7). When it was published it contained articles on art, literature and music.

They had a more analytical approach to art and wanted no divisions of the arts, as they felt the impulse to express emotions and ideas was beyond artificial boundaries. In one of his essays, Kandinsky wrote, 'That is beautiful which is produced by internal necessity which springs from the soul.' The artists who contributed to *Der Blaue Reiter Almanach* organised two touring exhibitions that tried to show 'the variety of ways in which the artist's inner wishes manifest themselves'. International artists, including Derain, Braque and Picasso, were invited to exhibit with them and the work was seen in the major cities of Germany and in Moscow.

Fig. 34.7 *Der Blaue Reiter*, 1911, by Wassily Kandinsky, 28cm x 22cm, Lenbachhaus, Munich. This is the final design for the cover of the almanac, which had important essays on art and music. It was illustrated with children's art and primitive art as well as the work of contemporary French and German artists.

Cubism

The two leading artists of the Cubist movement, Pablo Picasso and Georges Braque, worked together from the time they were introduced in about 1907 to just before the First World War. In this short time they explored ideas and methods of creating art that were highly influential in the 20th century. The initial influence was African art, particularly masks, and later the paintings of Cézanne.

Picasso's painting *Les Demoiselles d'Avignon* (see Fig. 34.13) is often cited as the first step towards Cubist painting. Braque was excited by the work and with Picasso tried to develop a new way of representing reality. They wanted to find an alternative to the European tradition of perspective. They also hoped to find a way of representing objects that was not limited by a single moment in time.

Analytical Cubism

* They tried to represent figures, landscape and still life as they might be seen from a number of different viewpoints.
* They wanted to show how a person might notice different characteristics of an object at different times.
* They began with a limited palette of earth colours and blue, which they eventually reduced to a range of warm greys.
* The Cubists did not follow a strict system, but liked to include everything that might be useful in producing a work of art.

Fig. 34.8 (left) *Still Life with Violin and Pitcher,* 1909–10, by Georges Braque, 117cm x 74cm, Kunstsammlung, Basel, Switzerland. The muted colours of the Analytical phase of Cubism kept the focus on form.

Fig. 34.9 (right) *Portrait of Daniel-Henry Kahnweiler*, 1910, by Pablo Picasso, 110cm x 73cm, Art Institute of Chicago. The geometric shapes hide rather than reveal the face of the sitter.

Braque's *Still Life with Violin and Pitcher* (Fig. 34.8), painted in 1909–10, can still be read quite easily. The violin, or its parts at least, and the pitcher can be found among the tightly painted planes of the surface. There is still a hint of traditional perspective in the description of space.

Picasso's portrait of the art dealer Daniel-Henry Kahnweiler (Fig. 34.9), who had introduced him to Braque, was painted late in 1910 and it went a step further. The two-dimensional surface of the canvas is hardly disturbed by the planes of Kahnweiler's face. Though he sat many times for the portrait, his hands and face are the only parts that can be seen easily.

Collage: Invented by Picasso and Braque, the word 'collage' comes from the French word *coller*, which means 'to stick'. It refers to the tickets, pieces of newspaper and pre-printed patterns that they stuck to their paintings.

In the following year, the paintings of both Braque and Picasso were almost completely abstract. A series of lines, marks and tones were applied in a painterly way to a flat surface. Having achieved this freedom from the description of reality, Picasso and Braque moved on to the second phase of their development.

Fig. 34.10 (above)
Collage 1913, 1913, by Pablo Picasso, 45cm x 48cm, National Gallery of Ireland, Dublin. Mixing real objects with painted shapes challenges the viewer's sense of reality.

Fig. 34.11 (right)
Young Girl with a Guitar, 1913, by Georges Braque, 130cm x 74cm, Musée National d'Art Moderne, Centre Georges Pompidou, Paris. Different angles of the face and guitar are contrasted with patches of wood grain and newspaper headlines, which challenge any sense of three dimensions.

Synthetic Cubism

Both artists had been using materials such as sand, sawdust, plaster, metal filings and even ash mixed with their paints to create surface texture. Then Braque added wood grain effects and Picasso introduced letters and numbers. Eventually they began to stick objects to the surface of the paintings – such as tickets, pieces of newspaper and printed images – which were 'real objects' and not representations.

Picasso's *Collage 1913* (Fig. 34.10), which includes part of a newspaper dated 1913, suggests angles of view and perspectives and then denies these perceptions by overlapping them with lines and shapes that suggest different viewpoints.

Braque's *Young Girl with a Guitar* (Fig. 34.11) from the same year includes parts of newspapers and wood grain that have been painted in imitation of collage.

There is frequently a light-hearted feeling to some of these paintings, as if the artists were playing visual games with the viewer.

Pablo Picasso (1881–1973)

A child prodigy, son of an art teacher/painter, Picasso mastered painting and drawing skills as a child and graduated from art college while still a teenager. Born in Malaga, he attended college in Barcelona and Madrid, absorbing influences from the Old Masters and modern painters. He was a member of the avant-garde in Barcelona before moving to Paris in 1904. This was his Blue Period, when he painted melancholy scenes showing the difficulties of life for ordinary people. *The Old Guitarist* (Fig. 34.12) shows this style, with hints of El Greco's elongated figures. The blue colouring adds to the sense of despair.

Primative art

He became interested in primitive art through the work of Gauguin, which he saw in a large exhibition in Paris in 1906, the same year that an influential exhibition of Cézanne's work was also seen. This interest in primitive art, particularly African masks, drew Picasso away from the European tradition of image-making to the freedom of ritual art, which included symbols and magic. This notion of the artist as maker of magic symbols occurs frequently throughout his career.

Les Demoiselles d'Avignon

Subject

Picasso worked on the idea for *Les Demoiselles d'Avignon* (Fig. 34.13) through sketches and smaller paintings. Early versions had male figures

Fig. 34.12 *The Old Guitarist*, 1903, by Pablo Picasso, 123cm x 83cm, Art Institute of Chicago. This was painted in Barcelona during Picasso's Blue Period.

as well. This painting was seen by friends and other artists from 1907 but did not go on public exhibition until 1916. Even friends and fellow artists were divided about it. Matisse did not approve. Braque disliked it at first, but after studying it for a time understood its importance. The five nude figures represent prostitutes from a brothel called Avignon in Barcelona.

Composition

The five figures are tightly arranged in the picture space. The eye is drawn from face to face in an oval movement. The two figures on the right are slightly separated in style and space.

Style

This painting is a step away from Expressionism towards Cubism. It has an emotional element that Cubism did not have. It is not fully Cubist, even though we are offered several viewpoints for some of the figures. The figure in the bottom right has her back to us, but her face also looks at us with features seen from different angles.

Technique

There is a mixture of areas of flat painting and strongly modelled areas with clear brush marks. This may show the experimental nature of the work, where Picasso is looking for the best way to express his ideas on representing shape and space.

Colour

The limited palette of earth red, blue, black and white follows into the Cubist period where Picasso was experimenting with form and found colour to be a distraction.

Influences

As noted above, the work of Gauguin and Cézanne interested him, as did the ancient primitive art of Spain, Africa and the Americas and the Spanish Mannerist artist El Greco. All these influences can be seen in the painting.

Fig. 34.13 *Les Demoiselles d'Avignon*, 1907, by Pablo Picasso, oil on canvas, 244cm x 234cm, MOMA, New York. The harsh drama of this painting relates more to Picasso's later work than the years of Cubist experimentation that followed.

* Cézanne's interest in breaking objects down into basic geometry can be seen in the angles of figures and background.
* Gauguin's paintings and sculptures from Hawaii have figures in simple forms in similar poses.
* The three figures on the left relate to the style of early Spanish sculpture.
* The faces of the two figures on the right are based on African masks.
* The blue and white background and the figure composition is said to relate to the work of El Greco, particularly his painting *The Opening of the Fifth Seal.*

Classical influence

At the end of the First World War, Picasso went to Italy to design sets for Diaghilev's Ballets Russes, which was performing in Rome.

Picasso's contact with classical art added another element to his range of work. While he continued to paint and sculpt in the Synthetic Cubist style, he also made drawings, etchings and paintings in a modified classical style. *Two Women Running on the Beach (The Race)* (Fig. 34.14), painted in 1922, provides an amazing contrast to *Three Dancers* (Fig. 34.15), with its abstract, surreal and Expressionist elements. These two styles existed alongside each other throughout Picasso's career. He chose whichever mode suited his needs at any particular moment.

Guernica

Subject

The bombing of the town of Guernica by the Fascists during the Spanish Civil War prompted Picasso to paint *Guernica* (Fig. 34.16), one of the greatest artistic expressions of the horrors of war. Considered by many to be his masterpiece, it combines symbols and allegories in an almost colourless composition of figures and shapes that describes the destruction and anguish of war.

Composition

The light/eye/sun at the top of the painting seems to be a focal point. Below this, a screaming horse tramples on a dismembered soldier. One of the soldier's hands holds a broken sword and a flower grows from it.

On the left of the canvas, a bull stands over a woman crying in anguish, holding her dead child.

The head and arm of a woman holding a lit lamp emerges from a space right of centre, towards

Fig. 34.14 (below)
Two Women Running on the Beach (The Race), 1922, by Pablo Picasso, 32.5cm x 41.1cm, Musée Picasso, Paris. These rounded figures based on classical sculpture appear in Picasso's work from the 1920s to the end of his career.

Fig. 34.15 (right)
Three Dancers, 1925, by Pablo Picasso, 215cm x 142cm, Tate Gallery, London. The flat areas of colour and angular figures are in a very different style to the more classical figures he used in other work.

Fig. 34.16 *Guernica*, 1937, by Pablo Picasso, matt household oil paint on canvas, 356cm x 782cm, Reina Sofia Museum, Madrid. The painting expresses the horror Picasso felt at the destruction of the Basque town of Guernica.

the top of the picture. Below her, a woman with outstretched arms staggers into the light, a look of disbelief on her face.

On the right, a woman is trapped with flames above and below her.

All the figures are trapped in a dark space. There seems to be no way out.

Symbols and images

When asked about the meaning of this painting, Picasso said, 'This bull is a bull and this horse is a horse…if you give meaning to certain things in my paintings it may be very true, but it is not my idea to give this meaning. What ideas and conclusions you have got I obtained too, but instinctively, unconsciously.'

In spite of this, critics agree on a number of ideas.

* Picasso painted in black, white and grey to create a sombre mood. He was greatly influenced by the reports on Guernica in the newspapers and newsreels at the time, which were all in black and white.
* The flames and destruction represent not just Guernica, but the destruction of war.
* The broken sword represents a defenceless people.
* The woman with the lamp may be throwing light on the war crime so the world can see.
* The delicate flower may represent a little hope.

Style

The style is Cubist and Modern, but it is full of emotions and symbols that are Picasso's own and are not defined by any style.

Technique

Picasso had a special matt house paint made so that the surface could be flat in every way. Brush marks and textures are kept to a minimum, but there are some scratch marks.

Picasso's range of expression and technique

After the war Picasso moved to the south of France, where he continued to work, choosing the medium and technique he thought appropriate. 'If the subjects I have wanted to express have suggested different ways of expression, I haven't hesitated to adopt them,' he declared. He painted, sculpted, drew, etched and produced lino prints, illustrations and ceramics in great numbers until his death.

Cubist development ended after the First World War, but it proved to be an immensely adaptable source for many of the movements that followed, including Futurism and abstract art.

Sculpture

Picasso experimented with ceramics and sculpture throughout his career. His early sculptures were conventionally modelled and cast, but around 1914 he began to experiment with found objects.

Many of Picasso's sculptures are witty and imaginative and often seem to be made for fun rather than as serious works of art. He exhibited very few of them during his lifetime.

Baboon and Young

Subject

The sculpture portrays a mother baboon and her baby. It is a playful assembly of found objects (Fig. 34.17).

Composition

This standing figure is fully three-dimensional and can be viewed from all sides. It stands on a base and is also supported by the tail. Our attention is first drawn to the head because it forms the apex of the assembly.

Style

Assemblage was a new idea of Picasso's, but the work is not in a specific style.

Technique and materials

Picasso was an innovator in everything he did. Assembling found natural and manmade objects together to make sculpture was an extension in three dimensions of the collages he had made as part of his painting practice.

* The face is made of two toy cars: one right way up, the other upside down.
* The ears are made of a number of cup handles.
* The body is a big ceramic pot. The handles make the shoulders.
* The spine and tail are made of a leaf spring from a car.
* All the other body parts and the baby were modelled in clay.

Fig. 34.17 *Baboon and Young*, 1951, by Pablo Picasso, 53cm x 33cm x 53cm, Musée Picasso, Paris. The found objects the sculpture is made from take a moment to be noticed.

* The assembly was cast in a mould and produced in bronze.

The development of abstract art

Artists most frequently arrived at abstraction through one of two basic routes: the reduction of natural forms and appearances to extreme simplification or the development of work from non-representational basic forms, like geometry.

Kandinsky is usually credited with having produced the first abstract picture around 1910. Robert Delaunay and other Cubists in Paris arrived at abstraction around 1913. At this time, Kazimir Malevich was producing Suprematist compositions in Russia. In 1917, Piet Mondrian and the De Stijl group produced abstractions in the Netherlands.

Abstract art: A term used to describe 20th-century work in which the traditional European concept of art as imitation of nature has been abandoned. Abstract paintings do not represent any recognisable objects.

Wassily Kandinsky (1866–1944)

Born in Russia, Kandinsky was a painter, printmaker and art theorist. He gave up a legal career after seeing one of Monet's haystack paintings in an Impressionist exhibition in Moscow, which showed him that painting was about something more than subject matter. He trained in Munich and encouraged an interest in French avant-garde painting in his fellow students.

He was involved in the *Blaue Reiter* almanac and exhibitions and produced an essay, 'The Spiritual in Art', which provided theories for abstract painting. He felt that art could be like music, free from the representation of reality. He used musical terminology to describe his paintings, compositions, improvisations and impressions.

Composition IV

Subject

Being an abstract painting, *Composition IV* (Fig. 34.18) has no subject other than its own shapes and colours, though in this case there are still some hints of human figures and landscape.

Composition

The eye is drawn to the purple area near the centre of the canvas, then right to the two 'figures', down through the two larger diagonal shapes to the bottom centre. The two vertical lines in the middle bring the eye up again, then left among the lines and colours and back to the bottom via the triangle on the bottom left. In this way the eye circulates around the composition, picking up more details and points of interest.

Style

This is a painterly abstract style using brush marks and blended colour to create a harmonious composition.

Technique and materials

Kandinsky's oil paintings use broad areas of blended colour overlaid with strong, dark line applied with a brush.

Colour

He moved away from the colours of nature to show that colour could have its own value and affect the viewer in the way that music does.

Complete abstraction

By 1914 Kandinsky had evolved a completely abstract style in which line, colour and shape

Fig. 34.18 *Composition IV*, 1911, by Wassily Kandinsky, 200cm x 275cm, Kunstsammlung Nordrhein-Westfalen, Germany. There are still traces of figures and landscape in these early compositions.

were used independently of each other and traces of subject matter had almost disappeared. At the outbreak of the First World War he moved back to Russia and became involved in the reorganisation of art education in the new Bolshevik state, but he soon found himself out of sympathy with the idea that artists should produce propaganda and designs for industry and not paintings.

He returned to Germany in 1921 and took up a teaching post in the Bauhaus, where he taught the foundation course based on an investigation of form. His paintings during these years were more abstract than his earlier experiments.

When the Nazis closed the Bauhaus in 1933, Kandinsky went to live in France, where the work of Joan Miró and Jean Arp had an impact on him.

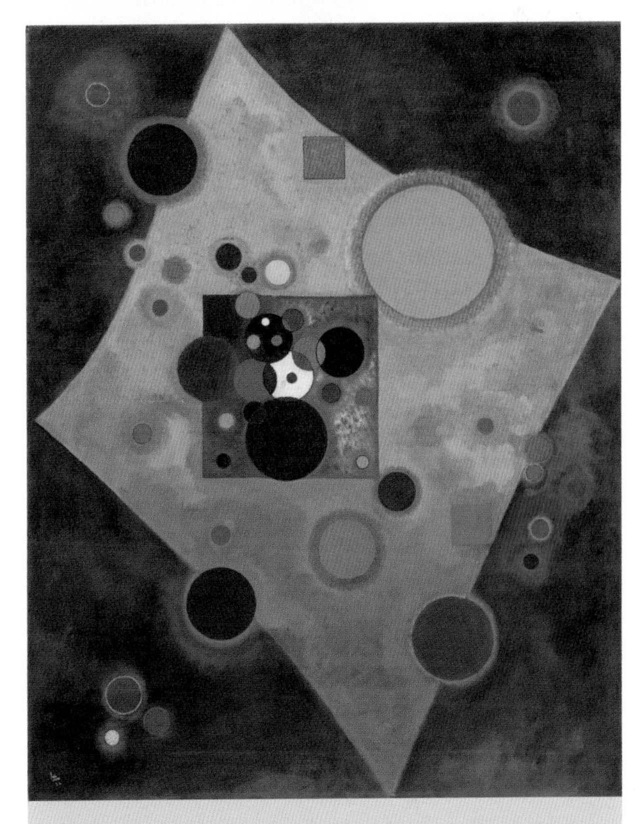

Fig. 34.19 *Accent on Pink*, 1926, by Wassily Kandinsky, oil on canvas, 101cm x 81cm, Musée National d'Art Moderne, Centre de Georges Pompidou, Paris. This is a painting without traditional subject matter.

Accent on Pink

Subject

Accent on Pink (Fig. 34.19) is a completely abstract work based on geometry. The free-floating shapes are nothing but themselves: harmonies in shape and colour.

Composition

The pink circle is the dominant element. It seems to light up its surroundings. The eye gradually moves out to the subtly coloured areas contained in and surrounding the other shapes. The big ochre rectangle with curved sides touches each edge of the canvas, holding everything together.

Technique and materials

This oil painting on canvas is painted in the most subtle brushwork and then contrasted with the hard-edge outlines of the geometric shapes.

Colour

A range of gently contrasting warm colours and tones on the dark purple background creates a gentle harmony, which makes the pink circle all the more dramatic.

Influences

The influence of the younger Russian artist Malevich is evident in this painting, though Kandinsky's feeling for colour and paint takes the work beyond simple geometry.

Dadaism

Dadaism was a complex international movement of artists, poets and writers who attacked artistic and political traditions. It was an anti-war movement that started in Zurich, Switzerland, among a group of artists and writers who performed at the Cabaret Voltaire. Their ideas soon spread to Paris, Berlin, New York and other cities.

Anti-war

The movement was anti-war. They blamed greedy capitalists and colonialists and social and intellectual conformity for allowing the war to kill millions. They abandoned 'reason' and 'logic', which they saw as part of the problem.

Anti-art

The very nature of Dadaism was anti-art. The artists chose non-artistic methods to make their work.

* **Collage:** Their collages were often made of rubbish (Fig. 34.20).
* **Photomontage:** They cut up words and images from newspapers and magazines and put unlikely or ridiculous elements together into one image.
* **Assemblage:** This was a three-dimensional version of collage. Unlikely combinations of objects were nailed, screwed or connected together to be viewed in the round or hung on the wall.
* **Ready-mades:** Manufactured objects with signatures or titles added were offered as art (Fig. 34.21).

Roots

Dadaism had its roots in Cubism and collage, the theoretical writings of Kandinsky and abstraction, and the intellectual poetry and critical writing of the time, which separated words from their meaning.

Events were organised that combined the simultaneous reading of several poems, music made from noises and exhibitions of found objects. Dadaist performances often ended in noisy debate or fighting, which was in fact the kind of controversy they were looking for, as it would draw attention to their theories on the need for change in art and society.

There are several accounts of how the name of the group was chosen. One version says that the French word '*dada*' ('hobby horse') was chosen at random from a dictionary as the name of the movement, partly for its nonsensical sound and also for its association with childhood freedom.

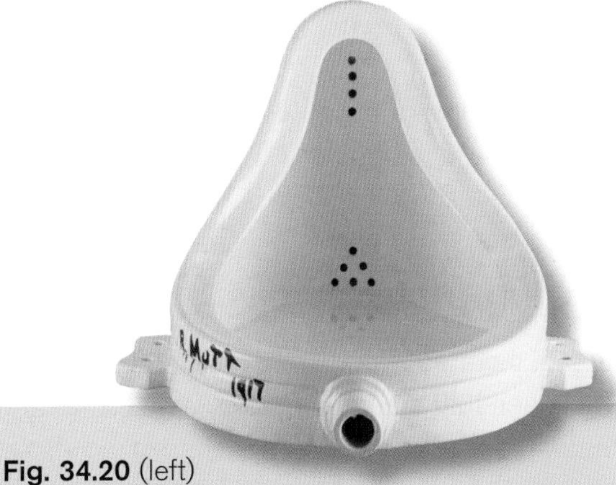

Fig. 34.20 (left)

Worker Picture, 1919, by Kurt Schwitters, 125cm x 91cm, Statens Konstmuseum, Stockholm. Dadaist collages were often made by throwing found objects on the floor and developing a composition from the chance or automatic arrangement that was found.

Fig. 34.21 (above)

Fountain, copy 1966, original 1917, by Marcel Duchamp, 30.5cm x 38.1cm x 45.7cm, Philadelphia Museum of Art. Presenting everyday objects as art was meant to challenge the art establishment who, the Dadaists felt, admired art for its monetary value rather than its beauty or truth as a work of art.

The importance of Dadaism

Many artists were associated with Dadaism throughout Europe and the US before it disbanded in the 1920s. Facts, reason and social order were shed in favour of imagination and randomness. This radical view of art and life was essential for the development of much 20th-century art, including the Surrealism of the interwar period and the action painting, Pop Art, conceptual art and 'happenings' from the period after the Second World War.

Surrealism

Surrealism was a movement that absorbed Dadaism. It was founded by the French poet André Breton in Paris in 1924. They looked for an alternative to the Realist or classical styles that had come to the fore in the 19th century. It was an art of the imagination and of dreams.

Roots

The Surrealists admired artists such as Bosch, Goya and Gauguin, primitive and naïve art and new 20th-century ideas such as cinema, detective novels and especially the research of Sigmund Freud as published in *The Interpretation of Dreams* in 1900.

The Dadaist movement and some aspects of Cubism had begun an anti-rational approach to art that the Surrealists took further, liberating the unconscious mind by giving up conscious control over their work.

Two approaches

Automatism

In Automatism, the artist drew freely, automatically, allowing his or her hand to move over the work with a minimum of conscious control using techniques like dribbling paint and making rubbings or scrapings and then responding to these marks. Miró painted in this way.

Dream pictures

Dream pictures were careful, realistic paintings of scenes that made no rational sense. Dali and Magritte preferred this approach.

Surrealism was one of the most influential art movements in the 1920s and 1930s. Large, dramatically publicised exhibitions, especially in London and New York in 1936, created an enormous impact. It provided an alternative to international abstract art, which was often not as well received publicly.

Salvador Dali (1904–89)

One of the best-known artists of the 20th century through his self-publicity, Salvador Dali, was born in Figures in the Catalonia region of northern Spain. His talent was evident early on and he had exhibited his work by the age of 15.

He went to art college in Madrid but was expelled before he graduated, accused of causing unrest.

His early work experimented with Impressionism, Fauvism and Cubism. He went to Paris in 1926 and was introduced to Picasso and the Surrealists by Miró, whom he already knew. He absorbed styles and techniques from classical Renaissance to the cutting-edge modern work he saw in Paris.

In 1929 he met Gala, then the wife of a poet friend, who became his muse and model. A Russian immigrant 10 years older than Dali, she became his most important influence for the rest of his life. They were married in a secret civil ceremony in 1934 and had a Catholic wedding in 1958.

He developed a carefully executed realist style to produce his 'hand-painted dream photographs'. He painted nightmare pictures of his own neurotic fantasies, following the Surrealist belief in revealing even the most difficult things from the unconscious mind.

Dali exhibited in Paris and New York and spent the war years in the US. His publicity-seeking behaviour made him one of the best-known contemporary artists. His face, with his flamboyant moustache, was recognisable worldwide.

In 1948 Dali and Gala returned to a house he built at Port Lligat near Cadaques in northern Spain, where he worked for most of the rest of his life, spending winters in Paris or New York.

Dali continued to paint until the end of his life. He also made sculptures and jewellery and he worked in theatre, film, fashion and photography. He wrote a lot and made public performances to promote his own work and demonstrate Surrealist ideas. He collaborated with other artists and produced prints of his own work.

Soft Construction with Boiled Beans (Premonition of Civil War)

This painting makes an interesting contrast with Picasso's *Guernica* (see Fig. 34.16). Both artists were deeply affected by the Spanish Civil War, though they supported opposite sides.

Subject

The dismembered figure of Spain tears itself apart – truly a nightmare image (Fig. 34.22).

Composition

The rectangle made by the limbs carries our focus from one place to the next. A claw-like hand tears at a breast. Ugly limbs grow out of each other. Everything is set in a barren landscape against a cloudy sky. This creature comes close to every side of the canvas, which adds to the tension and sense of discomfort in the composition.

Fig. 34.22 *Soft Construction with Boiled Beans (Premonition of Civil War)*, 1936, by Salvador Dali, 100cm x 100cm, Philadelphia Museum of Art. Dali's dream pictures can be all the more disturbing because of the realism of the painting. The changes in scale and logic can be disturbing.

The little man peering over the hand at the bottom left is Sigmund Freud, a key figure in psychiatry who was an inspiration to Dali. The little figure gives a sense of scale to the whole composition.

Style

This is Dali's mature Surrealist style. He called it 'my paranoiac-critical method', which was approved by the Surrealist group. All the parts are realistic but they are assembled in an unnatural arrangement and setting.

Technique and materials

Dali's oil painting technique was very accomplished. He painted in great detail and created a smooth finish in the style of the Renaissance masters he admired.

Colour

The colours in the sky and landscape are a little exaggerated but still realistic. The earth red of the foreground forms a solid area for the grotesque waxy-coloured creature that dominates the space.

The Hallucinogenic Toreador

Subject

The Hallucinogenic Toreador (Fig. 34.23) is an anti-bullfighting image made for Gala, who disliked the sport. Her face appears in the top left.

The image of the bullfighter is hidden in the negative spaces among the Venus de Milo figures. He wears a white shirt and green tie. His jewelled jacket and red cloak form his shoulders. The right breast of the second Venus forms his nose. The shadowed hip of the first Venus forms the outline of his face. The shoulder of the first Venus forms one eye socket. The head of the second Venus is the other eye.

Dali used this complicated illusionist imagery in many of his later paintings.

Composition

The upper edge of the canvas is framed with a wall with arches, which represents the bullring. The big orange space below this is the sand on the floor of the ring. The purple shadow on the left of this area creates an outline for the toreador's hat. The two dominant figures of the Venus de Milo on the right are repeated in a series of fading images to the left.

In the bottom left, below the brightly coloured circles that form part of the jewelled jacket, there is a bull's head described in a mesh of black and white. The head lies in a pool of blood, which doubles as a lake with a boat on it. A line of flies travels across the bottom to a little boy with a hoop in the bottom right corner (Dali as a child?). This is a very complicated composition and there are many more things to see in it. Can you find the dog?

Style

Dali's later style is still firmly Surrealist, but there is greater emphasis on visual tricks and illusions.

Fig. 34.23 *The Hallucinogenic Toreador,* 1968–70, by Salvador Dali, 398.8cm x 299.7cm, Salvador Dali Museum, St Petersburg, Florida. Dali hid images in the negative spaces of his paintings in his later career.

Technique and materials

This is a smoothly finished, realistic rendering of fantastic scenes.

Colour

Colours are cleverly used to reveal and disguise the toreador. A warm colour describes the face, which is also an area of sand. The draperies of the Venus figures become the clothes of the toreador. Colours and shapes are not what they seem.

The Bauhaus

The Bauhaus was the most influential art and design school of the 20th century. Its teaching programme and its approach to industry and society had a major influence on design education in Europe and the US long after it closed.

The school was founded in Weimar in Germany in 1919. Walter Gropius was its first director. Like the Deutscher Werkbund before it (see online material, page 408), it was a response to the need for modern design for industry so that Germany could compete with British and American industrial output.

In the beginning it operated a bit like the Arts and Crafts movement organised in Britain by William Morris (see online material, page 408). The intention was to unify art and design, combining architecture, painting and sculpture in a craft-based curriculum that would turn out craft workers and designers capable of producing beautiful and useful objects for manufacture.

By the mid-1920s, the craft-based approach gave way to designing for industry and mass production. They adopted a slogan: 'Art into Industry'.

In 1925, for political and financial reasons, the Bauhaus moved to Dessau. Walter Gropius designed the new buildings to house the school. These buildings, which were constructed in concrete, steel and glass (Fig. 34.24), became a standard form of modern architecture that spread through Europe and America after the Second World War.

The Bauhaus Building, Dessau, Germany

The Bauhaus Building is a flat-roofed building of steel and concrete construction. It has three wings arranged asymmetrically, which connect workshops and dormitories within the school.

The school was designed as a practical functioning structure, but it also manages to be elegant and beautiful. A feature of the design that was often imitated is the wrap-around glass façade that hangs outside the construction of the building, allowing views through corners, creating a lightness in its appearance (Fig. 34.25).

The preliminary course

The preliminary course was designed to introduce students from a variety of backgrounds to the principles of design theory. The course was based on experiments and problem-solving through the study of materials, colour theory and form. A number of famous artists taught the course, including Paul Klee, Wassily Kandinsky (see pages 388–90) and Josef Albers.

The cabinet-making workshop (furniture design)

Marcel Breuer, looking for modern approaches to the design of chairs, adapted the tubular steel construction of bicycles into lightweight, modern, stackable chairs that became a standard worldwide before suitable plastics were invented (Fig. 34.26). They used their own furniture and fittings throughout the Bauhaus Building.

Fig. 34.25 Bauhaus Building, 1919–25, by Walter Gropius. The glass curtain wall outside the construction of the building allows views through the corners, which creates a light appearance.

The metalwork studio

This studio designed light fittings and tableware for mass production, as well as one-off pieces that experimented with design principles.

Marianne Brandt, studio director from 1928, designed a silver and ebony teapot based on geometrical shapes (Fig. 34.27). The function of the design, from its non-drip spout to heat-resistant ebony handle, was just as important as its appearance.

The textiles and typography workshops had some commercial success producing designs that were taken up by industry.

Fig. 34.24 The Bauhaus Building at Dessau in Germany, 1919–25, by Walter Gropius. The Bauhaus Building created a new standard in modern architecture.

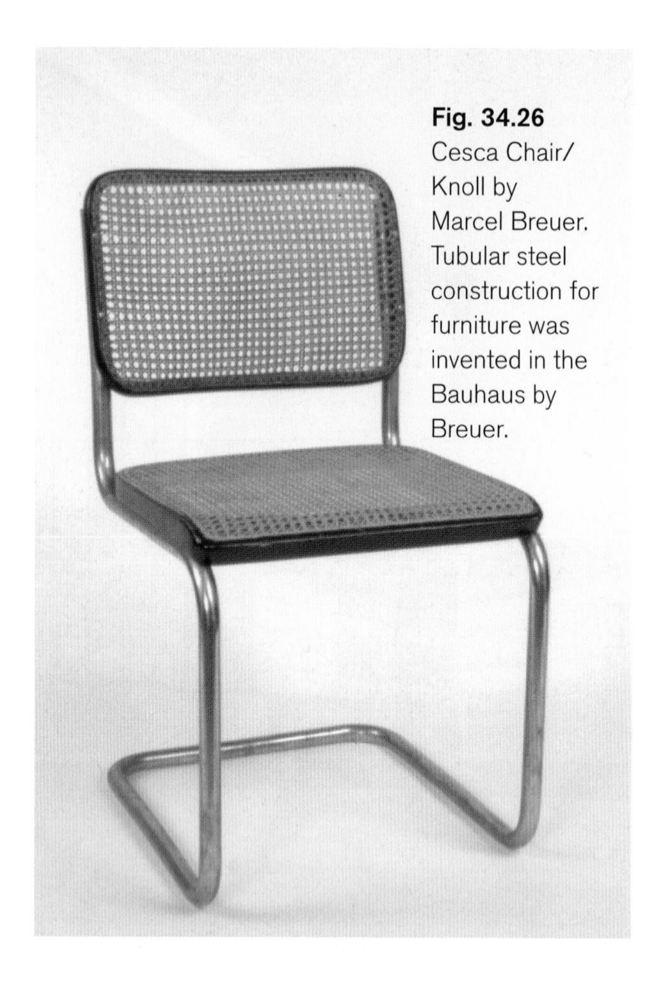

Fig. 34.26 Cesca Chair/ Knoll by Marcel Breuer. Tubular steel construction for furniture was invented in the Bauhaus by Breuer.

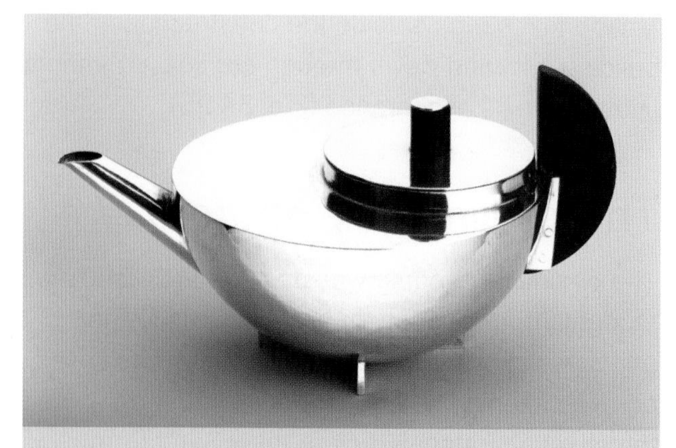

Fig. 34.27 Teapot in silver and ebony, c. 1924, by Marianne Brandt. The clean lines and simple geometric shapes of this teapot are typical of Bauhaus designs for industry.

The Bauhaus moved to Berlin in 1932, again for political and financial reasons, but it closed in 1933 under pressure from the Nazi Party. The staff emigrated to various countries, bringing the ideals of Bauhaus design and education around the world. America in particular accepted many of the leading architects and designers into their universities, which revolutionised their art and architecture courses.

The International Style of architecture

Many aspects of the International Style had already been worked out by the architects of the De Stijl and Bauhaus movements. Simple geometric design, steel and concrete construction and the extensive use of glass were the main characteristics of the style.

Reasons for the International Style

* In the early 1900s, buildings were still being decorated with features from historical styles (Renaissance, Gothic) in stone or brick, even though the internal structure was modern, steel and concrete.
* The increasing industrialisation of Europe created a need for large commercial and institutional buildings.
* New industrial processes made high-quality steel and plate glass cheaper and strong enough to use in bigger constructions. Steel-reinforced concrete technology was improved, allowing lighter structures to carry more weight.
* Designers wanted a modern style, without added decoration, that reflected the technology of the time.

Principles

During the 1920s, architects were trying to find a set of principles that would allow them to design buildings that were modern, honest and useful.

They wanted to create a harmony between the function of the building, the technology of its construction and its appearance.

Characteristics

* International Style buildings are usually made of simple rectangular forms.
* They have plain surfaces with no decoration.
* They have open-plan interiors.
* They are made of modern materials.
* They are modern and minimalist in appearance.

Ludwig Mies van der Rohe (1886–1969)

The third and final director of the Bauhaus from 1930 to 1933, Mies van der Rohe, emigrated to the US in 1938 and took up a position as Director of Architecture in the Armour Institute of Chicago (now the Illinois Institute of Technology), where he was a highly influential lecturer. He designed mainly private residences in Germany before the war.

Villa Tugendhat, Brno, Czech Republic

This was a revolutionary design built on an iron frame so that structural walls were not necessary (Fig. 34.28). Built on a slope, the house appears to be one storey tall on the street side but is three storeys on the garden side.

The living and social areas have a glass wall facing the garden. One wall in the living room is made of onyx and much of the furniture was specially made, so it was an expensive project. It is now a UNESCO World Heritage Site.

In the US, Mies van der Rohe had a successful private practice designing high-rise buildings in a minimalist style where the structure is often visible on the outside. He called it 'skin and bones' architecture.

Fig. 34.28 Villa Tugendhat, Brno, Czech Republic, 1928–30, by Mies van der Rohe. This view is of the garden front. It is a private house in iron, concrete and glass. The glass wall of the living area allowed people inside to feel part of the landscape.

Some of his quotes have become famous in the design world. 'Less is more' and 'God is in the details' are but two.

The Seagram Building, Park Avenue, New York

The Seagram Building in New York (Fig. 34.29) is considered to be one of the finest examples of modern high-rise building.

Mies wanted the building to be surrounded by a plaza set back from the street so that it could be properly appreciated. The ground floor is reduced in size, so the building seems to be standing on stilts and the public can interact with the structure.

The building has a complicated structure that includes several innovations. New York fire regulations would not allow him to expose the steel structure on the outside of the building as he would have liked, so he added bronze-toned I-beams running up the full height of the outside, surrounding the windows, to emphasise the structure. This idea of adding a non-structural façade to a steel and concrete skeleton is now common, but it was revolutionary at the time.

Attention to detail is a hallmark of his work. The blinds in the Seagram building can be fully open or closed or half-open, but they cannot be held in any other position. Mies did not like the look of buildings where blinds could be in any position, as he thought it made them look irregular.

The National Gallery in Berlin was his last design.

Spread of the International Style

The International Style spread throughout the world during the 1950s and 1960s. By the 1970s, buildings in the style had become so common that people said that they would not know what city they were in if they were dropped in the middle of the high-rise area.

Fig. 34.29 The Seagram Building, Park Avenue, New York, 1958, by Mies van der Rohe. This photo shows the full height of the building viewed from street level. Mies van der Rohe's skyscraper designs revolutionised large-scale building worldwide.

British art after the Second World War

Two of the major English artists of the post-war period – Henry Moore and Francis Bacon (see online material, page 402) – have Irish connections. Their work is often based on the human figure but tends towards abstraction.

Henry Moore (1898–1986)

Born in Yorkshire of an Irish father, Moore showed talent from an early age and was encouraged by his secondary school art teacher to apply to the local art college.

He volunteered for the army at 18 and was injured in a gas attack in 1917. He spent the rest of the war as a physical training instructor.

In 1919 he went to Leeds School of Art and got a scholarship to the Royal College of Art in London in 1921. He studied primitive art in the museums and galleries.

In 1924 he went travelling in Italy, where he saw the work of the Old Masters, Michelangelo, Giotto and others.

In Paris he saw a copy of a Myan sculpture, *Chacmool*, which greatly influenced him.

Back in London, he taught two days a week at the Royal College of Art and did his own work. He married Irina Radetsky, a painting student at the Royal College of Art, in 1929 and went to live in Hampstead, which was a kind of colony of modern artists at the time.

In 1932 he was appointed head of sculpture at the Chelsea School of Art.

His work gradually became more abstract and he began to have his work cast in bronze, working directly from clay and plaster maquettes rather than making sketches. During World War Two, the school moved out of London and Moore resigned his post.

He made drawings of the Londoners sheltering from the Blitz in the Underground. These drawings were bought by the War Artists Advisory Committee and taken on exhibition around America, which made Moore better known.

The Moores' home suffered bomb damage during the war, so they moved to a farmhouse in Herefordshire, where they remained for the rest of their lives.

After the war in 1946 he went to the US for a big retrospective exhibition of his work that was held in the Museum of Modern Art in New York. His daughter Mary was born the same year.

In 1950 he got his first large public commission for a bronze sculpture. Moore got more commissions during the 1950s and 1960s, including a bronze memorial to W.B. Yeats that you can see in St Stephen's Green in Dublin.

He continued to carve in stone and wood as well as working in bronze. By the 1970s he was becoming very wealthy and set up the Henry Moore Foundation to promote the visual arts.

Henry Moore was one of the most successful artists of the 20th century. His work is in museums and public places all over the world. The inspiration for the shapes he used came from simple natural things like stones, bones, shells and the human figure, which he simplified down to basic shapes.

Grey Tube Shelter

Subject

Grey Tube Shelter (Fig. 34.30) depicts people sheltering in the London Underground during the Blitz. Individuality is lost in the huddled mass.

Composition

The group is arranged in a low pyramid with taller figures for balance at the left and right sides. There are smaller triangular groups within the arrangement. The open space above and

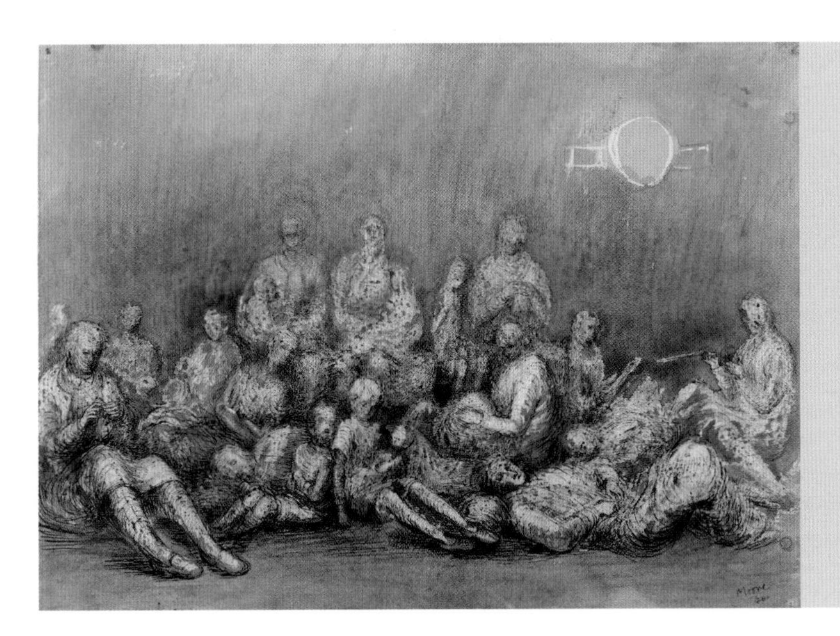

Fig. 34.30

Grey Tube Shelter, 1940, by Henry Moore, 279mm x 381mm, Tate Gallery, London. This is one of a series of drawings by Moore that recorded people sheltering in the Underground railway lines from the German bombing of London during the Second World War.

below the group emphasises their closeness. The light in the upper right casts an eerie light on the figures.

Style

Moore's drawing style is quite sculptural. The figure compositions look like his sculptures of family groups and reclining figures.

Technique and medium

This piece is watercolour, gouache, ink and chalk on paper. Moore works into a grey wash, adding lights and darks to create the figures. The watercolour runs off the chalk, creating dark dots on the white areas.

Colour

A few areas of yellow that represent the artificial light are the only relief from the grey, which seems to absorb everything.

Family Group

Subject

A mother, father and child are sitting on a bench (Fig. 34.31). The forms are simplified. They seem to be in the act of passing the child from one to the other.

Composition

Being three-dimensional, the composition will change as you walk around the piece. From the front it is mainly a group of soft-sided rectangles with spheres and cylinders making up the smaller parts. The quality of the work is abstract even though the figures are quite clear.

Technique and materials

The sculpture is cast in bronze. Moore made drawings and maquettes before working to full size.

Fig. 34.31 *Family Group*, 1950, by Henry Moore, Barclay School, Stevenage, Herefordshire, England. This was Moore's first large bronze public sculpture.

Large Reclining Figure

Subject

This piece is a large semi-abstract reclining figure (Fig. 34.32).

Composition

The figure seems to be in three parts even though it is cut from one large block of stone. Moore often separates parts so that their relationships change as you walk around them.

Technique and materials

Power tools and assistants would have been needed to carve the figure from the huge block of marble. Like many of Moore's pieces in stone,

Fig. 34.32

Large Reclining Figure, 1984, by Henry Moore, marble sculpture, Yorkshire Sculpture Park. Some of Moore's later work was completely abstract, but natural and human forms are often present.

bronze or wood, there is a beautiful smooth finish that makes you want to run a hand over it.

The 20th century

Change came more quickly in the arts, society and technology in the 20th century. There was a revolution in communications, which was felt in the arts.

Artists struggled to find a way to express the concerns of contemporary life. Abstract and conceptual art were completely new forms that became the dominant means of expression for leading modern artists.

The art idea replaced the art object as the point of expression for many artists, although the physical art object was still important for others.

Chapter review

* Does the Fauves' use of colour make sense to you? Could you imagine using colour in this way in your own work?
* Compare examples of Analytic and Synthetic Cubism. Which do you prefer?
* Look at some examples of the development of Wassily Kandinsky's work and see if you can observe the development of abstraction in it.
* What were the main influences on the development of Surrealism? Which style of Surrealism do you prefer?
* Some Bauhaus designs have become modern classics. Why do you think that is?

EXAM QUESTIONS

Ordinary Level (2015)

Choose one work you have studied by Pablo Picasso (1881–1973).

Answer (a) and (b).

(a) Name, describe and discuss your chosen work using the following headings:

- Subject matter
- Composition
- Colour and style

(b) Give some general information on Pablo Picasso.

Illustrate your answer.

Higher Level (2016)

Answer (a), (b) and (c).

(a) Choose and name **one** of the following:

- A painting by Mondrian (1872–1944)
- A sculpture by Henry Moore (1898–1986)

(b) Discuss a named work by the artist with reference to the artist, subject matter, style, composition, materials, technique and the period in which it was produced.

(c) Name and briefly describe and discuss **one** other work by the artist you have chosen.

Illustrate your answer.

FURTHER RESEARCH

www.tate.org.uk
www.metmuseum.org
www.theartstory.org

In addition to the artists featured in the book, you will find extra content on the following on **www.gillexplore.ie**:

Emily Nolde (1867–1956)
Franz Marc (1880–1916)
Georges Rouault (1871–1958)
Georges Braque (1882–1963)
Kazimir Malevich (1878–1935)
Piet Mondrian (1872–1944)
Joan Miró (1893–1983)
René Magritte (1898–1967)
Le Corbusier (Charles-Édouard Jeanneret) (1887–1965)
Francis Bacon (1909–92)

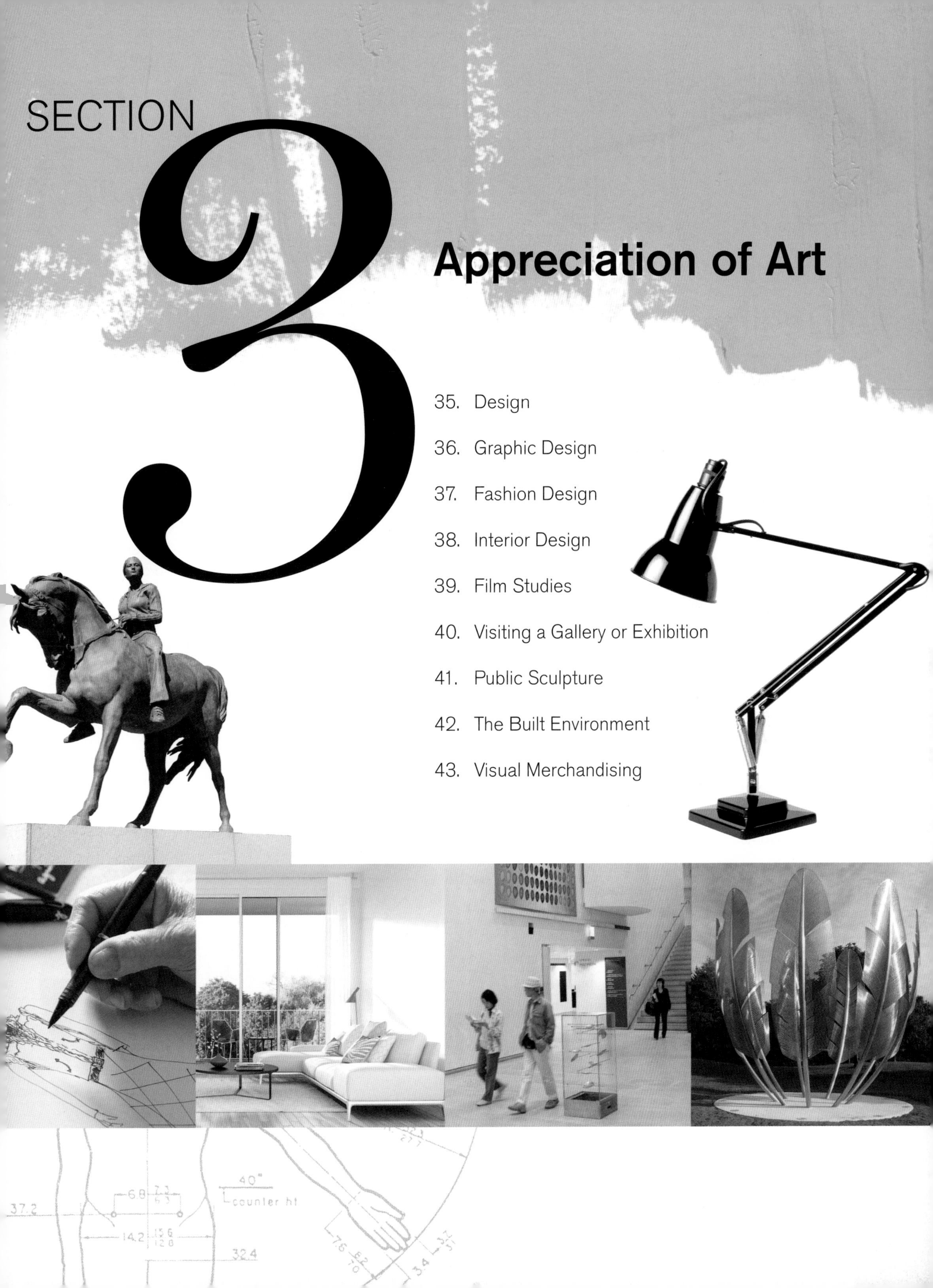

SECTION 3

Appreciation of Art

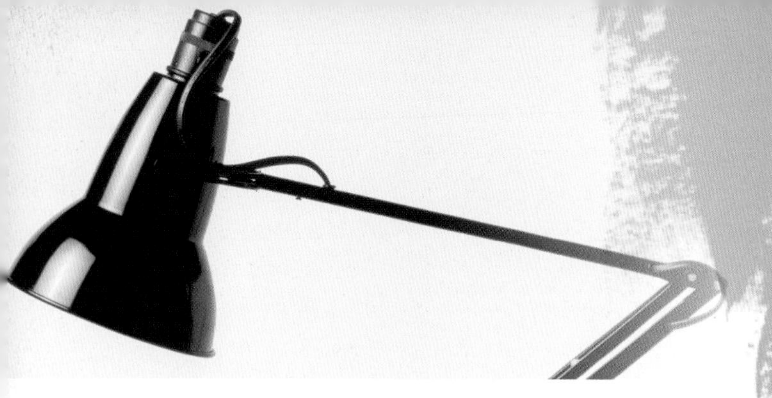

Chapter 35

Design

The term 'design' covers a wide area of activities, from architects and engineers, product and industrial designers to graphics, fashion, crafts and a number of other areas where people design systems and processes that may not closely relate to art. We will focus on the work of product designers, graphic designers, fashion designers and interior designers.

By the end of this chapter, I will...

* Know about ergonomics.
* Understand the changes brought about by modern materials and technology.
* Know the names of a few designers and examples of their designs.
* Have observed how the design process works.
* Know how to analyse a designed product using the four steps in the 'Examining a designed object' section. I need to practise this with a variety of products, such as mobile phones, kitchen tools and machines, electric equipment, furniture, electronics for entertainment, recycled materials, etc. The possibilities are endless, but the design principles are the important thing to know.

Go to page 408 for a list of extra content available on **www.gillexplore.ie**.

Product design

People have thought about the shapes and functions of the things that they make since the earliest times. The first pots, baskets, tools and weapons were made to fit a purpose, so we could say that they were designed. This type of project – where the designer and maker are one person – still goes on today in the areas of craft and 'one-off designs', which are produced directly for clients (Fig. 35.1).

Fig. 35.1 Modern craft pottery

The design process

The design process is a series of steps that designers use to help organise their work. Whether they are designing a building, a bicycle or even a computer game, this process helps the work to progress in an orderly fashion. Below is just one version of a range of processes used by different companies and individuals to help them with their design work.

Fig. 35.2 Product designer working with a computer-aided design (CAD) program

Pre-production

Most of the designer's work takes place before a product is manufactured.

Design brief

A design brief should state the goals of the project. For example, the designer might be asked to design an electric car for city use by young people, or an armchair with easy access for an older person. A detailed plan of the project will be written out with all the limitations in cost, materials, manufacturing and use. The possibilities in design and innovation that must be considered would also be noted. All these requirements should be discussed with the client (Fig. 35.3).

Fig. 35.3 Product design sketches

Research

Research into similar products and systems and related areas of design needs to be done. Simple sketches and notes should be made to create a variety of possible designs.

Presentation and choosing a solution

Fully worked-up drawings and/or models would be made of the preferred design solution, showing all the dimensions, materials and colours and highlighting any special features. These drawings and models would be shown to the client for their approval. At this stage a full set of technical drawings would be produced in consultation with engineers and technicians (Fig. 35.4). A manufacturer works from the technical information, selecting machines, materials and processes to carry out the project.

During production

Development and testing

The product should be developed and tested to improve the manufacturing process and to enhance the safety and the appearance of the finished item. With modern computer technology a good deal of testing can take place in virtual environments, which saves time and eliminates expensive changes to machinery and processes during production (Fig. 35.5).

Fig. 35.4 (left) Product design presentation for the Airvod media player by Cian and Matt O'Sullivan

Fig. 35.5 (right) Production line testing

Post-production

Implementation

Putting the product into use is the ultimate goal of the process. Evaluation and post-production testing help to discover if the process and the product were a success. Constructive criticism and suggestions for further improvement can be made at this stage.

Redesign

Redesign can happen at any stage of the process to make improvements and corrections.

Examining a designed object

There is a short account of William Morris online (see online material, page 408). He produced the first criteria for good design: truth to materials, fitness for purpose and form follows function. Let's restate these ideals here in simpler form and give some examples to help examine some products.

1. A product should suit the requirements of those for whom it was designed

This is where ergonomics comes into play. If you are examining something small, like kitchen utensils, then how they fit in the hand is important. They should be comfortable to use and do their job properly (Fig. 35.6). Larger items, like pieces of furniture, should be shaped to their purpose and materials. A dining chair or an office chair will have different requirements than an armchair. The body position of the user has to be considered. For larger items, like a car, there should be a comfortable and adjustable driving position and all switches and controls should be visible and easily accessible. The area of the market being designed for is also important. The specifications for a family saloon will be quite different from a sports car.

Fig. 35.6 OXO Good Grips kitchen tools are designed for people with limited grip

2. A product should function properly and efficiently

A product needs to be mechanically sound and safe. If we take the example of an electric lawnmower, it should obviously cut grass, but it should also be safe to use. On/off switches should be at the operator's fingertips. If it operates on a long flex, there should be an automatic cut-off in case it cuts its own cable, or, even better, it should have a rechargeable motor so that a cable is not necessary and does not present a hazard. Any product with switches and motors needs careful examination and assessment.

3. A product should be made of suitable materials

With modern developments in materials, a lot of equipment has become safer and easier to handle. For example, modern heat-resistant plastics have made domestic electric kettles much safer to use.

4. A product should look good in shape, colour and texture

This is where styling and colour choice are taken into account. What looks good can be very different in different times and places. Culture and fashion partly dictate what is acceptable, but well-designed objects should be ageless (Fig. 35.7).

Chapter review

This outline skims over some of the more obvious points. A full analysis of any design would need to be planned out and examined using the four points mentioned earlier a guide. The names of designers and famous design houses should be included in your analysis, where relevant, and you should include a little background for these too.

* Do you think the principles of good design that William Morris came up with are still valid today?
* How could the study of ergonomics help a designer to design an office chair or controls for a computer gaming console?
* Does computer-aided design (CAD) mean that designers are not needed as much as they were before computers?

Fig. 35.7 An Anglepoise lamp by the Terry Spring Company. Manufactured since 1932, they are still in production today.

EXAM QUESTIONS

Ordinary Level (2016)

Mobile phone cases come in a variety of styles and materials.

Answer (a) and (b).

(a) Describe and discuss the features of a well-designed mobile phone case under the following headings:

- Function
- Materials
- Style

(b) Design a personalised phone case. Give reasons for your design decisions.

Illustrate your answer.

Ordinary Level (2015)

'Upcycling' reuses old objects and waste materials to create useful and often beautiful items.

Answer (a) and (b).

(a) Describe and discuss the illustration on the accompanying sheet (a 50-gallon metal drum painted bright red and converted into a chair) using the following headings:

- Idea/function
- Shape/use of materials
- Colour

(b) Suggest a design to 'upcycle' empty tin cans. Describe the function of your design and list the steps that you would take to carry it out.

Illustrate your answer.

Higher Level (2012)

The Central Bank has recently issued a 10 euro silver coin. Discuss in detail the main considerations for the design of such a commemorative coin.

and

Outline your own design ideas for a silver euro coin commemorating Ireland's farming industry **or** architectural heritage.

Illustrate your answer.

FURTHER RESEARCH

www.vam.ac.uk – William Morris

www.eileengray.co.uk

www.idi-design.ie

www.ccoi.ie

You will find further content on **www.gillexplore.ie** on: origins of the designer, William Morris and the basic rules of good design, The Deutscher Werkbund, Bauhaus, The International Style, new technology, computer technology and design, and on:

Henry Ford (1863–1947)
Eileen Gray (1878–1976)
Henry Dreyfuss (1904–72)

Chapter 36

Graphic Design

Graphic design is the art of visual communication through typography, images, colour and space. The designer can work in a broad area, from advertising and company identity/branding to design for print (books, magazines, etc.), posters, billboards (large advertising hoardings), website graphics and art posters and prints.

Graphic design can be considered to be an ancient art, starting with the signs, symbols and writing of the ancient Egyptians, through the hand-lettered and illustrated manuscripts of the Middle Ages, to early printing and on to the 19th century, when it began to take on forms that we would recognise today.

By the end of this chapter, I will...

* Know the history and design of posters.
* Have looked at signs and pictograms.
* Know about company identity and logos.
* Have examined examples of advertising and packaging.
* Know about web design.
* Have learned how to examine a graphic design using the five points listed on pages 416–17.

Posters

The 1880s and 1890s were a high point in poster design. High-quality artists were involved and prints of their work are still popular today.

Jules Chéret (1836–1932)

Jules Chéret was an artist and lithographer. He developed a three-colour system for producing full-colour prints quickly and cheaply, which revolutionised poster design.

He designed posters for the music halls and cabarets of Paris in the 1880s. He went on to produce posters for advertising, drinks, perfumes, cosmetics and later for railroads and manufacturers. Chéret designed over 1,000 posters in his 30-year career. The effect of these bright posters seen around Paris made other artists want to get involved.

Palais de Glace (The Ice Palace)

This is typical of Chéret's posters, with a pretty young woman as the centre of attention (Fig. 36.1). His posters are credited with liberating young women to enjoy themselves in public.

Subject

The subject is a colourfully dressed young woman skating.

Fig. 36.1 *Palais de Glace (The Ice Palace)* poster, 1890s, by Jules Chéret. Chéret's young women became symbols for a new sense of freedom in France in the 1890s.

Composition

The young skater creates a diagonal across the page. This is balanced by the figures in grey tones behind her and the lettering at the top and bottom.

Typography/lettering

The artwork for lithographs had to be made by hand, including the lettering. The large blue letters were designed to be seen from a distance so that passersby could read them at a glance.

Colour

The warm oranges and reds of the clothing are lively and fun. They contrast with the blues and greys of the lettering and the background figures, which are there for balance.

Modernist poster design

In the early 1900s, Art Nouveau had lost its vigour. Artists working in Scotland's Glasgow School, Austria's Vienna Secession and Germany's Deutscher Werkbund were producing simpler, more modern and geometric work.

Bertold Löffler (1874–1960)

Bertold Löffler worked as a freelance illustrator in Vienna and taught in the Art School there. His

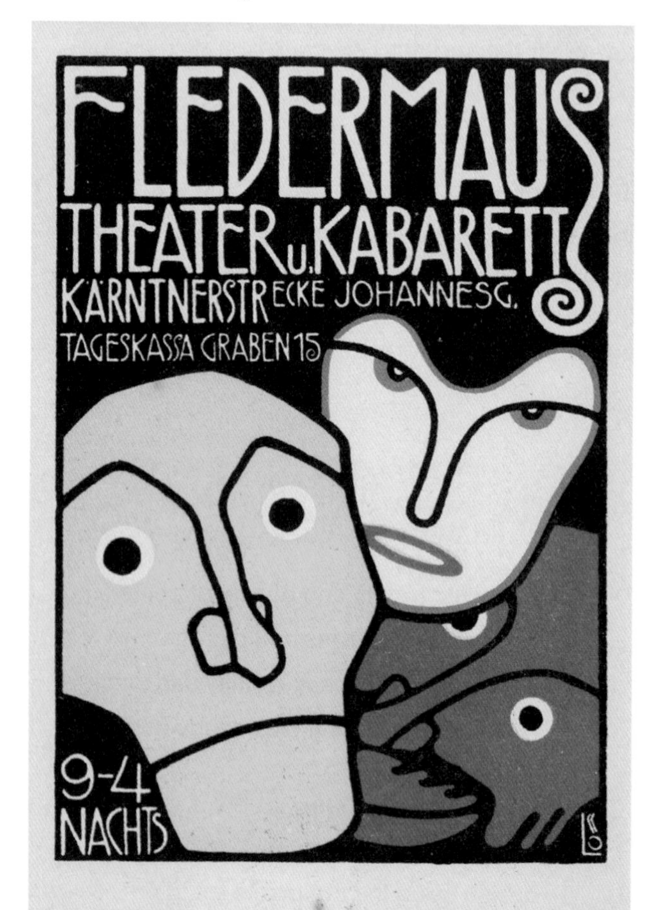

Fig. 36.2 *Kabarett Fledermaus* poster, 1907, by Bertold Löffler. Simple shapes and colours characterise the Modernist style.

poster designs for the Kabarett Fledermaus ('The Bat' Cabaret) look very different from the Art Nouveau work we have seen (Fig. 36.2).

Kabarett Fledermaus

Subject

A group of masks in a very simplified design is the focus for this nightclub advertisement.

Composition

Three overlapping masks take up the lower two-thirds of the space. Rows of lettering in decreasing size fill the upper third. The bright yellow mask on the front left dominates because it is larger and in front of the others. The simplicity of the parts and the way they appear to be squeezed into the space create a powerful image.

Typography/lettering

The tall, angular lettering is hand designed for the space it fills. It is strong and legible and it matches the simplicity of the images.

Colour

Flat primary colours are used against a black background. The white lettering on black takes second place to the bright masks.

A.M. Cassandre (1901–68)

A.M. Cassandre (his real name was Adolphe Mouron) was one of the great 20th-century poster designers. He worked in the style that is now called Art Deco after the Exposition des Arts Décoratifs et Industriels Modernes (International Exhibition of Modern Decorative and Industrial Arts) held in Paris in 1925 to celebrate modern life. The style is influenced by Cubism and Futurism.

Cassandre ran a commercial art studio and designed for many major French manufacturers and transport companies. He is quoted as having said, 'Designing a poster means solving a technical and commercial problem … in a language that can be understood by the common man.'

> **Art Deco** was the successor to Art Nouveau, although it was a very different style. Simple massive forms with influences from African, Aztec and Chinese art and Cubism were the basis for the designs. Luxury materials like lacquer, bronze, ivory, ebony and other precious woods and stones were often used by designers.

As the century progressed, design developed in a number of ways. Propaganda posters were used by all sides during the First World War. (Search the internet for 'images of World War One posters' to see the kind of work being done at the time.) After the war, commercial posters became more sophisticated because printing had advanced and designers were being trained in design schools all over Europe. The Russian Constructivist style influenced the Bauhaus and De Stijl groups.

Nord Express

Subject

This poster is promoting railway travel as fast and modern (Fig. 36.3).

Composition

A diagonal line from the top left to bottom right encloses the monster black steam engine. The upper right is blue sky with the tone reversed in a narrow triangle with white lines on it in the corner. The large letters are in the top centre and a frame is created by smaller letters running all around the edge of the paper. A list of connecting cities is printed over an image of crossing lines at the bottom. The lines symbolise connections. There is a vanishing point in the bottom right corner and all lines rush to it, helping to create the sense of speed in the image.

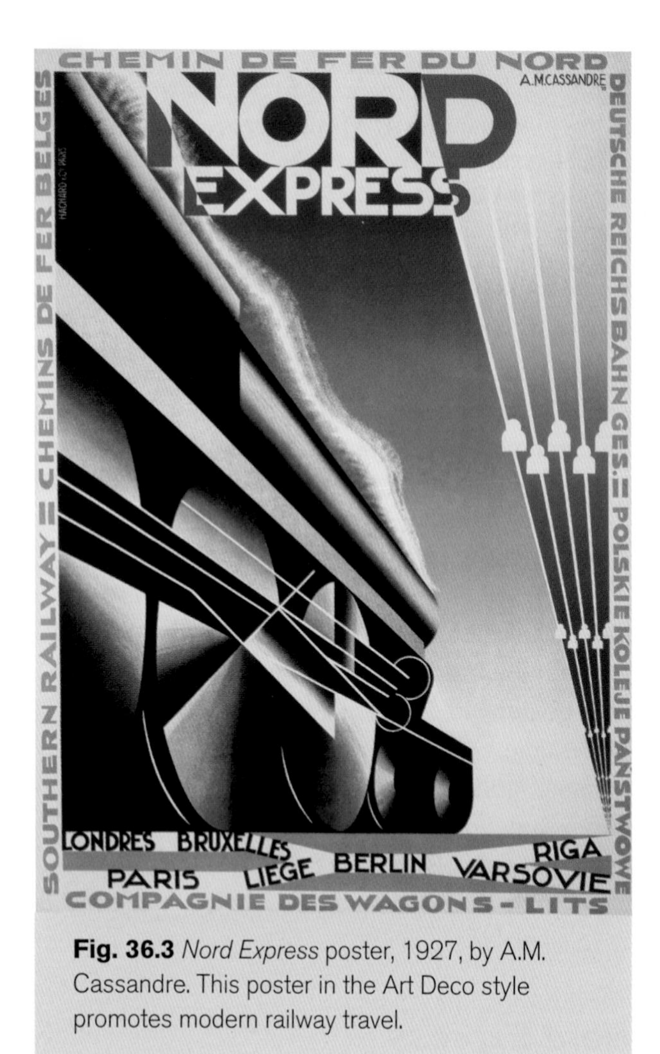

Fig. 36.3 *Nord Express* poster, 1927, by A.M. Cassandre. This poster in the Art Deco style promotes modern railway travel.

Technique

The artwork for this and most of Cassandre's other posters was done with an airbrush (a pen run on compressed air that lets out a fine spray of colour, allowing delicate changes in tone and colour) and stencils, which create the sharp edges where different areas meet.

Typography/lettering

Typography and images are always linked in Cassandre's work. He designed many typefaces that were popular in the Art Deco period. He always used capitals, as he felt they were more legible.

Colour

The shiny black train is the dominant image. The forms are simplified and the highlights create a sense of blurred movement and speed. The lettering is white when it is on a blue ground, but it turns red when the ground is white. The lettering around the border is in creams and beige, which are less dramatic and draw less attention. The sky blue that fades as it goes down the page is reversed in the narrow triangle on the right. This delicate fading of the colours is an effect of airbrushing.

Posters for the cinema

Film is one of the areas that still uses posters as part of their advertising. Film posters frequently combine photographic images with typography. In recent years, Irish films have done well on the world stage. In 2016 there were nine Irish connections with films nominated for Academy Awards. Lenny Abrahamson directed *Room*, a film based on the novel of the same name by Emma Donoghue, who also wrote the script.

Irish film on the world stage

Room

Subject

The subject is a photograph of a mother and child in blue tones (Fig. 36.4).

Composition

The mother and child are placed in the lower half of the page. Their outline almost makes a heart shape. The upper half of the space is a sky-coloured box with yellow and white lettering. The only area of the photographic image in sharp focus is the faces of the two characters.

Typography/lettering

The title of the film is in quite small yellow letters placed in a thin yellow rectangle against the actors' blue and grey clothes.

Fig. 36.4 *Room* poster by InSync Plus for the film by Lenny Abrahamson. Colour atmosphere is an important element in the design of this poster.

Colour

The dominant colour is the blue of the sky and the actors' clothes. The yellow letters stand out in contrast.

Signage

One important aspect of graphic design is signage: the letters and symbols that are used to inform the public on motorways, in hospitals, airports, factories and at public events. If we compare just two approaches to the same design problem, it may help your understanding of the process.

Olympic pictograms

The word 'pictogram' comes from Greek and Latin and means 'painted word'.

For the 1972 Munich Olympics, Otl Aicher produced geometrically inspired pictograms set in a square background, each a wordless depiction of a sport. The designs were a sensation. Many felt that they could not be improved upon and that they were clear to people from all cultures and languages (Fig. 36.5).

The designs for the 2016 Rio Olympics in Brazil grew out of the logo and the lettering designed by the London-based Dalton Maag type designers. They have designed lettering for Amazon, Nokia, BMW, Vodafone, Toyota and other international companies. The pictograms were designed with reference to the shapes of the letters by the Brazilian branch of the company. The fast gestures of the letters and images express the informal and joyous nature of Brazil.

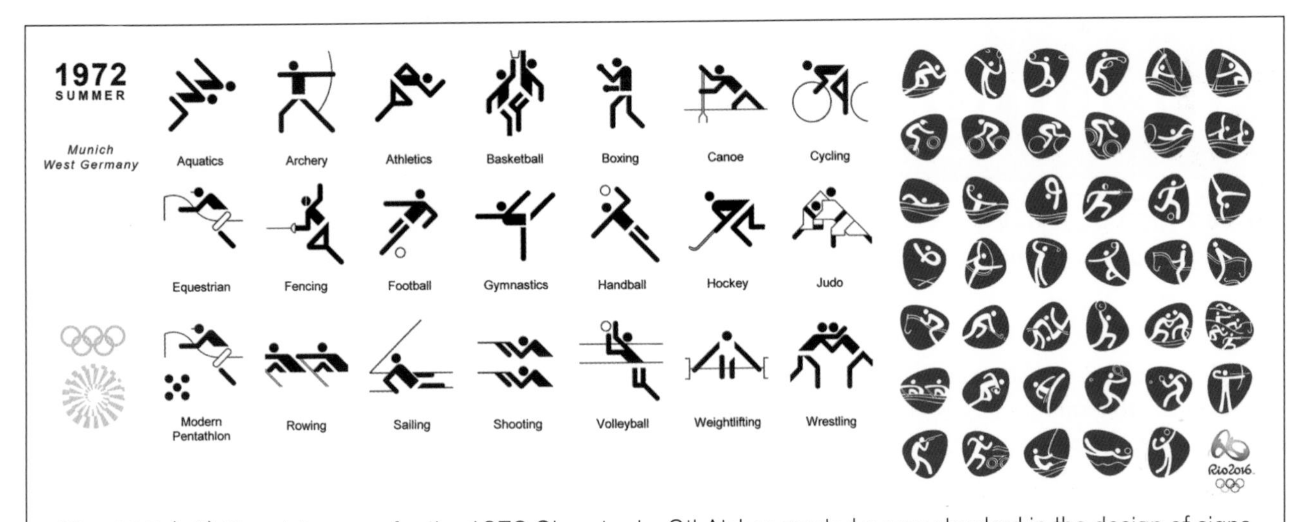

Fig. 36.5 (left) The pictograms for the 1972 Olympics by Otl Aicher created a new standard in the design of signs

Fig. 36.6 (right) Pictograms and logo for the 2016 Rio Olympics. It is interesting to compare the pictograms for different Olympic Games and note the changes in style and emphasis.

The designs began with pencil sketches, which were then computerised to standardise the thickness and curve of the parts. The pebble shape that encloses the pictograms is rotated to suit the action of the image and the sport (Fig. 36.6).

It is interesting to compare the two sets of pictograms separated by 44 years. Note the similarities and differences. Which do you prefer and why?

Company identity

There are many famous international companies with clear identities. The Coca-Cola lettering is recognised worldwide. The Nike swoosh and McDonald's golden arches are recognised without words. Most car manufacturers have a badge that people recognise.

Logos

Logos can be used in a variety of sizes and locations. For example, the Aer Lingus logo appears on letterheads, tickets, staff uniforms, signage, on vehicles, in their advertising and on the tails of their aeroplanes (Fig. 36.7).

Aer Lingus

Fig. 36.7 The Aer Lingus logo and typography have to fit a range of products, from small to large

A **logo** is a sign, symbol, trademark or badge that identifies the commercial enterprise, organisation or individual it represents. A logo that is made of letters, like the IBM logo, is called a logotype. A logo that is purely graphic, like the Nike swoosh, is called an ideogram.

Logos on computer interfaces have to be legible on large screens and on hand-held devices. The Twitter, Facebook and Google logos are good examples of this type of design.

Advertising design

Design for advertising usually links a range of media together. The images used in the print media (newspapers and magazines) will be repeated on television, roadside hoardings, packaging and the internet so that the viewer gets the same visual message and slogan wherever the product is mentioned.

Advertising campaigns like those made for Specsavers or Walker's crisps rely on humour and repeated messages to promote the product (Fig. 36.8).

Fig. 36.8 A Specsavers advertising campaign

Sponsorship

Sponsorship is another way that companies can promote their products. For many years, beer manufacturers sponsored rugby and Gaelic games. Their logos and the name of their product were used in all publicity for the sports.

There has been a negative public reaction in recent years to this association of alcohol with sport. Do you believe advertising can affect the choices people make?

Package design

Packaging has a number of practical functions as well as identifying or advertising the product.

Its first function is to protect the product, so a package should be made of a suitable material. Food products need to be kept clean and preserved for a time. Plastic wrappers, bottles, tins, paper bags and cardboard boxes can all be used for a suitable product. You could go on listing products and suitable packaging materials almost indefinitely – you need to think about what is suitable for any product you are examining (Fig. 36.9).

The designer has to put information on the package to identify the contents in an attractive way that will draw the customer's attention and help them choose the product.

Fig. 36.9 Packaging for Lily O'Brien's chocolates

Packaging is also point-of-sale design. The package should draw attention to itself on the shelf and be unique among its competitors.

Shopping bags or boxes that might be seen in the street can advertise the shop or business they came from.

Website design

Website design and layout are similar to design for print media. Designing a website involves a wide range of disciplines, including user experience design (interpreting the client's needs to make a more user-friendly website), interface design and development (coding). In practical terms, however, web design usually refers to the user interface (UI) design. This is the part of the website that users see, known as 'the front end'.

A UI designer starts their work in much the same way as any graphic design project: by sketching. A website sketch is called a wireframe (Fig. 36.10). It is concerned with the layout of the page contents. The sketch will usually show where the logo goes, how navigation is handled and how the contents are laid out. The layout is almost always based on a

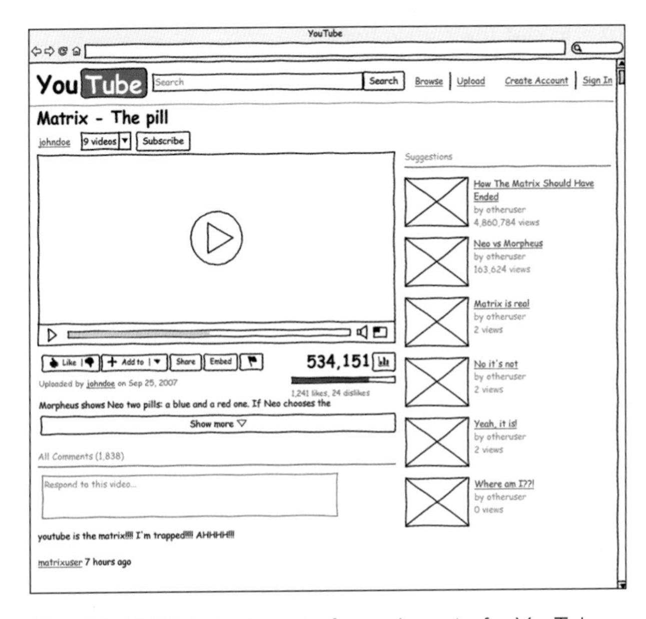

Fig. 36.10 Web design wireframe layout of a YouTube page

column grid (usually of 12 columns), as this helps the designer plan where content will move about on different devices with different screen sizes.

Once the layout has been decided on, the designer will start to work on a more accurate design on a computer. This will show the rest of the team the exact look and feel of the design. A final design is created for each unique screen on a site (the home page, a contact page and a shopping page, for example). The developers will use this final design to code the site.

Examining and planning a graphic design

Graphic designs can come in a wide range of shapes and forms, from posters and book covers to packaging and design for the internet, to company identity and signage. Yet all have some common elements when we examine them.

Concept/imagery

This is the idea behind the project. Who are we trying to communicate with? What images will we use to get their attention?

The work that AMP Visual did for Lloyds Pharmacy shows a well-thought-out approach to the project (Fig. 36.11). The colour scheme and visuals are used in all aspects of the design. The importance of people and services are highlighted in some information, while the illustrated poster shows the products that they offer, displayed in an interesting way.

Shape/form

What shapes or forms are we designing for (e.g. packages, signs, print media)? Will the product be three-dimensional or two-dimensional? Sometimes a whole range of products will be involved in designing for a large company like Aer Lingus.

Images and typography have to be flexible enough to look good on large and small objects, both flat and three-dimensional.

Layout/composition

Where will the design go on the product? It could be the paintwork on a transport fleet or delivery vans, or it might be the images and lettering on packages or bags.

On work for print or internet, how will words and images be combined?

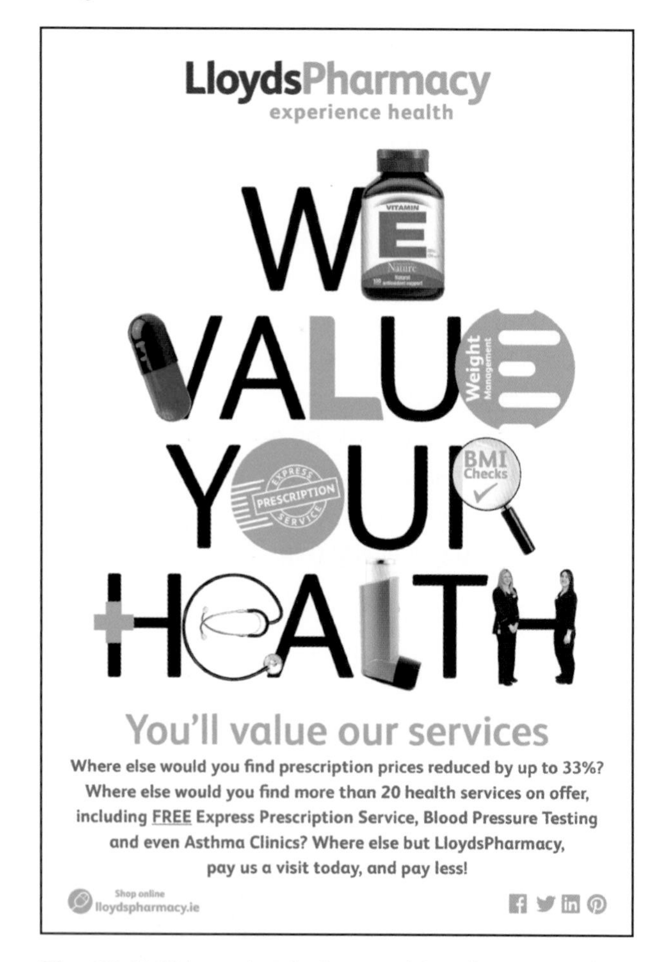

Fig. 36.11 This poster design combines humour and information to get the customer's attention

Fig. 36.12 Sometimes identity can be done with typography only

Typography/lettering

The shape, size and style of lettering need to fit with the images and ideas.

Some designs, like the website for spunout.ie by Treetop Studio, use typography without any images (Fig. 36.12).

Colour

Colour is often a key part of design work. It can create the mood and atmosphere and draw attention to special areas of the design. Most companies, like Aer Lingus and Lloyds Pharmacy, will have a colour scheme that runs through all their signs, designs and information.

Chapter review

* Do you think that posters are still an important design medium?
* What do you think are the main differences between designing a page for a website and the layout of a magazine page?
* Discuss the importance of typography in design. Give examples to support your arguments.

EXAM QUESTIONS

Ordinary Level (2016)

Answer (a) and (b).

(a) Describe and discuss the packaging for biscuits illustrated on the accompanying sheet under the following headings. (A photograph of a cardboard box designed to look like the hot plates of a gas cooker. There is a logo, Thelma's, in a script style, with a very simplified design of the upper half of an elderly lady with a tray of biscuits.)

- Colour/imagery
- Shape/form
- Lettering/logo

(b) Design a logo suitable for a pet shop. Give reasons for your decisions.

Illustrate your answer.

Higher Level (2015)

'Packaging is essential to marketing and can attract and entice a customer to buy a product.'

Discuss this statement, referring to the image illustrated on the accompanying sheet. (A photograph of five shopping bags for a shoe shop called '17' – each bag is white with a photograph of the front half of a Converse runner. The coloured string handles of the bag are the same colour and extend from the laces on the runner.) Refer in your answer to design concepts and the use of art elements.

and

Briefly outline your ideas for creating a packaging design for a shop that sells health food. Give reasons for your decisions.

Illustrate your answer.

FURTHER RESEARCH

www.artyfactory.com – Graphic Designers

www.hancocktimelineproject.weebly.com – The History of Graphic Design

Chapter 37

Fashion Design

Fashion design is an art form that tries to combine the natural beauty of fabrics and design to create clothing and accessories.

Fashion is influenced by culture and social attitudes and can be very different in various times and places.

Designers try to design clothes that function comfortably, as well as being attractive to their clients. They need to know who is likely to wear the garment and what situation it will be worn in.

By the end of this chapter, I will...

* Know the kind of work a fashion designer does.
* Have noted the different types of fashion.
* Know how to look at fashion.

The fashion designer

Designers can work in a variety of ways. They can work in a fashion house as an in-house designer, working with a team that produces designs for the house name, e.g. Chanel, Valentino (Fig. 37.1).

Freelance fashion designers can work in a number of ways.

* They can sell their designs to fashion houses, shops or clothing manufacturers who then produce the clothes under the buyer's label.
* They can set up their own label and design for individual clients.
* They can produce individual garments or small production runs for exclusive fashion shops, following fashion trends or creating original clothes, under their own label.

Clothing manufacturers employ most designers working in a team under a design director, e.g. Lacoste, DKNY (Fig. 37.2).

Fig. 37.1 (left) Models present creations for Italian fashion house Valentino

Fig. 37.2 (right) A model walks the runway at the Lacoste spring–summer 2016 fashion show

Fig. 37.3 Fashion design sketch

Designing a garment

Most designers begin with research into the theme they are working on. They might refer to fashion history or ethnic clothing. Nature often inspires the designer with colours, shapes and textures.

Designers often work out their ideas with sketches (Fig. 37.3). Some drape fabrics over a dress form to see how they look.

The designer makes a mock-up of the garment and consults a pattern maker, who makes a working version of the pattern out of cardboard or on computer.

A sample garment is made and tested on a model to make sure the design and pattern work.

Types of fashion

There are three main areas of clothing manufacture, although these can be broken down into more precise categories.

Haute couture

Haute couture is a French term meaning 'high sewing'. It refers to the standard of work that was expected. Until the 1950s, most clothes were made to measure for the client. Now, couture garments are made of expensive fabrics sewn with great attention to detail. Difficult and time-consuming handmade techniques often add to the cost and exclusivity of the garment. Fashion houses do not expect to make a profit from this type of work. They do it for publicity and prestige.

Ready-to-wear (prêt-à-porter)

These clothes are somewhere between haute couture and mass market. They are not made for individual customers, but great care is taken with the cut and choice of fabrics. Clothes are made in small numbers so that customers can feel they are buying something exclusive. These clothes and accessories are what most of the fashion houses make their money on.

Mass market

A wide variety of customers are catered for by mass-market design. Simpler manufacturing techniques and cheaper fabrics allow manufacturers to keep costs down. Clothes made for this area of the market follow the trends of the famous names in fashion, but with a time gap that allows manufacturers to see which fashions are most popular (Fig. 37.4).

Fig. 37.4 Mass-market clothing from Penneys

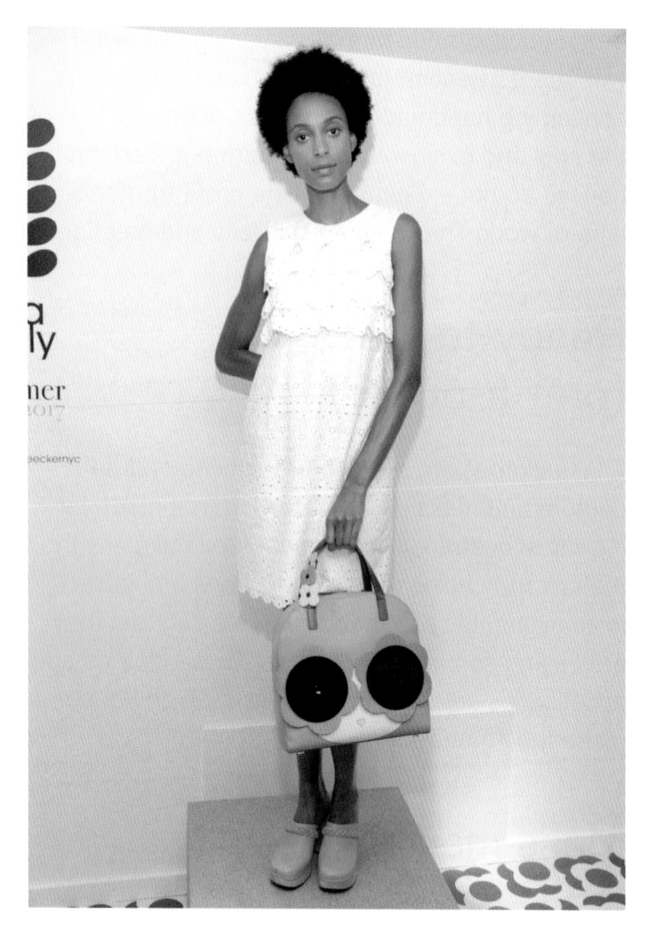

Fig. 37.5 A model poses with an Orla Kiely handbag

Accessories

Any item that adds to an outfit in a secondary way can be called an accessory. Accessories can be divided into two main categories: things that are carried and things that are worn.

Handbags and eyewear are the main accessories that are still carried by women (Fig. 37.5). In earlier times, fans, parasols and walking canes were used.

Jackets, boots, shoes, scarves, ties, belts, gloves, jewellery, watches, sashes, shawls, socks and stockings can all be worn to add to the look of an outfit.

Hats

Hats go in and out of fashion. There was a time when a lady would not go out of doors without a hat, but that time is long gone. These days, hats are worn on more formal occasions, often carefully matched to an outfit. Hats often appear on the runways at the big fashion shows (Fig. 37.6).

Fig. 37.6 Philip Treacy hats

Looking at fashion

Concept

* Who was the garment designed for: an individual, a certain part of the market, etc.?
* Where and when will it be worn? Every day or a special occasion?
* Is there a theme or idea behind the design, for example based on nature, fashion history or a design source?

Form

* What shape, cut, construction and materials have been used?
* Is it a stiff garment made of heavy fabrics? A light dress made of flowing material?

Technique

* Have the fabrics been dyed, sewn, knitted or constructed in some other way?

* Is the garment hand made or mass produced?
* Were high-tech methods used?

Details

* Some details are quite visible, like fastenings or added details such as jewels or sequins.
* Other detailing that might be part of the cut or construction may need closer examination.

Colour

* Colour is often the most striking part of a design.
* Note how colours are combined and contrasted.
* Colour may relate to current trends or it might be part of the design concept.

Chapter review

* Do you think that fashion is a way of displaying wealth and status?
* Can the large sums of money spent on haute couture fashion be justified?
* What do you think the place of accessories is in an outfit?
* What occasions justify wearing a hat?
* Has individuality been lost since so few clothes are now hand made?

EXAM QUESTIONS

Higher Level (2016)

'Traditional clothing styles from around the globe are a constant inspiration for the fashion industry.'

Discuss this statement with reference to the illustration on the accompanying sheet. (A photograph of models wearing Dolce & Gabbana black trouser suits beside a couple in traditional Spanish clothes.) In your answer, refer to design concepts, colour, shape and pattern.

and

Briefly outline your own design ideas for creating a wearable piece of fashion influenced by Irish pre-Christian art. Give reasons for your design decisions.

Illustrate your answer.

FURTHER RESEARCH

www.irishcentral.com – Top Ten Irish Designers Taking the World of Fashion by Storm

www.independent.ie – Our 12 Favourite Irish Fashion Designers

Chapter 38

Interior Design

Interior design is much more than room decoration. The designer needs to understand human behaviour and create spaces where people can function comfortably.

Interior designers frequently work with architects, engineers and building contractors to create safe and beautiful spaces.

By the end of this chapter, I will...

* Know about the work of an interior designer.
* Have some information and opinions on the points in the 'Looking at interior design' section.

The interior designer

In a small country like Ireland, interior designers work in most aspects of interior design. However, in larger cities, designers can specialise in a number of areas.

* **Residential:** Single rooms or whole houses, even patios and external spaces, can be included in a project.
* **Commercial:** Offices, reception areas, boardrooms and waiting areas can all be part of a design brief (Fig. 38.1).
* **Hospitality:** The look and function of lobbies, dining rooms, bedrooms, function rooms and even corridors can affect a customer's experience in a hotel or restaurant.
* **Healthcare:** The efficiency, cleanliness and safety of hospitals and clinics have to be considered at the design phase.
* **Exhibition spaces:** Museums, galleries and temporary exhibitions have to be carefully planned in terms of accessibility and movement of the public. Lighting and the location of the display are among the things that have to be considered.

Looking at interior design

The space

The first thing to consider is the function of the space to be designed. It might come under any of the previously mentioned headings.

Fig. 38.1 Signs in the Foundry, Google's first European Digital Innovation Centre in Dublin

Fig. 38.2 (left) A kitchen designed by Donaghy + Dimond Architects

Fig. 38.3 (right) The artificial lighting in this bedroom creates a calm atmosphere

Construction

The size of the space and the materials it is made of will limit what can be done. A small timber frame extension or an old stone house will have very different possibilities. Timber frame construction is easily changed but stone is not, so changing the location of doors and windows would be comparatively easy in one but not the other.

Changes to electrical wiring (lights, sockets, etc.) or plumbing (kitchen or bathroom fittings) would need to be decided on at an early stage. Any permanent fixtures or fittings (placing of doors, windows, roof lights or stairs) should be decided at the start.

Layout

Even within a room, some spaces will have different functions. In a kitchen there will be a cooking area, a washing-up area, a food preparation area, a fridge and a variety of machines. The designer will have to work out a flow pattern for the room so that the client can use the various areas without too much wasted movement (Fig. 38.2).

A teenager's bedroom might have a study area, a dressing area and a sleeping area, with the furniture arranged for the best use of the space.

Safety

In public areas like hotels and restaurants, space has to be created where people can move freely and exit quickly in an emergency. In all areas of design, materials and equipment should be chosen with safety in mind.

Ergonomics

We have already seen the use of ergonomics in product design (see also Fig. 35.6). In interior design, the heights of worktops, furniture, presses, doors and windows and the location of handles and switches are all based on ergonomics.

Lighting

The location of windows or roof lights is vital in a room. Light affects everyone and it is important for the atmosphere of a room. The designer may not be able to change a window, but he or she can use artificial light to improve the feel of the space (Fig. 38.3).

Lighting fixtures

There is a wide variety of lighting fixtures these days, such as flush with the ceiling, wall mounted, hidden lighting around kitchen units and pendant (hanging) lights. Spotlights (which can be tiny) can be used to pick out a feature in the home or an exhibit in a museum. Lighting in public areas has to be bright enough for people to find their way easily.

Movable lights

Table lamps and standard lamps can be moved around the room to create atmosphere or for reading or working. The range of colours, styles and sizes available makes choice the only problem.

Furniture

The choice of furniture to go in a space depends on many factors. In an older building, antique furniture might be needed to go with the style of the surroundings. Large pieces of furniture would be out of proportion in a small room. It is the designer's job, in consultation with the client, to select furniture that fits the purpose of the space and the overall style (Fig. 38.4).

Floor coverings

Not too long ago, people rarely looked beyond carpet to cover the floor in most rooms. With improved heating and insulation, however, houses are warmer and a wider range of flooring is available. Wooden floors in a range of types, and tiles of all sizes and colours are now more commonly used. Plastic tiles and linoleum also have a wide range of applications.

Decoration

There are so many possibilities in terms of colours, textures, patterns and ornaments that we cannot hope to cover them all here. A designer will sometimes work to a theme, such as a period from history or the colours of autumn. A client may have a preferred style, like Minimalist, Modern or Art Nouveau.

Paint and wallpaper

Paint comes in a wide range of colours and types. The choice depends on the purpose and the client's taste.

Wallpaper goes in and out of fashion. It is suitable in some situations, such as rooms in a period style, on an uneven wall surface or as an accent on one wall.

Fig. 38.4 A modern minimalist interior

Soft furnishings

Curtains, cushions and fabrics on furniture have to be co-ordinated (Fig. 38.5). The interior designer is responsible for all aspects of the project and needs to co-ordinate tradespeople and decorators, as well as producing the design and keeping the client happy. Designers often use 3-D computer modelling programs to plan their projects and explain the ideas to the client.

Fig. 38.5 The well co-ordinated soft furnishings in this room tie everything together

Chapter review

* Would you prefer living spaces in a home to be open plan or divided into rooms?
* What part do you think soft furnishings like curtains and cushions play in interior design?
* How should artificial lighting be used in a kitchen or a living room?

EXAM QUESTIONS

Higher Level (2016)

'Modern office design has evolved to create workspaces that can motivate employees and enhance their creativity.'

Discuss this statement with reference to the images illustrated on the accompanying sheet (a photograph of the lobby of the Lego offices in Denmark). In your answer, refer to function, space, layout and colour.

and

Briefly outline your own design ideas for a study or library space within your school.

Illustrate your answer.

Ordinary Level (2015)

A studio is a place where a visual artist can carry out creative work.

Answer (a) and (b).

(a) Suggest a design for a studio to be used by a student of visual art. Use the following headings in your answer:
- Layout/function
- Light/colour
- Storage/display

(b) Outline the types of furniture you would choose for this studio and give reasons for your choices.

Illustrate your answer.

FURTHER RESEARCH

www.houseandhome.ie

www.interiorholic.com

www.designbasics.com – Intelligent Traffic Flow

Chapter 39

Film Studies

Go to page 434 for a list of extra content available on **www.gillexplore.ie**.

Film, which some consider to be the most powerful art medium, is a relatively new art form. The combination of sound and vision makes it the most complete artistic experience available. It is also the most accessible, as it is available cheaply in public cinemas or at home on television, DVD or downloaded from the internet.

When looking at film we try to become aware of how the elements of sound, colour, lighting, camerawork, special effects, direction and editing affect our enjoyment of the film, as well as how the art director uses make-up, costumes, settings and props to support the storyline and atmosphere of the film.

By the end of this chapter, I will...

* Understand the technology of film.
* Have studied the different roles of the film professionals and how their work contributes to a film.
* Be able to make sketches of scenes and special effects for the films I have studied.

Genre

Genre is a word used in all the arts to describe the subject or style of the work. In film, different genres go in and out of fashion, but the following list gives an idea of what has been popular over the years: action, adventure, comedy, crime, documentary, drama, epic (historical drama), family, fantasy, horror, musical, mystery, romance, science fiction, sport, suspense, thriller, war, Western. Sometimes genres are combined, such as comedy-romance or horror-fantasy.

Professions and crafts

The scale of a production usually determines the number of staff and the levels of specialty that will be involved. One individual can make a complete film on their own, in which they are the producer, director, cinematographer, editor – the whole show. At the other extreme, hundreds of people can be involved in a production, from studio bosses through the layers of production and technical experts to actors and extras.

Some of the people involved in filmmaking are well known to the public. Actors and directors are often household names, whereas some of the others involved in key roles in the filmmaking process may never come to the public's attention, though they would be well known and respected within the industry.

The filmmaking process took on an industrial character in America from the early years of cinema. It includes the following roles.

Film production

The final responsibility for all aspects of the film lies with a production team. On big movies there would be executive producers, producers, production assistants and a whole range of financial and technical people responsible to them, all trying to turn the ideas in the story into profitable cinema entertainment.

Producer

The producer brings together the screenwriter, director, cast, financiers and production team in a creative environment. Producers are ultimately responsible for the success or failure of a film.

Director

The director is responsible for the creative vision and style of a film. Directors can start a film project working in a combination of roles, such as producer/director, writer/director or any number of roles. In smaller films the director can control the entire production process: writing the script, arranging finance, casting, filming, editing and looking for outlets to show the film.

Whatever the size of the project, the director is normally involved from an early stage, writing or commissioning the script or taking charge of the draft screenplay. The director takes charge of casting and will normally pick the leading actors, even in a large production where there is a separate casting director. The crew is also the director's responsibility. The director must also approve the choice of locations and settings for the film.

The director is the link between the production, creative and technical teams, and provides the ideas to turn the script into the images and sounds that the audience sees on screen. The direction of actors during rehearsals and filming is an important part of the work. The technical aspects of cameras, sound, lighting, design and special effects are also key to a successful film, so the director needs to motivate these teams to produce the best results (Fig. 39.1).

Fig. 39.1 Irish director John Carney working on the set for the movie *Begin Again*. He also directed *Once* and *Sing Street*.

When filming is over, the director works with the editor to produce the final cut of the film for approval by the production company and financiers. The director may also be involved in promoting and marketing the film, and has responsibility for the artistic and commercial success or failure of the film.

Art department

The art department is responsible for the visual world or setting of the film.

Production designer

The production designer comes up with ideas for how the film will look in consultation with the director.

Concept artists

Concept artists can be employed to provide illustrations for big-budget science fiction, fantasy and historical films, or films where complicated special effects may need to be visualised first. These illustrations can be used to help sell the idea for a film to production companies or financiers.

In *The Lord of the Rings* film series, concept artists played a key role in providing the images for characters, settings, colour and atmosphere. Their drawings may be used to decide what will be built and what special effects need to be commissioned.

Researchers

Sometimes researchers are used to check historical information or to look for images and references from works of art or from other films.

Storyboard artist

A storyboard artist can be used to produce a series of comic book-style illustrations that the director uses to show all the heads of departments what is needed in a scene. Whole films can be storyboarded if there is a lot of action or CGI or complicated chases, fights or battle scenes. The storyboard is designed from the camera's viewpoint, framing the shots as they would be seen on the cinema screen (Fig. 39.2).

Fig. 39.2 A storyboard

Art director

The art director works as a project manager for the production designer. They may be in charge of the creative vision for sets and locations, providing solutions for visual problems that can turn up during filming. The art director begins work long before filming starts, overseeing the production of sets, which are drawn up from a prop list taken from the script.

Draughtsmen

Draughtsmen draw up plans for sets and locations, which are then given to construction teams. The art director makes sure that all the settings are ready for filming and that the sets are 'struck' (dismantled) and locations cleared when filming is over.

Set decorator

The set decorator provides all the furnishing details on sets, as well as the action props that are used by the actors or involved in the action of a scene. Dressing props used for background atmosphere and to create the impression that the scene is a real location are also part of the set decorator's responsibilities. All the details of life – pictures on the walls, items left casually on tables and chairs, the contents of a fridge or a drawer – need to be included in a realistic scene.

Costume design

Costume design can be a separate department that designs, makes or hires costumes for the actors and extras. Costumes can be an important element in the overall look of a film. The designers make costume plots for all the actors and scenes

Fig. 39.3 Costumes for *Sing Street* (2016)

Fig. 39.4 Make-up being applied to Tilda Swinton for *The Grand Budapest Hotel* (2014)

to avoid clashes in style or colour and to ensure continuity. Costumes can highlight the emotional journey of the characters through the film. Colour palettes, sketches and fabric samples are checked with the production designer and the director (Fig. 39.3).

Hair and make-up

Hair and make-up people look after the design, application, continuity and care of hair and make-up during the production. The 'look' that is created can be contemporary or historical. Special prosthetics may be needed to change a face – noses and chins can be enlarged or scars and injuries can be added. Style can be an important element, matching the time, place and mood of costumes and sets (Fig. 39.4).

Camera department

Camerawork can tell us more about what is going on in a scene than dialogue or music.

Cinematographer

The director of photography, or cinematographer, helps to give a unique look to the film. He or she consults with the director and production designer to decide on the kind of cameras and lighting that are needed in the production.

The cinematographer is involved in pre-production. Working from the screenplay, he or she carries out research and preparation, considering style and technical aspects, as well as planning camera positions on sets and locations and the lights and equipment that will be needed for each shot. Camera cranes, steadycams, cameras on wires and filming from the air all have to be considered, planned and costed.

The cinematographer and director go through each scene, working out or 'blocking' where the actors will be in a scene and what movements the cameras or actors will make during the scene. During rehearsals, the actors walk through the scenes and the cinematographer works out camera moves and lighting. Each scene is marked up for focus and framing.

Teamwork is important during filming. The cinematographer may operate the camera on smaller productions, TV programmes, advertising and promotional work. Otherwise, separate people do these jobs.

Camera operator

The camera operator carries out the camerawork that was planned and may have creative input in reacting to what is happening in the scene or spotting an image that has not been planned. The camera operator also keeps the actors informed of what can and can't be seen on screen.

Grip

The grip builds, maintains and operates all the equipment and supports for the camera. These will include tripods and dollies, tracks and jibs, cranes, static rigs, etc. The grip also works for the cameraman during filming, moving dollies and operating jibs and rigs. In large productions there might be several camera crews operating together or at different locations.

Steadycam

The steadycam is a counterbalanced unit that allows smooth movement with a hand-held camera. It is a specialised piece of equipment that weighs up to 40kg and requires a strong and agile operator. It is used for shots that require complicated camera movements (Fig. 39.5).

Fig. 39.5 Director Gareth Edwards uses a steadycam to film a scene for *Rogue One: A Star Wars Story* (2016)

Drone operator

The drone operator controls the movements of the remotely operated flying camera that is used to get overhead shots and to follow cross-country action.

Editing and post-production

The raw material shot by the camera crew and recorded by the sound crew is edited together to form a completed film.

Filming frequently takes place out of sequence. The editor and director study the rushes each day and editing begins while filming is still in progress. An overview of how all the scenes fit together may not be available until all the filming is complete.

Editor

The editor works closely with the director to assemble shots into scenes. They check technical standards, continuity of lighting and colour and the actors' performance. An editor needs to be creative, noting opportunities and moments of spontaneity from the actors that might improve the story.

An editor's cut is made to see if the storyline fits together. This is examined closely with the director to spot flaws in the storyline or images and to plan any filming that might be necessary to fill gaps. A director's cut is a more complete version of the film, which is shown to the production company and financiers before the final cut is made.

The editing team mixes the sound, music and images, adding any special effects that are needed.

Special effects

Special effects can be mechanical/physical or visual. Computer-generated images (CGI), especially 3-D computer graphics, are now frequently used instead of building miniatures or hiring extras for big crowd scenes. CGI can also produce images that would not be possible otherwise. Blue or green screen can be used for human action that needs to be superimposed on an imaginary background or in a physically impossible location, such as Spiderman flying from building to building. Matte paintings, animation, miniatures, models and many other tricks are available to the special effects department.

Music department

The music department can be central to film production. In the case of a musical, it can be used as part of the storyline when an actor sings or performs on screen. The film score can be an important part of a film, creating atmosphere and defining characters, locations, period and nationality.

A composer is usually commissioned to write a suitable musical score that will help the director's vision of the film. The music should guide the audience through the story, creating an atmosphere, raising and relaxing tension, creating rhythm and setting a pace for the film.

The composer holds spotting sessions with the director to note particular locations for music in the film. The composer picks a style for the film and decides on the theme and the purpose of the music in the film. He or she works with the editor to match sound and images, making sure there is a smooth transition between scenes (Fig. 39.6).

Fig. 39.6 A scene from the film *Once*, which won an Oscar for best theme song, 'Falling Slowly', in 2007. It has now been made into a stage musical.

Analysing a film

It would be impossible to look at every shot in a film, so it might be better to break the film down into key scenes and sequences. The categories that are used at the Academy Awards might be a useful way to look at the various elements involved. Producers (best picture), writers, directors, actors, cinematographers, make-up artists, art directors, costume designers, editors, score composers and more receive awards each year.

Production

Production asks what sort of film this is. Is it a Hollywood blockbuster or a low-budget or experimental film? What is the target audience? Is it a commercial or artistic venture? These are some of the questions you might ask yourself about the production of a film you wish to study.

Writing

Writing is the starting place for most films. The script is not just the dialogue or story line – it includes stage directions, descriptions of settings, camera movements and the overall mood of the film. The Irish writer Emma Donoghue was nominated for Best Adapted Screenplay in 2016 for her adaptation of her own novel, *Room*.

When looking at the way the story is told in a film, the plot can be noted. It might be a linear plot, which means that the events described in the film happen in a natural sequence – one thing follows another in normal time. Or it might have flashbacks, cross-cuts or repetitions, all of which help to tell the story.

Direction

The director's role has been described on page 427. The director oversees all aspects of the film and determines how the screenplay will be interpreted on the screen.

It is worth noting whether the film has been made by a big name 'auteur' director who might bring a certain style or theme to the work. When you are writing about a film, you need to know the director's name and a little bit of background about them. The Irish director Lenny Abrahamson was nominated for Best Director for his film *Room* at the Academy Awards in 2016. The young Irish director Benjamin Cleary won an Oscar for his short (live action) film, *Stutterer*.

Actors

Actors can be an important element. Some films are made as a 'star' vehicle around the talents or marketability of a popular actor, while other films are made with comparatively unknown or even amateur actors.

The style of acting can also affect the film. Natural, melodramatic or deadpan performances influence the audience's reaction.

You should know something about the main actors in any film you study and what they bring to the style of the film. The Irish actor Saoirse Ronan was nominated for Best Actress at the Academy Awards in 2016 for her role in the film *Brooklyn* and Brie Larson won an Oscar for her role in *Room.*

Cinematography

Cinematography is the term used to cover all the techniques of motion picture photography. Framing, camera movements, film speed (slow or fast motion), film stock (black and white or colour; coarse grain, fine grain or digital), exposure, camera angles, lenses (deep focus, wide angle, zoom), shot selection (wide, medium, two shot, close-up), lighting (natural or artificial, high or low key) are all technical aspects that need to be considered.

In the classical Hollywood tradition, cinematography is designed not to be noticed but rather just to help the storyline. Modern filmmakers often push the boundaries of this convention.

It might be worth getting some background on the cinematographer in a film you look at, noting other work they have done and what they bring to the project.

Art department

The art department can be the largest contributor to the visual qualities in a film. If you look at the roles of the art specialists in the 'Professions and crafts' section on page 427, you can get some idea of the range of contributions made by artists in films. You can use all or some of these headings (production design, storyboard artist, art director, set decoration, costume designer, hair and make-up, etc.) when examining the visual content in a film.

Editing

Editing determines the pace and rhythm of the film by putting shots together and assembling sequences and scenes into the unfolding storyline. In the Hollywood tradition, continuity editing, which tries to make cuts invisible, is used to make a seamless visual and narrative storyline. Alternatives to this style are increasingly common. Montage theory, which was invented by the Russian director Eisenstein, proposed that two shots placed side by side in sequence without editing can imply ideas beyond the two images in the viewer's mind. Surreal images and jump cuts have also been incorporated into mainstream cinema from experimental films. When watching a film, you might try to work out why the various editing techniques have been chosen.

Sound

Sound, which incorporates spoken dialogue, sound effects, music and all heard aspects, is usually added artificially in post-production.

Diegetic sound is the sound that is heard by the characters and is part of the narrative, on screen and off screen. Sound is generally added artificially because of the control it gives the sound engineers, as natural sound is more unpredictable. Actors and directors sometimes rely on the post-dubbing process to improve vocal performance, smooth over flaws and hide gaps in the narrative.

Non-diegetic sound includes all the sound effects, voiceovers and musical scores that are produced after filming and matched to the visual track during post-production.

It can be interesting to play a scene from a film with the sound turned off to appreciate what it brings to the film.

Film analysis study guide

* Good film analysis avoids emphasising the obvious aspects, like retelling the plot, reproducing parts of the dialogue or simply listing visual techniques.
* Look for the meaning behind the film or the scene. Is there a message or a purpose? It might simply be entertainment or it might have a political, social, moral or environmental message.
* Look at the visual aspects of the film, such as the camerawork, special effects, colour, lighting, make-up, costumes and sets.
* Note the work of the professionals such as the director, editor and actors. What do they bring to the project?
* Use examples from the film to support your points.
* Draw sketches of key scenes and special effects to show your understanding of the filmmaking process.
* In the end, we take our own meaning from the moving images that we see, but it is always important to back up your ideas with evidence from the film.

Chapter review

* Pick a film and discuss the effect that colour and lighting have in describing the atmosphere. Look at two or three scenes where the effect is clearest. You could do this exercise with any other aspect of the language of film, such as framing, shots, camera angle, editing or sound.
* What does the work of the art department bring to a film?
* Look at a recently made Irish film and discuss the qualities of direction and editing. Pick scenes and events to support your observations.

EXAM QUESTIONS

Higher Level (2016)

'The exploits of characters from comics and graphic novels are brought to life by actors through the medium of film.'

Discuss this statement with reference to any named film based on a comic or graphic novel. In your answer, refer to costume design, set design, colour, special effects and camera techniques.

and

Briefly outline your visual concepts for a short film based on a historical character of your choice.

Illustrate your answer.

Ordinary Level (2016)

Answer (a) and (b).

(a) Name, describe and discuss an action film that you found visually interesting under the following headings:

- Location/setting
- Costume/make-up
- Camerawork/visual effects

(b) Design a storyboard for a short film based on a sporting event of your choice.

Illustrate your answer.

FURTHER RESEARCH

www.irishfilmboard.ie
www.entertainment.ie
www.ifi.ie

You will find further content on **www.gillexplore.ie** on: the technology of film and the language of film.

Chapter 40

Visiting a Gallery or Exhibition

An art museum or art gallery is designed to show works of art. They are for all to visit and enjoy in order to develop a greater understanding and appreciation of art.

Some art museums specialise in historical art, while some show contemporary artwork.

By the end of this chapter, I will...

* Understand the difference between an art gallery and a museum.
* Know where to find Ireland's National Gallery and other prominent art museums in Dublin and other cities.
* Know what to expect when visiting a gallery or art exhibition.
* Know how to look at art.
* Have the appropriate vocabulary to describe an art gallery and selected works of art.
* Be able to find the art centre in my local town or city.
* Know how to find out more about artists and their work.
* Know how to mount an exhibition in my school.

Art gallery vs. art museum

In Britain and Ireland, most public art museums are called galleries and are free to the public.

Art museums in large European cities can be quite expensive to visit but are usually free for students under 18 and older people (Fig. 40.1).

Fig. 40.1 The Rijksmuseum Museum, Amsterdam

Exhibitions

An exhibition is a special showing of selected artworks. It will have a theme and a title and might focus on:

* One artist from history
* The new work of a living artist
* A retrospective exhibition looking back over the artist's career

* The work of a group of artists who share a common theme, technique or subject matter

Retrospective means 'looking back'. A retrospective art exhibition looks back at the work that a living or recently deceased artist has produced over their entire career.

An exhibition will typically include:

* Paintings, drawings, sculpture, craft, film, an art installation, performance art or new media
* A selection of works from the museum or gallery's own collection (Fig. 40.2)
* Recent acquisitions (work bought in the recent past)
* Work relating to a theme, such as:
    * Art work created during a particular time in history
    * Art work that uses the same techniques or materials, such as printmaking or mixed media

Art installation: Installation art is used to describe mixed-media constructions or assemblages that are usually designed for a specific place and are only displayed for a temporary period of time.

Performance art: An art form that combines visual art with dramatic performance.

The collection

The museum will have its own collection of art works. These have been acquired by the gallery over many

Fig. 40.2 National Gallery of Ireland, Dublin

years. Some have been bought and some have been given to them by the artist or a benefactor.

A gift is called a bequest. The name of the person who made the bequest will appear on the label (Fig. 40.3).

Fig. 40.3 *The Umbrellas* by Auguste Renoir was a bequest to Dublin City Gallery The Hugh Lane by Sir Hugh Lane

Paintings are sometimes given to galleries and museums on permanent loan. For example, Caravaggio's *The Taking of Christ* is on permanent loan to the National Gallery in Dublin (see page 444).

Museums or galleries become known for important works, and people often travel specially to see them (Fig. 40.4).

Benefactor: A person who gives help to a person or cause.

Fig. 40.4 *A Sunday Afternoon on the Island of La Grande Jatte* is one of the highlights of the Art Institute of Chicago

Fig. 40.5 (left) *The Taking of Christ* from the National Gallery of Ireland was one of the key works in the *Beyond Caravaggio* exhibition, National Gallery, London

Fig. 40.6 (right) *The Dolls' School*, 1900, by Walter Osborne, watercolour and pastel on paper, 45.2cm x 59.5cm, National Gallery of Ireland, Dublin

Sharing works of art

Galleries will sometimes lend paintings to another gallery for an exhibition. The drawback to this is that for a short time its most famous works are not available and visitors can be disappointed. For example, the National Gallery in Dublin loaned *The Taking of Christ* to the National Gallery in London in October 2016 until January 2017 for an exhibition called *Beyond Caravaggio* (Fig. 40.5).

Caring for works of art – storage

Art works need to be stored very carefully because they can be delicate. For example, watercolour paintings have to be kept completely dry and protected from light to prevent dampness and fading (Fig. 40.6).

Conservation

Many art works are fragile and have deteriorated or been damaged over the years. For example, the varnish over an oil painting can darken, causing the work to lose its bright colours and subtle detail.

A **conservator** in the art gallery is a specialist who carefully cleans and restores this work so that it is as close as possible to its original condition.

Planning and mounting an exhibition

Exhibitions can take months and sometimes years to plan and develop. Designers, developers and a curator will be involved.

Curator

The person who makes plans and manages all the details of an exhibition is called a curator.

Each exhibition is unique. The curator's own ideas about what works to display and the choice of a theme and title are important.

Layout of the exhibition

The curator and his or her team will focus on two things:

* The message they want to communicate
* The audience that the exhibition is aimed at

Fig. 40.7
Space in an art gallery – the new wing at the Crawford Art Gallery, Cork

Visiting an exhibition

* Work out how much time you have to enjoy your visit.
* What is the theme of the exhibition? Who is it aimed at?
* Note the use of space. Is it calm and contemplative or is it noisy and oriented at children?
* How are light, colour and the shape and size of spaces used to make your visit more enjoyable (Fig. 40.7)?
* Use the 'Looking at art' section on pages v–xiv as a guide to evaluating the individual works of art.

NOTE! The permanent collection in an art gallery is also on exhibition, so the display and lighting arrangements are just as important.

The works of art

Take your time with the works of art, but if something in particular interests you, take extra time to enjoy and absorb its meaning.

Look at the painting and ask yourself:

* Is this an abstract or a realist painting?
* Is it figurative or non-figurative?
* What is the subject of the painting?
* If it is a portrait, does it seem to send you a message? If it is a modern painting or sculpture, can you tell what the theme is without looking at the nameplate?
* As you go through the museum, do you recognise any art from this book? How does the real work compare? Is it much bigger or does it look more colourful?

Look at the art elements:

* In a painting, how do the brushstrokes flow?
* Does the work seem to have sections?
* Are the colours spectacular or dull?
* What is the mood?
* Does the colour scheme affect the mood?
* Where is the focal point of the composition?
* What is the style?

At the end of the tour, try to revisualise what you saw. This will help you to remember it.

The gallery

When you visit a gallery or exhibition, note some of its important aspects.

- **The architecture of the gallery itself:** Is the building modern and designed specifically to show art or is this an old, historic building (Fig. 40.8)? What is the history of the building? Where can you find out more about the architecture? Check the gallery website for this information.
- **How is the gallery accessed?** By stairs (Fig. 40.9)? Are there lifts for people with a disability? Is the signage clear? Can you find your way easily? Is there someone friendly to ask?
- **Lighting:** Does the lighting focus on the work? Does it create a mood? Is the space bright or is it dimly lit to protect the works? Are there filaments over the windows to minimise the impact of daylight on the works?

Filament: A light material cover on a window to control brightness.

- **Colour scheme:** Are the walls white, dark or coloured? How does this affect the colour in the works of art?
- **How are the paintings hanging?** Are they well spaced and at a height that you can see them?
- **How are sculptures or ceramics displayed?** Are they on plinths? Is there a barrier in front of the work (Fig. 40.10)? How are the objects placed? Are they in display cases or are they in upright glass frames (vitrines)?
- **Labelling:** Is the labelling and other important information clear and easy to read?
- **Access:** Has access to the exhibition been controlled to avoid overcrowding? Can you see the work or are too many other people around it?

Fig. 40.8 Dublin City Gallery The Hugh Lane – exterior

Fig. 40.9 The Millennium Wing at the National Gallery of Ireland, Dublin

Fig. 40.10 (left)

Sculptural work at the Irish Museum of Modern Art, Dublin

Fig. 40.11 (right)

Art gallery information leaflets

Plinth: A heavy base supporting a statue or vase.

* **Interpretive media and technology:** Are there touchpad or other interactive audio and video devices to help you enjoy the works?
* **What type of experience does the exhibition provide?** Can you form your own opinions and thoughts or are you being given a particular viewpoint? What objects and themes get priority or prominence?
* **A guide:** Did you have a guided tour? Was it helpful? Did you understand the words your guide used? Did your teacher prepare you for the visit? Did your teacher act as a guide in the museum?
* **Support:** Do the leaflets, advertisements, e-communications and catalogues help to give you an understanding and appreciation of the art works (Fig. 40.11)?
* **Evaluation:** Did you like the art works? Why or why not?

NOTE! The question is not *whether* you liked the work, but rather, *why* you liked the work.

Small local galleries and art centres

Many of the thriving art centres in towns around the country regularly have small exhibitions by new and emerging artists. Sometimes they can also have work by established artists, especially if they live and work in the area. These are small exhibitions, but the work is often professional and of a high standard (Fig. 40.12).

Fig. 40.12 *My Minds i* exhibit by Janet Mullarney, Highlanes Gallery, Drogheda

Mounting a school exhibition

Most schools love to show students' artwork. This is often done for special occasions, like a visit

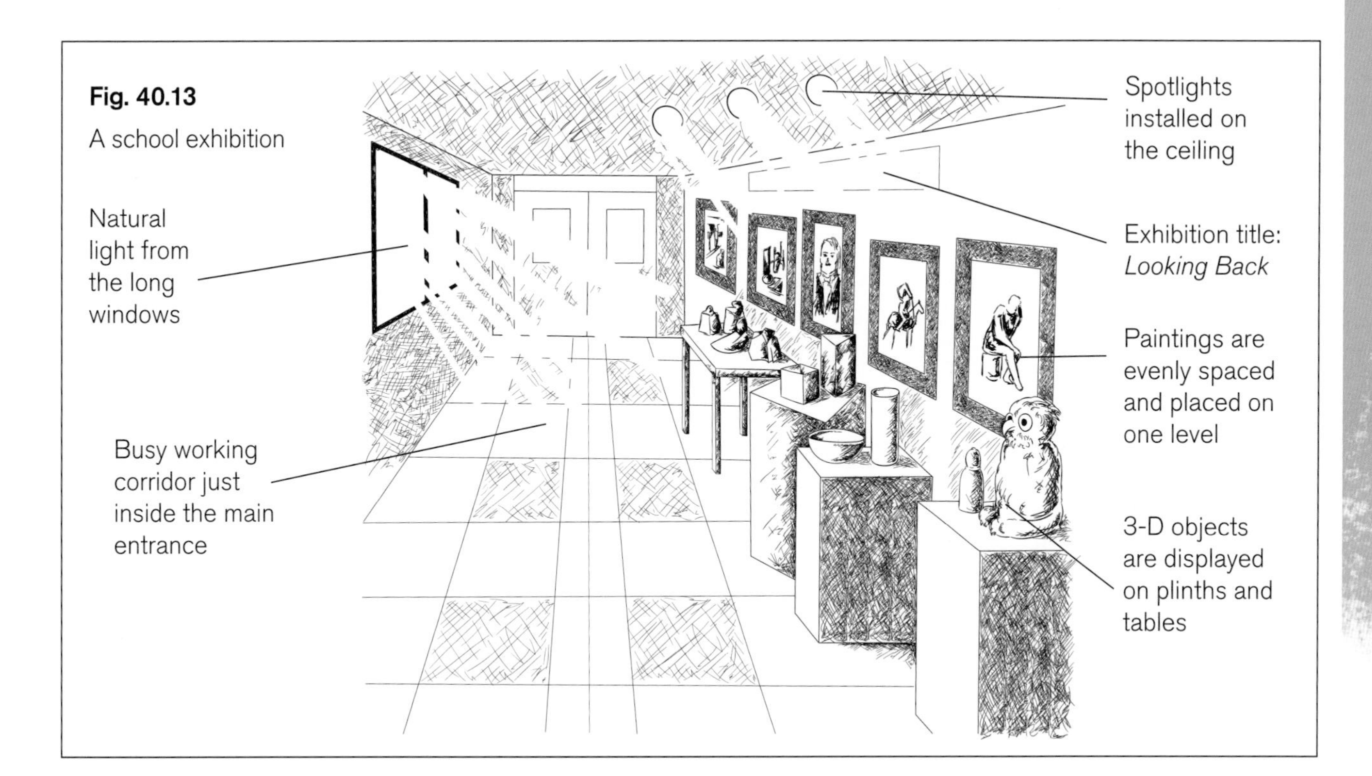

Fig. 40.13
A school exhibition

from a local celebrity or a school open night (Fig. 40.13).

To mount a school exhibition:

* Learn from your experience of visiting a professional exhibition in a major or small local gallery.
* One person should act as curator and then work as an organised team.
* Select an open, well-lit area well away from accidental damage by passing crowds.
* Choose a small amount of original works and do not overcrowd. Less is more. Quality work will look impressive when it is well displayed.
* Space the work evenly.
* Keep the work in groups of the same medium or style. For example, a series of colourful, imaginative paintings could look good opposite some life drawings in pencil or some prints in black and white.
* Hang the work carefully. Choose a line at eye level and centre the work around this. Smaller pieces can be placed above or below to act as a balance.
* Mount the work – this does not need to be expensive. Place the work on white paper, leaving a small margin all around. Mount this on black or another dark colour. Always use a guillotine to cut the paper neatly.
* Include some 3-D ceramic objects or modelling on plinths or on small tables. Paint the surfaces white or use white paper (tape this down to stop it from blowing away or falling off).
* Make sure everything is high enough and far back enough to prevent accidental damage.
* Label all the works clearly and give your exhibition a title.

Chapter review

* Looking at art and engaging with artists and their work is a rewarding and enjoyable experience. How do you think a visit to a major gallery in Dublin, Cork or perhaps even London or any of the major European art museums would compare with visiting a local gallery to see the work of new and emerging artists?

EXAM QUESTIONS

Ordinary Level (2016)

Answer (a) and (b).

(a) Name a gallery, museum or interpretive centre that you have visited. Describe and discuss how the work was displayed under the following headings:

- Layout
- Lighting
- Information for the viewer

(b) Design a smartphone application (app) to promote student visits to your chosen gallery, museum or interpretive centre. Give reasons for your design decisions.

Illustrate your answer.

Higher Level (2016)

'Architecture, floor plan, lighting and display techniques all influence the overall visitor experience and appreciation of works of art in a gallery or museum.'

Discuss this statement with reference to a named gallery or museum you have visited. Describe in detail two named works you found interesting and discuss how these works were displayed.

and

In your opinion, briefly outline **two** initiatives that would encourage young people to engage with works of art on display in museums or galleries.

Illustrate your answer.

Higher Level (2013)

Answer (a) and (b).
A curator's work involves planning all aspects of an exhibition, whether it is for display in a national or local gallery or museum.

(a) With reference to a named exhibition you have visited, describe and discuss the main steps taken by the curator when planning for and mounting this exhibition.

(b) If you were a curator, how would you go about curating an exhibition of Transition Year artwork in your school?

Illustrate your answer.

FURTHER RESEARCH

www.nationalgallery.ie – Art Appreciation: Visiting an Exhibition (PDF)

www.imma.ie – Visiting an Art Museum or Gallery (PDF)

www.ballinaartscentre.com

www.birrtheatre.com

www.crawfordartgallery.ie – Learn & Explore Secondary Resource Pack (PDFs)

www.dunamaise.ie

gallery.limerick.ie

www.galwayartscentre.ie

www.garterlane.ie

www.hughlane.ie

www.thelinenhall.com

www.mermaidartscentre.ie

www.westcorkartscentre.com

www.wexfordartscentre.ie – Janet Mullarney

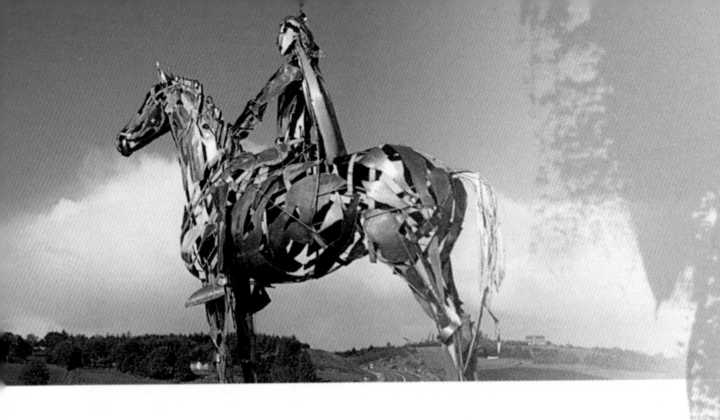

Chapter 41

Public Sculpture

Outdoor sculptural works can greatly enliven public areas. These permanent, prominent and site-specific works are a marvellous opportunity for the public to see and interact with high-quality works of art without restriction.

By the end of this chapter, I will...

* Be able to consider reasons why public sculpture has so captured the interest and imagination of the travelling public.
* Be familiar with the names of some public art works and the artists who designed them.
* Know how public art is funded.
* Know what an artist must consider when submitting a sculptural art proposal.

Roadside art

Roadside sculpture is the most visible form of public art and it has greatly captured the interest and imagination of the travelling public. Some people whose work means driving on the roads of Ireland on a regular basis are sharing their experiences by posting images and comments on blogs and social media.

Site specific

A site-specific piece of art is created to exist in a certain place. The artist will typically take the location into account when planning the work. They usually acknowledge the architectural, historical and environmental aspects of the area.

Irish horses

An Capall Mór ('*The Great Horse*') by Tighe O'Donoghue-Ross (Fig. 41.1) represents the type of warhorse used by Celtic chiefs in battle. The broken chains around its front legs signify freedom.

'The Unicorn', as it fondly known locally, has become a landmark on the N22 in Co. Kerry. Families have been known to drive specially along the route just to give their children the enjoyment of seeing it.

Fig. 41.1 *An Capall Mór* by Tighe O'Donoghue-Ross, N22 Cork to Killarney Road

Fig. 41.2 (left) *Misneach* by John Byrne, Ballymun. *Misneach* (which means 'courage' in Irish) was temporarily placed at the Trinity Comprehensive School in Ballymun. Upon completion of the Metro rail project, it will be moved to Main Street. The work will be installed on a new hand-carved stone plinth.

Fig. 41.3 (right) Lord Gough Memorial by John Henry Foley, Phoenix Park, Dublin

Misneach: A Monumental Celebration of Youth

In 2006, the sculptor John Byrne was commissioned by Breaking Ground, the Ballymun redevelopment scheme, to create a piece of public art for the town centre (Fig. 41.2).

He chose the statue of Lord Gough, 'The Conqueror of the Punjab', by John Henry Foley as his model. This had stood for many years in the Phoenix Park (Fig. 41.3) but was placed in storage in 1957 after militant republicans tried to blow it up.

The artist tracked down the statue to a relative in England and made a model of the horse.

The model

He then set out to find a young woman as a model. This was to assert the idea that people from all walks of life can be as heroic as the most celebrated – mostly male, mostly older – public figures.

Seventeen-year-old Toni Marie Shields was chosen after an audition. She travelled with the artist to London to undergo state-of-the-art 3-D body scanning.

The horse and rider

A wax model at one-and-half times life size was combined with the model of the horse and cast in bronze. It was transported to Dublin and *Misneach* was finally unveiled on 17 September 2010 in Ballymun.

Limestone horses

Michael Quane's themes are often centred on relationships between horses and people. One

Fig. 41.4 *Horses and Riders* by Michael Quane, Mallow, Co. Cork. Circling in a tight knot, the work conveys the connectedness of individuals through their culture and dependency on each other. When this was first installed, passing drivers would circle the roundabout just to take it all in.

of his most popular large-scale public works is *Horses and Riders* (Fig. 41.4) on the N20 Mallow roundabout in Co. Cork. It was carved from a 25 ton block into an 11 ton work.

The Gaelic Chieftain

The Gaelic Chieftain (Fig. 41.5) in Roscommon is a 5m-tall rider on horseback. It is possibly Ireland's most popular roadside sculpture.

Maurice Harron created this equestrian sculpture in 1999 to mark the 400th anniversary of the Battle of the Curlews that took place in 1599 between English forces and a rebel Irish force led by 'Red' Hugh O'Donnell.

Saints and Scholars

Saints and Scholars (Fig. 41.6), also by Maurice Harron, depicts four imposing figures standing tall at 7.5m each over the Tullamore by-pass.

Each holds a symbol representing the learning and sanctity of the nearby monastic settlements of Durrow and Clonmacnoise. One holds a book, one holds a chalice, one holds a staff and one throws aloft a flock of birds.

Fig. 41.5 *The Gaelic Chieftain* by Maurice Harron, Curlew Mountains, Roscommon. Made of stainless steel and bronze pieces welded together, the sculpture stands dramatically on a hill overlooking Lough Key.

Fig. 41.6 (left) *Saints and Scholars* by Maurice Harron, N52 Tullamore By-pass, Co. Offaly

Fig. 41.7 (right) *Saints and Scholars* detail

The semi-abstract patterns (Fig. 41.7) were inspired by ancient manuscripts like the Book of Durrow, but the material is modern stainless steel. The metal lattice gleams in the sunlight but changes with the weather and time of the day.

Public art in the city

One of Ireland's most eloquent contemporary artists, Rowan Gillespie, lives in Dublin. He works in bronze and does his own casting. He built a one-man workshop and foundry where he carries out this complicated process entirely alone.

Famine

His most famous work is *Famine* (Fig. 41.8) at Custom House Quay (see also Fig. 7.27 on page 145). This was commissioned by Norma Smurfit and presented to the City of Dublin in 1997. The commemorative work is dedicated to the Irish people who were forced to emigrate during the 19th-century Famine.

Fig. 41.8 (above) *Famine* by Rowan Gillespie, Custom House Quay, Dublin

Fig. 41.9 (left) *Famine* detail

Made of bronze, these life-sized figures look taller due to their gaunt, emaciated appearance and the linear quality of the drapery. Clasping their pitifully small bundles to their chests (Fig. 41.9), each haunting skeletal figure looks as if they could tell their own tale of suffering and loss. One man carries a limp child over his shoulders, and a woman at the rear stumbles forward, her hands hanging lifelessly at her side. This moving work draws attention to today's world poverty and suffering as much as it does to the Great Famine of 1848.

Linear: Arranged in or extending along straight or nearly straight lines.

Migrants

In June 2007, President Mary McAleese unveiled a second and equally emotional series of Famine sculptures by Rowan Gillespie. They were placed on the quayside in Toronto's Ireland Park to remember the arrival of these most miserable of refugees (Fig. 41.10).

Fig. 41.10 *Migrants* by Rowan Gillespie, Ireland Park, Toronto, Canada

Choctaw Indian Feathers

Sculptor Alex Pentek also remembered the Irish Famine with *Kindred Spirits* (Fig. 41.11), a giant stainless steel sculpture of nine eagle feathers in Midleton, Co. Cork.

The Choctaw people, a Native American tribe in the US, raised $710 and sent it across the Atlantic to Ireland during the Famine. The sculptor was very moved by the story of these downtrodden people who only a few years before had been stripped of their land in Alabama, Mississippi and

Fig. 41.11 *Kindred Spirits* by Alex Pentek, Bailic Park, Midleton, Co. Cork

Florida. Deprived of their homes, they were forced to march across mountains in the snow and many had died from starvation and disease.

Anna Livia

A fountain symbolising the River Liffey was placed on the central section of O'Connell Street in 1988 (Fig. 41.12). It immediately caused a storm of protests and became known as 'The Floozie in the Jacuzzi'.

The sculpture by Eamonn O'Doherty featured a woman sitting on a slope with bubbling water running past her. She was based on Anna Livia Plurabelle, a character in James Joyce's novel *Finnegans Wake*.

Controversy

The work attracted considerable hostile publicity as it became a target for litter, graffiti and washing-up liquid. Eventually it was removed and later relocated in the centre of a small lake in the Croppy Acre Memorial Gardens facing Collins Barracks on Dublin's north quays (Fig. 41.13).

NOTE! Use the 'Looking at sculpture' section on pages xiv–xviii to examine sculptural works in detail.

Art as a landmark

Outdoor works of art frequently function as important landmarks. A large ball called *Perpetual Motion* by Remco de Fouw and Rachel Joynt and covered in road markings on the Naas dual

Fig. 41.12 (left)
Anna Livia by Eamonn O'Doherty, O'Connell Street, Dublin

Fig. 41.13 (right)
Anna Livia today, in the Croppy Acre Memorial Gardens facing Collins Barracks, Dublin

carriageway is a sign for many that they have left Dublin and that the real journey south or west has begun (Fig. 41.14).

The Per Cent for Art scheme

Public art is paid for by public money. The Department of the Environment recognised the important contribution made by public art, and in 1997 introduced a new Per Cent for Art scheme. This placed a levy on building construction to include a sum for an Irish visual art project. The scheme has been a huge success for artists and has created an increased public awareness of art.

Planning a public work of art

Artists must consider the following:

* The work must be large enough to attract attention from a distance, but not large enough to distract a motorist driving at 120 km/hour.
* The public has not made an active choice to see it, so it cannot be offensive.
* It must survive weather, graffiti and, depending on the location, activity like children climbing on it.

Fig. 41.14 *Perpetual Motion* by Remco de Fouw and Rachel Joynt, N7, Naas, Co. Kildare

* The material must be strong because deliberate vandalism could also be a problem.
* Residents might object if they feel it will damage easily or become a gathering spot for anti-social behaviour.

The creative concept

The creative concept means the idea. Where does it come from? What influenced or inspired it?

The artist's proposal

The artist's proposal should include the following.

* **The title and description:** Its focus, concepts, thoughts and research methodologies.
* **Context:** This may include geographical, social and historical considerations.
* **Research and development:** Research and how the artist envisages developing a proposal.
* **Audience and public:** Consider who the proposal is intended for: the general public or a specific audience.
* **Costs:** A budget breakdown covering fees.
* **Materials and medium:** Information on materials with samples.
* **Location (the place or site):** Is it site-specific or a more open site?
* **Evaluation of the proposal:** Are there any maintenance or technical issues?

The artist's statement

This is a written description. It can be quite short, but it should be clear and informative. It should include:

* Why the artist made the work
* What interested them in creating it
* How media, materials, techniques and processes were used

NOTE! Use these guidelines and www.publicart.ie (advice for artists on preparing a proposal) to answer a Leaving Cert question that asks you, for example, to design:

- A piece of sculpture suitable for the entrance to your school or local youth club
- A public sculpture in your own area
- A sculpture that would enhance an outdoor space at your school

Chapter review

* Roadside sculpture has greatly captured the interest and imagination of the travelling public. Why do you think people are so interested in these works of art?
* Public art is funded by public money. Do you think this is money well spent?
* Indentify a public area in your city, town or countryside that you would like to see developed as an amenity for the public. If you were the artist, what would you have to consider when submitting a sculptural art proposal?

EXAM QUESTIONS

Ordinary Level (2016)

Answer (a) and (b).

(a) Describe and discuss *Kindred Spirits* by Alex Pentek (Fig. 41.11) under the following headings:

- Location/scale
- Form/shape
- Colour/texture

(b) Design a piece of sculpture suitable for the entrance to your school or local youth club. Give reasons for your design decisions.

Illustrate your answer.

Higher Level (2015)

'Site-specific sculpture on Irish roadsides gives the public an opportunity to view well-crafted contemporary works of art.'

Discuss this statement, referring to *Saints and Scholars* by Maurice Harron (Fig. 41.6 and Fig. 41.7). In your answer, refer to scale, materials and technique, colour/finish, context and visual impact on the environment.

and

Briefly outline your ideas for a sculpture that would enhance an outdoor space at your school. Give reasons for your design decisions.

Illustrate your answer.

FURTHER RESEARCH

clairedelabre.com – RoadArt: Travelling West

mauriceharron.com

www.corkcoco.ie – Public Art

www.dublincityartsoffice.ie – Public Art

www.irelandplanner.com – The Gaelic Chieftain Sculpture

www.irishartsreview.com – Everyday Heroes

www.publicart.ie – Commissioning – Preparing a Proposal

www.rowangillespie.com

www.youtube.com – John Byrne: Misneach (Courage)

www.youtube.com – Sculpting Life, A Documentary on the Work of Rowan Gillespie

www.youtube.com – The Art of Henry Moore

Chapter 42

The Built Environment

The built environment involves man-made structures like buildings, roads, pavements and the many artificial surfaces that are a normal part of our lives in today's crowded, urbanised world.

Good planning in cities and towns is essential for managing human activity and reducing its impact on the environment. This is because urban areas must be developed in a balanced, eco-friendly manner to facilitate a sustainable lifestyle for all.

By the end of this chapter, I will...

* Know the important aspects of design in building.
* Understand why planning is so important in urban development.
* Know why the prestigious RIBA medal was awarded to Irish architects.
* Know why conservation of historical buildings matters.
* Be able to discuss the importance of sustainable building in the countryside.
* Know the important design features needed for a children's playground.
* Be able to plan a garden or landscaped area.

Planning the built environment

Ireland's population has been growing steadily and in recent years there has been a significant trend towards urbanisation. Local councils therefore need to plan. Urban planning essentially has two functions:

* To manage development
* To plan ahead for future growth and development

It must take some of the following issues into account.

* **Environmental and aesthetic:** How will development impact on the environment or local community? How will it look?
* **Economic:** How will the development affect local business?
* **Legal and political:** Laws and national policies govern planning and land use.
* **Human and social:** How will people be affected?

NOTE! Planning affects everyone, so everyone is encouraged to become involved. Communities have a significant role to play in city or county development plans.

Architecture

Architecture is the art, the science and the business of building.

An architect is qualified to design and provide advice, both aesthetic and technical, on built objects in our public and private landscapes.

Aesthetic: Concerned with beauty or the appreciation of beauty.

Architects create homes, office blocks, schools, churches, sports stadia, bridges and urban spaces. As well as design, they need an awareness of social trends, a keen business sense, solid engineering skills and an understanding of the law.

An architect must consider function and form.

* **Function:** The design of a building depends on its function and the demands of climate. 'Form follows function' was a guiding principle in all kinds of modern design in the 20th century. This simply means that the shape of an object should be based on its intended function or purpose.
* **Form:** This refers to the shape of a building. Part of the design process is to take form and space into account.

O'Donnell + Tuomey

Dublin-based architects Sheila O'Donnell and John Tuomey received the world's most prestigious architectural award in 2014. Britain's Royal Gold Medal was awarded for their lifetime's work as a 'tour de force in Irish and British architecture'.

Personally approved by Queen Elizabeth II, the Royal Institute of British Architects (RIBA) gives the award to those who have had a significant influence on the advancement of architecture. The husband-and-wife team are only the third and fourth Irish citizens to win this award.

The couple started O'Donnell + Tuomey in 1988 after graduating from the UCD School of Architecture and a period of working together in London.

Their first major project, the Irish Film Institute on Eustace Street, Dublin, was praised for its dynamic reworking of the Quaker Meeting House (Fig. 42.1). More recent projects include the Saw Swee Hock Student Centre for the London School of Economics (LSE) (Fig. 42.2) and the Lyric Theatre in Belfast in 2012 (Fig. 42.3).

The team was also responsible for one of the country's most ambitious, complex and challenging school building projects. The redevelopment of the historic St Angela's College campus (Fig. 42.4) in Cork City won the Best Education Building Award in 2016 with the Royal Institute of the Architects of Ireland (RIAI), Irish architecture's equivalent of the Oscars.

St Angela's College

Four 19th-century buildings were refurbished and two new purpose-designed buildings were added: one for sciences and one for arts. The site for St Angela's had several protected historic buildings and is located in an Architectural Conservation Area. The confined site posed major challenges.

Lewis Glucksman Gallery, University College Cork

O'Donnell + Tuomey designed the Lewis Glucksman Gallery (Fig. 42.5) in the grounds of UCC in 2005. The timber building is raised to nestle among the treetops and an interlocking suite of rooms has selected views of the picturesque Gothic college buildings and the river. It is a must-see building for art, design and architecture fans.

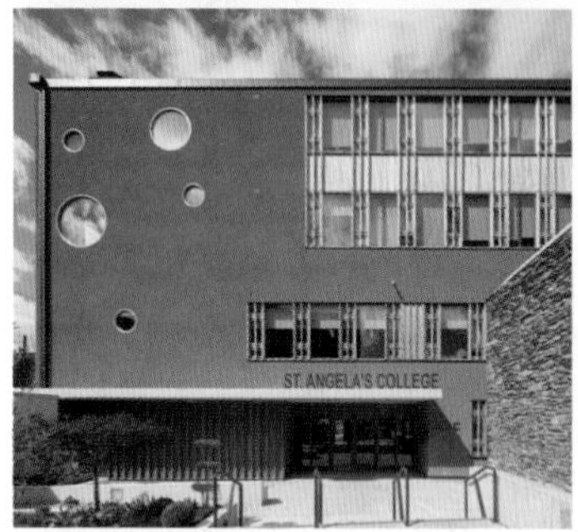

Clockwise from top left:

Fig. 42.1

The Irish Film Institute by O'Donnell + Tuomey, Eustace Street, Dublin

Fig. 42.2

The Saw Swee Hock Student Centre by O'Donnell + Tuomey, LSE

Fig. 42.3

Lyric Theatre by O'Donnell + Tuomey, Belfast

Fig. 42.4

St Angela's College by O'Donnell + Tuomey, St Patrick's Hill, Cork

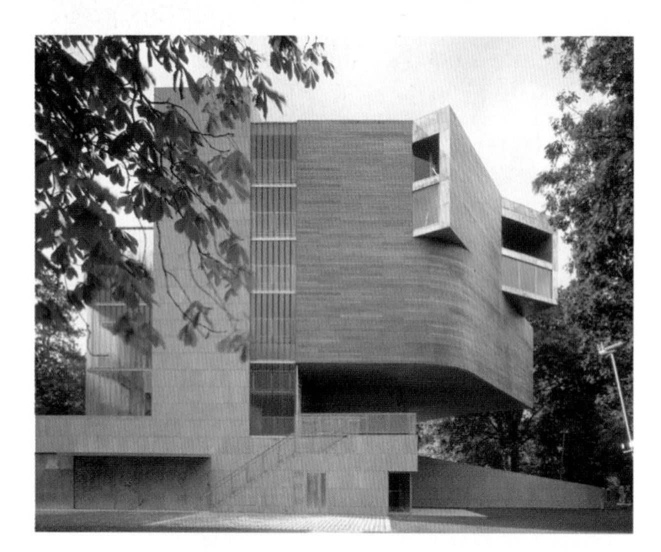

Fig. 42.5 The Lewis Glucksman Gallery by O'Donnell + Tuomey, UCC, Cork

UCD School of Architecture

O'Donnell + Tuomey continue to teach at the UCD School of Architecture, where John Tuomey is Professor of Architectural Design.

Looking at architecture

To analyse a building, consider the following.

* **Shape:** How surfaces and edges of a two- or three-dimensional object are placed together. Circles, triangles and squares generate volumes known as 'platonic solids'. Circles generate the sphere and cylinder. Triangles produce cones and pyramids. Squares forms cubes. Combinations of these platonic solids are the basis of most architectural forms.
* **Mass/size:** The size or the actual bulk of a building.
* **Scale:** Consider how the scale compares with something else, for example the human figure. The architect can use scale to make a building appear smaller or larger.
* **Proportion:** The relationship of one part to the other parts and to the whole building.

Clockwise from top left:

Fig. 42.6 Articulation in a building 1

Fig. 42.7 Articulation in a building 2

Fig. 42.8 The Guggenheim Museum by Frank Gehry, Bilbao, Spain

* **Rhythm:** The repetition of architectural elements like the structural bays that divide the building and windows establish rhythm in a building. Movement of people through a building like a school or an airport may also establish a pattern or rhythm of human movement.
* **Articulation:** Surfaces coming together to create form are described as articulation (Fig. 42.6 and Fig. 42.7).
* **Texture and colour:** Materials can greatly change the look of a building. For example, changing from a light to dark paint colour can make a room look smaller, or a rough brick finish can make a house look more solid.
* **Light:** The look of a building can change dramatically with changes in light and shade. For example, the Guggenheim Museum in Bilbao, Spain (Fig. 42.8), designed by Frank Gehry, is an example of articulation. A careful combination of a number of architectural qualities – shape, size, scale, articulation, texture and colour – come together.

Articulation: The way in which the surfaces of a form come together.

Architecture in engineering design

In recent times, architecture has joined with engineering in bridge design. This has brought a new level of artistic design to what were otherwise functional structures.

Fig. 42.9 The Millennium Bridge, Dublin

The Millennium Bridge

The Millennium Bridge (Fig. 42.9) opened in 1999. It offered the citizens of Dublin new views of the Liffey and quaysides from the old heart of the city.

Described as 'a simple symphony of water, light, movement and form', it is unobtrusive and restrained in its design.

A Millennium Project for Dublin Corporation, the design of the bridge was the result of a competition. Howley Harrington (architects) working with Price & Myers (consultant engineers) came up with the winning proposal.

Fig. 42.10 The Ha'penny Bridge, Dublin

The lightweight steel and concrete structure is a thoroughly modern take on its timeless neighbour, the Ha'penny Bridge (Fig. 42.10).

The Samuel Beckett Bridge

Spanish architect Santiago Calatrava designed this sleek, asymmetric structure (Fig. 42.11). It is a signature bridge for Dublin and is perfectly in tune with modern developments in the historic Docklands area.

Coolly contemporary in style but based on a traditional concept, the shape of the spar and cables suggests an Irish harp lying on its edge.

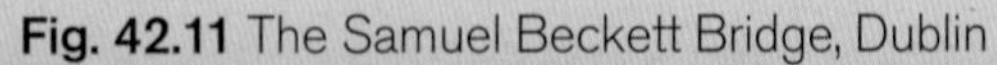

Fig. 42.11 The Samuel Beckett Bridge, Dublin

Heritage and conservation of old buildings

Buildings give character to both urban and rural spaces. They also define the landscape. Architectural heritage is a major aspect of heritage. Conserving historic buildings means that future generations can enjoy them.

The Heritage Council

The Heritage Council of Ireland supports the conservation of old buildings because reuse helps sustainable development. It may not always be easy, but careful planning in consultation with the local community and some creative thinking can produce interesting possibilities.

Tuar Ard Arts Centre

Tuar Ard (Fig. 42.12) in the small town of Moate in Co. Westmeath is a community-led project.

The building began its life as the Catholic parish chapel or the mass house of penal times in the 18th century before becoming a school for boys.

The new Arts/Enterprise Centre and coffee shop opened in 2000. Today it houses a theatre, art gallery, coffee shop, art/enterprise units and a conference centre.

Fig. 42.12 Tuar Ard Arts Centre, Moate, Co. Westmeath

The Irish Georgian Society

The Irish Georgian Society promotes awareness and protects Ireland's 18th-century architectural heritage and decorative arts.

It was founded in 1958 by the Hon. Desmond Guinness and Mariga Guinness. Castletown House in Co. Kildare (Fig. 42.13) was saved from falling into ruin by the Irish Georgian Society.

Fig. 42.13 Castletown House, Cellbridge, Co. Kildare

An Taisce

An Taisce is an independent charity. Founded in 1948, it is one of Ireland's oldest and largest environmental organisations. It holds a range of heritage properties in trust, including historic buildings and nature reserves.

Shop fronts

Ireland's traditional shop fronts are one of the country's most unique features. They underline the character and quality of shopping streets in towns and villages throughout the country (Fig. 42.14).

Kilkenny

Kilkenny city centre is famous for its beautiful handcrafted shop façades (Fig. 42.15).

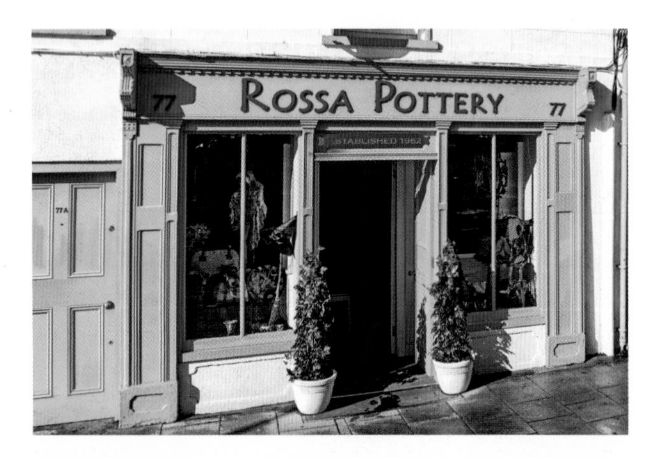

Fig. 42.14 Traditional Irish shop front

Fig. 42.15 Shop fronts in Kilkenny

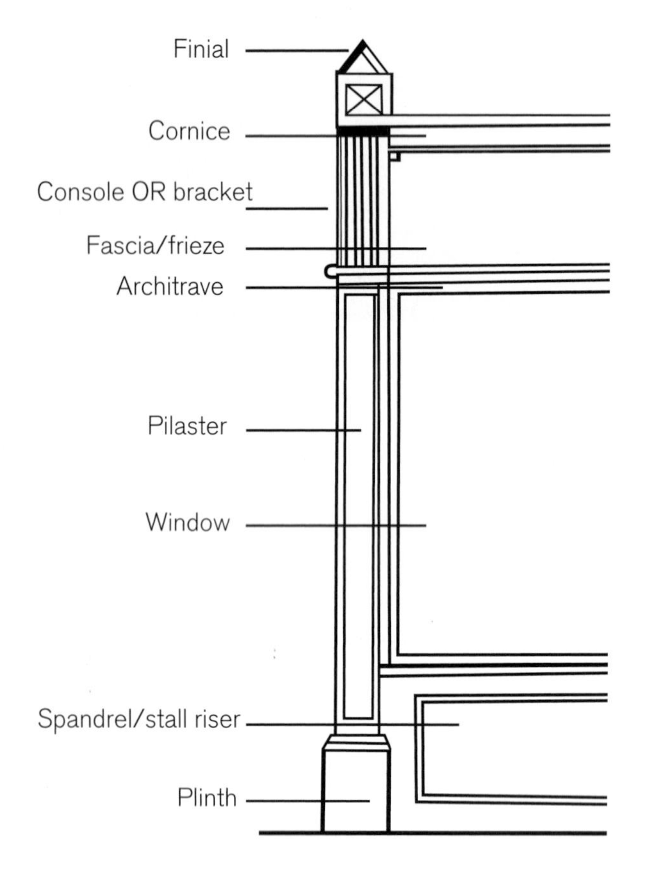

Fig. 42.16 Shop front design

The city is currently promoting its 'Medieval Mile' as a tourist attraction, so the city council has set up an Architectural Conservation Committee (ACC) to oversee the protection and enhancement of its historic streetscape. The ACC works with owners and tenants to make sure that old signs, relief lettering, sash windows and historic shop fronts are protected.

Important elements of shop front design

A shop front should:

* Reflect the architectural character of the overall building at ground-floor level
* Integrate successfully with the floors above

The essential elements of the shop front are derived from Classical architecture (Fig. 42.16). Those elements are:

* Cornice
* Fascia
* Pilasters
* Stall riser

Rural architecture

Some local authorities in Ireland publish rural design guides. These help to achieve:

* Better-designed houses for people to live in (Fig. 42.17)
* Well-located houses that improve the appearance of the countryside and are warmer and more comfortable (Fig. 42.18)
* The promotion of contemporary Irish design to incorporate regional characteristics of the local architecture (Fig. 42.19)

A rural guide will typically emphasise:

* **Stewardship/guardianship:** Responsibility towards the countryside and respect for the heritage for future generations.
* **A sense of place and community:** Building a new house in the countryside should be a positive addition to the rural environment. Much of the character and quality of the countryside relates to traditional buildings and their use of local materials.
* **Contemporary rural living and lifestyles:** Allowing for a modern lifestyle is vital so that rural living can be a comfortable alternative to suburban life.
* **The long term:** Because new dwellings permanently alter the landscape, the buildings should be durable and sympathetic to the local landscape.

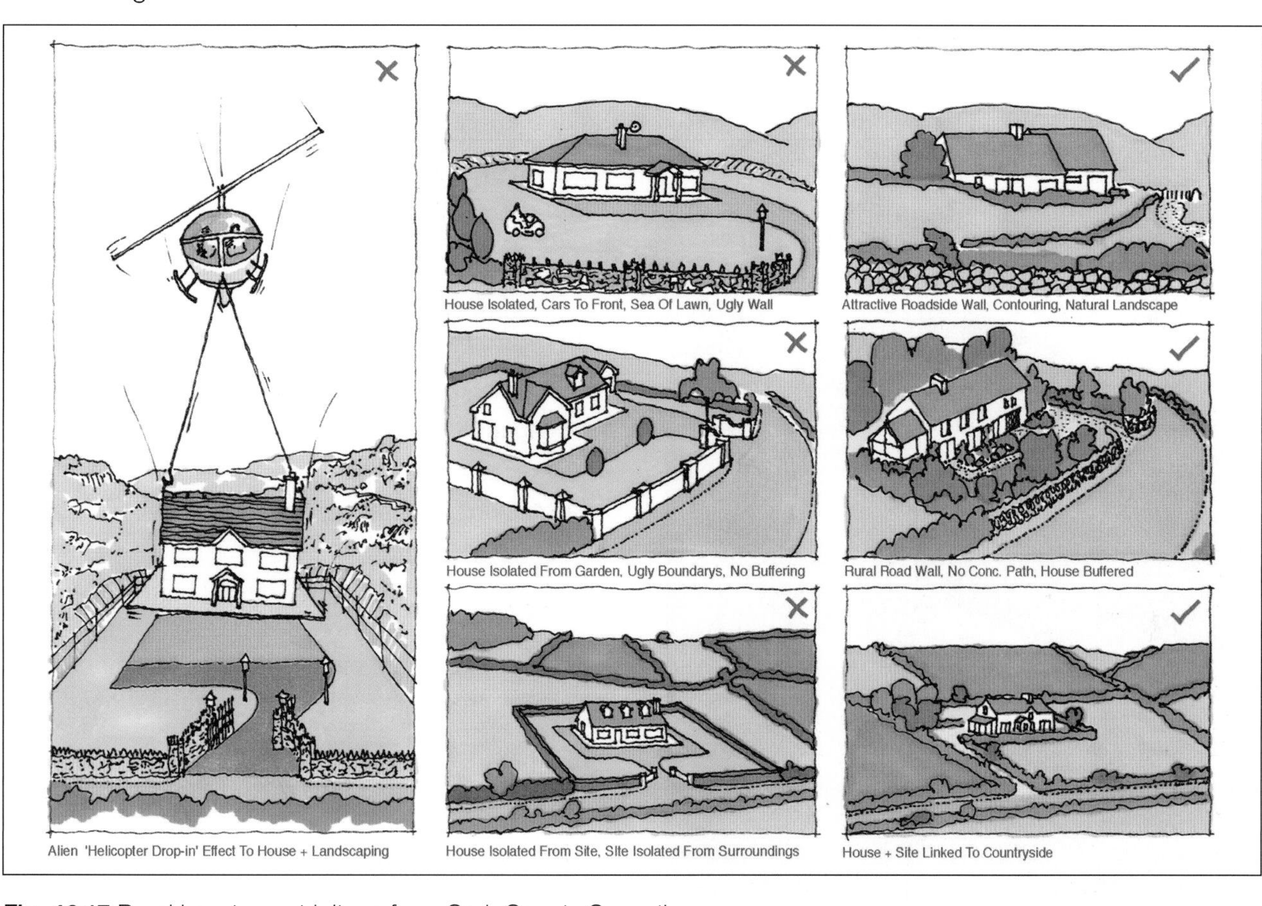

Fig. 42.17 Rural housing guidelines from Cork County Council

Fig. 42.18 Rural housing

Fig. 42.19 Rural housing

Garden designs

Diarmuid Gavin is a well-known garden designer. He won a bronze medal in 1995 in the Royal Horticultural Society (RHS) Chelsea Flower Show in London and won gold in 2011.

Irish Sky Garden

Gavin's Irish Sky Garden (Fig. 42.20) was the talking point of the show. Inspired by Oscar-winning Dublin animator Richard Baneham, who created the visual effects for *Avatar*, the centrepiece was a bright pink pod suspended 25m off the ground by a crane.

Fig. 42.20 Irish Sky Garden by Diarmuid Gavin, Chelsea Flower Show

Fig. 42.21 Carndonagh Town Park, Co. Donegal

Carndonagh Town Park

Under the Per Cent for Art scheme, Diarmuid Gavin Designs in partnership with Donegal County Council were invited to design a leisure park – a play park for the senses.

The landscape architecture project covers 4 acres on Barrack Hill, Carndonagh, Co. Donegal. It took several years to complete. The first stage focused on creating a special space for local children (Fig. 42.22).

The children's playground space was designed to engage children in more diverse ways than the traditional play area. The Carndonagh playground features:

* Soft ground and play equipment
* Places with changes in level, hiding places, trees and bushes
* An environment that tests the limits of capabilities through climbing, rolling and digging
* Places to stimulate the senses and the making of music in the natural environment
* Quiet places
* Colours and shapes, dark and bright places

The park, which serves as a hub for community activity, recreation and leisure activities, opened in 2015.

Fig. 42.22 Carndonagh Town Park drawing of the playground in the park

How to design a garden

Designing a garden should be a fun and rewarding experience, but gardens should be planned. A landscape architect could offer help and advice.

Combine function and aesthetics

A good design should emphasise a combination of function and aesthetics (appreciation of beauty) (Fig. 42.23 and Fig. 42.24).

Natural conditions

Consideration should be given to natural conditions, such as:

* Morning and evening sunshine (this will change significantly in summer and winter)
* Direction of the prevailing wind
* Rainwater drainage

Planting

The right plants and accessories can set the tone for the ideal outdoor atmosphere. Consider the location of:

* Lawns
* Colourful flowers
* Small trees
* Flowering shrubs

Fig. 42.23 Garden design

Designs might also include features like:

* Patios or decking
* Cobblestone pathways
* Small ponds, streams and water fountains
* Seating, stone walls, fences or screening
* A pergola (an arched framework) covered with climbing or trailing plants
* A gazebo – a small garden building (Fig. 42.23)

Gardens are personal. Like people, they evolve, grow and change with time.

Chapter review

* Well-planned cities and towns are essential to managing human activity. What are the most important issues a planner must consider to provide a sustainable lifestyle for all city dwellers?
* An architect has to take form and space into account as part of the design process. What other aspects of the environment do you think are important considerations?
* Ireland's traditional shop fronts are one of our country's most unique features. Should shop owners be compelled to protect, refurbish and maintain old signs? Should plastic signs be banned?
* A well-designed children's playground should engage children in a number of ways. How do you think traditional play areas could be improved?

Fig. 42.24 Garden design layout

EXAM QUESTIONS

Ordinary Level (2016)

Answer (a) and (b).

(a) Describe and discuss the shop front shown in Fig. 42.14 under the following headings:

- Visual impact
- Use of colour
- Signage

(b) Outline how you could improve this shop front in order to make it more attractive to its target market. Give reasons for your design decisions.

Illustrate your answer.

Ordinary Level (2016)

A public park is an area of land reserved for the enjoyment and recreation of visitors.

Answer (a) and (b).

(a) Design and discuss a layout for a public park to include the following amenities:

- Family picnic area
- Toddlers' play area
- Dog-walking trail

(b) Choose one of the amenities above and outline the health and safety features that this area would require. Give reasons for your choices.

Illustrate your answer.

Higher Level (2011)

'Bridges are functional structures that can have a strong sculptural presence, creating a lasting visual impact on their environment.'

Discuss this statement with reference to any named bridge, historical or modern. In your answer, refer to style, materials, function and visual impact.

Illustrate your answer.

Higher Level (2010)

'Groups such as the Irish Georgian Society and An Taisce work to highlight the need to preserve and restore our architectural heritage.'

Discuss this statement with detailed reference to two historical buildings, either local or national, that in your opinion should be preserved or restored.

Give reasons for your choices and outline the possible use for such buildings.

Illustrate your answer.

FURTHER RESEARCH

www.antaisce.org
www.bridgesofdublin.ie
www.buildingsofireland.ie
www.calatrava.com
www.corkcoco.ie – Cork Rural Design Guide
www.diarmuidgavindesigns.co.uk
donegalpublicart.ie – Carndonagh Town Park
www.glucksman.org
www.guggenheim.org – Guggenheim Museum Bilbao
www.igs.ie
odonnell-tuomey.ie
www.sdcc.ie – Shopfront Design Guide 2014
www.tuarard.ie

Chapter 43

Visual Merchandising

Visual merchandising (VM) is the professional term for retail design. It refers to anything a customer sees inside and outside a store, including displays, decorations, signs and floor layout. The overall purpose of visual merchandising is to attract customers into the shop and to sell the goods on display.

By the end of this chapter, I will...

* Know how visual merchandising is used in retail outlets.
* Understand why good display is a vital element in attracting shoppers.
* Know how design elements and principles apply to shop window displays.

Shop floor and window displays

Window and indoor displays are designed to capture not just the customer's attention, but their senses too. The designs will include elements like colour, lighting, space and product information; sensory inputs such as smell, touch and sound; and technologies such as digital displays and interactive installations.

Selfridges of London

The first store to use highly innovative selling techniques was Selfridges in Oxford Street, London. The store opened in 1909 and its founder, Harry Selfridge, wanted to make shopping a fun adventure. He emphasised the importance of creating a welcoming environment and placed merchandise on display so that customers could examine it.

Its window displays were like theatrical events. During preparation, they were covered with silk curtains and huge excitement built up in the days before they were dramatically unveiled. This helped to make the store one of the most famous in London. To this day, Selfridges window displays are renowned (Fig. 43.1).

Fig. 43.1 A Selfridges shop window display

How to create effective window displays

A professional window dresser will work with the following.

* **Fixtures and fittings:** These can either be custom built or ready made. A window dresser will know how to suit them to the product.
* **Mannequins:** A window dresser will know how to dress and place them.
* **Props:** A window dresser will know where to get props and how to use them.
* **Graphics:** A window dresser will know how to use text as a prop, as a visual aid or to provide information.
* **Lighting:** A window dresser will understand the importance of lighting and how best to use it.

Window displays should:

* **Have a theme:** This could be colours, the seasons or other celebrations and holidays.
* **Have a setting:** This could be a beach, a bedroom, a picnic, woodland, circus or anywhere that helps engage the viewers' imagination.
* **Tell a story:** For example, for Valentine's Day the theme could be 'how to mend a broken heart', featuring a jagged black line down a giant red plywood heart with hinges and chains attached and hardware tools nearby.
* **Use carefully chosen props to frame the display:** A few select pieces will help draw customers' attention.
* **Have a good composition:** The display should apply the elements and principles of design.
  - **Elements of design:** Line, shape, form, size, space, colour, value and texture.
  - **Principles of design:** Novelty, variety, harmony, unity, balance, proportion, emphasis, contrast, rhythm and pattern.
* **Be simple:** Less is more. Avoid clutter.
* **Use multiple layers of height:** This is to help the customer discover various items.
* **Be at eye level:** Not only for passersby, but also for passing cars.
* **Focus on colour and use at least three:** Contrasting colours, like black and white and monochromatic colours (tones of one colour), also create intriguing, eye-catching displays.
* **Create a focal point:** A good window display will have a 'hotspot' to direct the viewer's eye to an important point on the display.
* **Use lighting effectively:** Spotlights, uplights or coloured lights create the right mood for the display and draw attention to focal points. Lighting should also attract attention on city streets (or towns) at night.

Mannequins

Good-quality, classic mannequins are important for fashion windows (Fig. 43.2). These silent salespeople should be grouped like real people. Their clothing and gestures will create body language, which directs attention to the focal point or main character in the display.

Fig. 43.2 A shop window display

Mannequin: A dummy used to display clothes in a shop window.

NOTE! Goods can also be displayed outside on the pavement. This can include plants, but the area should be clean and free of clutter so that customers will be enticed to come in and explore.

Chapter review

* A bit of imagination and a few interesting props can turn a shop window into an eye-catching display that will have customers gazing at it in amazement. How, do you think, can the window answer that question: *Is it worth going in?*
* Visual merchandising refers to anything a customer sees inside and outside a store, including displays, decorations, signs and floor layout. How important, do you think, are these displays inside a shopping centre?

EXAM QUESTIONS

Ordinary Level (2014)

Shop window display can be an effective way of making goods attractive to the consumer. Answer (a) and (b), referring to the shop window display in Fig. 43.1 or Fig. 43.2.

(a) What makes this window display effective, in your opinion? Use the following headings in your answer:

- Composition
- Colour
- Theme

(b) Apart from the window display, describe and discuss the main elements that can make a shop front visually attractive.

Illustrate your answer.

Higher Level (2014)

'Shop window display (visual merchandising) is an important part of the sales and marketing process.'

Discuss this statement with reference to the clothing shop window display in Fig. 43.1 or Fig. 43.2. Indicate whether or not you find the window display effective and in your answer refer to theme, layout, props, colour and overall effect.

and

Briefly describe and sketch your ideas for a shop window displaying art supplies **or** mobile phones.

Illustrate your answer.

FURTHER RESEARCH

creativitywindow.com – 11 Surefire Window Display Ideas You Need to Learn About

creativitywindow.com – 11 Examples of Autumn or Fall Window Display Ideas

www.dit.ie – BA Visual Merchandising and Design Display

www.frameweb.com – Top 10 Shop Windows

www.selfridges.com – Shakespeare Windows

thebwd.com – Selfridges Store

SECTION 4

Preparing for the Written Exam

The written examination accounts for more than one-third of the marks for the entire Leaving Certificate art exam. As you can see, it is an important part of the examination. The written paper is worth 150 marks out of a total of 400 marks for the whole art exam, illustrated in the pie chart below.

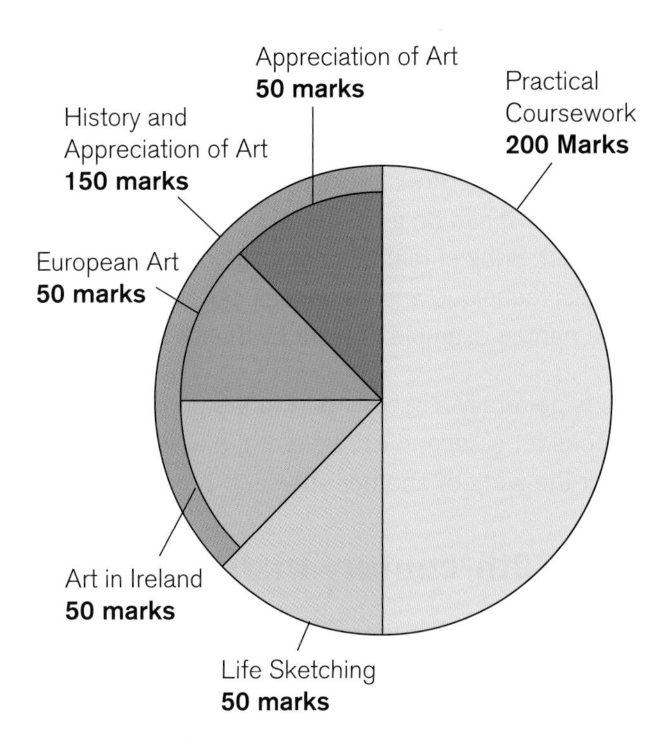

Marks in the Leaving Certificate art exam

The History and Appreciation of Art paper is divided into three parts:

* Section 1: Art in Ireland
* Section 2: European Art
* Section 3: Appreciation of Art

You must answer **one** question from **each** section. All questions carry equal marks.

When you are handed the paper in the exam, it will come in two parts. One part will be a booklet of **questions**. The other part will contain the **illustrations** that some of the questions refer to. About half of the questions have an illustration. This will be clearly noted in the question paper with a phrase in bold italics: ***illustrated on the accompanying sheet***.

NOTE! The style and content of examination questions change from year to year. The analysis below is based on papers from 2006 to 2016 and in no way predicts future trends in examination questions. Past examination papers and marking schemes are available on www.examinations.ie.

Higher Level

Section 1: Art in Ireland

There are normally seven questions in this section. You must answer **one**.

Q1. Pre-Christian art

The Stone Age, Bronze Age and Iron Age are looked at in Q1. Each year the question refers to one of the ages, but you cannot predict which age will come up in any particular year. In the past, both the Bronze Age and Iron Age came up in the one question.

In some years you might be asked to look at the development of design or a craft over the whole period. More often, though, an individual piece or style will be the point of the question. You may also be asked to refer to how the objects influenced later artwork from the Christian period.

Q2. Pre-Christian or Christian Celtic period

This can occasionally be a second question on the Pre-Christian period, but is more often a question on the Christian Celtic period from the 5th century AD to the 12th century AD.

Questions can be asked in a variety of ways on stone carving, metalwork or book painting. Again, the examiners avoid being predictable in the way they ask questions.

Questions can be asked on individual pieces like the Tara Brooch, Muiredach's Cross or the Book of Kells. Other times, the development of design or a craft over the period or comparisons between pieces might be looked for. Some questions also ask for influences from Pre-Christian art.

Q3. Christian Celtic art

This is a second question from the Christian Celtic period, usually in a different style to Q2. For instance, if Q2 was on an individual piece, then Q3 would be about the development of a craft or design over the period.

This question can sometimes include reference to the Romanesque period.

Q4. The Georgian period

The Georgian period is covered in Q4. Individual buildings or architects may be looked for. Public buildings or large country houses can be the topic.

NOTE! In Q1, Q2 and Q3 there is often a second part that looks for another example or another aspect of the topic being examined.

Examiners can look for a breakdown of information on an object into form, function, materials, decoration and techniques. This can be variable and the list may change to suit a particular piece.

Questions are often divided into parts, looking for information on structure and decoration and other examples by the same architect or in the same style.

Q5. A 19th- or early 20th-century artist

A 19th- or early 20th-century artist is usually the focus of Q5. It can be a painter, sculptor or stained glass artist. Subject matter, composition, style, materials, technique and influences can be looked for in a named example of work by the artist.

There is generally a second part to the question that looks for a second example of the artist's work or the work of another artist in a similar style.

Q6. A 20th-century Irish artist

A 20th-century Irish artist is normally the topic of Q6. Subject matter, composition, style, influences, materials, techniques and other criteria can be looked for in relation to their work.

A second part to the question usually looks for another example of the artist's work or work in a similar style by another artist.

Q7. Irish 19th- and 20th-century painters, sculptors or designers

A list of Irish 19th- and 20th-century painters, sculptors or designers is offered in Q7 and you have to choose **one**. You are generally asked to name and discuss **two** works by your chosen artist under the following headings: subject matter, style, media/materials, techniques and influences.

Section 2: European Art (1000 AD–present)

There are normally eight questions in this section. You must answer **one**.

Q8. Romanesque and Gothic architecture, sculpture, painting and craft

Romanesque and Gothic architecture, sculpture, painting and craft are generally the topics of Q8. The structure and decoration of named churches and cathedrals can be looked for. Named works of art and examples of style and technique can also be the focus of questions.

Individual artists like Claus Sluter and Gislebertus have also come up in exams.

Q9. The Early Renaissance

The Early Renaissance (Quattrocento – the 15th century) is the period generally covered in Q9. The emphasis is frequently on the development of realism in sculpture and painting.

Individual artists and their work are often the focus of questions. You would be expected to know subject matter, composition, style, materials and techniques for **two** works by **each** of the key painters and sculptors.

The background for the period is often looked for in a second part of the question.

Q10. The High Renaissance

The High Renaissance is the topic most frequently asked in Q10, but earlier and later work has also appeared over the years. Leonardo, Michelangelo and Raphael frequently appear, though this is not guaranteed by any means.

Most questions look for a second work to be named and described for each artist.

Northern European Renaissance artists have also come up in this question.

Subject matter, composition, treatment of the human figure, technique and the period are the headings most frequently looked for in questions from this time.

Q11. The 17th and 18th centuries

The 17th and 18th centuries are most frequently covered in Q11, although Renaissance artists and 19th-century artists have also appeared.

The question usually opens with a statement about an artist or a work of art, and asks for comments under the following headings: subject matter, composition, style, treatment of the human figure, materials and techniques, and the period.

A second named work is often looked for in a second part of the question.

Q12. The 19th century, Realism and Impressionism

The 19th century, Realism and Impressionism are most frequently asked in Q12, but a 17th-century artist appeared not too long ago, so there are no guarantees.

An opening statement about an artist or a work, illustrated or not, begins the question, followed by headings for you to comment under. Subject matter, composition, style, technique, materials, use of colour, treatment of the human figure and the period have been the most frequently used in recent years.

A second part to the question usually asks for a description and discussion of a named work by the same or another artist from the period.

Q13. The 19th and 20th centuries

There is a good deal of overlap between Q13 and Q12. Impressionist, Post-Impressionist and 20th-century artists and movements have all been asked in Q13.

The same form as the two previous questions is used here: an opening statement about an artist or movement, followed by headings to comment under. Subject matter, composition, style, techniques, influences, light and colour, and the period the work was made in are some of the more common headings.

Again, the second part of the question looks for a description and discussion on another work by the same artist or another artist from the same time.

Q14. List of artists

Q14 offers a list of artists. You are then asked to answer (a), (b) and (c).

* In part (a) you are asked to choose and name **one** work by an artist that you select from the list provided. The work can be a painting, a sculpture or a building, depending on the artist you select.
* In part (b) you discuss your chosen work in detail, making reference to the artist, subject matter, style, composition, materials, technique and the period in which the work was produced.
* In part (c) you name and briefly describe and discuss **one** other work by the artist you have chosen. The artists on the list can be from any era, from Romanesque to the 20th century. This can sometimes give you a second chance if an artist you have studied did not come up earlier in the paper.

Q15. Styles and movements in art

Q15 is a question on styles and movements in art that you must make a selection from. Answer (a), (b) and (c). This question has only taken its present form in the last few years.

* Part (a) asks you to select **one** style or movement in art from a list provided.
* In part (b) you discuss the main characteristics of your chosen style or movement.
* In part (c) you describe and discuss **one** named work by a named artist whose work is typical of this style or movement. Again, the style or movement can be from any time in the history of European art from the 10th to the 20th century, which may give you a chance to use information that did not turn up earlier on the paper.

NOTE! It is always a good idea to look over Q14 and Q15 in case something you have prepared is there.

Section 3: Appreciation of Art

There are normally five questions in this section. You must answer **one**.

The questions in this section do not follow a number order like they do in the previous sections. Questions can, and do, change from year to year. Some topics come up frequently, others not so often.

Gallery, museum or exhibition visit

A question on some aspect of a visit to a museum or gallery has been asked every year for the last

10 years. The examiner has looked for an account of the work of a curator, the layout, lighting and the information available on site and online.

You are frequently asked to give an account of **two** named works by named artists from the exhibition.

A second part of the question will often ask you to make your own plan for a suggested exhibition.

Film

There has been a question on film in eight of the last ten years. The question often opens with a statement about film and asks you to name a film and discuss it under a number of headings. The work of the director, set design, location, costumes, make-up, lighting, colour, sound, camerawork and special effects are some of the aspects of filmmaking that have been asked about.

A second part of the question often asks you for your own ideas on a film that you might make. Sometimes a title or a subject is offered for the student film.

Graphic design

There has been a question on graphic design in seven of the last ten years. Posters, packaging and book covers are the choices that turn up most frequently.

Some questions have an opening statement, but many are illustrated and you are asked to comment, frequently using headings. Design concept, art elements, imagery, composition, layout, branding, colour, typography and shape have been included over the years.

A second part to the question often asks you to come up with your own design ideas on a related topic.

Architecture and the environment

There has been a question on architecture and the environment in seven of the last ten years. Fitting buildings, in a successful way, into rural or urban environments is often the theme of the question. Restorations or changes of use for old buildings have also been asked about. Illustrations can be used.

Headings like scale, materials, site, colour/finish, exterior/interior features, landscape and impact on the environment have been suggested for the structure of the answer.

In a second part to the question, you can be asked to make your own suggestions for a similar project.

Product design

This was not asked about in the four years leading up to 2016, but it was asked in five of the previous ten years. Questions ranged from furniture and household equipment to coins and machinery.

Public art, sculptures, murals

This topic has come up in four of the last ten years. Opening statements and, sometimes, illustrations are offered for discussion. Headings like scale, materials, technique, colour/finish, context, visual impact and imagery have been suggested to structure the answer.

A second part of the question can give you a chance to make design suggestions for a similar project.

Interior design

There has been a question on interior design in three of the last ten years. An opening statement and sometimes an illustration give you a chance to discuss the topic under headings. Function, space, layout, colour, textures and patterns can be among the headings offered.

You usually have a chance to design your own space in a second part of the question.

Fashion design

This topic has come up in two of the last ten years, most recently in 2016. The question came with an illustration and a statement on fashion. Students were invited to discuss the statement under the following headings: design concepts, colour, shape and pattern.

A second part to the question asked students to come up with their own ideas for wearable fashion based on a theme.

One-off questions

One-off questions can be asked from time to time on almost any aspect of design. Visual merchandising, shop fronts, stage sets, crafts and other topics have come up over the years. They rely on your knowledge of basic design principles to offer an answer.

Ordinary Level

Section 1: Art in Ireland

There are seven questions in this section. You must answer **one**.

Q1. Pre-Christian Ireland, Stone, Bronze and Iron Ages

Pre-Christian Ireland, the Stone Age, Bronze Age and Iron Age are always the topic of Q1. There was an illustration with the question each year in the five years up to 2016.

This is a three-part question. You must answer (a), (b) and (c).

* In part (a) you name a place or object or describe its function.
* In part (b) you describe the object. Sometimes a list of headings is given, like location, structure, function (in the case of a tomb or sculpture) or how it was made and decorated (in the case of a metalwork piece).
* In part (c) you might be asked to name and describe another piece from the same period if the question is about metalwork. If the question is about Newgrange, you might be asked to describe an outstanding feature or decoration.

Q2. Pre-Christian period

A second question on the Pre-Christian period is most often asked here, but questions from the early Christian period have also been asked.

This question was illustrated for the five years before 2016.

This is a three-part question. You must answer (a), (b) and (c).

* Part (a) always asks for the function of the object in the question.
* Part (b) generally asks how it was made and decorated.
* In the three years up to 2016, you were asked to name and describe another object from the same time in part (c).

Q3. Christian Celtic period

The Christian Celtic period is covered in Q3. The most important high crosses, metalwork pieces or gospel books are generally asked for. This question is frequently but not always illustrated.

This is a three-part question. You must answer (a), (b) and (c).

* Part (a) generally asks for the function of the object in the question.
* Part (b) asks how the piece was made and decorated.

* Part (c) generally asks for another example of the type of object in the question.

Q4. The Georgian period

The Georgian period is generally looked at in this question, but not always. There was a question on the Book of Kells in 2014 and the Georgian question followed. This question is usually not illustrated.

This is a three-part question. You must answer (a), (b) and (c).

* Part (a) asks you to name an architect or a building.
* In part (b) you can be asked to describe the structure, decoration, exterior or interior of the building.
* Part (c) usually asks for an exterior or interior feature of the building, but you can also be asked to describe or compare it with another building.

Q5. A 19th- or 20th-century artist

A 19th- or 20th-century artist is usually the subject of Q5. Most years there is an illustration and the artist and work are named.

This is a three-part question. You must answer (a), (b) and (c).

* Part (a) generally asks you to describe the work. Headings like subject matter, composition, style and technique can be included.
* In the last couple of years before 2016, part (b) asked what the work was about. You also had to give reasons for your answer.
* In part (c) you can be asked to name and describe another work by the same artist, another artist working in the same style or with the same subject matter.

Q6. Another 19th- or 20th-century artist

Another 19th- or 20th-century artist is usually the subject of Q6. This question is occasionally illustrated.

This is a three-part question. You must answer (a), (b) and (c).

* In the two years before 2016, you were given the artist's name in part (a) and asked to name a work by them. Previously you might have been asked to describe the painting under headings like those in Q5.
* In part (b) you can be asked to describe the work. The most common headings are subject matter, composition, use of colour, technique and style.
* In the last couple of years before 2016, examiners looked for further information on the artist in part (c). Previously, other work by the artist in the question or other artists working in a similar way was looked for.

Q7. List of 19th- and 20th-century artists

Q7 offers a list of 19th- and 20th-century artists. You must choose **one** from the list.

This is a three-part question. You must answer (a), (b) and (c).

* In part (a) you name a work by your chosen artist.
* In part (b) you describe your chosen work under headings. Subject matter, form, composition, technique and use of materials are the most common headings.
* In part (c) you give some information about your chosen artist.

Section 2: European Art (1000 AD–present)

There are seven questions in this section. You must answer **one**.

Q8. The Romanesque and Gothic periods

The Romanesque and Gothic periods are the topics in Q8. It had been a three-part question up to the last few years, but most recently it only had two parts, (a) and (b). The question is sometimes illustrated. You can be asked about a specific building or sculpture, or sometimes asked to name a work of your own choice.

* In part (a) you may be asked to describe the work under headings. These can vary a lot depending on whether the question is on architecture or sculpture. The headings could be the exterior and interior of a building or the subject, composition and function of a sculpture.
* In part (b) you might be asked for the main features of Romanesque or Gothic architecture, the function of sculpture, or even how stained glass is made.

Q9. Late Gothic to High Renaissance artists

Late Gothic to High Renaissance artists can be part of Q9. It is generally about a named artist, like Giotto, and the artists of the Quattrocento, but not always. It is sometimes illustrated.

In recent years this has become a two-part question. You must answer (a) and (b).

* In part (a) you describe and discuss the work under headings like subject matter, composition, use of perspective, colour, treatment of the human figure and technique.
* In part (b) you can be asked to describe another work by the artist. Give some general information about the artist or describe the work of another artist from the same time.

Q10. The High Renaissance

The High Renaissance is usually the topic of Q10. Leonardo, Michelangelo and Raphael come up frequently, but not always. It is frequently illustrated.

This has recently been a two-part question. You must answer (a) and (b).

* In part (a) you discuss the work under headings. Composition, form, technique, use of materials, treatment of the human figure, light, colour and subject matter are among the headings offered.
* In part (b) you name and describe another work by the artist.

Q11. The 17th and 18th centuries

The 17th and 18th centuries were the topics of Q11 in 2015 and 2016. Before that, this was a question on Impressionism. Earlier again, it was a list of artists from the 13th to the 20th centuries. The list seems to have moved to the end of the section in recent years.

In the last few years this question has been illustrated and the name of the artist and the title of the work have been given.

This is a two-part question. You must answer (a) and (b).

* In part (a) you describe and discuss the work under headings. Subject, composition, style, light and colour have all been offered.
* In part (b) you name and briefly describe another work by the artist.

Q12. Impressionism and Post-Impressionism

Impressionism and Post-Impressionism has been the topic of Q12. Sometimes it is illustrated. You may be given an artist's name and asked to name and describe a work by them.

This is a two-part question. You must answer (a) and (b).

* In part (a) you describe and discuss the work under headings: subject matter, composition, style, colour and technique.
* Part (b) may look for general information on the artist or movement. You also might be asked to give another example of the artist's work.

Q13. A 20th-century artist

A 20th-century artist is the topic of Q13. It is a similar format to Q12.

This is a two-part question. You must answer (a) and (b).

* In part (a) you describe and discuss the work under headings. Subject matter, style, composition, colour, theme, medium and technique have all been offered in the question.
* In part (b) you may be asked to name and describe another work by the artist. General information on the artist or movement or some aspect of their work might also be asked for.

Q14. A list of artworks and artists

A list of artworks and artists has moved to this position on the paper in recent years. The work can be from any part of the European section, from the 11th to the 20th century.

This is a two-part question. You must answer (a) and (b).

* In part (a) you describe and discuss the work under headings. Subject matter, composition, form, style, colour and technique are among the headings used.
* In part (b) you are usually asked to name and briefly describe another work by your chosen artist.

NOTE! This question can often give you a chance to use some information that you have studied that did not come up earlier in the paper.

Section 3: Appreciation of Art

There are seven questions in this section. You must answer **one**.

Questions in this section do not follow a number order like they do in the previous sections. Questions can, and do, change from year to year. Some topics come up frequently, some not so often.

Gallery, museum or exhibition visit

There has been a question on some aspect of a visit to a museum or gallery every year for the last 10 years.

This is most often a two-part question. The content of the questions can vary a lot from year to year. Most often you are asked to name a gallery, museum or interpretive centre you have visited and to describe **two** works that you saw using titles and artists' names. You could also be asked to describe the layout and how the work was displayed.

A second part to the question can ask how you would display work in your school or even to design a phone app to promote gallery visits.

Product design

A question has come up on product design in nine of the last ten years. A wide range of products, from toys to mobile phone cases, can be examined in this question.

This is usually a two-part question. You must answer (a) and (b).

* In part (a) you are often asked to describe and discuss the product under headings. Overall design, safety, materials, colour, texture, function, form and shape have all been included.
* Part (b) can ask you to design something and to give reasons for your design.

Graphic design

There has been a question on graphic design in nine of the last ten years. Posters come up most often, but package design, T-shirts and other forms of advertising also appear.

This is usually a two-part question. You must answer (a) and (b).

* In part (a) you describe and discuss the design using headings. Imagery, composition, colour, shape, form, lettering and logo have all been used in recent years.
* In part (b) you can be asked to design a poster, logo or some other graphic on a suggested theme.

Film and TV

A question has been offered on film or TV in eight of the last ten years. Sometimes a theme like action or drama is offered to base your answer on. You can also be offered a free choice of film or TV series to choose from.

This is usually a two-part question. You must answer (a) and (b).

* In part (a) you describe and discuss the film or TV programme under headings. Costumes, make-up, camera work, special effects, location and sets can be offered to help you frame your answer.
* In part (b) you might be asked to describe **one** scene or to offer ideas for a film or TV programme of your own. Examiners have also looked for storyboards and ideas for TV ads.

Architecture and the environment

There has been a question on architecture and the environment in eight of the last ten years. This is a loose heading to group together topics like designing a children's playground, shop fronts, and upcycling second-hand materials into useful furniture or equipment.

This is usually a two-part question. You must answer (a) and (b).

* Part (a) asks you to describe and discuss the topic or illustration. Headings are given, but these vary so much that it would be pointless to give examples here.
* In part (b) you can be asked to design something based on the question or to look at safety features.

Public art

There has been a question on public art in six of the last ten years.

In recent years it has frequently been a two-part illustrated question. You must answer (a) and (b).

* In part (a) you are asked to describe and discuss the work of public art using the headings given. The location, size, shape/ form, colour, texture and its relationship to the environment have been given as points to help you form an answer.

* In part (b) you might be asked to design a sculpture for your school or some other public space. What you think the sculpture is about or how it might be lit at night are among the topics from the second part of the question.

Design for stage sets or live performances

There has been a question on this topic in five of the last ten years. Plays in theatres, performances, live bands and street festivals have all come up in this question.

This is usually a two-part question. You must answer (a) and (b).

* In part (a) you describe and discuss the performance under headings. Set design, scenery, colour, light, costumes, make-up or all the visual elements of a production can be looked for.
* In part (b) you may be asked to design a set for a play or concert, or explain why you found the production memorable using examples of the visual qualities that stood out for you.

Interior design

Interior design has come up in five of the last ten years. Designing a space for a purpose, like an artist's studio, a teenager's bedroom, a place to play music or carry out a hobby, has been the focus of questions in the past.

This is usually a two-part question. You must answer (a) and (b).

* In part (a) you are asked to describe and discuss a possible design for the space in the question using headings like function, layout, light, colour, floor space, storage and furnishings.
* In part (b) you might be asked to sketch a plan or describe the furniture and fittings you would like to use in your design.

Less frequent questions

These come up from time to time. Fashion, craft design, hairstyles, photography or almost any design topic is possible. The examiners rely on your knowledge of basic design principles to answer the question.

Marking schemes

Marking schemes vary a lot from year to year and it can be difficult to predict exactly where the marks will be awarded just by reading the question.

We will look at one Higher Level example and one Ordinary Level example from the 2016 papers.

Higher Level

Q1. 'By developing skills of working in gold, Bronze Age artists and craft workers ushered in a new period of culture and development in Ireland.'

Discuss this statement with reference to **two** named artefacts from this period. In your answer, describe and discuss form, function, materials used and decorative techniques.

and

Briefly describe and discuss where and how Bronze Age people in Ireland acquired the metals needed for their artefacts.

Illustrate your answer.

The highlighted parts of the question refer to the areas where points are awarded in the marking scheme below.

Q1		Marks	Notes
A	Discussion of statement and two named artefacts from this period	10	5 for discussion of statement, 3/2 names
B	Description and discussion of named artefact one under form, function, materials used and decorative techniques	10	
C	Description and discussion of named artefact two under form, function, materials used and decorative techniques	10	
D	Briefly describe and discuss where and how Bronze Age people acquired the metals needed	10	2 examples and information
E	Sketches	10	
	Total	**50**	

Most questions at Higher Level begin with an opening statement and/or an illustration. This introduces the subject of the question and often offers an opinion for you to react to.

* **Describe and discuss** are the words most frequently used to open the question. They often carry a lot of the marks – 25 marks in this question.
* **Name** is another word you will often see. There are usually marks on offer with it – just 5 in this question, but often more.
* The word '**and**' in bold letters separates a second element of the question. This second part can carry up to 15 marks – in this question it is 10 marks.
* **Sketches** carry 10 marks when there is no illustration (as in this question), 5 marks when there is one.

Ordinary Level

In the European section of the Ordinary Level paper, questions are usually divided into part (a) and (b). Part (a) usually carries more marks.

Q10. *Moses* by Michelangelo (1475–1564) is illustrated on the accompanying sheet. Answer (a) and (b).

(a) Describe and discuss this sculpture under the following headings:

- Composition/form
- Technique and use of materials
- Treatment of the human figure

(b) Name and briefly describe and discuss **one** other work by Michelangelo.

Illustrate your answer.

The highlighted parts of the question refer to areas where points are awarded in the marking scheme below.

Q10		Marks	Notes
A	Description and discussion of the illustration under headings	30	
B	Name, description and discussion of one other work by Michelangelo	15	5 for name 10 for discussion
C	Sketches	5	
	Total	**50**	

Many of the questions in the European section of the Ordinary Level paper are illustrated.

* The work and the artist are often identified. Part (a) of the question will ask you to **describe and discuss** the work under **three headings**. Thirty marks are awarded to part (a) in this question.
* Part (b) usually asks you to **name and briefly describe one** other work by the artist. This is worth 15 marks in this question.
* **Sketches** carry 5 marks with an illustrated question and 10 without. There are 5 marks available in this question.

How to structure your answer

The History and Appreciation of Art examination is 2.5 hours long (150 minutes).

Allow some time to read the paper at the start – maybe 10 minutes – and 5 minutes to review your answers at the end.

You should allow 45 minutes for each question:

* 45 minutes for Section 1: Art in Ireland
* 45 minutes for Section 2: European Art
* 45 minutes for Section 3: Appreciation of Art

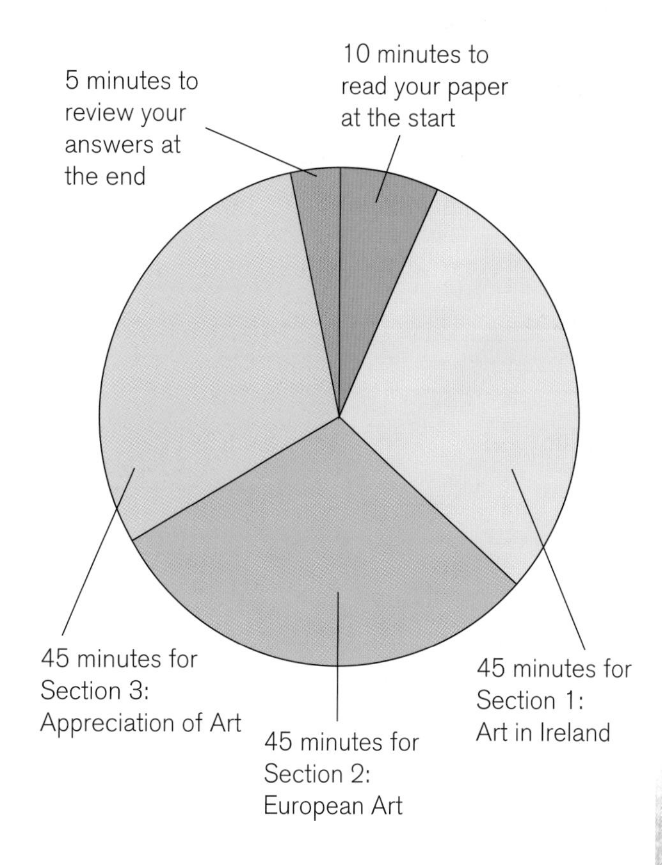

Structure your answer as follows:

* Spend the first 10 minutes reading over the paper to **identify suitable questions** in each section.
* Begin your answers by writing down the **key points** from the question. Note words like *describe*, *discuss* and *compare*, as they will identify the point of the question.
* Open your answer with an **introduction** to give the examiner an idea of the points you will cover. Refer to the opening statement or the illustration, if there is one.
* **Highlight references to the key points** in the question, maybe with a paragraph heading or a different coloured pen.
* **Opinions** are important. Back up your opinions with information.
* **Use separate paragraphs or even headings** to emphasise form, function, subject, style or materials so that the examiner can easily find your points and award marks.
* **Sketches** should be clear and simple. There should be two or three sketches with every answer. Use labels to clearly identify your sketch and include annotation in a different coloured pen to point out important features.
* **Add colour** where possible, especially when illustrating paintings.
* A **conclusion** should summarise your points and show their relevance to the question.
* **Check your answer** against the question at the end to make sure you have covered all the key points.

Summary

* Reading the questions carefully is very important. You cannot be given marks if your answer misses the point of the question. Note the important points of the question on your exam paper before you start and double check them before you begin your answer.
* Write your answers as if you were writing for someone with no experience of art history or appreciation. You must explain everything clearly. Write short, clear paragraphs.
* Avoid stock answers. It is unlikely that they will fit a question exactly and you cannot get marks if you miss the point of the question.
* Lists of facts are not enough. You must explain your points and put them in context.
* Make the information in your answer easy for the examiner to find. Put relevant headings on your paragraphs and use bullet points where they will help. Different coloured pens, markers or pencils can sometimes be used.

Glossary

A

Abstract art: Art that does not attempt to represent an accurate depiction of a visual reality, but instead uses shapes, colours, forms and gestural marks to achieve its effect.

Abutment: A structure built to support the lateral pressure of an arch, span or bridge.

Academy: Artist-run organisations whose aim was to improve the professional standing of artists as well as to provide teaching.

Aesthetic: Concerned with beauty or the appreciation of beauty.

Aisle: The side of a nave separated by a colonnade.

Allegory: Art that uses figures or objects to represent abstract qualities or ideas, often used to symbolise a deeper moral or spiritual meaning, such as life, death, love, virtue, justice, etc. Renaissance allegories frequently refer to Greek and Roman legends or literature.

Amber: Fossilised resin that is honey-yellow in colour.

Ambulatory: A walkway behind the high altar and around the apse of a large church or cathedral.

Anatomy: The science of the bodily structure of animals and plants. During the Renaissance, some artists dissected bodies to better understand their structure.

Antiquity: The classical age of Greece and Rome.

Apse: A semicircular vaulted space behind the altar of a church.

Arcade: A series of arches supported by piers or columns.

Architecture: The art or practice of designing and constructing buildings.

Archivolt: Moulding around the face of an arch, often ornamental.

Artefact: Something created by humans, usually for a practical purpose; an object of cultural or historical interest.

Articulation: A method of styling the joints in the formal elements of architectural design.

Ashlar: Hewn or cut square stone or stone facing.

Astronomy: The study of the stars and planets.

Atelier: A French word that translates literally as 'studio' or 'workshop'.

Austere: Severe or strict in manner or attitude.

Avant-garde: In art history, used for a group of people whose ideas are considered to be ahead of their time.

B

Baptistery: A detached part of a church where baptisms are performed. They are mostly round or octagonal in shape.

Barrel vault: A simple continuous vault, typically semicircular in cross-section.

Basilica: A building similar to a Roman basilica (public meeting hall), used as a Christian church. An important church, sometimes with special privileges from the pope.

Basin stone: A large stone carved into the shape of an open basin.

Bay: A division of a building, defined by features like windows, arches or columns.

Bifolium: A leaf of vellum or parchment folded to make two pages.

Blind arcade: A series of arches against a flat surface with no openings, usually a decoration on a wall.

Breakfront: A slightly projecting central section of a building.

Bronze: An alloy (mix) of copper and tin.

Buttress: A vertical structure of stone built against a wall that counteracts the outward thrust of the vault or wall.

Byzantine: Relating to or having the characteristics of a style of art and architecture developed in the Byzantine Empire, especially in the 5th and 6th centuries.

C

Capital: A separate wider piece at the head of a column, pilaster or pillar that provides a base for the structures above.

Cartoon: A full-scale preparatory drawing for a painting, tapestry or fresco.

Cast: A form created by pouring liquid material, such as plaster or molten metal, into a mould.

Chamber: A room or enclosed space.

Champlevé: Enamelwork where hollow areas made in metal sheet are filled with coloured enamels.

Cherub: A type of angel that is usually shown in art as a beautiful young child with small wings and a round face and body.

Chevron: An ornamental device made of a series of V shapes.

Chiaroscuro: Meaning 'light-dark' in Italian, the term refers to fine gradations from light to dark in painting.

Chi-Rho: A Christian symbol made up of the first two letters, Chi and Rho, of the Greek word Christos (Christ).

Choir: The part of a large church or cathedral between the altar and the nave used by the choir and clergy.

Cinquecento: An Italian word that means 'five hundred' but also refers to the 16th century in Italian art.

Cladding: A thin layer of one material used externally on a building.

Classical orders: The Doric, Ionic and Corinthian decoration of ancient Greek and Roman architecture.

Clerestory: A row of windows in the upper part of a church wall above the roof level of the aisles.

Cloisonné: Metal wires or strips soldered to a base, creating areas that are filled with coloured enamel.

Cloister: A covered walk or arcade surrounding a square enclosure, usually attached to a church or monastery.

Codex: A book made of separate leaves, as opposed to a scroll.

Colonnade: A row of columns supporting an entablature or a series of arches.

Column: A free-standing pillar, typically cylindrical, supporting an arch, entablature or other structure, or standing alone as a monument, often built in accordance with one of the orders of architecture.

Complementary colours: Any two hues positioned exactly opposite each other on the basic colour wheel. Complementary colours contrast with each other more than any other colour, and when placed side by side make each other look brighter.

Composition: The arrangement of elements within a work of art.

Concept: The idea behind a work of art.

Conservation (of art) and restoration: The preservation and repair of architecture, paintings, drawings, prints, sculptures and objects of the decorative arts.

Contrapposto: Meaning 'placed opposite'. In art it refers to a human figure standing with most of its weight on one foot so that its shoulders and arms twist off-axis from the hips and legs.

Corbelling: The process of making a dome or arch using overlapping layers of stones.

Cornice: The uppermost ornamental moulding that crowns an architectural composition.

Crossing: The area of a church where the nave is intersected by the transept.

Cruciform: In the shape of a cross.

Crypt: An underground chamber, usually vaulted, beneath the floor of a church.

Cupola: A small dome. An evenly curved vault on a circular or polygonal base.

Curator: Someone employed by a museum or gallery to manage a collection of artworks or artefacts.

D

Dado rail: A moulding that separates the lower part of an interior wall.

Damask: A rich, heavy silk or linen fabric with a pattern woven into it.

Decorative: Serving to make something look more attractive or ornamental.

Depict: To represent by a drawing, painting or other art form.

Diagonal: A straight line joining the opposite corners of a square or rectangle. A slanting straight line.

Didactic: Intended to teach, particularly in having moral instruction.

Diminuendo: Letters decreasing in size at the beginning of a passage in an Irish manuscript.

Diptych: Meaning 'folded twice' in Greek, this is an altarpiece made of two panels hinged together.

Distortion: Something put out of shape but still recognisable.

Divine: Of or like God or a god.

Divisionism: The characteristic style in Neo-Impressionist painting defined by the separation of colours into individual dots or patches that interact optically.

Dolmen: A megalithic tomb where large flat stones are laid on top of upright stones.

Drapery: Depiction in drawing, painting and sculpture of the folds of clothing.

Dressed stone: Smoothly finished blocks of stone.

E

Elongated: Something made longer, especially in relation to its width.

Enamel: An opaque or semitransparent glossy substance that is a type of glass. It is applied in powdered form to metal and is melted and bonded by heat. It is used for ornament.

Engraving: To cut or carve into a hard surface.

Entablature: The upper part of a classical building supported by columns or a colonnade, comprising the architrave, frieze and cornice.

Ergonomics: The study of people in their working environment. The interaction of people with structures and equipment.

Evangelist: A writer of one of the Four Gospels of the Bible: Matthew, Mark, Luke and John.

F

Façade: The front or main face of a building.

Fanlight: A window over a door, often semicircular, where the glazing bars look like the ribs of a fan.

Fascia: A long, thin board that covers the area where a wall joins a roof. The sign above the window of a shop where the shop's name is written.

Fibula: Usually means a type of dress fastener. Gold objects made of a bow and end cups or discs from the Bronze Age in Ireland were also called fibulae.

Figurative: Artwork that is clearly derived from real objects.

Filigree: Ornamental work in fine gold or silver wire.

Flamboyant: The last major style of French Gothic architecture. Elaborate flowing lines of tracery create flame-like shapes.

Flying buttress: An arched buttress that supports the upper wall of the nave in a church wall.

Foil: A leaf shape. A trefoil is three foils. A quatrefoil is four foils.

Foreshortening: The technique of depicting an object lying at an angle to the picture plane by using perspective devices.

Form: The visible shape or configuration of something.

Fresco: Wall painting on wet plaster.

Frieze: In classical architecture, the middle division of an entablature featuring a strip of decoration or figures. A decoration in painting or sculpture in a long horizontal format.

Frontispiece: The decorated entrance area on the façade of a building.

Function: The practical use or purpose of a designed object.

G

Gargoyle: A grotesque carved human or animal face or figure projecting from the gutter of a building, typically acting as a spout to carry water clear of a wall.

Genre: A style or category of art or film. In painting, it refers to small-scale paintings showing narrative scenes from everyday life.

Georgian: A style of architecture from the time of the English kings George I, 1714, to George IV, who died in 1830.

Gesso: The dense and brilliantly white ground used in tempera paintings.

Gild: To cover with a thin layer of gold.

Glaze: In oil painting, a thin coat of transparent colour laid over another.

Gouache: A type of water-soluble paint that, unlike watercolour, is opaque, so the white of the paper surface does not show through.

Gorget: A U-shaped gold collar from the Irish Bronze Age with a disc attached to each end.

Granulation: An effect that can be achieved with wash work when using colours with heavy pigment particles.

Greek cross: A cross where all four arms are of equal length.

Groin vault: A type of vaulting created by two barrel vaults intersecting at right angles.

Grotesque: A kind of ornament that refers to ancient Roman art found in caves. In medieval art it refers to twisted human figures, birds, animals and monsters.

Guilds: Associations of artists, craftsmen or tradesmen. These organisations regulated the financial, social and political interests of their members.

H

Hue: A colour or a shade of a colour.

Humanism: An intellectual movement in Italy that started in the 14th century. It suggested the ideal of an education based on Greek and Roman thought, emphasising the value, potential and goodness in humans, which turned away from medieval God-centred scholarship.

High relief: So deeply carved or modelled that the main elements are almost free from their background.

History painting: A painting with a serious narrative portrayed in a dramatic way, often with a moral message. The word 'history' relates to the Italian *istoria*, meaning narrative or story, and does not necessarily relate to actual events from history.

I

Iconography: The use or study of images or symbols in the visual arts.

Illumination: Decorations and illustrations found in medieval manuscripts.

Illusionist: A term used to describe a painting that creates the illusion of a real object or scene, or a sculpture where the artist has depicted a figure in such a realistic way that they seem alive.

Impasto: In oil painting, colour thickly applied (like paste) to a canvas or a panel.

Incision: Cutting into a surface with a point or blade.

Infrastructure: The basic equipment and structures (such as roads and bridges) that are needed for a country, region or organisation to function properly.

Initial: The first capital letter of a passage in a manuscript.

Installation (art): Used to describe mixed-media constructions or assemblages that are usually designed for a specific place and for a temporary period of time.

Insular style: The version of the La Tène style that developed in manuscript illumination and the decorative arts in Britain and Ireland in the 8th century.

Interlace design: Decorative patterns made by weaving strands together, like plaiting or basketwork.

J

Jamb: The side of a window, door or other wall opening. In medieval or classical architecture they sometimes contain columns or statuary.

Japonism: From the French Japonisme (first used in 1872), it refers to the influence of Japanese art, fashion and aesthetics on Western culture.

Juxtaposition: Two things being seen or placed close together with contrasting effect.

K

Kerbstone: In the Stone Age, the large stones that surrounded the base of passage mounds.

L

Lancet window: A tall, narrow window with a steeply pointed arch on top.

La Tène: A style of art developed by the Celts in Central Europe. It combines natural forms, leaf and vine shapes with spirals, scrolls and trumpet shapes into a flowing abstract art.

Latin cross: A cross where the vertical shaft is longer than the crosspiece.

Linear: A style that relies on line for its main effect rather than colour or tone.

Lintel: A horizontal piece of stone or timber inserted at the top of a door, window or other opening to take the weight of the wall above.

Lock rings: Ornaments made of gold wire and sheet metal formed into cone shapes. They may have been hair decorations.

Loggia: A gallery open at one or more sides.

Low relief: Sculpture that projects less than half its true depth from the surface.

Lozenge: Shaped like the diamond shape in playing cards.

Luminous: Giving off light; bright or shining.

Lunula: A sheet gold neck ornament from the Bronze Age, shaped like a new moon.

M

Majuscule: Large capital or uncial letters that are usually the same height. The Irish version has some small ascenders and descenders.

Mandorla: Almond-shaped stylised glory of light enclosing sacred figures like Christ.

Mannequin: A dummy used to display clothes in a shop window.

Medium: This can refer both to the type of art (e.g. painting, sculpture, printmaking), as well as the materials an artwork is made from.

Megalithic: A period in the Stone Age when people built monuments with large stones.

Millefiori glass: Meaning 'thousand flowers', this refers to little sections cut from multicoloured glass rods of enamel used to decorate areas in metalwork.

Modelling: The convincing representation of three-dimensional forms in two dimensions. The use of a malleable material like clay or wax to make a three-dimensional form.

Monochrome: A painting or drawing executed in shades of a single colour.

Monumental: Something great in size, ambition or importance, or serving as a monument.

Motif: A distinctive feature in a design. The subject of a painting.

Mould: A hollow container that gives shape to molten liquid (wax, plaster or metal) when it hardens.

Mythological: Relating to a collection of myths or mythology.

N

Narrative art: Art that tells a story.

Narthex: The single-storey porch of a medieval church.

Nave: The main area of the church between the aisles.

Neo-Classical: A style of decoration based on ancient Greek and Roman examples popular in the 1770s.

Neolithic: The new Stone Age, when polished stone axes and other tools came into use c. 3700 BC in Ireland.

Niche: A recess in a wall often used to hold a statue.

Nimbus: The disc or halo behind the head of a saint.

Non-representational art: Also called non-objective art, this style consisted of works that had no reference to anything outside themselves. In practice, it was mainly geometrically abstract.

Nymph: The word 'nymph' comes from Greek mythology. It described nature spirits in the form of young women, usually found in the woods.

O

Oil paint: A medium where pigments are mixed with drying oils, such as linseed. Oil paint became popular during the 15th century in Northern Europe.

Ogham: An alphabet of 20 characters consisting of parallel lines across a vertical line or edge. It was used in Ireland from the 3rd or 4th century AD.

Optical mixing: Pure primary colours in small touches placed close together so that they seem to merge, creating secondary colours in the eye of the beholder. This technique was used by Impressionists and Neo-Impressionists.

Outward thrust: Outward or lateral stress in a structure, such as that exerted by an arch or vault.

P

Painterly: Form is not represented by outline, but by the application of paint in patches of colour, resulting in the appearance of visible brushstrokes within the finished painting.

Palladian: In the style of the Renaissance architect Andrea Palladio.

Parchment: Animal skin, especially from a goat or sheep, prepared for writing.

Patronage: Financial or moral support given to an artist or craftsman by someone with wealth or power.

Pedestal: A base supporting a statue or other object.

Pediment: A gable-like decoration over a portico, door or window.

Pelta: An ornamental motif made of arcs, often elaborated on in Celtic art.

Penannular brooch: A brooch where the ring has an opening – it is not a complete circle.

Perspective: A method of representing a three-dimensional object on a flat or nearly flat surface. Perspective gives a painting a sense of depth.

***Piano nobile*:** The main floor containing the reception rooms in an Italian palazzo or a large townhouse.

Pier: A large, solid and freestanding support, usually square or round in section.

***Pietá*:** Meaning 'pity' in Italian, it refers to the representation of the Virgin Mary holding the dead Christ on her lap.

Pigment: The dry, usually powdered form of colour.

Pilgrimage: To go on a journey to a famous place. In medieval times, it was a place associated with a Christian saint.

Pillar: A freestanding upright in architecture, of any regular shape.

Pilaster: A rectangular column, especially one projecting from a wall.

Pinnacle: A small turret-like roof decoration. It is often richly ornamented.

Plane: A flat surface. Any distinct flat surface within a painting or sculpture can be referred to as a plane.

***Plein air*:** Meaning 'out of doors', this refers to the practice of painting pictures outside.

Plinth: A square base for columns, statues or vases.

Poesia: Sixteenth-century Italian paintings that have a poetic quality.

Pointillism: The theory or practice in art of applying small strokes or dots of colour to a surface so that from a distance they blend together.

Porcelain: A hard, fine-grained white ceramic ware.

Portal: A doorway. A portal was often set back several steps in Romanesque and Gothic architecture. This gave doors a considerable emphasis on the façade.

Portico: A structure consisting of a roof supported by columns at regular intervals, typically attached as a porch to a building.

Portray: To make a likeness of by drawing, painting or representing in a work of art.

Predella: A painting or carving beneath the main scenes or panels of an altarpiece.

Prefiguration: An early indication of something that will happen in the future.

Proportion: The relationship of a part to a whole object. In painting, sculpture and architecture, it can describe the ratio or ideal proportions of the various parts of the human body.

Proto Renaissance: Refers to the pre-Renaissance period (c. 1300–1400) in Italy and the activities of progressive painters such as Giotto.

Pseudo penannular brooch: A brooch that looks like a penannular brooch, but the ring is closed, usually with decoration.

Putti: Small naked little boys with wings engaged in playful activities.

Q

Quatrefoil: A form of tracery composed of four foils.

Quattrocento: The 15th century in Italian art. It was preceded by the Trecento in the 14th century.

Quill pen: A pen for writing with ink made from the flight feathers of a goose or other large bird.

R

Radiating chapels: Chapels leading off from the ambulatory and arranged in a semicircle.

Rayonnant: Radiating, a style in French Gothic architecture that was popular in the 13th and 14th centuries.

Relic: A part of a deceased holy person's body or belongings kept as an object of reverence.

Relief: A composition or design in which parts stand out from a flat surface. See also *high relief* and *low relief.*

Reliquary: A container, often richly decorated, for sacred relics, usually parts of a saint's body.

Repoussé: Metal hammered into a relief design from the back.

Representational art: Art that attempts to show objects as they really appear, or at least in some easily recognisable form.

Retrospective (exhibition): Retrospective means 'looking back', so a retrospective art exhibition looks back at the work that a living artist has produced over their entire career.

Ribbed vault: A vault composed on a framework of diagonal ribs.

Rococo: Light, sensuous, intensely decorative French style developed in the early 18th century after the death of Louis XIV and in reaction to the Baroque grandeur of Versailles.

Romanesque: A term used to describe pre-Gothic art and architecture from roughly the 9th to the 12th century. It is characterised by round arches and heavy construction.

Rose window: A large circular stained glass window divided into leaf-like shapes by spokes of tracery.